PENGUIN BOOKS

TWENTIETH CENTURY

J. M. Roberts, former Warden of Merton
College, Oxford, is the author of numerous
works of history, including *History of the
World* and *A History of Europe*.

J. M. ROBERTS

Twentieth Century

THE HISTORY OF THE WORLD, 1901 TO 2000

PENGUIN BOOKS

PENGUIN BOOKS
Published by the Penguin Group
Penguin Putnam Inc., 375 Hudson Street,
New York, New York 10014, U.S.A.
Penguin Books Ltd, 27 Wrights Lane, London W8 5TZ, England
Penguin Books Australia Ltd, Ringwood, Victoria, Australia
Penguin Books Canada Ltd, 10 Alcorn Avenue,
Toronto, Ontario, Canada M4V 3B2
Penguin Books (N.Z.) Ltd, 182–190 Wairau Road,
Auckland 10, New Zealand

Penguin Books Ltd, Registered Offices:
Harmondsworth, Middlesex, England

First published in Great Britain by Allen Lane The Penguin Press 1999
First published in the United States of America by Viking Penguin,
a member of Penguin Putnam Inc. 1999
Published in Penguin Books 2000

1   3   5   7   9   10   8   6   4   2

THE LIBRARY OF CONGRESS HAS CATALOGED
THE AMERICAN HARDCOVER EDITION AS FOLLOWS:
Roberts, J. M. (John Morris), 1928–
Twentieth century: the history of the world, 1901 to 2000/J. M. Roberts
p.   cm.
Includes bibliographical references.
ISBN 0-670-88456-1 (hc.)
ISBN 0 14 02.9656 5 (pbk.)
I. History, Modern—20th century.   I. Title.   II. Title: 20th century.
D421.R54   1999
909.82—dc21   99–41833

Printed in the United States of America
Set in Sabon

. . . The General added a very wise remark.

'Look here, you're always wanting to get things done,' he said to his companion reproachfully. 'And I admire you for it. But you ought to try thinking in historical terms for once.'

– Robert Musil, *The Man without Qualities*

Contents

List of Maps   xiii
Foreword   xv

BOOK I   THE WORLD OF 1901: INHERITANCES

  1   By Way of Introduction   3
      Our century – The weight of the past – The different
      pasts of 1901 – The 'civilized' world – Culture and
      hegemony – 'One-half of the human species' – Ideas with
      a future – The scientific legacy – Movers and shakers

  2   Structures   39
      Human numbers – The world's wealth – Commerce –
      States and governments – Monarchy – Non-western
      government – Islamic empires – The United States of
      America – Latin America – The international order:
      power and great powers – Potential for change

  3   The White Man's World   82
      Empire and imperialism – The European empires –
      Idealism, interests and imagination – Settlers and natives
      – Imperialism and international relations: the 'Scramble
      for Africa' – Asian and Pacific empire – The imperial
      United States – The South African war

  4   Shapes of Things to Come   111
      Long-term demography – The divisions of humanity –
      A century of growing wealth – An industrializing world –

New technology – Medical science – Communication –
Mass communication – Changing mentalities –
Acceleration and integration

BOOK 2   THE LAST YEARS OF THE EUROPEAN ASCENDANCY

5   European Exceptionalism   141
Europeans – Privilege and unrest – Socialism – Mass
politics and nationalism – Constitutional governments –
The German empire – Dynasticism – Religion in
European life – Tensions and strains – Women in Europe

6   Europe as a System of Power   175
International order – Alliances and entanglements –
The dissatisfied and dangerous – The appearance of
security – New alignments – Deepening divisions –
Young Turks – Russia's changing stance – Agadir and
after – The Balkan wars

7   Challenges and Challengers in the Making   207
Change and perceptions of change in Asia – The new
Japan – The end of the Chinese empire – The European
empires in the Far East – Indo-China and Indonesia –
India under the Raj – India enters the twentieth century –
Egypt and the end of Ottoman Africa – Ottoman empire
east of Suez – New actors in the imperial drama

8   The Great War and the Beginning of the Twentieth-
century Revolution   238
The last crisis – The end of an age – The Great War –
The changing world – 1917 – Revolutionary war –
Triumphs of nationality – The Ottoman collapse –
The end of the first German war

BOOK 3   THE END OF THE OLD WORLD ORDER

9   A Revolutionary Peace   271
The basis of settlement – The League – The

international economy – Economic disorder in
Europe – Democracy and nationality – Revolution
and counter-revolution – The new Germany –
International communism – The new Russian
empire – A new autocracy – A world divided

10 Years of Illusion   304
A last flourish of empire – Kemal Atatürk – Iran –
New currents in Europe's politics – An authoritarian
wave – New uncertainties – The optimistic years –
Locarno and after – An eastern enigma – The United
States

BOOK 4   WORLD REVOLUTION

11 An Emerging Global History   339
The world depression – Asia in the era of European
civil war – The sequel to the Chinese revolution –
Japan – The peace settlements and Asia – Chinese
communism – Japanese dynamism – Civil war in China
– The turning tide in India – The United States –
Latin America

12 The Path to World War   378
The approach to the abyss – The Manchurian crisis –
The China 'incident' – Indo-China and Indonesia
between the wars – The German problem – Adolf
Hitler – The German revolution – The crumbling
balance of power – Ideology's contamination of
international affairs – Towards a new German war:
the Spanish Civil War – Hitler moves beyond the
German lands

13 The Second World War   410
From Blitzkrieg to Barbarossa – German Europe –
World war – The conflation of wars – Global conflict
1941–5 – The meaning of victory

CONTENTS

BOOK 5   A NEW WORLD

14   Appearance and Reality   435
     Europe: amid the ruins – The framework of recovery –
     Reconstruction – Great power realities – Friction –
     The Truman doctrine and the Marshall Plan

15   The Cold War Unrolls   457
     Roots of conflict – The Berlin crisis and NATO –
     New nations: the beginnings of decolonization –
     Indian independence – The last throes of the Chinese
     revolution – Imperial realities in 1945 – Indo-China –
     The running sore of the Ottoman Succession – Cold
     and hot war in Asia: Korea – Stalin's legacy – A divided
     Europe in a dividing world

16   East Asia Reshaped   494
     After empire – The Indian sub-continent – The 'Third
     World' – Indonesia – The new China – China's
     re-emergence as a world power – The great steersman –
     Resurgent Japan

17   Africa and the Near East: Old and New Problems   521
     Past history, new facts – Pre-independence Africa –
     The independence process in Black Africa –
     South Africa and Rhodesia – Disappointment and
     disillusion – Arab and Jew – The Egyptian revolution
     and after – Algerian independence

BOOK 6   SHIFTING FOUNDATIONS

18   Changing Minds   553
     New ways of seeing the world – The management of
     the natural world – Power – Communications and
     information technology – The life sciences – Medical
     science – Space and the public imagination – Promise
     and misgiving – Facing new issues

19 New Economic and Social Worlds   584
In the long run – Europe's 'golden age' – Eastern Europe
– World contrasts – Changing lifestyles – The oil crisis
and after – Structural changes – Cultural consequences
in a wealthier world – Globalization

20 Authority and Its New Challengers   613
A liberating century – Dissolving certainty – Religion in
the later twentieth century – Government, democracy and
nationalism – Challenges to the state – Women – The
Pill – New waves – Women in the non-western
world – Youth

BOOK 7   A CHANGING WORLD BALANCE

21 The Cold War at Its Height   647
After Stalin – The second Berlin crisis – Latin America
enters world politics – Cuba – The aftermath in
Latin America – The changing USSR – The changing
United States

22 Vietnam and After   672
The American entanglement – The changing Asian
context – Oil and the Israel problem – The Iranian
revolution – Islam in international affairs – An uneasy
Latin America

23 The Reshaping of Europe   695
Seeds of unity – The division of Europe – National
interests – *Ostpolitik* – The path to Helsinki –
The British crisis

BOOK 8   THE END OF AN ERA

24 A World in Evolution   719
The last years of Chairman Mao – New patterns –
Japan: the new world power – The Indian democracy –
Africa's enduring problems

25 Crumbling Certainties   739
    Seeds of doubt – American misgivings –
    Disordered Islam – The last phase of Cold War –
    Changing eastern Europe – Polish revolution – The
    crumbling of the Soviet system – A new Germany

26 Post Cold War Realities   765
    The Gulf War – Persisting dangers – The end of the
    Soviet Union – A new Russia – New European security
    problems – The end of Yugoslavia – Nationality and
    ethnicity in the new Europe – European integration –
    Qualified re-orientation: the United Kingdom –
    Changes in China – Tiananmen

27 Fin-de-siècle   799
    Problems of peacekeeping – Europe after Maastricht –
    A common currency – Enlarging Europe – A troubled
    Far East – The Indian sub-continent – The United
    States at the end of the century – Pax Americana

28 Retrospect   829
    Historical importance – The great upheavals –
    The mythology of human happiness – Mastery of the
    material world – The first world civilization – Today's
    political world – Conclusion

    Appendix: The Exploration of Space   857
    Index   861

List of Maps

Imperial overseas possessions, 1901   40
Africa before the First World War   84
The Far East, 1901–14   208
The First World War in Europe   240
Territorial changes resulting from the First World War   272
Hitler's Europe, 1938–45   380
The Second World War   412
Cold War Europe   436
The Cold War World in 1962   458
The Post-War Recovery of Eastern Asia   496
Africa in 1999   522
South and Central America in 1999   648
The CIS in 1999   766
Energy consumption worldwide, 1998   830

Foreword

'There are great and obvious objections to contemporary history,' Macaulay once said, thinking of the events of his own lifetime.[1] He is not the only historian to have sensed them, even if the history of the form begins with the great work of Thucydides. It will always remain true that the closer we get to our own times, the harder it is to see what is the history that really matters. There is such a torrent of events – and we are so bombarded with information about them – that it is difficult to judge what is really important and what will seem trivial in 100 years' time. We lack perspective; we are not far enough away from the things we are looking at to see them in proportion to one another. This is even more true when people look at what has happened in their own lifetimes, and is therefore one of the special difficulties of the contemporary historian, as historians of their own or very recent times are often called. There are others, too. Often evidence about why things happened is not available until many years after the event, though for a variety of reasons we now know a great deal about why most events took the turn they did in the twentieth century, and certainly more than people knew about their own times in earlier centuries, even if gaps remain. In fact, the boot is nowadays often on the other foot: there is just too much evidence to handle. The hardest task of the contemporary historian is, therefore, to discriminate. That must appear all too clearly in the pages that follow. In them, I have tried to set out what seems to me to have been most historically important, what affected the largest numbers of

---

[1] Q. in G.O. Trevelyan, *The Life and Letters of Lord Macaulay* (Oxford, 1961), 1, pp.442–3.

human beings (whether directly or by creating new circumstances in which they had to live their lives) in this century, and to do so in a reasonably short book. The size of that task means that this can only be a reconsideration of facts established by others and not a work of original research. I hope, though, that it embodies considered and careful reflection.

Inevitably, the hardest decisions have been over the question of what to leave out. The book is intended to be a history of the world in a given period, yet not only can it not be factually complete, it must leave some history out altogether. It does not pretend to provide complete or even cover, any more than a guidebook pretends to give information about every part of the region it describes in uniform or equal measure. Take, for instance, the history of the Islamic republic of the Comoros Islands, which is by no means a long one. In 1975 the islands emerged from French colonial rule and became a sovereign independent state, a member of the United Nations on the same footing as all other members. In the twenty-four years since independence there are said to have been no fewer than eighteen *coups d'état* (by no means all successful), three of its four presidents have died in office (one by assassination), and French forces have twice returned to stabilize things. This is evidently a history *mouvementé* even by the standards of many post-colonial countries. Small though the republic is, moreover (its population is less than 700,000), it has had to face a problem of attempted secession (by one island that appealed to be returned to French jurisdiction unsuccessfully; France declined) and has experienced in local forms many of the most challenging historical trends of recent times – dependence on a narrow range of agricultural exports, rapid population growth, decolonization, modernization, Islamism. Its history, therefore, is not only turbulent and complex, but, in a certain light, exemplary and revealing of currents transcending its shores. Yet the Comoros Islands are not mentioned on any later page of this book. They do not impinge enough on its concerns, and in this resemble, I am afraid, many communities whose history has had to be set aside here, not as beneath the consideration of history (every human creation or phenomenon has its own history that demands and is worthy of proper study) but because their story neither illuminates nor contributes to the general themes of this particular book.

There is no principle of democracy to ensure equal treatment for states and nations in historical narrative, nor even for tragedies and disasters; they can only be touched upon as they relate to a world history whose nature in this book has to be very general. This is not an encyclopedia, and neither the name of every sovereign state that has existed in this century, nor that of every international institution it has spawned, nor those of all the persons who for a time captured the headlines of the international press, nor every event that has been brought to our notice by the mass media can be mentioned in it. This book is based on a personal selection of topics, though not one, I hope, which is capricious or indefensible. (The same might be said of the spelling and transliteration of proper names which follow; I have made my own judgement about what were likely to be the most easily recognized versions to employ and the result is not consistency. 'Peking', for example, is used in the earlier pages of the book, since that name was normally employed in western writing in the first half of the century, but 'Beijing' as a more familiar choice for the more recent period.)

In deciding how to set out the story, the most dangerous trap, potentially, was that of familiarity. All history is approached by the reader with certain expectations. I am very much aware of the pull of certain notorious dates. Some exercise an almost hypnotic effect, and shape our preconceptions without our being aware of it. As I began, there loomed ahead certain traditional and symbolic turning points – 1914, 1939, 1945, for instance – which could not be ignored. Yet these dates could easily be matched by others, once one slightly adjusted the perspective: 1904, 1905, 1917, 1931 were important, too. Arguments for saying so appear in what follows, but those dates themselves reflect the fact that some of the greatest historical themes of our century emerge because decisive historical action has in this century moved from the stage of European history to a wider stage, to, indeed, world history in the true sense. Some people saw this only a few years after the century began. That process leads to a conclusion that requires more than a mere coincidental assemblage of separate and distinct histories of different parts of the world. Within my formal and arbitrary dating, I have tried above all to trace that world history, what is general, what pulls the story together.

When I was born my parents may well not yet have heard the name of Hitler and we were only twenty-six years away from the Boer war, of which I heard a lot from them (as my children, I fear, forty years later, heard all too much from me about my adolescent memories of the Second World War). Our century has been so truly revolutionary that, as I thought about the structure of the book, I decided I had to begin by sketching the outlines of a forgotten world, one that is now no more, yet of which many of us through our parents and grandparents have some lingering and possibly very misleading impressions. After thus surveying the scene in 1901, my next step, I decided, should be to look ahead, to try to set out a summary view of some of the long-running forces for change that spanned the century or very large parts of it, and which are obscured when they are broken up into the shorter episodes that the history of public events imposes. After these glances at forces of inertia and movement visible at the outset, I felt I could embark on the narrative; this takes up most of the rest of the book. The canvas is a broad one and in organizing it I have had to court the danger of repetition. Many topics appear, disappear and then reappear in more than one context. They have had to be looked at from more than one point of view. At the end of the book, I have tried to look back on this century and to set out my view of its meaning and shape. This is, of course, the most personal and speculative part of all in what follows. Nevertheless, the outcome, I hope, will be a serviceable approach to nearly 100 years of more rapid, more sweeping, and more important change in human lives and prospects than there has ever been.

On some of the themes that embody these changes I have already written elsewhere. In talking about them again, I have not hesitated to reappropriate words I have already used when they seem to be the right ones. To some important aspects of human life, I have been unable to give the attention and space that some readers will undoubtedly feel is their intrinsic due. There is little, for instance, about art or music in what follows. There is more than one reason for this. It is partly because the sheer individuation that has overtaken and characterized them in this century even within a single tradition – the western – has shattered the frameworks within which they could formerly be meaningfully treated. It is partly, too, because of my ignorance of other cultures. It is partly because a world history cannot relate such matters to its overriding themes as can the histories of particular cultures, civilizations, or countries, partly because the numbers of human beings they decisively affect seem in the world context too few to spend space on them. Where 'mass' or 'popular' art forms are concerned, although their global importance may be more easily recognizable, I confess that I again remain too ignorant to proceed. Future historians of the twentieth century will no doubt do better. I am fairly confident, nonetheless, that the arts have shown no such implications for change in human life as those of, say, the unravelling of DNA, or the tapping of the energy of the atomic nucleus – and neither of those get a lot of space in what follows.

My wife read much of the typescript of this book in earlier versions, and I wish to thank her for labour going well beyond the normal boundaries of marital obligation. For all the other benefits I owe to her, both for their own sake and for the help they gave me in writing, this is not the place to thank her nor have I the space; I think, though, that she knows they are constantly present to me. Many friends and colleagues, too, have helped me in many ways, some so long ago and so fundamentally that I cannot hope to list them. Professor John Carey, Sir Martin Gilbert, Mr John Gooding, Professor Jack Gray, Dr C.A. Grocock, Mr Mark Roberts, Professor Chushichi Tsuzuki and Dr Jonathan Wright, though, were all kind enough to answer specific questions I put to them and some of them also scrutinized passages for me; I thank them all most warmly, as I do Lord Wright and Sir James Craig, who came to my rescue in a particular emergency at a very late stage. I owe special thanks to Dr Clare Griffiths, who much improved the quality of my references, and to Professor Tim Blanning, who read the whole text to its great benefit. I must particularly thank also Mr John B. Rhinelander for a stimulating conversation as we sailed down the Bosphorus a few years ago, and for his encouraging letters, and Professor H. W. Arndt for a most interesting communication. My editor at Penguin, Mr Simon Winder, has never failed to be helpful in his comments on drafts I showed him and in easing the processes of publication. To the University of Bristol I am much indebted for the access to its library that I have been granted. A special word of thanks, too, is due to an old friend and sometime undergraduate pupil, Mr Duncan Campbell-Smith, for urging that Penguin should publish this book. Finally, I must thank Mrs Jill Webber, who grappled valiantly and swiftly with the heavy tasks of typing and retyping sometimes very messy drafts. Neither she, though, nor anyone else save I, should be blamed for any of the shortcomings of what follows.

Like others of my books, this is intended for the intelligent layman and laywoman. When I began, I had hoped it would attract them by being shorter than it has turned out to be. It has been well said by one of the masters of my craft that 'if historians cannot reach that audience there is not a great deal of significance in what they say to each other. History only matters to non-historians.'[2] I believe that, too, and cannot put it more pithily.

J. M. R.
Timwood, June 1999

[2] Professor Norman Hampson, in his essay, 'The "Lessons" of the French Revolution', in *The Impact of the French Revolution on European Consciousness*, ed. H.T. Mason and W. Doyle (Gloucester, 1989), p.188.

BOOK I

THE WORLD OF 1901: INHERITANCES

I

By Way of Introduction

OUR CENTURY

Until quite recent times, peoples in different parts of the world looked at, thought about and organized the past in many different ways, and many (Muslims, for example) still do. Some have broken it up into the comings and goings of dynasties; others have thought of it in astronomical periods; yet others have picked great events, imaginary or historical, as markers. All such systems are arbitrary, as is the one more widely adopted than any other, that based on the Christian calendar and what came to be accepted as the date of birth of Christ. Since the Middle Ages, the two big divisions that that provides, BC and AD, have then been further subdivided into centuries of 100 years (and, by some, relabelled BCE and CE). This is like measuring an endless piece of string with a ruler – you pick a point for your own reasons and start there, measuring it off in metres or any other units you like. But the string is not naturally divided into metres or anything else. A metre is just a distance between two chosen points on a continuing line, and so, in relation to time, is a century. We should not be too impressed by a unit which happens to run from a year whose number ends in 01 to one which has a number ending in 00, for it is only a convenience. We give the centuries so defined special names according to where they come in relation to the supposed date of the birth of Christ and speak of the 'fifth century BC', for example, or of the 'twelfth century AD'. The twentieth century is properly the name for 100 years which began on 1 January 1901 and will end when 31 December 2000 gives way to New Year's Day 2001.

We sometimes talk of 'centuries' more loosely, to stress that many things that happened between a couple of days 100 years apart, or others close to them, seem to hang together comprehensibly and to give a special character to those years, as opposed to those which come before or after them, whether or not they exactly amount to 100 years of time. We have got used to speaking of some centuries in a kind of historical shorthand, as if they had identifying traits or qualities of their own. We even use them adjectivally, talking about (for instance) 'the eighteenth-century mind' or 'nineteenth-century morality'. This is to denote those eras which, for certain purposes and in some perspectives, may be described as having a special character. Such shorthand always implies many qualifications, but it is often useful in a pedagogic or expository way; I recall introducing undergraduates to a period of European and general history demarcated in the Oxford syllabus as 1715–1789 by getting them to write essays on the question 'When did the eighteenth century begin?' Professional historians sometimes make such qualifications explicit and specify 'long' and 'short' centuries (many books on the twentieth century begin not with 1901 but with 1914) in order to get away from the arbitrariness they associate with the formal dating, but this too is only a way of driving home the point that within certain spans of time events appear to have a unity and coherence which makes them good topics for study.

Even if we welcome the notion of a 'century', though, and use it rather than a vaguer word like 'age' or 'era' as an indication of what we are going to talk about, we must be careful. All such language is no more than a very rough and general way of speaking. No pair of dates, however carefully chosen, cuts off any part of history magically and absolutely from what came before it and what came after. Well after 1901 there were millions of people alive who for years, even decades, lived much as their grandparents had done well before that year; today, there are few in that position, even if we all live in ways and among problems and potentials that will not vanish at midnight on 31 December 2000 AD. It is partly for this reason that I have thought it best to treat the history of the twentieth century in a wholly conventional and formal way, as the story of what happened between 31 December 1900 and a date as near to 100 years later as I could manage before sending the typescript to the publisher.

4

That Procrustean decision once taken, one can still ask, nonetheless, whether there is something special, something characteristic, which would justify us in finding the twentieth century remarkable and worth examination for its own sake. To answer that question is one purpose of this book. It is not made easier by the banal fact that we have all, writer and readers alike, lived in it and, unless we are still in infancy, we can all remember in some degree our direct experience of it. This will not help us to achieve agreement about what it was and is. Indeed, shared experience is a constant temptation to misunderstanding. Direct experience shapes our valuation and judgement of what matters in it in very different ways. History (what is important about the past) varies according to the position from which you view it. In looking at the record, some will seek guidance in something that seems best to crystallize a general trend, some will scrutinize the immense variety of particulars for something that best typifies or symbolizes that very abundance. Some will look at the past in search of clues for understanding their own present problems and preoccupations.

Nothing in the past can be completely described or recorded; if we could do that we should relive history. There has to be selection; whether or not any particular selection is acceptable, it may enable others to select more defensibly. What must never be lost to sight is the fact that all pasts were, once upon a time, presents; all outcomes were, once upon a time, people's futures. History is made by people confronting predicaments, and those people were always individuals, always liable to escape from the big generalizations that have to be part of any general history. We are liable to judge them wrongly unless we try to keep in mind the limits to their own perception of what those predicaments were, and what they could and could not know at any given moment. Hindsight is always tempting us to forget this.

Hindsight, too, poses a special difficulty for what historians call contemporary history (itself not always a very helpful or immediately meaningful term; for a long time members of the French historical profession were quite content to define it as what had happened since the French Revolution of 1789 – which they saw as the culmination, of course, of 'modern' history). The history of yesterday, or of the day before yesterday, is the hardest history of all to get right because we know too much about it. Some think we know all about it, or at least about what matters most in it; once more, we come back to the fact that we have all experienced some of it. Yet the very impressiveness of some of the events we have witnessed threatens historical judgement. Canonical accounts of great events are quickly and all too easily established. The vividness of remembered experience imposes blinkers and mufflers, cutting out signals we need to see and hear, all the more dangerously because it so often does so without our being aware of it. It is not surprising that Americans who inherited a long tradition of isolation wanted to turn their backs on Europe after (they believed) coming to her help to win the Great War, or that Britons who lived through the great events of 1940 and the (at first dark and then victorious) years that followed found it hard later to recognize that their country was in the 1950s only a second-rank power. It is understandable that those who have battled valiantly for very fundamental political rights for women should often overlook the enormous extension in women's practical freedoms brought about more silently by technology and chemistry. But the historian has to try to do better than record his personal impressions. Trying to achieve a reliable impression of what men and women inherited from the past as this century began, and could not shake off, is a possible starting-point.

THE WEIGHT OF THE PAST

It is not hard to imagine life in 1901 if we are thinking of 'developed' countries (an expression that had not then been invented, incidentally). Many of us have talked to people who could easily recall it; there even are, after all, people still alive who were born before that year. This is the first century, too, during the whole of which it has been possible to make pictorial records other than with pencil or brush. We are able to look at the photographs that survive from its earliest years, and even at some flickering and jerky 'moving pictures' of them. Much of the language and idiom of the turn of the century is still perfectly comprehensible to us; we still read books written then with pleasure and profit and, for the most part, understanding. For these and many more reasons, those of us who are fortunate enough to live in the developed world are tempted to believe we know what the world was like as this century began. We may even think that we understand those who lived then, wrote its books and managed its affairs as we do not understand any earlier generation.

This is an illusion. There are no better grounds to believe that we easily understand the men and women of that age than there are to believe that we understand those who lived in the age of Leonardo da Vinci. We can only begin to approach understanding by recognizing how much they were not like us. Any history of the twentieth century must begin in a world deeply unlike our own. At least in the most 'western', developed societies, we are less like the men and women of 1901, and further distanced in our thinking and behaviour from them than, say, were they from their forebears of a century earlier. The African peasant or Australian aborigine of today may not be quite so remote from the experiences and thinking of their grandparents and great-grandparents, but people who live in the richer, developed or developing countries of the world – and that now means most human beings – perceive, think and feel in ways very different from those in which our own ancestors perceived, thought and felt their world as this century began. My father had only added English to his native Welsh a few years before this century began, when the first powered flight by a man in a 'heavier-than-air' machine had not yet been made; less than seventy years later, he could look at a television set and watch men bobbing about on the surface of the moon.

Not that there is any need to search the heavens for markers of change. In the cities and towns of those developed countries the photographic evidence is there to tell us that the world looked very different then as soon as one stepped outside one's front door. Nor was it only visually remote from our experience. A New Yorker, Londoner, Berliner or Parisian of 1901 would have awoken each morning to a world which smelt of horses rather than motor-cars, in which side-streets were still full of stable-yards, in which more straw than paper littered the streets (no plastic did, of course), in which milk, coal, beer and a hundred and one other necessities were delivered by horse-drawn carts and drays, and in which many more of his contemporaries would know how to ride or manage a horse than to drive a car. Outside those 'up-to-date' cities stretched a world that was unlike our own in much more striking ways, too, impossible to summarize in a phrase. Most of those who lived in it were shorter and slighter than their descendants today.[1] They also went without formal schooling and expected much less of life than we do today. Outside a few countries, few men and women expected long lives, or that their lives would be very different from those of their grandparents. Nowhere was more than elementary medication available to treat disease; rest, nourishing food and good nursing were the main advantages available to the rich when they were ill. Aspirin had only been invented a couple of years before[2] and, short of complete anaesthesia or morphine, pain had to be endured. Social classes could be identified at sight by the clothes they wore: drab, worn, ill-fitting for the mass, elaborate, carefully crafted and maintained for even the modestly well-off. One could go on listing such apparent differences and, of course, to do so would hardly touch many more significant ways in which the world of 1901 is now hard even to imagine, let alone understand.

The eighteenth-century idea of an *ancien régime* may be helpful. When the phrase was first coined it could be translated roughly as 'the old way of running things', or 'the former way of carrying on'. It has always since carried an implicit comparison: what has happened in the past is being contrasted with what has happened since. One only talks about the *ancien régime* when it is no more. Societies cannot be aware of having an *ancien régime* until something has actually changed. Then, people will have a fair chance of understanding what you mean because an *ancien régime* signifies a time when people behaved and thought differently from the way they behaved and thought in later times. In that sense, there was an *ancien régime* in 1901 and, indeed, there was more than one. People behaved and thought then in ways different from ourselves – not wholly differently, perhaps, but very differently. Most states in the world of 1901, for example, were governed by monarchs – emperors, kings and queens,

---

[1] There were, of course, important national differences: I recall the enthusiasm with which an elderly French friend once told me of her admiration and excitement at the appearance of the first American soldiers in Paris in 1917 because of their magnificent physique.

[2] In 1897.

princes, khans, shahs, sultans, rajahs and many more titles singled them out. That was the way things were when Queen Victoria, the oldest head of state in the world, died only a few days after the twentieth century began, and at her funeral two emperors and three other sovereigns, nine crown princes and heirs apparent, and forty princes and grand-dukes walked behind her coffin in respect. It is unlikely (though historians should never predict) that any future royal funerals will ever replicate such a display of the prevailing mythology about the way the world was run.[3]

The death of the old queen was for many of her subjects something of a psychological shock. Something, it was remarked, passed with her even if to some (mainly in high society) a change in the social atmosphere of the English court and aristocracy would have been all that was noticeable. In retrospect, though, Victoria's funeral came to seem a symbol of much more, perhaps the end of an era in the history of her country. The monarchs who attended her funeral went home afterwards to continue to reign; one of them, her grandson, the emperor of Germany, in whose arms she had lain on her deathbed, would still be on his throne in 1918. In spite of the sensation of a great change, nothing actually changed in 1901 which had any significant effect on the lives of those who had been her subjects. That the old queen was no longer on the throne did not alter the way they went about their work, thought about their families, worshipped and prayed, sought pleasure and suffered, nor did it improve or worsen their real incomes and standards of living. Although all those things were to change very radically in due course and sometimes quite rapidly, it was only in a somewhat superficial and misleading way that it could it be said that a British *ancien régime* came to an end with Victoria, far less that an age ended.

Queen Victoria was not the only head of state to die soon after this century began. Nine months later, the president of the United States of America was murdered. That did not mean any fundamental change either. Yet something of an immediately recognizable difference was

---

[3] An even more vivid evocation of a world that is gone, though, because of its far more medieval trappings, was the funeral procession, fifteen years later, of Franz Joseph, emperor of Austria and king of Hungary, and it, too, can be seen because recorded on film.

made to his country's history by his removal, because his constitutional role was so different from that of the old queen. Under the terms of the American Constitution, McKinley was at once succeeded in office by his vice-president, Theodore Roosevelt – 'that damned cowboy' as one enraged politician called him. Roosevelt was a man who liked to stir things up, and he used the powers of the presidency more vigorously to promote certain policies he favoured than his predecessor had done. That made a difference to American politics and policy, as the accession of Edward VII did not to those of the United Kingdom. Even so, Roosevelt's arrival in the White House was in no sense revolutionary, even if it somewhat changed the tone of American political life. Americans went on being American, just as Queen Victoria's subjects – who included not only Britons, but Indians, Fijians, Chinese, Matabele, Ashanti, Hottentots and many, many others – did not change their deeply rooted customs and went on being what they were. To the lives of all such people much greater change would come in due course from great wars, migrations and such technological innovations as the 'horseless carriages' and 'automobiles' of which early examples were beginning to trundle about the streets of a few cities even in Asia and Africa in 1901.

Even if changes in personnel make important differences to history in some circumstances and at some historical junctures, they only rarely make a difference so complete that one can say that some worlds are now no more, that they have truly passed into history as an *ancien régime*. The death of Adolf Hitler himself when it came at last was only incidental to the much greater historical transformation implied in the smashing of German military power. Yet changes truly revolutionary in their scope have occurred all round the world throughout the twentieth century. They are the main subject matter of its history. They are what have made this century one like no other century in the entire history of mankind, whether they are easily pinned down to a specific moment or – like most of the most important – prolonged over years or decades. Their gradual, incremental onset often makes them hard to recognize even in retrospect. To try to understand how almost unimaginably different was the world of 1901 from that of our own day is the first step towards measuring those transformations.

THE DIFFERENT PASTS OF 1901

One of the most important ways in which the world was different in 1901 was in the ways its societies saw the past, and the ways that shaped their perception of their present. Historians face an infinite number of past worlds. Few experiences except the most elemental are shared by all men and women in all parts of the world, even if there are more shared today than in 1901 (thanks to some of the biggest changes the century has brought about). Societies still have highly differentiated pasts, but they have shared shaping experiences to a greater degree in this century than ever in earlier times. The *ancien régime* of 1901 which has now disappeared was not the same thing in Europe as in the United States, nor was that of the Chinese the same as that of the peoples of India. It would only be a mild exaggeration to say that all those and many other societies in 1901 had in common as going concerns was that they were doomed to disappear within the next 100 years. The simplicities of rural North America, the still untouched traditional ways of Tibet, the life of the Berlin tenement-dweller – all these, and many more, have vanished beyond recall, except by historians and nostalgic novelists. No earlier century has ever brought about such complete, often swift and accelerating, change to humanity as has this one, nor change that has left it sharing so much common experience.

Just as today, what most people thought in 1901 was largely shaped by what they took for granted. That it was so unlike what we now take for granted may now be seen an obvious enough point, but perhaps it is still worth a moment's further consideration. Of the hundreds of millions of human beings that lived in Asia when the century began, for example, few except European expatriates ever thought about the continent where they lived as 'Asia'. That there was an entity corresponding to the word 'Asia' was a European idea, adopted only by a minority of Asians, not yet an idea most of them would have grasped. The slogan 'Asia for the Asians' had only just been coined by the Japanese in the 1890s; within 'Asia', that word was hardly known outside Japan, which had adopted European geographical nomenclature along with much else.[4] Of the inhabitants of the Indian sub-continent few ever thought of India as a whole, either, or as a geographical reality, let alone a social or political one; only a tiny minority of Indians had the idea that India might one day become the name of a country. Similarly, it was unlikely that many native-born Africans except those who were white would have had any notion that there existed an entity called 'Africa', the name given to the whole continent first by Europeans (who, of course, thereby also created the category 'African'). Europeans and North Americans, on the other hand, tended to be much more aware of the continents in which they lived. They had named them, too, after all. Nationhood or nationality was another European idea, even if there were non-European peoples – Han Chinese or Japanese for example – with strongly developed senses of their own ethnic and cultural distinction.

Given such contrasts, as well as others in the distribution of power and wealth, in habit and behaviour, our closeness in time to the men and women of 1901 can too easily deceive us; they took for granted much that we do not and could not conceive much that is commonplace to us. They felt the weight of pasts peculiar to them, and which are not ours, though parts of the landscape they laid out can still look familiar to us. They saw past time with the eyes of the nineteenth century in which they had been born (and they had experienced, of course, many different nineteenth centuries, according to where they lived).

The only futures that shape people's lives are imaginary ones that can stir them to action. For the most part, it is the past, real or mythological, which does most to shape – sometimes overwhelmingly – a present. Our ancestors on 1 January 1901 were heirs to hundreds of vastly different inheritances, varying in their detail according to when and where they were born: the world on the first day of the twentieth century was, as it is now, a complication of hundreds of millions of individual contexts set by hundreds of millions of pasts. Some of the

---

[4] 'Asia' – the name, originally of a province of the Roman empire – appeared first in Japan, it seems, in the seventeenth century in a book (which was not published until 1882), and also appears, written phonetically, on one of the earliest world maps produced in Japan, in 1786, along with the other European designations of sub-divisions of the globe's land-masses, Africa, the Americas, and Europe itself.

contexts thus formed were much more influential than others. It is not easy to grasp just what the world's peoples could in fact choose to assimilate or reject in the past history that confronted them.

Once away from the microscopic level, which can never be studied in its entirety, where each man and woman confronts his or her own destiny, it is nonetheless possible to make a start at a high level of generalization by recognizing the distinct pasts which belong to a few large collectivities. These provide the peaks and great mountain ranges of the historical landscape. One can distinguish, for instance, a number of historical cultures and civilizations that made up the world of 1901. They were as diverse in their essence as in their superficial appearance. In the Kalahari desert or in New Guinea there lived Stone Age peoples still untouched by civilization at a moment when Europeans were planning railways to span Africa from Cape to Cairo and link Berlin and Baghdad, or dreaming of a future in which air travel (by hydrogen-filled 'dirigibles' which were already beginning to appear in the skies of some countries) would be possible between the world's capital cities. Within the world historically shaped by Christianity, Russians were then just beginning to undergo the experience of industrialization that had come to western Europe from fifty to 100 years earlier, but were still following the pre-Christian Julian calendar which had been abandoned centuries earlier in western Europe. Buddhist Tibet was a country that only a handful of Europeans had yet even visited. Muslim Arabs from the Persian Gulf had only recently been forced to curtail a huge trade in slaves from east Africa; foot-binding was still normal for women in upper-class Chinese households. The Ottoman sultan, ruler of many peoples, Europeans among them, still maintained an official harem. Many more such oddities then existed which have long since ceased to be. They reflected age-old differentiation and global variety as this century began.

Our own world, of course, is also a very varied and highly differentiated place, but in the next 100 years such exotic variety was to be much reduced, if only at the level of superficial appearances and material circumstance.[5] Huge mental and moral differences remain

---

[5] Though some important changes came quite soon. Foot-binding was officially abolished in China in 1902, and in 1909 the Ottoman harem was officially dissolved.

between peoples, but nowadays we sometimes find them surprising, as our predecessors would not have done in 1901.[6] Such differences can suddenly erupt to complicate and sometimes poison our affairs after superficial similarities have misled us. People accepted in 1901 more readily than we always do that a shared humanity should not be trusted very far as a guide to behaviour, and said so more frequently than we are brave enough to do.

Whether or not intuition and experience seem to bear this out, it may at any rate be quickly agreed that as this century began the superficial differences between human societies around the world would at least have been even more obvious than they would be today. A traveller now punctuates his travel by sitting in identical airport 'lounges', takes similar taxis on emerging from them to travel along roads marked, wherever he or she may be, by traffic-lights sending the same messages as elsewhere and policed by public officials ostensibly intended to enforce similar driving behaviour, and does so in order to reach 'international hotels' aspiring to provide just what has been left behind in the last one. Fundamental and important differences in such trivial circumstances and even in the way people behaved were more apparent in daily life when this century began. Perhaps, too, they were more firmly anchored in identifiable public institutions than they are today; but this is harder to be sure about, and is perhaps better left for reflexion as the story unrolls. Different cultures and countries, we know, still differ profoundly about the way people should be treated; thoughts about the individual's proper relations with authority, social and economic behaviour in, say, Great Britain and Saudi Arabia, India and Australia, or France and Japan, can still clash even though more people in all countries now talk as if they believed in universal human rights than was the case in 1901.[7]

---

[6] Numerous persons in western countries were much startled in 1989 to discover that there were many Muslims who believed that blasphemy might properly be punished by death.

[7] Nearly a half-century after a declaration of human rights was adopted by the United Nations in December 1948 it was strongly and publicly criticized as inadequate (because presenting a partial, culturally determined view of rights) by a non-western politician, the Malaysian prime minister, Dr Mahathir Mohamed, at a meeting of Asian foreign ministers in July 1997.

Nonetheless, the past weighs a little less obviously on most of the world than once it did. The inheritances that people drew upon in their thinking and behaviour in 1901 often expressed the weight of centuries of virtually unquestioned authority. This was obvious in the way religions could then still be thought of as major categorizations of humanity. Most human beings still lived in the rich, complicated settings of ancient faiths – the main ones were Hindu, Buddhist, Confucian, Christian and Islamic – and adhered to them in practice, though what they believed is harder to say. It seems likely, though, that most human beings then still believed in some sort of supernatural world, and often in a two-tier model of a present, material sphere and another in which dwelt a god or gods, exercising real power and uttering authoritative commands. Within acceptance of some such theistic framework, though, different zones of religious observance had long somewhat overlapped and run untidily in and out of one another. Though people within its sphere still often used the word, Christendom was not so clearly defined in 1901 as it had been five or six centuries earlier. Its divisions had grown sharper and more plentiful in the last two or three centuries, too. Even in 1799, a German writer had been able to say that Christendom was no longer the same as Europe:[8] by 1901, the word indicated less a sphere of a particular faith than the world occupied by European stocks, who were assumed to be Christian. All round the world, too, Europeans had made converts to their historic religion (conversion rather than settlement had made South and Central America part of the Christian world), and even where they had not been very successful (as in India, or China), they had left many institutional and physical marks of Christianity in the form of churches, colleges, schools and hospitals. Europe itself, the Americas and the white settler lands of Australasia and South Africa, though, still thought of themselves as, above all, the heartlands of a Christian world. That notion would undergo radical change in the next 100 years, in which Christianity became predominantly a religion of non-European peoples.

Of the two other great monotheistic religions, Judaism was the best

---

[8] Novalis, whose significantly entitled essay 'Christendom or Europe' (*Die Christenheit oder Europa*) was written in that year, did not publish it in his own lifetime, though it circulated for some years in manuscript.

defined. It was also the most widespread; its adherents could be found worldwide, though their numbers were not very great. In 1901 most of the world's Jews lived in the relatively small part of Europe made up by the Russian Pale (which included much of what is now Poland) and adjacent central and east Europe. Islam, the other faith of believers in the God of Abraham shared by Jews and Christians, was (as it remains) as far flung as either Judaism or Christianity and had the allegiance of hundreds of millions.

Unlike Christendom, the world of Islam had not been defined by historic institutions like state or church: it was and is essentially what Muslims do and the way they live. They are united by a common attitude to God, this world and the next. Islam's footing in Europe had been dwindling in recent times; by 1901 Muslim minorities remained only in places that had been for two or three centuries parts of the Ottoman Turkish empire. They were few, too, in the Americas. The heartlands of Islam were the Arabic-speaking lands of the Near and Middle East.[9] But from them the Faith had spread, at first by conquest, west into Africa and Mediterranean Europe, east and north into Central Asia, India and as far as China. Then, in the nineteenth century, large Muslim communities had grown up in Bengal, Indonesia and Malaysia, to which Islam had been carried by Arab merchants favoured by the current and winds of the Indian Ocean. The outcome was a world of great social variety and numerous splinter groups and sects. The classical Arabic of the Koran is taught to many peoples with very different native languages, and even in the Arab

---

[9] These terms are so often used in what follows that they had better be explained here. I am not sure when the term 'Middle East' first appeared (some attribute it to the American writer Admiral Mahan), but it was in the early years of this century, well after peoples were used to distinguishing the 'Near East' (which meant the lands from Egypt to the Straits of Constantinople which were under Ottoman rule) and 'Far East' (which was a zone whose core was China). 'Middle East' came into use to cover some of the countries in between. It consisted at first of those forming the approach to India from the west: Persia, Afghanistan and (somewhat oddly) Tibet. By the 1920s, though, 'Middle East' experts in the British colonial office were also expected to deal with what had been Ottoman lands in the 'Near East' and it later became normal to confine it to these lands, as will be done in this book. It does not seem necessary to specify regional groupings further east other than in the case of the Persian Gulf (as in 'the Gulf region', or 'the Gulf states').

lands to some who only speak very colloquial and regional forms of Arabic.[10] In China and India, Islam encountered the more ancient cultural zones of Hinduism, Buddhism and Confucian civilization. The last still dominated China at the beginning of this century and lay also at the roots of Japanese culture, though in both countries it lived beside Buddhism, a more transcendentally orientated body of belief and practice, but associating more easily with Confucianism or Hinduism than the monotheistic beliefs of Islam. Buddhism sprawled across two distinct cultural zones in south and south-east Asia, the sphere culturally dominated by the Hindu influences emanating from the Indian sub-continent, and the Sinic sphere of the Confucian heritage.

THE 'CIVILIZED' WORLD

At any particular moment, human beings share visions of their world with others with whom they also share many other ideals and material realities. To categorize the world by major religious traditions was more helpful in 1901 than it would be today, but even then it was by no means the only way in which intelligent and informed observers might view it. Another distinction could be and was already drawn between what we might call the world of 'western', Europe-originated, cultures, and all the rest. In 1901 the inhabitants of one large part of the world could, had they wished to do so, have looked back on two, perhaps three, centuries of remarkable change. They were the Europeans or offshoots of European stocks in other continents. Among them, those who thought about the past at all would probably have said that it presented a picture of change for the better – that is, progress. European history since the Middle Ages was understood by many to look very much like a continuing advance to evidently worthwhile goals questioned by few. Whether the criteria were intellectual and scientific, or material and economic (even if they were moral

---

[10] In this respect, though like Christianity a missionary religion, Islam was different from it in not providing for a long time its sacred texts printed in local languages.

and aesthetic, some said, so persuasive was the gospel of progress), a look at the past assured them that they were set on a progressive course and further advance seemed to lie ahead. What is more, it looked as if they and their cousins in lands settled by Europeans beyond the sea were the only peoples who could plausibly make such a claim.

The leaders of what could already be called the 'western' world showed as the century began much the sort of confidence in the continuing success of their culture that the Chinese mandarin élite had shown in theirs a century earlier. Long before, their civilization had reached that degree of self-consciousness, of the possession of a particular and characteristic style, that always goes with an awareness of the distinctive inferiorities of other sections of mankind. The past, they were sure, proved them right. Only a few did not agree, and if those dissenters numbered in their ranks men of acknowledged standing and powerful minds, who argued that the civilization in which they lived had yet to reveal its self-destructive potential and sensed it to be drifting away from its moorings in religion and moral absolutes on the tides of materialism, democracy and barbarity, even they were clear that the civilization to which they belonged had been uniquely dynamic as a force in world history, and uniquely effective in shaping it. Most 'western' peoples, if they thought about such things at all, felt the future was full of promise; the past gave them grounds for confidence.

At the beginning of this century, for example, most of the non-western world had only recently, often somewhat grudgingly, begun to accept that slavery would have to disappear. Long taken for granted in every civilization the world had ever known, chattel slavery had first been denounced in Europe and then abolished by Europeans and nations of European origin overseas in their own possessions in the nineteenth century. The formal landmark of the completion of the process may be reckoned to be the emancipation of slaves in Brazil in 1888. By then, colonial governments and the British Royal Navy were pressing hard on the operations of Arab slave-traders in the African continent and the Indian Ocean; abolition was being imposed on the rest of the world by European force and diplomacy deployed in the good cause. Sharply contrasted attitudes towards slavery still existed in 1901 between the Europe-derived civilization and the rest of the world.[11] Like other such contrasts, this encouraged persons of European descent to view the rest of the world's inhabitants as somewhat backward, obviously needing the beneficent intervention of 'white' peoples in their affairs if they were to be liberated from sometimes evil and always encumbering tradition and released to follow the progressive road of true civilization, that of the white, formally Christian, peoples. After all, even if only after 300 years of large-scale and profitable slave trading across the Atlantic, European civilization and its derivatives had already in 1800 provided the only examples of countries ever to have eradicated slavery for themselves.

To such large perspectives we can conveniently return later; it is enough to note here that in 1901 the different ways in which other parts of the world related to the expanding vigour of western civilization made it easy to see that world not only as one of different traditions or religions, but also as one of different levels of civilization. One was that of the white peoples of western countries: Europe itself and the lands which European stocks dominated overseas. This was the 'civilized' world, in contemporary parlance, occasionally also called 'western', in spite of the confusion arising when that adjective was applied to countries scattered geographically around the globe. A second, accounting for most of the rest of the world, was that of the group of societies notably and increasingly influenced and shaped by that civilized world; Japan was an outstanding example, but there were others, some of them parts of European empires. They tended to display, in varying degree, some degree of modernization, by which was meant 'Europeanization' or 'westernization' of their native institutions. A third group of peoples still lived virtually unchanged by western influences. They were remarkably few in number and, in the eyes of western contemporaries, their cultures and behaviour were

[11] And went on doing so. It was only in 1962 that the crown prince of Saudi Arabia, on forming his government, while asserting that Saudi Arabia had been gradually working for years to eliminate slavery, acknowledged publicly that the time was now 'propitious' to complete its abolition in that country. See *The Annual Register 1962* (London, 1963), p.298. (This annual reference work is cited in what follows as *AR*, with the year that it covers, not that of publication. This citation, for example, would in shortened form read *AR 1962*.)

almost without qualification 'backward' (even if, like Ethiopia, they had centuries of Christian history behind them). For many reasons, some good, some bad, we no longer like such talk. We especially tend to shun the term 'civilized world'.[12] Yet the phrase was widely used and immediately comprehensible in most European languages to educated people at the beginning of the twentieth century. The phrase reflected a unique moment in world history, the culmination of a unique development, when one civilization among several had clearly emerged as the driving force of history in almost every part of the globe.

To define the civilized world as the world where European stocks were established in significant numbers was not very precise, but it was undoubtedly how many people saw it in 1901. People who confidently used the phrase could not easily see that there was much else deserving of the name of civilization in the world. When they looked for it, they tended to see among heathen, backward, benighted peoples only a few striving to join the civilized. The rest were the savage 'others' of the rest of the world, defining themselves by what they were not. A superior attitude towards them was not new; what were taken to be demonstrations of the inherent merits of their own ideas and values had for centuries nerved Europeans to fresh assaults on the world and thrown up fresh barriers to their understanding of it. Progressive and liberal values had come to provide new arguments for superiority to reinforce those originally stemming from religion. By 1901, Europeans had lost most of the respect they had once had for other civilizations. Their own seemed obviously superior to what they saw as the unintelligible barbarities to be found elsewhere. The advocacy of individual rights, a free press, a widening suffrage qualification, the protection of women, children (and even animals) from exploitation all showed it, they thought. So, many would still have said, did missionary Christianity. Such causes and ideals were to go on being promoted and pursued down to our own day by Europeans and Americans in alien lands, often wholly unconscious that they might be disruptive or inappropriate. This contributed to another of the special characteristics of our century, a more complete

[12] Though the British prime minister found it coming naturally to his lips in a radio interview broadcast by the BBC on 7 February 1998.

and successful universalization of values than any so far achieved in human history.

CULTURE AND HEGEMONY

In one way or another, most of the globe marched to European tunes and often under European flags in 1901 and responded to initiatives whose ultimate sources were European. This is more than metaphor. The flags and tunes were usually representations of a great fact, the occupation of most of the world's land-surface by the colonial empires and new nations of white people which had emerged from them. But such physical occupation was only one expression of hegemony. It had its economic and cultural components, too, and it operated as much through influence as overt control. There was observable worldwide a crucial distinction between the shaping, manipulative, sometimes aggressive forces stemming from countries which came to be called 'western' or 'westernized' and the peoples upon which they played. The latter were by no means always worse off as a result; they were sometimes clearly beneficiaries. They were, though, always equally clearly underdogs, members of societies that had always, in greater or lesser degree, to adapt to the alien ways of the 'civilized' world. Some of them adapted willingly, once subjected to the attractive force of the West's progressive ideals; sometimes the adaptation came about more subtly, when new expectations were aroused by alien teaching and example. Sometimes the alien western ways were simply imposed by force. Sometimes there were hints from those who experienced this that even if they were better than traditional ways, they were not necessarily the unquestionable good they were usually believed to be.[13]

The result even by 1901 was a world that could be envisaged

[13] 'We do not expect the European world to make us happier,' wrote in 1902 an Indonesian lady of aristocratic birth, one of the several wives of an Indonesian prince, who nonetheless opposed not only Muslim confinement of women in marriage, education and work, but also the colonial regime of the Dutch. She is quoted by Kumari Jayawardena, *Feminism and Nationalism in the Third World* (London, 1986), p.143.

culturally in yet another way, not quite corresponding to the categories of civilized, civilizing and uncivilized. To put it somewhat simply, it could be seen as a set of concentric circles reflecting power as well as culture. The innermost was old Europe itself (of which Russia and some of the new nations of the Balkans might or might not be thought parts, according to the strictness of the criteria applied). The countries of this region had during three centuries come to take control of and consume a larger share of the world's goods than numbers alone would have justified. Their peoples had shown increasing energy and skill in manipulating their environment and the other peoples with whom they shared it. Their civilization was all the time getting richer still; industrialization had confirmed its self-feeding capacity to open up and create new resources and the power generated by new wealth in its turn made possible the further appropriation of the wealth of other parts of the world. The profits of Congo rubber, Burmese teak or Indian cotton were for a long time not much to benefit those countries, whereas poor Europeans were long favoured by low prices for raw materials. The European peasant could buy cheap manufactured clothes and tools while contemporaries in Africa and India had still to live with, as it were, the technology of the Middle Ages.

Wealth was shared in large measure and power to some extent by the second circle where peoples of European origin exercised hegemony, that of the lands of European settlement overseas. The United States, Canada, Australia, New Zealand, South Africa and the countries of South America did not all stand on the same footing towards the Old World from which they were sprung, but shared important similarities, especially in their ideas and institutions, and in the ethnic origins of the dominant majorities of their populations. Of course, these were not all that had shaped them. They all had their distinctive origins and histories; they all had faced special environmental challenges and unique conjunctions of circumstances. But though different frontiers had reshaped their institutions in different ways, they provided certain shared responses to challenges; these lands were still all formally Christian (no one settled new lands in the name of atheism until the twentieth century), all regulated their affairs by European systems of law, and all had access to the mother cultures of Europe which gave them their languages.

These two zones together made up what has already been identified as the 'civilized world'; philanthropists and progressives long continued to be sure that its values should be offered, advocated and imposed as widely as were its medicine and sanitation. But there were native 'progressives' in many parts of the world who also often saw modernization and westernization as inseparable, tending benevolently towards the destruction of superstition and the bringing of such blessings as rational exploitation of resources, the provision of formal education and the suppression of bad customs. Only the blatantly reactionary and conservative overtly resisted the values of western civilization in favour of indigenous ones. That western values were often better is, of course, true. Unfortunately, the assumption that this was so usually went with a large obliviousness to side-effects they might have and to any merits of native institutions where they were introduced.

Alien peoples formed the third and outer concentric circle of this western (or Eurocentric) view of the world. Many of them were subject peoples, directly ruled by white-skinned superiors. Among them, it was usually believed, enlightened administrators toiled to bring the blessings of railways, western education, hospitals, law and order where local native institutions had clearly failed (it was taken as evidence of their inadequacy that they went down before the challenge and competition of a superior civilization embodied in empire). Beyond the subject peoples, though, lay others, alien but formally independent. They too were by no means untouched, and were sometimes shaped decisively, by western power. Sometimes their values and institutions were corroded by contact with it – as was the case in the Chinese and Ottoman empires – and this might lead to direct or indirect political interference (such as the capitulations first made with the Ottoman sultan in the sixteenth century to give protection to European merchants and their goods, or the intrusion of European officials to manage the customs services of China) and the weakening of traditional authority. Sometimes they were stimulated by such contacts, though Japan is the only example of a major nation clearly benefiting from this before the end of the nineteenth century.[14] To some countries,

---

[14] The special extra-territorial protection assured to Americans and Europeans in Japan by what were called the 'unequal' treaties earlier in the century was already abolished in the 1890s; this was not so elsewhere in Asia.

western values were transferred on the powerful wings of aspiration and envy. What was virtually impossible to achieve was immunity to western culture. The busy, bustling energy of the white trader itself made successful isolation rare and it did not need direct rule by white men to make western supremacy very visible. Geographical remoteness had been the best security and that had almost disappeared by the beginning of the century: even Tibet was to be invaded by the British in 1904. Ethiopia provided a solitary example of successful independence in Africa, having survived both British and Italian invasion in the nineteenth century; it had a special moral advantage in having been at least nominally a Christian country, albeit intermittently, for some fourteen centuries (its uniqueness should not be over-idealized: when it finally went under to European power in the 1930s, it was still a country of chattel slavery, feudal power and a substantial economic dependence on drug-trading).

Christianity had always been one of the most important agencies bringing European civilization to the rest of the world, because of the virtually limitless interest in all sides of human behaviour it had come to take in the course of nearly 2,000 years. The territorial spread overseas of the organized churches and the growth in their numbers of official adherents in the nineteenth century had made that the greatest age of Christian expansion since apostolic times. Much of this was the result of a renewed wave of evangelical activity; new Catholic missionary and teaching orders proliferated after 1800, and new societies for the support of overseas missions then appeared in Protestant countries.[15] Yet the paradoxical outcome was that a creed supposedly for all sorts and conditions of men had come to look more European than ever. In most of the receiving countries, Christianity was long seen as just one more aspect of white civilization, rather than as a spiritual message which might use a local idiom. A trivial example of the grounds for such a view was the excitement and concern missionaries often showed over dress. Whereas the Jesuits in the seventeenth century had discreetly adopted the costume of their hosts, the literati of China, their nineteenth-century Catholic and

---

[15] The Orthodox churches had shown notably less commitment to overseas missionary work.

Protestant successors had set to work with zeal to put Bantus and Solomon Islanders into European garments of outlandish and even freakish unsuitability. In this way as in others, Christianity brought with it more than a religious creed. Often, that included benign practices and material benefits: food in time of famine, agricultural techniques, hospitals and schools. Yet even such benefits could be disruptive. More ironically, missionaries at times prompted criticism of colonial regimes that protected and favoured them, doing so, sometimes consciously, sometimes unwittingly, by exposing gaps between the performance and the pretension of western civilization. Thus through their work too, the ambiguous effects of a progressive culture came to operate.

'ONE-HALF OF THE HUMAN SPECIES'[16]

It may seem to strain language somewhat in pursuit of a pedantic and formal point to say that the world can also be envisaged as divided in two halves by sex. Whatever the exact figures, and whether women did or did not then make up slightly over half the world's population, as they do today, it is nonetheless reasonable to say that their half of the human race was in 1901 for the most part in thrall to the other half. This was true round the world, in vastly differing degree and in many ways, but at every level of society. Overwhelmingly, and worldwide, human communities and cultures were at that time so engineered as to give immense advantages to men. Different societies have for a long time had different ways of treating women (it is odd that we so often put the point that way: we have rarely thought of societies as 'treating' the male sex in particular ways) and most of them for most of history have left their major decisions, including those about women, to be taken by men. Most countries have had their social and legal institutions biased towards men's interests, and have drawn their values from male-centred assumptions. This has not always meant they did not also have particular arrangements of

[16] A phrase used by William Godwin, 1798, in speaking of his wife, Mary Wollstonecraft, author of *A Vindication of the Rights of Woman* (1792), and defender of that 'one-half'.

positive benefit to women. Even those advantages, though, where they existed in 1901, have to be understood against a general background of overwhelming comparative disabilities standing in the way of most of the sex. Virtually nowhere could women be said to enjoy as much freedom or so high a legal status as men.

The French Revolution in its immense political fecundity had produced a 'Declaration of the Rights of Woman and the Citizen', but it was in the nineteenth century, in the wake of questioning that had already begun, that the first cracks had appeared in these structures and the assumptions that sustained them. They showed first in Europe and the United States. Eighteen forty-eight should be remembered not only for the revolutions of that year, but for the first Women's Rights Convention, summoned in the USA and traditionally seen as the foundation act of the world movement for women's suffrage. By 1914, two European countries (Finland and Norway) with New Zealand, the Commonwealth of Australia and eleven of the forty-eight United States had given women the vote. Some people had by then begun to speak of the 'liberation' of women from other sorts of traditional deprivations and constraints, too. Yet though what was called 'the woman question' had been posed in the nineteenth century in Europe and would soon be posed elsewhere, old practices and attitudes were still solidly entrenched worldwide as the century ended. By then just a few Hindu women had graduated from Indian universities, but virtually no Indian Muslim women had done so. Indeed, as the century began, Islamic society around the world showed no inclination to accept what might be thought to be the lessons of modernization in dealing with their womenfolk. Elsewhere, if the schooling of girls was firmly launched in Japan, even primary education had hardly touched their Chinese sisters; the first school in the country for girls opened in Shanghai in 1897, and within a couple of years it had closed again.

In the previous half-century, though, the area of debate over women's place in western societies had widened considerably, helped by general humanitarian concern and by pressure for individual rights and self-realization. In 1899 a congress had been held in London to consider the problem of what was called the 'white slave' trade, the international traffic in women for purposes of prostitution; in many countries the question of sexual exploitation of women was raised by people whose primary concerns might not be those of the women's movements themselves, but sprang from general moral and social principles and the claim of justice and equality before the law. The claims of women to education, to employment, to control of their own property, to moral independence, even to wear more comfortable clothes, were by then familiar and inflammatory themes for debate in western countries. Ibsen's play *A Doll's House* was interpreted as a trumpet-call for the liberation of women, though the author had intended only a plea for the individual in an unsatisfying marriage. The bringing forward of such issues at all reveals a real revolution already under way. By 1901, the words 'feminism' and 'feminist' had come (from France) to be well-established in English in association with the promotion of women's rights. The issues at stake awoke complex emotions, for they were linked to deep-seated ideas about the family and sexuality. They troubled and excited some men and women even more deeply than fears of social revolution or political democracy (a German 'League to Combat Women's Emancipation' was to be founded in 1912). People were right to see the question as one of large dimensions. In early feminism there was the seed of something of explosive content. Some men and women could see that even in 1901. Very few of them, though, were to be found outside the western world, and even within it the first feminists still formed a predominantly middle-class movement.

IDEAS WITH A FUTURE

The men and women of 1901 were the children of nineteenth-century parents, but it must be repeated that this meant different things in different places. In some parts of the world, the nineteenth century had merely maintained the prevailing assumptions of a more remote past. In some western countries, though, much of the material and mental reality which had made it possible to see the world as it could be seen in 1901 had only been put in place during the previous five or six decades. The nineteenth century had, indeed, been one of unprecedented historical change in every part of the world, a great creative and destructive era obliterating many old landmarks and throwing out much mental furniture. But this had been much more marked in the European-made world than elsewhere. Attitudes had changed more there than elsewhere.

The globe's physical unification had virtually been achieved in those years by men of European stock. Western geographical knowledge was almost complete; in 1847 Antarctica had been revealed to be a continent, even if the North and South poles were not to be reached by human beings until the early years of this century. But such knowledge, though soon available worldwide, was not used in the same way universally. By 1901, though, almost no part of the globe had been left undisturbed by western missionaries, explorers or soldiers. That meant that almost the whole of it had by then been mapped and penetrated by modernizing forces springing originally from Europe.

Communication across the globe had been revolutionized from the same source. The first steamship had crossed the Atlantic in 1819; in the next eighty years transcontinental railroads spanned North America and Siberia and the Suez Canal had been cut. Already by 1880 there were few areas far from the reach of the telegraph or a railroad. Twenty years later, cables crossed the floors of all the oceans, telephony was, if not universally familiar, at least well known in some countries, and radio-telephony was already emerging from the chrysalis of experiment. These innovations did not have the same disturbing force everywhere, but everywhere they were fundamentally disturbing to the status quo. To all intents and purposes the globe had become open to all humanity, and human beings were communicating and moving about in greater numbers than ever before. Technological progress helps to explain why there began after 1850 or so the greatest age of human migration that there had ever been in a comparable time-span, an age of wandering of peoples such as had not been seen for millennia, and on a much greater scale than ever before.

None of this meant that in 1901 any general ideas at all were shared by the majority of human beings. There were plenty of general ideas about, it is true, and they were often widely held among substantial segments of the world's population. That was a part of the reality of a world divided into still very distinguishable zones of civilization.

But there were very few, if any, except those shared by minorities and dominant cultural élites, that crossed all cultural boundaries.

Much less than today did different peoples share a common culture. One general idea held by numerous people in western countries, but almost nowhere else except by tiny numbers, was historically speaking very new; the twentieth century was almost certainly the first which opened with many people believing that what they might expect from life was change, rather than a continuation of things as they had been. Of course, mankind had long been used to the idea of sudden disaster; even in the nineteenth century there were many places where it was hardly a strange idea that a conqueror or raider might arrive, slaughter men in great numbers and carry off the harvest and the women.[17] Recurrent famine was still normal in many countries. But such local disasters were expected to be followed in due course by something of a resumption of old ways (unless, of course, a complete extinction of those who suffered them made that impossible). The warp and weft of daily life and the way people thought about it hardly changed much in predominantly agricultural and pastoral societies and the acceptance of occasional disaster was part of that.

In trying to express the weight of such facts, only the impressionistic truth of a sketch can be hoped for, not a scientific blueprint. This is not only because of the sheer scale of what we are trying to discuss, and its infinitely regressive detail, but because of inherent special difficulties in writing about the history of ideas. Just as greatly as – sometimes more greatly than – by material facts, general history is shaped by ideas. They shape it, nonetheless, in ways very hard to talk about, and at many different levels, some almost concealed from us. Traditionally, the 'history of ideas' emphasizes the rational and articulate (by no means always the same thing), and concerns itself especially with the thoughts of self-selected members of literate élites, intellectuals, writers and orators. This approach shades off sometimes to include ideas embodied in institutions – in law, for example – and those that are, in a currently fashionable term, 'structural'; the general notions that set terms to particular debates. They, in turn, bring us

---

[17] After a recession of these traditional dangers, they were, of course, to become familiar again in some African countries in the last quarter of the twentieth century.

to the edge of the vast, amorphous topic of generally and widely shared ideas and notions, often expressed as much in the behaviour as in the explicit utterance of large numbers of men and women. Such familiar features of the mental landscape can be summed up as 'the inherited conglomerate', to borrow a phrase from a different context.[18] It is impossible to say very much that is helpful about them, inherited or still in evolution, though their presence is easily recognized.

THE SCIENTIFIC LEGACY

Perhaps, though, it can be agreed that any attempt to say anything about states of mind and the influences shaping them in the twentieth century must give a dominant place to the intellectual and mythological importance of science. This is, or should be, as evident as, for instance, the dominance we can recognize being exercised by religion, or even magic, to shape history through culture in the past. Science is a ubiquitous, inescapable presence in modern history and it has moulded this century as no earlier one. Its influence now pervades most of the world and determines human behaviour as never before. It is as important to the cultural history of our age as to the material, and it is often woefully under-estimated, unrecognized or misunderstood. We have to recognize, in order to understand it, that its success is rooted in earlier centuries. Science was the most important part of the many creative legacies already in place in western societies as this century began.

Although the long view is once again the best one, to look back in detail to the roots of this phenomenon is not necessary, any more than it is necessary to look at the ultimate origins of the great religions or the invention of agriculture, important as they are. It is sufficient to recognize that one of the features that came to characterize western civilization was the emergence in it three or four centuries ago of the new form of knowledge that is science. This knowledge was built on investigation of the natural world and was always linked to aspirations to take more control of that world by understanding it. In the nine-

---

[18] It was used by the Australian scholar Gilbert Murray in a lecture of that title, reprinted in his book *Greek Studies*.

teenth century science came to acquire an intellectual primacy over most other forms of knowledge to which human beings had looked before that time. The word 'scientist' came into use to identify someone who explored the positive and measurable, gradually acquiring more and more knowledge whose significance was cumulative. Whether immediately of practical utility or not, what scientists, virtually all of them 'western', did in the nineteenth century was more than ever seen as a contribution to the further understanding of nature and as tending, in the end, to make her more manageable by humanity, even by laymen.

This lies behind the deepest change of all to which science was to contribute in this century, and the most difficult to trace as a specific process. Besides immeasurably enlarging our practised ability to control and exploit nature, it has helped to bring about an equally immeasurable expansion in countries all round the world of ordinary people's notions of what is possible. This most revolutionary change in the human mind was almost entirely the work of the twentieth century, and came about indirectly, largely through what was done by technology to show the difference science could make to human life. That is a topic of which much more will have to be said. But it was also important that science changed, first in the western world, and eventually in other cultures, the thinking of educated men and women. This had already begun long before 1901.

In the nineteenth century, ideas about the natural world were put forward which set out the basis for twentieth-century thinking about many questions of human life and behaviour, just as Copernicus and Newton in their day had set out ideas which came to dominate for centuries men's visions of the way the world worked. One of the few moments when such a change can be specifically seen to emerge came in 1859. An English naturalist, Charles Darwin, then published his most famous book, usually remembered by its short title: *The Origin of Species*.[19] It drew on work done by other men, and the word with which Darwin's name was always thereafter to be associated,

---

[19] Fully, *On the Origin of Species by means of Natural Selection, or the Preservation of Favoured Races in the struggle for Life*. The word 'Races', it may be helpful to point out, was not used here in reference to human variety. The entire first edition of 1,250 copies sold out on the day of publication and a second edition followed in 1860.

'evolution', was already familiar when he wrote (he did not use it in his own book until its fifth edition, ten years after first publication). Nevertheless, he set out, in a country and at a time which were especially propitious for excited debate on many associated topics, the most effective single statement of an evolutionary hypothesis in biology that there has ever been.[20] In essence, Darwin said that living things were what they were, and had the physical forms they had, because their forerunners had evolved from other and simpler forms, and that the process of such evolution was likely to have been very accidental, being determined by the selection imposed by climatic, botanical and geographical circumstance. The impact of this idea was all the greater when Darwin went on to emphasize that the evolutionary process embraced *The Descent of Man*, the title he gave to another book in 1871. He had been much impressed by the account given by Thomas Malthus at the beginning of the century of humanity's recurrent competition for finite resources (food, above all), and he put forward the view that the 'natural selection' which he had identified as the culling and conserving device which drove forward biological evolution worked through the presence or absence in plants and animals of qualities which favoured or disabled their possessors in potentially hostile environments.

This part of his teaching was vastly influential beyond the world of formal biology but all too soon was also often hideously misrepresented and misunderstood. In vulgarized form it was taken to imply something called the 'survival of the fittest' – a phrase Darwin did not use – and by the beginning of the twentieth century this notion was familiar enough to be widely misconstrued. It was, for example, widely taken to indicate a supposed superiority of white peoples over those of other colours. Yet great though even such a perverted impact might be, it was only secondary. Like other secondary impacts of his ideas it was almost certainly dwarfed in Darwin's own day and later by the almost casual blow he had given to the biblical account of creation, which had served Christianity as a central myth for 1,000 years. The ecclesiastical authorities that upheld or imposed this

[20] The first bibliography of books and articles on 'Darwinism' was published in Berlin in 1872. Though incomplete, it could already list 315 authors writing in all the major European languages.

account were bound to suffer with it. Far-reaching as this was, though, even this does not reveal Darwin's true importance; other scientists in other disciplines – geology, for instance – had already begun to undermine scriptural accounts of creation. Darwin's ultimate importance was scientific. He transformed biology as fundamentally as Newton had transformed cosmology. He provided the hypothesis that since his day has dominated and provided the ground plan of what are now called the 'life sciences'.

The other achievement of nineteenth-century science that had by 1901 already crucially changed views of the way the natural world worked had come in the physical sciences. It was collective; no single name dominates this story as Darwin's has dominated that of the sciences of life, though the work on electromagnetism done in the 1870s by James Clerk Maxwell, the first professor of experimental physics at the university of Cambridge, can be seen as the opening of the process. He made possible a cumulative supersession of physical theories that had served science well since the days of Newton. The classical view of the universe as essentially a system of lumps of matter, indestructible in essence and obeying a few well-observed laws, though capable of arrangement and rearrangement in various combinations, had now to be modified to allow for the existence of electromagnetic fields, thanks to Maxwell. The further investigations which solved the theoretical problems this raised were advanced by other nineteenth-century pioneers; in the 1880s Hertz provided experimental confirmation of some of Clerk Maxwell's ideas by discovering electro-magnetic waves, then came Röntgen who discovered X-rays, Becquerel who discovered radioactivity, Thomson who identified the electron, the Curies who isolated radium and, in the twentieth century, Rutherford who carried out the investigation of the atom's structure.[21] The physical world began to look different. The particles that were now shown to make up atoms (they began to look like tiny solar systems rather than solids) turned out to behave in a way that blurred the distinction between matter and electromagnetic fields. Moreover, the arrangements of such particles were not fixed, for in

[21] The first paper by Rutherford whose title included the word 'radiation' was presented in 1899, to the Royal Society of Canada.

nature one arrangement might give way to another and thus elements could change into other elements. Rutherford, in particular, showed that atoms could be 'split' because of their structure. Matter, therefore, could be manipulated at a fundamental level (though when as late as 1935 Rutherford said that nuclear physics would have no practical implications, no one rushed to contradict him).

The story of physics has to be taken just a little further and into the new century, for a new theoretical framework to replace the Newtonian order and take account of new experimental evidence was not achieved until the 1920s. By 1905 Max Planck and Albert Einstein had shown that Newtonian laws of motion could not explain a fact by then incontestable: energy transactions in the material world took place not in an even flow but in discrete jumps – quanta, as they came to be termed. Planck showed that radiant heat (from, for example, the sun) was not, as Newtonian physics required, emitted continuously and argued that this was true of all energy transactions; Einstein argued that light was propagated not continuously but in particles. Yet though Newton's views might be challenged by such new facts, there was still nothing to put in their place.

Einstein, after his work on quanta, published in 1905 the work for which he was to be most famed; though hardly widely understood, his statement of the theory of relativity demonstrated that the traditional distinctions of space and time, and mass and energy, could not be consistently maintained. He directed attention beyond Newton's three-dimensional physics to a 'space-time continuum' in which the interplay of space, time and motion could be properly understood. Soon this was corroborated by observation of astronomical facts for which Newtonian cosmology could not properly account, but Einstein's could. One strange and unanticipated consequence of the work on which relativity theory was based was a new formulation of the relations of mass and energy. The importance and accuracy of this theoretical formulation was not to be clear until much more nuclear physics had been done; it would then be apparent that the relationships observed when mass energy was converted into heat energy in the breaking up of nuclei also corresponded to this formula.

While these advances were absorbed, attempts to rewrite nuclear physics continued, and only in 1926 did a major theoretical break-

through finally provide a mathematical framework for Planck's observations. So sweeping was the achievement of Schrödinger and
Heisenberg, the two mathematicians mainly responsible, that it seemed
for a time as if quantum mechanics might be of virtually limitless
explanatory power in the sciences. The behaviour of particles in the
atom others had observed could now be accounted for. Quantum
mechanics seemed to have inaugurated a new age of physics, and
there, for the moment, the story can be left.

It remains hard for laymen and at the time was hard for many
scientists to grapple with such ideas. In other fields, too, nineteenth-
century science had great achievements to its credit – Mendeleyev's
formulation of a 'periodic table' of elements, and the establishment
(above all by Pasteur) of the germ theory of disease – whose implications would not yet be discerned. But in sixty years or so after 1870,
a great turning point in the history of the physical sciences was passed,
the most important since the seventeenth-century discoveries which
had culminated in the dazzling achievements of Newton, and this, for
all its confinement at first to a limited, scientifically literate world,
was to be as revolutionary in its effect as had been Darwin's work.
For all its mathematical complexity, Newton's universe had seemed
essentially and in principle simple. In part, it owed its sweeping success
in achieving domination over the western imagination and thought
to the fact that laymen could grasp a few fundamental laws. The
discoveries of twentieth-century science, though, were to remain baf-
flingly obscure. Laymen could not easily understand them even in
outline. The whole familiar notion of general laws, indeed, tended to
be replaced by the view that statements about what was statistically
probable were the best which could be hoped for in the way of general
views about nature. Science was to move away from the model of laws
and systems so influential in the nineteenth century. Paradoxically,
twentieth-century humanity was to be more aware of the importance
of science than its predecessors and to show more faith than ever
before in it, without any such hope of widespread understanding of
it such as past generations had indulged.

MOVERS AND SHAKERS

Only tiny minorities of Indians, Chinese and even Japanese would have been aware of the vigour of western science as the century began, or shared the idea that change was an inevitable feature of human history. Yet substantial numbers of people, overwhelmingly in Europe, North America and the white settler nations, already then took it for granted that the world was a dynamic place, and that change would be an inevitable feature of the future. For some of them already, this acceptance was quite conscious; it could be and was deduced by them from the evidence of what science and technology had already done to their lives and those of their immediate predecessors. The texture of day-to-day existence had been measurably and notably dramatically improved in many specifics since their grandparents' day; for example, they could expect longer lives. The moderately well-off, those most likely to reflect upon such things, could feel that their circumstances were more comfortable than a few years before, too, and they enjoyed great advantages of communication over their predecessors. They were tempted, often, to the complacent assumption that the benefits they enjoyed would be more and more widely shared (which they were indeed to turn out to be), and that this must be ultimately beneficial to mankind (which was by no means to be so unambiguously the case in the next 100 years).

The presence of this attitude was one of the cultural facts differentiating the 'western' world from the rest as this century began. It may well have been the most important. While many societies and cultures had throughout history from time to time thrown up minorities which believed in, announced, or prepared for coming change in the form of supernatural and apocalyptic events, and while millenarian sects had often briefly prospered, their influence had been marginal. Perhaps it was only in the eighteenth century that more than a significant few in Europe and North America had begun to sense that a new historical trend, different from the past, might lie ahead and that it would or ought to be brought on as quickly as possible by conscious human effort. In their eyes, the future had at last begun to look different — benevolent, and, above all, progressive. This was one of the most

important legacies of what is called the Enlightenment. In the nineteenth century, it encouraged specific demands for reform and
improvement; the anti-slavery movement was only one conspicuous
example, and hundreds of other particular goals were identified and
agitated by reformers in Europe and North America as the century
went on. They all helped to reinforce the assumption that historical
change was normal, and that it was likely to be progressive. By 1901
even a very few people in some parts of the non-western world were
beginning to share such ideas.

This may be regarded as the ultimate triumph down to that date
of the civilization that had spread its aspirations and hopes, as well
as its manipulative strengths, all round the world in the nineteenth
century. It was an extraordinary achievement, and one whose origins
and most of whose apparent strengths could still 100 years ago be
traced directly to their European sources. Some of its expressions were
unintended, ambiguous, such as those that followed the spread of
European languages. They brought with them European concepts and
opened to educated men and women in non-European countries the
heritage not only of Christian civilization, but of secular and 'enlightened' European culture, too. Even the simple urge to imitate (such as
was expressed in the adoption of European dress or, much more
importantly, in the conclusion already drawn by many who sought
to resist European hegemony, that it was necessary to adopt European
ways to do so successfully) spread this cultural contamination. Almost
everywhere, radicals and reformers advocated Europeanization. The
example of the Russian Peter the Great was a commonplace on the
lips of non-Europeans who sought to modernize at the turn of the
century as the ideas of 1776, 1789 and 1848 got to work in Asia and
Africa. This extraordinary one-way effect is too often overlooked
or undervalued. The balance sheet of cultural influence was to be
overwhelmingly one-sided. While the teaching of Marx has been a
force throughout twentieth-century Asia, the last non-European whose
words had any comparable influence in shaping the west was Jesus
Christ. The world gave back to Europe occasional fashions, but no
idea or institution of comparable effect to those Europe gave to the
world.

An Englishman coined the phrase 'movers and shakers' two-thirds or so of the way through the nineteenth century. He had musicians in mind, and could not have expected that his words would find new life and wider reference in common parlance over a century later, when his own name had been forgotten except by specialists.[22] It could already have been taken up, though, had they wished it, by thoughtful Europeans of his day, to apply to themselves. Their continent was at the beginning of this century still providing most of the dynamic of world history, just as it had done for three centuries or so since it launched modern history. The revolutionary repercussions of what went on in Europe had continued to roll round the globe and would still do so. Willingly and unwittingly, Europeans had forced the rest of humanity out of self-absorption and towards participation for the first time in a world history. The history of the twentieth century has therefore to be approached with (what is sometimes deplored) a 'Eurocentric' stance. In many ways, the world actually was centred on Europe when the twentieth century began. Much of that century's story is of how and why that ceased to be true before it ended.

[22] The poet Arthur Edgar William O'Shaughnessy, who wrote (in 'The Music-makers'): 'Yet we are the movers and shakers of the world forever, it seems'.

2

Structures

HUMAN NUMBERS

Whether we choose to see the world in terms of political, cultural, economic or any other divisions of the human race, we come in the end to numbers. Changes in the way population is distributed are the bedrock of general history. In each of the vast majority of the thousands of years recorded by human history the number of people alive has gone up: long-term growth is the predominant characteristic of global demography. Once the huge implications of the invention and spread of agricultural systems over most of the world had begun to operate (around the beginning of the Christian era), the process was almost continuous though for a long time a slow one. There were fluctuations in the rate and even sudden temporary setbacks lasting some years, such as the fourteenth-century 'Black Death' that brought about a steep fall in the population of northern and western Europe shortly after a comparable onslaught in China. Usually, though, a few generations were enough to repair even such grave demographic damage, and for growth to be resumed.[1] Over the last millennium there began a steepening and, lately, sharp rise in the rate of that growth. It appears first patchily and gradually in Sung China and late medieval Europe and then more rapidly and universally. In the last three or four

---

[1] An important topic that cannot be examined here, but for an introduction see W. H. McNeill, *Plagues and Peoples* (New York, 1976). This is perhaps also the place to draw attention to the essay by the same author in *The Oxford History of the Twentieth Century* (Oxford, 1998), an unrivalled starting-point for the consideration of twentieth-century population history, though it appeared after this book was written.

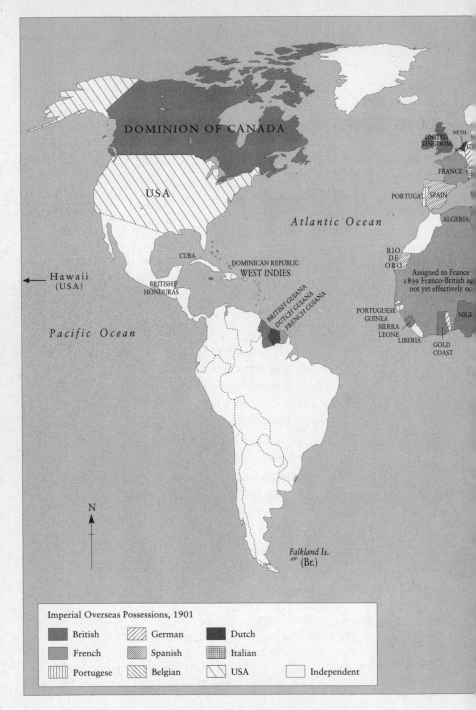

DOMINION OF CANADA

USA

Atlantic Ocean

United Kingdom
NETH.
G
FRANCE
PORTUGAL SPAIN
ALGERIA

CUBA
DOMINICAN REPUBLIC
WEST INDIES

Hawaii
(USA)

BRITISH
HONDURAS

RIO
DE
ORO

Assigned to France
1899 Franco-British as
not yet effectively oc

BRITISH GUIANA
DUTCH GUIANA
FRENCH GUIANA

PORTUGUESE
GUINEA
SIERRA
LEONE
LIBERIA

NIGI

GOLD
COAST

Pacific Ocean

N

Falkland Is.
(Br.)

Imperial Overseas Possessions, 1901

British

German

Dutch

French

Spanish

Italian

Portugese

Belgian

USA

Independent

Imperial overseas possessions, 1901

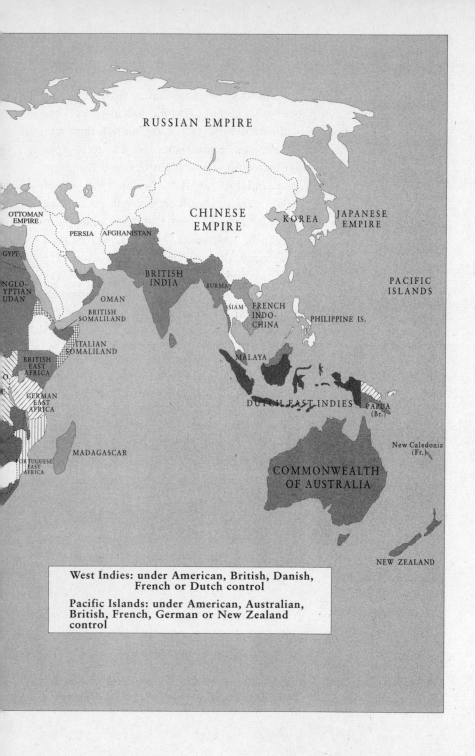

RUSSIAN EMPIRE

OTTOMAN
EMPIRE

CHINESE
EMPIRE

KOREA

JAPANESE
EMPIRE

PERSIA AFGHANISTAN

GYPT

NGLO-
YPTIAN
UDAN

OMAN

BRITISH
INDIA

BURMA

PACIFIC
ISLANDS

BRITISH
SOMALILAND

SIAM

FRENCH
INDO-
CHINA

PHILIPPINE IS.

ITALIAN
SOMALILAND

BRITISH
EAST
AFRICA

MALAYA

O

GERMAN
EAST
AFRICA

DUTCH EAST INDIES

PAPUA
(Br.)

New Caledonia
(Fr.)

MADAGASCAR

PORTUGUESE
EAST
AFRICA

COMMONWEALTH
OF AUSTRALIA

NEW ZEALAND

West Indies: under American, British, Danish,
French or Dutch control

Pacific Islands: under American, Australian,
British, French, German or New Zealand
control

centuries, rates of growth began to go up everywhere. In the course of the second half of the eighteenth century and the nineteenth, the total world population appears to have rather more than doubled, from about 720 million in 1750 to about 1,600 million in 1900. This was a huge speeding-up of the process of increasing human numbers but it was only a beginning; even more rapid increase was to follow.

Down to the end of the nineteenth century, Europe had for some centuries led the world in population growth. Before 1798, when Malthus published the epoch-marking book that began to change people's thinking on the subject,[2] it had recently been thought there that a rising population was to be welcomed. Malthus may be said to have turned round the accepted ideas of his day and society. He awoke a new concern that population might outrun food supply. Yet by 1901 fear of the demographic future had again somewhat subsided; increasing human numbers had been carried without apparent diffi-culty by growing resources in western countries, where growth in numbers had recently been fastest. Nonetheless, numbers would con-tinue to increase, and there were persuasive signs that they would do so at an accelerating rate. Uneasiness therefore continued to be voiced from time to time in western societies, and notably over such new concerns as, for example, the balance between what were then identi-fied as 'races' and regions. Some talked in 1901 about a 'Yellow Peril' whose basis was the sheer numerical preponderance of Far East Asians. Virtually no interest in population questions was shown, though, by anyone in the non-western world.

The 1,600 million or so human beings alive in 1901 were shared between the peopled continents roughly as follows:

[2] The first edition of his *Essay on Population* set out what Malthus took to be ineluctable laws of population growth and the pressure it was bound to exercise on growing but finite resources of food. Its influence was to go far beyond demographic science into, for example, economics and biology (Darwin had been much impressed by it).

	Millions	Percentage of total world population (to nearest 0.25 per cent)
Europe	390	24
Asia	970	59.5
Africa	110	6.75
South America and the Caribbean	64	3.9
North America	82	5
Australasia and Oceania	7	0.4

In that year nearly one in every four human beings lived north of the Mediterranean and west of the Ural mountains in the sub-continental peninsula jutting out from Asia, which had been for some centuries called 'Europe'. These were the Europeans proper. But overseas lived over a 100 million other people of European descent. Those in the United States and former British colonies were the 'English-speaking' peoples, wherever they might have come from and whatever languages they originally spoke. Most of the rest were to be found in Latin America. These countries had been the main recipients of what has been called the 'Great Resettlement' of Europeans in other continents, the culmination of an era of demographic history, and a fact of huge importance. Over the whole nineteenth century, about 60 million Europeans had emigrated to them. At the same time, a smaller, easily overlooked but also important movement overland towards the eastern provinces of the Russian empire (which nominally occupied one-sixth of the world's land surface, most of it empty) was going on. Yet the high tide of European emigration was still to come. In 1913 alone over a million and a half people left Europe to go overseas; over a third of them were Italians, nearly 400,000 were British and 200,000 were Spanish. Fifty years earlier, Germans and Scandinavians had loomed much larger in the passenger lists. The British Isles had always contributed heavily to the flow; from 1880 to 1910 8.5 million British subjects, many from Ireland, went abroad, most of them before 1901 to the United States, but the ratio changed in the new century in favour of the self-governing British colonies. By 1914 they were taking the majority of migrating Britons. Italians tended to prefer the

United States, though they (and the Spaniards) went to South America in large numbers, too. This diaspora profoundly influenced Europeans' ways of thinking about the world. It also confirmed a world map dominated politically in 1901 by the white peoples; large-scale resettlement was the final expression of those technical and governmental advantages over other peoples that the Europeans had begun to enjoy even in the sixteenth century.

The migration of European peoples was also a migration of ideas. They took with them to their new homes (and their descendants continue to this day to use) certain mental and cultural furniture that, whatever special arrangement or adaptations it underwent as they grappled with climate, topography, aboriginal inhabitants and economic opportunity, provided the basic structures of their beliefs and behaviour. Those structures therefore retained much that was European, with all its variety. It is of huge importance, for instance, that while the Christianity first introduced into Central and South America was that of the late medieval crusading Catholicism of reconquest Spain, that which shaped so much of North America was Protestant. It is of even greater importance, and possibly overlooked because so obvious, that *all* the Americas were captured by Europeans for Europeans. As a result, Christianity, whatever its local forms, long pervaded the dominant ideologies of American cultures, North and South, while its institutions provided much of their articulation. The world would be radically different today if the Americas had been colonized by Confucian Chinese, or Muslim Africans.

So far as continental Europe itself was concerned, its fastest population growth was over by 1901. By then it had slowed down in the continent's most developed and prosperous countries, where population growth (though it went on) had come to depend more and more on falling death-rates and less and less on the number of births. In such countries a few people had begun to accept that conscious restriction of family numbers was advisable, perhaps because it seemed more practicable than ever before. In much of eastern and Mediterranean Europe, though, those demographic trends were hardly yet observable; neither the attitudes, nor up-to-date knowledge nor the technical apparatus for effective contraception were available there, except among a very few. In the great agrarian slums of the Italian

Mezzogiorno and the valleys of the Danube and Guadalquivir, population went on shooting up well into the new century. Because there was always an outlet through emigration, and infant mortality was still high, the strains of over-population in the poorer parts of Europe did not become quite unbearable. Only a few pessimists worried about what would happen if emigrants ceased to be welcome in countries of European settlement overseas. Much more alarming reflexions, of course, occurred to those Europeans, probably even fewer, who speculated about what would happen when the agencies that had already so reduced death rates in Europe began to operate in Asia and Africa. Yet in the world that the nineteenth century had created, so much more interconnected than that of any earlier age, such influences and their effects could hardly be contained. Europe's very success in imposing its civilization on the world guaranteed the disappearance of the demographic advantage that had helped to spread its civilization in the first place as those agencies came to operate.

Besides emigration, Europe's rapid population growth had been buoyed up for a half-century or so by economic expansion and new employment. Larger numbers had been carried relatively easily by growing wealth. In the last thirty years of the nineteenth century, for example (and the first thirty of her life as a united nation), Germany's output of pig-iron, a very basic industrial commodity, had risen sixfold while her population rose by only about a third. In their consumption of goods and services, in their life expectation, and perhaps even in their general health, most people in the world's developed countries were better off in 1901 than their forebears had been a century earlier. That did not mean, of course, that Russian or Andalusian peasants shared equally in such an improvement with Pittsburgh steelworkers or British railwaymen; all such comparisons have little value except in the crudest terms. Nonetheless, even in poorer countries in the western world it seemed that the keys had been found to a growing prosperity that was more and more widely shared. The likelihood that this state of affairs would continue seemed high in 1901.

The Americas had been the greatest single recipient of European emigrants. Politics and persecutions had helped and rising populations always pressed on economic opportunities in Europe, as the nineteenth-century discovery of the phenomenon of 'unemployment' (and invention of the word) shows. In the last decades of the nineteenth century, too, when emigration was rising fastest, European farmers began to be seriously affected by overseas competition. There were obvious opportunities in the other continents where land was plentiful and labour was needed, at a moment when there were suddenly easier and cheaper means of getting there, too. The new possibilities offered by steamship and railroad began to show their greatest effect after 1880. Great Britain exported Irish peasants, Welsh miners and steel-workers and English labourers; she took in at the end of the nineteenth century Jews from eastern Europe. Many of these were to remain, though many more (above all from the Russian Pale) were to go on to settle finally in North America. Railways made temporary migrations of labour easier, too; to the seasonal migration of labour long characterizing, for instance, southern France, were now added longer-term movements as Poles came to Flanders to work in coal-mines and Italian waiters and ice-cream sellers became part of British folklore. There were even Italians in the first decade of the century who migrated seasonally across the Atlantic to help bring in the Argentinian grain harvest. As political change made the North African shore accessible, it, too, became the object of settlement from Europe; Italians, Spaniards and Frenchmen were drawn there to farm, or trade in the coastal cities of Algeria and Tunisia. There they created new societies with interests distinct both from those of the countries from which the migrants had come and from those of the native peoples beside which they had settled.

Nor was easier travel of benefit only to European migrants. There had been enough Chinese and Japanese settlement on the Pacific coasts of North America by 1901 already to provoke white local hostility. Japanese also went to South America and Chinese migrants down into south-east Asia (so frightening Australians, who already sought to pre-serve a 'White Australia' by limiting immigration by ethnic criteria). The British empire provided a huge framework within which Indian merchants and labourers spread round the world. But these movements, though important, were for a long time less striking than the last great *Völkerwanderung* of the European peoples, the greatest migratory fact of the nineteenth and early twentieth centuries and one as influential for the future as had been the Dark Age barbarian migrations.

THE WORLD'S WEALTH

Other than as a question of racial balance the problem of world population was also sometimes seen in Malthusian terms, as one of feeding the human race. Yet those who thought about these things could look back with growing reassurance, in spite of Malthus. There had been for half a century a huge rise in world food production, above all in the Americas, Australasia and those parts of Africa suitable for European settlement. It was achieved partly through better farming practice, partly through improved communications, partly through a vast increase in the area of cultivated and exploited land. The first of these trends looked set to continue, and was indeed to do so. Yet though this long story of improvement had already changed the face of much of the Americas, it had hardly begun to affect Asia and Africa except indirectly. Though there had already been many instances of the movement of vegetable and animal species between continents, agricultural habits and methods changed more slowly in the non-western world than in the western. For thousands of years farmers everywhere had edged their returns upwards almost entirely by clearing and breaking in new land, and millions of Africans and Asians were still doing that in 1901. But the agricultural revolution that had begun in late medieval Europe was, as the twentieth century began, still under way, speeding up faster than ever. Automation, chemical interference, genetic manipulation would be the twentieth-century chapters in the story that had begun with the terracing of hillsides, transhumance and enclosure, and had continued through better husbandry and selective breeding, clearance and draining, the first steam-driven agricultural machinery, and many other innovations. For most of its long history this process had been unplanned, casual and reactive. In the twentieth century it would be more consciously the product of public intervention, directed research and commercial decision. A process begun empirically centuries ago by observant European farmers would continue under the guidance of bacteriologists, chemists and engineers, to become worldwide and bring about a still more intensive and extensive utilization of the physical environment to produce food.

Not only had food supply grown, so had the supply of other resources. Minerals (iron, bauxite) and vegetable products (hardwoods and plant oils) for manufacturing economies, coal and petroleum oil for the world's power supplies were all commodities much in demand in 1901, vigorously searched for and rapidly exploited when found. Many of the basic materials needed by manufacturing industry, though, were at that date still supplied by the natural or agricultural resources of the manufacturing countries themselves. Both Europe and the United States were rich in virtually all the minerals their industries required; they were favoured in the geographical layout of the world's resources. Yet the demand for minerals would rise, and with it that for other material resources – rubber, scarce metals, vegetable oils – which would be consumed in enormous quantities by growing populations.

The possible dangers of unpredictable and uncontrolled growth did not much worry people in 1901. There was so much of the world still to exploit. Questions are now asked about the sustainability of societies and the levels of consumption to which we have become used, but of such concern little was heard as the century began. There are now nearly four times as many people alive as there were then, yet, in an age of rising expectations, rising consumption has been sustained by rising output. The needs of most have been met as never before. Broadly, this has been done by intensifying efforts to increase the production of food, fossil fuels and minerals and by engineering new energy resources. In 1901 successful prospecting was going forward all round the world and electricity produced by steam turbines and hydroelectric investment was already a major source of power.

COMMERCE

In 1901 there were already true global markets. Although they had been coming into existence over the previous three centuries, nevertheless, for the direct experience of most of the human race, this meant little; what mattered were very local markets. Though prices set far away might be in fact very relevant to rubber-growers in the Congo, or to peasants weaving their own fabrics in India, as individuals they were, like the great majority of Asians and Africans, unaware of what determined the prices they could get. Yet to sustain the system of exchange that governed the distribution of the world's resources, the most elaborate, geographically widespread commercial networks ever yet seen had come to maturity in the nineteenth century. Their centre and focus was by 1901 Europe. The obvious broad distinction of world roles between industrial manufacturing and primary producer countries (the second tending to meet the needs of the increasingly urbanized populations of the first) springs to the eye, but it is much too crude to be unqualified. The outstanding example of a country that did not fit it was the United States, in 1914 a huge primary producer, the world's leading manufacturer and a great debtor nation. Its industrial output in that year already equalled those of Great Britain, France and Germany combined.

Nor did distinctions of primary producers and manufacturers run solely between nations of European and non-European culture. Japan and Russia were both industrializing faster than China or India in 1914, but Russia, though European, could certainly not yet be regarded as a developed economy, and most of the Russian labour force (like that of Japan, or, for that matter, though in lesser degree, of France) worked in agriculture. Most western European peoples were not then predominantly engaged in manufacturing; nor could a developed economy in a modern sense be found anywhere in Balkan Europe. It can safely be asserted, though, that a nucleus of countries then already existed whose social and economic structures were very advanced and different from those of more traditional societies, and that these were the core of the group of nations that had long been the centre of the world's commercial system, and the richest among them.

London focused the financial services sustaining and lubricating world trade and a huge amount of the world's business was transacted by means of sterling bills of exchange. An international gold standard sustained confidence by ensuring that the main currencies remained in fairly steady relationships with one another. There might be small fluctuation but, for example, the pound sterling would usually buy from \$4.80 to \$4.90 in United States currency. Most major countries had currencies redeemable in fixed amount of gold, and all of them minted gold coins; travel anywhere in the world was possible with a bag of gold sovereigns, five-dollar pieces, gold francs or any other major currency without any doubts about their acceptability.

By 1901, the United Kingdom's gross manufacturing output was less in some ways than that of either the United States or Germany, but she retained in one economic respect world leadership: she was the greatest of trading nations, importing and exporting more than any other country. She was also the only one sending more of its manufactures to non-European markets than to European. The bulk of the world's shipping and carrying trade was in British hands. So was most of the world's commercial insurance business. As the world's biggest exporter of capital, Great Britain also drew a huge income from overseas investments, notably in the United States and South America. Her special role gave much of international trade a roughly triangular shape. The British bought goods, manufactured and otherwise, from Europe and paid for them with their own manufactures, cash and overseas produce. To the rest of the world they exported manufactures, minerals and capital and sold services, taking in return food, raw materials and cash. This complex system itself illustrates how little the European relationship with the rest of the world was merely a matter of exchanging manufactures for primary produce. And there was, of course, always the unique instance of the United States, little involved in exporting agricultural commodities, but gradually commanding a greater and greater share of its own domestic market for manufactured goods, and still a capital importer. In money value, most international commerce was carried on, as it still is, between the most developed countries.

British economists and businessmen still tended to say that the prosperity of this system and the increasing wealth it made possible demonstrated the truth of the Free Trade doctrine that had triumphed in debates between their nineteenth-century forebears. Their own country's prosperity had grown most rapidly in the heyday of the idea that non-interference with commerce, and the reduction of tariffs and duties on the movement of goods, was bound to advance general prosperity. British foreign policy had often been directed to the opening of countries and regions closed to trade, for that was where the road to prosperity was deemed to lie. For a while in the middle of the nineteenth century it even seemed that other governments might be catching the Free Trade infection, but that era passed. By 1901 Great Britain was the only major nation without tariffs for protection. Nevertheless, the economic world of the early twentieth century was one of great economic freedom in contrast both to the not-so-distant past and to what was soon to follow. A long peace between great powers had provided a stability in which trading connexions could mature. Sound currencies assured great flexibility to a world price system; exchange controls existed nowhere in the world. Freight and insurance rates had grown cheaper and cheaper, food and other commodity prices had gone down, long-term and real wages had gone up. Interest rates and taxation levels were low.

As this system had grown to incorporate Asia and Africa it helped to diffuse ideas and techniques originally European, but soon acclimatized in other lands. Joint stock companies, banks, commodity and stock exchanges spread round the world by intrusion and imitation, supplementing or displacing traditional and local structures of commerce. The building of docks and railways, the infrastructure of world trade, together with the beginnings of industrial employment, had already begun in some non-western countries to turn peasants into waged proletarians. Sometimes the effects of involvement in the new patterns of world trade could be bad for traditional occupations and interests: the cultivation of indigo in India, for example, had more or less collapsed when synthetic dyes became available in Germany and Great Britain. Non-commercial relationships were being transformed, too; the canal opened at Suez in 1869 not only affected British commerce but British strategy, giving the Mediterranean new historical importance, not this time as a centre of special civilization, but as a route. Soon, in 1914, a canal would open across the isthmus of Panama, and direct communication by railway would be possible from Europe to Vladivostok.

The world of 1901 was indeed a rich place in comparison with even a century earlier. It was not hard to predict that it would become richer. It would have been much harder, though, to envisage the sheer scale of the next 100 years' increase in wealth and the startling contrasts that would open up in the consumption of world resources. Today, roughly one half of mankind consumes about six-sevenths of the world's production; the other half shares the rest. Things were not quite as skewed as that in 1901, for all the violent contrasts reflected in, for instance, mortality rates and life expectancies.

STATES AND GOVERNMENTS

Another very visible and accomplished fact of the world of 1901 was the presence worldwide of a particular form of political organization: the territorial sovereign state. It was still not universally the dominant political form at the outset of this century. In some parts of the world the ground plan of international organization and government was set in remote, even ancient, history. In a merely formal sense, China was still what she had claimed to be for millennia, an empire containing the largest body of population governed as one entity anywhere in the world. Most of the world's political units were much younger than that. The oldest political institution in Europe was the Roman Papacy, but England, France, Spain and Portugal all proudly traced their territorial and national histories back into the Middle Ages. Even the United States of America, with more than a century of independent life behind it, was older than most European states in 1901.[3] The Ottoman empire had been a political reality longer than any of its neighbours and could be traced back to the fourteenth century (or, even earlier, to the adoption of the title of sultan by its ruler). It still

[3] Setting aside such tiny antiquities as Monaco, San Marino, the bi-principality of Andorra and the grand duchy of Luxemburg, eleven of the other sovereign European states were younger than the USA in the sense that their constitutional arrangements had been settled later than 1788 (when the American constitution came into operation): these were Belgium (1830), Sweden (incorporating Norway since 1815), Greece (1830), Serbia (1878), Romania (1878), the German empire (1871), Italy (1859–70), Montenegro (1799 or 1878), the Dual Monarchy of Austria–Hungary (1867), the Swiss Confederation (1848), the Third Republic of France (1871). But of these, of course, France and Switzerland had enjoyed general recognition as national entities for some centuries, though under different constitutional arrangements. The position of the Papacy was a special one: until 1929 no pope would recognize the arrangements imposed on it in 1871 by the government of Italy, although they provided for their sovereign control of the territory of the Vatican City.

covered a huge area even after grave losses (suffered above all in Europe) since the early eighteenth century began.

History, as ever, set out the main lines of world politics and the structure within which the statesmen of the early twentieth century would have to work, but they were not the state structures facing their modern successors, nor did they look to the same sources for their legitimacy. The nineteenth century had given new political maps to much of the world. In Europe, the recently united German empire and kingdom of Italy were respectively only thirty and just over forty years old. A number of south-eastern and Balkan new nations had not existed at all a century earlier: Serbia, Montenegro and Romania had all only become fully independent states in 1878. Needless to say, though, this did not prevent such countries from making large claims for historic roots going much further back. Bulgaria had enjoyed a particularly spectacular medieval history before being absorbed in the Ottoman empire, of which it remained still formally part in 1901 (though then already enjoying substantial autonomy), and without full legal independence until 1908.

While multi-ethnic empires (Habsburg Austria–Hungary, Romanov Russia, Germany under the Prussian Hohenzollerns and Ottoman Turkey) still presided over much of eastern and south-eastern Europe, they had all been obliged to make concessions, great or small, to the idea of nationality, the most successful principle of political legitimacy to emerge in the nineteenth century. Its heart was usually the negative proposition that it could not be right for a nation to be governed against its will by members of another nation. This opened a huge door for argument about what a 'nation' might be in many particular cases, but as self-recognition was the essence of the matter, such argument was (though often lengthy) almost always finally irrelevant: the fact was usually established by circumstance. The principle also sustained a wide and varied spectrum of political behaviour. At one end of it could be found the authoritarian pursuit of power and superiority: at the other, determined defence of cherished tradition as a badge of identity. Broadly speaking, nations were rediscovered and celebrated by intellectuals, poets, linguistic scholars and historians, and even occasionally invented by them, before being brought to birth and exploited by bandits, agitators and politicians.

During the nineteenth century, dramatic concessions had been made to national claims. In the 'Dual Monarchy' of Austria–Hungary, the Habsburgs had been forced in 1867 to give way to those of the Magyar Hungarians, who after achieving a constitutional revolution had won a privileged place for themselves among the empire's nationalities (which left them all the better able to oppress other peoples within historic Hungary). German Austrians and Magyars together, though, made up less than half the population of the Dual Monarchy and had to face the claims of Czechs, South Slavs and Romanians – to mention only a few – within the imperial structure. Even the Russian tsars had conceded a measure of autonomy to Finland (though Nicholas II's government was striving to take it away as the twentieth century began) and the German empire could be said to have been made by Bismarck as a concession to German nationalists willing to pay the price of Prussian domination within Germany in order to defend German culture and civilization against the threat from Slavdom. Great Britain, too, had got to the brink of giving 'Home Rule' to Ireland. As for the story of the Ottoman empire in Europe, after long being one of sheltering communal diversity better than later rulers were to do, it had become in the nineteenth century little more than one of giving ground to nationality, and it was from former Ottoman lands that the new states of the south-east had been made. Nothing like the same concessions had been made by the multinational Chinese empire, which had given way to external force in Sinkiang, Burma and Siam (and on the coasts of mainland China itself) but had never conceded anything to nationality in principle.

The victories of nationality had spread in the 'New World' of the age of discoveries, too. Setting aside the 'new nations' of South and Central America, the principle had triumphed most obviously in 1865 in the United States, when the end of a bloody civil war settled that the southern states of the USA should not be allowed to break away by secession from the national Union. Like most triumphs of nationality, of course, this could also be viewed as a defeat for a different nationality, in this case the Confederate states of the South; whether they were themselves a nation was one point in dispute. Even in conservative Japan, the cause of national self-assertion was harnessed as the century progressed to an ancient monarchy in a new and in many ways western-looking national state. Among former European colonial possessions, Canada and Australia were confederations that linked together earlier scattered settlements in 'new nations' (the Commonwealth of Australia actually came into existence on the first day of the twentieth century). By the end of the nineteenth century there were very few states in the western world which had not in one way or another been driven to confront the demands of national integration even if none of them had done so at the cost of such bloodshed as the United States. Though not yet complete, there had already come about by 1901 a growing strong association between the idea of nationalism and that of the territorial sovereign state worldwide. Nation-states were to be the chief actors on the twentieth-century diplomatic stage.

Within the countries concerned, this often implied psychological and cultural change. Few countries had to face such actualities of nationalist unrest, rebellion and terrorism as plagued Russia and the Ottoman empire or simmered under the surface in the Habsburg lands. But even old nation-states, settled in their ways and increasingly civilized in their collective lives, had to recognize new needs. French conservatives were agitated by the rise of international socialism and flirted with ideas of what was called 'integral' nationalism, while their radical but nationalist opponents strove to make a different kind of Frenchman and Frenchwoman – that is, good democratic republicans – with the instrument of a national and secular education system. In Italy and Germany the problem of making Italians and Germans was the more visible because the national unity was in those countries even more troubled by loyalties of Catholics to Rome than it was in France. Though Scottish and Welsh nationalism barely existed, even England's leaders were slowly coming round as the century began to accept that the Irish were not just a different sort of Englishmen, but an alien people who happened to be under the Crown. That recognition, though, did not settle whether Irish nationalism should be killed by kindness or contained by force.

Externally, the assumption that the world should be (as it was for the most part) organized in a system of sovereign, independent jurisdictions called states carried with it a new tightness of territorial definition, whether the boundaries thus set recognized national claims or not. States theoretically occupied specific areas within which their agents alone were normally entitled to use force, and frontier posts, flags and other symbols indicated the extent of their authority and the reality of their government. Infringement of sovereignty so expressed was usually taken to be tantamount to an act of war. There existed a body of international law that in theory bound their governments when they had entered into agreements, and treaties that were enforceable, though the degree to which major states could be coerced into accepting the authority of such law was always a matter of circumstance and, therefore, uncertain.

Nonetheless, there were some grounds for believing, as some people did in 1901, that there was a growing if still limited respect for international law. There had been some notable instances of successful international arbitration of disputes and other diplomatic successes in negotiating complex international problems during a long peace between major powers since 1871. A permanent court of arbitration had been provided for after a 'peace conference' met at the Hague in 1899 (though its use remained voluntary). In the long perspective, like the ideas of state and sovereignty themselves, such notions were creatures of the modern age: they could not have been understood or recognized in, say, 1500, nor were they yet in those many parts of the world where dominion and dependency still took other forms at the end of the nineteenth century. The exercise of unchallenged authority by the state within its territories often implied revolutionary change; earlier rulers had not been able to benefit from an idea which was essentially the creation of post-Renaissance European history (even if its roots in jurisprudence went back to ancient Rome). If an inter-state order, or, as it had come to be called, an 'international' order, existed, states were the fundamental units which made it up, the atoms, so to speak, of its chemistry.

MONARCHY

However power might be distributed and wherever their actual rulers might be, few people anywhere in the world outside the USA or France had any formal say in the choice of their heads of state.

The other individual states of the western world were governed in well-established and, in the main, monarchical forms; only in the American continents (outside the remaining British and Dutch dependencies there) had republicanism swept the board by 1901.[4] France, Switzerland and San Marino were the only republics in Europe (though Portugal was to join them after a revolution in 1910). Yet the basis of monarchy and the context in which it operated had much changed since the early nineteenth century. The name concealed much variety. Monarchy's formal prevalence in Europe was little guide to where power really lay in individual countries.

Great Britain was exceptional in having a monarchy based on revolution and nearly two centuries of contractual and limited – indeed, decreasing – authority behind it. Her example had been influential in winning support elsewhere in Europe for the idea of 'constitutional monarchy', that is to say, monarchy whose power was checked by laws and representative institutions. In varying degree, most European monarchies outside Russia paid at least lip-service to this idea in 1901 in so far as they often had written constitutions and some even observed them. Growing nationalist feeling did not often clash with monarchy in constitutional states, though the British faced an independence movement in Ireland, and the Norwegians decided to break away peacefully from the Swedish crown in 1905. The British monarchy had a long and successful association with nationality and patriotic feeling behind it, though its throne was occupied by a dynasty German in origin (as was the Danish). But such political acuity was unusual. During the nineteenth century, though, both the nomenclature of rulers ('king of the Hellenes' was one example) in new states, and their strenuous identification of themselves with national prestige and interest reflected a trend which left the high dynastic doctrine of old monarchical houses more and more exposed to criticism.[5]

Even in the German empire, the most developed of the dynastic

---

[4] The last South American monarch was the emperor Dom Pedro II of Brazil, deposed in 1889.

[5] Famously, legend says that when Franz Joseph (who, since 1867, had formally ruled under a modicum of constitutional restraint in both halves of the Dual Monarchy) was told that a certain officer was a 'patriot', he replied, 'Yes, but is he a patriot *for me?*'

empires, with a freely elected federal Reichstag and a wide suffrage qualification, little concession had been made to democracy by 1901. Some recognition of what respect for national symbolism required of the figureheads of nations in performing symbolic acts was usually as far as the Habsburg, Romanov and Hohenzollern monarchs went in concession to mass feeling. There was still some divinity hedging kings then, even in Europe (and much more in Asia). In Europe, too, there was something like an international society of royal families, knowing one another, visiting one another's palaces and, above all, marrying one another, and constituting something of a caste apart. This did not apply among oriental monarchs like those of China and Japan who, for many reasons of history, culture and geography, were still remarkably remote from their subjects, nor, indeed, to the many subordinate monarchs who retained their offices within alien empires, such as the Indian princes of the British Raj, or the khans, sheikhs and sultans whose allegiance was claimed by Romanov, Manchu and Ottoman.

NON-WESTERN GOVERNMENT

Although many of its components might be only just surviving and were sometimes only fictionally independent entities, the theoretical and legal organization of the world as overwhelmingly a structure of sovereign states reflected the way it had been deeply shaped by Europe. Formal diplomacy was in itself a very visible sign of the influence of one civilization on the history of the rest of the world. A complete and universal domination of the idea of the territorial state was not to come until late in the twentieth century when, paradoxically, it became a benchmark of Europe's political decline; it was by organizing themselves as national states on European lines that non-Europeans sought and sometimes successfully forged defences against western power. Such diffusion of the state model was in part a matter of ideas, in part a matter of technical devices. In 1901, though, much of the world was not actually made up of such uniformly similar institutions, nor were such ideas universally accepted, even if international law was based on the notion of the sovereign state.

Most strikingly, there were still Chinese in 1901 who believed that their emperor was ruler of the world. It was a traditional view in that country that the world was a great monarchy and that a 'Mandate of Heaven' had been conferred on the Chinese emperor, the ruler of a 'Middle Kingdom', to preside over ever-widening but concentric circles of peoples in varying degrees of subordination. All mankind was supposed to be in greater or lesser degrees of dependence upon the emperor, and to owe him tribute. The status of those peoples in their outermost reaches was thought to be merely that of 'barbarians' who, it was hoped, might lose some of their rawness through contact with the superior civilization of China – a point of view not unlike that from which many white people, with a very different institutional framework in mind, looked at the rest of the globe.

Yet it was a picture far removed from Chinese reality as the century began. The empire had expanded in the eighteenth century, but in the nineteenth it had lost huge areas of China itself to foreign predators, had been forced to watch its satellites fall into the sphere of European empires, and been obliged to permit intrusions of its domestic life in the form of traders and missionaries that had been unthinkable in 1801. All the western powers (except Russia) accepted, not very meaningfully, the British 'Open Door' principle urged on them by the American secretary of state: to maintain the Chinese customs tariff and levy equal dues in the harbours and on the railways of their respective 'spheres of influence', so offering equivalent conditions to all foreign merchants. But the phrase 'open door' was itself revealing.[6] China had proved incapable of generating the strength needed to hold off the predator; she had not been able to close the door to them though she wanted to. This had led a few Chinese officials already to think that the white barbarians had been too successful in bullying, harassing and exploiting the Middle Kingdom for the last sixty years or so for their institutions not to be worth study. Yet Chinese government was still little influenced by western ideas in 1901. Though a few among the educated mandarin class had come round to the acceptance of certain western devices as perhaps needful to secure the

[6] The background to the episode of the American Note on the 'Open Door' is too complicated to explore here but was conveniently unravelled in 1951 in lectures by the American diplomat and scholar George F. Kennan, then published by him as *American Diplomacy 1900–1950* (London, 1952), esp. pp.21–37.

empire's defence, there was hardly any recognition that radical change might be needed to assure independence. Even after humiliating defeat in war by the Japanese in 1895, pressure for it had scarcely begun to affect the actual conduct of Chinese government. Railways might be allowed to be useful for moving soldiers about, but they were looked at askance when they ran into violent local opposition on grounds that they disturbed ancestral graveyards or troubled the spirits of the land. The mandarin class was still recruited by the system of examination in traditional classical learning that had for centuries indeed provided a remarkable consistency in the management of a huge and diverse country. More recently, though, traditional assumptions seemed sadly unable to promote traditional goals. As a working system, the empire was a shattered relic of what in theory at least had been a once-aspiring totalitarianism.[7] In western eyes, it was chiefly characterized by corruption, neglect of the people's well-being and the grotesque cruelty of its punishments.[8]

A few Chinese intellectuals and civil servants had founded in the 1890s a society for the study of 'self-strengthening' to consider Western ideas and inventions that might be helpful. Its leaders pointed to the example of Peter the Great of Russia as a modernizer and, more significantly, to what was then going on in Japan. Yet even these would-be reformers still sought to root change in Confucian tradition, albeit one purified and invigorated. Members of the gentry administrative class, they sought to work within the traditional framework and machinery of power to bring about reform and technological innovation without compromising the fundamentals of Chinese culture and ideology. Unfortunately this meant that what came to be known as the 'Hundred Days of Reform' of 1898 was almost at once entangled in court politics. Reform edicts were swiftly overtaken by a *coup d'état* by the dowager empress, Tzu Hsi, who locked up the

---

[7] Another word still uninvented in 1901.

[8] For example, the traditional punishment of death by slicing (which became part of the western stereotype of Chinese backwardness as the 'death of a thousand cuts'). It was ordered, in fact, for K'ang Yu-wei, a man termed the 'Rousseau of China', and a major advocate of intellectual and governmental reform in the 1890s. He avoided his fate by taking refuge in British-governed Hong Kong.

emperor whose ear the reformers had sought. Their failure was in part the outcome of the provocation offered by their inept political behaviour; yet it was something that 'self-strengthening' had been advocated at all in so conservative a culture. The example was to stimulate wider and deeper thinking in the future.

One handicap to Chinese government was popular resentment of the Manchu dynasty, still seen (after two and a half centuries of its occupation of the throne) as alien by many Han Chinese. Intermarriage between Manchu and Chinese was still forbidden in 1901. There was a substantial predominance of Manchu appointees in the imperial service. Their hegemony had the support of the dowager empress, who was the effective ruler of China as the century began. There seemed, though, to be little likelihood of popular support for change. Indeed, the reverse was true. China was in upheaval as the twentieth century began, but in a reactionary not a revolutionary sense, and the country was to all intents and purposes out of control of the government at Peking. A xenophobic and popular rising against foreigners (celebrated as the 'Boxer' rebellion because of its participants' pursuit of traditional martial arts) had resulted in invasion by a multinational expeditionary force against the rebels (the only instance in history of a combined, if reluctant, military effort by all the great powers of the day) under a single commander, a German, which had led to a declaration in June 1900 by the Chinese government that it was at war with the entire world.

Two other East Asian empires had to be taken into account in Far Eastern affairs in 1901, though in very different ways. One of them was technically only three years old: the ruler of Korea had only taken his title of emperor in 1897; only in 1901 did his government first decide to send resident representatives to foreign countries (even the Chinese had already done this). Several nations had interests in Korea: the Americans and British had long encouraged the 'opening' of the country to trade and reform (as they saw it), the Russians and the Japanese competed there for political supremacy and possibly territorial aggrandizement, and (in theory as the suzerain power but actually increasingly powerless in Korean affairs) the Chinese went on claiming that Korea was a dependency of the Middle Kingdom. This was one reason for the Japanese (who had successfully occupied

Seoul in the mid-1890s during a war against China) to promote 'westernizing' influences in the court and among officials.

The empire of Japan was much more important. It was a new addition to the western state system and the portent of a new dynamism in East Asian affairs. Once, Japan had appeared as resistant to change as China, locked into patterns of life set centuries before. That impression was superficial and misleading. As the nineteenth century began, Japan had already been a semi-developed, diversifying society, with a money economy, large commercial cities and the beginnings of a quasi-capitalist structure in agriculture. In the 1850s and 1860s the pace of change speeded up, spurred by alarm over the further overt encroachments of western powers in China, the imposition on Japan of 'unequal' treaties and the intrusion of western diplomatic representatives and businessmen. Amid complicated factional struggles between powerful clans and aristocratic connexions that had, in effect, ruled the country for three centuries, there followed a radical change of direction, usually summed up as the 'Meiji restoration' (taking its name from the Meiji emperor who presided over it), which, while a process taking several years, can be arbitrarily dated to 1868, when a previously secluded emperor formally resumed his place and power at the centre of the national life. With this, Japan's rulers set about entering into the modern world.

By 1901 Japan had assumed not only the trappings and style but also the status of a western state. Her army (German trained) and navy (British trained) had performed brilliantly in a war of 1895 against China which announced that Japan, too, was going in for overseas expansion (Taiwan, then known as Formosa, was her main prize at the peace). Her economy was beginning to develop a modern manufacturing sector, whose major expression on the world stage was the production of cheap textiles, and she had an unusually high credit rating in the eyes of foreign investors. The traditional ethnic pride of the Japanese was harnessed to the new state's needs and a state Shintoist cult, often in the past hostile to foreign religious influence, stressed and enhanced the role of the emperor as the embodiment of the divine origins of the nation. The demands of loyalty to him were in due course to turn out to override the liberal-sounding principles of the new European-style constitution. Assessments of the character and tendency of the regime had to take into account not only its modernizing rhetoric, but also the authoritarian and repressive behaviour of the imperial police. Japan's nineteenth century closed not only with the presentation to the Diet (parliament) of a petition asking for universal suffrage, but also with the passing, shortly afterwards, of a fierce Public Order Police Act. The reconciliation of constitutionalism and imperial authority was in the end only to be possible after a national disaster.

Modernizing the Japanese economy required strong governmental initiatives and harsh fiscal policies. There had been for a time a grave danger of opposition and disorder. Centuries before, the imperial power had gone into eclipse, unable to control over-mighty subjects; its restored authority faced new dangers in a new age. Not all conservatives could be reconciled to the new model Japan. Discontented *ronin* or retainers – rootless and masterless *samurai*, the traditional fighting class – had been one source of trouble.[9] Another was peasant misery; in the first decade of the Meiji era there had been scores of agrarian revolts, but reform had created unconditional private ownership in land and many tenant farmers were to benefit from it. There had also been a last feudal rebellion, but the energies of the discontented *samurai* were gradually siphoned off into the service of the new state; building their interests into it, though, only intensified an assertive nationalism in certain key sectors of the national life. It was soon expressed not only in continuing resentment of western power but also in support for imperial ambitions directed towards the nearby Asian mainland.

Unlike the empire of Korea (where the most urgent of her ambitions were focused), Japan had to be taken into account internationally; she was going somewhere. Her leaders knew it, and were happy that firm government should take them there; her people seemed willing to accept it, too. She was emphatically one of those nations that a British prime minister had referred to only a few years before as

---

[9] One important early symbolic step towards modernity was a decree in 1876 that forbade the wearing of the traditional two swords tucked into the sash of members of the *samurai* class, the old sign of their privilege and of the brutalities of the feudal society. Henceforth only policemen and officers of the new armed services could wear swords in public.

'living', in contrast to the 'dying' (a category which certainly included Korea).[10] In south-east Asia, it might have been more difficult to classify the still independent kingdom of Siam at that moment as either.[11] It was weak and, as it had been for some decades, under pressure from France, whose first missionaries had arrived there as long ago as the seventeenth century. But the British had a strong interest in keeping Siam going as a buffer state, insulating France from Burma and the approaches to India except for a short shared Burma–Indo-China border, and Siam was to survive the threat of western imperialism. The regime was also seeking modernization; symbolically, 1901 brought the opening of its first railway. One hundred and sixty-five miles long, it had taken some eight years to build and over 7,000 lives, the overwhelming majority of them Asiatic.

ISLAMIC EMPIRES

In the Islamic world of the Near and Middle East and the Maghreb, the Ottoman empire had for centuries stood out as the leading power. It was a subtle qualification of that status, though, that the idea of an autonomous state did not necessarily mean much to Muslims (and therefore did not to the majority of the millions of its subjects). They saw the world, rather, as divided between the brotherhood of the faithful, who followed Islam, which united people owing allegiance to many different rulers, and the unbelievers (themselves divided between the Christians and the Jews on the one hand, who at least worshipped Allah, though in their own mistaken ways, and mere pagans). If there was an overriding focus of Islamic loyalty it was presumed to be found in the Caliph, the spiritual successor to the Prophet. Since the eighteenth century he resided in Constantinople, in the person of the Ottoman sultan. The Ottoman Arab lands respected the Caliphate's claim to spiritual leadership and British officials in India bore it in mind when thinking

---

[10] Lord Salisbury's distinction was drawn in a speech in London's Albert Hall in May 1898.
[11] Siam changed its name to Thailand in 1949.

64

about Muslim subjects of the Raj.[12] The governance of the Ottoman empire thus still had a theocratic element about it.

In 1901 it still extended to three continents, and though it had many Christian and Jewish subjects in each of them, most of those it ruled were Muslims. This did as much as bureaucracy to give a framework and measure of order to lands which had stretched at one time in Africa from the Maghreb to the Sudan. By 1901, though, they no longer included Morocco, Algeria or Tunisia and only formally retained Egypt. Elsewhere, they still embraced the Yemen and Mesopotamia, and still had a foothold in Europe. As the twentieth century began, few among the peoples of this vast area had begun to take up western ways or ideas. A few had begun to do so in the early nineteenth century even under Mehemet Ali, technically the vassal of the Sultan, but in reality an independent potentate who had sought to modernize Egypt. The influence of European and North American missionary education had also produced some Egyptians who hankered after modernization and national independence. But the pace of political change had been slow until the end of the nineteenth century.

The Ottoman empire had begun its history as a 'plunder machine'.[13] Once it ceased to advance territorially, the plunder had to be extracted from its own subjects who, with time, grew restless and, with increasing success, broke away in rebellion. In the nineteenth century it was still an open question whether the empire could become more than this, and take on the characteristics and viability of a modern state. Though in 1876 (a year when two sultans came and went within months) the Ottoman government conceded a constitution on western lines and proclaimed the freedom of the press, it soon proved a dead letter; the general election held the following year, the first in the history of any Islamic country, was to be the only one of the century. In its last months there opened the institution which was to become the university of Istanbul, 'the first truly indigenous modern university in the Muslim world', as one authority has called it, but this hardly offset the

---

[12] Yet no Ottoman sultan except the last ever made the pilgrimage to Mecca, and he did so only after being driven into exile. Alan Palmer, *The Decline and Fall of the Ottoman Empire* (London, 1992), p.268.

[13] I borrow this useful phrase from E. L. Jones, *The European Miracle* (2nd edn, Cambridge, 1987), p.185.

reputation of the Ottoman regime for corruption, inefficiency and a nervous and haphazard cruelty.[14] These characteristics helped to explain the well-established status of the empire in western eyes as 'the sick man of Europe', though few in 1901 would have said that implied its likely demise in Asia. Nonetheless, Salisbury would not have thought of the Ottoman state as one of his 'living' examples.

Elsewhere in the Muslim world, Persia and Morocco were both obvious candidates for inclusion in the moribund category. Both were historic Islamic monarchies which seemed likely before long to undergo absorption into European empires. Yet this was not quite to happen. Though very much a focus of great power rivalry and bullying, Persia was to survive with her formal independence intact. As the century began, the country was even more an old-fashioned despotism than Ottoman Turkey and had as yet undergone no conscious or enforced westernization; she had her modernization still to come. Persia was a multilingual, multireligious, very rural society (there were less than eight miles of railway in the country and the two largest cities, Tehran and Tabriz, had only 200,000 inhabitants between them in 1901), whose Muslim teachers and preachers, the *ulema*, provided the main channel for the expression of an often turbulent popular feeling. Morocco, too, still awaited modernity. It looked fragile, for though the USA and the leading European powers had recognized its independent status as recently as 1880, a violent border with French Algeria, and the practice of some of the Sultan's more unruly subjects of kidnapping Europeans and Americans and holding them to ransom, often threatened to provoke foreign intervention. International rivalries would nonetheless help to preserve the independence of Morocco and Persia, as they did that of Siam.

[14] B. Lewis, *The Emergence of Modern Turkey*, 2nd edn (London, 1968), p.182. This seems a good point to note one symptom of the political realities of the empire – the cautious practice of the Ottoman press in avoiding any reference to the assassination of rulers. The murder of the empress of Austria was reported as a death from pneumonia, that of the French president Carnot as due to apoplexy, McKinley's as due to anthrax, and, most fancifully of all, the double assassination of the king and queen of Serbia as death from indigestion (Lewis, p.188).

THE UNITED STATES OF AMERICA

The American continents, north and south, contained the largest contiguous area of the world's land-surface not ruled by European nations in 1901, but they were emphatically shaped by European origins. North America was then divided almost as it is today between Canada and Newfoundland (then two distinct entities) and the United States. The first two were self-governing, but legally ruled by the English monarch, while the last was a republic. Two of them were of huge territorial extent, but Canada counted for much less in the balance of continental power, with a population of only just over 5.5 million against the 76 million of the USA.

Two great historical facts determined the pattern of historical development of the United States. First, the Louisiana Purchase of 1803 released the young republic for continental expansion. The Civil War of 1861–5 then settled that the United States would survive as a single political entity. In the scales of world history this may well be thought the most important military and political decision of the century. America's constitutional arrangements had by 1901 a far longer continuous history, therefore, than those of any major European state except Great Britain or Russia. Yet the continuing arrival of new Americans long helped to give the United States the characteristics and psychology of a new nation. A need to integrate her new citizens encouraged the expression of strong patriotic feeling. But because of geography, political origins in a rejection of Europe, and the continuing domination of American government and business by élites formed in the Anglo-Saxon tradition, American nationalism was hardly likely to matter much outside the western hemisphere. Even in 1914, the United States was still a young giant waiting in the wings of history. Her full international weight would only come to bear when Europe needed to involve her in its quarrels. Though potentially the greatest of all powers, distance and a tradition of isolation meant that she normally played no part in Europe's affairs, and European powers were not much interested in her. Once the Canadian boundary had been settled by negotiation with Great Britain and those of California

and Alaska with Russia,[15] there was little reason for European governments to have much diplomatic business with the United States except
over commercial matters in the western hemisphere. Americans
showed little concern with the world outside it, except in the Far East.
Their politicians normally still sought to follow the counsel of their first
president, who had warned his own generation to avoid entanglement
with Europe's affairs. The likelihood of further European intrusion
in the hemisphere was slight and American diplomacy had long taken
account of any such danger in the comforting knowledge that no British
government would permit any fresh establishment of a European great
power in Central or South America outside the few small colonies
remaining there.

As the century opened, the United States could also look back on
a century of phenomenal growth. This, too, helped to give her people
great confidence, and perhaps justified them in appropriating to themselves specifically the name of 'Americans'. Their numbers had multiplied more than twelvefold since 1800. They had secured the whole
northern continent between the Canadian border and the Rio Grande
under one government, a great national and imperial triumph. Once
the crisis of the Civil War had been successfully negotiated, their
constitution and democratic institutions had proved able to handle
all their domestic problems peacefully.

The constitution was not the only advantage, of course, which the
young country had enjoyed. There had been a huge opportunity
to exploit. Geographical remoteness meant that no potential rivals
confronted Americans in the hemisphere once the Russians had gone.
There was, too, the enormous benefit of steady recruitment of millions
of enterprising European immigrants. Tempest-tossed and poor
though they might be, 'the huddled masses' (as the verse inscribed at
the base of the Statue of Liberty put it) turned out to be a rich source
of enterprise, vigour and ability. More than 33 million Europeans
took their ambition, energy, intelligence and skills to the USA between
1820 and 1950. Foreign investment, too (notably British), found the
United States attractive, and had provided the capital for the creation
of much of the industrial and agricultural infrastructure: at the begin-

---

[15] The last in 1867.

ning of the century the United States already had more than 200,000 miles of railway track – more than all Europe. She was the world's greatest debtor nation, but seemed easily to carry that burden.[16] By 1914 she would have the greatest manufacturing output in the world (although manufacturing was not to employ most of her labour force until the next decade). The number of motor-cars on her roads reached 1 million for the first time in that year. Huge damage had been done along the way to securing her economic triumphs. Vast forests had disappeared and millions of acres of the Great Plains had been turned into desert by exploitative farming: virgin land was already in danger of running out in the 1890s.[17]

History does not everywhere move at the same pace or countries' histories within the same synchrony, and it is convenient at this point to look ahead a little at the changing United States in the first years of the new century, when its citizens continued to pursue successfully the greatest experiment in democracy and republican government yet seen, within a federal framework that still gave the national government far less power than was taken for granted in other civilized nations. This structure channelled potentially bitter divisions through its electoral machinery, and provided conditions in which variety could flourish at lower levels. The political organization of the mainland was completed when Oklahoma in 1907 and New Mexico and Arizona in 1912 joined the Union as states.[18] So there came under democratic government from sea to sea the largest area yet to be dedicated to that principle in history. Within it there were notable political experiments and innovations Women's suffrage in local government existed in some places even before the nineteenth century was over,

[16] The massive foreign debt of the Americans and their complete political independence combine to provide perhaps the best simple refutation of the view expressed in the works of J. A. Hobson (*Imperialism*, 1902) and Lenin (*Imperialism, the Highest Stage of Capitalism*, 1916), that overseas investment was the heart of European imperialism. See as an old general book still of great value H. Feis, *Europe, the world's banker 1870–1914* (New Haven, 1930).

[17] For an impression, see the maps of virgin forest areas in *The Atlas*, Vol. XIV of *The New Cambridge Modern History* (Cambridge, 1970), pp.208–9.

[18] The last state to be admitted in the nineteenth century had been Utah in 1896 (after its inhabitants ceased to provide a legal endorsement of polygamy); the outliers, Hawaii and Alaska, were to be added to the Union later, in 1959.

socialist mayors could be found in office in the years down to 1914, and some states became famous or notorious for their social welfare legislation at a moment when federal government was notably inactive and even hostile in that area. The first regulation of minimum wages for women and children in the United States was enacted by the state of Massachusetts (the Supreme Court was still willing, though, to invalidate a statute from New York in 1933). One popular social experiment had an important future ahead, though it was not in the end to turn out very happily: in 1901 five states prohibited the public sale of alcoholic beverages and two-thirds of them did so by 1917.

As industrialization surged ahead in the years after 1865 it had been sustained by a widespread acceptance that few restraints should be placed on the process; government had shown itself unwilling to intervene to prevent the weakest being driven to the wall. Slowly, other interests – organized labour, farmers, regional and sectional interests – won leverage in a system that at first favoured above all the controllers of finance and industrial capital, sometimes at the cost of serious exploitation and suffering. There was ample material for would-be reformers to get their teeth into in the early twentieth-century United States. Yet for all the violence of American life (visible in frequently bloody industrial disputes) there was no sign of a revolutionary danger to democracy. In every presidential election from 1892 onwards there were 'socialist' or 'socialist-labour' candidates but they never polled a large share of the votes cast (5.97 per cent in 1912, their best year). American socialism was always a very different thing from its European counterpart. Wholly alienated Americans were always a tiny minority; for a long time, too, they had no shared focus, they were a number of minorities rather than one.

It had once briefly looked otherwise. An agrarian-based populist movement had come to a climax in the 1890s. The plight of the American farmer had steadily worsened since the Civil War. He had seemed to be moving inexorably towards poverty; some talked of him declining into peasant status.[19] 'Populism' was the last great challenge

---

[19] The number of farms grew and their average acreage much decreased during 1860–1900, while more and more of them came to be held on tenancies.

of rural America to the coming United States of the twentieth century. It attempted briefly to link in common cause the western farmer, the northern industrial worker and the poor white of the South. In 1896 it had succeeded in securing nomination of its leader as the Democratic presidential candidate, and a passionate crusade followed against the power of the eastern banks, the railroads, the supporters of industrial tariffs and the cities. But he was not elected. Farming, with occasional breaks of short-lived temporary prosperity when world prices went up, was to go on being the most depressed section of the American economy well into the mid-century. Radicals were more successful in the years before 1914 in getting action (not only through federal legislation and more often through state or local government) on other matters, though progress in social reform was slow and halting by comparison with European countries. There was much dissatisfaction still waiting to be mobilized and by 1901 the old safety valve of migration to free land had long since ceased to be available. There were all too evident evils in the (still growing) concentrations of economic power represented by trusts, corporations and holding companies, in their use of political influence (and corruption) to obtain favourable legislation. A twelve-hour working day was then the rule in US Steel, the huge combination that dominated American metallurgy. Millions of minors were still working in factories. 'Muckrakers' exposed in the periodical press and a flood of books scandal after scandal, corruption in government, exploitation of the weak, the ruthless use of economic power, the exploitation of women, slum housing conditions and much else.[20] Industrial relations were almost continuously turbulent down to 1914.

The general current of reform that consolidated as a response in these years is remembered as 'Progressivism'. Its adherents were broadly speaking interested in a wide range of specific political and administrative reforms. They believed that better government would eradicate great evils, and that better government would follow from

[20] 'Muckrakers' was the name given by Theodore Roosevelt to the writers and journalists who specialized in such exposures – slightly surprisingly, given his own reforming instincts. He took the name from the suggestion provided by Bunyan's depiction of the 'man that could look no way but downwards, with a muck-rake in his hand' in the second part of *The Pilgrim's Progress*.

more popular participation (including, for many progressives, that of women), would lead to cheapness and efficiency and would end corruption, a much-denounced because notorious evil. Progressives were to be found in both of the two great historic parties, the Republicans and the Democrats. The former was the Grand Old Party that had preserved the Union and freed the slave – or so mythology ran; the latter was the party of the defeated South. Democrat domination of that impoverished and backward section was tolerated by Republican administrations in return for acceptance of the South's lack of power at the national level. Roosevelt had been a reforming governor of his state (New York) and both his presidencies (he was elected for a second term in 1904) showed Progressivism's influence in his advocacy of reform, which did much to change the national mood in its favour. His successor, Taft, was another Republican president. Though not a man of innovative temperament, important measures were passed during his presidency, including a constitutional amendment permitting the imposition of a federal income tax. Taft looked and sounded more conservative than he really was. More suits were brought to the courts against business under anti-trust legislation during his tenure of office than that of any of his predecessors.[21]

Nineteen-twelve, though, brought a political change of far-reaching impact and Progressivism's greatest triumph. When Theodore Roosevelt failed to be chosen by the Republicans as their presidential candidate that year, he decided to run instead as a Progressive. The result was a six-cornered contest (though only three candidates really mattered). In it, the Democratic candidate Woodrow Wilson, an academic who had gone into politics to become Governor of New Jersey, was elected, though with a minority of the popular votes cast, on a reform programme with strong Progressive support. It transcended old divisions. For the first time in more than ninety years, Massachusetts and Virginia had both voted for the same presidential candidate. The Republican party had been split by Roosevelt but there had been a convincing majority of votes cast for two men who might be called progressives; there had been little to choose between what was

[21] Eighty, in fact; there had been thirty-three under Roosevelt and three under McKinley.

offered by Roosevelt and Wilson. The lines of a new twentieth-century American politics now begin to be discernible. The Republican party was now to turn away from radical policies for a half-century or so. A Democratic alliance of southern social conservatism with northern reform was shown to be possible. Wilsonian democracy also had its ideological roots in history; the president was always happy to draw refreshment from the deep well of Jeffersonian rhetoric and principle. Presbyterian and Southern in origin, Wilson saw politics as a moralizing activity, a conflict of good and evil (so, ironically, did Roosevelt).[22]

A couple of years after his inauguration, Europe was at war and Wilson's fellow-citizens felt grateful to him for firmly keeping them out of it. Neutrality was in tune with virtually all Americans' instincts. For a long time yet, American history was to continue in its own rhythms and under its own compulsions. Internal problems, too, would help prolong American exceptionalism. Deep in her culture, too, still far from emerging in its full immensity, lay a problem within a problem, that of the negro, as the black American was then called. It was hardly visible as a national question when Woodrow Wilson came to office, let alone in 1901. It was contained at that moment within the southern states, the poorest and politically least powerful region of the United States. Racial inequality was nevertheless to reveal itself a half-century later as a major qualification of the global prestige the United States would come to enjoy. It would have to become a national and very visible problem, though, before American government really addressed it. Few Americans were much troubled by it in 1914.

The domestic history of the United States is worth more reflexion in other countries than it has usually been given and very few foreign observers discerned the potential importance of that history as the century began. European statesmen, for their part, were still apt to reflect only that the United States was a long way away, preoccupied with interests hardly likely to concern most other nations. Only a few of them grasped deeper truths. One who perhaps did so was Bismarck; he is said to have once remarked that that the same language was

---

[22] Symptomatically, Wilson's political hero was the British Victorian prime minister W. E. Gladstone.

spoken by the Americans and British was the most important political fact of his age.

LATIN AMERICA

A common language – Spanish – was also a tie between most of the nations of 'Latin America' (a term invented in the middle of the nineteenth century by an imaginative ruler of France to describe what lay south of the Rio Grande), but this fact obscures the huge diversity of Central and South America, let alone the Caribbean islands. The independent political entities that had emerged there had their roots for the most part in the colonial empires of Portugal and Spain. The southern Europeans drawn to them as immigrants in large numbers in the nineteenth century found much on their arrival that was familiar. Catholicism provided the framework of cultural and social life, anti-clericalism much of South American politics. Other than Spanish, Portuguese (in Brazil) was the only widely spoken language. Political and legal institutions, too, still reflected an imperial past shared by European countries of emigration and the American receptors alike. They and the assumptions that went with them had survived the old empires of Spain and Portugal, whose collapse at the beginning of the nineteenth century shaped most of the political map of modern South America. Yet geography and topography also imposed huge differences on the peoples who lived in this vast area. For all the hopes of the great hero and emblematic leader of the Wars of Independence, Bolívar, no United States of Latin America had emerged from the independence struggles. Too many circumstances, economic, social and military, added to physical facts to tell against unity. There was also an absence of either a danger or an opportunity that might make unity desirable. In 1823 the president of the United States had declared, in what became known as the 'Monroe doctrine', that the Americas should not in future be regarded as zones for further imperial acquisition by European governments. As the British agreed with him, this meant that Latin America was henceforth safe; the Royal Navy would see to that. The few colonial footholds that lingered on in the Caribbean posed no threat to the rest of the continent.

As in Africa 150 years later, the removal of colonial rule in Central and South America revealed that geography and community did not always match the political units that emerged from old administrative divisions. The new big but thinly populated states were fragile. Some soon crumbled away. Some had to face ethnic problems. Social tensions were not removed by independence. In Argentina, the relatively small Indian population had undergone near-extermination at the hands of the army by the end of the century; that country was thenceforth notable for an unchallenged domination of European strains in its population. At the other extreme, Brazil had a population the majority of which, originally of slave origin, was black and, at the time of independence, still in slavery. Yet after slavery's demise, intermarriage was not frowned upon as it was in the post-slavery United States, and the result is a population that may well be the most successfully integrated ethnic mix in the world today. Usually in Latin America, though, social and economic distinctions went on reflecting ethnic divisions: Indians tend to be at the bottom of the pile, *mestizos* (those of mixed blood) a little higher up, and *creoles*, persons of dominantly European descent, at the top.[23]

The new Latin American states had no such self-governing tradition as the former English colonies to their north. Their colonial administrations had been absolutist. For new political principles, the leaders of the young republics had often looked to the ideas and rhetoric of the French Revolution, but that did not help much when the continent's tiny ruling élites did not even share among themselves agreement about acceptable practice or show mutual tolerance. Worse still, revolutionary principles quickly brought the Church into politics, a development which was perhaps in the long run inevitable, given its huge power as a landowner and popular influence, but one which in some countries added a violent anti-clericalism to already turbulent politics. In these circumstances, it was hardly surprising that during most of the century the republics that had emerged from the wars of independence often found their affairs drifting into the hands of *caudillos*, military adventurers and their cliques who controlled armed

---

[23] Even though Mexico had an Indian president as early as 1861, and a *mestizo* in office as the century began.

forces sufficient to give them sway until more powerful rivals came along.

The cross-currents of civil war and wars between the new states – some very bloody – had produced by 1901 the political structure that was, with a few boundary changes, largely already that of today. Mexico, the most northern of the former Spanish colonies, had lost over half its territory to the United States in the nineteenth century. Four mainland Central American republics had appeared, and two island states, the Dominican Republic and Haiti, before Cuba achieved independence from Spain in 1898. To the south lay ten other republics, of which Brazil was the largest and youngest (twelve years old) in that year. Most of them had survived civil war and much disorder to enjoy very different degrees of stability, constitutional propriety, and economic well-being; some had engaged already in bloody conflicts with one another. In 1901 itself, Colombia and Venezuela were (though not formally at war) fighting one another, and Chile and Argentina were believed to be on the brink of collision, each accusing the other of invading its territory.[24]

Many South American states were enjoying a growing prosperity as the century began. The continent had rich and potentially very important natural resources that had become even more valuable as Europe and the United States industrialized. Argentina's spaces included some of the finest pasture in the world: the invention of refrigerator ships made her butcher to the world. She also exported grain and was the richest of the Latin American countries in 1901. Chile had nitrates and Venezuela had oil; both would grow in wealth and economic importance because of them. Mexico had minerals, and oil was discovered there in exploitable quantities in 1901 itself. Brazil was to prove to have practically everything except oil; she also supplied the world with two-thirds of its coffee. The list could be prolonged but reflects the fact that Latin America's wealth came from primary produce, especially food, and world prices were to provide advantageous terms of trade until the end of the 1920s. The capital to exploit these resources often came from Europe, above all the United Kingdom, but

[24] The (nominal) arbitration of the British king, Edward VII, happily resolved the Chilean–Argentinian border dispute in the following year.

Americans were heavily invested in sugar and banana plantations in the Caribbean and Central American republics, as were Germans in coffee.[25] Growing wealth sharpened social and economic inequalities. An apparently Europeanized urban élite lived lives very different from those of the Indian and *mestizo* masses. For all the dynamism of some countries, millions of Latin American peasants still lived at subsistence level. This was not in itself remarkable in the world of 1901; everywhere then the rich and well-born lived lives almost unimaginably unlike those of the poor.

Latin America's ruling classes were in a sense underwritten by foreign creditors seeking security for their investments. They by no means always got it, but the search for it tended to lead them to support the existing social and political authorities, who thus enhanced still further their own wealth. It would take only a few years of the twentieth century for this to produce graver instability than hitherto in Latin America. Meanwhile, in the eyes of the 'civilized' world the states of Latin America had a somewhat ambiguous standing as the twentieth century began, for all the importance of international commercial and financial ties. Rooted in European culture, tied to Europe by economics but politically disentangled and geographically remote from it, they stood, so far as Europeans were concerned, on the superior side of the great distinction between those within the pale of western or European civilization and those outside it. But they were not of great concern to Europe. Most European and North Americans, indeed, thought only of men and women of European descent, an urban, privileged minority, not of Amerindians and blacks, when they thought of 'Latin America' at all.

[25] Because of this, Lenin dogmatically termed Argentina a 'semi-colony'. For the real state of affairs, see H. S. Ferns, *Britain and Argentina in the Nineteenth Century* (London, 1960), p.488.

THE INTERNATIONAL ORDER: POWER AND GREAT POWERS

Some governments in 1901 were more concerned with the power they possessed inside their own countries than with their place on an international spectrum, but most politicians had to take a broader view. In constitutional states they were ultimately responsible to electorates, but even Russia's rulers usually felt that they should in some measure take account of 'public opinion', whatever that might mean (and they were often wrong in interpreting it). This raised questions about comparative international standing. Even if sovereign states were formally and legally equal, recognition had always to be given to what really mattered, to differences of influence and weight in international affairs, and how these were regarded at home as well as abroad.

Some countries were acknowledged to be 'great' powers. This long-current phrase has already been used in these pages but deserves a moment's explanation. The roots of the idea of great powers lay in the business of peacemaking at the end of the Napoleonic wars, when the real decision-makers were recognized to be Russia, Great Britain, Austria, Prussia and France. Though many other states and rulers had been represented at the Congress of Vienna in 1815 these countries had the last word there, and they and their successors were thereafter conceded to be the Great Powers, exercising more weight than others and with resources able to assure that they would go on doing so. They dominated international affairs in the course of the nineteenth century, constituting from time to time what some liked to call a 'Concert of Europe', for if they could agree, no diplomatic problem was beyond solution, at least for a time. Such a concept shaped the outcome of the Congress of Paris of 1856 that wound up the issues of the Crimean war and that of the Congress of Berlin of 1878 (which endeavoured to settle the problems presented by a declining Ottoman empire). By then Prussia had defeated the Austrians in war, had been merged in a new German empire, and had become a greater power still. Another nation that had not existed in 1815, Italy, was also reckoned to have joined the great power club by the end of the century.

The realities of power, though, are often far from completely expressed by the language and culture of diplomats, historical formations that are always likely to be out-of-date. The realities change more rapidly in time. Imperial Russia provides a good example. In an age when no army in the world could move faster than a man could march on his own feet, and when the best weapons available were muzzle-loaders, her vast numbers of soldiers undeniably gave Russia great power. By the Crimean war, this was already shown to have much diminished; at a moment when no railway line ran south of Moscow and the supply of Russian reinforcements and supply to the Crimea posed great logistical difficulties to her generals, British and French commanders could deliver by sea sufficient force to wrest from Russia her main Black Sea naval base. In 1901 there were still question-marks over Russia's true strength, although it had much recovered since mid-century. With over 35,000 miles of railway track (mainly in her western provinces) her superiority in numbers was once again formidable, a matter of much concern to the German General Staff. The Russian army and navy had, too, been re-equipped with up-to-date ordnance and ships. Yet Russia was still in many ways a backward – and very obviously backward – country. Setting aside the question of her political stability, notoriously liable to disturbance by recurrent rural disorder and terrorism, two-thirds of her population (of over 100 million as the century began) was illiterate. Most of it worked in agriculture and by comparison with western Europe (though not with their neighbours in Bulgaria and Romania) most Russians lived in miserable poverty.[26] Russia's gross industrial output, it is true, was the fifth largest in the world, but for so huge a population and given the qualifications which had to be made for the special characteristics of Russian manufacturing (much of it still came from non-factory, cottage and peasant producers), that was not very revealing. It was an inadequate base on which to carry the high military expenditure of a great power. Yet the growth rate in the manufacturing sector was high, running at about 8 per cent per annum

---

[26] For a brief discussion of relevant matters, see M.E. Falkus, *The Industrialisation of Russia, 1700–1914* (London, 1972). He suggests (p.11) that even in 1914 national income per capita in the United Kingdom was still four and a half times larger than Russia's, Germany's three times, and Italy's double.

in the 1890s. Though the pace slackened for a time in the early 1900s, it again began to rise rapidly from 1907 onwards. In the countryside, the benefits of the emancipation of serfs a half-century earlier were by then beginning to work through at last. At a moment when international interest rates were low, borrowing abroad (mainly in France) to finance industrial and infrastructure was easy and the cost tolerable. The completion of the Trans-Siberian railway was begun, as well as major railway building in the west. Such facts (and there were others which could be cited) were impressive, even in 1901. They tended to worry Russia's neighbours. Even if it was still hard to be assured of Russia's exact strength as an international competitor, it was clear at least that she was much nearer to realizing her vast potential than she had been fifty years earlier.

POTENTIAL FOR CHANGE

As diplomats strove to look forward into a new century, they would not have found it hard to identify certain areas and countries where change might be expected. Two (upon which imperial Russia had long looked with covetous eyes) were to be found in the Ottoman and Chinese empires. So far as the first was concerned two centuries of decline had already assured it a place always near the centre of the international stage. There had already been many wars of the Ottoman succession, and seemed likely to be more. Though still vast in extent, the Ottoman empire was certainly not a great power. For all its potential resources, its ability to control its subjects and to protect its territories from predators fell far short of its aspirations and did so only too obviously. Though less and less a European power as time passed, it was always likely to be in the forefront of the calculations of European statesmen, in part because its further decay would be bound to provoke rival claimants to the booty. China, too, presented what could still be seen in 1901 as similar potential and Russia was a well-established predator in Asia. Other nations, too, had of course taken a growing interest in China and in the Far East as a whole as the nineteenth century went on, but a more recent change that they had to consider as they surveyed Asia was the emergence of modernizing Japan. By 1901, most diplomats also accepted that she was bound to have a significant role in the world card pack, though some thought it might be as joker: Japan's weight varied according to the particular circumstances with which she was confronted. She was nonetheless bound to be regionally important. Some thought Commodore Perry might have uncorked a bottle containing a particularly muscular and unpredictable genie.[27] This was an over-simplification, but Japan's assertion of an independence to pursue her own interests and escape the bullying which China underwent was bound to revive her interest in areas of mainland Asia in which other great powers were interested, too, above all, Korea. This would trouble her relations with other powers.

Japanese intentions remained uncertain but increasingly pre-occupying and help to explain why a coalition of European great powers in 1895 forced her to forgo some of her gains when she made a victorious peace with China. France, Russia and Germany sensed a growing threat to their own Far Eastern interests. In absolute terms in the scale of power, so far as such a thing could be measured, Japan might not yet weigh greatly but no individual European great power (except, perhaps, Great Britain, which took no part in coercing her, or Russia, which did) was likely to be able to bring much strength to bear against her. The main concerns of most of the great powers were still in Europe, and that is where the resources of most of them had mainly to be deployed. Japan's success and the notice taken of it was the outstanding illustration of a truth still to wait decades for its full demonstration, that European power, for all its magnificent certainty and apparent irresistibility as the century ended, was not absolute. It was limited in the Far East by circumstance (above all, geographical circumstance) as it was limited in its relations with the United States. That country, of course, was potentially the greatest power of all, but what this would mean could hardly be guessed in 1901.

[27] Perry was the commander of a United States naval squadron sent in 1852 to Japan with a message from President Fillmore requesting a treaty with the isolated empire. One was negotiated on Perry's return to Japan in 1854 and is conventionally regarded as the beginning of the process of 'opening' Japan to intercourse with western countries.

3

The White Man's World

EMPIRE AND IMPERIALISM

The way in which of the world order of 1901 is most obviously different from both that of 1801 and that of our own day is the extent to which its fate either was or appeared to be in the hands of what were called white peoples. Most of the globe's land surface was in that year in the outright physical and legal possession of European nations or their overseas offshoots, new nations like Canada or Australia, or of yet older offspring of empire, such as the American republics, north and south. Non-western, independent states based on their own historic institutions took up much less of the world's inhabited lands, even allowing for the huge size of China. Japan was a serious and viable contender for her own independence (and provided an example of non-white overseas imperialism on the mainland of Asia and in Formosa). Korea, Siam, Afghanistan and Persia were nominally independent, but all owed their survival less to their own strength and viability than to their position and utility as historic buffers between territory occupied by imperial overlords. These over-lords were sometimes menacing neighbours; they were also all Euro-pean, except in Korea, though there the nominal suzerainty of China was largely ignored by the Russians and the Japanese. In Africa north of the Zambezi, only Liberia and Ethiopia had escaped direct rule or 'protection' by Europeans. Morocco, independent but looking temptingly disordered as the century began, was seen as an area of great potential for expansion by both Spain and France. In southern Africa two independent republics both dominated by European stocks and settlement were just surviving in 1901, though about to go under in their war with Great Britain: the South African Republic, usually known as the Transvaal, and the Orange Free State. Imperial high-handedness was soon to be shown again, too, in a new vigour of interference in the affairs of its Caribbean neighbours by the United States.

Great empires were the most spectacular features of the world's political landscape in 1901. They divided between themselves most of its land surface. They were of two kinds: old agglomerations of largely contiguous territory (the east European and Ottoman empires, and China, were the most obvious examples) and the newer empires of colonial possessions overseas (of which the British was the outstanding instance). All of them ruled alien peoples. The second class still seemed to be expanding and expressed in its most obvious form the world hegemony of the white minority of mankind. The impact on history of what the nineteenth century came to call 'imperialism' – the positive advocacy and promotion of particular forms of their supremacy – has generated an immense body of scholarly writing and probably even more diatribe. Selective use of evidence for and against, conscious censorship and simple prejudice have all encumbered the recovery of the truth and helped to sustain *a priori* positions. Very little is agreed by all commentators, except the most obvious points: that empire and imperialism were very important facts of modern history, and that the phenomena which expressed them were hugely varied in both their nature and their appearance.

For most of this century, though, imperialism has tended to get a bad press. Strong cases have many times been made for seeing the whole story as simply one of domination at its most gross, as the most obvious way in which white peoples exploited others. The ills of independent countries, thirty or forty years after their emergence to statehood, are still often attributed without qualification to what was done (or not done) which should not (or should) have been done in colonial times. Yet there have also always been those who have seen the colonial era as in greater or lesser degree objectively beneficial to those ruled by the colonial powers. Though a minority, they too have pointed to undoubted truths – for instance, that white rule ensured peace as never before over sometimes large areas of the world's surface (India is the most notable example) and that it can hardly be plausible to say that no good at all came of that. The introduction by colonial

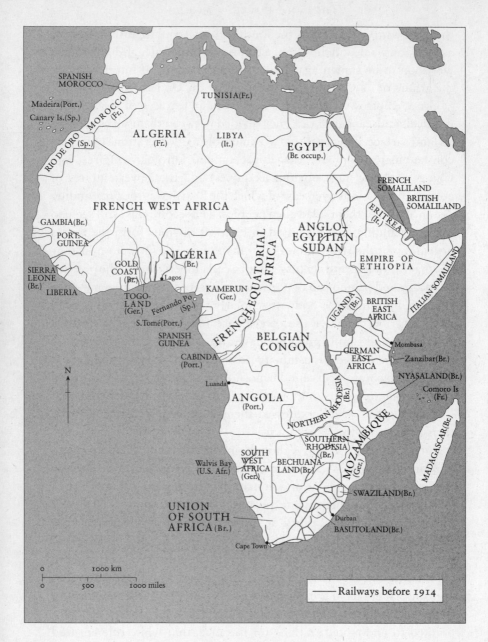

SPANISH
MOROCCO

Madeira(Port.)

Canary Is.(Sp.)

RIO DE ORO
(Sp.)

MOROCCO
(Fr.)

ALGERIA
(Fr.)

TUNISIA(Fr.)

LIBYA
(It.)

EGYPT
(Br. occup.)

FRENCH
SOMALILAND

BRITISH
SOMALILAND

ERITREA
(It.)

FRENCH WEST AFRICA

GAMBIA(Br.)

PORT.
GUINEA

SIERRA
LEONE
(Br.)

LIBERIA

GOLD
COAST
(Br.)

TOGO-
LAND
(Ger.)

NIGERIA
(Br.)

Lagos

Fernando Po
(Sp.)

S.Tomé(Port.)

SPANISH
GUINEA

KAMERUN
(Ger.)

CABINDA
(Port.)

FRENCH EQUATORIAL AFRICA

ANGLO-
EGYPTIAN
SUDAN

EMPIRE OF
ETHIOPIA

UGANDA
(Br.)

BRITISH
EAST
AFRICA

ITALIAN SOMALILAND

Mombasa

Zanzibar(Br.)

GERMAN
EAST
AFRICA

NYASALAND(Br.)

Comoro Is
(Fr.)

BELGIAN
CONGO

Luanda

ANGOLA
(Port.)

NORTHERN RHODESIA (Br.)

SOUTHERN
RHODESIA
(Br.)

MOZAMBIQUE
(Ger.)

MADAGASCAR(Br.)

N

Walvis Bay
(U.S. Afr.)

SOUTH
WEST
AFRICA
(Ger.)

BECHUANA-
LAND(Br.)

SWAZILAND(Br.)

UNION
OF SOUTH
AFRICA (Br.)

Durban

BASUTOLAND(Br.)

Cape Town

1000 km

500   1000 miles

——— Railways before 1914

Africa before the First World War

rulers of modern medicine, education, or the provision of investment in infrastructure in the form of communications or irrigation (for example) can also be seen as blessings, even if not unqualified; at the very least, it has been argued, they were a preamble to (or aspects of) a modernization which brought advantages and progressive improvement to peoples who needed them. Such facts, of course, have sometimes been applauded in just as crudely indiscriminate a way as unqualified condemnations of colonial rule have been mounted because of the careless social disruption they seemed to imply.

In recent years, greater subtlety has been brought into what began as a very crude debate. There has been closer and more careful observation of what actually happened in different societies and more attention paid to the immense variety of what can only misleadingly be thought of as 'the colonial experience' as a phenomenon uniform, or largely so. The social disturbance and destabilization brought about by the introduction of alien ways and institutions can now sometimes be acknowledged to have been great, while at the same time bringing benefits with them. Conversely, for all the spread of western forms and the conscious zeal of white administrators in imposing them, it has often been pointed out that in some colonies they left life virtually undisturbed, that their efforts often produced no more than superficial change, and that deep patterns of indigenous culture remained intact.

No over-arching generalization is possible. 'Empire' and 'imperialism' (and, for that matter, 'colonialism') were words invented to allow western minds to come to grips with certain topics. They mean little, except in specific contexts. In each of thousands of different sets of circumstances the facts of conscious direction and formal government (where it existed) operated in distinctive ways, responding to different local conditions and to different preoccupations and assumptions among imperial rulers themselves. This had been true even at the start of the European onslaught on the world centuries earlier, and would never be more evident than as the western imperial age was coming to a close in the twentieth century. The prime example of an overseas empire in 1801 had already been that of Great Britain; that was still true 100 years later, but the British empire had by then dramatically changed in its nature and extent. The crumbling of the Spanish empire so soon after the rebellion of the British thirteen colonies had led many people to expect that the Canadian and Australasian settler colonies of the British empire would throw off the rule of London, too. This indeed happened, but by no means as anticipated. As the nineteenth century was ending, volunteer contingents were arriving in South Africa from other colonies to fight for the British in the war for empire there. A century earlier, no one would have dreamed that a single colonial soldier would ever be available to help the 'mother country' in her wars.

To understand the nature of empires and imperialism in 1901 it is best to recall at the outset how short-lived an historical phenomenon it turned out to be. A huge recession of alien, white-race rule is one of the most important facts of the history of this century. Today only Russia among European states rules much more of the earth's surface than it did in 1400 (and that is a somewhat artificial comparison: we can, after all, hardly discern something geographically and politically recognizable as 'Russia' in medieval Muscovy, whatever cultural continuity may suggest). From the fifteenth century to the early twentieth, though, the tide of empire flowed continuously with only local and occasional checks, growing confidence and seemingly swelling success. Some of the new nations of European settlement overseas (the United States of America is the outstanding example), which came into existence in those centuries, now occupy territories much larger than anything conceivable when they first appeared and they have made their own imperial and colonial acquisitions since their foundation. The American republic continued to grow in geographical extent well into the twentieth century, and has never felt it needed to 'decolonize' its mainland territory or to return any of it to the descendants of the aboriginal native Americans,[1] far less to the Mexicans, from whom much of it was taken in the nineteenth century.

This century's great reversal of the imperial tide is now taken for granted, though. As a result, it can be difficult to recognize the degree to which things were once otherwise, how natural a state of affairs people could then find domination over others, and how confident some could be (even withing living memory) that imperialism was

[1] Though some continue to enjoy special advantages and protection under federal law.

still the wave of the future. Why this was once credible is a vastly ramifying, complicated story, not to be summarized here. General explanations are generally unhelpful. Once again, it was often a matter of very specific and particular local circumstances, the work of distinctive individuals and their distinctive purposes. The legacies which imperialism left to the future were also very varied, whatever superficial resemblances they sometimes seem to share. Specific timings and sequences of change mattered a lot, notably in the Americas, where the events of 1776–83 in the British colonies had important repercussions in the independence struggles of Latin America only a quarter of a century later that mark the first era of decolonization.

THE EUROPEAN EMPIRES

Clearly, the imperialism of Europeans is another of those stories that cannot be taken up suddenly in 1901. Old empires had gone on growing in the nineteenth century. The outstanding example, territorially, was the Russian. At first sight, its linkage of growth overland with demographic diffusion makes it look somewhat like the expansion of the United States. Both countries acquired huge contiguous tracts of land empty of all but a few aboriginals, establishing new populations in them. Both also seized big tracts of the territory of neighbouring states, Mexico in the one case, Persia and China in the other. From a different standpoint, Russian imperialism also somewhat resembles British expansion in India: much of the nineteenth century was spent by soldiers and statesmen in search of viable frontiers by overthrowing, overawing or patronizing native rulers. The outcome was in the one case the domination of much of Central Asia and its great caravan cities and a huge despoliation of China, and in the other the subjugation of the sub-continent of India and, eventually, Burma (indirectly also a despoliation of China, though more marginal than Russia's, since Burma was supposed to be only a tributary of Peking).

Russian imperialism was in yet another way special. At the end of the nineteenth century her rulers still had lingering imperial dreams to the south and south-west in the region of the Black Sea, the Caucasus and the Danubian lands. It was unlikely, given her partners in the crime of the eighteenth-century partition of Poland, Hohenzollern Prussia and the Habsburg monarchy, that she could hope for or need fear any change in the state of affairs in that country. Further south, on the other hand, temptations to adventure were always likely to spring up in the long-enduring, but weak, Ottoman empire. Such temptation had taken Russia into the Crimean war with Great Britain and France (and almost with Habsburg Austria). In the closing decades of the nineteenth century, a vision of a Russian Constantinople and with it control of egress from the Black Sea, capital of an ancient empire reclaimed for Christianity and under the flag of the old double eagle the tsars had borrowed from Byzantium, still hung about in the daydreams of Russian diplomats and strategists, though at that moment obscured by their empire's spectacular territorial advances in Asia. On the Caspian, in Armenia, Central Asia and, above all, the Far East, Russia had already added vast new territory to her empire. Russians had advanced beyond the river Amur (the boundary with Manchuria established in 1858) to take more from China, and had completed by 1901 a rail link of European Russia with the Far East as far as Chita, beyond Lake Baikal. Soon the tracks would reach Vladivostok, the capital of the province beyond the river Usuri, cutting across Manchuria to provide a link with Port Arthur, the naval base that Russia had secured on lease from China in 1898.

Among the old nations with overseas empires, Great Britain and France had waxed fattest in the nineteenth century, as changing maps make clear. The pattern of British acquisition reflected a growing British preoccupation with sea routes to Asia and a deepening involvement in India. By 1850 the sub-continent was no longer just a great trading prize, important though that was; much of the rest of the empire had by then only been acquired because of India. British control over the subcontinent itself was almost complete. The Raj was already the centrepiece of British empire and communications with it gave the Near East new importance. Without formally contesting the Ottoman claim to suzerainty there, the British had in 1879 begun an occupation of Egypt – which soon led to them effectively ruling that country – and were in that year given a protectorate in Cyprus as well. Their installation in Egypt especially enraged the French, who had found North Africa a growing temptation as the nineteenth century went on. Their conquest of Algeria had begun as early as 1830, and with it a long partition of Ottoman Africa.[2] The French seemed almost inevitably drawn forward in North Africa if only for reasons of geography, and though the making of Algeria took decades, there were soon conflicts with Morocco and Tunis. The latter became a French protectorate in 1881 while Morocco was increasingly to come under French influence and 'protection'. To the North African ports there began to flow European immigrants, not only from France, but also from Spain and Italy. European settlement did not, of course, mean that local inhabitants were eliminated; the day when they might have suffered the fate of the Aztec, North American Indian or Australian aborigine was long past. Moreover, Muslim North Africans were part of a civilization that had once contested Iberia with Christendom, ruling half that peninsula; they had important cultural resources to sustain their sense of identity. Nonetheless, the peasants of the Maghreb suffered gravely, above all economically, as the introduction of alien notions of land law broke up traditional usages, impoverished the peasantry, and led to profound social changes. Meanwhile 'Algeria' was imposed by France as a framework on diverse peoples, Arab, Berber and European, and was given a departmental and administrative structure integrated with that of the metropolitan country itself.

IDEALISM, INTERESTS AND IMAGINATION

To explain the vigour of what has sometimes been called the 'imperialist wave' of the nineteenth century is no simple matter. By 1914, more than four-fifths of the world's land surface outside Antarctica was under either a European flag, or the flag of a nation of European settlement. Part of that story is one of the sheer momentum of accumulated power. The hegemony of the strong became more and more irresistible, for it built upon growing strength. Technology had added to that strength, and not only by providing weapons. As paddle steamers pushed up the river valleys of the 'Dark Continent' of Africa

[2] Though Ottoman rule in North Africa was at one moment actually extended by the seizure of Tripoli in 1835.

to penetrate its interior, its full exploitation began to be feasible at last. Medicine began to fight back effectively against tropical disease (even if only slowly) and made it easier to establish permanent bases in hitherto hardly touched regions – notably sub-Saharan Africa, in territorial extent the main theatre of empire-building after 1870.

Usually, hopes aroused by such new capacities were ill-founded; they were often disappointed. Yet late imperial expansion continued to have, as empire always had done, important random factors in its working which make it hard to generalize. Among them were individuals, some of them popular heroes, for this most active phase of European imperialism coincided with a growth of popular participation in public affairs, even if merely superficial. By buying newspapers, voting, or cheering in the streets, the masses of the advanced countries could enjoy imperial competition as a spectator sport. A new cheap newspaper press dramatized exploration and colonial warfare.[3] Novelists and travellers wrote best-sellers about both. Some politicians thought that social dissatisfactions might be soothed by emigration or even just by pride and excitement as the national flag was hoisted over new areas (even when experts knew that nothing was likely to be forthcoming except expense). As a motivation of the most enterprising, sheer greed was important. But cynicism is not the whole story, nor is the profit motive. Idealism inspired some imperialists and salved the consciences of others. Men who believed that they possessed true civilization were bound to see the ruling of others for their good as a duty. When Rudyard Kipling urged Americans to remember new responsibilities they were acquiring towards Filipinos, he told them to take up 'the White Man's Burden', not the White Man's Booty.

The dark side of the balance sheet of empire has so often been set out that there is mercifully no need for further elaboration on the many wickednesses it contains. Yet glib acknowledgement should not be the last word on the subject, either. The problem of self-justification always presented itself: many Europeans and Americans witnessed terrible things happening in colonial territories. Some of them per-

---

[3] Not only in the West, either; when Japan went to war with China in 1894, her sixty-six newspapers sent 114 correspondents, eleven artists and four photographers to report the fighting.

petrated their own evils. Others did nothing to stop them. Some administrators saw their task only as one of ensuring that western settlers and visitors could extract whatever advantage they had sought in coming to colonies in the first place. It is too simple to explain this, though, by saying they were all bad and greedy. The work of missionaries, humanitarians and defenders of native rights among them by itself makes the harshest judgements untenable. There is a special state of mind to be recognized; it took for granted the moral superiority of the culture of the colonial power. Furthermore, even Europeans who could recognize that the native populations could be damaged by contact with whites could not be expected at that time to understand the full corrosive effect of their own arrival when it was benevolent in intention. This required an anthropological knowledge and insight still to be achieved.

Such insight was all the more difficult when a lot of native culture looked indeed like simple savagery. North African and Indian peasant cultivators could be accepted as a level above that, but head-hunting, cannibalism and human sacrifice definitely could not. The European's missionary confidence was strong, he (or she) *knew* they were on the side of Progress and Improvement and many saw themselves as on the side of the Cross, too.[4] Great moral confidence ran through every side of European hegemony, whether in white settler colonies, directly ruled possessions or the arrangements for protectorates and privileges made with dependent societies. Those who no longer possess that confidence face an obstacle to understanding an age that did. The assured sense of belonging to a higher civilization was not only a licence for predatory habits (as Christianity itself had often been), but was the nerve of an attitude akin, in another way, too, to that of crusaders. Imperialists were usually sure that they brought something better than what indigenous cultures could offer. All too often, this

---

[4] Notable, too, was the missionary zeal of Americans. President McKinley, who presided over the annexation of the Philippine islands to the United States, confessed to agonizing about what to do with them until he realized that his country's duty would be to 'uplift and Christianize' the Filipinos (most of whom, of course, were Catholics, thanks to 300 years of Spanish rule). For his prayerful hesitations see his words quoted in S. E. Morison, H. S. Commager and W. E. Leuchtenburg, *The Growth of the American Republic*, vol. ii, 6th edn (New York, 1969), pp.257–8.

would blind white men and women to the actual and material results of turning hunters and gatherers, whose possessions were what they could carry, into wage-earners, or peasants used to communitarian agriculture into hired field hands by substituting individual freehold for collective rights.

The ideological confidence of those men and women, though, also rested on the knowledge that in the last resort they could not be kept away, even from countries that they did not colonize. There appeared to be almost no part of the world where they could not, if they wished, impose themselves, if necessary, by armed strength (this had been shown in the Americas, north and south, as well as in the European overseas empires). Nineteenth-century weapons had much increased their relative advantage. At the battle of Omdurman in the Sudan in 1898 a British regiment opened fire on its opponents at 2,000 yards' range with the standard rifle of the British army of the day; a few minutes later, shrapnel shell and machine-guns were shredding to pieces the masses of a native army that never reached the British line. By the end of the battle, 10,000 Sudanese were dead, but only forty-eight British and Egyptian soldiers. True, the Khalifa had machine-guns of his own at Omdurman, as well as telegraph apparatus to communicate with his forces, and electric mines to blow up the British gunboats on the Nile. But none of these things was usefully employed; not only a technical, but a mental transformation was required before non-European cultures could turn the instrumentation of the Europeans against them. The result was a huge imbalance of power. In 1905 the tiny German armed forces and settler population in Tanganyika virtually lost control of their colony for months in the Maji-Maji rebellion. But the outcome was hardly in doubt. Seventy-five thousand Africans died in the repression of the rebellion and subsequent famine. It was only one of scores of examples of a ruthless use of force against indigenous peoples by imperial power.

SETTLERS AND NATIVES

Great Britain had for centuries provided the outstanding example of a country used to planting colonies of its sons and daughters far away across the oceans. Like the *creoles* of Spanish America and the Dutch settlers who arrived in the Cape of Good Hope in the seventeenth century, the British had in due course given birth to new nations. So had evolved what might be called new 'native' peoples, white and distinct from the aboriginal inhabitants. In British official circles, one outcome had been, broadly speaking, a certain coolness towards what were still thought of as 'settlers'. They made expensive claims on the 'mother country', their actions could embroil her in diplomatic quarrels with other nations, and there was always the uncomfortable and humiliating memory of 1783 at the back of the official mind. Colonies tended to have disturbed frontiers, too, which led them to further territorial advances and Westminster to the unwilling acquisition of new responsibilities for alien peoples. Settlers gave empire a bad name among administrators who tried to tackle colonial affairs with an eye to economy and the avoidance of trouble; the Spanish could count themselves lucky, it was thought in London, in having shed the responsibility for most of their former settler possessions well before 1901.

In the huge spaces of Canada and Australia history led, somewhat stormily, to the union of individual colonies in North America and Australasia in federal structures with responsibility for their own government. Though still, in 1901 owing allegiance to the crown, the British colonies were somewhat hybrid governmental forms with practical, even if not completely formal, independence. They had their own currencies and armed forces, while still seeing themselves parts of the British empire. The Commonwealth of Australia (which came into existence with this century on 1 January 1901) had been preceded by the granting of responsible government to originally distinct colonies, as had happened earlier in Canada before its confederation in 1867. There had been difficulties; in Canada, there was a French-speaking community in the province of Quebec, in Australia, clashes of interest between settlers and convicts in the early days. Canada and Australia were huge and still, in 1901, thinly populated; a sense of nationality could only slowly be generated in them. New Zealand was also to achieve full independent status in 1907, but one less decentralized, as befitted its smaller extent. Interestingly, as the new century began, New Zealand's government was already showing remarkable independence and vigour in the pursuit of advanced social welfare policies; women had the vote there, and the eight-hour day and old age pensions had both been introduced in the 1890s – as was a stiffening of controls on Asian immigration.

In 1906 a Colonial Conference in London decided that the name 'Dominion' should in future be used for the British self-governing dependencies, which meant, in effect, the colonies of white settlement. No other colonial power except France had overseas possessions with such substantial white populations as those of the British crown. Attempts to encourage settlement by Germans in south-west Africa and Tanganyika, or by Italians in Eritrea and Somaliland, achieved little, numerically speaking. Dutch residents in Indonesia had been established there a long time, but were comparatively few.[5] France remained a special case only because of Algeria, which was not technically a colony at all. Some of the European immigrants there settled on the land but many more in the cities. Nevertheless, a revolution in the countryside had followed them. The French introduced new crops, and also bought under favourable land laws land that had previously been communally owned. Antagonism with the bulk of the native peasantry inevitably followed.

The growth of humanitarian and missionary sentiment in England and the well-founded Colonial Office tradition of distrust of settler demands made it harder to overlook the native populations of the British colonies than it had been for the nineteenth-century Americans who flooded into the unorganized west and the lands acquired from Mexico after the Louisiana Purchase to sweep aside their own native American 'Indians', as they were then called. Modernity, though, often made a disastrous impact on very primitive societies. Some of them were at a stage of achievement low enough to be called Neolithic

[5] The population of the Netherlands Indies born in Europe (which was not quite the same thing as the European population) was said to be 14,316 in 1895 (J. S. Furnivall, *Netherlands India – A Study of Plural Economy* (Cambridge, 1939), p.233).

if not Palaeolithic, and were very vulnerable. The impact on them of the white man's arrival – yet alone the imposition of his government – could be catastrophic. In Canada, the Indians and Eskimos were relatively few, and presented no such military obstacle to the exploitation of the west and north-west as had done the Plains Indians in their struggle to keep their hunting-grounds in the American West. The story in Australia was bloodier. The hunting and gathering societies of the aborigines were fatally disrupted by settlement, tribes were antagonized and provoked into violence by the uncomprehending brutality of the white Australians, and new imported diseases fast cut into their numbers. The early decades of white Australia are stained by the blood of massacred aborigines; in this century there was notorious neglect, bullying and exploitation of the survivors. No other population inside once British territory underwent a fate so like that of the American Indian as did the aboriginal Australians. In New Zealand, the arrival of the first white men brought guns to the Maori, who employed them both on one another, and then in later wars with the settlers. The essential issue was the displacement of the Maori from their lands and, once again, the indigenous people were the losers. When the fighting ended, the government took steps to safeguard the tribal lands from further expropriation, but the introduction of English notions of individual ownership led to further disintegration and their virtual disappearance by the end of the century. The Maoris, too, declined in numbers, even if not so violently or irreversibly as did the Australian aborigines. In South Africa, an old Dutch settler country, the story is a mixed one; British protection enabled some of its native peoples to survive into the twentieth century living on their ancestral lands lives which changed only slowly. Others were driven off or exterminated.

In all cases, though, in South Africa, as elsewhere, the crux of the situation was that the fate of the original inhabitants was never in their own hands, they suffered whether this was intended or not. What was at stake was almost always land. Alien notions of freehold and transferability played havoc with traditional peasant societies based on customary allocations of grazing and cultivation. The fates of native peoples were to be shaped in future by different local balances of governmental interest and benevolence, settler needs and ideas, economic opportunities and exigencies. In the short run they could sometimes present formidable security problems but they could never in the end generate from their own resources the means of effective resistance. For non-European peoples to do that, they would have to Europeanize.

IMPERIALISM AND INTERNATIONAL RELATIONS: THE 'SCRAMBLE FOR AFRICA'

European governments had quarrelled with one another outside Europe at least since the sixteenth century. The later nineteenth century brought extra-European issues even more visibly and frequently into play. 1901 is not a significant date within this process. Yet though European nations in the nineteenth century often bickered about their interests overseas, and though the United States went to war with one of them in 1898, the partitioning of much of the non-European world was carried out in an amazingly peaceful manner. One reason was the lingering *Pax Britannica* imposed by British naval supremacy, which for the whole nineteenth century presented an obstacle to the European powers fighting one another for mastery of the non-European world just when the greatest extension ever of direct colonial rule was going on. There were no repeat performances of the colonial wars of earlier times. The final outcome, indeed, when a Great War at last broke out in 1914, was that Great Britain, Russia and France, the three nations which had quarrelled most over imperial difficulties in the previous thirty years, found themselves on the same side. Overseas colonial rivalry cannot explain that conflict, though it contributed to it psychologically. Quarrels over non-European affairs before 1914 were in fact often positive distractions from the more dangerous rivalries of Europe itself: perhaps they even helped to preserve European peace.

This had been most strikingly shown in the historical process remembered as the 'Scramble for Africa': a spreading of European power into the non-European world unrivalled in extent and pace since the sixteenth-century Spanish conquests in the Americas. Outside Algeria or South Africa, for most of the nineteenth century only a little of Africa beyond a few coastal enclaves had been in European hands. In 1879 the arrival of a British army in Egypt registered yet another setback for the Ottoman empire, of which that country remained formally a part, and also a change in the continent's fate; to the south, even before the century ended, Anglo-Egyptian rule had been pushed deep into the Sudan. Elsewhere, southwards from Morocco round to the Cape of Good Hope, the African coastline was by the beginning of the twentieth century entirely divided between Europeans (British, French, Germans, Spanish, Portuguese and Belgians) with the exception of the isolated black republic of Liberia. The empty wastes of the Sahara and Sahel became nominally French, as was the basin of the Senegal River and much of the northern Congo; Tunisia was a French protectorate. The Belgian king enjoyed as a personal estate (and his agents governed atrociously) most of the rest of the Congo, which was soon to prove some of the richest mineral-bearing land in Africa; the Belgian state was to take over responsibility from him for what was called the 'Congo Free State' in 1906. Further east, apart from the Boer republics of Transvaal and Orange Free State over which the British government claimed suzerainty, British territories ran almost continuously from the Cape of Good Hope up to the Rhodesias, which were hemmed in by the Belgian Congo and German and Portuguese East Africa (Tanganyika and Mozambique). The last two cut them off from the sea, but further north, from Mombasa, Kenya's port, a belt of British territory stretched throughout Uganda to the borders of the Sudan and the headwaters of the Nile. Somalia (divided between the British, Italian and French) and Italian Eritrea isolated Ethiopia, the only African country other than Liberia still to escape European domination. This ancient Christian polity was ruled by the only African monarch of the nineteenth century to avert the European threat by a military success, the annihilation of an Italian army at Adowa in 1896. Other Africans could not prevail, as the Anglo-Egyptian conquest of the Sudan in 1898, and, in the next century, the Portuguese mastery (with some difficulty) of insurrection in Angola in 1902, the British destruction of the Zulu and Matabele in 1907, and, most bloodily, the German quelling of Tanganyika in 1907 and massacre of the Herrero of south-west Africa in the same year, were to show.

A colossal extension of European power in Africa had thus been brought about, for the most part in the last twenty years of the nineteenth century. By 1901 the Scramble was virtually over, and African history had been transformed. It had in twenty years drawn in previously non-imperial countries – Belgium, Germany and Italy – to join the old colonial powers of Great Britain, France, Portugal and Spain.[6] The bargains of European negotiators, the accidents of discovery and the convenience of colonial administrations were now to shape the modernization of Africa. The suppression of inter-tribal warfare and the introduction of even elementary medical services released population growth in some areas, but distortion of the local economy and the introduction of new diseases cramped it in others. The sandflies which came to Angola from Brazil in the 1850s had spread continent-wide by the end of the century and were contributing by then to a series of demographic disasters.[7] As in America centuries earlier, though, the introduction of new crops also made it possible to feed more people. New docks and railways began the reorientation of trading patterns. Much followed from what often began in almost casual encounters, decisions often haphazardly arrived at or fashioned by circumstance, but with little danger of international conflict once Europeans had settled the main lines of partition.

Different colonial regimes had their special impacts. Long after the colonialists had gone home, distinctions survived between countries where, say, French administration or British judicial practice had taken root.[8] Statutory labour days were used in French and Belgian Africa to raise revenue: poll tax was the preferred instrument elsewhere. All over the continent Africans found new patterns of

[6] Though today there are still some Spanish possessions on the Moroccan coast, they are all that is left of an empire which in 1901 still included Rio Muni and associated islands in the Gulf of Guinea, and Rio Oro (Spanish Sahara), acquired in the nineteenth century, but before the Scramble.

[7] See J. Iliffe, *Africa, The History of a Continent* (Cambridge, 1995), pp. 210–11, on this topic and the difficulty of talking about general patterns of demographic damage in Africa at the turn of the century. Professor Iliffe suggests as 'a knowledgeable guess' that the population of the Belgian Congo fell by a third or even a half in 1880–1920.

[8] For first-hand observation and an agreeable introduction to the realities of different systems of colonial rule, see Geoffrey Gorer, *Africa Dances* (London, 1935).

employment, observed the mysterious ways of Europeans, sometimes learning something of them through European schools or service in colonial regiments, and saw different things to admire or hate in what had now come to regulate, directly or indirectly, and in varying degree, their lives. Even when, as in British possessions, emphasis was placed on rule through traditional native authorities, such institutions had henceforth to work in a new context. Tribal and kinship groups would go on asserting themselves but more and more would do so with or against the grain of new structures created by colonialism. These structures helped the task of the Christian missionary, whose shaping influence it is impossible not to recognize, though hard to measure. Christianity may well have changed Africa more than colonialism. The first book printed in every African language was almost always the Christian Bible. European languages, Christian monogamy, entrepreneurial attitudes, new knowledge and concepts all contributed finally to the legacy that would in the end be left to independent Africa, and thus to a new self-consciousness; they made possible new notions of identity, a new individualism, and created new native élites. Such changes corrupted and undermined local cultures. From them, though, would emerge the new Africans of the twentieth century, shaped by the literacy and education provided by missionary, as well as official, efforts. Without imperialism, for good or ill, it is hard to believe that such influences could have been so effective so fast, or perhaps effective at all. How much weight should be given to them as facts offsetting the suffering and exploitation colonial domination often brought with them is another matter.

Europe, by contrast, was hardly changed by African adventure except, perhaps, psychologically. Empire and imperialism were influences shaping self-identity, and in an age of growing popular participation in politics, that mattered somewhat. In that process, then, the Scramble had its part. It was a colourful spectacle which attracted much public interest and struck popular imagination through the ease with which, it seemed, Europeans could lay their hands on yet more easily exploitable wealth. Yet before 1939 probably only Belgium drew resources from colonial Africa that made a significant economic difference to its national future; France never made a financial 'profit' on its colonies.[9] Increasingly, what was done in Africa aroused political criticism in Europe, too. An age proud of its humane civilization did not like what it heard some of the new *conquistadores* were up to. The administration of the Congo by the Belgian king Leopold (which caused outrage across Europe) and forced labour in Portuguese Africa were notorious examples; refugees from the rural round-ups in Mozambique sought refuge and even found better working conditions by fleeing to South Africa. There were many instances of Africa's natural resources – human and material – undergoing ruthless exploitation or despoliation in the interests of profit by Europeans, often with the connivance of imperial authorities. This stimulated anti-colonial movements and lobbies in Europe, where bad consciences were hard to silence.

Some European nations recruited African soldiers (the French hoped to employ them in Europe itself to offset the weight of German numbers; the British and Germans saw their *askaris* rather as local security forces). Some countries envisaged outlets for emigration that would ease social problems, but the opportunities Africa presented for European settlement were very mixed. There were large blocks of old white settlement in the south, and more were established as the British opened up the Kenyan and Rhodesian lands suitable for white farmers. Apart from this there were the Europeanized cities of French North Africa where most of a growing immigrant population settled, and increasing numbers of Portuguese in Angola. The hopes later entertained of Tripolitania as an outlet for Italians, on the other hand, were disappointed, and German emigration to both south-west and east Africa was tiny and proved for the most part temporary. Only a few Spanish lived in the sixteenth-century *presidios* of Melilla and Ceuta. Some European countries – Russia, Austria–Hungary and the Scandinavian nations – sent virtually no settlers to Africa at all.

[9] See H. Brunschwig, *French Colonialism, 1871–1914: Myths and Realities* (London, 1966), esp. pp.185–6.

ASIAN AND PACIFIC EMPIRE

The last phase of expansive imperialism changed other parts of the world, too. By 1901 no independent political unit survived among the island peoples of the Pacific.[10] In mainland Asia, above all in the Chinese sphere, the French had established themselves in Indo-China; the British followed suit in Malaya and Burma in order to safeguard the approaches to India from the French. The British went on to launch an expedition to Tibet in 1904, still with the old worries about Indian security from Russian advance in mind. Most of these areas, like much of the zone of Russian overland expansion, were claimed by the Chinese to be under their suzerainty. The story of the crumbling Chinese empire has many parallels with the corrosion of Ottoman, Moroccan and Persian power by European influence, though it was to prove one with even greater importance for world history. At one moment it looked as if a Scramble for China might follow that for Africa, but for the present it is convenient to notice merely that one important way in which the imperialist wave in the Chinese sphere (as in the Pacific) was significantly different from that in Africa was that Americans had a special interest in it. They did not, it is true, join in the sudden rush to acquire leases on Chinese mainland territory in the form of ports and their immediate hinterland which was a feature of 1898 (though they made an abortive attempt to annex a port a couple of years later). Within a few months in 1898, Wei-hai-wei and the New Territories of Hong Kong had been acquired by Great Britain, Tsing-tao on the Shantung peninsula by Germany, the Kwantung peninsula on which Port Arthur stood by Russia, and Kwangchow by France. These were further aggressive impositions on China after those of a half a century and more.

All the European great powers and almost all the overseas European peoples except the South Americans took part in the last great seizures of territories by white peoples. Even the Queenslanders tried to annex New Guinea, and the Italians to pick up something in China. By 1914

[10] The last, the Christian kingdom of Tonga, placed itself by treaty under British protection in 1900.

a third of the world's land surface was under only two flags, those of the United Kingdom and Russia (though how much Russian territory can properly be regarded as colonial is indeed debatable). In that year the United Kingdom ruled 400 million subjects outside its own borders, France over 50 million and Germany and Italy about 14 million each. Yet there were already a few signs that overseas imperialism might at last be running out of steam. China was proving a disappointment after all, for all the talk of her partition. There was little left of the world to divide (though Germany and Great Britain had discussed the possibility of sharing out the Portuguese possessions in Africa, which seemed likely to follow the Spanish empire in America into history). The most obvious area left for further European imperialism was the decaying Ottoman empire, whose final dissolution had long been awaited by would-be beneficiaries. Its partition seemed unlikely, though, to be so peacefully manageable as had been that of Africa: much more crucial issues would be at stake in it for the great powers, because more of them were directly interested in the Balkans (where in 1901 there were still Ottoman lands in dispute) and the Near East.

THE IMPERIAL UNITED STATES

The United States had its own part in the last surge of imperial expansion. In the 1890s America's territorial maturity could be thought to have been achieved. A continuous frontier of domestic settlement no longer existed; the continent had been filled up. Contemporaneously, massive growth had given new importance to the influence of business interests in American government, often expressed in the rhetoric of economic nationalism. By 1898 there could be observed a change in national psychology and mood, which gave a new tone to American policy at the end of the century. For a time even Americans were, it appeared, not immune to currents stirring older nations. It was vividly caught in 1898 by one newspaper's observation that 'a new consciousness seems to have come upon us – the consciousness of strength – and with it a new appetite, the yearning to show our strength . . . whatever it may be, we are animated by a new sensation. We are face to face with a strange destiny. The taste of Empire is in the mouth of the people even as the taste of blood in the jungle. It means an Imperial policy . . .'[11] These currents and this mood helped to swell a uniquely overt burst of American overseas imperialism as the nineteenth century drew to a close. Traditional restraint on the acquisition of new territory overseas seemed to be for a time set aside. For the first time other powers began to recognize that the United States had to be taken into account outside her own hemisphere.[12]

This was something of a novelty. Outside the continent they had long regarded as God-given to them, Americans had been uneasy and distrustful over acquiring territory. The very creation of their country had been by successful colonial rebellion. Even at its most arrogant, imperialism had to be masked, muffled and muted in the republic in a way unnecessary in Europe. The constitution contained no provision for the ruling of colonial possessions and it was always very difficult to see what could be done with new territories that could not be expected in the end to move towards full statehood within the Union. Yet although much of the nineteenth-century territorial expansion of the United States was blatantly imperial, imposed by force on aboriginal Americans and Mexican neighbours alike, Americans had not recognized their imperial activities when packaged as a 'Manifest Destiny'. The development of new American interests in the Far East and the Pacific went beyond this, though, and had in fact begun before the Union had acquired its Pacific coast in 1848. California grew rapidly in population in the next few decades. From the 1840s onwards, the evident crumbling of China's ability to fend off foreign intruders gave that country a new importance in the eyes of Americans, too. One outcome had been Commodore Perry's celebrated expedition to Japan in 1854. There followed the purchase of Alaska, the acquisition in 1878 of a naval base in Samoa, and a few years later agreement that the United States should join the British and the Germans in

[11] From the *Washington Post*, q. in S. E. Morison, H. S. Commager, and W. E. Leuchtenburg, *The Growth of the American Republic*, vol. ii, 6th edn (New York, 1969), p.245.
[12] Though with only 65,000 soldiers (see *The Statesman's Year-Book 1901*, London, 1901) as this century began the United States had an army less than a third of the size of the British, and fewer battleships than Great Britain, Russia or France (*All the World's Fighting Ships*, ed. F. T. Jane, London, 1901).

parcelling out those islands between them. Then, after two decades of growing intervention in its affairs, Hawaii had been annexed to the United States as a Territory, in July 1898.

At that moment, to the south, in the Caribbean, the United States was engaged in an imperial war. For years the Spanish government had failed to master rebellion in Cuba; some Americans thought the Spanish unworthy of retaining American possessions, and the American government had sought to mediate between the two sides (an offer the Spanish government unsurprisingly rejected). When, in February 1898, a mysterious explosion destroyed an American cruiser, the USS *Maine*, in Havana harbour, American passions were aroused and the United States went to war with Spain. Thanks to the extent of the Spanish empire (which had been the first of which it was said, truthfully, that on it the sun never set), the war was to be worldwide, fought both in the Caribbean and the Philippines. That fact made the task of the Spanish navy impossible; it could not defend Spain's possessions in the Far East and Cuba. When peace was made at the end of 1898, American rule replaced Spanish in the Philippines. But the Filipinos soon turned against their supposed liberators. The long and difficult process of disentangling the United States from her first Asian possession opened in guerrilla war.[13] Americans soon discovered that they had little taste for the White Man's Burden in the version thus confronting them, but given the apparent fragility of the Chinese empire, it seemed best in Washington not to withdraw precipitately; naval bases in the Philippines might be useful. On 4 July 1900, the islands were handed over to civilian government. Elsewhere in the Pacific, Guam had gone to the United States at the peace, while in the Caribbean Puerto Rico became effectively American territory and Cuba obtained its independence on terms that assured its domination by the United States. 'It has been a splendid little war,' remarked the United States secretary of state.[14]

There now followed the building of an isthmian canal to connect the Caribbean and the Pacific, a project canvassed since the middle

[13] As, it may be remarked, had done the Japanese seizure of Formosa (now Taiwan) where operations of pacification (lasting from 1895 to 1902) cost the Japanese as many casualties as the war with China which had led to invasion of the island.
[14] Q. in Morison, Commager and Leuchtenburg, p.256.

of the nineteenth century, and once attempted by the French. The half-century's talk of building one was coming to a head when the Spanish-American war broke out. American diplomacy negotiated a way round the danger of possible British participation; all might have seemed plain sailing, had not a snag arisen when, in 1903, a treaty with the United States providing for the acquisition of a canal zone from Colombia was held up by the Colombian legislature. A revolution was more or less overtly engineered in Panama, the area of Colombia where the canal was to run, and the revolutionaries were given United States naval protection against the Colombian government. A new Panamanian republic duly emerged which gratefully bestowed upon the United States the necessary land together with the right to intervene in its affairs to maintain order. Work at last began in 1907 and the canal was duly opened in 1914, an outstanding engineering triumph. The capability it created to move warships swiftly from the Atlantic to the Pacific and back transformed American naval strategy. A deep distrust had been sown, too, in the minds of Latin Americans, about the ambitions and lack of scruple of American foreign policy.

The canal in fact changed American hemisphere policy. Once it became central to American naval thinking, it was more important than ever to assure protection of the Canal Zone by United States influence over stable Caribbean states. In the past, the irritation and disappointment of foreign investors who could not collect debts due to them had led sometimes to diplomatic conflicts and even to threats of armed intervention in the region. Attempts to collect debts hardly amounted to a revival of colonialism, but when Great Britain, Germany and Italy together instituted a naval blockade of Venezuela and seized that country's warships in 1902 in order (amongst other things) to collect money owed to their subjects, the president of the United States decided he must go beyond the Monroe doctrine in the interests of hemisphere security and, particularly, that of the Caribbean. Though in political terms by then hardly significant, the hemisphere's financial and economic links with Europe suggested prospects of future trouble. North Americans, too, were among the investors in Latin American countries, notably in Mexico, by 1914 the only country where they outweighed European investment. President Theodore Roosevelt therefore announced in 1904 that the United States would be prepared to intervene in the affairs of any state whose internal affairs were so disordered as to tempt non-American powers to action there in defence of their interests.[15] This came to be called a 'corollary' to the Monroe doctrine.

The outcome was for a time a certain American heavy-handedness and even a show of arrogance in the Caribbean. The Roosevelt corollary was almost at once given effect in Cuba and the Dominican Republic. American forces were to come back to occupy Cuba from 1906 to 1909 under the terms of the treaty, and again in 1917. They still occupy an enclave sheltering a naval base there. An American president sent marines to Nicaragua in 1912 under the terms of the corollary, and yet another, President Wilson, who was later to win a great repute as a defender of small nations, announced in 1913 that if the rebel general who then dominated the Mexican scene did not retire by force of circumstances 'it will become the duty of the United States to use less peaceful means to put him out'.[16] Wilson went on in the following year to occupy the Mexican port of Vera Cruz as a way of coercing a Mexican government (its main revenues came from the port's customs dues). In 1915, too, he established by treaty an American protectorate over Haiti that was to last forty years.

THE SOUTH AFRICAN WAR

If the Spanish-American war was an episode in the history of a once-great empire in decline, another war going on as the century opened was made by an old and great empire still expanding. Great

---

[15] 'If' (said Roosevelt in his message to Congress) 'a nation shows that it knows how to act with reasonable efficiency and decency in social and political matters, if it keeps order and pays its obligations, it need fear no interference from the United States. Chronic wrong-doing, or an impotence which results in a general loosening of the ties of civilised society, may in America, as elsewhere, ultimately require intervention by some civilised nation, and in the Western Hemisphere, the adherence of the United States to the Monroe Doctrine may force the United States, however reluctantly, in flagrant cases of such wrong-doing or impotence, to the exercise of an international police power.' *AR 1904*, p.429.

[16] See the circular to American embassies q. in *The Diplomacy of World Power: the United States 1889–1920*, ed. A. S. Link and W. M. Leary (London, 1970), p.88.

Britain had been installed since 1814 in the former Dutch colony at the Cape of Good Hope, and thousands of British settlers had gone there within a few years. Though outnumbered by the Dutch 'Boers' (whose ancestors had been there since the seventeenth century), they had the backing of the British government in introducing British assumptions and law. A period of what the Dutch farmers saw as the whittling away of their privileges began. In particular, the Boers were excited and irked by reductions of their freedom to exploit the native African as they wished. Their indignation was specially aroused by the general abolition of slavery in British territory. A great exodus of Boers from British territory accordingly took place in 1835, the 'Great Trek' north across the Orange River; among the trekkers was a ten-year-old boy who would be president of the Boer republic of the Transvaal sixty years later, and would cherish a deep dislike of the British and their ways in consequence.[17] Boer self-awareness began the forging of a new identity as 'Afrikaners' (as the Boers came to call themselves), who were to be in the twentieth century the most successful of African peoples (Afrikaans became a written language in 1875). Before that could happen, Anglo-Saxon and Afrikaner struggled for most of the nineteenth century to live in Africa sometimes apart, sometimes together, but always found it uncomfortable to do so. The decisions they made dragged in their train the fates of others, above all those of black Africans.

Easy relations had never been likely; circumstances changed and made them more difficult. South Africa's history was complicated by changes sought by neither Boer nor Briton. New interests emerged as a result of economic and technological development. The Transvaal was industrialized after the discovery of gold there and a great influx of foreigners followed. These *uitlanders* soon outnumbered the native Afrikaner in Johannesburg. They appeared to present a real threat to Afrikaner ways and values should numbers ever give them political power. Meanwhile, foreign investors and adventurers behaved foolishly and provocatively. Another part of the background was the Scramble for Africa, which stiffened London's determination that nothing must shake the British presence at the Cape, deemed essential

[17] Paul Kruger.

to the control of sea-routes to the East. Strategists worried, too, that the Transvaal republic might gain independent access to the Indian Ocean through a port not under British control.

The outcome of such divers forces was a peculiar vulnerability in British policy to the pressure of special interests. After a couple of decades of increasing bitterness an oddly-assorted crew of idealistic imperialists, Cape politicians, English demagogues, shady financiers and hired bravoes who had their own ambitions and visions of the future in South Africa supplied such pressure and the outcome was a confrontation that ended in an ultimatum from the Transvaal's president, Paul Kruger, and the outbreak of war in 1899. As one British politician put it, the essential question was 'is British paramountcy [in South Africa] to be vindicated or let slide?'[18]

Of the outcome there could be no doubt, for all the early incompetence of British generalship and quality of Boer marksmanship; Queen Victoria showed better strategic judgement than some of her subjects in remarking that the possibility of defeat did not exist. The war could be isolated by British sea power; no other European nation could help the Boers. It could only be a matter of time before greatly superior numbers (the total Afrikaner population of the two republics was fewer than 250,000, although their field forces at the outset outnumbered the British on the spot) and resources were brought to bear upon them. Yet the first war of the twentieth century proved the most costly fought by the British since 1815. Some £250 million was spent and some 450,000 British and imperial soldiers had to be sent to South Africa (four times as many as had gone to the Crimea), of whom over 20,000 died.[19] Initial humiliating defeats and a drawn-out struggle aroused much bitterness in British domestic politics. Nor did they do any good to imperial Great Britain in the eyes of the outside world. The Afrikaners were almost universally regarded as an oppressed nationality and so saw themselves, though the liberal obsession with nationality in this case as in others blinded observers to some of the

---

[18] Q. in I. R. Smith, *The Origins of the South African War 1899–1902* (London, 1996), p.420, the best recent study.

[19] Three-quarters from disease, but this was proportionately a much better record than that of the American campaign in Cuba in 1898, where fewer than 300 men were killed in battle and thirteen times as many died from disease.

shadows it cast. It also concealed complications that the traditional label, 'the Boer war', has obscured. Many South Africans, British and Afrikaner alike, strongly sympathized with the other side; technically, Cape Province (the major area of British settlement, though more Afrikaners lived there than in the two republics combined) never took part in the struggle, but remained neutral. As for South Africans of non-European stock, at least 15,000 of them died in the war, to what benefit to their own peoples it remains difficult to see. In the end, British statesmanship recovered itself sufficiently to make a generous settlement in 1902 after victory in the field and the diplomatic obliteration of the republics. Its generosity was directed towards the Afrikaners: exclusion of black and 'Coloured' South Africans from political rights, except in Cape Colony, was part of the peace treaty.

This was an ironic outcome. By 1906 the Transvaal again had a responsible government of its own which, in spite of the large non-Afrikaner population attracted to it by mining, the Afrikaners controlled after an electoral victory the following year. Almost at once they began to legislate against Asian immigrants, mainly Indian (a young Indian lawyer, Mohandas Gandhi, made his entrance to politics there as the champion of his community). When, in 1909, a draft constitution for a federal South African Union was agreed, it was on terms of equality for the Dutch and English languages and provided for government by an elected assembly to be formed according to the electoral regulations decided in each province. In the former Boer states the franchise was confined to white men. In 1910 the Union came into being as the youngest self-governing Dominion of the British empire.

At the time, the settlement was welcomed by most liberal-minded men. It embodied the essence of the British war aims of 1899: the establishment of a federation strong enough to secure government for the white South African under British influence. When people then spoke of a 'racial problem' in South Africa they meant the problem of British and Afrikaner relationships with one another and the need to conciliate them. They tended to be seen as parts of a greater whole; as one writer put it when considering what should be in the nature of a post-war settlement, 'finality [was] imperatively required' in ordering those relations so as to 'promote the fusion of the European race in South Africa in furtherance of the higher mission of the race the world over'.[20] The defects of what was agreed would take some time to appear. Yet the South African war had created many new Afrikaner grievances. Thirty thousand farms had been burnt by the British in the last anti-guerrilla phase of the war and civilian deaths (largely from epidemics in the camps in which much of the Boer population was concentrated) outnumbered the combatant deaths on both sides combined. Afrikaners were angered bitterly, too, that the British had armed some native Africans against them. The historical sense of Afrikaner identity was thus further strengthened: it was to prove tougher than the optimists of 1910 had hoped.

Meanwhile, the transformation of South African society by industrialization could not be halted and would give irresistible momentum to the issue of the black Africans, by sucking labour to the cities. By 1914 Johannesburg was a city of 250,000 inhabitants. South Africa's future was already caught up, like that of other 'settler' countries, in world economic processes. Some of these new nations found agricultural staples able to sustain economies more viable than those permitted by the tobacco and indigo of the seventeenth-century plantations. South Africa was one that benefited from her own farming exports but was above all important as a producer of minerals. The beginnings of the revelation of this fact had been the appearance of a diamond industry, followed by the Rand gold discoveries. Development then sucked into Africa capital and expertise which made possible the eventual exploitation of other minerals. South Africa provided not merely a real return to its companies and shareholders, but also an augmentation of the world's gold supply, and that stimulated world commerce.

[20] M. J. Farrelly, *The Settlement after the War in South Africa* (London, 1900), p.9.

4

Shapes of Things to Come

LONG-TERM DEMOGRAPHY

Besides a sense of the past, most people also have a view of the future, even if it is only an expectation that things will go on much as before. At the beginning of this century, those among them who already thought, on the contrary, that further and dramatic change was likely soon turned out to be right. Yet even so, their ideas fell far short of the reality of what was to come. The twentieth century was to bring with it change of unprecedented scope and scale. Most of the rest of this book attempts to make sense of a torrent of events, and in trying to rise above it there is a danger of forgetting that what happens is always happening to people whose time horizons are close, whose lives are short, and who have little reason to care about the long run in which we are all dead. It is easy to lose one's bearings and any sense of general tendencies and it is worth trying to discuss one or two of them before immersion in the flow.

We can go back again to population, the outstanding instance where the long-term view forwards and backwards is helpful. We can only estimate to within one or two hundred millions how many people are now alive but we can be fairly sure that while about 850 million were added to the world's population between 1750 and 1900, it took another fifty years – a third of that time – to add rather more than that figure again. In 1950 the population of the world would stand at about 2,500 million. Even more strikingly the next 850 million would be added in less than another twenty years, by the middle of the 1960s. It took roughly 50,000 years, the pre-historians say, for *homo sapiens* to multiply to a world population of 1,000 million (a figure reached in 1840 or thereabouts) but the last 1,000 million of our species to be added to it have joined it in only fifteen years or so. Though growth rates in some countries have fallen since the 1960s, up-to-date estimates say the human race is still growing by 1.63 per cent per year. We shall number over 6,000 million as this century ends.

Unsurprisingly, such figures have sometimes quickened the spectre of Malthusian disaster, which seemed so much more remote in 1901. In 1974 the first world conference on population ever held met in Romania; for the first time the human race was uneasy enough about its future for its representatives to come together to talk about the demographic outlook. The unwilled, seemingly uncontrollable and accelerating rise in world population which has gone on for the last couple of centuries is now seen as a phenomenon requiring attention, perhaps as a global problem, even if much about its exact nature remains uncertain. Perhaps fortunately, though, Malthus himself said that 'no estimates of future population or depopulation, formed from any existing rate of increase or decrease, can be depended upon.'[1] One reason for this is human intervention, though that was not what he primarily had in mind.

Several societies have during this century tried to take control of, or at least to affect, their shape and size, but for the most part in Europe, and with the aim of encouraging, not restraining, births.[2] Recently, attention has switched in poorer parts of the world to trying to reduce birth rates. Of course, there have always been parts of the world where infanticide and abortion have been acceptable ways of keeping down demands on scarce resources. Babies were exposed to die in medieval Japan; female infanticide was widespread in India a century and a half ago and has recently emerged again (or perhaps been again acknowledged) in China.[3] Abortion now appears to be favoured, unofficially, as a major form of birth control by Russians (a country whose population now actually appears to be falling). But

[1] See *An Essay on Population* (Everyman Library edn., London, 1914), i. p.311.
[2] France, Germany, Italy and the USSR all tried to achieve this in the 1930s, for example.
[3] The current ratio of boys to girls in China is 118:100. The natural rate is 106:100 (*Independent*, 12 January 1998).

it is new that some governments are now putting resources and authority behind more humane means of population control; their aim is to achieve positive economic and social improvement, instead of just the avoidance of family and personal misfortune.

Yet over the century human numbers have gone on rising more dramatically than ever before. At a fertility rate of 2.1 children per family, say demographers, population will stabilize. But to engineer that outcome worldwide is at present inconceivable, even if agreement is reached that stability is desirable. There are too many difficulties in the way of consciously shaping population growth through human agency. This makes it possible to wonder whether population will ever stabilize without major disasters. For good or ill, growth, though worldwide, does not everywhere take the same form. Its variety reflects limits set not only by material conditions but also by knowledge and ignorance, by social and personal attitudes. Such facts are hard to identify, hard to measure, and harder still to manipulate. Some non-European countries have followed the nineteenth-century European trend of falling death rates while birth rates remained high, but it would be very rash to prophesy that they will go on to repeat the next set of patterns that followed that. We cannot simply expect declining natality shown in one place or one society to be repeated elsewhere. The best that can be said is that neither should we be confident or fearful that they will not be.

At present, most countries have not achieved demographic equilibrium. In the near future, it looks as if most of them will find it hard to do so, though some of them may within three or four decades if present conditions continue. Those last four words require emphasis. In rich and developed countries, natality began to drop even before 1901, when it became more attractive to significant numbers of men and women to have smaller families. Few of today's fastest-growing countries are yet anywhere near that point. Further medical, nutritional and sanitary progress will almost certainly make population pressure worse by increasing life expectancy. Though advance in such matters has been colossal, yet there are many countries where mortality still waits to be cut as dramatically as it was in Europe in the nineteenth century. If, when, and where the operative factors come into play (in much of the Middle East, for example) that have already operated in western countries, numbers may be expected to rise faster still if there is no offsetting force.

Infant mortality therefore still remains a good rough indicator of potential for further population growth. For a century before 1970 it fell dramatically in developed countries from an average of about 225 per 1,000 live births to under 20. Yet discrepancies between poor and rich countries persist, and some of them have tended to widen since 1901; in 1988 the comparative figures for Bangladesh and Japan were 118 and 5. There are comparable differences in life expectancy, too. In developed countries, life expectancy at birth rose from rather more than 40 in 1870 to slightly over 70 a hundred years later. It now shows a remarkable evenness. Life expectancy at birth in the United States, Great Britain and the USSR in 1987, for example, was 76, 75 and 70 years respectively; the differences between them were negligible by comparison with Ethiopia (41), or even India (58). But these things can change rapidly; we are now told that male life expectancy in Russia has fallen below the sixty years mark, after dropping rapidly in a decade. On the other hand, a Russian baby now faces prospects enormously better than those of 100 years ago. So does an Indian baby, now much more likely to survive infancy than was a French baby in 1789. Given the prospect of further improvement in infant mortality in many countries, it is at least unlikely that the steam will go out of population growth in the near future.

Complicated as it is, the long-term demographic perspective reveals another great change. As far back as we can go, human societies resembled pyramids with large numbers of young people at their bases and a few old at their pinnacles. Now, in the developed world at least, societies are beginning to look more like slowly tapering columns. The proportion of older people in them is much bigger than in the past. Poorer countries still show the older pattern: half Kenya's population is under fifteen, and two-thirds of China's is under thirty-five. What this may imply is too complicated for speculation here, but it shows that overall population growth does not say much about demographic reality. The world's population was to grow mightily after 1901, but in very different ways and with very different effects in different parts of the globe. It remains, though, a good starting point for understanding our century to bear in mind throughout that human beings have almost quadrupled in numbers while it has been going on.

THE DIVISIONS OF HUMANITY

There have also been major shifts in the balance of peoples since 1901. Europeans have roughly doubled their numbers, but Europe now contains only about a tenth of humanity. China by itself now accounts for as big a share (nearly a quarter) of the world total as Europe did when the century began. More than half the human race is now Asian. Nearly 1,000 million people live in the Indian sub-continent, against 300 million or so in 1901. Some countries have grown even faster. Malaysia and Singapore have multiplied their combined populations sevenfold in this century,[4] and Thailand has almost done the same.

Such figures make international averages uninformative except in the very long run. Brazil's population growth in the early 1960s was already running at more than double the annual world average rate of about 1.6 per cent per annum and Brazilians increased in numbers sixfold between 1901 and 1975. Over the same period Mexico's population quadrupled and Colombia's quintupled. Argentina, though, seems to have outstripped them all over the century (but her rising numbers also owed much to immigration). Simple single explanations (one often cited in the Latin American context is the attitude of the Roman Catholic Church towards contraception and legal abortion) rarely seem adequate to account for such fecundity. The attitudes of Latin American males and the social arrangements and traditions that impose large families on Latin American women were long shaped by heavy and complex historical legacies of which religion was only one. This must be remembered in many other parts of the world where public policy struggles with rising numbers. Some of the most threatening growth rates are to be found in Islamic countries. Jordan's, at 3.9 per cent a year, implies a doubling of population in sixteen

---

[4] Modern Malaysia comprises units that were linked in different ways to the British crown in 1901, Singapore being, with some others, part of the crown colony of the Straits Settlements at that date.

years. But Iran is growing at 3.5 and the much smaller Saudi population at 5.6 per cent annually.

What government has done or can do to influence demography remains hard to say; its absence or inaction was probably more important for the first half of this century, outside Europe. Even after 1945, Communist states for a long time frowned on ideas of population stabilization or reduction, but both China and the USSR began in the 1960s to encourage people to delay marriage and have smaller families. In China this has had some evident success, the crude birth rate halved between 1970 and 1996 if official statistics are to be believed. Legal regulation, tax incentives and social pressure were the main methods employed but female infanticide re-emerged as an unwelcome by-product. Other poor countries have tried propaganda and education in contraception, the western answer to over-population. Indonesia imposed a very authoritarian family planning programme in 1970 and it is now said that its population will stabilize (at 230 million) in forty years' time. In India large sums have been spent on promoting contraception and (voluntary) sterilization, with measurable but not yet very large effect. Neither revolutionized by industrialization (like Japan) nor by a political attack on its social traditions and institutions (as was China), India is still a predominantly agrarian society, for all the change she has undergone in this century. Indian government, like the British Raj before it, has respected social traditions, so making population management very difficult. Outside a tiny élite, vast and traditional inequalities still determine status and employment pros-pects for Indian men and women. Were attitudes towards women taken for granted in western countries (and frequently denounced there as inadequate) even slightly more prevalent in India, they would be likely to raise dramatically the average age of women at marriage, and therefore to reduce the number of children in the average family. But such a change would presuppose a revolution in habits in India's slums and villages, redistributing power in a much more radical break with the past than independence in 1947. No country should be expected easily to shake off so much.

A CENTURY OF GROWING WEALTH

During the nineteenth century one sign of rapidly growing human numbers was the spectacular rise in the number of European and North American and, to a lesser extent, Latin American and British colonial city-dwellers. In this century, the trend to urbanization became world-wide. Now none of the twelve largest cities in the world is in Europe or North America. Growing urbanization is another indicator of growing wealth in the form of food supplies that can carry larger non-agricultural populations. Many have starved since 1901, but many more have lived. To speak of them as enjoying wealth may well seem paradoxical to any visitor struck with dismay on discovering the slums of Cairo or Calcutta. Yet humanity now has at its disposal a greater abundance of resources than ever. It has in this sense grown richer in this century with only occasional interruption. If the world had not been able to feed a growing population human numbers would be smaller. Though millions have died in the famines which television has brought vividly to the consciousness of the well-fed, there has been no worldwide disaster, and we now live in a world of agricultural surpluses.

We owe this to 100 years of growth in food supplies. The consequences, if this should go on, are for futurologists to debate. So is the likelihood of success in making surpluses available to those who need them. In such matters, we enter the realms of speculation. Yet the very existence of such possibilities and the hopes and aspirations they arouse should concern historians, for it says something about what *is* – the present and actual state of the world. This is because what is believed to be possible helps to determine what actually does happen. That the world has been able to feed itself in this century is one of the most persuasive facts at work on our minds – or ought to be. It should have broadened our notion of what is possible and stimulated our dreams of Utopia; perhaps it has done so even without many people being aware of it. The facts, after all, are uncontroversial and have already been touched upon. They are not hard to summarize. Agricultural development is an historical topic, like population, where the long run matters, and in this century scientists have pressed forward with work which has added to our food resources as never before.

They have bred plant strains better able to resist disease and produce greater yields from smaller areas of land; they have produced better fertilizers that render soil more productive and prevent its exhaustion. Pest control has been transformed in many countries where herds used to be decimated and crops ruined before they could be harvested. Now scientists are further improving crops by direct intervention with genetic structures instead of by earlier, cruder methods of cross-pollination and grafting. The results have been astonishing.

Chemical fertilizers had been the first sign of what could be done and an unprecedented rate of replacement of nitrogen in the soil has been the most basic way of obtaining greater yields in this century. Though effective herbicides and insecticides did not begin to be available commercially until the 1940s and 1950s, their use then spread rapidly and very widely. In a single decade, from 1930 to 1940, the yield of grain in the United States went up a third, thanks to the introduction of new 'hybrid' strains – and thus, ironically, contributed to an unprecedented long fall in world grain prices, which harmed poor farmers everywhere (and most of the world's farmers were poor). Well before 1939, wheat was being successfully introduced to lands in which, for climatic reasons, it had never been grown hitherto; the evolution of new strains of cereals was one of the first twentieth-century scientific contributions to agriculture which clearly outstripped the trial-and-error 'improvement' of earlier times. In the 'Green revolution', as it was sometimes called, of developing specific and related strains of seed and better fertilizers for use in poorer countries, lie hopes of feeding those who at present rely on grain imported from countries of advanced agriculture.

The use of machinery has been another force transforming agriculture. In 1901 human and animal muscles, supplemented in some activities and areas by wind and water, were the main sources of power on the world's farms. Centuries ago this had begun to change with improvements maximizing the energy derived from these sources, but the greatest difference only came with the internal combustion engine[5] – above all deployed on the land in tractors. As a source of

[5] An internal combustion engine uses energy produced from heat when gas is burned inside a cylinder to drive a piston (instead of generating steam for the cylinder by using an external flame). The gas burnt is usually obtained by mixing some form of

power for other machinery it was quickly shown to be far more mobile and flexible than the steam engines of the last century. The working horses which dominated even the most advanced agriculture in 1901 are now hardly to be seen in developed countries except as interesting curiosities, or for certain restricted uses where the rising cost of fuel does not justify the use of a tractor as a prime mover. Combine harvesters, invented in the United States, and soon self-propelled, were another important mechanical innovation. But power did more than perform traditional tasks more efficiently: it broke in new land. It has been estimated that in this century 30 million acres of land in the United States hitherto only available for pasture were opened by the tractor to cultivation. Nor was it fields alone that were mechanized. Electricity has made possible automatic milking, better grain drying and threshing, and the heating of animal sheds in winter. Now, the computer and automation have begun to reduce dependence on human labour even more. Everywhere in the developed world for a century or so the agricultural workforce has fallen while production per acre has risen.

Many of those advances have brought with them new costs: big energy inputs are now needed to sustain the productivity of advanced western agriculture. For all the advances, too, there are probably more subsistence farmers in the world today than in 1901, because there are so many more people. Their relative share of cultivated land and of the total value of what agriculture produces, though, has fallen. In Western Europe the peasant has almost ceased to be the typical cultivator, as he ceased to be in Great Britain 200 years ago. But the benevolent changes that have brought this about are unevenly spread and easily disrupted. Russia has traditionally been a great agricultural producer, but as recently as 1947 suffered famine so severe as once more to generate reports of cannibalism. In many years in this century, India has suffered grievous famine. In the 1960s, millions of Chinese starved to death. Local disasters can still devastate countries with large and rapidly growing populations where subsistence agriculture is the norm and productivity remains low. Just before the First World

---

petroleum vapour with air, though the first machine to work in this way (in 1860) ran on coal gas.

War, the British got more than two and a half times as much wheat
out of an acre than did the Indians; by 1968 they were getting roughly
five times as much – as Indian yields had gone up, too. Over the same
period the Americans raised their rice yield from 4.25 to nearly 12
tons an acre, while that of Burma, sometimes called the 'rice bowl of
Asia', rose only from 3.8 to 4.2. In 1968, it was calculated that in
Egypt slightly more than one family could be provided for by one
agricultural worker, while one New Zealander could supply over
forty families.

Not only is much more food grown than in 1901, but its international
availability has immensely increased. Only in the long-term
perspective, once more, can that easy availability be understood.
Building railroads to move grain from western Canada and the
American prairie states to the Atlantic ports, and cattle from the
ranges of Texas to the stockyards of Chicago, or sheep from the
Antipodean farms to Sydney and Wellington, had by 1901 already
done as much to ensure Europeans were fed as the raising of
gigantic harvests and the breeding of huge herds and flocks. The
refrigerated food-store and ship, pasteurization and effective canning
processes were already in service, and made Argentina, Uruguay
and New Zealand butchers to the world. Improved, refined and
added to, such innovations have made possible the banal abundance
of the western supermarket, and have changed the ways in which
different parts of the world are related to one another. Countries
where there is most need to improve agricultural productivity
because of population growth have found it very hard to produce
crops more cheaply than richer, developed countries. Ironic paradoxes result: Russians, Indians and Chinese buy American and
Canadian wheat, and Europe and North America now export more
food than ever, while their domestic markets are over-supplied from
domestic resources.

AN INDUSTRIALIZING WORLD

There can be very few countries, if any, whose GDP has not risen
over this century though there are some where it has fallen in recent

years.[6] To that rise, agriculture made huge contributions, but even so it did not outdistance those made by manufacturing and extractive industry. Even by the standards of the revolutionary nineteenth century, when industrialization was first recognized as a major historical phenomenon, the changes it has brought about in this century have been colossal. They have also been worldwide: the old distinction of a world of industrial nations and another of primary producers has been blurred, even if this has not always been much noticed.

Once again, it is in the long run that the most basic facts best stand out. Increases in wealth-production have been neither steady nor continuous, nor universally shared over the century. Caveats must be entered at the start of any discussion of the subject. A world in which, down to 1914, inflation was low, manufacturing productivity rose each year and there was continuous growth in world trade gave way in that year to a period not only of physical destruction in two World Wars, but of distorted investment patterns, upheaval in markets, undependable currencies and an appalling world depression. That time of economic troubles also passed, though, and between 1945 and the early 1970s humanity enjoyed over a quarter-century of virtually uninterrupted and global wealth-creation. This achievement was only slightly qualified by the economic history of the closing decades of the century, though relative positions between the beneficiaries of the process then changed considerably.

A table complied for a recent study is helpful.[7] It shows average annual growth rates per cent of GDP per capita in terms of 1990 dollars for the period 1900–1992 and for sub-periods within that.

---

[6] It may be useful to distinguish at this point two terms that crop up from time to time in what follows. Gross *Domestic* Product (GDP) is product generated within a certain defined area (usually a country, or group of countries); Gross *National* Product (GNP) is the same with an addition, that of income from abroad (which may, of course, be a negative figure).

[7] Taken from G. Toniolo, 'Europe's' golden age, 1950–1973: speculations from a long-run perspective', *Economic History Review* (1998), LI, 2, p.253. The table does not include Japan in the ten countries making up the 'Asia' group, 'Europe' consists of the current fifteen EU members plus Switzerland, the 'Western offshoots' are the United States, Canada and Australia, and only seven Latin American countries are taken into account. The most obvious absences from the table are Africa, the former USSR, and Eastern Europe. Nonetheless, it is revealing.

	Europe	Western offshoots	Latin America	Asia
1900–1992	1.9	1.8	1.7	1.7
1900–1913	1.1	2.0	2.2	0.7
1913–1950	0.9	1.5	1.5	0.0
1950–1973	4.1	2.6	2.6	3.6
1973–1992	1.8	1.4	0.6	3.5

The actual processes lying behind these figures are much too complicated to set out here. Among the most obvious, though, were an enormous increase in the productive capacity of well-established industries, the migration of those industries worldwide (often to countries that knew nothing of them in 1901), a transformation of technology (much of which led to the emergence of manufacturing sectors that did not even exist in 1901), and a diffusion and integration of processes on a global basis.

Thus the twentieth century transformed all sorts of economic relationships. Some showing this most strikingly were micro-economic, those between the individual worker, his tools and his working environment. Others were between employed and employer. Some were between countries and regions, though in that respect it has to be noted that some relativities changed little: throughout the whole century, the largest share of international trade was generated by developed countries trading with one another (about four-fifths of international trade goes on between them at present). Until mid-century or so, the developed world was largely self-sufficient (thanks to the presence inside it of the USA and USSR) in meeting its main industrial needs for energy, metals and major minerals, vegetable fibres and hides.[8] This changed, and the consequential new economic interdependencies of the second half of the century have to be included among its great transformations.

[8] Until the 1920s the Americans alone were capable of meeting most of world requirements for oil, for instance.

NEW TECHNOLOGY

Technological applications explain much of the shape taken by the industrialized world. As they had done in the nineteenth century, too, they presented the world with the most acceptable and easily recognized evidence of the power of science. Far away from those intellectual milieus where tiny minorities consciously confronted the problems posed by, say, the theory of relativity, they were at work changing minds by their direct impact on human life. They, above all, were the way in which larger numbers of people than ever before became aware of science and its power. This is not to underrate the importance and power of the high, specialized science that in the nineteenth century established the distinction between organic and inorganic chemistry, placed thermodynamics at the centre of physics, launched the exploration of the laws of electromagnetism, identified the phenomenon of radioactivity, and laid the foundations of microbiology and immunology. All these great steps also bore fruit in applications, some quite soon and some in major industrial outcomes. Even in the world's most developed societies in 1901, though, it is unlikely that many people had any clear notion of them; ideas of what science could do were to be found most easily in the evidence of material change going on in daily life.

The nineteenth century had been the age of steam and iron. Steam had become its major source of power and as such was only just beginning to be challenged by 1901. Iron had been used in larger and larger quantities in the previous century to build the machines and make the steel for which it found more and more uses. Recently, electricity had joined steam as a source of power, usually generated by coal-fired steam turbines. Electricity had been recognized as a natural phenomenon and studied accordingly in the eighteenth century, but the nineteenth had made it usefully available; by 1901 its effects were already obvious in lighting, transport, the siting of manufactures in all developed economies. It had already begun by then to make its mark outside the developed countries, too.[9] In the twentieth century, electricity was to change the world, transforming the appearance of cities, banishing darkness from their streets at night as coal-gas had not been able to do, giving those who lived in them new possibilities of timetabling their day, and offering new scope to architects. With the electric tram and train (both widespread before 1901) urban geography began to change again, as it became easier for workers to live further away from their work and to travel to it. Electricity was by then already changing the place of work itself; factories no longer had to be sited with easy access to waterpower or to railways to bring coal to their engine-houses. With the new century, electricity began to transform the homes of the rich, and, in the western world, those of the not-so-rich. It was soon providing not only light and heat, but power for machines to lighten the housewife's drudgery. In the final year of the nineteenth century a British engineer had invented the inaccurately but arrestingly named 'vacuum cleaner' and an electrically powered washing machine was put on the market in the USA in 1907. The domestic refrigerator appeared in 1926. Since then dozens of new appliances have come to be taken for granted (subtly influencing, among other things, changes in women's roles and minds).

Other technological changes in the structure of daily life, too, were already under way. One of the most striking contributions of directed research in industrial processes came in the chemistry of devising new, man-made materials to replace natural ones. The first 'plastics' were made in the nineteenth century, and the Germans for a long time led in this field, but in the 1920s a British firm produced the first plastic fibre, 'Rayon' – or 'artificial silk', as it was sometimes called – and it was the beginning of a revolution in the provision of cheap and attractive clothing. It began the narrowing of the gap between rich and poor in dress, as well as dealing a heavy blow to the Japanese silk industry. In 1938 an American company launched 'Nylon', a fibre in many ways superior to Rayon. Later refinements have made possible the mass supply of cheap clothing on a scale that would not have been

[9] It affected more than the human world: of the 16,000 horses pulling trams in England as the century began, there were fewer than 1,000 left in 1914.

possible had mankind been able to draw only on the traditional natural materials.

Some new materials were invented with warlike ends in view. In the 1930s, when European nations were beginning to rebuild their armed forces, new materials were sought either to replace metals in short supply, or to perform tasks for which known metals were in one way or another inadequate. Aluminium alloys for aircraft were among these, and by the end of the 1930s magnesium alloys, too. Since 1945, even more refined and specialized metals have been produced as the demands of first jet aircraft and then space rockets set chemists new goals. These have resulted in new materials usable for a wide range of industrial products quite unconnected with the purposes for which they were originally devised.

MEDICAL SCIENCE

Even in 1901, when they could achieve very little, few people in developed counties would have questioned that doctors could be helpful in looking after health. Yet by comparison with what was to come, at that date very little had actually been done by medical men to deploy new scientific knowledge. Almost certainly, the major reductions in mortality so spectacularly evident in the nineteenth century in some countries should be attributed to public health regulation, improved drains, purer water supplies, cheaper and better clothing, soap and better nourishment, rather than to progress in scientific medicine. Almost the last great contribution it had made had been the introduction of vaccination and inoculation in the eighteenth century. A hundred years later, in some countries, the definition of a properly qualified medical profession had still yet to emerge. Although Lister had dramatically reduced surgical infection and so transformed surgery in the 1860s, and though Pasteur had created a sensation by his successful treatment of rabies, and his Institute (founded in 1888) had gone on to study diphtheria, infectious disease was, for the most part, still largely incurable well into the twentieth century. All that could be provided once it had taken hold was careful nursing, something much more likely to be available to the rich than to the poor.

In 1901, there were hardly any drugs available to doctors for selective treatment of infection (that is, by attacking its specific origin). By 1920, only two or three more had been added to the quinine (used in treating malaria) and mercury (used in treating syphilis) primarily available. Nowadays, there are hundreds; the advance has been the result of organized scientific effort.

The first 'magic bullet' (as it was called because it singled out the specific target of one infection) was Salvarsan, discovered in 1909 by the chemist Ehrlich after he had synthesized and tested hundreds of compounds, of which Salvarsan was the six hundred and sixth. Overlooked by one of his assistants when first tested, it nonetheless proved effective against syphilis. A few years later, another scientist, Alexander Fleming, spent much of his spare time while working in a field hospital in France during the Great War looking for ways to kill bacteria that infected wounds. Twenty years later, in London, he noticed an unfamiliar mould growing on an old culture dish which had been set aside after an experiment; on examination, it proved to have destroyed a colony of bacteria. Fleming's observation was followed up at Oxford and in 1941 the tiny quantity of 'penicillin' available was used for the first time there with dramatic results. By 1944 it was being manufactured on a large scale (in time to be of decisive importance in treating war wounded). The first antibiotic had become one of the most powerful weapons modern medicine had in its armoury. Within a half-century or so, indeed, medicine had for the first time become dominated by the ideas and methods of science.[10]

COMMUNICATION

For moving people and things about quickly or easily, steam was in 1901 still only beginning to be supplemented by electricity. Nineteenth-century civil engineering, steamships and railways had laid down patterns of surface communication that would dominate long-distance

[10] A wise and very senior medical colleague once expressed to me in the 1950s his satisfaction with the progress of medicine in his lifetime, saying that when he qualified in the early 1920s, 'medicine was ten per cent science and the rest magic: now it's at least twenty-five per cent science'.

transport well into the next half-century. Technical changes had virtually perfected the steam locomotive by 1914, though other sources of rail motive power, based on the diesel engine and electricity, were by then in use. Railways had spread not only over all the industrial nations, but much of Asia and Africa, too. Regular shipping routes came to link continents; in some of them, steamers sailed up rivers still unexplored only a few years earlier. By 1910, the Russian Trans-Siberian railway was almost complete; India had an excellent railway network and even in China the building of railways was under way. The Japanese had quickly adopted railways among other technological importations from the European world. There had long been talk of 'Cape-to-Cairo' and 'Berlin–Baghdad' routes, and few areas of the inhabitable world could not be approached to within a reasonable distance by rail when the century began. This affected the movement of goods as well as that of people, and particularly goods in bulk, and therefore the growing of crops and location of industry. Coal and ore were especially important. For the first half of this century, rail still carried the bulk of goods moved on land.

The development of the machine that would change this, the auto-mobile, had also begun in the nineteenth century. The first machine propelled by an internal combustion engine appeared in 1885. Nine years later a French inventor, Panhard, built a four-wheeled vehicle that is recognizable as the ancestor of the modern car. Such contrap-tions remained unusual, rich men's toys, until automobile pre-history gave way to history in 1907. In that year the American Henry Ford set up a production line for his Model T, a cheaper car than any hitherto built. Deliberately planned for a wide market, it cost only $950 – about £180 at the then current exchange rate. This was still a substantial sum; in England at that time a house could be bought at that price. In the next twenty years it came down to less than $300; demand had risen so rapidly that even by 1915 Ford was producing a million cars a year. Something previously regarded as a luxury had become an everyday article and Ford had changed the world. People of modest incomes could, thanks to him, move about as freely as millionaires fifty years earlier. The motor-car (like the coming of railways in the nineteenth century) also created a new and rising demand for other commodities, for steel, for oil and for rubber for tyres (the pneumatic tyre had been invented in 1888).[11] Political results would also follow. Car-owners in the industrialized countries soon demanded better roads, vested interests appeared in jobs in the automobile industry, and new economic foci developed in places where deposits of oil were discovered. Much of this lay far in the future.

It was not long after the century began that the still comparatively young internal combustion engine took to the skies. For a long time – thousands of years, perhaps – men had dreamed of learning to fly. In the eighteenth century they began to do so in balloons, but for a long time the only lifting agents available were hot air and other gases generated by burning materials directly under the balloon. These 'lighter-than-air' machines (they were, of course, heavier than air, though their lifting agent was not) had by the end of the nineteenth century begun to get their buoyancy from gases such as hydrogen which required no heat. The size and shape of such machines had changed as men sought to do more than simply drift downwind in them, but the first real 'dirigibles' – that is, airships which could be steered – were by then available, thanks to internal combustion engines which could provide the power for them to change direction. In the most advanced, such as those of the German pioneer Count Zeppelin, the simple inflatable bag of the early balloons was replaced by rigid construction, with an envelope built around a light frame, eventually of metal. The biggest 'Zeppelins' could by 1914 carry a couple of dozen passengers.

Yet the search for a means of flight that could dispense with the buoyancy provided by bags of gas had never stopped. Of the strange contraptions built in the closing decades of the nineteenth century one or two 'flew', in that they could glide briefly when launched downhill or by a fast tow. But once in the air they had only their own inertia to work for them; they could not accelerate as speed fell off and soon had to descend. Attempts to emulate bird-flight in 'ornithopters' with mechanically flapped wings came to nothing. At last the internal combustion engine provided a light enough source of power. On 17 December 1903 the first power-driven flight in a

---

[11] By John Boyd Dunlop, a Scottish veterinary surgeon, as a result of his son's complaints about his tricycle's solid rubber tyres.

man-carrying flying machine was made at Kitty Hawk, North Carolina, by Orville Wright, one of two brothers who had built the first successful aeroplane. He was in the air for less than a minute but within a few years some aircraft were flying for hours non-stop. Soon the English Channel was crossed by air, a very important symbolic achievement, and some multi-engined, if very odd-looking, machines capable of carrying passengers were built in the next few years. With smaller aeroplanes, a degree of control had been achieved by 1914 which made possible the carrying out of what was called 'aerobatics'.

For the whole of history before the nineteenth century human beings had been able to go no faster on land than a good horse could gallop, no faster on water than wind could move them. From this to transatlantic liners making twenty knots, to trains travelling at eighty miles an hour and, finally, to controlled flight was a huge jump that came very quickly. In the lands of bullock-carts, sleds and camel-trains and in the countryside of Europe animal muscle still remained the main source of power for transport even in 1914. Though they moved large armies by rail over long distances in that year, European generals had given more thought to horse-fodder than to petrol-dumps in planning their campaigns, and hansom cabs, milk-floats, brewers' drays and coal carts still meant that large populations of draught animals were kept in even the most up-to-date cities. But a new age of physical transportation had begun.

The nineteenth century had also fundamentally transformed the communication of information, and after 1901 the effects of that, too, were soon to be truly revolutionary. It has often been pointed out that Napoleon's couriers could not much improve on the speeds maintained across Europe by those of Julius Caesar. Heliographs and smoke signals were woefully inadequate supplements. A faster way of transmitting information had indeed appeared at the end of the eighteenth century in a few places, where semaphore telegraphs were worked by pulling ropes that wagged wooden arms up and down to deliver a coded message. Under the best circumstances, messages could be thus sent even faster than by carrier pigeons, but required chains of signal towers – between Paris and the Belgian frontier, for example, or, on the other side of the Channel, between Portsmouth and the Admiralty in London. Semaphore was geographically restricted, dependent on good weather, and unable to handle any great volume of traffic. The true revolution in communications technology can be dated to Samuel Morse's simple idea that an electrical impulse sent along a wire could be treated as a signal. Once the equipment had been designed and he had devised a satisfactory code, the age of telegrams and cables could begin. By the end of the century, poles carrying lines for the electric telegraph were commonplace. By 1914 there were few parts of the world outside the polar regions that were not within reasonable distance of a telegraph station. Diplomacy, journalism and business life had by then all been transformed by this invention. Yet the telegraph was still not so swift as direct communication by human voice; in 1876 Alexander Graham Bell patented the first practicable telephone and by 1914 the telephone, though still a somewhat cumbersome and even, to modern ears, primitive instrument, had ceased to be a novelty in major cities.

Telephones, like the telegraph, required lines and cables. The greatest break in principle with existing communications methods came with the invention of 'wireless' transmission in 1895 by the Italian, Marconi. The transmitter and receiver of a message needed no longer to be physically connected. In 1901, the first year of a century that was to be revolutionized by his applications of the fundamental electromagnetic science of Clark Maxwell and Hertz, Marconi sent the first message across the Atlantic by this means; this century is therefore the first during virtually the whole of which radio signalling has been available. In 1914 it was still very much a luxury affordable only by governments and major shipping lines; radio signalling between ships at sea had been one of the first widespread uses of it, and helped to save passengers cast adrift by the *Titanic* disaster of 1912, when the largest passenger ship ever built sank on her maiden voyage. The general public had already become aware in 1910, though, that something very special had been added to communication when Dr Crippen, a murderer who had fled from Great Britain, was arrested on arrival in Canada, a wireless message having been sent from England to alert the captain of the ship in which he was crossing the Atlantic.

MASS COMMUNICATION

In the nineteenth century, the whole world had been affected and already often changed out of recognition by railways, steamships and the telegraph. The appearance of the first true world markets presupposed that a need for information could be met as it had not been met hitherto. The speeding up of the flow of information was still proceeding, and at an accelerating pace, as the twentieth century began. A merchant conducting business with the Far East in 1801 had been obliged to wait at best for four or five months for a question to be answered. His successor in 1901 could have his answer within twenty or thirty minutes, if he needed it.

The nineteenth century had brought about the first and simplest improvements in communicating written ideas and information as steamships and railways speeded up their movement. By 1914, letters were already being carried by air. Quicker transport enormously increased the volume of the world's correspondence (most governments had set up postal services before the nineteenth century was over). Printed material was soon going by post in increasing volume; much more was being printed, above all in newspapers. This was in part a function of the spread of literacy in the western world of European origin. More and more people were going to school and so obtained at least a basic skill capability to read and write. The result was a huge rise in the number of books and periodicals published (not only in western countries), many of them specially aimed at the new literate populations of the big cities. The most obvious example was the spread of cheap popular newspapers, aimed deliberately at as wide an audience as possible.[12] They reported and commented on news in a much livelier – and more superficial – way than the older-established newspapers whose dense columns of small print provided hours of reading but deterred many readers (as did their prices, too, for they were not cheap). Early in the century, both the

[12] Some examples, with their years of first publication, were *Le Journal* (1892), the *Daily Mail* (1896), *Berliner Morgenpost* (1898) and the *Daily Mirror* (1903).

English *Daily Mail* and the French *Petit Parisien* had daily sales of over a million copies.

More solid and traditional newspapers survived, though, for they had their own assured market among men of affairs, and they profited, as did their newer rivals, from the technical advances of the period. The *Times* newspaper of London had been the first in the world to install steam-driven printing presses. Then came rotary printing, using cylinders, instead of flat beds of type, and thus printing a continuous roll of paper. With this method, machines producing 96,000 pages an hour had come into use in the 1880s. Improvements making possible colour printing and automatic typesetting (the linotype machine was first used by a major newspaper, the *New York Times*, in 1886) followed. Quality of production was by 1914 already much higher than even in 1901. Journalism by then had become a huge business. Large sums of money were invested in it and the printing of advertisements that could reach a large public became the basic support of newspaper finances. Journalists found their task eased with the coming of typewriters, trains, steamships, cars and even bicycles, but they profited even more from the new ways of transmitting information through media other than the written word, the telegraph, telephone and, finally, radio.

The great age of radio had to wait for the 1920s. The principle of 'broadcasting' – transmitting radio programmes to listeners at large, rather as farmers had for centuries sown their fields by scattering seed broadcast – then at last took hold (some had hitherto thought it a disadvantage of the new medium that people other than designated recipients might pick up and eavesdrop on messages). Millions of receiving sets were soon being sold worldwide. By 1930 most people who owned receivers had ceased to believe that windows had to be kept open while they were in use in order to allow the broadcast 'waves' to reach them. Most major countries had by then regular radio broadcasting services in operation.

Another important new form of mass communication was visual: the cinema. The first motion pictures or 'movies' were made in the 1890s and were at first seen only as exotic and curious entertainment, rather than a new medium for mass communications. The first commercial performance was given in Paris in 1895 and the French pioneers quickly found imitators and audiences; by 1914 there were 3,500 cinemas in Great Britain and many more in other European countries. 'Talkies' – films with recorded soundtracks synchronized with the image projected on the screen – became the general rule from 1930. By then, huge film industries were at work in many countries around the world, and not merely in the United States and Europe. Film (with radio) was a new fact changing social habits and ideas, sometimes intentionally, sometimes unintentionally, and politicians, governments and businessmen were using it to promote their wares. It is difficult to believe that the twentieth century's unprecedented expansion in literacy, primary schooling and the newspaper press did as much to spread knowledge among millions of what life had to offer in material terms as did radio and the cinema. Moreover, although important contributions were made to both by the USSR, India and Japan, where film industries made very distinctive films for local consumption, the cinema for a long time tended to spread ideas and standards based on the lives of North Americans and Europeans.

The story must be taken just a little further to maintain perspective. Cinema and radio have gone on shaping ideas and aspirations, but after 1945 were joined and in a measure replaced by television. Crude transmissions of pictures by radio waves had been achieved by a German in 1911 and the first demonstrations had been made of the devices on which television was based in the late 1920s. The first successful regular broadcasts were begun by the British Broadcasting Corporation (BBC) in 1936 and by the French in 1938 but only after the war did the new medium really take hold for the first time, above all in the United States. It is now influential far beyond the rich western countries where it made its first impact. President McKinley's murder in 1901 had only been captured in a still photograph, but in 1963 millions of people worldwide were watching the assassination of another American president on their screens within a few hours of its occurrence. By 1970, there was roughly one television set in the televisual country *par excellence*, the United States, for every four citizens (the corresponding figure for India was one set for every 100,000 Indians) and by 1990 well over 90 per cent of American homes had sets. People are still arguing about the precise nature of the impact television has had on society, but one that was quickly obvious was its challenge to other kinds of mass communication. At the beginning of the 1950s the average Briton went to the cinema twenty-eight times a year; by 1970 the figure was less than five times. Television inaugurated a new age of communication through images, a qualitative historical change in the history of culture greater even than the coming of print; just as there are now more people alive than ever, there are now more who can be reached by a combination of spoken word and the visual image (especially since the introduction of satellite transmission) than ever by the printed word.

Changes in communications affect many sides of human life. Like the coming of print, much more was implied than merely the replacement of one technology by another, while such changes as came with radio and the cinema helped to liberate humanity from forces previously restricting it. They could also work in other ways; as the fate of Crippen shows, radio lengthened the reach of justice. Governments were enormously strengthened by the communications revolution. Armed revolt became a much less dangerous threat when the telegraph could summon help to be delivered at a few hours' notice and soldiers sent by railways. Like other technological advances, many of those in communications contributed to a growth in the coercive powers of the state during this century.

CHANGING MENTALITIES

It was said soon after they made their appearance that popular newspapers, and later the cinema and television, undermined religious faith, often in very gross ways. In Europe this was not a new charge; there it had been levelled in the past at any likely source of more plentiful information (such as printing in its first centuries), and any new source of innovative ideas. Such innovations had rarely taken place within the ambit of other civilizations and when they had done so (in, for example, the appearance of printing in China) they seemed of little effect. The weakening of the claims of revelation and the authority of priest and clergyman in Europe and its offshoots before 1901, though, was agreed by believers and non-believers alike to owe much to growing freedom to print and publish. The damage done in this way, though, was as much the work of implicit challenges as of explicit. The growing prestige of science was a case in point.

It had been one of the most effective, though often indirect, forces undermining traditional popular belief. But it was not what scientists published that impressed the masses, but the effectiveness and power that showed themselves more clearly than ever in new applications in the early twentieth century. By 1914 in the western world, when 'wireless' radio messages were being sent across the Atlantic, aeroplanes were commonplace, petrol-driven motor-cars were beginning to crowd city streets, and educated people could take for granted anaesthetics, steam turbines, harder and specialized steels, telephones, and many more marvels which had not existed even half a century before, minds were changing even more rapidly in the same direction. Science had come to shape the way the world was seen by millions, just as great religions had shaped the mental landscapes of the past. It had come to be more than just a method for exploring and manipulating nature; it was a mythology. Some even looked to it for guidance about metaphysical questions, the aims men ought to pursue, the standards they should employ to regulate behaviour. None of this, of course, had any intrinsic or necessary connexion with science as scientists knew it. But the upshot in the end in the western world was a civilization many of whose leaders had, except vestigially, no dominant religious belief or transcendent ideals and whose masses were relaxing more and more into an unconscious materialism (even if minorities vigorously sought to keep popular religion alive).

As in other ways, western civilization was in this respect unique; no earlier civilization had yet dispensed with an articulated religious foundation, nor did other cultures for a long time begin to show similar trends. In the twentieth century, though, the core of western civilization, articulated or not, would come to lie in belief in the promise of manipulating nature. In principle, that civilization now asserts that there is no problem that need be regarded as insoluble, given sufficient resources of intellect and money; it has room for the obscure, but not for the essentially mysterious. This was already implicit in many of its attitudes before 1914.

ACCELERATION AND INTEGRATION

While long-term changes in demography, well-being, attitudes, technology and communication can no more than be hinted at, they
provide continuing themes spanning a century's history, moving it
along almost without reference to its politics. Even brief glances ahead
into the long run help also to emphasize how hard it was for men and
women anywhere as the twentieth century unrolled to take in the
significance of much that was bringing change to their lives. There
was indeed to be plenty to distract them from fundamental reflexion
as time passed. For hundreds of millions of people, the century would
prove far from benevolent; the prolongation of many people's lives
that it made possible was often a prolongation of misery, it now
seems. Those who seek to judge it good or bad have to balance the
enormous and obvious amelioration shown by such facts as population
growth, increases in expectancy of life or the elimination of diseases
which had long been scourges, against the wretchedness and deliberate
brutality suffered by so many people along the way as the century
unrolled. It would be nonsense to rush to judgement. Moreover, to
weigh the happiness of those with access to commodities available to
them as never before against the unhappiness of those disturbed by
social change or by the criticism of traditional ideas is impossible.
Acceptable evaluative judgements may well be finally unattainable;
at this stage, certainly, any attempt to weigh good and evil should be
set aside until the record has been examined at least a little less
superficially than in the facts set out so far.

One final forward-looking comment can, nonetheless, be made. The
century brought a new pace of change. Since 1901 it has been quicker
and more widespread than ever before. Not only change but accelerating
change has been a leading fact of recent history, though one first appearing a long time ago. From the discovery of fire and the mastering of its
use, to the application of it to refining and shaping metals (the invention
of metallurgy), took hundreds of thousands of years. It took less than
10,000 to get from that point to the invention of the steam engine. From
the steam engine to the steam turbine producing electricity took only
a couple of centuries. A half-century or so later still, the turbine often

gets its steam from nuclear power. Our scientists are now trying to tap that power in the form of fusion, too.

Some people have in this century found recent acceleration not exciting, but appalling. They fear that it is now too rapid for mankind's habits of mind and standards of behaviour to adapt to it. Fortunately, historians do not have to predict – and, indeed, they should not, for all they know about is the past, and that is full of examples of predictions that turned out badly. They can agree, nonetheless, on the fact: acceleration in historical change of all sorts has seemed to increase exponentially since this century began. Technology shows it most obviously. In 1901, the fastest ships took just under a week to cross the Atlantic, but now it can be flown on a commercial flight in three and a half hours by men and women born before the first man-carrying flight took place. They have lived to see, too, on television, a new kind of traveller variously called an 'astronaut' or 'cosmonaut' stepping on to the moon; the first journey by men from earth to land on the moon, it is worth recalling, took four days – slightly less than the transatlantic 'liners' of 1901 were taking to get from Liverpool to New York.

Such a technological change should remind us that the twentieth century brought to completion the integrating of the globe that began a few hundred years ago. Humanity truly now lives in one world. Technology, politics, economics and, more and more, culture have all tied it together, even if many people do not seem to recognize it or to behave accordingly. The process bringing that about was launched by Europeans and it was a part of the achievement of supremacy by the peoples of European origin over the whole globe. So far as that supremacy was political and military, it is over: much of this book is about the ways in which the empires of yesterday have crumbled to become 'one with Nineveh and Tyre', as Rudyard Kipling feared they might when he wrote at the end of the nineteenth century. Curiously though, this recession of power has been accompanied by even greater success for European culture and civilization, taken up and exploited as never before by non-Europeans, often at one remove, through a generalized 'westernization'. That did not come about, though, in ways that would have seemed at all likely as the century began, when Europe's evident and continuing world mastery could still seem an unquestionable, unchanging fact.

BOOK 2

THE LAST YEARS OF THE
EUROPEAN ASCENDANCY

5

European Exceptionalism

EUROPEANS

Even North Americans, aware as they rightly were of their specially happy lot as citizens of the world's greatest democracy, would not have disputed when this century began that the European nations from which most of them sprang were the leading players on the world stage. Europeans could be kept from interfering politically or militarily in the affairs of the western hemisphere, but elsewhere, for two or three centuries, their story had been one of their growing world power. Whatever might be the potential of other parts of the globe for the future, it was from Europe that capital came to finance international commerce and economic enterprises all round the globe; the local cultures of Americans, Australasians and many Africans on which rested western civilization outside Europe were, after all, all European in origin; to a remarkable degree the creativity of western art, music, science was still most marked in their old European cradles. The greatest empires were European. Of Europe's importance in the world, there could be no dispute.

Once away from such generalities though, it was as hard in 1901 as it is today to pin down exactly what the entity that was so influential might actually be. The very meaning of the word 'Europe' is still debated. So is the content of the history of Europe. So, even, is its geographical definition; the peninsula to which we give the name blurs physically into something else, Asia, and exactly where it does so has long been and still is open to argument even as a matter of climate or topography. Exactly how that area, however defined, is coterminous with a certain culture, style of life or even civilization remains more contentious still. Discussion of such questions is liable to be passionate and confused; there are too many interests cluttering it up for things to be otherwise.

Yet it is undeniable that an immense role has been played in the world by ideas and institutions stemming from the thoughts and deeds of peoples living in a particular part of the world called Europe. Those ideas and institutions are no longer distinguishable from others essential to a 'western' civilization now spread round the world, and a certain blurring was already evident early in this century. 'In this period,' (meaning his own) wrote an historian in 1910, 'the History of Europe becomes in a sense the History of the world.'[1] Yet the possibility of distinguishing something called Europe was still one more widely taken for granted than today, even if most of the millions of Europeans then alive would neither have had much sense of it, nor of sharing in any collective historic role. But only a small minority would have then felt they had any personal impact on public events at all except, at most, in so far as those events concerned their families or local communities. Most Europeans still lived in the countryside, locked into traditional ways, almost buried in their ignorance, illiteracy, and what Karl Marx once called 'rural idiocy'; like the other millions who lived in Europe's cities, they could hardly have any real picture of other cultures, let alone the movements of world history. What some among those millions may well already have observed or simply intuited, nevertheless, is that they lived in a world of change in many ways very unlike the one into which their grandparents had been born. They could listen, if they wished, to those grandparents' stories of the ways in which daily life had much changed since their own youth; the likelihood that even the country-dweller would travel and know something of a world beyond his or her nearest village or city had much increased and was increasing, and in many other ways the contexts in which people lived could stimulate in them new ideas and responses to the world. New facts had bred and were breeding new assumptions about what was possible, what was desirable, and

[1] S. Leathes, in *The Cambridge Modern History*, vol. xii, *The Latest Age* (Cambridge, 1910), p.1. He also thought it worth noting (p.5) that 'the whole world is now the sphere of European activity'.

even what was the due of millions of people, most obviously the city-dwellers.

Such shorthand blurs colossal differences. The immense diversity behind such words as 'Europe' and 'Europeans', or 'city-dweller' and 'peasant', must never be lost to sight. Nevertheless, a majority of Europeans shared something important: they lived in societies changing faster than those of most of the rest of humanity. This was also true of their cousins in the countries founded by expatriate Europeans overseas, and was to be seen in the humblest circumstances of everyday life. For decades a flow of commodities at first available only in (relatively) tiny quantities had been changing the lives of the mass of Europeans. In the nineteenth century, a vast new range of goods had come into existence that they could buy. Paraffin oil (kerosene), coal gas and electricity had joined coal, wood, wind and water as sources of energy and had begun to light their homes and cook food for their tables. Railways, electric trams, steamships, motor cars and bicycles had given millions a new freedom from their immediate environment, making travel easier over long and short distances.

Doubts came too, inevitably perhaps, with such new advantages and practical freedoms. Even if what might happen in the future were ignored, contemplation of the cost of new levels of consumption and doubts about the social justice of its distribution troubled thoughtful and responsible minds. Most Europeans in 1901 were by modern standards very poor, whether or not they lived in rich countries where the incongruity of this seemed more striking than in earlier times. Poverty was coming to appear all the more afflicting when society had such obvious power to create new wealth. There were to be seen, though, the dim beginnings of what would prove to be revolutionary changes in expectations; already, most of the richer European countries had imposed restrictions on hours of work, albeit within broad limits. There were other changes, too, which presented new threats and evils. If it was unsurprising that men (and in the European world at least it was still the presumption that men, not women, would provide the main income of the household) should sometimes be without work, it was new that situations should suddenly arise in which the operation of blind forces of boom and slump produced almost overnight millions of men without work in the new great towns. This was 'unemployment', the new phenomenon for which a new word had come into use in England in the 1880s. Some economists thought it an inevitable concomitant of capitalism, and that life was bound to be hard for the poor.

Many Europeans indeed lived in a poverty that left them unaware of the advantages they enjoyed over their predecessors; their conditions hardly encouraged them to such reflexions. Millions lived in cramped, ill-housed agglomerations, under-provided with schools and fresh air, let alone amusement other than that of the streets, though often in sight of the wealth their society helped to produce. 'Slums' was another idea (and word) the nineteenth century had invented. Two converging conclusions were often drawn from their existence. One was fearful; many sober statesmen at the end of the nineteenth century deeply distrusted the cities as centres of revolutionary danger, crime and wickedness. The other, held by those on the extreme Left of the political divide, was optimistic: the condition of the cities assured those who wished to lead the 'damned of the earth' (as a socialist anthem had it)[2] that revolution against the injustice of the social and economic order was inevitable. Both responses were drawn from the same evidence: both also overlooked other evidence suggesting, on the contrary, that revolution was becoming less likely, in western Europe, at least.

PRIVILEGE AND UNREST

Europe was ruled in 1901 by the powerful and rich, but that is not a very helpful statement. The Swiss burgher was unlike the Prussian *Junker*, the French industrial *patron* or the Spanish grandee. The powerful and rich differed greatly from country to country. Everywhere, though, the ruling class still included substantial components from the old, sometimes very old, hereditary hierarchies of blood and noble status, as well as representatives of the plutocracy and professions. It is safe to say, too, that land still played a large part

---

[2] The words of the *Internationale*, the hymn of the socialist Internationals (see below), by Eugene Pottier, member of the Paris Commune of 1871.

even in the most developed countries in sustaining the incomes of the wealthy and a more important one than it does today. The continent was large; it could present a rich variety of social custom and many idiosyncratic distinctions among the ruling élites. The conduct of some aristocrats in central and eastern Europe still followed conventions that would be today regarded as at least outlandish and perhaps barbaric.[3] When all such facts are given due weight, we have to fall back in the end on some such bland generalization as the statement that political power in Europe in 1901 was shared by varying combinations of aristocracy and the higher bourgeoisie, and that meant people with a high degree of respect for private property.

That does not explain very much about any particular country. Even to the eye – in the persistence of local costume, for example – Europe was much more varied than it is today. There were parts of it only a few hours by railway from capital cities where modern life was in full swing, where the dominant classes could still be found living in a mental world which was pre-nineteenth rather than pre-twentieth century. Over much of eastern Europe, quasi-patriarchal relationships and the traditional authority of the landowner over those who lived on his estates were still intact. Poland, Hungary, the Baltic lands still produced aristocratic conservatives who were opposed in spirit not merely to encroachments upon the material privilege rooted in often huge estates but also to the values and assumptions of any modern society. At the other extreme were examples such as could be found in the United Kingdom, where aristocracy was long used to the idea of legal equality, whatever the realities of social and economic power might be, and where landowners, though hugely and disproportionately influential still in politics and society, yet had to exercise that influence in a context of democratically elected institutions, and to share it with businessmen, bankers, and even a few workmen.

The European ruling classes of 1901 had lived through decades haunted by memories of a century of revolutions and, above all, by

[3] The realities of life on a Hungarian estate in 1901 are strikingly set out in O. Jászi's classic account of *The Dissolution of the Habsburg Monarchy* (Chicago, 1929), pp.234–5 (repr. edn 1961), and (no less startlingly, but more light-heartedly) in the *Memoirs of Michael Karolyi* (London, 1956), pp.31–2. Jászi's story of the nudity of the Archduke Otto, p.237, is also worth a moment's consideration.

those of the Paris Commune thirty years earlier. It is unsurprising, therefore, that their fears continued to be fed by sporadic outbreaks of violence well into the twentieth century. Sensational headlines were often made by attacks on heads of state and members of royal families in these years.[4] Strikes and demonstrations could become violent in industrialized countries, whether they had revolutionary traditions or not; France, in whose politics revolutionary rhetoric always played a large part, was well used to seeing soldiers deployed in industrial disputes before 1914 but even in Great Britain there were violent deaths in riots and soldiers were at times ordered to open fire to prevent threats to persons and property. In Eastern Europe, though, the countryside was potentially more dangerous than the cities: it took artillery and cost 11,000 dead to put down a Romanian peasant rising in early 1907. Rural Spain and Italy, too, were violent places. In Russia, while there was a continuing revolutionary movement which from time to time broke out in terrorism (and as recently as 1881, a tsar had fallen victim to it), recurrent agrarian disorder was more menacing than anything a comparatively few terrorists, however determined, could do; peasant attacks on landlords and their bailiffs in fact reached their peak after 1901. When such violence was followed by defeat in war at the hands of the Japanese and the momentary shaking of the regime's confidence, the result in 1905 was, for the first time, a Russian revolution.

Such upheavals, combined with the sporadic and well-publicized activities of terrorists, kept policemen and respectable citizens on their toes. True, some of the spectres that troubled them had little substance. There was much baseless fright at the end of the nineteenth century about the work of non-existent 'secret societies', for example.[5] 'Anarchists', too, had great success in pressing themselves on the

[4] President Carnot of France had been stabbed to death in 1894, the Spanish minister was assassinated in 1897 and the empress of Austria in 1898, the king of Italy in 1900, the president of the United States in 1901, the king and queen of Serbia in 1903, the king and the crown prince of Portugal in 1908 and another Spanish prime minister in 1912; there was no logical connexion between these events, though some were carried out by self-proclaimed anarchists, but their occurrence in relatively rapid succession was striking, and to some, alarming.

[5] See J. M. Roberts, *The Mythology of the Secret Societies* (London, 1972).

public imagination, and their acts of terrorism and assassinations during the 1890s received wide publicity; the importance of what they attempted transcended any success or failure they might have because the growth of the press had meant that great publicity value could be extracted from the explosion of a bomb or a dagger-stroke.[6] In using such methods, not all anarchists shared the same aims, but they were all children of a turbulent epoch, protesting not only against the state, but also against a whole society that they judged unjust.

SOCIALISM

Though well-publicized acts of terror ensured the anarchists notoriety, they were wrongly but easily and often confused with others on the Left whom they usually despised, the socialists, to the chagrin of the latter. Almost everywhere, socialists had by 1901 come to mean Marxists, and their rhetoric helped to keep fears of revolution on the boil.[7] Though Karl Marx had died in 1883, his ideas make him, like Darwin, another of those nineteenth-century figures who decisively shaped the twentieth century. Important working-class traditions and mythologies other than Marxist existed only in two countries: England, where the early growth of a trade-union movement and the possibility of working through one of the major established political parties produced a non-revolutionary radicalism which proclaimed socialist goals, and, to a lesser degree, in France.

Official Marxism, as defined by events in Karl Marx's own lifetime and its key texts, had hardened into something of which he himself appears not wholly to have approved in his last years. Marxism was treated by many socialists as a set of dogmatic principles purporting

---

[6] 'Anarchy is a crime against the whole human race; and all mankind should band against the Anarchist,' proclaimed President Roosevelt in his first message to the United States Congress after taking up office. *AR 1901*, p.415. His predecessor's murderer had been an anarchist.

[7] The spread of Marxism outside the western world was largely a matter for the new century; in 1901 it was still overwhelmingly a European phenomenon. Marxists made little impact in the USA. The first Japanese translation of *The Communist Manifesto* was published in 1905 (in a newspaper that was at once shut down by the authorities).

to rest on a reading of history so as to give guidance about the way that history was going and would inevitably continue to go. Debate has raged about the role played in the development of Marx's ideas in this sense by his friend and collaborator, Friedrich Engels, after the older man's death, about the validity of the arguments involved, about their fidelity or otherwise to the master's own views, and many other matters. This is not relevant, though, to our concerns. What is certain is that the dominant and dogmatic versions of Marxism already in place when the twentieth century began rested in fact on articles of faith that proved able to sustain revolutionary political activity well into the twentieth century, and that for most of that time Marxist socialism characteristically presented an authoritative and inelastic style when confronting other tendencies in the politics of the Left.

Of the Marxist articles of faith, the most important were that history was progressive, that it progressed by 'dialectical' confrontation and conflicts, that such clashes were ultimately the expression of the economic interests of classes, that they were unavoidable and bound to take revolutionary forms, that a final confrontation between the bourgeois masters of capitalist society and the proletarian workforce they exploited was at least in sight, and that once a 'dictatorship of the proletariat' had been deployed to eliminate the last vestiges of class conflict a classless society would come into being in which economic exploitation would not exist. This was heartening and bracing for those who sought to correct injustice and set the world to rights. It is not hard to discern in it a quasi-religious content: the Judaic notion of the Chosen People. The proletariat was to march like Israel in the desert (or like the early Christian Church through a hostile world and vale of tears) to an apocalyptic end in salvation (revolution) and the promised land of socialism. It was a faith of consolation, vengeance and promise. It appeared to explain why things were as they were, to identify the enemies to be overthrown and to assure the faithful that history was on their side. To borrow a phrase as yet unknown, socialists were made to feel that they were the wave of the future. For three-quarters of a century or so, huge resources of energy and self-sacrifice were marshalled in support of Marxist causes and were poured out in advancing them. In those years Marxism was to prove the most successful evangel of the age, and its most convincing mythology. For many it would retain its emotional excitement and glitter long after its fire had declined into the sullen glow of the propaganda of bureaucrats intent on defending their vested interests.

The supremacy of Marxism in continental European socialism had been enthroned in 1893, when the 'Second International', an international working-class movement set up four years earlier to coordinate socialist action in all countries, formally excluded the anarchists who had until then belonged to it.[8] In 1900, the International had opened a permanent office in Brussels. Numbers, wealth and theoretical contributions made the German Social Democratic Party (since 1890 officially Marxist) preponderant within it. In spite of police persecution, socialism had prospered in Germany in an era of rapid industrialization: by 1901 it was an established fact of German politics, and, indeed, provided their first truly mass organization. Numbers and wealth alone would have made it likely that the official creed of the German party would be accepted by socialists elsewhere. But Marxism's religious and mythical appeal mattered more, even if intellectuals preached endlessly about the 'scientific' nature of the doctrines they called Marxist, deliberating their niceties like medieval schoolmen. Marxism's real strength was as a faith, and its greatest formal triumph was yet to come, when nearly a quarter of the human race would be formally ruled in its name and China learnt to revere the name of a German philosopher who had rarely spoken of Asia but with contempt and had never gone further east than Prussia in his life, while his ideas remained rooted in German idealist philosophy and British political economy.

Although the mythology of socialism frightened the wealthy and troubled the established order as the century opened, it should have been easy to see that recent history by no means obviously justified such fears. As some intelligent Marxists noted, industrial workers had manifestly been able to improve the material standards of their lives within the capitalist system. The unfolding of that system in all its

---

[8] As late as its London Congress of 1896, though, the president of one session, an English trade unionist, said he would call the police to eject anarchists who were 'shouting and stamping' (James Joll, *The Second International 1889–1914*, rev. edn London, 1974, p.74), so falling back on a threat of which, of course, any good bourgeois would have approved.

complexity had not simplified and sharpened class conflict in the way Marx had predicted, but had produced institutions helpful to the working class. This was at first and above all obvious in Germany, but also later in England.[9] Elected parliaments provided opportunities to win concessions and advantages, many working-class leaders did not want to ignore the power of the vote while waiting for the revolution. Some of them sought to restate official Marxism so as to take account of such trends; they were called 'Revisionists'. Broadly speaking, they advocated a peaceful advance towards the transformation of society by socialism. That transformation when it came would be, they were sure, in its objective reality, a revolution, but not necessarily a violent one. This theoretical position and the conflict it provoked soon entangled itself with a practical issue of politics at the turn of the century: whether socialists should or should not sit as ministers in 'capitalist' governments if the chance of doing so came up – as it did in France.

The debate on revisionism took years and fizzled out ambiguously in the end. The Second International explicitly condemned it in theory and socialist rhetoric continued to be about revolution while national socialist parties, notably the German, continued to act as revisionists in practice, making deals with the existing system as suited them. Some socialists hoped that revolution might be made a reality by refusing to fight as conscripts if their governments tried to make them go to war. One group, the majority in the Russian socialist party, continued vigorously to denounce revisionism and to advocate revolutionary violence: this reflected the peculiarity of the Russian situation, where there was no opportunity at all for effective parliamentary activity before 1905 and a deep tradition of revolution and terrorism. Its adherents were called Bolshevik, from the Russian word meaning a majority.

[9] The political setting was very different in the two countries, of course, for all that they were both countries with formally constitutional and representative government. As an Irish observer (George Bernard Shaw) noted in 1896, 'The Germans with their compact Social Democratic Party in the Reichstag are apparently far ahead of us. But then their leader . . . is going to prison for a speech which Mr Arthur Balfour [a conservative minister] might make to the [conservative] Primrose League with the approbation of England.' Q. in Joll, p.76.

Socialists claimed to speak for the masses. Whether they did so or did not, by 1901 many conservatives already worried that the advances gained by liberalism and democracy in the nineteenth century would prove revolutionary, whether slowly or swiftly, and thought that their further advance should be resisted even, if necessary, by force. In some countries, government was much influenced by aristocratic conservatives opposed in spirit not merely to encroachments upon their material privilege, but also to the values, commonplaces and assumptions of what might be called 'market society'; they did not accept that they had interests in common even with the non-noble rich. But this line became more and more blurred and, for the most part, conservative thinking had by 1901 tended to fall back upon the defence of capital, a position which, of course, would half a century earlier have been regarded in many places as radically liberal, because individualist. What this could mean varied much from country to country: Great Britain had never been without an income tax since 1842, but French governments had still not succeeded in introducing one by 1914. Capitalist, industrial conservatism opposed more and more vigorously the state's interference with wealth, an interference that had nonetheless grown steadily, if slowly and irregularly, in the previous half-century as states had taken on more and more tasks and military and naval expenditure had risen.

MASS POLITICS AND NATIONALISM

A broadening of the franchise was an essential part, but still only a part, of the advance of constitutional government in Europe. The growing incorporation of the masses in politics had other manifestations, too. In the last quarter of the nineteenth century the modern political party came into being to organize electoral support. It simplified issues in order to present them as clear choices, it evolved a bureaucratic apparatus for the delivery of votes at the polls, and it sought out and cultivated special interests.[10] Party was to spread round

---

[10] The first serious study of the phenomenon was M. Ostrogorski's book, *Democracy and the Organisation of Political Parties* (London and New York, 1902).

the world. Old-fashioned politicians deplored it in its new model; they saw it, correctly, as another sign of the coming of mass society, the corruption of public debate and of pressure on traditional élites to adapt their politics to the ways of the man in the street. The 'public opinion' that party sought to address was far less novel (the first history of the phenomenon had been published as early as the 1820s) but its importance had grown in the nineteenth century. Even Bismarck, the quintessential conservative statesman, had felt bound to give way to popular outcry and heed mass sentiment. The manipulation of public opinion seemed to have become much easier as the century went on (or so, at least, many newspaper owners and statesmen believed). Mass education had been accepted as necessary in order to civilize the masses for the proper use of the vote. What seemed to be the consequence of rising literacy, though, was that a market was created for a new cheap press which pandered to emotionalism and sensationalism, and for the sellers and devisers of advertising campaigns, another nineteenth-century invention.

The political idea which had the greatest mass appeal at the end of the nineteenth century was nationalism. Since the 1790s it had been a dynamic force in European politics and international relations. It encouraged the creation of notions of collective identity – or, rather, identities – which were distinct from allegiances to personal rulers and it had increasingly remade the map of Europe as one of national states. This was most obvious in the dynastic empires. In what had been Ottoman Europe, the sultan's lands had been largely broken up into national states by 1901, but important ethnic demands still remained unsatisfied (above all, at that moment, in Macedonia). Within the Russian Empire, Poles, Jews, Ukrainians and Lithuanians felt themselves oppressed by the Russians. In the Austro-Hungarian empire nationalism presented a real revolutionary threat; the rulers of the Hungarian half of the monarchy, a Magyar minority, lorded it over Poles, Jews, Ruthenes, Slovaks, Germans, Croats and Romanians alike and in the Austrian half, a German-speaking minority struggled with the aspirations of Czechs, Slovenes and Italians in the Trentino.

As for constitutional Great Britain, she faced two nationalist problems in Ireland. That presented by the southern Catholic Irish was the more obvious though by 1901 agricultural reform and better economic conditions appeared to have drawn much of the venom from the issue of 'Home Rule'. Yet it had only recently been reinflamed by another Irish nationalism, that of the Protestant majority of the province of Ulster, some of whose members threatened revolution if the government in London gave Home Rule to their Roman Catholic compatriots.

All those who supported unsatisfied nationalisms believed themselves with greater or lesser justification to do so on behalf of the oppressed. But great powers, too, claimed to embody the national principle. France had been psychologically deeply wounded by Germany's seizure of Alsace and Lorraine in 1871. French politicians whom it suited to do so long and assiduously cultivated the theme of *revanche* for that despoilation. Nationalism in France gave extra bitterness to many domestic political issues, notably to struggles over anti-clerical legislation which seemed to raise questions of loyalty to national institutions or an external power, the Vatican. Different though they were in resources and strength, too, the short histories of both united Germany and united Italy made their rulers especially sensitive to internally divisive forces and willing to court chauvinistic feeling as national cement. Some of Italy's leaders hankered after and occasionally indulged colonial adventures that they thought would appeal to their countrymen, while keeping alive suspicion and unfriendliness towards Austria–Hungary. The Habsburg monarchy was formally Italy's ally, but it remained the ruler of territories still regarded by Italians as *irredenta*, 'unredeemed' as other lands acquired in the unification of Italy had once been, and therefore an enemy.

Even the British, in no sense a 'new' nation, whose rhetoricians and cartoonists liked to dwell on their countrymen's supposed steadiness and political sobriety (unless they were talking about the Irish), could easily become over-excited about national symbols. There was a brief but vigorously expressed enthusiasm for the empire in the 1890s that had its impact in support for the South African war. There was also great popular sensitivity over the preservation of British naval supremacy, when it appeared to be threatened by Germany, a power whose alarming economic dynamism was also thought by some to challenge British primacy in world commerce. That both countries appeared to many of their subjects to have interests opposed in many specific ways was more important than the reality that they were one another's best customers. Things were made worse by the stridency of German official rhetoric and the irritated personal outbursts from time to time of the Kaiser, Wilhelm II. When, for instance, he showed enthusiasm for building a battle fleet (as he often unwisely did) the British could hardly fail to feel that it must be intended for use against them.

Whatever influence popular national feeling might have, though, few states in Europe even in 1914 had truly democratic constitutions in the sense that the mass of the population had, even formally, the last word in politics. France and Switzerland were the only republics of significance. Elsewhere (a few curious fossils such as Andorra or San Marino excepted) hereditary monarchies and often a hereditary component in the legislature provided the prevailing constitutional forms and retained substantial powers, even if some countries had big electorates and representative arrangements which could be reasonably termed democratic. In 1912, when the powers agreed to set up an independent Albania as a last extension of the national principle in the Balkans, they decided as a matter of course to give it a prince on its emergence from the Ottoman heritage the following year.[11] But respect for the utility of monarchy permitted much variety in the way it worked. Few monarchs regarded the institution with the consistency of England's Edward VII, whose respect for it extended to the native rulers of the South Pacific; his nephew, the German Kaiser, said he did not believe the British monarchy really to be a monarchy at all. Yet, of the constitutional but hereditary monarchies, the British was undoubtedly the leading example; others were Belgium, the Netherlands, Scandinavia, Italy, Spain, Portugal and some of the new Balkan creations of the nineteenth century, Greece being the oldest. Within this group, the real distributions of political power varied a lot, whatever the formal arrangements. There were some unpromising examples of the genre among the newer creations (especially in the Balkans). Constitutional monarchy was nonetheless a

---

[11] He was to hold his throne for less than two years.

widespread, successful, recognizable and recognized institution in the Europe of 1901.

CONSTITUTIONAL GOVERNMENTS

Constitutional government, and its associated principles of representation, a broad franchise, and substantial freedom of expression, had been for much of the nineteenth century seen as the wave of the future. Yet it was only too evident in 1901 that it had its problems. Even in the United Kingdom, as the old century closed, there was coming into sight what was in a few years to become a major political crisis. Rising bills for government (to pay for armaments and welfare services) confronted what was already the most highly taxed nation in the civilized world. At its heart was the issue of the state's larger and larger role in the regulation of society, and its power to override particular interests within it. It came to a climax in 1911 in a peaceful transformation of the constitution by crippling the power of the House of Lords to restrain an elected House of Commons. In the background there were other issues, too; it was not just the higher taxation of the rich to pay for social services that was in question. These, in the end, strained British constitutionalism more than the struggle over the powers of the House of Lords. The violence of Ulstermen and the 'suffragettes' who sought the vote for women led to speculation that parliamentarianism itself might be under threat. There was less sense than in the past of a sustaining political consensus. This would have a bearing on international affairs in 1914, when some foreign observers were misled into thinking that the country would be inhibited from strong action on the continent by the danger of civil war. As it turned out, that proved to be fanciful; there was still a huge solidity about British institutions and political habit. Parliamentary monarchy still seemed able to carry through and adapt itself to vast changes in the land of its birth.

If, in the end, advocates of constitutional government could feel encouraged by the example of Great Britain, they were less likely to be when considering the other major constitutional states of Europe. France was the only republic among them; in a sense, its very creation in 1871 had established a new ideological fact of international life. In the wake of the Paris Commune and the troubled years in which the Third Republic was slowly established, though, there had been more than one occasion when the survival of republican institutions seemed in doubt. In 1901 itself, political France – which was usually taken to mean Paris – was in uproar over allegations of injustice that raised deep issues of principle. The victim was Alfred Dreyfus, a Jewish regular officer of the army who had been court-martialled on trumped-up evidence for espionage, stripped of his commission and sent off to imprisonment in a penal colony.[12] The subsequent struggle to obtain justice for him was obstructed by antisemitic prejudice, the professional solidarity of many of the soldiers involved in the case, and an outraged sense of nationalism, aroused by what were believed to be dangers to the security of the nation if the army were not supported. As public interest grew, French society became more and more bitterly divided by the 'Affair', as it was called; what it seemed to show was that many Frenchmen were not yet reconciled to the Revolution of 1789 and the republic that was its heir.[13] Some Catholic clergy behaved very imprudently in the attacks they made on Dreyfus and the support they gave his accusers. This helped to revive radical anti-clericalism and poisoned the atmosphere in which governments approached the settlement of long-running quarrels with the Church (the eventual outcome was the unilateral ending of the Concordat made by Napoleon I a century earlier, which had guaranteed the legal position of the Roman Catholic Church in France).

The opening years of the new century therefore presented a spectacle of violent ideological and political division within the country that *par excellence* represented the cause of democracy among the great

[12] Dreyfus had been condemned at a court-martial in 1894. Four years later, the celebrated novelist Emile Zola publicized the injustice done to him in a famous newspaper article entitled 'J'accuse . . .'; this detonated the public debate, though Dreyfus's supporters had already been hard at work to have his case reviewed. Only after a second court-martial – that again found him guilty but with 'extenuating circumstances', a nonsensical decision – was the injustice corrected and Dreyfus restored, with promotion, to the army in 1906.

[13] These divisions explain the title of a book which an outstanding French reactionary, Charles Maurras, wrote about the Affair, *Quand les Français ne s'aimaient pas* (Paris, 1906).

powers.[14] It did not enhance French prestige abroad and even revived old doubts about the ability of the Third Republic to survive. The regime turned out, though, to be more firmly grounded in the loyalties of the French than sometimes appeared from the heated rhetoric of the politicians. Revolutionary socialism did not prove to be a serious threat in a country where the rural population had for so long regarded itself as a beneficiary of the Revolution of 1789. The Republic would in fact survive all internal challengers and finally succumb in 1940 only to military defeat and invasion. France's Latin and monarchical neighbours, Spain and Italy, also found clericalism and anti-clericalism presenting them with recurrent political problems. They were, though, also faced with others, much more serious. It could not have been said that the prospect for continuing constitutional government looked promising in either country in 1901. Both countries were much poorer than France. Both had major regional problems exploited or ignored but always exacerbated by unrepresentative and oligarchic politicians. Until 1902, no prime minister of Italy had ever visited the backward South while in office; the *Mezzogiorno* was a region where in the 1860s more Italian soldiers had died repressing 'banditry' than in all the wars of the *Risorgimento*. Since then, conditions in the region had grown worse by comparison with the rest of the country. Nor had years of peaceful alternation of liberal and constitutional governments at Madrid (which indeed marked an improvement on the record of coups and revolution of a few years earlier) done anything to prevent the alienation of Catalonia and the entrenchment there of an anarcho-syndicalist movement that spurned constitutional Spain, or to alleviate the appalling rural poverty of, for instance, Andalucia. Spain and Italy were countries in the course of modernization, somewhat limping, financially weak (one of the few consolations of Spaniards for the loss of Cuba in 1898 was the reduction in military and administrative expenditure that it made possible), and repeatedly troubled by popular outbursts of violence.

In 1898 Italy had undergone something that looked like near-revolution, with thirty of her provinces under martial law, some of her greatest cities in a state of siege and 400,000 soldiers under arms.

[14] France had first introduced universal male suffrage as long ago as 1793.

In 1909, in the 'Tragic Week' of Barcelona, when riots had followed the mobilization of Catalonian reservists to go and fight in Spanish Morocco, nearly 200 people were shot in the streets by the army and police. A few years later, in 1913, much of central Italy went out of control of the government in a 'Red Week' provoked by a general strike; several towns declared themselves independent communes, and a republic was proclaimed in the Romagna before order could be restored. Revolutionary socialists had not provoked the movement, but made themselves prominent in it when it was under way. So did revolutionary journalists, among them one of whom more would be heard, a young socialist called Benito Mussolini.

Much could be said about the diversity of circumstances and structures, as well as of historical legacies, between Italy and Spain, and their formal constitutional similarity should not be allowed to conceal it.[15] The negative essence of the difficulties facing them was, nonetheless, the same: neither had a general will able to sustain the regime. Class and ideological divisions, and the artificiality of a political system almost entirely confined in each country to a small and oligarchic political class that manipulated the constitutional procedures to its own benefit, meant that the majority of Italians and Spaniards had hardly any constitutional and moral assumptions about the state in common. It was a Spanish statesman who said in 1909 'either we make the revolution from above, or it will be made for us from below'.[16] France did better; for all the concern to which her turbulent politics gave rise, they were much more a matter of froth and rhetoric than of fundamental insecurity. But all the constitutional states shared a flexibility in approaching their problems in comparison with more authoritarian regimes.

[15] Though Spain had introduced universal male suffrage in 1890 and Italy (for those men over thirty) did so only in 1912.
[16] Q. in *Historia Social y Económica de España y América*, ed. J. Vicens Vives, iv, part ii (Barcelona, 1959), p.396.

THE GERMAN EMPIRE

In many ways the most interesting example of the deceptiveness of constitutional appearances in early twentieth-century Europe was to be found in the German empire, a federal structure of four kingdoms, five grand-duchies, six duchies, six principalities and three free cities, to say nothing of the 'imperial territory' of Alsace-Lorraine. All these components except the last had a degree of real local power. There was no centralized imperial police, for example. The national Reichstag was elected by secret ballot on the basis of universal male suffrage; it was free to outvote the government's proposals if it wished. The courts upheld the rule of law. The German people were by any comparative standard well educated and orderly and could look back in 1901 on thirty years of continuing growth in prosperity. Those years had also delivered to many Germans unprecedentedly generous welfare provision, for which Germany was admired abroad. Yet this was, in fact, a sham constitutionalism. In spite of its formal constitution, an empire that was parliamentary in form did not have parliamentary government. The head of the government, the chancellor, was appointed by the emperor and was responsible solely to him. The Reichstag could not remove him or the ministry. Its role was unreal. It could not control the executive. Moreover, because of the fragmentation of the Reichstag by party divisions, chancellors could usually manage to pull together majorities on specific issues or necessary financial legislation round a conservative core of deputies deeply antagonistic to both the Catholic Centre party and the Social Democrats – the 'enemies of the empire' (*Reichsfeinde*) as the great Bismarck had called them. Those parties, though strong in numbers and popularly based, were nonetheless sundered from one another ideologically; clericals and atheists could not join forces. Thus the nightmare of conservatives, a 'red-black' coalition, never became a reality. Yet the SPD in the 1912 elections became the largest party in the Reichstag, with a good prospect of winning a majority next time round, and that, to some conservatives, looked like a revolutionary threat.

Institutions were not the only reason why constitutional government was not a reality in Germany, though. Deep cultural and historical forces also worked against it. Even when (as occasionally happened) the chancellor's proposals were voted down by the parliamentarians, there was no collective will that could span their divisions and turn a tactical defeat for the executive into the winning of the initiative by the legislature. That was not the way parliamentarians had been taught to think of their role in the day of the all-competent Bismarck. Furthermore, certain interests and pressure groups were particularly strongly placed to bring effective force to bear on the chancellor (of whom only two held office between the beginning of the century and the outbreak of the Great War). Local electoral arrangements, for instance, ensured that Prussia's parliamentary representatives would be dominated by the *Junker* landowners of the east. They provided the backbone of conservatism that resisted progressive taxation and any political concession to the Left. Nor was there to be a conservative element with a different base to offset the agrarians' influence; there was to be no German re-run of the great Corn Laws battle that had changed the face of British politics in the nineteenth century. The major industrial interests that might have been expected to oppose the agrarians were, in fact, willing to concede the tariff concessions that the agrarians wanted to protect their incomes against cheap Russian grain; in return industry got support for the major armaments programmes that nourished it. Industry had a strong disposition to support the old army and (much newer) naval lobbies. Above all, in default of strong leadership from executive government the soldiers and sailors usually had the ear of the emperor; Wilhelm II, unhappily for his country, conceded so much to them that he was unable to resist them even when, belatedly, he wished to do so. Such political facts were the reality of sham-constitutional Germany. They help to explain the comment of an English observer known for his own sympathies with and understanding of the German nation and its culture: 'in this highly organised nation, when you have ascended to the very top storey you find not only confusion, but chaos'.[17] For all its impressive appearance, Imperial Germany was not in the end an efficient state in any but a merely bureaucratic sense. It had not

---

[17] Viscount Haldane, *Before the War* (London, 1920), p.71.

by 1914 been able to deliver lasting solutions to national problems inevitably posed by its social and economic development.

DYNASTICISM

Germany may also be categorized as one of the three major European states embodying and based upon political principles of a bygone era. In constitutional states, whether they were monarchical or republican in form, and whatever old-fashioned attitudes might survive among their ruling classes and courtiers, heads of state were in the last resort agents and representatives of their peoples, however great their personal authority might be. In Romanov Russia, the Habsburg empire (sometimes called the Dual Monarchy) and in Hohenzollern Prussia, the theory of the state was quite different. It can conveniently be called dynastic and it rested on prescriptive right and claims to divine approval. In such states, in theory completely and to some measure also in practice, national and social interests were never supposed to override the rights and interests of the ruling monarchs themselves. The dynastic states were still what most European states had been 300 years earlier, personal possessions, agglomerations of lands belonging to a family. All three of them had another bond in that they ruled over more than one people (and all three, conspicuously, over large numbers of Poles). If it was true that by 1914 they had made some concession to constitutionalism, it had been very slight and only very recent in Russia,[18] had real limits in the Dual Monarchy, and only had some degree of reality in Germany. There, too, the nature of the restraints on the emperor was not such as to provide reliable constitutional checks. Adulation was heaped on him, his authority was the subject of much rhetorical exaggeration (not least by himself), and he was king of Prussia, in a *Reich* dominated by that state since 1870. Nonetheless, the internal reality of the Prussian monarchy, for all the incense burnt to the 'War Lord', had much cynicism and make-believe about it. The king could not move far

[18] Even Russia acquired its first representative, though only consultative, assembly, in 1905.

outside the parameters that the Prussian ruling class would tolerate. In all three dynastic empires, evidently, the personality and temperament, and the incapacity or capacity, of the monarch was likely to be a decisive factor.

Two political Europes can thus be differentiated. Not everyone, and few other monarchs, would have put it as did the German Kaiser in 1903 in a private letter to his cousin, the tsar: 'the democratic countries governed by Parliamentary majorities, against the Imperial Monarchies', but there was a grain of truth in his excited language.[19] Everyone knew that the personalities of rulers had more weight in the three great multi-ethnic empires than in the constitutional states, even if some Englishmen seemed to have felt a special *frisson* of loyal excitement in toasting their own 'King-emperor'.[20]

It is the essence of empire that it rules over many peoples, and all the dynastic states did this in Europe. They had long been troubled, in consequence. Russia and Austria–Hungary each faced truly revolutionary dangers. Germany probably did not. Her ethnic divisions were more manageable. Her problems expressed themselves in different ways, in managing a foreign policy that seemed to be more and more an impatient search for the impalpable and slippery prizes of respect and prestige – a 'place in the sun', as some Germans put it – or in the growing difficulties of reconciling the economic and social forces spawned by rapid development with a conservative constitution which gave so much weight in imperial government to a semi-feudal agrarian aristocracy. In comparison, a few discontented Danes did not matter much, as it did not that Alsatians continued to show no great willingness to behave like Prussians. Germany's worst minority problem was to be found in Prussian Poland, where the antagonism of Teuton and Slav was vigorously alive.

More than any other states the ruling houses of Russia and the

---

[19] *The Kaiser's Letters to the Tsar*, ed. N. F. Grant (London, 1920), p.99. Wilhelm II did not like parliamentarians and spoke of his own Reichstag as a 'troop of monkeys and a collection of blockheads and sleep-walkers'. See G. A. Craig, *Germany 1866–1945* (Oxford, 1978), p.292. For the curious psychology of Franz Joseph, see Jászi, pp.91–2 and 117.

[20] The dual title arose from Queen Victoria's assumption of the title of 'Empress of India' in 1876.

Dual Monarchy still tended to behave in the old *ancien régime* style, as if governments were the natural enemies of their subjects, though the servants of the Habsburgs were perhaps more cautious (and even emollient) in style than those of the Romanovs. Yet, both empires had been changing in recent decades, for all their conservatism and apparent continuity. The hyphenated Habsburg monarchy was itself the political creation of the successful nationalism of one of its subject peoples, the Magyars, only as recently as in 1867. In the early years of the twentieth century, though, there were signs that it was going to be more and more difficult to keep together the two halves of the monarchy that that so-called 'Compromise' had defined without provoking other nations inside it beyond endurance. In the Dual Monarchy, too, industrialization (in Bohemia and Austria) was beginning to add new tensions to old. Nor had Magyar separatism been put to sleep for good in 1867. A quarrel with Vienna over economic interests in the 1890s evolved into a dispute about Magyarization of the army in the early years of the twentieth century and the invocation by the monarch of the ultimate deterrent, the threat to introduce universal suffrage. This would end Magyar domination over the Slav and Romanian majority in the kingdom of Hungary. The politicians in Budapest came to heel; Hungary in 1914 was still a feudal monarchy ruled by landowners. By then the Austrian lands had for seven years enjoyed a system of universal adult male suffrage – though none of the governments presiding over it had ever had the support of parliamentary majorities.

Russia's condition was hard to assess (and this became even more true after her explosion in political revolution in 1905). Autocracy and terrorism between them had destroyed the liberal promise of the reign of Alexander II, the 'tsar liberator' who had ended serfdom, but they had not hindered industrialization. A Russian economic revolution was under way as the century began. Fiscal and tariff policies designed to exact grain from the peasant provided exports to pay interest on foreign loans. The country at last began to show truly significant economic advance even if it was still not able to compete with leading industrial countries: in 1910 Russia produced less than a third as much pig-iron as the United Kingdom and only about a quarter as much steel as Germany. But such levels had been achieved very rapidly and were continuing to rise. By 1914 Russia would have the fourth largest industrial economy in the world, though well behind those of the USA, Germany and Great Britain. There would even be indicators that Russian agriculture might at last have turned the corner and be capable of producing grain harvests that would grow faster than population (and it was still grain that was Russia's most important export). A determined effort was made by one minister, Stolypin, to provide Russia with a class of prosperous independent farmers whose self-interest was linked to raising productivity, by removing the last of the restraints on individualism left behind after the abolition of serfdom. Yet there was still much backwardness to overcome. Urban growth had been rapid but in 1914 less than a fifth of Russians lived in towns and only about 3 million worked in industry (in a total population that had risen to over 170 million). Russia might have a giant's potential, but was still entangled with grievous handicaps. The general level of culture was low and unpromising; a civilized society and industrialization would both demand a better-educated people. The autocracy governed badly, reformed unwillingly and opposed most change. Liberal traditions were weak; the terrorist and absolutist traditions were strong. Russia was still dependent on foreign suppliers for the capital she needed and was still Europe's largest debtor nation in 1914. Partly because of the costs of servicing this debt, and the fiscal policies which resulted, the lot of the poor peasant – that is, of most peasants – had not improved as Russia underwent a renewed industrial boom in 1907–13. But the country was on its way to realizing its economic potential at last.

Nowadays, because of the terrible simplifications they imposed upon public reactions, we tend to think the strains inside the dynastic monarchies must have been fatally threatening even at the beginning of this century. Yet this is not necessarily so; rational patriotism and intransigent nationalism can be distinguished. Moreover, those who felt confident about the international system could point to the diminution of international violence in the nineteenth century; when European great powers had gone to war since 1871, it had not been with other European great powers. In 1899 and again in 1907 there were international congresses to try to halt competition in armaments; though they failed in their aim, they were not wholly unpositive in their outcome and that they had taken place at all could be seen as a good thing. Acceptance of the practice of international arbitration had grown and restrictions on the brutality of warfare had been increased. When the German emperor, stirred to anger by reports of atrocities against Europeans, saw off his contingent to the international force fielded against the Chinese Boxers and urged his soldiers to behave 'like Huns', the phrase was thought excessive and stuck unpleasantly in people's memories. Its real interest, though, is that he should have believed such a recommendation was needed. Nobody would have had to tell a seventeenth-century army to behave like Huns; it was then broadly taken for granted that they would. By the twentieth century, though, European troops were not expected to behave in this way (even if they sometimes did in colonial warfare) and had therefore to be told to do so. So far had the humanizing of war come. 'Civilized warfare', a nineteenth-century concept, is far from a contradiction in terms. In 1899 it had been agreed to forbid, albeit for a limited period, the use of poison gas, dum-dum bullets and even the dropping of bombs from the air. Oddly, such attempts to humanize conflict and limit its effects took place without much support from the organized churches.

RELIGION IN EUROPEAN LIFE

By 1901 Christendom was no longer a significant political term. Christian churches had long lost any plausibility as a potential check to Europe's governments except perhaps in the United Kingdom, where evangelical feeling could sometimes influence specific questions of colonial or foreign policy. This was not, of course, altogether new. Restraint arising from religious belief or affiliation had never exercised any dependable control over kings in their dealings with one another; even the hope of any such check had already been virtually non-existent as the nineteenth century began and, by its end, religion was as a significant international force at best a palliative, at worst an inflammation of conflict; Orthodox Russians and evangelically minded English Protestants could easily be worked up against the Turk when he was massacring Christians, and sectarianism was taken for granted as a basis of politics in Ireland.

Many Europeans nonetheless continued to believe that organized religion had a social and political role. They saw religious belief and discipline as prophylactics against social disorder and what they feared was moral decline. Consequently, the evident recession at least in the most developed countries of the power and influence of organized churches alarmed them. Whatever might be alleged about religious belief, religion as a matter of observance was visibly in decline. Fifty years earlier, Charles Dickens had already pointed out that it was not the workers of Coketown who filled its many churches and chapels. Yet in 1901 many millions of Europeans, most of them Christian, still regularly attended religious worship.[21] Disagreement flourished about the roots and agencies of the decline in Christian church-going, too. Some sought explanation in human agency, blaming freemasons or Jews, or even the Protestant Reformers. All such explanations were too simple. Some Europeans of 1801 may well already have thought somewhat differently from their sixteenth-century predecessors about heaven and earth, the way nature worked and might be used, the way they got their living, their relations with one another and with authority, all of which had been matters once inseparable from religious belief, but for many different reasons. By 1901, things had gone much further. Many of them had by then come to believe that progressive improvement was a universal tendency of mankind, and some that no supernatural agency was needed to explain *any* aspect of human life. Thoughtful people were troubled by the implications of geological and biological discoveries. Others worried over what scholarship was doing to call in question the inerrancy of scripture. Some simply found the notion of any religious authority at all an unacceptable affront to the liberal, individualizing tendencies of the age.

Well before the nineteenth century was over the German seer and philosopher Nietzsche had already announced that 'God is dead'; religious faith, he believed, was no longer possible for an intelligent human being, and the spirit-and-body dualism so long taken for

---

[21] In the United Kingdom there was even a revival – the last of its kind – about to begin in the non-conformist churches at about that time.

granted in European culture could no longer be sustained. Whether this was true, and, if it were, whether it was the result of a general loss of religious belief or of a changing view of what religion might be thought to imply and require is a harder question to clarify. So far as ecclesiastical authority went, almost all the Christian communions seemed in a measure touched by the intellectual blight of one or other of these trends. If many Europeans could be found who still retained simple and literal beliefs in the dogmas of their faiths and the narratives of the Bible, so could others who contested the claims of revelation and questioned the authority of priest and pastor, and did so more and more strenuously and publicly. Traditional belief may indeed well have been most consciously and explicitly threatened and challenged among Europe's élites themselves. Educated men and women had often held 'Voltairean' ideas of a generally irreligious and sceptical nature, and among those who did not there was usually little willingness to revive old repressive devices such as censorship to meet new intellectual challenges, even if the Syllabus of Errors was only forty years or so old.[22] The nineteenth century had also brought into play other ideas corrosive of faith, not least those of a science-fed materialism that might at first have been the concern only of élites, but that gradually reached wider audiences thanks to cheap printing and the spread of mass literacy.

The Orthodox and Roman Catholic churches were the most obviously affected by intellectual criticism, but the legal standing of ecclesiastical establishments was also under attack in the politics of several countries, as they had often been in the past. Broadly speaking, in Orthodox Russia and the Balkans, Catholic Poland and the Protestant United Kingdom (except in Ireland) this was not so. Religion was not a major jurisdictional issue in them; their churches did not conflict with patriotism and national sovereignty. In France, Germany and Italy (and, in due course, in republican Portugal after 1911) things were different. Jurisdictional, fiscal and educational debate in states

[22] The Syllabus was a papal pronouncement of 1864 defining the Roman Catholic Church's opposition to many key notions of the age, above all to the proposition that 'the Roman Pontiff can and ought to reconcile and harmonize himself with progress, liberalism and recent civilization'. These words became notorious, and a gift to anti-papal writers and agitators.

newly conscious of the respect they believed to be owed to the nation had led politicians to reopen old quarrels of Church and State in many Roman Catholic countries. Such issues were given new importance with the spread of the franchise. The Roman Church, which had made so many new ideological and intellectual demands on credulity as the nineteenth century went on, was ill placed to resist alliances of politicians and secularists. Like other churches, too (a few successful innovators like the Salvation Army apart), it did not seem able to exploit new techniques and devices such as the new mass-circulation newspapers, which might have helped it; indeed, it long positively proclaimed its distrust of such developments.

Under Leo XIII (who had become pope in 1878) the political position of the Roman Church had improved in some countries, but anti-clericalism and priest-baiting were still prevalent as the new century began, notably in France. Governments had by then much encroached upon areas where the Church had earlier been paramount – above all, education. A burst of activity in the founding of Catholic schools and 'free' universities in the last decades of the nineteenth century was one response. Quarrelling bred intransigence and in France the eventual outcome in 1905 was the ending of Napoleon's century-old concordat with the Papacy and the separation of Church and State. The Vatican's relations with the Italian state, on the other hand, improved under Pius X, who succeeded to the throne of St Peter in 1903. Though participation in the public life of constitutional Italy remained formally forbidden to Catholics, there was relaxation in practice as the Church came to appreciate the growing power of socialist voters.

It was becoming clear, too, that whatever view intellectuals might take of the teachings of the Roman Church, and whatever figures for attendance at mass might show, it could still draw on much loyalty among the European faithful. Indeed, the nineteenth-century liberation of the Papacy (which had sometimes seemed the most threatened of all religious institutions) from its responsibility for the government of large areas of Italy made it easier for some Roman Catholics to feel uncompromising loyalty towards it. It was noted hopefully that the faithful were still being recruited by conversion in the mission field overseas (where, of course, they were to be added to in still greater numbers by demographic trends). Though none of the churches made much progress among the growing numbers of city-dwellers of Europe, untouched by inadequate ecclesiastical machines and paganized by the slow stain of the secular culture in which they were immersed, the nineteenth century had turned out to be the greatest missionary age since that of St Paul. Technology and the *pax Britannica* had both been on its side. Christianity was far from dying, let alone dead, as a political and social force once one looked beyond Europe. It was only there that it appeared violently to affront the spirit of the age. Liberal presuppositions had no room for reiterated assertions of the inerrancy of scripture,[23] renewed persecution (in new definitions) of heresy,[24] or (for that matter) for the grim identification of church and regime in Russia during a quarter-century of supervision by the notoriously reactionary K. B. Pobedonostev.[25]

TENSIONS AND STRAINS

In the years before 1914, an ill-defined sense of strain was becoming apparent in some very visible aspects of European civilization. Its double-sidedness made it easy to overlook or misunderstand. If it showed most blatantly in the way it seemed to challenge traditional religion, it had other subtly destructive aspects, too. In determinisms such as those many men drew from thinking about Darwin, or through the relativism suggested first by anthropology, by the study of the human mind, or by physics, science itself was sapping the confidence in the values of objectivity and rationality which had been so important to it and to intellectual liberalism since the eighteenth century. This was a paradox. By 1914 there were signs that the values of liberal,

---

[23] As in the Bull *Providentissimus Deus* of 1893.

[24] The 'Modernism' condemned in Pius X's Bull *Pascendi* of 1907 was to all intents and purposes an intellectual creation by the persecutors of a very diverse array of Catholic theologians, social reformers and historians who never saw themselves as a group or party.

[25] Procurator of the Holy Synod, the committee administering the Russian Church, from 1880 to 1905.

rational, enlightened Europe were as much under strain as were those of traditional, religious and conservative Europe.

Doubt must not loom too large, though. On the eve of a great calamity of whose closeness very few had any inkling, most educated Europeans still believed in progress. The few who felt pessimistic were, perhaps, more numerous than ten years earlier, but one cannot be sure. It is hard to form more than an impressionistic view. As it turned out, neither optimists nor pessimists were wholly right, perhaps because their eyes were glued too firmly to what they thought were the countries which best embodied European civilization. They looked to the inherent powers, tendencies, or weaknesses of cultural forces in those countries for guidance about the future. Not many of them paid much attention to the way that civilization was changing the world outside the lands of the European peoples, though that was how the balance between the major centres of civilization was once again to be altered, and there, perhaps, that key European assumptions were as yet least questioned. This did not mean that in many ways the cultural gap between Europe (and many of the European lands overseas) on the one hand, and the non-European world on the other, was not wide. It may have been wider between 1901 and 1914 than ever before, or after.

Most Europeans still then took for granted, often complacently, ordered civil life and international peace. Among their intellectual and cultural élites, scholarly and scientific knowledge of other civilizations and experience of them was more widely shared than ever, but that, paradoxically, separated Europeans and non-Europeans more than ever. Europeans knew better than they had done for centuries how special they were and how different from Asia and Africa, whenever they thought about those continents. Few, however well informed, felt that alien cultures had anything to teach them, even if they could provide them with new sources of aesthetic satisfaction. In material life and expectations, the difference between Europeans and non-Europeans was almost certainly greater than ever before. Many Europeans had already grown used to an access to material goods unknown to most of the other inhabitants of the globe. Psychologically and politically, then, different worlds on the same planet operated in ways still starkly contrasted in 1901, for all the improved physical contact between them. Yet the corrosive power of European ways had already begun to eat into the life of millions of non-Europeans while European power settled many of its practical circumstances.

A few thoughtful Europeans were not complacent about such apparent success. A decade into the new century, the signs of strain inside European civilization were being increasingly commented upon. Yet in so far as they thought at all about the world and its history, most educated Europeans were then still likely to be self-conscious and self-congratulatory. They were, in their own eyes, still the heart of the civilized world. Though divided by nationality and class, historical experiences and myths, they shared spectacular and splendid accounts of the past, reminiscences of Christendom, racial ideas about the superiority of European stocks (whatever distinctions might in practice be drawn between them), similar institutions and ideas, and an enormous confidence in the superior manipulative power of their culture. 'Europe' was for them a way of looking at the world, a state of mind, rather than the name of a certain portion of humanity. It was, one might say, a way of behaving and thinking, rather than a physical fact.

Few institutions attempted to transcend national boundaries to give form to such a unity. The European Postal Union, or the Scandinavian or Latin monetary unions, had been matters of agreement and convenience, as were international bodies for the regulation of great rivers, or of European interests outside Europe. Only a few enthusiasts occasionally dreamed that federal Germany or federal Switzerland might provide models for a future federal Europe. Subjectively, though, that hardly mattered. Europe was a familiar and comforting idea for many who would not have dreamed of trying to act so as to express its reality.

WOMEN IN EUROPE

European men and women were alike sensitive to the cultural currents of the age, but they could differ importantly in their responses. In the first place, although it is virtually impossible to measure, it is likely that fewer women than men were affected by growing and conscious uncertainty about old assumptions. Those people who showed such uncertainty were an educated minority, and among them the traditional shape of education for women almost certainly meant that most of them were men. Church-going provides a guide to the prevalence of conservative attitudes among women; in all denominations and churches, pews and seats were more usually occupied by women than men. In considering that fact, too, the focus shifts away from the educated minority, and it is hard to believe that most girls and women, whether in the industrial towns or the countryside, were likely to question traditional and customary views about their roles, potential and, above all, standing in relation to the other sex.

Yet important changes can be discerned at the same time as, at least, qualifying old rigidities and restrictions. They were to be of slowly growing but eventually gigantic importance in undermining many of women's practical servitudes. Long ago, the earliest days of modern industrial society had seen the creation of new wage-earning jobs (notably in textile mills) which gave women incomes potentially, at least, their own. A woman able to earn her own living could take a small step down the road to freedom from other constraints laid on her by tradition; marriage was no longer essential to economic survival. Economic development thereafter brought about a major, if quiet and unthreatening practical shift of economic power. The maturing in scale and complexity of the advanced capitalist economy was providing by 1914 great numbers of new jobs – as typists, secretaries, telephone operators, factory hands, department store assistants and teachers – for women in some European countries (and North America) almost none of which had existed a century earlier. Women, of course, have long been deeply involved in the daily labour of society, even in simple agricultural systems, and there is nothing new in the gainful employment of women as such. But in India, or Africa, a country woman is even today likely to toil as a field labourer on the family plot, very much under the control of the menfolk of her family, and exploited in the interests of others. For growing numbers of girls in a few European countries even at the beginning of the century, a job as secretary or shop assistant already offered a chance of liberation from parental regulation and the trap of married drudgery. Most European women still had not so benefited by 1914, but there was an accelerating process at work, and such developments were already stimulating other demands (for example for education and professional training).

A second great transforming force even further from showing its full potential to change European women's lives by 1914 was contraception. Early in this century, though little discussed, it had already begun to affect demography in a few countries even if, perhaps, not more than abstention from sexual activity. What lay ahead was a revolution in power and status as more women took in the idea that they might resist the demands of bearing and rearing children which had throughout history dominated most women's lives; beyond that lay an even deeper change, hardly discerned in 1901, as some women came to see that they could seek sexually satisfying lives without necessarily entering the obligation of lifelong marriage.

To the third great tendency moving women imperceptibly but irresistibly towards liberation from ancient ways and assumptions it is much harder to give an identifying single name, but if one force drove it, it was technology. It was not quite confined to the developed economies though most apparent in them and, therefore, a phenomenon common to Europe and the USA. A vast number of innovations, some of them slowly accumulating already for decades, all tended to cut into the iron timetables of domestic routine and drudgery. Their effect was for a long time little more than marginal. The coming of piped water, or of gas for heating and lighting, reduced drudgery in the home; electricity's cleanliness and flexibility was later to have even more obvious effects. The great stores which made their appearance in the nineteenth-century cities, as well as smaller shops able to offer wider ranges of choice, had been the advance guards of big changes in retail distribution providing a notion of luxury to people other than the rich, and making it easier to meet household needs. As refrigerated, imported food, and better processing and preserving became available, they changed patterns of family catering once based – as they are still often based in Asia or Africa – on daily or twice-daily visits to the market. The world of detergents and easily cleaned artificial fibres still lay in the future in 1901, but soap and washing soda were available far more easily and cheaply then than 100 years earlier, while the first domestic machines – gas cookers, vacuum cleaners, washing machines – had begun to appear in the homes of the rich.

All such developments foreshadowed an often almost silent revolution for millions of women. The gap between the ways in which women are treated in the developed world and those countries where tradition retained its grip was, in fact, to widen enormously in this century. It was one of many reflexions of the growing differences in wealth between two sorts of society. Even in western countries, too, the implications of such humble household instruments as cookers and washing-machines did not strike many people at the beginning of this century (and perhaps still do not strike many historians sufficiently); labour was still cheap. More attention was given to the noisy campaigning of 'suffragettes', as women who sought the vote were called in England (but they were to be found in other countries, too). There were heroines among them, but fanatics, too; they attracted ridicule, as well as hatred and fear. The evident liberalization and democratization of political institutions in the interest of men argued powerfully for them, though. Logically, democracy could hardly fail to cross the boundaries of sex when France, Germany and several smaller European countries had universal adult male suffrage, and Great Britain and Italy had mass electorates of many millions. The question was bound to be brought forward: if uneducated men could do so, should not women vote in national politics? Soon after 1901, the issue was causing uproar in England. But by 1914 only Finland (then part of the Russian empire) and Norway had admitted women to Europe's parliamentary electorates. The issue was to remain open in Switzerland for another sixty years. But there were other signs of change. In 1913, only a few weeks after the rejection by the House of Commons of a bill to give women the vote, the first woman magistrate in the United Kingdom was appointed.

6

Europe as a System of Power

INTERNATIONAL ORDER

When we read about international relations nearly a century ago, we should pause carefully before judgement. We take for granted an international framework and setting for them that is entirely unlike that of our own day. They took place in a world in which the United States still played only a more or less marginal, and geographically highly restricted, role in them, and when what went on outside their continent could hardly concern most Europeans unless their own governments fell out over it. As 1901 began, international affairs did not seem particularly ominous. Europe was at peace. German troops in China were carrying out punitive expeditions to stamp out the dying embers of the Boxer rebellion, Americans were suppressing rebellion in the Philippines, and European peoples were fighting one another in South Africa, but all this violence was a long way away from Europe, even if European great powers were involved. When the first war of the century between two major states took place in a few years' time, it, too, would be in the Far East, far from Europe, even if between Japan and one European power, Russia. There was very little going on that appeared to threaten an international order still focused above all on Europe and its affairs as the century began.

Once again, hindsight may be an obstacle to historical understanding. It is very difficult but crucially important to make another imaginative leap in order to understand what happened between the opening of the century and 1914, a date that is of outstanding significance on any reading of the history of this century. It was, nonetheless, one whose approach awoke little concern at all in the minds of the vast majority of human beings until the very last moment. To grasp why this was so, we have to penetrate the assumptions of an era which no statesman or diplomat alive in 1901 dreamed would shortly come to an end. Far less could they then have believed that a whole civilization would be mortally wounded in the process. Our hindsight, and the enormous historical effort which has been poured into seeking out the origin of that disaster (almost from the moment when the Great War began), stand in the way of seeing things with their eyes. What happened in 1914 and the next few years left such deep marks on collective and individual memory that even now it overhangs all accounts of early twentieth-century history. We still tend to see the story moving ineluctably towards Armageddon; whether as drift, slide or march, does not much matter. Because war destroyed the old Europe, a huge effort is now needed to realize that until a very late moment before it broke out, such an outcome was unthinkable to most responsible people. For twenty years after 1914 historians would scrutinize facts and events which might demonstrate – or seem to demonstrate – why war between the European great powers had been inevitable, or at least logical. Yet there was no such inevitability and no inescapable logic, as many successful passages of diplomacy showed, until a very late stage, if even then.[1] Circumstances, some accidental, created the logic, and many of those circumstances did not appear until very late in the day.

Indeed, anyone visionary enough to grasp the possibilities which might be released by a breakdown in the system of international relations would have had to counter powerful argument from those who looked at events with more optimistic eyes. Allowing for a very few individual exceptions (perhaps fewer, too, than in earlier times), the diplomats and statesmen of the age were manifestly neither incompetent nor unintelligent. Since 1856 they and their immediate predecessors had managed to avoid war between great powers over the booty provided by the Ottoman Empire as it slipped further into decay, posing dangerous conflicts of interest and problems about what should take its place. They had successfully and peacefully partitioned

---

[1] The lively speculative essay by N. Ferguson, 'What if Britain had "stood aside" in 1914?' in the collection he edited under the title *Virtual History: alternatives and counterfactuals* (London, 1997) is an interesting starting-point for reflexion.

Africa. They had managed without bloodshed their disputes with one another over the fate of China and other parts of Asia. They had, in fact, for the most part discharged their tasks not only with probity, responsibility and skill, but also with success within a structure all took for granted and none of them wished to destroy in its essentials.

ALLIANCES AND ENTANGLEMENTS

The main elements in that structure were the six great European powers. Convention and diplomatic good manners notwithstanding, though, the United Kingdom, France, Russia, Germany, Austria–Hungary and Italy formed a very disparate group of states. Among them, Germany was a 'new' nation less than a half-century old, and strong by any standard. Militarily, she had overtaken France, once and for so long the continent's dominant power. Great Britain was the world's greatest naval and colonial power. Russia was of uncertain though certainly major weight. Her ancient rivalry with the somewhat ramshackle Austria–Hungary in the Balkans was at least in abeyance and possibly had gone away for good, some thought, given that Russia had been for a couple of decades vigorously and successfully building up her position as an Asian power. Of Italy, Bismarck had rudely remarked that she had a big appetite but poor teeth. Besides these six great powers, Spain and Portugal were still treated with formal courtesy as old historic monarchies and imperial nations, but carried little weight when it came to fighting-power or wealth, as Spain's defeat in 1898 had most recently shown. For most of the time, the six great powers settled between them the affairs of the globe outside the western hemisphere (where, *de facto*, North Americans would have the last word) and there seemed to be no reason why they should not go on settling them successfully. Japan had already to be taken into account, of course, in the Far East, but that was again a faraway region. It was all but inconceivable that Europe would not continue to be the centre of the world's affairs, the greatest concentration of political power in the globe and the real shaper of the destinies of most of it. If the relationships of the European powers with one another now seem to have absorbed the attention of European statesmen as the century began, we must remember that few of them had anything else so important to worry about.

From time to time, groupings had come and gone among the six. There had once been a conservative tie between the three multinational eastern empires, formerly embodied in a 'Three Emperors League', the *Dreikaiserbund*. Logical and historically comprehensible though it was, it had nonetheless come to an end in the 1890s even if individual monarchs liked to think they still shared anti-liberal and anti-democratic principles and interests which ought to influence their countries' policies. Two other connexions still alive in 1901 had cut across such ideological links in the 1890s: a Triple Alliance of Germany, Austria–Hungary and Italy, and an alliance between France and Russia. Each was something of an ideological and political paradox. The first associated two strongly dynastic states with the constitutional Italian monarchy whose success was built on a history of revolution and anti-Austrian aggression; united Italy would not have been there but for wars with the Habsburg Empire. The other linked the most reactionary and autocratic of all Europe's monarchies with her only great republic, France, for many Frenchmen and foreigners alike, the heiress of the Revolution and champion of the Rights of Man.

At first sight, the Franco-Russian alliance had changed little in Europe. Bismarck's Europe was crumbling away in the 1890s. The great chancellor had sought to keep Europe in equilibrium, with Germany at the centre of its diplomatic arrangements, and France (which he identified as the main danger to peace) at their periphery, isolated and with no temptation to embark on a war of revenge for 1871. After the *Dreikaiserbund*'s disappearance, he had, it was true, come to believe that in the last resort he must back Austria–Hungary should conflict between her and Russia arise. The Triple Alliance had added Italy to this choice. But Bismarck had always kept a line open to St Petersburg. His successors did not. When, in 1892, Russia became the ally of France the road had merely opened towards a possible division of Europe into two camps. German policy under Wilhelm II subsequently made it easier to take it. German military planning was quick to do so because it had crystallized in an offensive mode. His generals now accepted that if they fought the Russians they would need to fight a two-front war and had better begin it with a swift overthrow of France before the slowly mobilized resources of her Russian ally could be brought into play. Quite separately, German naval planning, too, had begun in the 1890s to be shaped by officers who forecast a clash of interests with England as inevitable for a Germany seeking power and a global role through *Weltpolitik*. They believed a challenge to the old supremacy exercised by British naval power required the building of a fleet big enough to persuade England to accept Germany as an equal.

The terms of the Franco-Russian and Triple alliances were not completely known to the world. Each had arisen in special circumstances to meet different needs. They did not imply at first any automatic or necessary division of continental Europe in two camps. If, though, circumstances developed in some ways rather than others, they might tend to produce such a division in the end. They provided a diplomatic framework that had at least to be taken into account by countries that stayed outside the alliances, of which the most important was the United Kingdom. The alliance partners, in any case, all had other interests formally unaffected by their commitments to one another in addition to those that the alliances were meant to safeguard. Many historic circumstances seemingly remote from the interests of the five land powers linked by the two alliance systems have to be taken into account in understanding the way European affairs actually worked.

The United Kingdom in particular had special interests and policies with deep historic (indeed, prehistoric) roots: as one of her prime ministers memorably put it, '*nous sommes des poissons*'.[2] In saying he and his countrymen were fishes, Lord Salisbury meant that England, as an island, had inevitably and predominantly maritime concerns. They were, indeed, oceanic. That was one among many reasons special to her which explained why, in 1901, she should be engaged in her most expensive war for nearly a century to the almost universal disapproval of the other European powers. They could do nothing about it, though; Britannia ruled the waves. The South African war was also marginal to the real interests of most of Europe, even if it brought into focus a number of the irritants which excited public

[2] *German Diplomatic Documents*, ed. E. T. S. Dugdale, vol. I (London, 1928), p.249.

opinion and thus, indirectly, the conduct of diplomacy. Neither the origin of the war nor its conduct showed British imperialism in a very good light and there were those who thought that it had demonstrated a dangerous diplomatic isolation, too. The British prime minister did not agree: in a confidential memorandum in 1901 he dismissed the supposed perils of isolation as 'a danger in whose existence we have no historical reason for believing'.[3]

While none of the European states had any direct interest in the issues that had brought about the South African war, all of them except, perhaps, Austria–Hungary could find plenty elsewhere in the world to bicker about with the United Kingdom, if diplomats were not careful. There had appeared to be a real danger of an Anglo-French war in 1898. Yet traditionally, the United Kingdom had stood clear of European entanglements and commitments. This had proved, it seemed to Lord Salisbury and many others, an advantageous stance on the whole; she had exercised unquestioned power during most of the nineteenth century through predominance at sea, wealth, technological primacy and the prestige of success itself. By 1901, though, her sun was beginning to set. Others were beginning to rival her economic and technical prowess and relationships in Europe were changing. There were signs of growing uneasiness about Great Britain's relative economic strength. Some businessmen were sure that Germany was a major commercial rival and feared that her technological sophistication and efficiency would inevitably mean German industry would prove superior to that of the United Kingdom. Some British diplomats, too, thought they should look round for continental friends.

So far as the British government was aware in 1901 of any lively history of antagonism with other countries, though, it was with France and Russia, as it had long been. Those two powers were already linked by more than the formal undertakings of their alliance. Most of the foreign borrowings that sustained Russia's modernization, for instance, came from her ally. This was odd, some thought, given that the Third Republic stood for liberalism and constitutionalism among Europe's great powers and Russia for despotism. Yet Frenchmen, in

[3] *British Documents on the Origins of the War*, ed. G. P. Gooch and H. Temperley, vol. ii (London, 1927), pp.68–9, Memorandum by Lord Salisbury of 29 May 1901.

spite of the intellectual vitality their country showed and its wealth, were uneasy about their national strength and conscious of demographic weakness. The overthrow of France by Germany in 1870 had left the realists among them fearful and often sure that on their own they could not beat the German army. Since defeat in that year, the disparity between the two countries had grown ever greater as French manpower had fallen further still behind that of her neighbour. In economic development, too, France had been distanced by her neighbour. In 1913 she would be raising only about one-sixth as much coal as Germany, would make less than a third as much pig-iron and only a quarter as much steel. If there was ever to be a return match for 1870, Frenchmen knew they would need allies. The consciences of most of them became easy about alliance with a tyrannical autocrat who, nonetheless, could raise the largest armies in the world.

France had a great overseas empire, as far flung if not so large as the British, and this had imposed its own distractions and commitments. Yet the major focus of French foreign policy was bound to be Europe. The recovery of Alsace and Lorraine was the overriding obsession of many (politicians said a majority of) Frenchmen. In retrospect, the French government's decision not to press matters to war with Great Britain after a dangerous confrontation on the upper Nile at Fashoda in 1898 can now be seen as a turning-point. Though there was still a violent explosion of anglophobia at the time of the South African war, it was implicitly recognized by the directors of French foreign policy that imperial adventure in remote places might jeopardize France's freedom of action in Europe and make unnecessary enemies. Yet in Europe, where weakness tied her down, France was a dissatisfied power.

Besides being an obvious candidate for courtship by France in Europe, Russia was also the only power comparable with France and Great Britain in the range of her imperial interests. They did not much impinge on those of France but often awoke concern and even alarm in London, especially when Russian policy had come to show more interest in Asia and in the Far East. No country had gobbled up more of the Chinese empire in the last 100 years. Russia had pursued her ambitions especially in central Asia, Manchuria and, more recently, Korea. In the buffer lands between her and India, there was, too, a long-standing and frequently renourished rivalry with the British and an enduring suspicion on both sides over their respective influence in Afghanistan and Persia. On the other hand, the Russian government could never forget south-east Europe with its substantial Slav populations and Orthodox Christian communities. Russian public feeling over Slav brotherhood had to be taken into account. This meant that the ambitions of fellow-Slavs in the Balkans – the Serbs, for example – might well confront the tsar's ministers with emergencies requiring Russian responses. What was more, should further revolutionary changes occur there, or should the Habsburg monarchy become the undisputed dominant power in the Danube valley, then Russia might be cut off from an old dream – of control of the Straits of Constantinople – and even lose any egress from the Black Sea. That mirage had helped to bring on the Crimean war nearly a half-century earlier. By 1914 it would have new significance, too, because through the Straits and the Dardanelles went more than four-fifths of Russian grain exports, the country's major earner of foreign currency.

Further disturbance in the Balkans or unsteadiness in the Ottoman empire would thus be likely to ruffle relations with the Dual Monarchy. Nevertheless, those relations had for some years been managed with some care and success. Although the *Dreikaiserbund* had lapsed and the Triple Alliance left out Russia, neither of the two great multinational empires wished to disturb the status quo set by the Berlin settlement of 1878 and somewhat modified by later agreement. The Russians tolerated Austrian occupation of the still formally Ottoman provinces of Bosnia and Herzegovina (where particularly vociferous pro-Serb nationalists were to be found) and, at least in Europe, Russia seemed a satisfied power with no wish to rock the diplomatic boat, though continuing to brood carefully over its ancient and modern ambitions and interests at the Straits. Her diplomats were able to cooperate successfully with the Habsburg monarchy when a bloody insurrection against Ottoman rule broke out in 1902 in Macedonia, where Serbians, Greeks and Bulgarians squabbled with one another as well as with the sultan.

THE DISSATISFIED AND DANGEROUS

At Vienna, there was an awareness that the Magyars of Hungary, who were beginning to play a more influential role in the foreign affairs of the Dual Monarchy in the early years of this century, might cast something of a shadow over the future. Ruling as they did in their half of the Monarchy large numbers of non-Magyars to whom they denied equitable treatment, they saw Habsburg foreign policy as above all a matter of containing national ambitions among those they ruled. Magyars particularly feared their Slav subjects. Most of the Dual Monarchy's Croat subjects lived in its Hungarian half. Serbia, a Russian satellite and client state, was the focus of the hopes of South Slavs for unification – which was likely to mean unification in an enlarged Serbia. The Magyars were anxious therefore to show that other Slavs could hope for nothing from the Serbs. The Austrian half of the Monarchy also contained Slavs (Poles, Slovenes, Croats and, notably, Czechs) whose political demands, though less strident than in the Hungarian lands, troubled its own predominantly German ruling class and bureaucrats. Altogether, the domestic politics of the Habsburg empire contained plenty of material that might affect external relationships, above all with Serbia, but possibly also even with Russia.

Balkan peoples had nursed their dissatisfactions and anguish for nearly a century. Some of those dissatisfactions had been expressed and institutionalized in the new nations set up during European diplomacy's long efforts to contain the effects of Ottoman decline. Their creation began in the Serbian revolt of 1804–13. As they emerged, the new nations stabilized themselves with massacre and forced expulsion of the ethnic groups they had seen as enemies. The Serb Muslims had taken their revenge in 1813 on the Christian peasants who had attacked Muslim communities supposed to support the Ottomans, the Greeks massacred the Muslims of the Peloponnese in the 1820s – and so a story opened which has gone on to this day, complicated by the many diplomatic arrangements and concessions that jumbled ever further the ethnic jigsaw with new political divisions. The failure of Ottoman government lay at the root of the problem. There came back again and again to trouble the diplomats the same question: what was to take its place? The great powers had their own fish to fry, their own great power interests to assert. Their manner of doing so could easily create new hatreds and divisions, encourage dangerous clients and raise the stakes.

One simmering problem was posed in the Ottoman provinces of Bosnia and Herzegovina. Serbians saw those provinces and the Austrian occupation of them since 1878 as barriers to their own access to the sea.[4] Bosnian Serbs correspondingly looked to Belgrade for succour. They saw a Greater Serbia as the key to the future organization of the Danube valley. Romania was another new nation that had recently emerged from Ottoman rule. Its rulers were interested in the fate of the 3 million of their countrymen who lived in Transylvania, part of the Kingdom of Hungary. Possibly the most troubled part of the Balkans in 1901, though, was Macedonia, still under Ottoman rule and chronically disordered. Serbs, Bulgarians and Greeks watched greedily over the sufferings of their co-nationals there; Albanians cherished hopes of a state of their own. Greece also cast covetous eyes on Crete and had gone unsuccessfully to war with the Turks after proclaiming union with the island in 1897. Such dangers, all arising at bottom from the facts of Ottoman weakness and decline, were familiar to European diplomats. They had been nonetheless handled with comparative success for decades by concerted action by the powers, however grim things had looked at times; there seemed no special cause for concern about them as the century began. If there was anything to worry about, it was that tensions between the Balkan succession states about Macedonia (still under Ottoman rule) might be harder to resolve than quarrels between great powers.

Italy was another dissatisfied nation. Yet she, too, seemed in 1901 to present no danger to international peace. The completion of her unity by the occupation of the papal city of Rome in 1870 had left her government facing formidable social and political problems to think about at home. Abroad, no Italian could think of quarrelling with the British, old friends and patrons of Italian unity and possessors

---

[4] As was, also, the Austrian occupation of the Sanjak of Novibazar, south of Herzegovina, preventing contact between Serbia and Montenegro, another Slav kingdom.

of naval power of which their long coasts made Italians especially aware. But Italy bickered with another former patron, France, over North Africa and cherished ambitions on the Dalmatian coast that gave her an interest in the fate of the Habsburg and Ottoman empires, too. Above all, many Italians did not think the *Risorgimento* complete, and it troubled them that they were linked in alliance with Austria–Hungary which still held lands in Venezia Giulia, Croatia and the Trentino (these were the *Italia irredenta* of patriotic rhetoric). Fortunately, many Italian statesmen, too, knew that their country's teeth were poor and that they should not take risks.

Prussia had been one of Italy's allies in helping her towards unity and the new German empire had welcomed Italy into the Triple Alliance. By 1901 this great state was no longer the Germany of Bismarck, carefully conservative, assiduous in preserving, if possible, good relations with Russia, and intent on avoiding war. Germany instead looked increasingly like an unstable and unpredictable element in the European system. In the 1890s, a 'New Course' in foreign policy had by no means obviously brought her solid benefits and had caused diplomatic strains where they might have been easily avoided (in, for instance, relations with the United Kingdom). Much of the seeming restlessness in German foreign policy had its roots in psychological facts, some collective, some personal,[5] rather than in coldly calculated national interest or *Realpolitik*, such as some Germans liked to advocate. The ambiguities which surrounded the actual location of power and decision-making in Germany made matters worse, for particular interests exercised great influence, and the emperor Wilhelm himself was an unpredictable, destabilizing force in policy-making. Within a few years a minister in Vienna would ask the question 'Who rules in Berlin?' and it was far from clear who might have the last word there. Nevertheless, there was no particular issue of interest to Germany in agitation in 1901 that might pose a threat to European order, and her restlessness was not seen as immediately dangerous.

In the chancelleries of Europe in 1901, in fact, little attention was

[5] 'Foreign policy you can leave to me!' said Wilhelm II with characteristic (but unjustified) confidence to Bülow, the outgoing chancellor in 1901 replaced by Bethmann Hollweg, of whose grasp of foreign affairs Bülow was sceptical (q. in Craig, p.287).

being given – because there was no reason to do so – to any of the matters in which might be discerned the origins of a great war fourteen years later. Far from prefiguring a radical change in the European system, a Franco-Russian military convention renewed as recently as the previous year still envisaged the possibility that the two allies might find themselves fighting Great Britain. Russia was at that time still preoccupied with the Far East (and would in due course find herself at war there, though not against a European power). Other European powers, too, even Italy, had their eyes on the possibilities that appeared to be opening up as a result of China's multiplying domestic troubles. The French were consolidating their positions in North Africa. The Balkans were quiet, except in so far as the inadequacy of Ottoman rule continued to tempt Macedonian revolutionaries (sustained by help from Sofia) to terrorist adventures. Outside Europe, the Ottoman empire seemed unlikely to throw up unanticipated troubles after navigating the disapproval caused by official sponsorship of massacres of its Christian Armenian subjects in the 1890s. As for wider, global, horizons, little anxiety was felt by European statesmen when they thought of the two extra-European great powers. Even if there were signs for those who could interpret them that the United States would before long be capable of dwarfing Europe's strongest powers as the most powerful nation in the world, and that the Japanese portent would almost certainly cause future trouble with Russia, these seemed matters of at best remote implication as the century began.

THE APPEARANCE OF SECURITY

The fact that there was some dangerous tinder about, and even some smoke which might prefigure dangers in the indefinite future, did not, then, make the European statesmen who were the main custodians of early twentieth-century world order uneasy. Many things had to happen before a major disaster could break. One was a change in the psychology of some of the continent's leaders and that of the circles from which they were drawn. In the next decade, many more of those influential persons than in 1901 (though not necessarily a majority) would come to feel that the chances of any war they could imagine might offer better prospects than continuing peace. The change was particularly notable in the ruling circles of Germany, Austria–Hungary and Russia, but it could be detected in a few individuals in Whitehall and Paris, too. As a background to such a shift in the way some of those who ruled Europe thought and felt, the complicated ties, obligations and interests which so involved most of the great powers with one another had by then lessened the chance that any conflict that broke out could be limited to two or three of them. Nevertheless, new diplomatic and material facts that would change the minds of politicians and soldiers about the desirability of peace and war took a long time to appear.

It clearly made for instability that some small countries enjoyed special relations with great powers. This could constitute a dangerous freedom to make decisions that could compel the attention and even force the hands of the patron states. This delicate situation was made more dangerous by public opinion and the changing atmosphere in which statesmen had to work. Mass emotions were easily aroused in those years, in particular by nationalist and patriotic stimuli. In most countries, there was a curiously widespread glamorization of war and the military spirit in the abstract, and an almost total ignorance of its likely reality. When possibilities were publicly discussed, few except professional soldiers envisaged that European war would be much different from what was remembered of the Franco-Prussian war of 1870. Most Europeans overlooked the face which modern war had shown in prolonged slaughter and huge costs in Virginia and Tennessee only a few years before that, even if the professional soldiers did not. Everyone knew that wars could be destructive and violent, to be sure, but that very belief tended also to make them believe, too, that in the twentieth century wars would soon be over.[6] The very cost of armaments was believed to make it inconceivable that civilized states could sustain them for long; the war in South Africa had been expected to cost the British tax payer £10 million, but the bill in the end was

[6] Although one hero of German unification, the great chief of the general staff, Von Moltke, told his countrymen in 1890 that another European war would be a Thirty Years War as horrible as that of the seventeenth century. 'Woe to the man who sets Europe ablaze,' he said.

£230 million. Such reflexions diminished misgivings about courting danger. There were even some vocal Europeans who claimed to be bored by their lives in 1914 and welcomed war for its promise of an emotional release purging away a sense of decadence and sterility.[7] Revolutionaries, of course, usually hoped for international conflict because of the opportunities they thought it might offer to bring down the existing order. But very few people could, in fact, imagine a war like the one that eventually unrolled for four years after 1914.

Perhaps the long success of diplomats in negotiating grave crises without war was itself a fundamental danger. Their machinery had worked so many times that when in due course it was presented with facts more than ordinarily recalcitrant, their significance for a time seemed to escape many of those who had to confront them. In 1914 itself, on the very eve of general conflict, some statesmen were still finding it difficult to see why another conference of ambassadors or a European congress should not extricate the great powers from their problems. At the beginning of the century it might even have been thought that some of the steam was running out of the bickering of European powers. Outside Europe, there was little left of the world to divide other than the dying empires (Germany and Great Britain were driven to discuss the possibility of partitioning Portugal's colonies). True, the final dissolution of the Ottoman empire seemed at least possible but although its partition seemed unlikely to be manageable in so peaceful a way as had been the partition of Africa it did not seem immediately threatening as the century began. Much more crucial issues would be at stake in it for the great powers than there had been in the scramble for Africa, it was true, because more of them were vitally interested in the Balkans, the eastern Mediterranean and the Near East than any had ever been in sub-Saharan Africa. But so long as Habsburg and Romanov did not fall out

[7] This is a very difficult phenomenon to assess. Men of letters who thought in these terms achieved, of course, easy publicity for such views and there is, therefore, a risk of exaggerating their popularity. Nonetheless, poets like Brooke and d'Annunzio make the point. So, more amusingly perhaps, did the Italian Futurist Marinetti, who designed (and showed off in Paris) an 'anti-neutralist' suit to deplore standing aside from the conflict of 1914 when it came.

(and they were about to embark on a fruitful period of cooperation over the problems presented by Macedonia) any grave danger was remote.

NEW ALIGNMENTS

The dynamic that drove a new phase of international relations between the European powers in fact began outside Europe. The United Kingdom was instrumental in releasing it. Preoccupied with empire rather than Europe, the British government, like the Japanese, had been alarmed by Russian advances in the Far East in the 1890s, notably in Manchuria, which both countries saw as a danger to Korea. By 1900, the naval balance in the Far East between the British fleet on the one hand and the Franco-Russian combined fleets on the other was held by Japan, and the ships built for her in many British yards.[8] This led in 1902 to a remarkable step, the first alliance the British had made in peacetime for over a century. Japan and the United Kingdom promised one another benevolent neutrality should either find itself obliged to defend by war its interests in the Far East and, should a third power enter such a war, each agreed to come to the engaged partner's assistance. Clearly, both had in mind as possible enemies Russia and her ally, France. Great Britain's reasons for making the alliance had nothing to do with the balance of power in Europe. They were rooted in a long history of clashes with both France and Russia over imperial ambitions and interests, not only in China and Chinese waters, but also in Egypt, central and western Africa, central and south-eastern Asia, and the Pacific. Anglo-German skirmishes on overseas questions had been more easily managed than these, even if relations had occasionally been prickly.

Already, though, a way had been opening for better Franco-British relations. For all the resentment Fashoda awakened in France, Delcassé, the man who was foreign minister of France from 1898 to 1905 while cabinets came and went, was realistic. He took the crisis to have shown that France could not contemplate war with Great

[8] I. H. Nish, *The Anglo-Japanese Alliance* (London, 1985) p.36.

Britain. He came to be sure that quarrels over imperial and secondary issues must be set aside: imperial ambitions (which were in any case always a matter of special lobbies and particular, rather than true national, interests) had to be subordinated to the improvement of France's position in the European balance of power. France should seek, he thought, to ease Anglo-Russian relations and reduce the dangers of conflict between her ally and the British. But that meant forgetting old antagonisms.

After the anglophobia shown in France during the South African war had died away, popular feeling in London and Paris was flattered by an exchange of personal visits between the French president and the English king. Meanwhile, officials began to consider business of mutual interest. The outcome was an Anglo-French agreement in 1904. It wound up a number of long-running disputes between the two powers. West Africa, the Newfoundland fishing grounds, Siam, Madagascar and the South Pacific all provided matters for resolution. The British were pleased to heal sores that had run so long. But the core of the agreement lay in North Africa. The British assured the French of their willingness to see the development of French interests in Morocco (the British were sure it was another 'dying empire'), and the French undertook that there should be an end to their long efforts to hinder and embarrass the British in Egypt. In Morocco the French had ambitious ideas of future possibilities. In Egypt, the crux of the issue was the determination of British governments to maintain secure imperial communication with India through the Suez Canal. The French were given a green light to proceed to add 'the finest part of North Africa' to their empire;[9] the British had thrown off the political and financial handicaps with which the French had so long hampered their control of Egypt.

Even its geographical comprehensiveness and its closure of very long-running disputes, though, does not reveal the full importance of the convention which registered the agreement. It was a starting-point for a process of association and a seed from which would grow *entente* – 'understanding' on other matters – or, as a later generation might

[9] The phrase of A. J. P. Taylor in *The Struggle for Mastery in Europe 1848–1918* (Oxford, 1954), p.415. He also remarks, aptly, that 'French had paid cash down, the British with a promissory note' (p.417).

put it, a special relationship. The implications of *entente* were to remain vague, undefined, never incorporated in treaty form, and perhaps should have been suspect for that reason. But in 1904 that all lay in the future. Even if some officials glimpsed such a possibility, a special tie had not been part of the intention of the French and British governments, but rather the removal of grievances.

DEEPENING DIVISIONS

What diplomats do is not always important but the complex interests they are meant to defend and represent always are. Well-defined exchanges of notes and dispatches and the congresses, conferences and interviews can easily disguise this, just because of the well-nourished record material they often provide. Nonetheless, there are times when the actions and reactions of the diplomatic process not only provide an intelligible narrative thread but also are major facts in the way the story develops. So are the perceptions and priorities to which they give rise. An important instance arose as a consequence of the Anglo-Japanese alliance, which released Japanese ambitions from some restraints, and led, in 1904, to a Japanese attack on the Russian empire.[10] Among other things, Russian defeats in the war that followed provoked revolution at home and a reorientation of Russian foreign policy. Its traditional interests in the Danube valley and the Straits were requickened and expansionism in the Far East was set aside. The discomfiture of her ally at the hands of the Japanese was important for France. It is a part of the background of a process in which Anglo-French settlement hardened into more than a clearing away of old grounds for dispute. But that this happened was largely occasioned by German diplomacy.

The Anglo-French agreement had already irritated Berlin. It should not, perhaps, have come as a surprise that Wilhelm II and some of his officials would feel any settlement of Morocco's future that did not include the consultation of Germany (or indeed, of any other government except the Spanish) was a slight to their country. It was

[10] For fuller details, see Chapter 7 below.

decided that France should be shown that Germany expected to be taken into account in such matters. A gesture should be made and Wilhelm was willing to be the man to make it.[11] When he happened to visit Tangier in March 1905, he made a provocative speech stressing Germany's commercial interests in Morocco and, when he visited the sultan, assured him of Germany's support in maintaining his independence under French pressure for reforms. This caused consternation, all the more because no one was quite sure what the emperor meant. Germany's economic involvement in Morocco was far less substantial than Great Britain's, let alone that of France. Out of what was intended as a reassertion of outraged dignity and an exercise in prestige grew a crisis. In its resolution, Germany won a pyrrhic victory. An international conference met at Algeciras in 1906, thus implicitly conceding that Europe had a collective interest in management of the fate of Morocco. But Germany obtained nothing else of substance and she had gone unsupported at the conference except by the Austrians.

Some British officials had by then come round to the view that they would have to concern themselves for the first time in decades with the European balance of power. They – and, in some measure, British public opinion was with them – were awakening to the United Kingdom's interest in supporting France, if the balance of European power was to be maintained and Germany was not to demand a decisive voice in every question that arose. On the day after the Algeciras conference opened, secret military talks began with the French about what might be done to meet a possible German invasion through Belgium. At the end of the road opened by these discussions lay an outcome that no one foresaw: Great Britain's acceptance once again of a role as a major land power on the continent. The country had not put its major weight into prolonged military effort on the mainland of Europe since the days of Marlborough.[12] Yet it was still not inevitable that it should do so; the Morocco crisis of 1905 was not the point of no return on the road to 1914, but was one of the several moments

[11] Though it has been alleged that some German officials were in fact actually seeking to provoke a war with France at this moment. Craig, p.318.
[12] Important though it was strategically, the Peninsula campaign against Napoleon did not make demands on British resources comparable to those of continental fighting in the wars of William III and Queen Anne.

at which certain conjunctures became more likely. A British foreign secretary would still be insisting a few days before his country went to war in 1914 that military conversations were not an alliance; they did not bind the British government to any specific course of action. Nonetheless, they registered the end of what had seemed to be a period of British isolation in Europe and in the assumptions of British policy. The agreements of 1902 and 1904 had been meant to look after British interests overseas; Morocco brought British policy back to the European balance of power. A corner had been turned; on one side of it lay the 1904 agreement on specific issues and on the other, *entente*. Groundlessly, Germany had suspected a secret Franco-British alliance; she had now driven the two countries closer together and had perhaps made one more likely.

Another significant rapprochement took place in 1907. An Anglo-Russian convention then settled a number of contentious issues between the two imperial powers. Persia, nominally independent, was divided into Russian and British spheres of influence. The neutrality of Afghanistan, an old area of competition, was provided for, and each government agreed not to interfere (as the British had in fact just done) in the affairs of Tibet, where China's suzerainty was recognized by them both. This range of decisions, like those of 1904, was extra-European, limited and provided real advantages to each participant. In Berlin, though, the agreement aroused more suspicion of what it was becoming fashionable there to see as 'encirclement'.

German fears of encirclement were the more unsettling because they accompanied increasingly blatant and acknowledged naval competition between Germany and Great Britain. For some years, Germany had been building a battle-fleet to challenge the supremacy of the British – there was no one else there to challenge – in the North Sea. The British could not understand against whom a German fleet was intended to be used unless it was against themselves. One British response had been the launching in 1906 of HMS *Dreadnought*, a vessel whose size, speed and, above all, big-gun armament (ten twelve-inch guns, instead of the four usual to the most powerful pre-dreadnoughts) at a stroke made all existing battleships obsolete. But other nations could build dreadnoughts, too, and several soon started to do so. The very large British superiority in numbers of pre-dreadnought battleships at once lost much of its value, therefore. In 1907 the British made an offer to Germany to cut their own naval construction and the British naval estimates of 1908 were indeed reduced. The Germans, though, would agree to reduce their building plans only in return for an unconditional promise of British neutrality in the event of a war between France and Germany. This was impossible after Algeciras. Yet a threat to British naval hegemony was bound to alarm British public opinion, deepen the often-uncomprehending exasperations of British politicians and officials with German policy, and impose new tax burdens in each country.

YOUNG TURKS

It was thus in a more dangerous, even a somewhat poisoned, atmosphere, that Balkan tensions began to revive. Though there was recurrent and indirect violent intervention by outsiders (above all, Bulgarians), and though Macedonia had exploded in insurrection in 1902, Austria–Hungary and Russia had at that time cooperated successfully. They produced schemes for an international policing of Macedonia. This was reassuring. Ottoman rule was no better, but perhaps no worse, in the early years of this century than it had been at any time since the Congress of Berlin. Nor were great power sensitivities specially inflamed, even if at Constantinople itself a growing German influence was evident (and perhaps recklessly so, given the canons of Bismarckian diplomacy). Macedonia was not to be the detonator of the next diplomatic confrontation between great powers in the Balkans.

In July 1907 a revolutionary movement of 'Young Turks' forced the sultan to renew the constitution he had briefly granted thirty years earlier. This was more than a milestone in the unhappy story of the struggles of liberalism and constitutionalism in the Ottoman empire; it was also the first in a story of growing demand for modernization which would restore strength and dignity to an empire the Young Turks saw as humiliated and despoiled by the powers. For a little, it looked as if they might put the Ottoman empire back on its feet as a major power. Their choice of name echoed the language of an earlier age of west European nationalist fervour. Their purpose was simple, though their ways were devious. As one of them put it, 'we follow the path traced by Europe . . . even in our refusal to accept foreign intervention'.[13] The first part of this meant that they wished to end the despotic rule of the Sultan and hence the re-inauguration of the liberal constitution of 1876. But Young Turks sought this less for its own sake than because they thought constitutional government could revivify the empire by making modernization possible and ending the process of decay.

This was a very western-looking programme, but was also a symptom of political hostility to Europe. The Young Turks resented the way the great powers had interfered in Ottoman internal affairs (notably in the management of finance, the securing of interest on debts to foreigners, and the coercion of the sultan's government to accept Austro-Russian decisions on Macedonia) and deplored the long and humiliating retreat of Ottoman rule in the Danube valley and the Balkans which they blamed on European bullying. When, after a series of mutinies and revolts, the sultan gave way to them and the constitution was restored, liberals abroad smiled on the new Turkey: it seemed that misrule was at last to end. But instead there was an attempted counter-revolution. The deposition of the sultan Abdul Hamid followed and from 1909 to 1913 a confused politics operated behind a façade of constitutional monarchy. The culmination of this period was an outright Young Turk dictatorship (by a triumvirate), set up to rule in the sultan's name. When a Young Turk announced that there were no longer Bulgars, Greeks, Romanians, Jews and Muslims, a new, Ottoman nationalism was in the making. This was, though, somewhat ominous: it suggested the end of a centuries-old multinational and cosmopolitan regime.

With the passage of time, the Young Turks seem easier to understand than they once were. They were among the earliest of many twentieth-century modernizers in non-western countries. They faced problems like those of other patriotic rebels in other places and from necessity, imagined necessity, admiration or simple ambition, they turned to violent methods. In this, too, they were later much emulated. They

[13] B. Lewis, *The Emergence of Modern Turkey*, q. p.203.

threw themselves into reform of every branch of government and brought in European advisers to help them do so. But they sought modernization as a road to a powerful state rather than westernization for its own sake. They proposed advances in female education and legal emancipation, but did not prevent the religious authorities from warning against the wearing of European dress by Muslim women. Because they took power in the middle of a succession of external humiliations their appeal was sapped by apparent failure to navigate them successfully and they came to rely more and more on force. They had no compunction about hanging opponents. It was soon apparent that the post-reform harmony of peoples within the empire to which liberals had looked forward was a chimera. Religion, language, social custom and nationality continued to fragment the empire. The Young Turks were driven more and more to assert one nationalism among many, that of the Ottoman Turks. This produced new strains. The result was once more massacre, tyranny and assassination, the time-honoured instruments of rule at Constantinople; from 1913 they were deployed by the collective dictatorship. The bad old Ottoman ways returned and would in the end produce new massacres that cost hundreds of thousands of lives. Yet though they had disappointed many of their admirers, the Young Turks had the future on their side. They represented ideas (nationalism and modernization) that would one day remake the Ottoman heritage, even though they did much evil with them. They even – willy-nilly – did something towards advancing them by losing most of what little was left of the empire in Europe, thus releasing themselves from a burden.

The Young Turks quickly began to contribute to international instability. Any prospect of reform in the Ottoman empire was bound to jeopardize the interests of its neighbours – or so many of those neighbours thought. The Young Turk revolution therefore encouraged Balkan governments to attempt further changes in the status quo while they could still do so. The Habsburg monarchy, whose military occupation of the Turkish provinces of Bosnia and Herzegovina had hitherto been acceptable to the other powers, including Russia, drew a similar conclusion. It now seemed desirable to turn occupation into outright annexation. This was not altogether unexpected. Speculation about such a possibility had been in the air since the 1890s. It had been clear for some time that Russia would go along with such a further modification of the 1878 settlement if she received an appropriate consolation prize. When the Young Turk revolution startled Habsburg policy into action, the Russian foreign minister believed he had been given a promise by his Habsburg opposite number that would assure adequate compensation for the gain to the Dual Monarchy.

Unhappily, bad management by the Austrians (and, to a lesser degree, the Russians) led to this proposal going badly wrong. The foreign ministers of the two countries had left the crucial meeting with different ideas of what had actually been agreed – or so they later said. A diplomatic explosion therefore followed when the Austrian annexation of the province took place on 6 October 1908, not quite a month after they met, the Russians protesting strongly when it became clear that they were not to have compensation they had expected (Austrian support for a strengthening of Russia's influence at the Straits). Partly thanks to the annoyance it felt at that moment over the recent Anglo-Russian convention, the German government gave unconditional and noisy support to the Austrians. It believed Russia would recognize that she could not fight Germany and the Habsburg empire if they stood together. In such a war the French would not wish to take part, it was believed in Berlin, and there was a chance that Serbia, Russia's protégé, might disappear altogether.

The Russians had to give in. They accepted the accomplished fact, formally acknowledging the validity of the annexation without obtaining compensation. But their foreign minister was soon at work advocating a Balkan league, including the Ottoman government, to resist further encroachments on the 1878 settlement. This reflected the way in which the Straits had come to matter much more to Russia since it was made, and in a different way. Once, the great dream of Russian policy had been of a new 'Greek' – that is, Orthodox – empire based on Constantinople which would revive the glories of Byzantium. There was now a new, more urgent concern, over the security of the lifeline for Russian grain exports through the Straits, and a growing German influence in Constantinople alarmed Russians more than it would have done in earlier times.

It was a further ominous consequence of the annexation that the Dual Monarchy acquired more Slav subjects, though it already had enough discontented subject peoples, especially in its Hungarian half. More and more under pressure from the Magyars, the government in Vienna had in recent years shown increasing hostility to Serbia, to which many of those Slav subjects already looked for moral and might look for military support. That Serbia aspired to be the nucleus of a future state embracing all South Slavs had come to be feared and believed in Vienna. Serbia's rulers seemed unable (and perhaps unwilling) to restrain South Slav revolutionaries who used Belgrade as a base for terrorism and subversion in Bosnia. Lessons from history are drawn more frequently than people think, and are often drawn wrongly; such was now the case. Vienna was only too ready to conclude that Serbia would seek to imitate Sardinia in the Danube valley.[14] Unless the serpent were scotched in the egg, it was believed, another loss of Habsburg territory might follow. After exclusion from Germany by Prussia and from Italy by Sardinia in the previous century, the empire might be excluded from south-eastern Europe by Serbia in the twentieth. A potential South Slav state (a 'Yugoslavia') would cut it off from the lower Danube valley, too. This would mean the Monarchy's end as a great power, and an end, too, of Magyar supremacy in Hungary, for a triumphant South Slavdom would insist on fairer treatment of Slavs who remained in Hungarian territory.

A potential destabilization might have been avoided and yet another compromise managed without disaster had both Habsburg and Russian policy still sought as a primary goal to preserve the Balkan status quo. The two empires had cooperated well enough to contain the Macedonian question when smaller nations tried to rock the boat, after all. Yet Habsburg policy had already veered away from caution by launching a tariff war against Serbia in 1906. Russia had not been prepared at that moment to identify her interests with Serbia. After defeat by Japan in the Far East, though, she began to take a renewed interest in south-east Europe. The Bosnian annexation was then decisive in changing her attitude. Russia would stand behind Serbia after 1908 determined henceforth that there should not be another settlement like that in Bosnia at the expense of herself and her protégé.

---

[14] The second-rank Sardinian kingdom had, with French and Prussian help, unified Italy at the cost to the Habsburgs of their territories there between 1859 and 1866.

Other powers, too, were to be pulled into Balkan problems by interest, choice, sentiment and formal undertakings, though the last may have been less important than was once thought. The alliances defined conditions on which countries would go to war to support one another, and later critics thought that had cramped diplomacy. Yet none of them in fact ever operated as planned.

RUSSIA'S CHANGING STANCE

Instead of concessions that might meet the aspirations of their Slav subjects the Habsburg government believed it had solved the South Slav problem by excluding Serbia from Bosnia and Herzegovina and blocking any outlet for her in the Adriatic through Montenegro. Just as the British ten years before had feared the acquisition of a port on the Indian Ocean by the Boers, so the Dual Monarchy feared a Serb port on the Adriatic. The annexation had produced the additional benefit, some Habsburg officials thought, that they could now seriously take in hand the terrorist problem in Bosnia. Moreover, as the newly annexed provinces would not form part of the kingdom of Hungary, but of the Austrian lands of the Monarchy, Habsburg rule could show its ability to manage Slavs properly when Magyars were not involved. Yet the South Slav problem remained unsolved. Indeed, it got worse, and so did the publicity given to the shortcomings of Habsburg government. A group of Croat leaders was convicted in 1909 at Zagreb of plotting with Serbia; when the conviction was soon shown to rest on forged evidence from the Austrian foreign office, they were acquitted on appeal, to the discredit of the Dual Monarchy in international opinion. The terrorists began to get more clandestine help from Belgrade; Austrian officials in Bosnia were soon being attacked.

Russian officialdom, meanwhile, was deeply wounded by the way Germany had so bluntly proclaimed in 1908 that the old Berlin–St Petersburg connexion was finally gone and by German efforts to ingratiate themselves in Constantinople. A major programme of reorganization and re-equipment of the Russian army was begun so that no such blow to the autocracy's prestige as Bosnia could ever occur again, nor any doubt arise that Russia could not in a future crisis stand up for her Slav brothers. The moral defeat (as it was seen) of 1908 does not by itself, though, provide a deep enough perspective to understand the role of Russia in the remaining years of peace. Her standing as a power was all the time changing as the slow process of modernization went forward. Things would have moved faster, had not Nicholas II been one of the most unimaginative of tsars.

For a time, liberals inside and outside Russia had felt hopeful about constitutional progress after a revolution detonated by defeats in the war with Japan. A consultative council called the Duma had been set up in 1905 and it looked as if the long-delayed training of Russians in self-government could begin at last. Unhappily, it was to have only a few years of life, and those studded with frustration. Yet by 1914 Russia's growing strength was unquestionable. The improvement of her strategic railway system was begun in 1912 and would be complete by 1918. Though economically far weaker than Germany or Great Britain, her rate of growth was faster than that of either. Her rulers were again confident that the army's numbers and modern weapons, supported by an expanding industrial base, could sustain her great power role. There were even signs that at long last Russian agriculture might have turned the corner. Agrarian unrest had diminished. New laws registering the final disappearance of the legal restraints on individualism imposed at the time of serf emancipation a half-century before had accelerated the emergence of a new class of peasant-farmers – *kulaks* – whose self-interest improved productivity. Yet Stolypin, the minister who presided over this hopeful development, was strongly disliked by the tsar and tsarina. Characteristically, they did not grieve when he was assassinated in 1912.

Stolypin's murder was a portent of backwardness, of the inability of the regime to extinguish the revolutionary and terrorist tradition, and, therefore, of its political failure. These enduring weaknesses were usually overlooked by Russia's rulers. Though some of them, at least, were European in their aspirations, they presided over a country of which some components had not yet achieved nineteenth-century, let alone twentieth-century, levels of civilization. Russia could still display a poverty of Asiatic horror. She was dependent on foreign capital. Institutional concessions to liberalism were stunted and puny. Religion was still mixed up in government and society in a way long unknown in most of western Europe. She had one or two good universities and schools and some distinguished scientists and scholars, but the overwhelming majority of the tsar's subjects were ignorant and superstitious peasants, for the most part illiterate. Russia was still a country, too, where government rested in the last resort on a metaphysical concept increasingly at odds with the age, the supposedly God-given power of the autocrat. For all her strength, she was still a modernizing, not yet a modern, state.

Yet Germany's rulers felt menaced by Russia. German generals took the view that she might become militarily invincible after the completion of her strategic railway systems. That hardly means, though, that international relations were therefore irreversibly set on a path to general war already after the Bosnian crisis. It took six years to show it, if it were true, and much could have happened otherwise in that time.

AGADIR AND AFTER

The next milestone in international relations did not come in the Balkans, but once again in Morocco, though not until 1911, and again precipitated by Germany. Though the French had consolidated their position and special influence there, talk of Morocco's mineral potential had helped to keep international interest in that country alive. In 1909 there had been a Franco-German agreement affirming Moroccan independence but recognizing French political and German economic interests there. When a rebellion against the sultan in 1911 provoked disturbances against foreigners and resulted in a French expedition to occupy Fez, the capital, the German government protested. It decided to establish a position from which it could make a strong claim for compensation if any permanent extension of the French role in the country followed, as now seemed likely. A German warship was sent to the Moroccan port of Agadir, ostensibly to protect German nationals there (there were none). The real aim was to show that Germany meant business and to frighten France into agreeing to compensation for her.

On 1 July the gunboat *Panther* dropped anchor at Agadir.

Gratuitously provocative, this gesture soon turned out also to have been ham-fisted. A government in Paris which had recently been disposed to be conciliatory now found it very difficult even to make friendly noises, let alone concessions, to Germany, because of the patriotic feeling aroused among Frenchmen by the *Panther*'s leap; it could not allow itself to appear to be weak in defending French interests. Agadir had also startled British opinion. Although the Admiralty did not seem much concerned, the Foreign Office was troubled and the press and parliament were excited by the alleged danger of a German naval base being set up on the Moroccan coast (the Germans had in fact no intention of creating one). It was felt in London that a gesture was needed to show British concern. A speech was made by a minister, which, whatever it was intended to mean, was taken as a warning that if France found herself at war with Germany, Great Britain would support her.

In due course, diplomacy negotiated the second Moroccan crisis, as it had the first. Germany in effect gave France a free hand in Morocco (a formal French protectorate followed in 1912) and was given a little more African territory (far away in the Congo) as a sweetener. But the importance of the crisis was that it had occurred at all. It had made the *entente* much more popular in France and Great Britain. Once more, it stirred up the old British alarm over the German naval threat, for the gap in size between the two fleets was narrower in 1911 than it had ever been (or was ever to be again). German anglophobes, on the other hand, believed Germany had suffered 'humiliation' as a result of British threats. When this bore fruit in the following year in an announcement of an even larger German building programme, the British withdrew the Mediterranean Fleet to home waters (while later in the year the French fleet was moved to Toulon) and increased their own capital ship building. Clearly, British naval strategy now envisaged only one potential European enemy, Germany. By 1914 British naval superiority in the North Sea in capital ships was greater than it had been at the time of Agadir.

These were not the only repercussions of the crisis. Italy had long cherished her ambitions on the east coast of the Adriatic and had resented the annexation of Bosnia as a gain for the Habsburgs, her formal allies but old enemies. Her diplomats began now to talk of 'compensation' for French ascendancy in Morocco. The obvious place to look for it was the Ottoman empire, where, if the Young Turks had their way, the process of decay might before long be arrested. In September 1911, after declaring war on the sultan, Italian troops landed in Tripoli; later they opened another front in the Dodecanese. For the first time since the Boer war, a European power had deliberately chosen war as a solution to its problems, and diplomats in several countries found this frightening.

THE BALKAN WARS

The Italians turned out to have done much more than merely make a belated grab at Ottoman territory. They had also launched a new Balkan crisis. By setting about the further demolition of the Ottoman empire in Africa they provoked others to think the time might have come for its final elimination in Europe. Greek and Bulgarian bandits had for years been terrorizing Macedonia and now the hopes of the governments which encouraged them revived. When the Straits, too, were closed by the Ottoman authorities after a bombardment of the Dardanelles by the Italians, the Russians felt bound to take precautions. They began to look for help to safeguard their interests. Contradictory but cumulative doubts (about the Ottoman capacity to survive) and fears (that the Young Turks might succeed in making survival possible) led to Russian encouragement of an alliance between Serbia and Bulgaria in 1912. It was hoped that this would give the Turks something to think about and might help to check German influence at Constantinople. The new allies were then joined by Montenegro and Greece. The smaller nations then began to plan their own 'compensations' for Tripolitania. The Russians did not want to appear to be failing to support other Slavs, and so found themselves drifting into the position of underwriting a possible war against the Ottoman empire by smaller nations.

What is known as the First Balkan war was finally started on 18 October 1912, after an ultimatum had been delivered to the Ottoman government a few days earlier. With Montenegrins, Bulgars, Serbs and Greeks lined up against them, the Turks hastily made peace with

Italy at the cost of their North African possessions. The great powers speedily awoke to the dangers of the situation. The Dual Monarchy still believed it dared not let Serbia acquire new territory. The Russians were soon alarmed that the Bulgars might fight their way to Constantinople and take it for themselves. These worries made concerted action possible. A conference of ambassadors met in London and averted the danger of the war spreading further. The Ottoman empire had to give up almost all its remaining territory in Europe, keeping only part of Thrace. To keep Serbia away from the sea, an independent Albania was created; this was the last new nation to emerge from Ottoman Europe (and the belated recognition of a bloodily suppressed insurrection against Ottoman rule in 1910). Albania was a reassurance for Austria, and Russia found the outcome acceptable. At last, too, the Ottoman empire gave up its long-contested rights in Crete (which had in fact proclaimed its union with Greece in the wake of the Bosnian crisis).

Unfortunately, the victors soon fell out over the spoils. This caused another war of the Ottoman succession, the Second Balkan war, but this time between different antagonists. Serbia was attacked by Bulgaria with the aim of turning Serbian forces out of Macedonia, which they had invaded. A further Bulgarian attack followed, this time on Greece, once again over claims to Macedonia. Once again, it seemed a good moment for outsiders to speculate on the chances of war; Romania chose the moment to attack Bulgaria while she was preoccupied in the west, with the aim of detaching from her the Dobrudja. The Turks meanwhile quickly retook Adrianople. When the great powers did not intervene, Bulgaria lost almost everything she had gained in the First Balkan war except some of Macedonia, the rest of which was now divided between Serbia and Greece. It did not appear, though, that the Macedonian question was permanently solved. Only Germany felt obliged to make a gesture: Wilhelm II insisted that the Austrians send an ultimatum to Belgrade over a Serbian incursion into Albania. The Serbs withdrew.

This is a tangled story that would hardly need re-telling here were it not for what it revealed. These episodes in faraway countries, of which most of the newspaper-readers and inhabitants of the capital cities of the great powers knew little that was either detailed or wholly true, once again demonstrated the potential for future trouble which was lying about. Obstreperous smaller states had followed the Italian lead and taken the initiative in a further despoiling of the Turks. The great powers had not been able to prevent further infringement of the now much tattered territorial settlement it had been supposedly their interest and duty to defend. Not much of it, indeed, was now left. Serbia had gained a million and a half more inhabitants but with her hopes to reach the Adriatic thwarted she was more embittered against Vienna than ever. The savage fighting and accompanying atrocities of the war emphasized the endurance of deeply rooted ethnic, religious and cultural division in the Balkans and built up new resentments for the future.

Above all, worries in Vienna and Budapest about Serbian ambition continued to grow. Something of a parallel, though in no sense one that is perfect, can again be drawn between the Dual Monarchy's nervous desire to settle with the Serbians and that of a British government fifteen years earlier to settle with the Boers (the difference was that Africa was not Europe, and no other power in 1899 thought its vital interests involved, so the British had been able to act without endangering international peace). The Bulgarians now had new grudges to nurse against their neighbours and an unsupportive Russia. It was a small off-setting factor that there at last appeared to have been a slight improvement in Anglo-German relations as the two powers worked together in the London Conference which ended the Second Balkan war. They negotiated secretly over a proposed railway from Berlin to Baghdad and the possible fate of another supposedly crumbling empire, the Portuguese (paradoxically, it was in the end to prove the longest-lived colonial empire of all). Unhappily, German officials did feel reassured by this. Taking the responsiveness of the British on these matters to mean they lacked confidence, they hopefully speculated that Great Britain might not, after all, be serious about backing France, should Germany attack her.

Such an attack had by this stage long been an essential element in German strategic planning. In 1913, the Kaiser confided to the Austrian chief of staff that he was no longer against a great war (by which he meant one between several powers) in principle. One of his ministers even felt able to talk to members of parliament of the 'coming world

War'.[15] In an atmosphere of excited patriotism (it was the centenary of the so-called 'War of Liberation' with Napoleonic France) a special army bill was introduced that year into the Reichstag. The Russian modernization and rearmament programme (to be completed by 1917) had certainly alarmed the German soldiers. But by itself this can hardly explain the psychological deterioration in Germany that had brought about so dangerous a transformation of German policy as the acceptance of the inevitability of conflict with Russia – and therefore with France – if Germany's due weight in Europe was to be assured.

Many Germans felt that 'encirclement' frustrated the exercise of German power, and should be broken, if only for reasons of prestige, too, and that such a step must involve a confrontation – though not necessarily war – with Great Britain. But this was not all that was happening in Germany in the decade before 1914. There had been a major inflammation of nationalist (and conservative) thinking and agitation in those years. It showed in the growth of societies and pressure-groups with different aims – safeguarding of the social hierarchy, antisemitism, patriotic support for armaments – but all contributing to a xenophobic and authoritarian atmosphere. Some Germans thought positively of possible territorial and material gains in the east and brooded on a supposed historic mission of Teuton to dominate over Slav. Some were troubled by the colonial questions that had been so contentious and prickly before 1900 (yet colonies had proved disappointing and colonial rivalry played virtually no part in the final approach to war). Germany was dangerously ready psychologically for conflict, even if, when war came at last, it was to find its detonator in the South Slav lands.

[15] Words used by the German secretary of state in confidential discussion with members of the Reichstag in April 1913. See F. Fischer, *Germany's Aims in the First World War* (London, 1967), p.3.

7

Challenges and Challengers in the Making

CHANGE AND PERCEPTIONS OF CHANGE
IN ASIA

The Indian Census Report of 1901 recorded that just under 300 million Indians were governed by about 900 white civil servants. Roughly speaking, there was also about one British soldier in India for every 4,000 Indians. Were all the Indians to have spat at the same moment, a Victorian observer had once remarked, the British in India would have been drowned. Yet, facts and fancies alike set aside, European supremacy in India and Asia looked very solid. The imperial rulers felt secure. Only in the last few years, most of them had picked up more territorial booty in China. All of them had then sent contingents to join the international expeditionary force sent against the Boxers, which was imposing an often relentless vengeance on the areas of rebellion, and would in due course obtain substantial financial penalties from the Chinese government as a result. A Chinese partition seemed a possibility.

With the advantages of the false perspective provided by hindsight, the confidence felt about such acts now looks strange. We know that barely half a century of life was left to the European Asian empires and wonder that Europeans could feel so sure about the foundations of their world power. After all, a few straws in the wind already visible should have suggested that things were changing. Liberal certainties and claims that their values were Christian or universal had encouraged self-doubts among Europeans about their right to rule subject populations, even for their own good; democratic and nationalist ideology provided other grounds for new reflexion on such matters.

The Far East, 1901–14

A few people, too, sensed changes of other kinds. As the century opened there had been talk of a 'Yellow Peril' as well as of 'dying empires'. In 1908, in his novel of the future, *The War in the Air*, H. G. Wells depicted British, American and German air fleets slogging out their battles over the Atlantic but the Japanese reaping the benefits of victory.[1] His hero witnesses the destruction of the German airfleet's flagship, the *Hohenzollern*, by the Japanese (the wreck is swept over the Niagara Falls) and sees its fate as a symbol of that of Europe, as the abandonment of his world 'to Asia, to yellow people beyond Christendom, to all that was horrible and strange!' Yet such sensational and occasional evidence of excitement should probably be given no more weight than the enthusiasm of a minority of European artists for Japanese prints and screens a couple of decades earlier, or than the more popular pleasure provided to the French when a great international exhibition in Paris in 1900 revealed to it the exotic variety of the French empire and its peoples. Europe was very self-absorbed in the years before 1914.

It mattered greatly, though, to the calculations of officials, generals and admirals that in 1902 a European power, Great Britain, had allied with Japan in order to safeguard her interests in the Far East. This was recognition of Japan's new strength. There were soon other signs that European powers ought to tread cautiously in the Far East, too. The revolutionizing of Asia had produced defensive reflexes among its peoples, many of them of the Europeans' own making, that had to be taken seriously by 1914. Colonialism, cultural interplay and economic power were catalysts of modernization, channelled through local and Asian forces and beginning at last to speed up the pace of the Hundred Years War of East and West which had begun around 1840. By 1921 a South African statesman was only slightly anticipating events in saying that 'the scene had shifted away from Europe to the Far East and to the Pacific'.[2] Twenty years later, his judgement was

---

[1] R. Wohl's account of Wells's book in *A Passion for Wings. Aviation and the Western Imagination 1908–1918* (New Haven and London, 1994) reproduces some evocative illustrations from the first edition, and cites the passage quoted (p.93).
[2] The former Boer leader Smuts was speaking to fellow delegates at the British Imperial Conference of 1921. Q. in G. M. Gathorne-Hardy, *A short history of international affairs 1920–1939*, 4th edn (London, 1950), p.146.

borne out. Even before 1914, the grounds for it had been there for those with eyes to see. Yet Europe's leaders found it hard to recognize coming realities (some Americans were by then a little more perceptive, encouraged as they were by a newly-founded Californian 'Japanese and Korean Exclusion League'). Hypnotized by ever-present but familiar problems in their own continent, few of them were even beginning to sense as the century began that their difficulties soon might not be confined to it.

THE NEW JAPAN

Modernization and westernization are threads running through the story of the undermining and final disappearance of western hegemony in Asia. Resistance to European political domination, even when the participants were slow or unwilling to recognize it, increasingly required Asians to choose what should or should not be adopted from the West, and between ways of responding to its civilization. In Japan, the first Asian country whose rulers gave much thought to these matters, many startling choices had been made by 1901. By then, whatever her approach towards 'civilization' might appear to merit in praise and applause, few Europeans and Americans concerned with Far East affairs felt unequivocally easy about a modernizing Japan. After her victory over China in 1895, they realized they confronted a new power at least in regional terms.[3]

Once the Japanese felt strong enough to join the western predators, China had always been likely to be their victim, at first in her satellites and dependent territories. Mainland Asia was nearest to Japan at the Tsushima Straits. Along with Russia, Japan threatened Chinese suzerainty above all in the ancient kingdom of Korea, long a tributary of Peking. In 1876 the Koreans had agreed to open three of their ports to the Japanese and to exchange diplomatic representation with them. The statesmen of the Meiji Restoration made haste slowly. Japan did not embark upon her first major modern war, with China over Korea,

[3] Symptomatically, the Dutch administration of Indonesia in 1899 decided to treat the Japanese as Europeans in their legal relations (the Chinese were not so treated). Furnivall, p.240.

until 1894. Japan's armed forces were then sweepingly successful. Yet national humiliation followed when Russia, France and Germany forced Japan to go back on the advantageous terms she had imposed on the Chinese (which had included a declaration of Korea's independence and the cession of the peninsula on which Port Arthur stood) and accept a much less triumphant treaty. Japanese resentment of white power now fused with zeal for imperial expansion in Asia. Popular dislike of the 'unequal treaties' exacted from her earlier in the century by western powers had always run high amid the turmoil of Meiji modernization. The 1895 disappointment brought it to a head. Slowly, the western powers would now awake to the fact that dealing with Japan was a very different matter from bullying China. She was, it soon came to be accepted, not to be treated like other non-western countries, and had to be recognized as a 'civilized' power. One symbol of the change was the ending of a humiliating sign of European superiority, extra-territoriality and the privilege of western residents to be tried only before special courts. An agreement with Great Britain was the first of several which brought this system to an end in 1899. Another signal was Japanese participation in the international anti-Boxer expedition. Then, in 1902, came alliance with Great Britain.

Behind this lay Russian action, too. Russia had long been the most adventurous and aggressive European power in the Far East. Her continuing territorial advance and railway building,[4] the development of Vladivostok and Russian commercial activity in Korea – where domestic politics were little more than a struggle of pro-Russian and pro-Japanese factions – all increased Japanese alarm. Of these foci of antagonism, Korea was much the most important. Its future awoke in Japan much popular concern, which brought together political and economic ambition with traditional Japanese ethnocentricity. Imperialism was always to be a popular cause until checked by military

---

[4] The Japanese attempt to seize Port Arthur in 1895 was in part a response to Russian railway-building and the Russian wish to acquire an ice-free port, which was accomplished by obtaining the lease of Port Arthur in 1898. In the following year, St Petersburg was connected by the Trans-Siberian railway with Chita, a couple of hundred miles east of Lake Baikal (which had at that time to be crossed by ferry). In 1903 a line through Chinese Manchuria established direct connexion with Vladivostok, Peking and Port Arthur.

defeat. In 1901 Japanese patriots formed an aggressively expansionist organization called the Amur River Society.[5] It quickly won support in military circles; this was significant because of the special constitutional place the armed services had come to enjoy in Meiji Japan. Shortly before the new century began it had been settled that the ministers from the army and navy should always be drawn from officers on the active list and that their appointment should be made by the emperor, not the prime minister.

By then, the first Japanese overtures for closer cooperation had been made to the British. Second only to Russia in her Asian imperial interests, the United Kingdom had not taken part in the bullying of 1895. For a long time, Japanese naval cadets had been sent to Great Britain for training. British experts and officers had worked in Japan in advisory and instructing roles, and most of the Japanese fleet had been built in British yards. During the Boxer episode. British pressure had ensured that the Japanese should form part of the international expedition (and eventually Japan provided its largest single contingent). Though at first the Japanese speculated whether as much could not be obtained from the Russians as from the British in securing their interests in Korea, the Russians would not give ground sufficiently. Accordingly, the Japanese turned elsewhere and on 30 January 1902 the Anglo-Japanese alliance was signed. It safeguarded the interests of both powers in China – the maintenance of whose 'independence and territorial integrity' in the context of 'Open Door' policy was explicitly asserted – and the Yellow Sea region, but precisely stipulated that Japan was 'interested in a peculiar degree' in Korea.[6] Each party undertook to be neutral if the other became engaged in a war in defence of its interests, and to come to the aid of the warring party should a third nation enter the struggle against her. It was the clearest indicator yet of the acceptance of Japan as an equal by a western power. Japan, it was said, had joined Europe. The practical effect

[5] Sometimes referred to and possibly better known outside Japan as the Black Dragon Society, a name which was to give rise to much excited misunderstanding. See R. Storry, *The Double Patriots, A study of Japanese nationalism* (London, 1957), p.13, for helpful clarification.

[6] The text is conveniently available in *Key Treaties of the Great Powers 1814–1914*, ed. Michael Hurst (Newton Abbot, 1972), II, pp.726–7.

was that she had been released to fight the Russians alone over Korea, if she wished.

Japan's attitude towards them at once stiffened. When a promised withdrawal of Russian forces from Manchuria was not forthcoming and preparations were made to strengthen the Russian Far Eastern fleet, the Japanese government decided that war was unavoidable. This was justified to the emperor of Korea, when he was notified of the decision, as a step 'to ensure the survival of the East Asian people', on the grounds that the Russians were among those 'who resort to violence and aggression in competition for the survival of nations'. The Japanese emissary went on to say of them 'they are enemies of civilization. They are barbarians, and we should drive out barbarians.' This was an ingenious blend of traditional attitudes and the commonplaces of western political thinking.[7]

Having broken off diplomatic relations with St Petersburg two days later, on 8 February 1904, the Japanese launched a torpedo boat attack on the Russian squadron based at Port Arthur, crippling it. A Japanese army landed in Korea, marched north across the Yalu River and entered Manchuria. Port Arthur was besieged. A year's hard land fighting followed, and further Russian humiliation at sea when the Baltic fleet, sent half-way round the world to win naval supremacy in the Yellow Sea, was annihilated in the battle of the Tsushima Straits, the first decisive battle of the twentieth century in a war between great powers.[8] It ensured Japanese victory in the first defeat of a European power by non-Europeans in a major war since the Middle Ages. The moral, political and strategic repercussions were immense.

For many Japanese, though, they did not at once offset another disappointing peace. The cost of victory had been great in both men and money. The Japanese had made the first overtures to the president

[7] I owe this reference and the translations to Professor Csuchichi Tsuzuki, who refers me to *Ito Hirobumi Den III (The Life of Ito Hirobumi*, vol. III) (Tokyo, 1940), pp.639–42.

[8] The Japanese commanding admiral, Togo, who became a national hero, had been a cadet at the British Royal Navy academy at Osborne, and flew his flag in a battleship built at Barrow-in-Furness. It was incorrectly believed by many Russians that he had also been assisted by the presence of British gunnery officers on his ships.

of United States to suggest that he might broker the process, but the terms of the subsequent Treaty of Portsmouth (New Hampshire) of September 1905 nonetheless angered Japanese patriots; there were riots in Japanese cities, some with loss of life, and martial law was imposed in Tokyo. Nevertheless, Japan's major war aim had been achieved: the Russian will to contest supremacy in the Far East had been broken. The tsarist monarchy turned away to grapple with the problems presented by the revolution at home which the war had touched off and back towards old foreign policy concerns in south-eastern Europe. It explicitly acknowledged the Japanese special interest in Korea in 1907, and so did the United States in return for Japanese recognition of its own special position in the Philippines. The war itself had *de facto* given Japan a high local degree of practical control in Korea in spite of native Koreans' hostility towards the Japanese army. After taking over the representation of Korea in her external affairs, Japan disbanded the Korean forces (but this added embittered Korean ex-servicemen to the ranks of those who were by now actively resisting the Japanese take-over).[9] In 1909 the Japanese resident-general was assassinated by a Korean patriot, and less than a year later, in August 1910, Japan formally annexed the ancient kingdom, the emperor and his family being incorporated into the lineage of the Japanese royal house. Another 'dying empire' had gone and the international community remained unmoved. A renewal of the alliance with the United Kingdom for ten more years in 1911 assured the Japanese even more specifically than 1902 had done a green light for further consolidation in Korea.

THE END OF THE CHINESE EMPIRE

We can now see the formal annexation of Korea, and a Chinese revolution in the following year, as milestones. They mark a turning-point and the end of the first phase of Asia's modern response to the West. The reactions to western challenges of Japan and China, the two states that were to be the great Asian powers of the second half

---

[9] By 1910 nearly 20,000 Koreans had died in Japanese police operations.

of the twentieth century, had been strongly contrasted. Japan had sought safety through inoculation with the western virus of moderniz-ation. Her reward had been recognition as a great power. China's response to western influences had been more complex and much less effective. Having struggled longer from a more vulnerable position against growing western harassment, and far from succeeding by 1901 in shaking off the toils of foreign domination, the imperial regime had by then achieved virtually nothing by way of domestic modernization. With several ports in foreign hands and a British inspector general of customs the Chinese empire, though never formally a colony, was in effect semi-colonized.[10] Its claims in Burma and Indo-China had been swept aside by the British and French in the 1880s. China then had to give up Formosa to the Japanese, and the old paramount influence in Korea was seeping away. China's partition seemed very much on the cards as the century opened. Soon, in 1904, the British would invade Tibet.

At that moment China seemed even to be in the throes of a violent reversion to older ways. The Boxer movement, exploited by the dowager empress Tsu Hzi and given official encouragement, was essentially backward-looking and reactionary. Missionaries and con-verts were murdered, and the foreign legations at Peking were besieged (and a German minister was killed) in a wave of xenophobic violence. The Boxers revealed and released a hatred of foreigners which was waiting to be tapped, but their rebellion also showed how little could be hoped for from the old empire, which it served further to discredit in western eyes. After its suppression, further diplomatic humiliation was visited on China; an enormous indemnity was settled on the customs revenue, whose management was to be henceforth under foreign direction.

Yet the bullying of China which had seemed so likely to prove fatal to that empire was now in fact to dwindle away. Though foreign

---

[10] After the Sino-Japanese war of 1894–5, the Japanese had been forced to return the Liao-Tung peninsula to China, but in 1898 besides Russia, which obtained a twenty-five-year lease on Port Arthur, the Germans obtained a ninety-nine year lease on the port of Kiaochow, France one on Kuangchow, the British one on Kowloon (opposite Hong Kong island) and another on Wei-hai-wei. The Chinese were successful in resisting the demands of Italy to join the list of beneficiaries, though.

garrisons took up new posts on her railways the empire conceded no more territory to European imperialists. Indeed, in 1907 it resumed the administration of Manchuria, which had been in Russian hands. European statesmen were beginning to see that the time for acquiring new footholds or dreaming of partitions of the Sick Man of the Far East was over. China had turned out to be a disappointment. It would suit everyone better to turn to the old British policy, the assurance of an 'Open Door' through which all countries might seek their own commercial advantage – an advantage which, in any case, showed signs of being less lucrative than had once been thought.

The Boxer episode had also changed the mind of the empress, who, after thwarting reform in the 1890s, had clearly backed the wrong horse. Reform had failed but so had reaction. The adoption of western ways might be needed after all, she thought, but in the cause of defending the established order in its essentials. Her choice of means was unsystematic and idiosyncratic – inter-marriage between Manchus and Chinese was now permitted, foot-binding (a Chinese not a Manchu custom) was discouraged, and it was indicated that schools should be promoted. But such symbolic acts did not go far. Tzu Hsi proclaimed the principle of constitutionalism while failing to introduce it. There was official talk of reform, but it was clear that it was only to be tolerated while taking the imperial system for granted.

Officers of the Chinese army (beginning now to be trained on western lines) began to think about more fundamental change and even to see revolution as the way ahead for China. Students in exile were already meeting and discussing their country's future, above all in Tokyo, to which some thousands of them went in the early years of the century. Given their own imperialist thrust, the Japanese could see the potential advantages and usefulness of subversive movements that might weaken their neighbour. They had already in the 1890s offered Chinese and other dissidents the slogan, 'Asia for the Asians', which emerged from an 'East Asia Cultural Union' set up in Tokyo. Its journal, *Asia* (appearing under that title 1891–4), promoted the idea of a possible special role for Japan in a continent disputed between white and yellow peoples. Though among the fiercest of recent predators on China, the Japanese nonetheless enjoyed great prestige in the eyes of young Chinese radicals as Asians who had evidently escaped from the trap of traditional backwardness which seemed to be about to engulf their own country.

Some students looked for support to China's long-enduring secret societies, among them a young man of peasant origin called Sun Yat-sen. He was schooled by missionaries, studied medicine in British Hong Kong, never prepared for the traditional and literary test of the official examinations, and was more influenced by foreign, western influences than any previous Chinese reformer had ever been. His achievement was to be exaggerated by his followers, but he remains a central and symbolic figure. He attempted revolution ten times altogether before in the end finding himself in the right place (that is, abroad but able to return to China) at the right time. In the 1890s, Sun Yat-sen, like many others, was asking only for a constitutional monarchy, though that seemed a very radical demand at that time. Some of the Chinese businessmen abroad (of whom there were many, for the Chinese were great traders throughout Asia) helped Sun Yat-sen to form in 1905 in Japan a revolutionary alliance aiming at the expulsion of the alien Manchu dynasty and the initiation of native Chinese rule, a republican constitution, and land reform. Subsequently expelled from Japan at the request of the Chinese government (it also attempted to kidnap him in London, an incident that gave him helpful publicity in the west), Sun Yat-sen had already sown in this way the seed of the nationalist party that would eventually emerge as the Kuomintang (KMT) and the dominant force in the later Chinese Republic. He sought to conciliate western liberal opinion, at this stage a wise tactical move, and his programme showed the influence of western thinkers (notably, of the English radical John Stuart Mill and the American economic reformer Henry George); thus the West was again providing stimulus and ideological baggage to a Chinese revolutionary movement, as it had done in the Taiping rebellion half a century earlier.

In 1905, the traditional imperial examination system was abolished. As much as any other institution, it had held Chinese civilization together for centuries, making possible the creation of a bureaucracy of great internal homogeneity and cohesion. Its influence would not quickly wane. Yet a crucial distinction between the mass of Chinese subjects and the privileged ruling class disappeared with it. Some progress was made in additional educational provision, but not enough.[11] Meanwhile, students returning from abroad dissatisfied with conditions in China were no longer under the necessity of accommodating themselves to them by going through the examination procedure if they wished to enter government service. This was a new disturbing influence, advancing the irradiation of China's élites by western ideas. Together with the soldiers in a modernizing army, more and more of the young were looking to revolution for a way ahead.

Several unsuccessful risings took place (some directed by Sun Yat-sen from Indo-China with French connivance) before Tzu Hsi and the emperor she had dominated and manipulated both died on successive days in 1908. The new emperor was a child, on whose behalf there governed a reactionary prince regent, and the change made little difference. The Manchu government continued to drag its feet over reform. Though there were some concessions and the flow of students abroad was increased, it still failed to achieve any decisive break with the past or even to surrender any of the Manchu privileges; the long-standing sense of grievance over the over-representation of Manchu in government posts both at the centre and in the provinces still festered. A new dowager empress intrigued against the prince regent, who continued to favour Manchu over Chinese and maintained a regime notably nepotistic and corrupt even by traditional standards. Still dependent upon the traditional official class, the dynasty was slowly ceasing to be able to provide effective government throughout China. As gentry officials sought to see to their own interests, it appeared that little but the energy of the old dowager empress had kept the imperial system going. Some attempted reforms – for instance a little more freedom for the press – only further weakened it; a system of licensing was successful in reducing opium smoking somewhat, but also alienated the loyalty of farmers whose livelihood centred on poppy-growing (and opium tax revenue, too, declined).

Stalemate produced by internal faction fighting was a traditional sign of the waning years of a dynasty, as were natural disasters, and early 1911 brought plague and flood. They drove vast numbers to

[11] It has been estimated that there were 65,000,000 children of school age in China in 1910, but that only 1,600,000 were enrolled in government schools. See M. E. Cameron, *The Reform Movement in China 1898–1912* (Stanford, Calif., 1931), p.86.

despair and destitution. Nationalists fumed over fresh rumours of partition by the great powers. Provincial interests were further antagonized by a well-meant railway centralization programme; the wrath of the national assembly (its institution had been approved in 1908 and it met first in 1910) was further aroused when it was proposed to seek foreign capital for this and other economic developments. The moderate success of the anti-opium campaign, the proclamation of a new constitution (based on the Japanese), reforms in the army and the beginnings of a national school system were now not enough to save the Manchu regime. In October a revolutionary conspiracy was discovered at Hankow, when a bomb went off by accident in the Russian concession there. Revolts earlier in the year had been more or less contained; the Hankow discovery at last precipitated a successful revolution. The outcome was settled by the defection from the regime of its military commanders. When the most important of them, Yuan Shih-kai, turned on the Manchus, the dynasty was lost. The Mandate of Heaven had been withdrawn and this time there was no alternative dynasty at hand. On 12 February 1912 the six-year-old Manchu emperor abdicated and with the dynasty that had reigned over it for over two centuries went the age-old empire itself. Sun Yat-sen, whose name was used by the early rebels (and for whom the revolution was to mark the end of his long political apprenticeship), was taken by surprise; he returned to be elected president of the 'United Provinces' of China at the end of 1911 by a provisional national assembly.

Within a few months, though, Sun Yat-sen resigned the presidency to Yuan Shih-kai. This tacitly acknowledged that power in the new republic actually lay with the man who controlled its military. For the immediate future, an ineffective constitutional regime at Peking would dispute the practical management and exploitation of China by warlords. China had still a long way to travel before she would be a modern nation-state. Nonetheless, she had now begun a forty-year-long march towards that goal and the recovery of the independence she had lost in the nineteenth century to foreigners. Like Japan, she was to translate old attitudes and collective consciousness into a new idiom and language, that of European nationalism, but with very different results.

THE EUROPEAN EMPIRES IN THE FAR EAST

While the emergence of Japanese power was already a fact of major interest for Western diplomats and strategists, and the Chinese revolution might clearly be regarded as a portent of future change in the global distribution of power, the European empires themselves in Asia still looked reassuringly solid in 1914. Yet even within them there were some signs that the old assumption of the durability of European power was no longer to be relied upon. Some subtly self-destructive forces had been nurtured by European influences, by the rich variety of suggestive innovation, educational initiatives, exemplary practice, economic disturbance and disinterested missionary zeal that flowed into the European empires from the western world. Such stimuli awoke support in them for the twentieth century's most successful political principle, nationalism (which, in 1901 still had its greatest triumphs to come in Europe itself). Asia was now to take up the doctrine that only a regime which could be plausibly represented to be self-made by an indigenous people could provide government with real legitimacy. But simple resentment probably mattered more as a subversive force.

Not all colonial regimes behaved in the same way. The British encouraged nationalists in Burma but viewed those of India with growing alarm, while the Americans doggedly pursued a benevolent paternalism in the Philippines after their ugly suppression of the insurrection launched originally against their Spanish predecessors. Those same Spanish, like the Portuguese elsewhere in Asia, had for centuries vigorously promoted Christian conversion and so had left the Philippines strongly Catholic, while the British Raj still remained cautious about interference with native religion in India and was resented by religious lobbyists in London because of this. Different imperial styles shaped the history of colonial Asia and, therefore, its future.

INDO-CHINA AND INDONESIA

By the end of the nineteenth century, the French had acquired overall control of Indo-China, a substantial part of south-east Asia. Cochin China they took outright. Cambodia, Laos and Annam were turned into protectorates. Enough French residents established themselves there to exercise some political weight in Paris. The Third Republic formally operated through existing native rulers, though administration in the Napoleonic tradition soon made it clear that the independence of indigenous government in Indo-China was a sham. French practice sapped local institutions without replacing them with others that might win the loyalty of the people, a dangerous course. It also brought with it French tariff policy, which slowed down industrialization. The inspiring motto to be found on official buildings and documents, 'liberty, equality and fraternity', soon led Indo-Chinese businessmen to wonder in whose interests their country ought to be run. French law and notions of property meanwhile broke down the structure of village landholding and threw power into the hands of money-lenders and landlords. With a growing population in the rice-growing areas, this built up a potential for future unrest. The conception of an Indo-China which was integrally a part of France, whose élites should be turned into Frenchmen, also brought problems to the deeply Confucian Indo-Chinese dominant class.

Vietnamese nationalism had a long history of rejecting foreign rule. Antipathy to China, which had long claimed suzerainty over the country, soon transferred itself to the French. There had been rebellions and bitter campaigns of 'pacification' before the acquisition of Laos in 1893 completed the physical structure of French Indo-China. The Japanese victory over Russia led several young Vietnamese to go to Tokyo, where they had met Sun Yat-sen and the Japanese sponsors of an 'Asia for the Asians'. After the Chinese Revolution of 1911, one of them organized a society for a Vietnamese republic. None of this much troubled the French, who were well able to contain such opposition before 1914, but it made them wary of the dangers of education, and their unwillingness to promote it was another cause of grievance among the mandarin class and its sons. Though a university was opened in 1907, it had to be closed almost at once because of fears of unrest (and it remained closed until 1918). An important section of Vietnamese opinion was thus deeply alienated from French rule within a couple of decades of its establishment.

The French could nonetheless feel unafraid of opposition by the old dominant classes seeking to maintain the Confucian order, for they also found collaborators among them. It was the young men who went to Tokyo who indicated the presence among Vietnamese youth of other forces looking for the way to modernization and the liberation they believed would come with it. They were attracted by the example of their host country. It can hardly have been irrelevant, either, that during the Great War something like 100,000 Indo-Chinese soldiers served in the French army in France (sometimes on security duties among the French population), where they must have seen a very different face of French empire from the one it presented in Saigon or Hanoi. Paradoxically, such modernization as was being delivered by the French (like that delivered by the British in India) was itself likely to encourage and promote the emergence of new pressures for change. These were to be found increasingly in the rising numbers of professional and business entrepreneurs in modernizing cities like Saigon and Hanoi. Even French contributions to the improvement of public health increased the potential for change; population had begun to rise early in the century and this exacerbated the effects of colonial policy over land.[12] The French had steadily undermined the traditional arrangement of communal land-holding by introducing the notion of outright possession, and encouraging, by grants and administrative benevolence, the consolidation of large estates and plantations. These were in the hands of French entrepreneurs and Vietnamese collaborative with the colonial regime. On them laboured growing numbers of peasants working for often tiny wages.

The other great European empire in the East was the Dutch. It was well established in Java and Sumatra since the seventeenth century. Unlike Indo-China, Indonesia and its islands belonged to the historic Hindu cultural sphere, not that of China (though it contained large

---

[12] The population of Indo-China more than doubled from about 15 million in 1900 to over 30 million at mid-century.

Chinese communities). Its population was large and (somewhat nominally) Muslim; Islam had arrived in the eighteenth century. Some Dutch had begun by the end of the nineteenth century to feel uneasiness about the conduct of their colonial government, which was confronted by a diversity of challenges to its rule, and had to respond to economic pressures arising from the new importance of Indonesian markets to the Netherlands. This culminated in an important change of attitude; in 1901 a new 'Ethical Policy' was announced that focused on the welfare of the native population as well as vigorous state action to promote economic expansion and efficiency. It brought some administrative decentralization and a campaign to achieve improvement through village management. It was accompanied by the successful pacification of North Sumatra after a long war, but proved so paternalistic and interventionist that it, too, stimulated a hostility that was soon utilized by the first Indonesian nationalists. In 1908 they formed the first nationalist organization, the 'Glorious Endeavour'. Three years later an Islamic association appeared. Its early activities were directed as much against Chinese traders as against the Dutch but by 1916 it was going so far as to ask for self-government while remaining in union with the Netherlands. Before this, though, in 1912 a true independence party had been founded in the name of native-born Indonesians of all races; one of its three founders was Dutch. In 1916 the colonial government took the first step towards meeting some of its ambitions by authorizing an Indonesian representative assembly with limited powers. It was at this point still used as much by Indonesians of Dutch blood as by those of native stock to promote what were still conceivable as common interests.

INDIA UNDER THE RAJ

India was the largest and most spectacular of all the European overseas possessions. Expressions of discontent with white government there before 1914 were bound to be especially significant. The sub-continent contained the second largest population in the world under one sovereign power, which ruled through a variety of constitutional arrangements. The British governed some provinces outright through the

Indian Civil Service, others indirectly, through special arrangements with native rulers advised by official Residents at their courts. Since the middle of the nineteenth century India had thus been effectively united by the British Raj as never before, a huge achievement, given the variety of peoples, languages, terrain and economic potential it contained. By the end of the nineteenth century the benefits in security and innovation this brought with it had already made it impossible to conceive of a future for the sub-continent which did not include a measure of modernization. But that was bound to be disruptive, just as it was in many parts of other European empires. In India, as elsewhere, for instance, the introduction of European notions of absolute property in land were to change history. And so did many other things introduced by imperialism. In the sub-continent, as throughout Asia, Europeans brought with them (sometimes unwittingly, sometimes consciously) ideas such as those of nationalism and humanitarianism which were in the end bound to weaken their political hegemony. The teaching of Christian missionaries threatened the dislocation of local custom and belief and of established hierarchies. In India such forces slowly helped to crystallize an awareness of a new sense of being exploited in ways not sanctioned (as in earlier times) by tradition.

The Mutiny of 1857 is something of a marker in the story of the way modernization came to India, a primitive, almost blind, response to it (like the Boxer rebellion). It was an uncoordinated sequence of outbreaks against the authority of the East India Company, which then governed British India, beginning with a mutiny of Hindu soldiers of the Company's army who feared the polluting effect of using a new type of cartridge, greased with animal fat. That specific provocation is revealing; much of the Mutiny was an outburst of spontaneous and reactionary response to innovation, supplemented by the irritations of native rulers, both Muslim and Hindu, who regretted the loss of their privileges and thought that the chance might have come to recover their independence. The British were after all very few.

The response of those few was nonetheless prompt and ruthless. With the help of loyal Indian soldiers the rebellions were crushed, though not before there had been massacres of British captives and a British garrison had been besieged in rebel territory for some months. The reports of these horrors and difficulties (and their later mythologizing and exaggeration) provided a disastrous myth of the Mutiny for the future Raj. Like many episodes important in the making of nations, what was later believed of it mattered more than what it actually was. It not merely became for some later Indian nationalists what it had never been, a national liberation movement, but its truly disastrous and deepest effect was negative, the wound it gave to British goodwill and confidence. Whatever the expressed intentions of British policy, most British who lived in India henceforth never forgot that some Indians had once proved almost fatally untrustworthy. New and harder policies and a new discrimination and social exclusiveness were the unhappy outcomes. In more than one way, therefore, the Mutiny thrust Indian history more firmly still in a direction to which it already tended, the tightening of British control.

The East India Company disappeared into history and India now became the responsibility of a British cabinet minister, operating through the Queen's viceroy. Anglo-Indian trade was after the opening of the Suez Canal also locked more closely than ever into that of the general expansion of British manufacturing supremacy and world commerce. By 1900 the volume of British trade with India had more than quadrupled since the Mutiny. But Indian industrialization was probably retarded by British competition, which, without anyone so intending, virtually destroyed Indian manufacturing for export.

In 1877 parliament had made Queen Victoria 'Empress of India'. She appears much to have enjoyed her new dignity; some of her British subjects laughed, and a few disapproved, but most of them seem not to have been much concerned. They took the British Raj to be permanent or near permanent and held that only firm government was able to prevent another Mutiny. Others, more thoughtful, would nonetheless have agreed with the British viceroy Lord Curzon who declared as the twentieth century began that 'As long as we rule India, we are the greatest power in the world. If we lose it, we shall drop straightaway to a third-rate power.'[13] The Indian taxpayer could be made to pay for the defence of much or most of the British empire;

---

[13] In a letter of 3 March 1901 to the Conservative minister A. J. Balfour, q. by David Dilks, *Curzon in India, I, Achievement* (London, 1969), p.113.

Indian soldiers sustained British policy from Malta to Hong Kong and constituted the empire's strategic reserve.

This was not all the nineteenth-century history that was to shape twentieth-century India. Human beings do not find it easy to pursue collective purposes without some sort of myth to justify them. Many British in India eagerly sought one and found it in seeing themselves as the heirs of the Romans whom their classical education taught them to admire, stoically bearing the burden of a lonely life in an alien land to bring peace to the warring and law to peoples without one. Others believed their Christianity was a precious gift with which they must destroy idols and cleanse evil custom. Some never formulated any clear views at all, feeling no need to go beyond the simple and plausible conviction that what Great Britain brought to India was better than what it found there, and therefore that what they were doing was good. At the basis of all these views there was the conviction of European superiority, plausible as it was at first sight and reinforced as it was in the later nineteenth century by fashionable racialist ideas and a muddled reflexion of what was believed to be taught by current biological science about the survival of the fittest. Such ideas helped to justify the social and political separation of the British in India from native Indians. Nor until the very end of the century did a few elected Indians enter the legislative branch of government. Moreover, though Indians were by then allowed to compete to enter the civil service, there were major practical obstacles in the way of their ascent to the ranks of the decision-makers. In the army, too, Indians were kept out of the senior commissioned ranks.

It was a matter of prudence, too, that after the Mutiny the British Raj assumed that Indian life should be interfered with as little as possible. Female infanticide, since it was murder, was to be rooted out, but there was to be no prohibition of polygamy or child marriage (though after 1891 it was not legal for a marriage to be consummated until the wife was twelve years old, a virtually unenforceable prohibition). The line of the law was to run outside most of what was sanctioned by Hindu religion, even if the prohibition of *suttee* (the self-immolation of a Hindu widow on her husband's funeral pyre), which had been promulgated by a British governor-general as long ago as the 1830s, was maintained. A politic conservatism was also reflected in a new attitude towards native Indian rulers. In the Mutiny most of them had been loyal and their rights were afterwards scrupulously respected. The princes were left to rule their own states (in which lived one Indian in five) independently and virtually irresponsibly, checked only by their awe of British political officers sent to reside at their courts. The British also cultivated the native aristocracy and the landlords, though that sometimes meant leaning on those whose own leadership positions and power were also already being undermined by social change. Reciprocal benefits followed for the participants in innumerable tacit agreements with other client groups, too. Yet no more than any other imperial government was the Raj able to stave off change. Even its successes could tell against it.

The suppression of warfare in the sub-continent removed a check on population – there followed more frequent famines. The building of the Indian railway network was essential to the infrastructure of a slowly modernizing economy, but in breaking down, however slightly, divisions of region and locality it was one of the forces easing the way to national politics.[14] Meanwhile, the provision of ways of earning a living other than by agriculture (and therefore of possible outlets from an over-populated countryside) was not easy. There had always been landless labourers in India, but there were more of them under the Raj. Nor did the slowly growing class of Indian industrialists feel warmly towards government. There was also a small but growing number of Indians who were educated along English lines and subsequently had been irritated by the contrasts between what they had learnt and British practice in India. Indians who had studied at Oxford, Cambridge or the Inns of Court could find this especially galling: there were even Indian members of the House of Commons in the 1890s, at a time when in India Europeans could still not then be brought to answer a charge before an Indian magistrate. Some simply pondered what they read in books that reached India; John Stuart Mill and Mazzini were to have a huge influence on the rhetoric of Indian radicalism, and, through its leaders, in the rest of Asia.

---

[14] In 1901 India had thirty-five times China's railway mileage.

INDIA ENTERS THE TWENTIETH CENTURY

Bengal was the historic centre of British power and Calcutta the capital of India. In 1905 the province was divided in two; there was henceforth to be a West Bengal where a majority of the population was Hindu, and an East Bengal with a Muslim majority. Rage over this administrative decision detonated explosive materials long accumulating. A new political factor had now to be taken into account. The crisis was the first to show the importance of the significantly-named Indian National Congress, a political organization, the initiative for which had come from an Englishman, formerly a civil servant, with encouragement from the then Viceroy. Europeans had been prominent, too, in its management when Congress was set up in Bombay in 1885. Many delegates to the foundation conference symbolically attended wearing European dress and indeed in morning-suits and top hats of comical unsuitability to the climate of their country. By 1905 Congress was an established Indian institution, though. The second adjective of its name showed that a European idea had been introduced to the arena of Indian politics even if one at first sight ill-matched to Indian realities. Congress had soon committed itself to the exotic and hitherto unfamiliar goals of national unity and regeneration, but did not at first aspire to self-government. It had proclaimed its 'unswerving loyalty' to the British crown and only after twenty years, in which much more extreme nationalist views had been circulated among its members, did it begin to discuss the possibility of independence. Attitudes had by then been soured and stiffened by British residents who vilified them as unrepresentative and by administrators who preferred to work through more traditional and conservative social forces. Extremists became more insistent after the inspiring victories of Japan over Russia.

The partition of Bengal provided the issue for an open clash. In the eyes of government, partition would be doubly beneficial: it would be an administrative improvement and might help to weaken Bengal's nationalists by division. Within Congress a split was avoided by agreement on the aim of *swaraj*, a word of uncertain scope, which in practice might mean independent self-government such as was enjoyed by the white dominions of the British empire. The extremists, though, were heartened by anti-partition riots and an effective new weapon deployed against the British, a 'boycott' of British goods.[15] It was hoped these might be extended to other forms of passive resistance such as non-payment of taxes and the refusal of soldiers to obey orders. By 1908 the extremists were excluded from Congress and some of them were already turning to violence. Russian revolutionary terrorism now joined Mazzini's writings and Garibaldi's inspiration as formative examples. Assassination and bombing were met with special repressive measures, and extremists argued that political murder was not ordinary murder.

A third consequence of partition was perhaps the most momentous of all, the launching of the modern political division between Muslim and Hindu. Indian Muslims had for a century began to feel more and more distinct from Hindus, with whom they had lived easily in earlier times. Distrusted by the British because of attempts made in 1857 to revivify the Mogul empire, Muslims had subsequently had little success in winning posts in government or on the judicial bench. Hindus had responded eagerly to the educational opportunities offered by the Raj; they had more commercial weight and more influence on government, too. Yet Muslims had found British patrons and allies. They had established an Islamic college to provide the English education Muslims needed to compete with Hindus, and had helped to set up Muslim political organizations. Intensification of Hindu ritual practice such as a cow protection movement (Muslims were beef-eaters) was not likely to do anything but increase the separation of the two communities at a popular level. Some English civil servants began to sense a potential for balancing Hindu pressure, though Congress still kept its ranks open to the two communities alike and proclaimed itself non-communitarian.

Only in the partition debate did the split emerge clearly at last into the subcontinent's politics, albeit one still far from displaying its full potential. The anti-partitionists campaigned with a strident display of Hindu symbols and slogans but the British governor of eastern

---

[15] 'Boycott' was a word and device that had only recently entered British political consciousness from another land of struggle between imperialism and nationalism, Ireland.

Bengal favoured Muslims in his province against Hindus and strove to give them a vested interest in it. He was dismissed, but not before his inoculation had taken: Bengal Muslims deplored his removal, while what was taken to be an Anglo-Muslim *entente* further inflamed Hindu terrorists. To make things worse, this all took place, from 1906 to 1910, while prices were rising faster than at any time since the Mutiny. Political reforms conceded in 1909 did not mend matters. They provided for the first time for Indians to be appointed to the council which advised the British minister responsible for Indian affairs, and more important, for more elected places for Indians in provincial legislative councils. But the elections were to be made by electorates that, though limited, had a communal basis; the division of Hindu and Muslim was thus institutionalized.

In 1911, for the first and only time during the Raj, a reigning British monarch visited India. A great imperial Durbar was held at Delhi, the old centre of Mogul rule to which the capital of British India was now transferred from Calcutta. The accession of George V as king and emperor that year had been marked by symbolic acts of princely grace, of which the most notable and politically significant was the reuniting of Bengal. The princes of India did personal homage to the emperor. Congress still did not question its duty to the throne. If there was a moment at which the Raj was at its apogee, this was it. Yet India was far from settled; neither concession nor the display of imperial might had been effective. Terrorism and seditious crime continued. The year after the Durbar the viceroy himself was wounded by a bomb. Hindus remained resentful that the Bengal partition had ever happened while Muslims now felt that the government had gone back on its understandings with them in withdrawing it. They feared that a more representative system meant they would be swamped numerically in the province. Hindus, on the other hand, took the concession as evidence that resistance had paid and, sure that numbers favoured them, began to press for the abolition of the communal electoral arrangements which the Muslims prized.

Indian Muslims who had favoured cooperation with the British were increasingly under pressure from disillusioned co-religionists who responded to the violent appeal of a pan-Islamic movement. The pan-Islamists alleged that the British had not only let the Muslims down in Bengal, but also in Tripoli, by failing to help the Ottoman sultan when the Italians attacked that part of his empire in 1911, and in the Balkans in 1912 and 1913 when, once again, Christian peoples attacked him. Constantinople was the seat of the Caliphate, the institutional embodiment of the spiritual leadership of Islam. Great Britain was, indisputably and self-proclaimedly, a Christian – that is, an infidel – power, and was clearly behaving in a way hostile to Islam. The intense susceptibilities of lower-class Indian Muslims were excited to the point at which even the involvement of a mosque in the replanning of a street could be presented as part of a deliberate plot to harry them. When in 1914 Turkey went to war with Great Britain, though the Muslim League remained loyal, a few Indian Muslims began to prepare revolution against the Raj. They were less important for the future, though, than the fact that not two but three forces were now contending in India's constitutional politics: British, Hindu and Muslim.

EGYPT AND THE END OF OTTOMAN AFRICA

In 1901, the first example of a 'dying' empire which was likely to spring to a European's mind was the Ottoman; it had been moribund for a long time. In Europe, it had lost territory since 1683 with only temporary reversal or respite; there was now little left to give up north of the Straits of Constantinople. It could easily be believed that the last stage was at hand in the long story of the partition of Ottoman Europe. But in the previous century its grip had slackened in Africa, too. The basic causes were the same as they had been in Europe, the predatory activities of European powers, and the growth of nationalism, though they operated in the Maghreb and Egypt in different degree and to different timetables. By 1901, though, almost all the former Ottoman territories and client rulers in Africa had already slipped from the sultan's effective grasp, even if they did not enjoy formal independence of him. By then nationalist agitation both in Egypt and in the Maghreb countries had come to be directed more against Europeans than against the Ottomans.

Nationalism, whatever its ethnic or other roots, was a western idea which had already been at work within the sphere of Islamic civilization for a long time. Mehemet Ali, an Albanian, had established himself as a virtually independent governor of Egypt in 1805. He admired European civilization and believed Egypt could benefit from it (though he himself never went west of his birthplace, Kavalla, in Thessaly) and had launched the process of opening the Near East to modern European (especially French) influence, sometimes through educational and technical institutions. The old-established French interest in the trade and affairs of the Ottoman empire was important, too, and French was soon the second language of educated Egyptians and a large French community appeared at Alexandria. Borrowings from the western source of modernization can rarely be confined to technical knowledge and young Egyptians soon began to pick up European political ideas. They began to draw the same lesson as would Indian, Japanese and Chinese modernizers: the European disease had to be caught in order to generate the necessary antibodies against it. So modernization and nationalism became, as elsewhere, tangled.

Such ideas were for a long time the creed only of a few, and of élites in societies whose masses lived in Islamic cultures still largely uncorroded by western influence. It was the most 'Europeanized' Egyptians (and Europeanized Syrians and Lebanese) who were the first nationalists in the Middle East. It was among Christian Arabs of Syria, too, that there seems first to have appeared the idea of pan-Arabian or Arab nationalism (as opposed to Egyptian, Syrian or some other version). The claim that all Arabs, wherever they were, constituted a nation was of course not the same as saying they all shared the brotherhood of Islam. Moreover, not only did Islam itself embrace millions of non-Arabs, but it excluded many non-Muslim Arabs, among them important Christian communities in the Levant. The implications and potential complications of this would take time to appear.

The opening of the Suez Canal in 1869 was another landmark in westernization. More than any other single fact it doomed Egypt to prolonged foreign interference, though it was not the immediate occasion of further European intervention. Finance was. Under the khedive Ismail (the first ruler of Egypt to obtain from the sultan that title in recognition of his substantial *de facto* independence) the Egyptian national debt shot up, multiplying nearly fifteen times to a total of almost £100 million in thirteen years, a colossal sum for the era. When in 1876 the khedive's government went bankrupt, foreign managers of its debt were put in. Two controllers, one British, one French, were to make sure that Egypt was governed (nominally by Ismail's son) so as to keep up revenue and pay what was owed the European bankers. Though they worked in the khedive's name, they and their subordinates looked like European imperialists. The literate class, moreover, was offended by steps on which the controllers insisted in their search for economy – such as the reduction of government salaries.

The outcome was discontent, xenophobia, conspiracy and ultimately revolution. Amid the mounting hubbub, some Egyptians began to talk about not only the plight of their country but also the possibilities of the reform of Islam, of unifying the Muslim world, and of pan-Islamism. Some still saw Istanbul's formal suzerainty over Egypt as a problem. But ideas mattered less in fanning hatred of the foreigner than the arrival in 1882 of a British army after a successful Egyptian nationalist revolution in that year. British policy, even under a Liberal prime minister who favoured new nations in other parts of the Ottoman empire, dare not risk the security of the Canal route to India. The British, having defeated the nationalists, said they would withdraw as soon as a dependable government was available, but none acceptable to them appeared. Instead, in the absence of the French (who had refused to support British policy), their administrators took on more and more of the government of Egypt. Egyptian resentment deepened. France was affronted. Relations with that country reached their nadir after Fashoda and the proclamation of an Anglo-Egyptian condominium over the Sudan in 1899.

That British interference reduced public debt, and promoted irrigation schemes which made it possible to feed a growing population (it doubled to about 12 million between 1880 and 1914) is not in doubt. The British continued to antagonize Egyptians, though, by cutting down jobs in the government service, by collecting high taxes and, of course, by being foreign. The twentieth century brought growing unrest and violence. The British and the puppet Egyptian government proceeded firmly against agitation, and continued to seek ways out of the morass of imperial involvement. Administrative reform came first and led in 1913 to a new constitution, providing for more representative elections and a legislative assembly with real powers. But the assembly met only for a few months before the outbreak of war in 1914 brought its suspension. The Egyptian government was then pushed into war with its formal suzerain, the Ottoman sultan. The khedive (suspected of anti-British plotting) was removed, and at the end of the year a British protectorate of an Egypt under its own sultan was proclaimed. Given the earlier seizure of Libya and Tripolitania by the Italians, this was the end of Ottoman empire in Africa.

OTTOMAN EMPIRE EAST OF SUEZ

The government of the Ottoman sultan had long ruled huge Asian provinces, largely Muslim in religion and its largest remaining block of territory in 1901. They sprawled across a large and strategically very important area. From the Caucasus, frontiers with dependent territories and with Persia ran down to the Gulf near Basra, at the mouth of the Tigris. On the southern shore of the Gulf they ran round Kuwait (an independent sheikhdom under British protection) and then back to the coast as far south as Qatar. From there the coasts of Arabia right round to the entrance of the Red Sea were in one way or another under British influence, while the whole interior and the Red Sea coast were in theory Ottoman. Under British pressure the Sinai desert was surrendered to Egypt in 1906, but the ancient lands of Palestine, Syria and Mesopotamia, the heartland of historical Islam, were still ruled by the sultan. Even within this historic Arabic-speaking and Islamic region, though, there were signs well before 1914 that new political forces were at work. Some of these, as in Egypt, stemmed from the western cultural influences which operated in Syria and the Lebanon even more strongly than in Egypt, thanks to American missionary efforts and the foundation of schools and colleges to which there came Arab boys, both Muslim and Christian, from all over the Arab world. The cities of the Levant were culturally advanced and highly literate. On the eve of the world war over 100 Arabic newspapers were published in the Ottoman empire outside Egypt.

Something of a political crystallization of opposition to Ottoman rule followed when the Young Turks came to power in Constantinople. Secret societies and groups of dissidents began to form among Arab exiles, notably in Cairo. In the background was another uncertain factor: the rulers of the Arabian Peninsula, whose allegiance to the sultan was shaky. The most important of them was Hussein, sherif of Mecca: by 1914 the Istanbul government had no confidence in him. A year earlier, there had been an ominous meeting of Arabs in Persia to consider the possible independence of Iraq. The Turks could really only hope that the divisiveness of the different interests represented among the Arabs would help to ensure the status quo.

Although they did not present an immediate danger, one other significant community of new converts to the religion of nationalism was about to step on to the Near Eastern stage. The history of the Jews had taken a new turn in 1897. A Zionist Congress had then been set up whose aim was the establishment of a national home for Jews. In the long history of Jewry in Europe assimilation had usually been the goal of Jewish leaders since the liberating years of the French Revolution. Yet real assimilation was still largely unachieved in some countries, notably the Dual Monarchy and Russia. It was now to be replaced as an ideal by that of territorial nationalism. The desirable location for a Jewish state had not at once been clear; Argentina, Uganda and Madagascar were all suggested at different times, but by the end of the century Zionist opinion had come to rest finally on Palestine. Jewish immigration to it had begun before 1914, though still on a small scale. About 85,000 Jews lived there in that year.

A curious parallel existed between the Ottoman and Habsburg empires in 1914. Their rulers, in each case, in the end came to see war as a possible solution to their problems, yet both contained too many people inside and outside their borders who would see in war an opportunity to bring these empires down. Moreover, the Russians, historic enemies of the Ottomans, had been held in check in the past only by the long resistance of the British and French to the establishment of tsarist power at the Straits of Constantinople; now, though, France and Russia were allied and Great Britain had an *entente* with the first. The French would have their own Middle Eastern fish to fry, too, if war broke out. Evocations of St Louis and the crusaders with which some enthusiasts made play need not be taken too seriously, but undeniably, French governments had for 100 years claimed and exercised (with the acquiescence of other powers) a special interest in the protection of Catholics in the Ottoman empire. It was clear by 1914 that both they and the British would now have to take account as never before of autonomous forces in the area.

NEW ACTORS IN THE IMPERIAL DRAMA

Two themes dominate what would within a few years prove only too evidently to have been the last of European world supremacy. The first is the dialectical interplay of western imperialism and the forces which were undermining it. In Asia, that would be evident by 1914: non-western peoples were beginning their schooling in nationalist thinking and were being encouraged in aspirations to modernization, with all its inevitable dislocations. By 1914, British governments had already set out on a road leading away from post-Mutiny despotism towards effective representation of Indians in government. By their alliance with Japan, too, the British had conceded implicitly that they could not single-handed sustain their empire in Asia in all circumstances. Such signs were portentous: as were events within China, or, very differently, in Japan, or in the other European empires in Asia. In North Africa and the Middle East, similar processes were at work, but as yet much less evidently.

The second was the degree to which the timing and chronology of imperial decline was shaped almost incidentally by the relations of the European powers with one another. In the nineteenth century, their rivalries (and others with the United States, too) had fuelled the scramble in China, and first alarmed and then tempted the Japanese. The Anglo-Japanese alliance had assured Japan's rulers that they could strike at their great enemy, Russia, and would find her unsupported. A few years later and Japan and China would be looking to gain advantages by participating in an essentially European quarrel. Meanwhile, Japan's example and, above all, its victory over Russia, were inspiring other Asians; they had been given serious grounds to ponder whether European rule was bound to be their lot. In 1905 an American scholar could already speak of the Japanese as the 'peers of western peoples';[16] what they had done, by turning Europe's skills and ideas against her, might not other Asians or Arabs do in their turn? In the perspective of world history, white domination was to turn out to have been only briefly unchallengeable and unchallenged.

[16] See the *American Journal of Sociology*, xi (1905–6), p.335.

8

The Great War and the Beginning of the Twentieth-century Revolution

THE LAST CRISIS

As 1914 began, the Russian foreign ministry was less concerned with the Balkans than with the Straits. The old rivalry with the Dual Monarchy had again receded somewhat. German influence was clearly dominant at Constantinople, though. She alone among the great powers had never taken an inch of former Ottoman territory. In 1913 a German general was appointed to command the Ottoman forces at the Straits; a German military mission had by then reorganized the Ottoman army. German investment and mercantile interests were active and successful.

By then, too, German official opinion was broadly accepting the inevitability of war with Russia. This gave even greater importance in German eyes to the old ally, the Dual Monarchy. At the very least the long Habsburg frontiers would pin down large Russian forces in the event of a war. Germany's leaders had done nothing, therefore, to restrain Vienna from confrontation with Russia. On the contrary, they had encouraged Austrian irritation with Serbia and applauded the determination to crush her. Such support, it was hoped, would ensure the Dual Monarchy's presence at Germany's side in the anticipated conflict with France and Russia. Of course, by itself this still did not make a great European war inevitable, nor settle when it was to be. Neither Germany nor any other power wanted a war unless they could win it. But if any local conflict were actually to begin, then the nature of earlier military planning made the involvement of at least four of the great powers likely and there were plenty of dangerous materials lying about.

As late as June 1914, indeed, they were still being added to. Magyar government of the Hungarian lands continued to worry Vienna. Not only were there many discontented Slavs in the Kingdom of Hungary, but there were 3 million or so possibly discontented Romanians. Hungarian leaders had been courting them half-heartedly and unsuccessfully for a couple of years when a Russian minister on a visit to Romania ostentatiously crossed the frontier to Transylvania to see how these subjects of the Dual Monarchy lived.[1] There was much alarm in Budapest and Vienna. The planning of a visit of the heir-apparent, the Archduke Franz Ferdinand, to Sarajevo, the Bosnian capital, accordingly went ahead against the background of heightened feeling in both capitals that Serbia and Romania should both in some way be shown the danger of backing irredentist movements inside the Monarchy. Paradoxically, the Archduke was believed to be an advocate of conciliatory policies towards both its Slav and its Romanian subjects.

On 28 June, when the visit had barely begun, the Archduke and his wife were both shot dead by a young Bosnian Serb terrorist. The circumstances were strange. The assassin was one of a gang of conspirators who had failed earlier that day to carry out the deed in the manner they had planned (with a bomb); it was pure accident that he suddenly found himself able to remedy that failure when the Archduke's car drew up in front of the café at which he sat and presented him with (literally) a sitting target. At that moment, hardly a diplomat in Europe could have anticipated the consequences of the murder, but it was at once felt in Vienna that the moment had come for a reckoning. Serbian agents were presumed to be behind the affair and in touch with the terrorists (as indeed some were, though not necessarily with the authorization of the Serbian government). Counsels of prudence were silenced when enthusiastic German support was at once forthcoming for an ultimatum to Belgrade (characteristically, Wilhelm II and his chancellor offered this support without consulting the German foreign minister). It was hoped that Russia would feel unable to support her Slav brothers and (as in 1909) would accept the outcome.

[1] See K. Hitchins, *Rumania 1866–1947* (Oxford, 1994), pp.215–30, for the complex background to this story and A. J. P. Taylor, *The Struggle for Mastery in Europe*, p.517, for Romania's diplomatic position in July 1914.

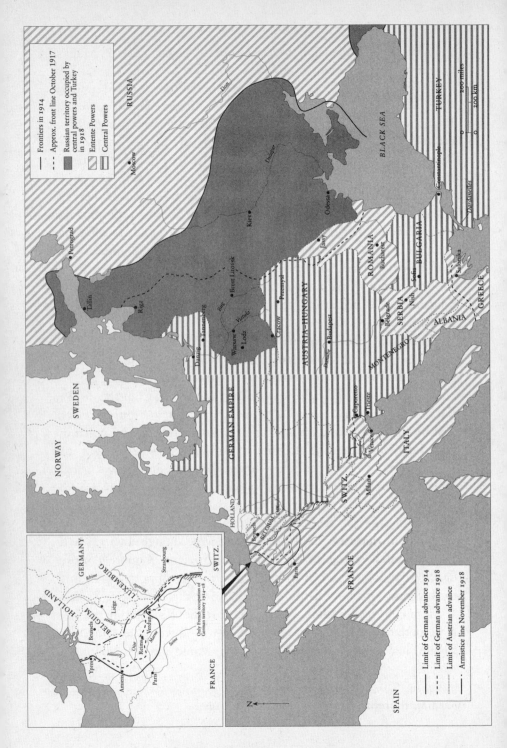

The First World War in Europe

If she did not, though, the German generals were ready to fight at Austria's side the war they had long thought necessary against Russia.

After almost a month, on 23 July the Austrians presented a humiliating ultimatum to Serbia which demanded action against South Slav terrorism on a scale amounting to detailed intervention in Serbia's internal government. Russia advised the Serbs not to resist; Great Britain had offered to act as a go-between. Serbia accepted almost all of the terms. Without waiting, though, for further clarification, the Dual Monarchy, determined now to crush Serbia once and for all, declared war on her on 28 July.

German encouragement to the Austrians had produced this outcome. Yet it was still not clear who would join in the war or what would follow. German military planning had always taken it for granted that if Germany went to war with Russia, the Franco-Russian alliance would operate sooner or later. The German generals had drawn from this assumption the logical conclusion that if Germany had to fight on two fronts, it would be desirable to overthrow France before Russia's slow mobilization could provide effective help to her ally. In the east, space and Russia's administrative and material backwardness would for a time favour Germany. The man who was chief of the German general staff from 1891 to 1905, Schlieffen, had planned, therefore, an immediate sweep into France with the aim of defeating her even more quickly than in 1870. But this required a huge outflanking movement through Belgium, whose neutrality was under international guarantee. This raised the possibility of a British intervention to defend Belgian neutrality. The 'Schlieffen Plan' accepted this danger, and with it the German general staff had therefore accepted the risk of a widening of the war. The plan and its strategy had never come before (let alone been considered by) civilian ministers.

Once the Austrians had declared war on Serbia, Russian mobilization began. It was at first deliberately restrained; only those armies which might be needed to intervene against the Dual Monarchy were to be put on a war footing. Even with this self-imposed handicap, though, it was too much for Berlin, from which came a menacing message to the Russian foreign minister: this had the effect only of stiffening Russian resolve. Full Russian mobilization was resumed. German mobilization was ordered on 31 July and on the following day Germany declared war on Russia – at a moment when her ally Austria–Hungary was not at war with Russia, but only with Serbia. The German government asked France for a declaration of neutrality. The reply was considered insufficiently provocative; an alleged French air raid on Nuremberg was therefore said to justify a German declaration of war on France on 3 August. Germany was now at war – on her own initiative – with two great powers, Austria–Hungary still with none. Great Britain at once warned Germany that naval operations in the Channel against France would not be permitted, but that was all. Though many thought that the country should go further in standing up to Germany, many did not and the French, expecting more of the *entente*, were dismayed. A German ultimatum to Belgium on 3 August, demanding unobstructed passage for her armies across that country, resolved the British government's difficulty. On the following day, it demanded that Belgian neutrality, of which Great Britain was a guarantor, be respected by Germany. This was ignored and a British declaration of war on Germany followed on 4 August. Thus Germany acquired a third great power as an antagonist. Austria–Hungary still had none at war with her.

Tragic though this sequence of events was, it was rich in paradoxes. The Franco-Russian alliance had never come into effect after all; the Germans had declared war on France before it could do so. The British on 4 August still had no obligations under treaty to France or Russia, whatever may be thought to have been their moral commitment to the first. The Anglo-French military conversations had only been given reality by German military planning, which offered the British government a chance to enter the war without serious division and at the head (in so far as these things are ever possible) of a united public opinion, in defence of international law and the rights of small nations. These were grounds wholly irrelevant to the antagonisms that so often in the past had seemed to bedevil the possibility of friendship between England and Germany, and were in no way connected with formal alliances. Finally, the central issue of so much worried diplomacy in the last decade and more, Austro-Russian rivalry, had almost dropped out of sight as the final crisis unrolled. It was not until 6 August that a declaration of war on Russia at last came from Vienna. Six days later the British and French went to war against the Dual Monarchy too.

THE END OF AN AGE

The Great War had been made in Berlin and was to be the first of two twentieth-century wars about German power in Europe. The huge damage done by these two German wars contributed decisively to the ending of Europe's political, economic and military supremacy.[2] Each of them began over what was essentially a European question, and the first always had a predominantly European flavour; though it sucked into itself other conflicts and jumbled together many issues, Europe was the heart of it. In the end, self-inflicted damage would deprive her of her world hegemony. This was still not completely accomplished when the Great War ended and would become undeniable only in 1945, at the end of a Second World War that was, so far as Europe was concerned, the second German war. Considered in that longer perspective, to speak of the years from 1914 to 1945, as a whole, as a European 'civil war' is not a bad metaphor, provided we bear in mind that it is no more than that. The containment of internal disorder is the fundamental presupposition of government: Europe had never achieved that and could not therefore have a true civil war. Nor had she ever for long been wholly free from war. Even during the long peace between her great powers before 1914 there had been plenty of intermittent fighting in the Balkans. But the continent was the source and seat of a civilization that could be envisaged as a unity. Whether through simple ignorance and prejudice, or in the case of more educated Europeans, through awareness of cultural realities, Europeans thought they had more in common with other Europeans (and with European peoples overseas) than with black, brown or yellow peoples. Europe's member states were tied together, too, in a measure of economic interdependence. Such facts (all of which were to vanish by 1945) make the metaphor of civil war both vivid and acceptable. Their disappearance signifies the self-destruction of a civilization and the coming of a revolution in world affairs.

That revolution, taking more than thirty years to be completed,

[2] Of course, other names can be, and have been, given to the first German war. It might be called the Third Balkan war, or counted as yet another of the long series of wars of the Ottoman succession.

closed the historical era in which European history had been an identifiable and autonomous subject, and that is why, though only a few guessed it at the time, 1914 remains a marker in world history. What began then was to change the destinies of peoples far away from the European battlefields where the war was to be fought most bloodily. It would sweep away the European system of power that had been the basis of international order in 1901, a gigantic historical change. The whole process was ragged and untidy, revolutionary not merely in its transformations of politics and society, but in the upheavals in ideas and even personal behaviour that it brought about, too. Paradoxically, while the twentieth century has been notable for wider and wider, and more and more enthusiastic adoption of European ideas, institutions and standards in the non-European parts of the world, at the same time it deprived Europeans of confidence in much which lay at the very roots of their civilization. In these huge transformations, some of whose origins lie very deep indeed, what came to be called the 'Great War' was a major catalyst. It was the bloodiest, most intensely fought, and most costly struggle that had ever taken place. These uniquenesses explain its other striking features, its unprecedented psychological and cultural effects, as well as its name.

THE GREAT WAR

Those uniquenesses and effects were not totally unanticipated, even if only very few people had glimpsed any of them. Yet it is still striking and puzzling to read of the enthusiasm that accompanied the declarations of war in so many European capitals. Criticisms of what rulers had or had not done and warnings of what was to come were drowned in the cheering of the crowds that engulfed the newly mobilized reservists as they marched to their railway stations to entrain for the front. Hindsight is again a handicap to understanding. Sheer ignorance of what was to come was the deepest of the negative forces at work. But there were others, some much more positive in their effect. Europe had, after all, been prepared for war by the first age of mass education and literacy, by the first mass newspapers, and by decades of the propagation of ideals of patriotism. When it started, the Great War, which was to reveal itself as the most democratic in history in its nature, may well also have been the most popular ever. Nor was it only a matter of popular delusion. In every country there were members of the ruling classes and directing élites who welcomed the prospect of final solutions to old problems, and who responded to the 'strange temper in the air' noted by the British minister Winston Churchill.[3] A German politician, even from the sad vantage-point of 1918, recalled the first weeks of the war as 'great and unforgettable'; the moment was for him a 'ringing opening chord for an immortal song of sacrifice, loyalty and heroism'.[4] Such sentiment swept across political divisions, engulfing left and right alike. One socialist minister resigned from the British government, but the Serbian and Russian parliamentary socialist parties were the only ones to vote against the war credits asked for by their governments. Even before that, in 1913, the German socialists had been unable to prevent the passing by the Reichstag of a huge increase in the military budget, while their French comrades had not been able to stop an extension of the obligatory period of military service. The news of Russian mobilization swept away the last hesitations and restraints on the patriotism of the German SPD; the old myth of the Teuton–Slav cultural confrontation was too strong for the international ties of the working class to hold (and, anyway, Marxist doctrine provided sophistries that could justify a war against the tsar).[5] The socialists, too, usually shared the assumption that another short, sharp struggle of a familiar type lay ahead.

In its scale and the way it was fought, though, the war begun in 1914 was to be different from anything anyone had experienced before. It lasted over four years. This itself was unusual and unexpected, but not without precedent. There had been even longer wars in earlier centuries. Yet they had not been wars of such continuous and such

---

[3] W. S. Churchill, *The World Crisis*, I (London, 1923), p.188.

[4] Walter Rathenau, q. in James Joll, *Three Intellectuals in Politics* (New York, 1960), p.90.

[5] 'The overthrow of Tsarist Russia, the elimination of the Russian empire, is . . . one of the first conditions of the German proletariat's ultimate triumph,' Engels had written in 1875. See *Karl Marx, Friedrich Engels. Collected Works*, Vol. 24 (London, 1989), p.103.

intense fighting. The longest of them had been wars of relatively short campaigns with long pauses while armies rested and drew breath and the Franco-Prussian war of 1870–71, the last between European great powers, had lasted only a few months. The South African war had been drawn out for two and a half years, but its closing fifteen months or so, though expensive, were of low-intensity guerrilla and anti-guerrilla operations. Only the American Civil War had remotely prefigured the Great War, in which millions of men faced one another day after day, year after year, striving to grind their enemies into submission.

Nor was this new intensity of conflict confined to land. From the start the struggle at sea was fierce and became fiercer as each side tried to starve the other by blockade. The air, too, became a true place of battle, though it was not the first time aeroplanes had been used in war. Early in 1911 an American pilot had made a reconnaissance flight over a besieged Mexico City and later that year aircraft appeared over the battlefield in Tripoli when they were used by the Italians to drop bombs. Balloons had first been employed for observation over a century before, by the French in the Revolutionary wars, but in 1914 for the first time the skies became a zone of combat.[6] Almost at once, aircraft were being used for reconnaissance and to carry war to targets behind the enemy's lines. A few clear-sighted people had seen that this might happen, but the scale and rapidity of the change was striking. In 1914 the major combatants each had a little over 100 aeroplanes at their disposal; by the end of the war these puny forces had become huge. The British Royal Flying Corps had been set up only in 1912; its successor, the Royal Air Force, had over 20,000 machines in 1918.

This was only one sign of the new importance of technology in war. In the nineteenth century railways had moved and supplied bigger armies than ever before. Huge numbers now intensified logistical

[6] C. F. Snowden Gamble, *The Air Weapon* (Oxford, 1931), p.138. It appears that the first aerial combat took place in 1914 over the Chinese port of Tsingtao, when pistol shots were exchanged between Japanese aircraft and the only German machine in the area. Air operations over Tsingtao subsequently included also the first night-bombing. For further details, see C. B. Burdick, *The Japanese Siege of Tsingtau. World War I in Asia* (Hamden, Conn., 1976), pp.132, 160–61.

needs. Traction on the battlefield itself was transformed. A few steam tractors had lumbered about the veldt dragging supply-wagons and guns for the British army in the South African war. By 1914 robust petrol-driven engines were available in quantity and four years later, trucks and tractors were as important as horses to the soldiers in the field. As for weapons, they improved terrifyingly in four years, though ordinary firearms had already been brought to high perfection by 1914. The ordinary British infantryman then already had a rifle with which he could hit a man-sized target at ranges of up to half a mile, its sights graduated up to 2,000 yards. But by then, too, infantry in most armies were already supported by machine-guns firing 600 rounds a minute, field guns firing three or four times a minute at ranges of 10,000 yards or so, heavier guns which enlarged the battlefield by bombarding targets six or seven miles away, and a few monsters capable of even greater range.

Such refinements (if that is the word) led to another revolutionary change of scale: slaughter more terrible than ever expected. No one has ever exactly computed the numbers of killed and wounded, but in proportion to the numbers of total populations and combatants they were colossal; once more, they had been anticipated only in the American Civil War. For four years, about 5,000 men died on average every day, most from wounds inflicted by shellfire. In only one paradoxical way could this balance sheet be read with anything but horror; for the first time since reliable records were available, most of the military casualties of the war were being caused by direct enemy action. In all previous wars the worst killer had been not the other side, but disease. Large numbers of men, cramped together in makeshift conditions, with temporary sanitation, probably contaminated water supplies and little fresh food, had always presented ideal conditions for epidemics of dysentery, cholera, smallpox, typhus. Sickness had killed three times more British soldiers than the Boers had done between 1899 and 1902. Armies had better health records in the Great War, not just because the treatment of sickness itself had improved, but because more was known about prevention, and because industrial societies could feed, supply and maintain huge numbers in the field better than their predecessors. This did not help civilians much, it is true. Even outside the battle zones, they suffered heavily. Poorer feeding and disease became more common as the war went on and each side tried to starve the other into surrender. Children and old people were notably less able to stand up to under-nourishment and sickness than the armies, composed for the most part of men in the prime of life. Where, too, conditions were more primitive and the resources of modern societies were not available to support the armies, the old wartime killers were at work as for centuries past. Serbia, the country over which, ostensibly, Europe went to war, in the end lost a quarter of her 1914 population, the highest proportionate loss of any participant.

Just as the war soon outran all expectations in its duration and intensity, so it did in its geographical spread. Japan and the Ottoman empire joined in soon after the outbreak; the former on the side of the Allies or, as they were sometimes called, the 'Entente' (France, Great Britain, Belgium, Serbia and Russia) and Turkey on that of the Central Powers (Germany and Austria–Hungary). The years 1915 and 1916 brought anxious searchings for new allies. Italy did not join her Triple Alliance partners but in 1915 plumped for the Allied side in return for promises of Austrian and Ottoman territory. Other efforts were made to pick up new supporters with post-dated cheques to be cashed after a victorious peace; on that basis Bulgaria joined the Central Powers in September 1915 and Romania the Allies in the following year. Greece followed Romania in 1917. Portugal's government had talked of entering the war in 1914, but internal political troubles supervened. She was finally faced with a German declaration of war in 1916, after her government had requisitioned German ships then in Portuguese harbours. In Europe, only Spain, Switzerland, the Netherlands and the Scandinavian countries remained neutral throughout the struggle.

Thus, the issues of Franco-German and Austro-Russian rivalry came to be mixed up in other struggles. In south-eastern Europe the Balkan nations were fighting again over the Ottoman succession in Europe. The British, some argued, had used the excuse of the violation of Belgian neutrality to fight a war they had long desired against German naval and commercial power. Many Italians believed they were fighting the last war of the *Risorgimento* and a crusade to evict Austria from the unredeemed soil inhabited by those of Italian descent or speech; others thought there would be spoils going and that Italy should have a share of them. Outside Europe, the British, French, Russians and Arabs all came in the end to be engaged in a war of Ottoman partition in the Near East while the Japanese seized an opportunity to take another, smaller-scale, but cheap and highly profitable step in the assertion of their power over China. Even the Chinese republican government joined in the war, though in the hope rather than the certainty of a profitable outcome. Finally, in 1917 when the United States became an 'associated power' of the Allies, the war truly became worldwide.

The war had quickly shown every sign of bogging down in an unexpected stalemate, once the German sweep into northern France failed to achieve the lightning victory that had been its aim. It could be argued that with that failure Germany had lost the war, for she had disposed of neither France nor Russia, and now had to face an unanticipated enemy in Great Britain. She nonetheless held all but a tiny scrap of Belgium, and much French territory besides; victory for the Allies would have to mean at least the recovery of those areas. In the east, the Central Powers had stopped the initial Russian offensives. Thereafter, though more noticeably in the west than the east, the battlefields settled down to siege warfare on an unprecedented scale.

Military operations were dominated by two facts. One was the huge killing-power of modern weapons; small-arms fire and barbed wire could by themselves stop any infantry attack not preceded by pulverizing bombardment. When human targets were not visible, they were nonetheless open to destruction by the formidable power of modern artillery. Huge casualty lists showed it. By the end of 1915 the French army alone had lost 300,000 dead; a seven-month battle before Verdun in the following year added another 315,000 to this total. In the same battle 280,000 Germans died. While it was going on, another prolonged struggle further north, on the Somme, produced a bloodletting that has never been exactly computed. Yet it is clear that it cost the British 420,000 casualties, the Germans about the same, and the French about half that number, while the first day of that battle, 1 July 1916, remains the most tragic in the history of the British army. At that time still a wholly volunteer force, it suffered in a few hours 60,000 casualties, of whom more than a third were killed.

However weary of war their peoples were by the end of 1916,

though, the combatant nations amply demonstrated a capacity far greater than had been imagined not merely to kill and incapacitate their enemies but to conscript and organize their peoples to endure. Alone among the European great powers, the United Kingdom had not had a conscript army before the outbreak of the war, but in 1916 her government imposed conscription (outside Ireland, where it was not applied until April 1918), a step which had a revolutionary impact on the British political system and national psychology. The armies of all the great powers had larger needs of material, too, than ever before. Boots, uniforms, mess tins, water bottles, barbed wire, timber for building, picks, spades and shovels, cooking utensils, sandbags and sacks – all were needed on a scale unimaginable a few years earlier. Though millions of animals – horses, mules, carrier pigeons and even dogs – were employed by the armies, trucks and tractors swallowed fuel as avidly as the larger animals swallowed vast quantities of fodder. Of weapons and ammunition, there seemed never to be enough. The demand was enormous: in 1914 the establishment of a British infantry battalion provided it with two machine-guns; a few years later it had over fifty, and that meant, of course, an enormous and wholly unanticipated increase in the use of small arms ammunition. As for artillery, this used shells at a rate that in the first year of war left supplies far behind. When enough became available, colossal bombardments took place; that before the battle of the Somme was delivered for seven days by nearly 2,000 guns on a ten-mile front, and the cannonade was heard on Hampstead Heath, 300 miles away. Even this, though, was surpassed by the fire of 6,000 guns on a forty-mile front that opened the final German offensive in 1918.

Economic organization on the scale needed to supply such extravagance made nonsense of the once-cherished belief that long wars were economically unendurable, though there had been little planning for it. On the eve of war, Germany had still been exporting grain; she had no food regulations or plans for the management of industry. 'Even our ammunition was not planned for a large-scale war,' said one German politician of the country with the most admired military leadership in Europe.[7] Two years later, whole industrial societies were

[7] Friedrich Naumann, quoted in Henry Cord Meyer, *Mitteleuropa in German Thought and Action 1815–1945* (The Hague, 1955), p.123.

engaged against one another, their lives organized for war virtually from top to bottom. The international solidarity of the working class might never have been dreamed of; unions and socialist parties could not resist the mobilization of war-making power by the state. Nor, though, did the common interest of the ruling classes in holding revolution at bay assert itself.

Inability to batter one another into submission on the battlefields thus led diplomats to seek new allies and generals to seek new fronts. Turkish participation in the war had enormously enlarged the potential theatre of strategic operations. The Allies in 1915 mounted an attack at the Dardanelles in the hope, not to be realized, of knocking the Ottoman empire out of the war and opening up communication with Russia through the Black Sea. The same search for a way round the deadlock in France later produced a Balkan front at Salonika to replace that which had collapsed when Serbia was overrun in the first weeks of 1916, and in the same year Romanian entry to the war on the Allied side held out for a moment the prospect of a successful invasion of Transylvania, but then gave way to defeat at the hands of the Central Powers, who occupied Bucharest and were henceforth able to tap new resources of wheat and oil.

Colonial possessions, too, meant there was fighting all round the globe, even if much of it was on a small scale. Most of the German colonies could be picked up fairly easily, thanks to the British command of the seas, though those in East Africa required lengthy campaigning. The most important and considerable extra-European operations, though, were in the east and to the south of the Ottoman empire. The Russians threatened it in the Caucasus and Armenia. A British and Indian army landed at Basra in 1914 to safeguard oil supplies from Persia (the Royal Navy's new capital ships were by now all being built with oil-fuelled engines), while another force advanced from the Suez Canal towards Palestine. In the deserts of Hejaz, the beginnings of an Arab revolt against Ottoman rule appeared to provide some of the few colourful episodes with which journalism could relieve the brutal squalor of the war in Europe.

THE CHANGING WORLD

The mills, factories, mines and furnaces of Europe worked as never before. So did those of the United States and Japan, the former (until it entered the war) accessible to the Allies but not to the Central Powers, thanks to British naval supremacy. This helped to bring about one of the earliest of the many distortions and disruptions of the pre-war world trading system as old economic relationships between countries were transformed. The United States ceased to be a debtor nation as the Allies sold their transatlantic investments to pay for what they needed and became debtors in their turn. British exports halved in value during the war, and German overseas exports all but evaporated, but Indian industry received the fillip it had long required and that of Japan and China prospered. The war brought boom years to the ranches and farms of Argentina and the British dominions. The repercussions of the vast increase in demand rolled through society in other ways, too. They led everywhere in Europe in some measure to greater government attempts to achieve control of materials, production and conscription of labour, to a transformation of the ideas and reality of women's employment, to the introduction of new health and welfare services to support the industrial worker and the soldiers' families. As for the movement of manpower, the Allies brought hundreds of thousands of soldiers to Europe and the Near East from the British dominions, India and the French colonies, while other British imperial forces fought the Germans in their colonies. The South African government also had to suppress a rebellion against the Crown in 1914; they were careful to use Afrikaner, not British, troops to do so. The consciousness of what the war had cost them in blood helped to mature a sense of nationality in Canada, Australia and New Zealand.

Technical advances continued to make war more remorseless and terrible. This was not only because of the scale of slaughter and maiming they permitted nor even because of new horrors such as poison gas,[8] flame-throwers and tanks, all of which made their appear-

[8] Poison gas was first used on the eastern front by the German army at the end of 1914; it was available in huge quantities to both sides by 1918.

ance on the battlefield as the soldiers strove to find a way out of the deadlock of barbed-wire and machine-guns. It was also because the fact that whole societies were engaged in warfare made all their members targets for warlike operations. In this sense, the assumptions of civilized warfare that civilians might only accidentally or in areas of guerrilla warfare be submitted to the full force of conflict was fatally undermined. Increasing desperation brought the launch of what was later called 'total' war. Previously unimaginable attacks on the morale, health and efficiency of civilian workers and voters were now possible, and became desirable or necessary, according to your point of view. When such attacks were denounced, the denunciations themselves became blows in propaganda campaigns aimed at civilian and neutral audiences. The possibilities presented by mass literacy and the recently created cinema industry supplemented and overtook such old standbys as pulpit and school in this kind of warfare. To British charges that the Germans who carried out primitive bombing raids on London were 'baby-killers', Germans looking at the rising figures of infant mortality could retort that so were the sailors who sustained the British blockade.

At the end of 1916, after failing to win the summer's battles in France, with Russia still in the field against them in the east, and after strategic defeat (in spite of inflicting heavier losses on the British than those sustained by the German fleet) in the greatest naval action of the war,[9] the German High Command concluded that Germany would lose the war because of the British blockade, if something were not done quickly. Famine in the Balkans might be ignored, but there were people starving in the suburbs of Vienna, German city-dwellers were hard pressed and food riots and strikes were becoming more frequent. German infant mortality was rising towards a level 50 per cent higher than that of the previous year. The French had by then suffered 3,350,000 casualties in the field, and the British over a million; on the other side, German casualties were nearly 2.5 million. There was no reason to suppose that the German army, still divided between east and west in the war on two fronts the Schlieffen plan had been meant to avoid, would be any more likely to achieve a knockout than had

[9] The battle of Jutland, 31 May – 1 June 1916.

been the British and French, though it was more favourably placed to fight on the defensive than they, given the lie of the land and the extent of its occupancy of enemy territory.

Unwilling to risk again the German battle fleet whose building had done so much to poison pre-war feeling between the Germans and British, the German High Command now decided to employ in a new way the submarine, a weapon whose possibilities had hardly been glimpsed in 1914.[10] Given that attacks could be made without warning and on unarmed vessels, a submarine offensive might be launched not only at Allied shipping but also against that of neutrals who were supplying the Allies, with the aim of starving Great Britain out of the war. Unrestricted submarine warfare had first been attempted as early as 1915, but few submarines were then available and they did not do much damage. There had been a great outcry when a British liner was torpedoed that year, with the loss of 1,200 lives, 128 of them Americans. The campaign had then been called off by the Germans in the interests of diplomatic relations with the greatest of the neutral countries. But in October 1916, more desperate counsels prevailed. Against the wishes of Bethmann-Hollweg, the German chancellor, a resolution of the finance committee of the Reichstag approved the introduction of unrestricted submarine warfare whenever the High Command thought it fit.

1917

The actual decision was forced on the chancellor in January 1917 by the High Command. It was likely to bring about a truly revolutionary transformation of the war, by causing the entry into it of the United States. The German generals knew this to be almost certain, but gambled on bringing Great Britain to her knees – and thus forcing France to give in – before American numbers could be decisive. For a couple of months it looked as if they might be right. American opinion, favouring neither one side nor the other in 1914, had come

---

[10] Though the first successful attack by submarine on a surface vessel had been made as long ago as 1777.

a long way since then, though. Allied propaganda and purchases had helped; so did the borrowing of money by the combatant powers, the Allies taking the overwhelming majority of the loans made.[11] The early German submarine campaign of 1915 had a notable effect on some Americans' views. President Wilson might suspect (and certainly did not approve) the war aims of both sides, but he was clear that what he called 'Prussian militarism' presented greater risks to a civilized post-war world than a British or French victory (though that made many of his countrymen suspicious that he might lead them into war). Nonetheless, Wilson campaigned to be re-elected in 1916 with the slogan 'He kept us out of war' in what was arguably the first American presidential election since 1860 to be of world historical importance. He was helped to victory by southern and western voters attracted by a broadly Progressive programme, and almost at once invited the belligerent powers to set out terms for a peace that they would see as satisfactory. When this proved fruitless, Wilson's next step would be to formulate 'Fourteen Points' on which a 'peace between equals' could be established with American cooperation. By then, though, the United States was at war.

On 31 January the American government was informed by Germany that from the following day unrestricted submarine warfare – the sinking at sight of all merchant vessels within a zone around the British Isles and in the Mediterranean – would begin. Diplomatic relations were at once broken off by Washington. The German decision was a direct threat to American interests and the safety of her citizens. When it was also revealed to the American government by British signals interception that Germany had been hoping secretly to negotiate an alliance with Mexico and Japan against the United States, the hostility aroused by the submarines was confirmed. Soon, a number of American ships were sunk without warning. On 6 April 1917 the United States declared war on Germany. The Allies could now be sure of eventual victory, if they could hold on long enough for the as yet unformed American armies to reach France.

The impossibility of breaking the European deadlock by means

---

[11] By Easter 1917 Allied governments had borrowed $2,000,000,000 in the United States, as against only $27,000,000 borrowed by the Central Powers.

short of total war had sucked the New World into the quarrels of the Old, almost against its will. For the first time since the Ottoman onslaught of the sixteenth century, Europe now faced a settlement of its fate by non-European power. Immediately, though, the Allies faced a gloomy year; the rest of 1917 was even blacker for Great Britain and France than 1916 had been. Not only did the submarine take months to master (by the adoption of convoy at sea, which did not begin until May 1917), but a terrible series of battles in France (usually lumped under the name of an obliterated Flanders village, Passchendaele) inflicted an ineffaceable scar upon the British national consciousness and cost another 300,000 dead and wounded to gain five miles of mud. Worn out by its heroic efforts the year before, the French army meanwhile was undergoing a series of mutinies. Worst of all for the Allies, the Russian empire collapsed.

Both the tsarist monarchy and the regime that followed it were destroyed by war. In the 1905 revolution all the socialist factions had failed and as 1917 began Lenin, the leader of the Bolshevik socialists (then in exile in Switzerland), had said that his generation would not live to see revolution in Russia, much as he, like many another European socialist, had hoped the war would bring one about. By then, though, the tsarist regime was mortally wounded. The German armies were the real makers of a revolution that erupted in February 1917.[12] The fighting had in the end broken the hearts of even the long-enduring Russian soldiers. The Russian army had shot its bolt in a final great offensive against the Austrians in 1916. It lacked supplies and weapons to do more, while soldiers' families were starving at home because of the breakdown of Russian transport. The Allies had only been able to help Russia in a small measure through Arctic ports frozen for much of the year, or through Vladivostok, 6,000 miles from the front line and connected to it only by (for the most part) a single-track railway line. Mismanaged conscription had taken skilled workers from Russian industry (and, in any case, much of Russian industry was located in Russian Poland – the major battle zone). Over

[12] Until 13 February 1918 the Russian (Julian) calendar was thirteen days behind the western European (Gregorian) calendar inaugurated in 1582. Hence the 'February' revolution (25–28 February) occurred, in contemporary Russian style, 10–13 March.

this disaster ruled an incompetent and corrupt government that, as 1917 opened, still feared constitutionalism and liberalism as much as it feared defeat.

By then even its security forces could no longer be depended upon. In February, food riots in Petrograd were followed by mutiny.[13] The autocracy was suddenly seen to be powerless. A provisional government of liberals and socialists was formed and the tsar abdicated; a grand-duke nominated to succeed to the throne declined the position and a provisional government of liberals and socialists took power. It assured the western Allies that it would stand by the treaties made by the tsarist regime but could not. It was attempting the impossible, to keep Russia in the war. Russians wanted peace and bread, as Lenin saw. His determination to seize power from the government added to its problems. Presiding over a disintegrating country, administration and army, still facing the unsolved problems of privation in the cities, it was swept away in a second change, a *coup d'état* carried out by the Bolsheviks, to be remembered as the October Revolution.[14] Together with the American entry into the war this marks 1917 as a watershed between eras. Previously, Europe had settled its own affairs; now this was no longer true. The United States would be bound to have a large say in its future and in Russia there had come into being a state committed by the beliefs of its founders to the destruction of the whole pre-war European, and indeed, world order.

REVOLUTIONARY WAR

The Bolsheviks consolidated their success by dissolving (since they did not control it) the only freely-elected representative body based on universal suffrage Russia was ever to know until 1990 and by

[13] St Petersburg had been renamed Petrograd during the war because of the Germanic flavour of the old name. For similar motives the British royal family took the name 'Windsor' and ceased to be known as the house of Saxony-Coburg-Gotha.
[14] 6–8 November in the then operative Russian style; in the Gregorian style, later adopted by the USSR, the revolution was dated 25–27 October.

bidding for the peasants' loyalties with promises of land and peace.[15] This was essential if they were to survive; the backbone of the party that now strove to assert its authority over Russia was the very small industrial working class of a few cities, exercising its power through the *Soviets* (workers' and soldiers' councils) which were dominated by the Bolsheviks. Only peace could provide a safer and broader foundation. At first the terms demanded by the Germans were thought so objectionable that the Russians broke off negotiation; they had, though, finally to accept an even more punitive outcome, the treaty of Brest-Litovsk, in March 1918. This imposed on them losses of vast tracts of territory which included about a quarter of the population and three-quarters of Russia's coal and metallurgical industries, and an obligation to deliver a million tons of grain a year (it was an indication to the Allies of what a German victory in the war might mean for them). Nonetheless, it gave the new order peace and the time it desperately needed to tackle its internal troubles. It created a new strategic situation, too. The Allies were furious. They had not been against a Russian revolution *per se*, provided Russia kept in the war, but they saw the Bolsheviks' action as a treacherous defection. At first they misunderstood it as the work of German agents, a by no means implausible view; Lenin had been sent back to Russia with German help in 1917, the Germans provided funds to the Bolsheviks as they undermined the provisional government, and were still doing so in 1918. In August that year, in a supplement to Brest-Litovsk (and the first exercise in secret diplomacy by the communists) the Bolsheviks gave the Germans authorization to crush Allied forces in south Russia if they could not do so themselves.

Things were made worse by the revolutionary propaganda soon being directed against their former allies by the new regime. The Russian leaders believed a revolution of the working class was on its way in the advanced capitalist countries. This gave an extra dimension

[15] The 'Constituent Assembly' met on 5 January 1918. The Bolshevik delegates (and some others) withdrew from it the same day, the Assembly adjourned in the early hours of 6 January, was prevented by force from meeting again later that day, and was declared dissolved on 7 January by the 'Soviet Central Executive Committee'. Of its original 707 members, only 175 were Bolsheviks. No other election as free was to be held in Russia for seventy years.

to a series of military 'interventions' in the affairs of Russia mounted by their former allies. Their original purpose had been strategic and non-ideological; they were conceived as a way of stopping the Germans from closing down their eastern front. They were soon interpreted, though, by many people in other countries and by all Bolsheviks as anti-communist crusades. Worse still, Allied forces became entangled in a Russian civil war that seemed likely to destroy the new regime. Even without the doctrinal filter of Marxist theory through which Lenin and his colleagues saw the world, such armed interventions would have been likely to sour relations between Russia and her former allies. To Marxists they seemed to confirm the essential and ineradicable hostility of 'capitalist' states. Myths about intervention were to dog Russian attitudes for the next half-century. They strengthened the case for the new regime's eager recourse to authoritarian government and brutality; fear of the invader as a restorer of the old order and patron of the landlords combined with Russian traditions of autocracy and police terrorism to stifle any liberalization of the regime.

TRIUMPHS OF NATIONALITY

The Bolsheviks seemed to have been prescient: in its last year, the war's revolutionary potential indeed became plain. It had been foreshadowed almost from the start; the Russians were bidding for the support of the Poles with promises of post-war autonomy even in 1914. German encouragement of disaffected Irishmen and of revolutionary Ukrainians, Jews and Finns – as well as of Lenin's followers – provided further indicators. Increasingly, too, the revolutionary potential of the war showed itself in national, not class, forms. To that extent, the Bolsheviks were badly wrong. It was in exploiting nationalism that the Allies became revolutionaries in Europe too (they had been encouraging rebellion against the Ottoman empire long before this), provoked as they were by the bleak military outlook as 1918 began. It was obvious that they would face a German attack in France in the spring with no help from a Russian army to draw off their enemies to the east, and that it would be a long time before American troops could arrive in large numbers to help them. But they had their own revolutionary weapon. In a declaration published in January they appealed to the nationalities of the Austro-Hungarian Empire and in April a 'Congress of Oppressed Austrian Nationalities' opened under this benevolent auspice in Rome. This strategy had considerable success, as well as having the advantage of emphasizing further in American eyes the ideological purity of a cause no longer tied to tsardom. When the Allied governments began to talk about reconstructing post-war Europe in a way that would safeguard the interests of nationalities, their utterances about war aims had become more agreeable to Wilson and to 'hyphenated' Americans.[16] Subversive propaganda was directed at the Austro-Hungarian armies and encouragement was given to Czechs and South Slavs in exile. As a result, well before the nerve of the German generals gave way, the Dual Monarchy was beginning to dissolve as national sentiment swelled among its subject peoples.

The exiled Czechs were the first to benefit. The Italian government in particular was happy to patronize them because any subversion of the Dual Monarchy they might help to bring about was unlikely to queer its pitch over *Italia irredenta*, unlike changes in the Adriatic and South Slav lands in favour of Serbs or Croats which might do so. Italy's was the first government to recognize a new Czechoslovak national council; the British, French and Americans followed suit during the summer. The Czechs also had the valuable asset of actually having an army to contribute to the Allied cause. This was the 'Czech legion', recruited formerly by the imperial Russian government from among their prisoners of war; in 1918 it was inconveniently placed, it is true, in the middle of Russia, but hopes were entertained that a way might soon be found for it to be brought out along the trans-Siberian railway to Vladivostok and eventual deployment on the western front.

Events were soon moving too fast in central Europe for there to be time for this. The long unsuccessful Allied campaign in the Balkans based on Salonika at last began to provide victories. When a last Austrian offensive collapsed in June, the defeat of the Dual Monarchy

[16] Some of the latter, that is; German-Americans responded less warmly than Polish-Americans.

began to come into sight. Efforts were soon made by Vienna to open peace discussions independently of its ally in Berlin. These were rebuffed, but the political structure of the whole area bounded by the Urals, the Baltic and the Danube valley was now in question, as it had not been for centuries. All certainties seemed to be in the melting pot. The Germans had patronized a Polish national army as a weapon against Russia, while the American president had announced even before the American entry to the war that an independent Poland should be a goal in any peacemaking. Multinational empire, already implicitly identified as unjustifiable in the Fourteen Points, was dissolving in the Danube valley under the impact of defeat and revolution, as well as in the former tsarist empire after the Bolshevik seizure of power (though this was to turn out to be only a temporary aberration).

THE OTTOMAN COLLAPSE

Another long familiar issue over which there still hung huge uncertainty as the last year of the war began was that of the oldest of all the empires, the Ottoman. By 1914 it had become predominantly a non-European entity. The empire had entered the war because of Young Turk optimism, the Germans' military and diplomatic influence at Constantinople and the unplanned arrival of a couple of German warships in the Straits in September 1914 which probably tipped the scale in Ottoman official opinion. When these ships took part in a bombardment of some Russian ports the Allies had declared war on the Ottoman government. From this were to flow major upheavals. The Ottoman empire's geographical spread, let alone its military weight, was bound to give it immense strategic significance – not least as an obstacle to Allied communication with Russia through the Black Sea. Once Great Britain was committed she abandoned the last remnants of her historic support for the sultan against Russia. Turning their backs on nearly a century and a half of diplomacy, the British and French joined in secret agreements with Russia that she should have Constantinople and much of eastern Anatolia at the peace. Other allocations of future Ottoman booty followed. French patriots still liked to recall a tradition of a special French role in the Levant, and this offered them some diplomatic leverage. The cultural presence evinced by a wide use of the French language in the Levant, and a large investment of French capital, were also matters not to be overlooked. In 1914, though, the main military antagonists of the Ottoman empire in the field outside Europe were Russia in the Caucasus and Great Britain in the Sinai desert. Defence of the Suez Canal was the bedrock of British strategic thinking about the Near and Middle East, and it soon became clear that it was not in danger from the Turkish army. But there were soon signs that other, new, strategic factors were entering the equations. One was the beginning in Mesopotamia (later called Iraq) of an interplay of oil and politics in the historical destiny of this area, though it would take decades to mature. Fighting began there at the end of 1914 when an Anglo-Indian expedition landed at Basra. Another was a British decision to seek to use Arab nationalism, or what might pass for it.

The attraction of striking at Germany's ally became all the greater as fighting went on bloodily but indecisively in Europe. When the attempt to force the Dardanelles and take Constantinople by combined naval and land operations in 1915 bogged down, some thought that sowing dissidence among Ottoman subjects might be more productive. The duplicities of Russian policy made it impossible to exploit Armenia whose Christian people was left to undergo a calculated attempt to exterminate them by the Young Turk government, an early exercise in what would later be called 'ethnic cleansing'. But there were now Arabs sure that the Turks were alien oppressors, rather than brothers in the faith. There was a limit to what could be offered by the Allies to win new friends in the Near East, and the French had their own fish to fry in Syria. Nevertheless, agreement was eventually reached between Paris and London on spheres of influence in a partitioned Ottoman empire. It left much still undecided for the future, including the future status of Mesopotamia, but settled that there should be an Arab national state, to be set up after the Allies' victory. An Arab nationalist political programme had thus become a reality.

Hussein, sherif of Mecca, with whom the British finally came to an agreement in 1916, had at first demanded independence for all the Arab lands up to about eighty miles north of a line from Aleppo to Mosad – in effect, the whole Ottoman empire in Asia outside Turkey itself and Kurdistan. This had been much too much for the British to take at the gallop. The French had to be consulted and when British and French spheres of influence in a partitioned Ottoman empire were at last agreed, much was still left unsettled about the post-war Arab lands, including the future status of Mesopotamia. Meanwhile, a revolt in the Hejaz had begun in June 1916 with an attack on the Turkish garrison of Medina. It was never meant to be more than a distraction (a 'side-show' was the expression then in vogue) but it prospered as a symbol and became a legend. Soon the British felt they must take the Arabs more seriously; Hussein was recognized as 'king' of the Hejaz. In 1917, British, Australian and Indian forces began to defeat the Ottoman armies and pressed forward into Palestine, taking Jerusalem. In the following year they were to enter Damascus, together with Hussein's forces. Before this, though, other events had further complicated the situation.

One was the American entry into the war, following which the Fourteen Points had spoken of the United States favouring 'an absolutely unmolested opportunity of autonomous development' for the non-Turks of the Ottoman empire.[17] The other was the Bolshevik publication of their predecessors' secret diplomacy early in 1918, which revealed the Anglo-French proposals for spheres of influence and the concessions to Russia that they involved. Another part of those proposals had been that Palestine should be administered internationally; that cut across Arab expectations.[18] A still fiercer irritant to Arab feeling, though, had been a third fact: a unilateral British announcement in 1917 that British policy favoured the establishment of a national home in Palestine for the Jewish people. This 'Balfour Declaration' was not strictly incompatible with what had been said to the Arabs (and President Wilson had joined in the good work of obfuscation by qualifying it with proposals to protect Palestinians who were not Jews), yet it is almost inconceivable that it could ever have operated unchallenged. In due course, further British and French

---

[17] *Speeches and Documents in American History*, ed. R. Birley, IV, *1914–1939* (Oxford, 1942), p.41.
[18] The main texts published by the Bolsheviks were re-published in English in April 1918 by a political movement, the Union of Democratic Control, after first being published in a newspaper, the *Manchester Guardian*, and so given wide circulation.

expressions of goodwill towards Arab aspirations followed in 1918. Nonetheless, the declaration can be accounted Zionism's greatest political success down to this time. On the morrow of Turkish defeat, the outlook was thoroughly confused. Once again, the old and protean 'Eastern Question' was taking a new shape.

THE END OF THE FIRST GERMAN WAR

The last crucial battles in France were thus fought out against a revolutionary and increasingly portentous world background. Even in 1917, it had been clear to some that the tide was now running against Germany; the question whether she could escape it remained unanswered. In July that year, the Centre (Catholic) party had joined the parties of the Left who were by then in favour of concluding peace as soon as possible. As 1918 began, the general staff were sure they had to win that year in the west if Germany was not to be defeated in 1919 by numbers and superior allied resources.[19] Transferring to the western front large numbers of men after the Russian collapse, the Germans launched a last great series of attacks in March 1918. For two months they hammered away, only just failing to break the British and French armies.

For the first time (and before the commander of the American expeditionary force wished), American formations were thrown into the struggle, too. By the summer, though, the Allies had managed to bring the German offensives to a halt. The huge gains of ground made by the Germans had not been enough, and they had been made at great cost. When the Allied armies began to move forward victoriously in their turn, the German army began to crumble. The German generals now began to seek an end; they feared defeat in the field would be followed by revolution at home.

Finally, both the Central Powers asked for an armistice on the same

[19] At the end of the war, for instance, the German army had 45 tanks; the Allies 3,500. For 1919, the prospect was even worse; a few months later, it was being planned that 100 American divisions would be available in France then. See H. H. Herwig, *The First World War: Germany and Austria-Hungary, 1914–1918* (London, 1997), p.420.

day, 4 October 1918; significantly and ominously for the Habsburgs they had made their request on the basis of an acceptance of the Fourteen Points as a starting-point for negotiation. A few days later the emperor Charles (who had succeeded the aged Franz Joseph in 1916) announced that the Austrian lands of the monarchy were to be reorganized as a federation. This acknowledgement of the nationalist tide came too late, though. Before October ended the Czechoslovaks had gone beyond demands for recognition of their right to self-determination and had proclaimed their independence. They were followed by Slavs who already spoke of themselves as 'Yugoslavs', while a 'German National Council' had appeared in Vienna to promote the cause of the German-speakers of the Habsburg lands. On 1 November an independent Hungarian government had been set up in Budapest.

The Allies granted an armistice to the Habsburg monarchy on 3 November, a month after it had asked for one. Three weeks later a 'kingdom of Croats, Slovenes and Serbs' was proclaimed at Zagreb. After deposing their king (who disliked the idea of playing second fiddle to the king of Serbia, the head of the new South Slav monarchy) the Montenegrins joined up to found what was to become Yugoslavia. By then the last Habsburg emperor of the Dual Monarchy had abdicated, and independent Austrian and Hungarian republics were in being. The latter, it was soon clear, was not likely to survive untroubled for long without further modification; at the beginning of December a national assembly of the Romanians of Transylvania was already voting for incorporation in the kingdom of Romania.

At the end of October sailors at Kiel had mutinied, refusing to go to sea to fight the Royal Navy; their example spread to other German ports. On 7 November came the proclamation of a republic after a rising in Munich. There had already been demands for the Kaiser's abdication. When it was announced, at last, on 9 November, there came to an end the last of the east European dynastic empires.[20] The Hohenzollerns had only just survived their old rivals. A new, republican, German government requested a suspension of fighting;

[20] Although Wilhelm did not sign a document of abdication until 28 November.

an armistice was rapidly granted and the fighting on the western front came to an end at 11.00 am on 11 November 1918.

Out of former German, Austro-Hungarian and Russian territory there were to emerge in the end three new Baltic republics (Latvia, Lithuania and Estonia), a resurrected Poland, a new republic called Czechoslovakia, an Austrian republic, a much reduced Hungary (still a kingdom, but without a king) and a new South Slav kingdom, but the details of so huge a change took years to settle. That there would be a new map of eastern Europe organized round these new states or something like them was certain well before the peacemakers met, though, and it was not a prospect that pleased everyone. Many people, indeed, bitterly resented it and even those who might have been expected to approve nevertheless would find much to dislike in its detail. Nevertheless, the victory would seem to settle a lot of questions that had been troubling people for much of the previous century and it had brought multinational empire to an end at last in Europe itself. Many of the nationalist demands of the past were satisfied; it was not at once clear that others still remained, and that many fresh ones had been created. It seemed at the very least, for good or evil, a triumph of the principles of national self-determination and representative democracy.

The cost of the Great War has never been adequately computed though its scale is clear enough; over 10 million men died as a result of direct military action. As for disease, typhus probably killed another million in the Balkans alone. Nor do even such terrible figures indicate the unprecedented physical and psychic toll in maiming, blinding, the loss to families of fathers, husbands and sons, the spiritual havoc in the destruction of ideals, confidence and goodwill. Europeans looked at their huge cemeteries and the long list of those who were, as the British memorials recorded, 'missing', and were appalled at what they had done.[21] The economic damage was immense, too. Starvation ravaged much of Europe in the winter of 1918–19. A year after the war, the continent's manufacturing output was still nearly a quarter

---

[21] The Thiepval memorial in north-western France alone records the names of over 70,000 British and Dominions soldiers killed in battles on the Somme of whom no trace was found, and to whom, therefore, no burial could be given, the Menin Gate memorial the names of 50,000 similarly lost in the Ypres Salient.

below that of 1914, while Russia's was only a fifth of what it had been. Transport over any distance was in some countries almost non-existent. The complicated, fragile machinery of international exchange had been smashed. At the centre of this chaos lay, exhausted, a Germany that had been the economic dynamo of central Europe. 'We are at the dead season of our fortunes,' wrote a British economist. 'Our power of feeling or caring beyond the immediate questions of our own material well-being is temporarily eclipsed . . . We have been moved already beyond endurance, and need rest. Never in the lifetime of men now living has the universal element in the soul of man burnt so dimly.'[22]

[22] J. M. Keynes, *The Economic Consequences of the Peace* (London, 1919), pp.278-9.

BOOK 3

THE END OF THE OLD
WORLD ORDER

9

A Revolutionary Peace

THE BASIS OF SETTLEMENT

The best-known fact about the peace settlement which followed the Great War is that it failed to prevent another and greater war. As a starting-point for understanding it, though, that is liable to mislead; it is another of those perspectives flawed by hindsight and self-righteousness. Though it was to become the fashion to emphasize the failures of the peace, the men who made it were but human; others' failures at later times, and the recognition of the magnitude of their tasks should by now impose a certain sympathy for them, even if not respect for what they did. They faced the greatest exercise in peace-making since 1815 and had to reconcile great expectations with stubborn facts, many of them still unrecognized as they began their task.

Not least, the peace settlement had to be a world settlement. It not only dealt with territories and peoples outside Europe – earlier peace-makings had done that – but many voices from outside Europe were heard in its making (and there were several that, though they sought to be heard, were excluded). Of twenty-seven states whose representatives signed the main treaty, seventeen were non-European. The United States was the greatest of them; with Japan, Great Britain, France and Italy she formed the group described as the 'principal allied and associated' or victorious powers. For a world settlement, though, it was ominous that no representative attended from the new Russia, the only great power with both European and Asian frontiers.

Decision-making was remarkably concentrated: the British and French prime ministers and the American president dominated the negotiations. These took place between them, the victors; the defeated

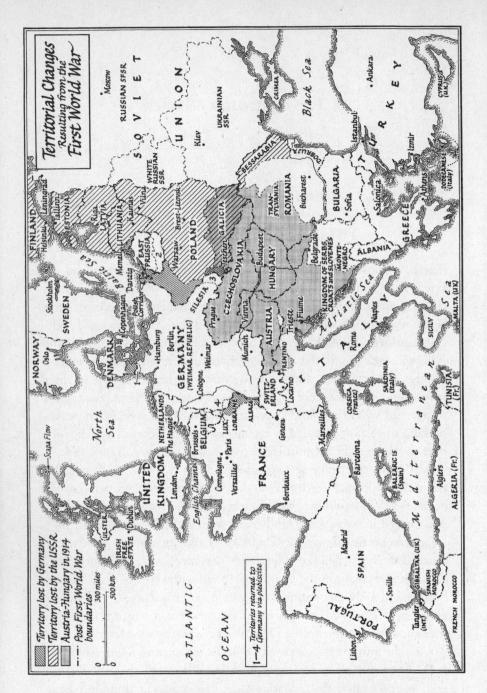

Territorial changes resulting from the First World War
(from *Dark Continent*, Mark Mazower, Allen Lane, 1998)

were subsequently presented with their terms. In the diverging interests of France, aware above all of the appalling danger of any third repetition of German aggression, and of the Anglo-Saxon nations, feeling no such peril, lay a central problem of European security, but many others surrounded and obscured it. Technically, the peace settlement consisted of a set of distinct treaties with Germany, with Bulgaria, the Ottoman empire and the 'succession states' which claimed the divided Dual Monarchy. Of these a resurrected Poland, the enlarged Serbia later called Yugoslavia and an entirely new Czecho-slovakia were taken to be on the winning side and were present at the conference as allies. A much-reduced Hungary and old Austria, though, were treated as defeated enemies with whom peace had to be made. All of this posed difficult problems, and it took over a year to draw up and sign the five main treaties. But the main concern of the peace conference was the settlement with Germany embodied in the Treaty of Versailles signed in June 1919.[1]

This was deliberately punitive. It explicitly stated that the Germans were responsible for the outbreak of war and that turned out to be a source of future resentment and danger. But the Treaty's harshest terms lay not in this moral condemnation, nor did they arise from it, but from the French wish, if it were possible, so to tie Germany down that any third German war was inconceivable. This was the purpose of imposing heavy economic 'reparations', which were to become one of the most deplored parts of the settlement. Not only did they embitter Germans, making the psychological acceptance of defeat even harder, but they were also economic nonsense. Nor were the economic penal-ties they laid on Germany for years to come supported by effective arrangements to ensure that Germany might not one day try to reverse the decision by force of arms. This angered the French. They did not get much more reassurance than an undertaking that the German bank of the Rhine should be 'demilitarized' and a temporary Allied occupation of certain zones. Germany's territorial losses, it went without saying, included Alsace and Lorraine, which were returned

---

[1] After that of Versailles came four other treaties with the 'defeated': that of St Germain with a new Austrian republic (10 September), of Neuilly with Bulgaria (27 November), of the Trianon with the Kingdom of Hungary (4 June 1920) and of Sèvres with the Ottoman empire (10 August 1920).

to France. Otherwise, Germany lost most in the east, to Poland.

It was a leading characteristic of the peace that it took for granted the validity of the principles of self-determination and nationality. Sixty million people were now to live in states they could call their own. This owed much to the convictions of Woodrow Wilson, but in many places, of course, these principles merely recognized existing facts; Poland and Czechoslovakia had governments of their own even before the peace conference met, and a new South Slav monarchy was already then crystallizing round what had been Serbia and Montenegro. By the end of 1918, these principles had already appeared to triumph over much of the territory of the old Dual Monarchy (and were soon to do so also in the former Baltic provinces of Russia). In that year, Thomas Masaryk, the Czech national leader, had published a book entitled *The New Europe* which interpreted the war as a struggle of democracy; though this was not an idea for which any of the belligerents of 1914 had gone to war, it was one that the leaders of the Allies had come to advocate as the fighting dragged on, their task much eased when the February revolution rid them of the moral encumbrance of tsarism. Some of the states formed as the Habsburg empire crumbled away were to survive (if with interruptions) for most of the rest of the century. At least at the outset, too, they appeared to represent democratic national entities. The principle of self-determination was also followed in tackling certain frontier problems by plebiscite. Yet such beneficent steps actually imposed upon much of Europe the assumptions of an alien ideology. This was particularly clear in the provisions made in the treaties for the protection of national minorities within new states. Nationalist-minded Poles in particular saw no reason why outsiders should insist on special protection for the collective rights of their 3 million Jews and 1 million Germans.[2]

The principle of nationality itself could not be applied consistently and plebiscites did not always produce helpful solutions. Geographical, historical, cultural and economic realities cut across the divisions they suggested. When political principle prevailed over social and

---

[2] The minority provisions of the peace settlement were soon evidently unenforceable, but continued to breed resentment.

economic realities – as it did in the destruction of the economic unity of the Danube valley – the results could be bad; when it did not, they could be just as bad because of the aggrieved feelings left behind. What the Italian prime minister termed a 'thorough Balkanization' left over 20 million people in eastern and central Europe living as national, cultural and religious minorities embedded resentfully in nations to which they felt no allegiance. More than a third of the population of the new Czechoslovakia consisted of Poles, Russians, Germans, Magyars and Ruthenes; an enlarged Romania soon contained well over a million Magyars, three-quarters of a million Germans and about as many Jews. In some places, the infringement of national principle or aspiration was felt with especial acuteness as an injustice. Germans particularly resented the existence of a 'corridor' connecting Poland with the sea across formerly German lands now in thrall to Slavs, Italy was disappointed of Adriatic spoils promised to her by her allies when they had needed her help, the Austrians (now the citizens of a largely German-speaking republic) were forbidden to unite with Germany, and the old Irish problem (though soon to be thought settled) was not touched by the Treaty.

Outside Europe, the most obvious question to be settled was the fate of the German colonies, but that posed few serious difficulties. Old-fashioned colonial aggrandizement was distasteful to the United States; partly for this reason, tutelage for non-European peoples formerly under German or Turkish rule was provided instead. 'Mandates', or trusteeships, were given to the victorious powers to administer these territories and to prepare them for self-government (though the United States declined any).

THE LEAGUE

A new 'League of Nations' that authorized those changes was the most imaginative idea to emerge from the settlement, even though in some instances its mandates did little more than provide fig-leaves of respectability for the last flowering of European imperialism. The League was nonetheless far more than the mandate system; it was a great creative idea. It owed much to Wilson's enthusiasm, and he ensured its Covenant – its constitution – pride of place as the first part of the Versailles Treaty. In that respect at least the settlement transcended the idea of nationalism a little and the dream of a new international order which was not an empire seemed for a moment to achieve some reality. The League also transcended the idea of Europe; it is another sign of the new era that twenty-six of the original forty-two members of the League were from outside Europe.[3] It was, in fact, the ultimate expression of the logic of Wilson's ideas about war aims. Uniquely among the victors and ideologists his war had not been subordinated to the goal of defeating Germany and preventing her resurgence but was focused beyond that, on making the world safe for democracy. He sought to build a new world order. Tortuous (and, in the end, a matter of circumstance created by others) though America's path to war had been, Wilson in 1918 became the first of her presidents to turn United States foreign policy firmly away from the belief in isolation and interest drawn from Washington's Farewell Address, and to identify the national interest with that of a world based on new principles. He strove to speak and plan for humanity as a whole. His was a grandiose and perhaps an arrogant illusion, but it was also a noble one. Wilson failed, but whether, given time, he could have sustained an American foreign policy grounded in ethical principle is impossible to say; it would have implied – as tensions inside American policy-making were to show again and again in the next eighty years – a national willingness to act to prevent wrong-doing or correct its effects which might never have been forth-coming except in felt emergencies. Wilson, though, was never to have time to find out. Because of domestic political circumstance that he had not taken into account and illness that he could not have foreseen, the United States was not to join the League. Disabled by paralysis at the end of 1919, the president lived on in retirement until his death in 1924, with the doubtful consolation of a Nobel peace prize.

America's absence was the League's greatest weakness, but there were several others. Perhaps from the outset they made it impossible for the League to satisfy the expectations it had aroused. Perhaps all

[3] The British empire provided from the start five members other than the United Kingdom: Canada, Australia, New Zealand, South Africa and India.

such expectations were unrealizable in principle, given the actual state of world political forces. Nonetheless, the League was to have its successes. Several matters were handled by it which might have proved much more explosive without its intervention, above all the question of Upper Silesia, disputed between Poles and Germans. After a settlement in 1922 (greeted by the German Reichstag draping itself in black), the territory remained reasonably peaceful until 1937. The Aaland Islands, disputed between Finland and Sweden in 1921, were also the subject of successful mediation by the League. It did its best in Vilna to reconcile Poles and Lithuanians, but failed (fighting between them spluttered on there until 1927), and it was blatantly divided over the administration of the Saar in 1923. Its authority was flouted, too, as early as 1923 when the Italians bombarded and then occupied the Greek island of Corfu. If exaggerated hopes had been entertained that it might do more, though, it does not mean the League was not of practical benefit as well as an imaginative idea.

It was another weakness of the League that the Union of Soviet Socialist Republics (USSR)[4] was not a member, and was therefore absent from its deliberations, just as she had been from the peace conference. The latter, though, was probably the more important. The political arrangements to shape the next stage of European history were thus made without consulting the new Russia, though in eastern Europe they required the drawing of boundaries in which any Russian government was bound to be vitally interested. The Bolshevik leaders did all they could to provide excuses for their exclusion. They envenomed relations with the major powers by revolutionary propaganda directed at their peoples, believing that the capitalist countries were determined to overthrow them. The British prime minister, Lloyd George, and Wilson were in fact more flexible – even sympathetic – than many of their colleagues and electors in their approach to the new Russia, and certainly more willing to give its government the benefit of any doubt than Clemenceau, the French prime minister. Passionately anti-Bolshevik, Clemenceau had many French ex-

[4] The Union of Soviet Socialist Republics officially came into existence under this new name in December 1918, when the 10th All-Russian Congress of Soviets so resolved.

servicemen and irritated investors in Russian bonds behind him. But however responsibility for the USSR's absence from the making of a new Europe is allocated, the outcome was that the European power which had, potentially, the greatest weight of all in the affairs of the continent, whatever her temporary weakness, was not consulted. Any government of Russia that took account of the country's historic experience and strategic needs would be bound eventually to join those seeking to revise the settlement or overthrow it. Worse still, her rulers detested the social system the peace was meant to protect; they were, after all, self-proclaimed world revolutionaries.

The hopes entertained of the peace settlement turned out to be not merely unrealistic, but to be undermined by revisionists and in the end blown away by events. In spite of this, the settlement had many good points; when it failed, it was for reasons that were for the most part beyond the control of the men who made it. In the first place, as Wilson's decisive role showed, the days of European world hegemony were over. Whatever its formal terms, the decisions of 1919 could not settle much of the future of the world outside Europe except in the Near East and Africa, and there only for a few years. Secondly, the old imperial policemen were now too weakened to do their job inside Europe, let alone outside (and some of them had disappeared altogether). The United States had been needed to ensure Germany's defeat. Unhappily, Americans had begun to withdraw into an artificial isolation even before Wilson (already disabled by a stroke) was replaced in 1921 by a Republican and isolationist. As for Bolshevik Russia, her rulers did not wish to help stabilize the continent in the next few years – indeed, they often loudly proclaimed the opposite. The isolationism of one great power and the sterilization of another by ideology thereafter left Europe to its own inadequate devices, and dangerously unstable. When no revolution broke out in Europe, the Soviet rulers turned in on themselves; when Americans were given the chance by Wilson to be involved in Europe's peace-keeping, they refused it. Both decisions are comprehensible, and may even be regarded as inevitable, but they were fertile in bad consequences. One of them, paradoxically, was that colour was lent to the survival of the illusion that European autonomy was still a reality, and could still provide an adequate framework for handling its problems. What is more, this unhappy illusion was to persist into an era when clear thinking and a firm grasp of realities were needed more than ever.

THE INTERNATIONAL ECONOMY

Some of the most taxing difficulties facing the peacemakers of 1919 lay outside their remit, although their decisions would impinge upon them. The economic repercussions of the war had been very different in different parts of the world. European countries had been badly damaged, while many non-European economies had prospered. New ties and relationships between different countries had appeared but much of the network of trading, investing and financial links that had bound Europe together commercially before 1914 was torn to shreds. Broadly speaking, non-Europeans had not done badly out of the war. The young industries of Japan and India received an enormous boost; they had provided clothes, boots, equipment, ammunition and arms for the Russian armies through Vladivostok, ammunition, food and beer for the British fighting in Mesopotamia and Egypt against the Turks. Agricultural production had fallen in Europe as the armies took men from the fields, but farming countries beyond the oceans enjoyed a boom; there was almost limitless demand for meat from South America, Australia and New Zealand and grain from North America to feed the Allied armies. Countries supplying primary products needed by industry also enjoyed boom conditions. Malayan tin and rubber, North American lumber, iron ore and oil from the United States,[5] bauxite and nitrates from South America, jute from India – all these and a thousand and one other commodities were swallowed in growing quantities as the war dragged on.[6]

Above all, the United States prospered. Already in 1914 she had

[5] In 1914 most of Europe's oil requirements were met from the USA; even at the end of the war, the potential of the Middle East was far from apparent.
[6] The sandbag is one of the humbler and less exciting instruments of war, but a growing demand for it makes the point: the British army expected in 1914 it would require 250,000 a month, but by May the following year, with the war not yet twelve months old, it was asking for a monthly supply of 6,000,000.

been the largest manufacturing power thanks to her huge and growing home market, but the Great War made her a great exporter of manufactures as well as of agricultural produce. Between 1914 and 1916 her exports of munitions during her years of neutrality had risen in value more than thirty-fold, from $40 million to $1,290 million. In theory, as a neutral she had been able to supply buyers on both sides. But since Britannia ruled the waves there was little chance of the Central Powers getting much through the British naval blockade, though there were one or two dashing attempts to run small quantities of goods through it by submarine. The Allies were the main customers of American industry and farmers; Allied spending fuelled an economic boom in the United States. That transformed the whole picture of world trade in a few years. Before 1914, Great Britain, Germany and France had been exporters of capital and the United States had been a capital importer. The war reversed this. The Allies had to pay for the things they bought, and in theory could do so by exporting their own goods, but the Americans had not wanted many of them and, in any case, British and French industry was busy meeting orders from their own governments. Allied bills for arms and commodities bought in the United States had to be settled, therefore, in dollars or some other acceptable currency (which in the end meant gold, since that was what made currencies acceptable in those days). To raise the dollars, the British steadily sold off their large pre-war investments in the United States to Americans. After that, they borrowed money there. It had been hoped that reparations would help the European allies to pay off their wartime debts to the United States, but by the middle of the 1920s their total indebtedness had been much swollen by new borrowing. Thus the United States, which had ceased in the war to be a debtor nation, paying interest on capital it borrowed from abroad, became even more decisively a creditor, exporting its own capital. Gold flowed across the Atlantic to American vaults in quantities no longer reflecting the normal course of trade. The United States had assumed a new economic role in the post-war world, and a puzzling one for those who still thought of 'normality' as a restoration of the pre-war patterns of international trade.

ECONOMIC DISORDER IN EUROPE

Europe's plight had thus to be tackled against a new world economic background. Mortal damage had been done to the continent's internal economic order. Everywhere its resources were in some measure stricken or distorted by the war. A great tract of France was physically blighted and ravaged by fighting more intense than any previously seen; the Germans had systematically flooded mines, looted factories for machinery and torn up roads and railway lines, had even ringed the fruit trees in orchards and left them to die. In eastern Europe, devastation was less intense, but there had been less to destroy in the first place. Sowing and harvesting had been interrupted again and again over wide areas, and in many places agricultural production had collapsed. The railways were often in ruins; until they were put right, Europe's grain growers could not feed starving cities even if they could lay their hands on the seed corn and labour to restore production quickly. Europeans were poorer also because they had used up capital that ought to have been ploughed back into investment. Productivity had declined, too, as labour had been taken from farm and factory to serve in the armies. It was calculated that the war cost Europe eight years of growth at pre-war rates. No European state was able to satisfy its basic needs in 1918 as many had done four years earlier. Between 1913 and 1920 the continent's manufacturing output had gone down by almost a quarter.

Germany had been Europe's greatest pre-war industrial nation, Great Britain's best customer and a great consumer of the agricultural produce of Russia and the Danube valley. But the terms of the peace, which imposed indemnities on Germany to pay for the damage the war had done, were a severe obstacle (though only one of several) to any restoration of her prosperity. Russia, Germany's greatest potential market, was cut off behind her new distrust of and ideological enmity towards the capitalist world and could no longer play her important pre-war part in the smooth working of the European economy either as a customer for manufactures and capital, or as a supplier of grain. Austria–Hungary in 1914 may have been a political anachronism, but it had given economic unity to much of the Danube valley. The new democracies had before the war been part of larger economic units that had eased their economic problems, but now old economic ties were not rebuilt at the end of a long period of (in some areas) almost continual fighting, prolonged in some places well after 1918.[7] For months after the end of the war, much of central and eastern Europe was actually starving. Among the new units into which it had fallen apart some were so weak economically that they dared not even allow such rolling-stock as was left on their railways to cross frontiers in case it should not come back, so that goods had to be unloaded and reloaded at border stations. The health and resistance of peoples had been undermined by years of shortages and belt-tightening; the soldiers returned to labour markets which could not offer them jobs knowing that their children and old folk were likely to die from disease or malnutrition if they could not obtain work. The saving and *rentier* classes saw the inflation of the war years suddenly and disastrously steepen and found themselves deprived of much of their wealth.

The first attempts of young governments and regimes to grapple with these problems may well have made things worse. New nations strove to protect their infant economies by throwing up tariffs and instituting exchange controls. Bigger and older nations tried to repair their own shattered and enfeebled and almost always distorted industries behind protection. Inflation swept away healthy currencies. Germany, potentially central to European recovery, was saddled with what looked like an indefinite burden of reparation in kind and in cash which, as well as distorting her economy and delaying its recovery, also took away much of the incentive to rebuild the economy, while adding to the problems soon presented by an appalling collapse of her currency. These difficulties were to be gradually overcome with the help of American money, which Americans were willing to lend (though they would not take European goods in return, and had

---

[7] Czechs and Poles fought over Teschen in 1919, Hungary went to war with Czechoslovakia and was herself invaded by Romanians (who occupied Budapest) that same year, Albanians had to repel Yugoslav incursions, bands of Bulgarians terrorized Macedonia, the Soviet Union went to war with Romania and Poland (1920–21) and invaded the Baltic states and Finland.

retired behind their own tariff walls). But this implied a dangerous dependence on the continued prosperity of the United States.

DEMOCRACY AND NATIONALITY

To this day the peace settlement of 1919 retains the distinction of being the only one in history made by great powers all of which were democracies. Whatever may be thought of the foresight of those who negotiated it, they were aware as none of their predecessors had been of the dangers of disappointing electors. Allied propaganda before victory and the rhetoric of peace-making made many think that there had been a great triumph of principle. After all, four autocratic, undemocratic, anti-national empires had collapsed, and the fact that so many other institutions of the *ancien régime* had also disappeared made many people optimistic about the prospects for democratic government, long seen by progressives as the wave of the future, and newly respectful of self-determination. Easily confused with democratic processes, self-determination was the master-idea of the settlement. Liberal optimism also drew strength from the ostentatious purity of Wilson; he had done all he could to make it clear that he saw the role of the United States in the war as essentially different from that of the Allies, being inspired (he irksomely reiterated) by high-minded ideals and his own belief in democracy, a matter of some importance in safeguarding his electoral support at home.

Against this background, new states, most of them republican, but all with democratic constitutions and parliamentary arrangements, had appeared all over eastern and central Europe.[8] Not all were the creations of the settlement. The independence of Latvia, Lithuania and Estonia had been recognized in the treaty of Brest-Litovsk. Two defeated countries, Austria and Germany, had reincarnated themselves as democratic republics, and the roots of independent Poland lay in

[8] It is interesting that there were brief attempts to set up new constitutional monarchies (in Finland and Lithuania in 1918) and, of course, the new Hungary, after a brief republican interval, was proclaimed a monarchy in 1920, although its throne was never to be successfully occupied by the man who had been the last Habsburg emperor and king, Charles.

its leaders' successful exploitation of German offers and the situation created by the Bolshevik revolution during the war. Democracy made new advances in western Europe, too, where two constitutional monarchies, Great Britain and Italy, widened their electorates in the aftermath of the war to include all adult males (this almost trebled the British electorate); some women, too, were given the vote in Great Britain in 1918 (all of them would be in 1928). It at first looked promising, too, when the League took an active interest in the protection of minorities and the victorious Allies had imposed terms in some of the peace treaties that were intended to give their rights security. Finally, there were the plebiscites that settled a number of questions left over from the peace negotiations at Versailles. All this looked like and should have meant a huge extension of democracy and civilized political practice, embodied in representative institutions and legal provisions for the protection of rights.

But democracy had to operate in a world in which it had many enemies, old and new. It had not been a widespread form of government before 1914 and many Europeans were soon regretting the passing of the regimes under which they had previously lived; Croatians quickly began to complain about the way Serbs treated them in the new state of the South Slavs, Magyars about their plight in a now Romanian Transylvania. There were many old-fashioned conservative opponents of democracy in the east and central Europe, too. Others, whatever their feelings in the abstract about democracy, lost by it – those who had been in the minority in plebiscites, for example, and now found themselves living under governments they did not like, with official languages they did not naturally speak and neighbours who now behaved unpleasantly towards them, instead of the other way round. Satisfying some nationalists had almost always meant irritating others. Poland might be revived to the delight of patriotic Poles, but a third of the inhabitants of the republic did not speak Polish as their mother tongue. Czechs and Slovaks might agree to live together in a new and democratic country, Czechoslovakia, but the Germans of Bohemia did not want to do so; they would have preferred to go on living under the Habsburgs, or, at least, under government by fellow-Germans. South Slavs and Romanians might be pleased to have done with Magyar rule, but Hungarians felt bitter over their huge territorial losses in the treaty of the Trianon.

There were old and troublesome questions to be settled, too, that had no intrinsic connexion with peacemaking but now re-emerged to plague politics. In 1914, the British government had finally conceded the principle of Home Rule in Ireland. This step (which was to prove to be only the beginning of a process of disaggregating the United Kingdom that was to go on until the end of the century) was nevertheless not to become effective until after the war. Well before that, the patience of some Irish patriots was exhausted. At Easter 1916 they had attempted a rising, which was quickly suppressed, German help for the rebels proving of little avail. In 1919 the nationalist Sinn Fein ('ourselves alone') party refused to take seats it had won electorally in the imperial parliament at Westminster. Instead, it organized its own assembly, proclaimed Ireland's independence and launched a new rebellion against the British. That ended in a British concession of two parliaments to a divided Ireland, one in the Protestant-Unionist north, one in the Catholic-Nationalist south. The nationalists then fell out between themselves over acceptance of the principle of partition.

At the end of 1921 an Anglo-Irish treaty set up a new Irish Free State in the south, with Dominion status inside the British empire. There followed civil war between the pro- and anti-partition nationalist factions, assassinations of Irish politicians and a violent repression of Sinn Fein by the new nationalist government. More Irishmen were killed by Irishmen in this struggle than were killed in the 1916 and 1919 rebellions by the British. The partitioners won. Irish politics crystallized for years (in so far as their volatile mix can ever be said to have done so) around the issue of the parliamentary oath of loyalty to the English king still required from Irish members of parliament. It was to remain an obligation until 1933, to the chagrin of many patriotic Irish. Meanwhile, the country's leaders hastened to join the League of Nations, a symbolic assertion of the independence they now exercised as the government of a British Dominion (and, indeed, they established a permanent mission to the League in Geneva before any of the other Dominions did so).

It was not only in the defeated states of the peace settlement, then, that there was dissatisfaction with the 'democratic' post-war world, and it was soon to appear that in this respect the foundations for optimism about the peace settlement had been much less secure than many believed when it was made. Though democracy survived until 1939 in Ireland and Czechoslovakia, it did not do so in many other countries where it was newly introduced. Within ten years it was clearly in retreat almost everywhere except the United States, France, Great Britain and the smaller countries of Scandinavia and Western Europe. Since the peacemakers had been obliged to do much more than enthrone liberal principles – they had also to safeguard their own national security, pay debts, protect vested interests, and take account of intractable facts of popular sentiment and mood – those principles had been much qualified in practice. Above all, they had left much unsatisfied and even outraged national feeling about (particularly in Germany). Perhaps this could not have been otherwise, but it was a soil in which things other than liberalism could and would grow. Launched as they had been into an unfriendly economic context of poverty, hardship and unemployment,[9] the political struggles of young democratic and constitutional institutions could never have had an easy future before them.

REVOLUTION AND COUNTER-REVOLUTION

Revolution was under way in several countries as the fighting came to an end, and there seemed every likelihood that it would persist in eastern Europe. Politicians there confronted long-standing problems, acute in many countries where there had long been widespread and grinding rural poverty. Some attempted to deal with this in the 1920s and 1930s through land reform and redistribution. Such schemes, though, proved only partial remedies to deep-seated ills and usually created new political difficulties as the details were hammered out, in particular where ethnic minorities stood out among the old landowning classes. True, immediately after the war circumstances seemed

[9] And, added to them in 1918–19, the additional disaster of a worldwide influenza pandemic which cost between 5 and 10 million lives in Europe (and probably 15 million in India).

propitious for change (and some thought it inescapable) if the contagion of communist revolution was to be avoided. Romania carried out major land reforms between 1919 and 1921 (beginning with the confiscation of all royal property), Poland and Estonia also passed measures of redistribution in that year, and Finland in 1922. Altogether, over the years from 1920 to 1939, something like 60 million acres of eastern Europe changed hands, a total area rather greater than that of the United Kingdom. The effects varied very much, both on the dispossessed (usually compensated with state bonds) and the peasants who took up new holdings. There were about three-quarters of a million new holdings established in Poland in the end, but such a number indicates that the average size of each was not large, although 6.5 million acres in all were redistributed.

Though this brought striking changes to agricultural economies dominated for centuries by very large estates, success varied from country to country. The exact social and economic impact was bound to take time to emerge and still remains hard to assess, because of a worldwide fall in agricultural prices in the 1930s which meant that by 1939 the problem of rural poverty seemed as intractable as ever. Frequently, too, the creation of very small farms led to plunges in agricultural productivity; Romania's was in 1939 only a fifth of that of Switzerland. Most of south-eastern Europe was a region of high population growth with only slow urban and industrial development to soak up its abundant labour supply. As for the political consequences of reform, it led in several countries to the emergence of new peasant-based agrarian parties, predominantly conservative and protectionist. Rural unrest was a disturbing force, another contributor to a Europe-wide malaise and restlessness which revolutionaries of different stripes could exploit. The communists believed that history had cast them for this role and were happy with what looked a promising situation.

Communism, or 'Bolshevism' as it was often called, had indeed appeared to pose an immediate threat to the new Europe even before the peace settlements were made. Internally, most European countries soon had their own revolutionary communist parties. In the post-war years the communists actually effected little that was positive (they were too few to do so), but they awoke great alarm nonetheless. More importantly, they also hindered the emergence of strong progressive and left-wing parties, committed to constructive change. The fundamental explanation of this goes back to the huge disappointment of 1914. The outbreak of the Great War had shattered the Second International. For years socialists had sworn that the workers whom they claimed to lead would never go to war to uphold the interests of their rulers, but patriotism had triumphed over the illusory solidarity of the international working class. Socialists were bitterly divided by the recriminations that followed. Although the Second International lived on in form after 1914, it never really recovered from the wound it received that year. The success of left-wing movements in 1918–19 was, in part because of this, to prove ephemeral and great opportunities were lost. Those movements registered fatal divisions in what had been preached to its followers and the world as a truly international cause.

The Russian Bolsheviks had adopted firm anti-revisionist principles and had stuck to extreme revolutionary positions in the pre-war years. When 1914 came, they had opposed their own country's part in the war (and had been joined by their bitter enemies, the Mensheviks, in the vote against war credits in the Duma). They therefore had much appeal for socialists in other countries disillusioned by the failure of international working-class solidarity as the horrific struggle came to an end. At the end of 1917 they had at once launched a propaganda campaign for a general peace, at a moment of great war-weariness in every combatant country. There was much immediate popular and liberal sympathy for the one country in the world with a socialist government in power (and soon, it seemed, under attack by 'capitalist' enemies).

When the formal closure of hostilities did not end economic hardship in central and eastern Europe, and children and old people continued daily to die of hunger and cold, intransigent revolutionaries felt they had fuel for revolution to hand and could prevent the restoration of the old order. Pressed both within and without as the Bolsheviks felt themselves to be, it is hardly surprising that they sought to exploit that situation. If they were in danger of outside attack, nothing could be more logical than to encourage revolution in the ranks of their likely enemies. Moreover, ideology reinforced self-interest; as the Bolshevik leaders looked west from Moscow (to which the government had moved in 1918) they were confident that the revolution in the capitalist countries predicted by Marx was in fact about to begin in Germany, and they were not alone in this.

THE NEW GERMANY

As 1918 drew to a close, German generals and officials believed they had made peace only just in time. They had discerned signs that the country was beginning to break up before the armistice could be agreed. The naval mutinies at the end of October had been followed by a rising in Munich and defections from the government of garrison troops in several north German cities. On 9 November, two days before fighting stopped in the west, the chancellor resigned, to be succeeded in his office by the leader of the Social Democrats. Even before the Kaiser left for exile in Holland later that day, a socialist deputy had enthused a mass meeting outside the Reichstag with the words 'long live the great German republic'.[10] When a formal imperial abdication came on 28 November, all the hereditary rulers of the other German states had by then given up their thrones. So the empire Bismarck had made came to an end amid disorder and the threat of revolution and Germany began a new phase of her history as a nation state under a republican government.

That government was only accepted by many Germans *faute de mieux*. 'Either Wilson or Lenin', was supposed to have been the quip of the man who drafted their new constitution.[11] The new Germany is remembered as the 'Weimar republic' because Weimar, Goethe's city, was where its constitution was drawn up. It had to contend with grave disadvantages from the outset. In the eyes of violent patriots, the republic was only there at all because Germany had been defeated. They thought its founders had helped to bring about that defeat: there was talk of a 'stab in the back' to the army.[12]

[10] Q. in Craig, p.402.
[11] Hugo Preuss, q. in M. Mazower, *Dark Continent: Europe's Twentieth Century* (London, 1998), p.8.
[12] In the music-drama *Götterdämmerung*, Wagner's hero, Siegfried, is murdered by a spear thrust into his back by his enemy, Hagen. The image was evocative for many German patriots.

The republic would have to agree peace terms or face invasion and starvation; they were bound to be unpleasant and the regime would be blamed for them. On the other hand, many people wanted the revolution that had attended its birth to go further and accordingly attacked the new order's other flank. 1919 opened with a left-wing rising in Berlin that the republicans called upon the army to crush; the Supreme Command had offered its support to the new government on the very day of the Kaiser's departure in return for an undertaking to oppose 'Bolshevism' and there was at first nothing else which was reliable to which the socialist leaders could turn. They did not win a Reichstag majority in the election of January 1919 and in the next few months there were further risings in the capital and in Bavaria (where a Soviet Republic was briefly established), and a separatist Rhineland Republic supported by France was briefly proclaimed. In due course 1920 brought an attempted right-wing *putsch*, followed a few days later by a communist rising in the Ruhr. All these attempts were put down, sometimes ferociously, but disorder and political murder (overwhelmingly the work of the Right rather than of the Left) continued well into the new decade.[13] Amid all this, Germany's new rulers had to face the awful practical problems of defeat: the demobilization of the troops when no jobs were available, the feeding of the cities while the Allied blockade was still in force, getting business and industry going again, and stabilizing the currency.

At the outset, then, the socialist politicians who formed the first, socialist-dominated governments of the new Germany had a poor hand to play. In the circumstances they did not do badly. They tried to give Germany a democratic and liberal constitution, though this meant they would be attacked by radicals who wanted, instead, a revolutionary republic based on workers' and soldiers' councils like the Bolshevik Soviets. For a few months the issue had hung in the balance but in the end the much-reduced German army and the 'free corps' raised by former officers were decisive. The international socialist movement had by then consummated its split. Divisions in the German Left had been especially bitter even before a German

---

[13] Political murders included those of the former Reich finance minister Erzberger in 1921, and of the foreign minister Rathenau in the following year.

Communist party looking to Moscow for leadership was founded. From the start a rival of the old Social Democratic Party, it was bitterly opposed to the socialists and the republic they had created. The Weimar republic had therefore to continue to fight off enemies both on the Right and on the Left. The Allies meanwhile had made things worse for it. Though they at last called off the blockade in July 1919, the peace treaty's insistence that Germany was responsible for the war – Germans strongly disagreed – together with the deprivation of Germany of much of its former territory in the east, the intrusion of garrisons in parts of west Germany, and the decision that for many years Germany was to pay economic 'reparations' for the damage done in the war caused bitter resentment. The country appeared to have been condemned to perpetual poverty by the last while, as Germany was to be permitted only very small armed forces, and no battleships, submarines or weapons of other special types, there seemed no likelihood she would ever regain her former international status. Yet the republic's government had signed the peace treaty: it could not do otherwise.

INTERNATIONAL COMMUNISM

While a left-wing German revolution still looked possible, a 'Comintern', or Third Socialist International, had been set up in Moscow in March 1919 to provide leadership for the international socialist movement and prevent it rallying again to the old leaders whose lack of revolutionary zeal was blamed for a failure to exploit the opportunities of the war. Lenin made adherence to the Comintern the test of loyalty to the socialist revolution. The Comintern's principles were deliberately rigid, disciplined and uncompromising, in accordance with his view of what an effective revolutionary party should be. In almost every country, this further and more bitterly divided former socialists. Those who now adhered to the Comintern usually took the name communist; others, though sometimes claiming still to be Marxists, remained in the rump socialist parties and movements and competed with the communists for working-class support.

Soon, nervous governments in other countries began to see the

Comintern and its agents behind every disturbance (and there were several other than those in Germany; in Hungary a communist government took power in 1919 and survived for some months). The revolutionary threat on the Left appeared all the more alarming because there was so much discontent and misery for communists to exploit. Yet communist policy made radical reform and united resistance to reaction more difficult, because it frightened moderates with its revolutionary rhetoric and reputation for conspiracy. In the east, too, the social threat was also seen as a national threat. Poland was the most anti-Russian by tradition, the most anti-Bolshevik by religion, as well as the largest and most ambitious of the 'new' nations of central and eastern Europe. But all Russia's neighbours felt threatened by any recovery of her power, which now seemed to mean social revolution as well as a renewal of Russian empire. The Baltic states of Lithuania, Latvia and Estonia all underwent Bolshevik invasion in 1918–19, but, with German help, drove out the intruders. Finland, which the new Russia had already recognized as independent, nevertheless fell out with her in 1919, and the two states went briefly to war over a territorial dispute.

The Comintern quickly came to be a mere instrument of Russian foreign policy. The Bolshevik leaders assumed that the future of world revolution depended upon the preservation of the first socialist state as a citadel of the international working class, and that it must be defended at all costs. In the early years of civil war and slow consolidation of Bolshevik power in Russia this was bound to mean the deliberate incitement of disaffection abroad at a moment when Bolshevik prospects seemed especially promising in eastern and central Europe. The final territorial settlement remained in doubt long after the Versailles treaty and fighting did not finish there until March 1921 when a Polish–Russian war in which, at one time, Warsaw itself had appeared to be about to fall to the Red Army, came to an end. The peace treaty between the USSR and the Polish Republic provided frontiers between the two that would last until 1939.

By the time Polish–Russian peace was established, Soviet power had recovered control of many parts of the old Russian empire that had slipped into independence briefly in the confusion of defeat and civil war. Armenia, Azerbaijan and Georgia, for instance, had all declared their independence in 1918; the end of the Polish war opened the way to dealing with the civil war in southern Russia and the Caucasus, whose briefly independent states were all absorbed into the new USSR in 1922. There followed a normalization of diplomatic links between the Soviet Union and the outside world. Official relations were established between the USSR and Great Britain in 1924 (Italy and France soon followed suit), and there was a noticeable relaxation in east Europe's tensions. This was linked to the Russian government's own sense of emerging from the acute dangers it had faced. It did not much improve its diplomatic manners, and revolutionary propaganda and denunciation of capitalist countries did not cease, but the Bolsheviks could now turn with some confidence to the rebuilding of their own shattered land.

THE NEW RUSSIAN EMPIRE

Though Russia's new rulers after 1917 were Marxists and their ideology shaped what they did with their new power, even a Bolshevik state could not be just the outcome of Marxist theorizing. The circumstances in which they had to operate mattered just as much as doctrine. They could not wipe the slate clean, willing as they were to try to do so. They had to start with a country that was in Marxist terms not ready for revolution: it was the most backward of all the great powers, still overwhelmingly a rural, peasant society, illiterate and even primitive. The new regime claimed and had to try to govern peoples of many different nations, ethnic stocks and tongues, too; some of them at once broke away, or at least tried to. It was an advantage that the mass of Russians was used to the idea that government was a brutal business. They took autocratic and ruthless responses to its problems for granted. In tsarist days, only powerful individuals had ever expected to have their rights respected (and even then they might find they were not) and such continuities as press censorship and a secret police were accepted as part of the normal state of affairs under the new Soviet order.

Though they at first went carefully with non-Bolshevik Russians who sided with the revolution, the winners of 1917 nevertheless believed that history was on their side and this, in their view, justified using their power to crush opposition to the triumph of their party, which proclaimed itself the vanguard and guide of the industrial proletariat. But the proletariat was itself only a small part of the Russian masses. An immediate step had therefore been taken to win the support of those living in the countryside. A decree passed by the Congress of Soviets the day after the seizure of the Winter Palace declared all land to be the property of the people; over the next few years this led to the transfer of over 500 million acres of land to the poorer peasants, and the wiping out of the estates of the old landowning class, the Church and the royal family. A huge majority of Russians were thus given a stake in keeping the new regime going, even though Bolshevik influence itself was weak outside the towns.

Meanwhile, the civil war went on savagely; atrocities mounted up and every day more of the country's precious economic resources were destroyed. Some parts of the old empire had already broken away from the USSR; some (Poland, Finland, the former Baltic provinces) were to be successful in maintaining their independence, others with would-be independent governments (the Ukraine and Armenia, for example) would prove not to be. When it was necessary to confiscate food supplies from the peasants to feed the towns, this led to more resistance to the regime and opposition in the countryside and therefore to even more brutal exercise of Soviet authority. But brutality fitted Lenin's view of what dictatorship meant: 'authority untrammeled by any laws, absolutely unrestricted by any rules whatever, and based directly on force'.[14] Even some of those who had first supported the Bolsheviks turned against their harsh rule. At the Baltic naval base of Kronstadt in 1921 a sailors' revolt promoted demands for democratic elections, freedom of speech and the press, and the release of all political prisoners. The rising was mercilessly repressed by the Red Army under Trotsky's direction, surviving mutineers being swiftly and ruthlessly shot.

The Bolsheviks were all the more ruthless in the civil war because it was unpleasant for them to think about what would happen to them if they did not win. A terrible food crisis was another incentive

[14] Q. in Mazower, p.10.

to terror; the cities had to be fed, if necessary, by force. The Bolsheviks had quickly replaced the old tsarist secret police with one of their own, at first called the *Cheka*, and the Kronstadt episode showed their mercilessness towards opposition on the Left. This continued: by 1922, not only had anarchist and other left-wing politicians been locked up but the Communist party itself had been purged of about a fifth of its members. It is difficult to believe, though, that it was only the circumstances of crisis that explains the regime's readiness to shed blood. There was plenty of sheer indulgence of the possibilities of power: in 1922 Lenin himself said 'the more members of the reactionary bourgeoisie and clergy we manage to shoot the better'.[15] Nor did the ruthless spare those who were on their own side.

The introduction of a 'New Economic Policy' (NEP, for short) then brought a relaxation in political as well as economic life. The central aim of NEP was to encourage peasant producers to take their goods to market by allowing them to get market prices for them. This relaxation was necessary after stringent measures of 'war communism' (forcible requisitioning of food, savage rationing) had been adopted in the economic crisis which followed Brest-Litovsk. Nearly half Russia's grain-growing areas were then out of production, occupied by the German army or in revolt. Livestock numbers had gone down by over a quarter and cereal deliveries were less than two-fifths of those of 1916. On to this impoverished economy there fell in 1921 a drought in south Russia. More than 5 million are said to have died in the subsequent famine, in which the miserable sufferers fell back on eating straw from roofs, leather harness and sometimes one another. But industrial Russia was in no better shape than the rural economy. In 1921 Russian pig-iron production still ran only at about one-fifth of its 1913 level, that of coal at a tiny 3 per cent or so, while the railways had less than half the locomotives in service with which they had started the war.

Communist die-hards disliked NEP, but its liberalization of the economy brought about revival. By 1927 both industrial and agricultural production were nearly back to pre-war levels. In 1928 they achieved

[15] Q. in O. Figes, *A People's Tragedy. The Russian Revolution 1891–1924* (London, 1996), p.749, where the violence and cruelty of the new regime is amply illustrated. The tsar and his family had already been murdered in July 1918.

them. Large industry had been nationalized but new private enterprises had emerged under NEP. Clearly at that moment the USSR was much less powerful than had been tsarist Russia in 1914, and much former tsarist territory had been lost. Yet a vast change had in fact begun. The country was again on the road to modernization she had entered upon under the tsars; the revolution had given her a government which, however barbaric in western eyes, clearly enjoyed or knew how to win the support of the people as the tsarist government in its last years had not. Much of the old empire was recovered; even if Russian Poland, Finland and the Baltic provinces were gone, the Ukraine was safe. The universal diffusion of the Communist party's apparatus through the republics of the USSR would contain the nationalist danger in the future.

It was a part of the world outlook of the Soviet leaders to be sure that the socialist cause of which they were the vanguard was destined to triumph worldwide. True or false, this was an encouraging belief. They could draw also on old-fashioned patriotism among those who were not communists but who felt that what they were doing was in the best interests of a country whose potential wealth in minerals, timber, agricultural land and sources of power was vast – if it could be tapped. The revolution had triumphed in a backward and poverty-stricken land (and that did not fit Marxist predictions) but one that had been a great power and might become one again.

A NEW AUTOCRACY

Yet at this moment, the regime was showing uncertainty in its leadership. In the early years of the new state, Lenin had dominated the government and the Bolshevik party. A brilliant speaker and debater, he seemed more than once to have been proved right by events, and even those who disagreed with his policies respected his indubitable personal devotion to the cause and his ruthlessness in promoting it. From 1921 onwards, though, he was often ill after being wounded by a would-be assassin. This had made it easier for personal rivalries and divisions to develop among his colleagues. Some were already apparent before Lenin died in 1924, but the removal of a man whose acknowledged ascendancy kept forces within it in a balance of sorts opended a period of uncertainty. There was debate within the Communist party leadership over economic policy; tactics and personal rivalry gave it extra edge. The centralized, autocratic nature of the regime that had emerged from the 1917 revolution went unquestioned, of course. No Bolshevik thought political democracy conceivable or that the use of secret police and the party's dictatorship should or could be abandoned in a world of hostile capitalist states. About the use of the state's power, though, there emerged, broadly speaking, two viewpoints. One emphasized that the revolution depended on the goodwill of the masses, the peasants; they had first been allowed to take the land for themselves, then antagonized by the attempts of 'war communism' to feed the cities at their expense, then conciliated again by NEP and allowed to make profits. The other viewpoint recognized similar facts, but set them in a different perspective. Continuing to conciliate the peasants would slow down industrialization, it was held, which the Soviet Union needed to survive in a hostile world. The party's proper course, argued the supporters of this view, was to rely upon the revolutionary militants of the cities and to exploit the still non-Bolshevized peasants while pressing on with industrialization and the promotion of revolution abroad. The communist leader Trotsky, whom some saw as a possible successor to Lenin, took this view. His view was in fact to prevail – not, though, as a result of open victory in debate, but because a new political leader decided to enforce the industrialization programme.

This new leader who emerged triumphantly from the rivalries and contentions was a member of the party bureaucracy, Joseph Stalin. He has been found less attractive intellectually then either Lenin or Trotsky, but he was just as ruthless, and turned out to be of greater historical importance. Two years after the end of the civil war, it has been said, Soviet society lived under his 'virtual rule, without being aware of the ruler's name'.[16] As Commissar of Nationalities, Commissar of the Workers' and Peasants' Inspectorate, Member of the Politburo and, finally, General Secretary of the Communist Party of the Soviet Union (CPSU), he had quietly armed himself with bureaucratic

---

[16] I. Deutscher, *Stalin* (2nd edn, London, 1967), p.228.

power. He was now to use it against former colleagues and old Bolsheviks as cold-bloodedly as against his enemies. Stalin was to carry out the real revolution to which the Bolshevik seizure of power had opened the way and would create a new élite on which a new society could be based.

Stalin was a Georgian; some people have likened him to an oriental monarch, but the analogy of Russia's own great despots, Ivan the Terrible or Peter the Great, seems more helpful in understanding him. He was cunning and secretive, good at masking his intentions and feelings until the moment came to strike, and then using his power remorselessly and perhaps even with pleasure. Carefully, he out-manoeuvred the one major figure who might have displaced him; in 1927 Trotsky was expelled from the party (later he went into exile, and was assassinated in Mexico in 1940 by an employee of the Soviet secret police).

For Stalin, industrialization was the key to the future. The road to it lay forcing the peasant to pay for it just as he had paid for it through taxation in tsarist days. Now he was to be made to supply the industrial workers with grain. After the ending of NEP and the ending of chances of a good profit many farmers tended to consume more of their produce themselves. A violent new departure in Soviet policy was probably detonated by a grain crisis in 1927 that preoccupied the party's fifteenth congress, held in December that year. Besides rounding on Trotsky and others, Stalin dwelt on the danger of imperialist attacks, and the need for 'collectivization' on the land and the develop-ment of heavy industry. From 1928 onwards, two 'Five Year Plans' announced and carried out an industrialization programme whose roots lay in what was in effect a war against the peasants, who were to be dragooned into providing food at less than cost to the cities. The party now at last conquered the countryside though by means which in practice, though not in theory or presentation, ignored the Plans. To make the peasants give up their grain, land in all the main grain-growing regions was brought into huge collective farms. There was tenacious resistance, sometimes far from passive. The crushing of it was undertaken by the secret police and army. Millions of poorer peasants – as well as the better-off smallholders, the *Kulaks*, who were now vigorously denounced – were killed or starved to death in what was virtually a second civil war while their grain was carried off to feed the industrial cities, where bread rationing was introduced in 1929. Famine, particularly in the Ukraine, followed massacres and mass deportations.

In seven years, 5 million families disappeared from European Russia. It seems likely that the huge round-ups of the collectivizations also launched what was to become a very distinctive feature of Soviet society, its development of the old tsarist system of forced labour on an unprecedented scale. In 1929 the term 'labour camps' began to be used, and the mass arrests of the next few years appear to have provided a population of 2.5 million prisoners in labour camps and other special settlements by 1933. This total was to rise even higher. It provided a labour force under the direct management of the security services that carried out huge construction tasks; on the eve of the Second World War whole industrial areas (often in particularly unpleasant environments) depended on slave labour while new industrial cities had been constructed by it, and the security service is said to have been responsible for about a quarter of the building work of the whole Soviet Union.

Stalin was soon blaming his henchmen for going too far (a few years later he was to tell a British prime minister that collectivization had been a trial as harsh as the Second World War) and argument continues about what precisely happened and the costs that were incurred. Even official Soviet figures admitted that in every year down to 1940 gross agricultural output was lower than it had been in 1928. The livestock population had been virtually halved as angry peasants slaughtered their animals rather than give them up to the authorities. But the aim of getting food from the land at less than the true cost of production by holding down the peasant's consumption was achieved. Although grain production fell, violence assured that deliveries to the state organs went up in the 1930s, and the towns were fed. The police apparatus kept consumption down to the minimum in them. A fall in real wages pressed heavily on all Soviet citizens, but by 1937, 80 per cent of the industrial output of the USSR came from plant built since 1928. The urban labour force tripled in about the same time. By 1940 (claimed the official statisticians) the 1928 level of steel production of 4.3 million tons had more than tripled while the coal mined mounted from 35.5 to 165.6 million tons. Industrial production was said to have risen by 852 per cent overall in the same period. Russia was again a great power, and for the first time an industrial one.

Whatever the true figures, the achievement was very great.[17] The price in material terms had been colossal; for everyone except the party bureaucrats and directing élite, whose privileges increased, consumer goods remained in short supply and housing was woefully inadequate. This was only partially offset by improvements in educational and social services. Above all, industrialization confirmed the authoritarian and, indeed, totalitarian aspect of the regime. Very little space was left for private life in the USSR. Methods of government even more brutal but also more effective than those of the old autocracy make Stalin a somewhat paradoxical claimant to Marxist orthodoxy, which taught that the economic sub-structure of society determined its politics. The Soviet Union he created precisely inverted this; Stalin showed that if the will to use political power was there, the economic sub-structure might be revolutionized by force. By 1939 there existed a new Soviet society, in which huge numbers had been shifted from agricultural to industrial employment, great strides had been made in overcoming illiteracy, and a new élite within the party had shouldered aside those who had made the Bolshevik revolution. Seventy per cent of the party in that year had joined it since 1929.

A WORLD DIVIDED

In 1917, said a historian of the French Revolution, 'Russia – for better or worse – took the place of France as the nation in the vanguard of history'; she became a great mythological symbol and, in many eyes, the bearer and guardian of revolution.[18] In the 1920s and 1930s there

---

[17] With the collapse of the Soviet regime, it seems likely that more accurate and refined figures will be available to measure it. There is a helpful condensation of information about various estimates which have been made (taking 1928 at 100, eight different western indexes of figures for 1940 are cited, ranging from 263 at the lowest to 462 at the highest) in S. de Mowbray, *Key Facts in Soviet History*, I (London, 1990), pp.231–3.

[18] F. Furet, *Interpreting the French Revolution* (Cambridge, 1981), p.6.

were contemporary observers in many countries, by no means all of them communists, who already held up Soviet Russia, of which they had a very rosy picture, as an example of the way in which a society might achieve material progress and a revitalization of its cultural and ethical life. The establishment of the USSR and the dividing of Europe in a new way were preliminaries to the eruption of new ideological divisions in almost every society in the developed world. The single civilized world of 1914, with its shared assumptions at many levels among developed nations, had gone. With it had also gone much of the unanimity of progressive intellectuals in pursuing similar goals. Now, for only the second time in European history, there existed a state that claimed to be opposed to the principles on which every other state was based. Though with hindsight we may now think that there was little likelihood in the 1920s that Soviet armies would spread revolution (they were not yet powerful enough to do so anywhere except, perhaps, in a few immediately contiguous areas), the Soviet government proclaimed its support for revolution everywhere. The reality of the threat this presented may not have been great, but the psychological impact was immense. The rulers of other countries had to live with the knowledge that the USSR regarded them at bottom as irreconcilable, and would try to undermine them whenever possible. Even those who were not communists but who clung to courses that had since the Revolution traditionally been associated with the political Left could now look hopefully to Moscow for support for them.

The USSR quickly took up new media opportunities for propaganda. At home, the cinema was put into service as an instrument of political conditioning. Abroad, radio broadcasts were aimed at other countries in which communist aims were set out and offers of help made to those who were seen as oppressed. Much of this propaganda was addressed to the peoples of colonial countries, so that their politics began to be affected, too. For a time, it did not seem as if it had much effect (though it deepened British officials' suspicion of the USSR, worried as they were always ready to be about India and the Arab world). But it was a clear sign of a new fact in world history – the appearance of a centre for the promotion of revolution everywhere.

In this way the Russian revolutions of 1917 left a deep mark on the age. Here lies their largest significance. The February revolution had cleared the way for the Bolshevik coup which in the end created a citadel and chief place of arms (as well as providing many of the leaders and general staff) for world revolution. That there should be such a centre at all was unprecedented, at least since the days when French revolutionaries offered fraternal aid to all peoples seeking to throw off the yoke of tyranny. Russian foreign policy appeared for a time to have shed its old pan-Slavist and vestigial religious overtones. Another new world-historical fact was the provision by the USSR of a mythology to sustain the process of modernization and industrialization in other backward societies as an alternative to the mythology of liberal, capitalist society. It appeared to the borne out by evident success. Of course, both Marxism and liberalism were European creations. Though its immediate disruptive effects were greater in Europe than anywhere else, the Russian revolution was another demonstration that European history was becoming impossible to distinguish from world history.

It may nevertheless be the case that the Russian revolution delayed much that would have been likely to come about more quickly without revolution. We cannot know, but had imperial Russia escaped defeat and been among the victorious allies of 1918, with her old rival Austria–Hungary in a state of disintegration and Germany disarmed, she would have been likely within a few years to have assumed the continental predominance which the USSR was to display only in 1945. Her massive potential had been hinted at, after all, even in 1815, in the pre-industrial era of the Holy Alliance. It may be (to take speculation just a little further still) that the failure of the Dardanelles campaign cost Russia a quarter-century of exclusion from the European role it might have expected to play, since failure to overcome virtual isolation from effective material support by her allies entailed the military and economic defeat which made possible the Bolshevik seizure of power. Undoubtedly, too, the revolution slowed down Russia's recovery from the damage done by the war to its economy, for it closed the USSR to foreign investment and so delayed the onset of rapid industrialization until the 1930s. Stalin then put the country back on the road to it with more ruthless energy than the tsarist regime had ever shown and enormously increased Soviet power. Yet it still remains hard to be sure whether the USSR could have survived on its own the German onslaught that was to come. Certainly there is no indisputable evidence that Soviet development had by 1941 made that certain. Counter-factual history can be fascinating and informative, but it is ultimately unsatisfying because logically without boundaries; perhaps, though, it can justify the speculation that the failure at the Dardanelles settled much of the history of the world in the rest of the century.

IO

Years of Illusion

A LAST FLOURISH OF EMPIRE

Well before 1939 Europe's troubles were providing plenty of evidence that in other parts of the world her governments could no longer operate as effectively as they had once done and that European history was no longer an autonomous process, to be narrated in purely European terms. Yet one very obvious part of Europe's world domination still seemed intact. One colonial empire, Germany's relatively recent creation, had disappeared in 1919, but the overseas empires of other European powers had not. For a few years some were actually to be bigger than before the Great War: Italy's in the Aegean, for example. Although there were former German colonies to be divided in Africa, the Pacific and the Far East, the process of imperial extension was most marked in the Near and Middle East, in the lands of the old Ottoman empire. There, the British and French had set about remaking the map to suit their own interests even while the war was still going on; Great Britain formally annexed Cyprus, for example, on Guy Fawkes' Day, 1914, thus ending an agreement with Ottoman Turkey for British occupation of the island in 1878. But what were regarded as the Arab Ottoman lands mattered more, and in the process of settling their fate French and British alike involved themselves in complex relations with the Arabs whom they had conjured on to the stage of world politics, while the Arab leaders quarrelled among themselves.

Little was clear in the Middle East in 1919 except that the Ottoman empire, the only power that had ever given the region a period of prolonged peace, had disappeared. But, it seemed, so had the vestiges of Arab unity that had briefly flickered above the surface during the war. The Russian threat in the Middle East had also disappeared (for the moment), so of the great powers in the region only the British and French really mattered, though Italy had sought to be a player, too.[1] In spite of much mutual distrust, agreement between them was possible, roughly on the basis that if the British had their way in Iraq (as Mesopotamia came to be called after the war), the French could have theirs in Syria. This arrangement was legitimized when the League of Nations awarded mandates for Arab lands; Palestine, Transjordan and Iraq then went to the British and Syria and the Lebanon to the French. The latter had to install themselves in their mandate by force after a national congress had asked for independence or at least a British or American mandate instead of a French one. They went on to govern high-handedly, evicting the king the Syrians had chosen (Hussein's son). Subsequently there was a full-scale insurrection against them, but the French were still holding their own by sheer force in the 1930s, though there were signs by then that they would have to make concessions to the nationalists. Meanwhile, Syria soon provided yet another instance of the disintegrating power of nationalism when the Kurdish people of the north revolted against the prospect of submergence in an Arab state. Here was another Middle Eastern problem that had not been resolved by the collapse of Ottoman rule and still with a long life before it.

The Arabian peninsula was meanwhile racked by a struggle between Hussein and another Arab king with whom the British had negotiated a treaty, and whose followers, to make things still more difficult, were members of a particularly puritanical Islamic sect. Thus sectarian was added to dynastic and tribal conflict between Arabs. Hussein was in due course displaced and in 1932 the new kingdom of Saudi Arabia emerged in the place of the Hejaz. Hussein's sons by this time sat on new thrones in Iraq and Transjordan so this created fresh tensions. In 1928, Transjordan had been recognized as independent by the British, though they kept some military and financial powers there. In Iraq, a rebellion had shown the difficulties that might lie ahead,

[1] The United States clearly signalled its unwillingness to be involved in the region when the Senate refused to take up a mandate in Armenia.

and the British moved as fast as they dared towards ending their mandate, seeking only to secure their strategic interests by preserving an air force presence there with sufficient ground support to defend its bases. In 1932, Iraq entered the League as an independent and fully sovereign state.

Palestine proved much more difficult. In 1921 there were anti-Jewish riots by Arabs alarmed over Jewish immigration and Jewish acquisition of Arab land. After this, that unhappy country was never long at peace. More was at stake than merely religious or national feeling. Jewish immigration brought fresh westernizing and modernizing forces, changing economic relationships and imposing new demands on traditional societies. The British mandatory power was soon to be piggy in the middle, caught between the outcry of Arabs if it did not restrict Jewish immigration and the protests of Jews if it did. But Arab governments now had to be taken into account and they occupied lands economically and strategically more than ever important to British security in an age of oil and growing tensions in the Far East. World opinion was becoming involved, too. The question became more inflamed than ever when there came to power in Germany in 1933 a regime that set about persecuting German Jews and destroying the legal and social gains they had been making since the French Revolution.

For centuries before the establishment of Ottoman hegemony, the collapse of a paramount power in the Arab lands had often been followed by disorder. What was unclear after the most recent fragmentation was whether disorder would be followed – as earlier periods of anarchy had eventually been – by the establishment of a new hegemony with its own attendant benefits and evils. The British did not want a new empire; after a brief spell of imperial intoxication in the aftermath of victory, they sought only to safeguard their own most fundamental interests in the area, the protection of the Suez Canal and the growing stream of oil from Iraq and Iran. Between 1918 and 1934 a pipeline was built from northern Iraq across Transjordan and Palestine to Haifa. This gave another new twist to the future of these territories. Oil consumption in Europe was not yet so large that there was any general dependence on Middle Eastern supply, nor had the great discoveries yet been made which would again change the political postion in the later twentieth century. But the Royal Navy had turned over to oil for its ships and car-ownership was growing in the western world. A new factor was thus emerging.

The British still believed Suez could be best be secured by keeping a garrison in Egypt, but the Great War had intensified local feeling and armies of occupation are never popular. When the war sent up prices, too, they had been blamed. Egyptian nationalist leaders attempted in 1919 to put their case to the Paris peace conference but were prevented from doing so; a rising against the British was then quickly put down, but the occupying power was already morally on the defensive. The British protectorate was declared at an end in 1922 in the hope of getting ahead of nationalist feeling, but this hardly helped. The new kingdom of Egypt that now came into being had an electoral system which returned parliaments containing nationalist majority after nationalist majority, and it soon became clear that no Egyptian government could survive if it offered safeguards for British interests that any British government would find acceptable. The result was prolonged constitutional crisis and intermittent disorder. In 1936 the British retreated another step and agreed to be content with a right to garrison the Canal Zone for a limited number of years. An end was also made to the jurisdictional privileges of foreigners resident in Egypt.

This was a reflexion of a worldwide overstretching of power and resources. British foreign policy was beginning to be preoccupied elsewhere. Changes far from the Middle East were beginning to shape the history of the Arab world, notably through the strains the Far East placed on British naval resources (especially once the Japanese alliance had been allowed to lapse, as it was in 1922).[2] Another novel factor was Marxist communism. Russian radio broadcasting to the Arab countries encouraged the first Arab communists, though in spite of the worry they caused communism showed no sign of sweeping the Islamic world. The strongest revolutionary influence of the area continued to be Arab nationalism, and its focus had come by 1938 to be Palestine. Arab governments began to interest themselves in the Mandate as riots, murders, Arab terrorist attacks on Jewish

[2] See Chapter 11 below.

settlements and pitched battles disturbed it. By 1939 a British army was pinned down trying to contain an Arab insurrection there. In the previous year a congress had been held in Syria to support the Palestinian Arab cause, and as well as the Arab outcry against the British, Arab resentment of the brutality of the French in Syria was swelling too. Some thought pan-Arabism might in the end even override the divisions of the Hashemite kingdoms.

KEMAL ATATÜRK

Turkey was the first nation to obtain a successful revision of the peace settlement imposed on her by defeat. It was to prove, too, to be the longest-lasting revision. A new Turkish nation emerged from the multinational Ottoman empire. Once again, Allied agreements during the war complicate the story. In the course of 1914 and 1916, the Russians, British, French, Greeks and Italians had all agreed on the ways they would share out not only Syrian and Mesopotamian, but also Thracian, Anatolian and Dodecanese booty after victory. The only subsequent change to the fate awaiting the old empire was the elimination of the Russian claim to Constantinople and the Straits when that country collapsed in defeat and revolution. But this was not much. Its back to the wall in the face of invasion by Greeks and Italians in Anatolia, and an invasion of Cilicia by French forces from Syria, the Ottoman government signed the humiliating Treaty of Sèvres in 1920. Large territorial concessions were made to Greece, Armenia was to be an independent state again, while what was left of Anatolia and the tiny European remnant of Turkey was divided into British, French and Italian spheres of influence. To drive home this exercise in blatant imperialism, European financial control was re-established together with the humiliating 'capitulations'.

The 'Great Idea', as the Greeks called it, of an imperial Greece which would include western Anatolia did much to reawaken Turkish martial and ethnic feeling. The annexations were not to last, nor was the treaty of Sèvres; it was overturned, largely, thanks to the leadership of one man, Mustafa Kemal. A former Young Turk and an outstanding soldier, he had been one of the few victorious Ottoman commanders, first at Gallipoli, then in the Caucasus. In 1919 he still identified himself with the Ottoman regime, establishing himself at Ankara at the end of that year, before Sèvres had decisively discredited the old order. He then launched in the following summer an onslaught on the Greeks, winning the crucial battle on the Sakarya in August. The French and Italians then came to terms with him. Adroitly cooperating with the Bolsheviks in what he and they called 'the common struggle which both peoples have undertaken against the intervention of imperialism',[3] he first crushed the Armenians who, after their brief emergence as an independent nation, once again returned to the margins and shadows of history as subjects of the new Turkey and the USSR, and then completed the recovery of Anatolia from its invaders.

The British (influenced, among other things, by the opposition of the Dominions to fighting the new war with Kemal that seemed likely to be the price of upholding the Sèvres treaty) decided to negotiate. Accordingly, a second peace treaty with Turkey was signed at Lausanne in 1923. This registered the triumph of Turk nationalism over the decisions taken three years earlier. It was the only part of the peace settlement to be negotiated between equals and not imposed on the defeated, and was also the only one in which Soviet negotiators took part. These facts no doubt help to explain why it was to last better than any of the other peace treaties. The capitulations and financial controls disappeared. The Straits were demilitarized. The reparations imposed at Sèvres were cancelled. Turkey gave up her claims to the Arab lands and the islands of the Aegean, Cyprus, Rhodes and the Dodecanese. Armenia was not mentioned. A massive, internationally supervised exchange of Greek and Turkish populations took place with sad but unsurprising accompanying atrocities which ensured that the hatreds of these peoples for one another would have new memories to brood over.[4]

The Ottoman empire had by then already come to an end. The sultanate had been abolished on 1 November 1922; the caliphate

[3] Words used in the Turco-Soviet treaty of 1921 and quoted by B. Lewis, *The Emergence of Modern Turkey*, p.283.
[4] Nearly 400,000 Muslims left Greece to go to Turkey and 1.3 million Christian 'Greeks' went the other way. Many of the latter settled in Macedonia, and in the eyes of patriotic Greeks, completed the long overdue 'hellenization' of that land.

followed the empire, in 1924. This was the end of Ottoman history. For the first time in five or six centuries the Anatolian Turks were now the majority people within their state borders. The Arab lands had gone, and the 'ethnic cleansing' of the population exchanges and the earlier massacre and deportation of Armenians in 1915 seemed to have removed the dangers of rival nationalisms in the new republic of Turkey, a national state based at Ankara under the dictatorship of Mustafa Kemal. He rapidly proved to be one of the most effective of the century's modernizers. Kemal was to be what Mehemet Ali could not be, the first ruler to transform an Islamic state by modernization. Already in the 1920s his regime was attracting the condemnation of the scholars of the university of Al Azhar in Egypt, the most famous of all centres of Islamic learning. He remains strikingly interesting; until his death in 1938 he showed a determination not to let his revolution congeal and the result was the creation of a country at that date in some ways among the most advanced in the world, let alone the Islamic sphere.

Kemal, as he tended to call himself (the name meant 'Perfection' and the National Assembly conferred on him the name of Atatürk, or 'Father Turk'), had something of the ruthless style of a Peter the Great (though he was not interested in territorial expansion) as well as something of that of an enlightened despot. The abolition of the caliphate began the attack on Muslim theocracy. Turkish law was secularized in a code on a Swiss model, the Muslim calendar abandoned, and in 1928 the constitution was amended to remove the statement that Turkey was an Islamic state. Polygamy was forbidden. Primary education became obligatory and schools ceased to give religious instruction. A Latin script was introduced in 1928, and the written use of Arabic characters for the Turkish language ceased. In 1935 the weekly day of rest, formerly Friday, the Islamic holy day, was moved to Sunday and a new word entered the language: *vikend* (the period from 1.00 p.m. Saturday to midnight Sunday). Wearing the fez was made a criminal offence; although it was in origin European (it came from Bosnia), it was considered too Muslim. The veil, though, was not forbidden, even if Kemal voiced his personal disapproval of it. He was conscious of the radical nature of what he wished to achieve and such symbols mattered to him. They were signs of something very important, the replacement of an Islamic view of society by a European one. A national past was set out in the schoolbooks; it was claimed that Adam had been a Turk. In 1934 Turkish women received the vote; they were encouraged to enter the professions, too. In Turkey, a much greater break with the past was involved in giving a new role to women than in Europe. The most obvious problem Kemal left to the future (and in some measure aggravated) was that of Kurdish nationalism. The Kurds, though, were to continue long after his death to be fatally handicapped by their dispersion over the territory of three new nations – Turkey, Syria and Iraq.

IRAN

Before 1914, the most important other Islamic country neither under direct imperial rule by Europeans nor by Ottomans had been Persia. It could look back on a long imperial history of its own even if in the nineteenth century its power had evaporated. The British and Russians had then begun interfering in Persian affairs and continued to do so, agreeing in 1907 over respective spheres of influence in the country. When Russian power lapsed with the Bolshevik revolution, British forces continued to operate against them on Persian territory until the end of the war. Local resentment against them was excited when a Persian delegation was not allowed to state its case to the peace conference (though Persia soon became one of the first members of the League). In a confused period the British struggled to find means of maintaining resistance to the Bolsheviks after their withdrawal of their forces; there could be no question of retaining Persia by force, given the over-taxing of British strength. Almost by accident, a British general had already discovered the man who was to do this, Reza Khan, an officer who carried out a *coup d'état* in 1921.

He at once used the Bolsheviks' fear of the British to win a treaty from them conceding all former Russian rights and property in Persia and the withdrawal of Soviet forces. Reza Khan then went on to defeat separatists who had British support. The ruling shah left the country, never to return, and in 1925 Reza Khan was given dictatorial powers by the national assembly. A few months later he was proclaimed by the old imperial title, Shah of Shahs. He was to rule until 1941 (when British and Soviet forces together turned him off the throne) somewhat in the style of an Iranian Kemal, and with a determination to achieve independence through modernization. In 1928, the capitulations were abolished, an important symbolic step; meanwhile industrialization and the improvement of communications were pressed forward. The abolition of the veil and religious schools showed Reza Shah's secularist aims, though they were not pressed so far as those of Kemal. A close association with Turkey was cultivated. Finally, the Persian strong man won in 1933 the first notable success in a new art, the diplomacy of oil, by cancelling a concession held by the Anglo-Persian Oil Company. The British government took the question to the League of Nations, but there only followed another concession more favourable to Persia. This was Reza Shah's most remarked victory and the best evidence of the new independence of his country. It suggested that a new era had opened in the Gulf, fittingly marked in 1935 by an official change of the name of the state: Persia was renamed Iran.

NEW CURRENTS IN EUROPE'S POLITICS

Initial optimism only intensified dissatisfactions and disappointment felt with constitutional and liberal government in Europe when it seemed to fail, and in some countries signs of failure appeared quite soon. When people sought explanations and scapegoats, there were plenty to choose among, though it was tempting to over-simplify. In truth, the recession of democracy in Europe between two world wars (like its failures in post-colonial Africa thirty or forty years later) was a very diverse and complicated matter, influenced much by circumstance and personality, as well as troubled by vastly different historical legacies of weakness, ambition and grievance.

Amid the problems confronting liberals were new political forces. Bolshevik communism was not all that was on offer to the radically discontented as an alternative in the 1920s. In Italy, a movement called fascism came to power whose name was to be given also to a number of other and only loosely related radical, anti-liberal and anti-Marxist movements in other countries. Fascism could draw on support from elements on both sides of the traditional political dichotomy of Left and Right that had come to dominate European politics in the nineteenth century. Constitutional Italy had been badly strained by war. Poorer than the other great powers in 1914, she had then still been a young and uneasy nation, whose rulers were aware that their state rested on some shaky foundations. Her constitutional politics, based on an electorate much restricted by a literacy test, faced a double challenge. Many of the industrial and agricultural masses looked to revolutionary socialism for satisfaction of their needs, and the turbulence of the Italian cities and parts of the countryside had often shown it. As for Catholics, since 1870 the Papacy had never accepted its loss of the Temporal Power and of its former territories to the Kingdom of Italy and the pope had ostentatiously remained a 'prisoner in the Vatican', never leaving it even to visit his own cathedral as bishop of Rome. In 1914 there had been only a partial relaxation of the injunction to the faithful to support the claims of the Holy Father by abstaining from participation in constitutional politics.

Then had come the Great War. Italy's share of fighting had been disproportionately heavy and cost her nearly half a million dead; it had often been unsuccessful, and on land all of it had been on her own territory. Inequalities had accentuated social divisions as fighting went on and then peace had brought further and more rapid inflation. The owners of property, agricultural or industrial, and those who could ask higher wages because of a labour shortage, were better insulated against it than the middle-class professionals and those who lived on investment or fixed incomes (especially if their savings were in government bonds, much depreciated by the war). Yet it was they, on the whole, who had provided the most convinced supporters of the unification completed in 1870. They had sustained a constitutional and liberal state while conservative Roman Catholics and revolutionary socialists had long opposed it. They had seen the war Italy entered in 1915 as an extension of the *Risorgimento*; a muddled, unscientific, but powerful idea focused on the acquisition of *Italia irredenta* after victory. Peace brought them disappointment and disillusion as nationalist dreams were left unrealized and costs were counted. Moreover, as the immediate post-war economic crisis deepened, the socialists grew stronger in parliament; that seemed more alarming than ever now that a revolutionary socialist regime existed in Russia. Disappointed and frightened, alienated by left-wing anti-nationalism, many Italians began to turn away from liberal parliamentarianism and to look for new ways out of Italy's disappointments. They were sympathetic to intransigent nationalists (for example, to the poet-adventurer d'Annunzio who seized the Adriatic port of Fiume when the peace conference had failed to give it to Italy and then declared war on the Italian government when it failed to support him) and to violent anti-Marxism at home. The second was always likely to be attractive in a Roman Catholic country, but new leadership against Marxism was to come by no means only from the traditionally conservative Church.

Benito Mussolini had been a nationalist journalist and an extreme socialist until the war turned him into a fierce advocate of Italian intervention. After serving in the army he formed in 1919 a new political movement based on the *fascio di combattimento*, which can be roughly translated as 'union for combat'.[5] It sought power by any means, including violence. Groups of its young thugs were let loose at first on socialists and working-class organizations, then against elected authorities. They wrecked premises and beat up individuals and their movement prospered particularly in northern Italy. The constitutional politicians could neither control fascism nor tame it by cooperation. Soon it was in some places enjoying official or quasi-official patronage and protection from local authorities and police. Gangsterism was thus semi-institutionalized. By 1922 fascists had not only achieved important electoral success but had virtually made orderly government impossible in some areas by terrorizing their political enemies on the Left, driving out the communist municipal government of Bologna (though they also drove d' Annunzio's regime out of Fiume). In that year, other politicians having failed to master the fascist challenge, the king called Mussolini to form a government; he did so, on a coalition basis, and the violence came to an end. This was what was called in later fascist mythology the 'March on Rome'.

[5] The word *fascio* was not new in Italian politics. It had been used of radical associations in Sicily in the 1890s.

It was not quite the end of constitutional Italy. Mussolini did not at once turn his position into a dictatorship. Not until 1926 were elections suspended and government by decree begun. There was, though, little significant opposition as a second European great power followed Soviet Russia into dictatorship – perhaps partly because Italy still kept the forms and trappings of constitutional monarchy.

The new regime had terrorism in plenty at its roots, and explicitly denounced liberal ideals, yet Mussolini's rule was far short of totalitarian. It was less brutal (sometimes despite his efforts) than that of Lenin and the Bolsheviks of whom he sometimes spoke admiringly. He undoubtedly shared with many of his followers an emotional attraction to revolutionary change, but in practice the 'revolution' side of fascism turned out to be largely window-dressing. As much as a truly radical ambition, Mussolini's own temperamental impatience with an established society from which he felt excluded lay behind it. Office revealed fascism's conservative potential and lack of radical creativity. In practice and theory it rarely achieved coherence; it tended, rather, to reflect more and more the power of established and vested interest, and the volatile, disordered personality of its leader. The state, though, remained formally a constitutional and hereditary monarchy.

Fascism's greatest domestic achievement was to make peace by diplomatic agreement with the papacy. In return for substantial concessions to the authority of the Church in Italian life (which persist to this day), the pope at last officially recognized the Italian state. For all Mussolini's revolutionary rhetoric the Lateran treaties of 1929 which embodied this agreement were a concession to the greatest conservative force in Italy. 'We have given back God to Italy and Italy to God,' said the pope.[6] Just as conservative were the results of fascist criticism of free enterprise. The subordination of individual interest to the state boiled down to depriving trade unions of their power to protect their members' interests. Few checks were placed on the freedom of employers and fascist economic planning was a mockery, even if agricultural production somewhat improved.

[6] Q. in A. C. Jemolo, *Church and State in Italy 1850–1950* (Oxford, 1960), p.232.

AN AUTHORITARIAN WAVE

There were similar divergences between style and aspiration on the one hand and achievement on the other also to be seen in movements elsewhere which have been called fascist.[7] Though indeed reflecting something new and post-liberal, in practice such movements almost always made compromising concessions to conservative influences. This makes it difficult to speak of the phenomenon 'fascism' at all precisely; regimes appeared in various places which were authoritarian in aspiration, intensely nationalist, and anti-Marxist. But such ideas did not make them fascist, and fascism was by no means the only source of such ideas. The governments that emerged in Portugal and Spain, for example, drew much more upon traditional forces than upon those arising from the new phenomenon of mass politics. In such states, true radicals who were fascists often felt discontented at concessions made to the existing social order by successful authoritarians. Only in Germany did a movement sometimes called 'fascist', but with very special national characteristics, succeed in bringing about a revolution that mastered historical conservatism. For such reasons, the label of fascism can confuse as much as it clarifies.

So many nuances and political shadings exist, and the strong nationalist and patriotic tendencies of so many of the most authoritarian governments to appear in Europe in the years 1919–39 are so markedly individual, that it is fruitless to try to categorize the extent of an identifiable 'fascism' in these years. It is safer merely to emphasize the recession of democracy and constitutional rule. By September 1939, no constitutional regime survived east of the Rhine except in the Netherlands, the Scandinavian countries and perhaps Yugoslavia and Finland. In every country, moreover, movements that could be called or were self-proclaimed fascist had appeared, and in some resistance to them had led to bloodshed. In several countries, traditional anti-semitism played an important part in upholding reactionary governments; in some, where peasant-based agrarian parties were strong,

[7] Much has been written on this theme. For an introduction, the essays in *European Fascism*, ed. S. J. Woolf (London, 1968), are still very suggestive.

agrarian reform entrenched new conservative forces. In all eastern Europe a violent anti-Marxist current can be observed, usually resulting at least in anti-communist legislation.

Perhaps it is best merely to emphasize the distinction between two phenomena separable in the twenty years after 1918. One is the appearance (even in stable democracies such as Great Britain, France or Belgium) of ideologists and activists who spoke the language of a new, radical politics, talked of class-cooperation, idealism, willpower and sacrifice, and looked forward to rebuilding society and state without respect to liberal ideas, vested interests or concessions to materialism. Such radicalism, though widespread, triumphed without foreign help only in two major states, Italy in 1922 and Germany just over ten years later. In each, economic collapse, outraged nationalism and anti-Marxism lay at the roots of its success. If one word is wanted for this, let it be fascism. In other countries, often underdeveloped economically, it might be better to speak of authoritarian, rather than fascist, regimes, especially in eastern and southern Europe. There, large and poverty-stricken agricultural populations had long presented social problems some of which were further aggravated by the peace settlement or the post-war movements of world markets. Sometimes alien minorities appeared to threaten the state and exacerbated tensions at a very local level. Liberal institutions were only superficially implanted in many of the new countries where traditional conservative social and religious forces were still strong. For some of them the physical closeness of Bolshevik Russia was a potent and enduring source of fear. As in Latin America, where similar economic conditions could be found, constitutionalism tended to give way sooner or later to the rule, overt or indirect, of strong men and soldiers. This proved the case before 1939 in the new Baltic States, Poland and all the successor states of the Dual Monarchy except Czechoslovakia, the one democracy surviving in central Europe or the Balkans until its overthrow by foreign invasion. The need of these states to fall back on such regimes demonstrated the unreality of the hopes entertained of their political maturity in 1918.

Such pressure operated also – though less acutely – in the Iberian peninsula: there, the influence of old-fashioned conservatism was even stronger and Catholic social thinking and a tradition of military authoritarianism counted for more than the modernizing creed of fascism. In Spain, there was at work a special historic factor: resentment of the centralizing rule of Castile, particularly in the Basque country and Catalonia.[8] Though a constitutional monarchy, and one operating successfully a parliamentary system based on alternations between two major parties in office and opposition as the century began, Spanish politics had been riven increasingly by issues arising from the disaster of 1898, by anti-clerical feeling, and by the unpopularity of military commitments in Morocco. In 1912, the liberal prime minister was assassinated. Politics fragmented (between 1909 and 1923, Spain endured thirty-four evanescent governments). Another disaster, in Morocco in 1921, led to violent criticism of the army, and a coup by a general in 1923 that sought to protect the soldiers against parliamentary censure. From that year Spain was governed by Primo de Rivera as a military dictator almost uninterruptedly until the installation of a republic – Spain's second – in 1931. The concessions then made to Catalan autonomy, a burst of anti-clerical legislation, a general secularizing style among the republic's supporters on the Left which had an abrasive, disturbing effect in many communities, and an apparent slide into disorder all boded ill for the survival of Spanish democracy, especially after a much-resented 'Popular Front' coalition of the Left, containing Marxists and anarcho-syndicalists, came to power after the elections of February 1936. What looked like a traditional military *pronunciamiento* then took place. As for Portugal, with a population that at the end of the Great War was still two-thirds illiterate, her politics were studded by attempted coups which led to the overthrow of the constitutionally democratic state as early as 1926 and the emergence within a few years of a dictator who was to hold office undisturbed until 1968; only then, and after suffering a stroke, did Dr Salazar retire to die peacefully.

---

[8] This was hardly a novel phenomenon: it is said to have been a seventeenth-century Spanish statesman who, bemoaning the realities of Castilian absolutism, remarked that 'if death came from Madrid, we should all be immortal'.

NEW UNCERTAINTIES

Many cultural and institutional changes evidently already at work in world (and especially western) history before 1914, and whose origins lay in the nineteenth century or even earlier, resumed their progress after 1918. Some of them troubled some people. Among them was growing evidence of the mass nature of modern society and the demands it made. This was not just a matter of the evidence of the changes brought to politics by bigger electorates and the advance of universal suffrage, important as these were.[9] Mass action expressed itself in other ways than through the ballot box. Politicians had to adapt themselves to such new facts as the general literacy achieved in most European countries through compulsory education, the deployment in politics of cheap newspapers, and the introduction of 'wireless' (as a generation of Englishmen emerging from the nineteenth century much aware of the electric telegraph had now learnt to call it) broadcasting. In the 1930s, the growing cheapness and availability of 'receiving sets' put new power in the hands of those who controlled or could enjoy access to radio, as the history of (notably) Germany and the USA was to demonstrate. The other new mass medium of communication was the cinema, first silent and then accompanied by sound. It had been much exploited by propagandists during the Great War. Mass communication had, of course, cultural, economic, social implications that by far transcended even its political potential. Its most famous institution, the British Broadcasting Corporation (BBC), demands discussion in any study of British domestic history and the view the British took of themselves in the inter-war years, and can even be said to have had international influence. Fittingly, when in 1937 the man who first sent messages by radio, the Italian Marconi, died, British broadcasting stations paid him the unique tribute of two minutes' silence after making the announcement; he had truly been one of the makers of twentieth-century history.

In considering the possible implications of such material changes,

[9] The United Kingdom at last achieved universal adult suffrage in 1928 – peers, lunatics and convicted felons were the only adults henceforth excluded from the privilege of voting for a member of parliament.

a degree of measurement is possible in principle. Hard, or allegedly hard, facts can be set out about such matters as the numbers of newspapers printed and sold, the accessibility of cinemas and the ownership of wireless sets. But beyond this fairly firm territory, it is very hard to find and hold a footing. Not only were the messages delivered often laden with unnoticed and perhaps unintended assumptions (though film censors tended to show a lively if not very discriminating awareness of the dangers some films shown to colonial peoples might present), but they were received in very different environments by very different audiences, above all, outside the western world. In the Far East, Japan's popular culture was highly literate; China's was not, and the different history of newspapers in each reflected that. It is impossible, too, to believe that western, urbanized filmgoers received the same message from a Hollywood film as those who saw it in open-air performance in an Indian village with a commentary by the village schoolmaster as their guide to what was going on. Nor, for a long time, were the same messages actually being built into the films made by the new cinematography industries of India or Japan.

It was in western countries where it had been dominant that the recession not only of liberal politics but also of liberal civilization between the wars was best observable. This was the world in which it is easiest to guess at what was going on in high culture, where an ample documentation suggests that long-term disruptive forces at work before the Great War operated even more powerfully in the 1920s. In 1914, Europe was already experiencing profound intellectual and cultural innovation. The war struck a blow at its self-confidence such as had never been struck by any external force; after 1914–18 it was impossible ever again to equate civilization merely with Europe. Yet it remains hard to go further, or to say confidently or precisely what such statements mean.

One clear fact is that the declining years of European world hegemony were accompanied by the questioning and qualifying of established ideas and values as never before, and, in particular, of ideals and values highly prized in the past, even if they had never been without their conservative critics. One example might be the old liberal idealization of the individual. It is less clear, but equally certain, that the behaviour of the 'masses' in developed countries appears also to have been changing in ways which showed the crumbling of support for old ways such as that implied by such values. At least the city-dwelling proletariat seemed more anxious to enjoy freedoms long reserved only for the better off than to overthrow them. Clearly, though, as old systems of thought and old values were increasingly undermined after 1918, new claimants for adherence and intellectual allegiance appeared, and found outlets for their claims in mass media. In extreme cases, scepticism about the past and its values even blossomed as a denial of the possibility of absolute standards at all. Yet it is also true that a huge cultural inertia prevailed in many western societies (to say nothing of the non-western world).

In 'high' culture, the innovative power of the nineteenth century once again seems to have been the seed-bed. Although it is often hard to distinguish between the explicit utterances of intellectuals and educated minorities on the one hand, and attitudes and behaviour of society at large on the other, the roots of what looks like cultural disintegration in western civilization can be traced back to the critical questioning actually begun before 1901. Exaggeratedly, one man's name came for many to symbolize this, that of Sigmund Freud. Already as this century began, he had set out a language in which to explore human behaviour and to promote confidence that it was in the study of some of its most neglected aspects that the key to much of the state of western society could be found. In so doing, he founded 'psychoanalysis', an allegedly therapeutic technique to which many would deny the status of a science, although that was how it was promoted by its founder. Freud's place in the history of culture, though, does not depend on the difference he made to science (manifestly he was no system-making Newton or Darwin and many have denied that he was any sort of scientist at all). He was not the only influence changing the way humanity saw the natural world; yet he was redefining its limits. More than any other person, he changed the way educated people looked into themselves, whether or not they explicitly accepted his ideas. He provided a new cultural mythology, a way of understanding behaviour, and an idiom in which to express it.

By the 1920s, many of Freud's ideas and much of his phraseology were making their way into ordinary speech: the special meanings we now give to the words 'complex', 'unconscious' and 'obsession', and familiar terms like 'Freudian slip' and 'libido' speak for the fact. His influence spread into literature, personal relations, education and politics. What he said was often distorted, but what he was believed to have said and was understood by many people to mean was vastly more important than his specific words or clinical studies. His influence, like that of Newton and Darwin before him, ran far beyond science and the illumination of the natural world. Like those giants, he offered laymen a new vision, and like those they had offered (or that of Marx) his was to prove to have highly corrosive effects. Some welcomed 'Freudianism' because it looked like one of those nineteenth-century determinisms that had so often been in vogue, captivating many of the intellectual élite. Whatever Freud himself believed, the message laymen drew from his teaching was that the unconscious mind was the real source of behaviour, that moral values and attitudes were consequences of the influences which had moulded this unconscious, that, therefore, the idea of responsibility was at best a myth and probably a dangerous one, and that perhaps rationality itself was an illusion. It did not matter much that Freud's own assertions would have been of none but symptomatic interest had this been true, or that this left out many of the qualifications with which he attempted to defend his conclusions. What mattered was what many people believed (and some still believe) he had shown. Such ideas called in question the idea of the rational, responsible, consciously motivated individual – a key notion of western civilization and a presupposition of the right of society to impose morality.[10]

Freud even appeared to say that much previously thought good was bad. Conscience (by whatever name you might call it) had hitherto been thought of as a fundamentally beneficent force; even if it made cowards of us all, it regulated and checked in individuals not only conscious wickedness, but evil impulse. Now, people were asked to confront the startling idea that moral self-control might be a source of danger to their mental health. We need not exaggerate. Freud's teaching was not the only intellectual force contributing to the loss of certainty and the sense that men had little firm ground beneath

---

[10] Freud's most celebrated publications all came out before 1914, but in 1923 he published *The Ego and the Id*, the book which more obviously than any of his others promoted the psychoanalytic approach to the moral life.

their feet. But along with Marxism (another often-misunderstood body of ideas) it was one of the most obvious and fashionable messages about traditional culture in western intellectual life in the inter-war period that told against liberal civilization.

What men and women took from Freud added to the pressures building up in other ways against individualism, freedom of speech (liberals always expressed great respect for rational argument), property rights as expressions of personality and guarantees of freedom, and many other great nineteenth-century received ideas. The huge human and material mobilizations called forth by the Great War had given greater plausibility than any earlier human experience to the claims of socialists that society might be rationally planned. Some conservatives had never abandoned their basic tenet of the innate wickedness and corruption of sinful humanity, and the conduct of the war amply supported their reservations about liberal optimism, too. At the same moment, moreover, individualism was under fire from the collective values of communism and fascism, the idolization of class, *volk* and nation. Intellectual and cultural relativism combined with them to strike – like Freud's teaching – at the core assumption of liberal civilization, the moral and mental autonomy of the individual.

Perhaps the only area of western culture after 1918 where individualism was still claiming an unrestricted sovereignty was that of the arts. Yet they, too, had since the century began been showing symptoms of cultural dislocation and dissolution. For two or three centuries after the age of humanism most Europeans who thought about such things at all had implicitly believed that art expressed aspirations, insights and pleasures accessible in principle to ordinary men and women. Artistic productions might be of such exceptional degree of fineness in execution, or so especially concentrated in form, that sometimes only the educated could wholly appreciate them. But it was always thought possible that those whose taste was cultivated by time and study could enjoy and discriminate among the arts of their day if they sought to do so. The arts were presumed to be cumulative expressions of a shared culture and shared standards, undergoing ups and downs, but essentially unfolding in a continuing story. This idea began to be undermined in the early nineteenth century, when the Romantics came to idealize the artist as genius and formulated the notion of an *avant-garde*. But this was nothing to the fragmentation that followed in the triumph of what was (in retrospect) to be called 'modernism'.

The notion of modernism has always been difficult to deal with because of an inherent lack of definition and continually shifting boundaries in its usage. It was European in origin (another of the seminal creations of that continent's nineteenth century) and one of those cultural transformations that rolled out to shape intellectual and artistic attitudes worldwide and far from its roots. It was a shift in the focus of the arts to the subjective, from the object depicted or the story narrated to a vision, a state of mind and primal reaction, above all to the state of mind of the artist, whether it was comprehensible or not to anyone else. The shift could already be found in the poetry of Baudelaire, or the painting of the French Impressionists, but soon they were left far behind by others, and even by 1914 trained eyes and ears could find much difficult to recognize as art (and some things that were already incomprehensible) in what was offered to them by the artists, poets and musicians of their day.

A particularly recognizable instance of this (there is no space for more) was the abandonment of the figurative tradition and a new dislocation of the image in painting in the work of up-to-date painters. Some shed any vestige of the representational. There persisted a recognizable but a tenuous link with western painterly tradition as late as Cubism, and its abandonment of perspective and the illusion of depth. By then, though, the link between what many painters saw and what had been traditionally shown had long ceased to be easily apprehended by the average cultivated person, if, indeed, such still existed. Artists retired into a less and less accessible chaos of private visions, whose climax (if such a metaphor has any meaning) was reached after 1918 in the world of 'Dada' and 'Surrealism'. They entered new levels of distintegration; in Surrealism even the notion that there was an object disappeared, let alone its representation; 'real' objects might be shown in works of art, but only in a context set by the unconscious mind, to which access had been achieved by some kind of psychic insight or automatism. As one Surrealist put it, the movement meant 'thought dictated in the absence of all control exerted by reason, and outside all aesthetics or moral preoccupations'.[11] Through change, symbolism, shock, suggestion and violence the Surrealists sought to go beyond consciousness itself. In so doing, they were only doing what many writers and musicians were trying to do, but perhaps, for the general public, even more startlingly; their work was, after all, easier to illustrate in the popular press.

Striving to grapple with Freud's alarming (or, to some, liberating) suggestions – or with the chaos of the arts, or with the practical feebleness and seeming intellectual inadequacy of twentieth-century Christianity in developed societies, or with the incomprehensibility of a natural world that suddenly seemed unintelligible in a universe of bending space and relative time – people looked about confusedly and worriedly for new bearings. Perhaps this influenced and benefited new irrationalisms in politics, and gave fresh violence to older ones (such as nationalism), but this is not a topic on which it is easy to know what is significant evidence. At least, the conscious intellectual life of Europe seemed to indicate that little excitement could still be aroused by tolerance, democracy, or the old liberal absolutes set up to protect the individual. Though many still clung to old shibboleths, the élites that led thought and opinion seemed to be giving up old foundations they no longer thought firm. For a long time, only a minority of Europeans, even in Roman Catholic countries, had been regularly attending religious worship. The masses of the industrial cities lived in a post-Christian world of growing paganism. Whether or not the decline of church-going made much difference to their daily lives, a mass-entertainment industry was at work destroying or transforming much of the structure of festivals and commemoration embodied in the traditional calendar, and public law was cutting into or by-passing the experience of the great traditional rites of marriage and baptism. Reference points long understood and providing direction for society were becoming incomprehensible. The liberal ideas that had helped to displace Christianity in the past were now being displaced in their turn. In the 1920s and 1930s, sweeping changes could be sensed on every side. The liberal certainties of the autonomy

---

[11] See André Breton's *Le Manifeste du Surréalisme* (1924), printed in P. Waldberg, *Surrealism* (London, 1965), from which the quotation is taken (p.72).

of the individual, objective moral criteria, rationality, the authority of parents, and an explicable mechanical universe all seemed to be crumbling away. It was a deep paradox that such changes were worrying so many of the élites of the European world just at the moment when so many of the old European certainties – democracy, nationalism, Marxism, the positive faith in science as a liberating force – were beginning to be taken up in non-western cultures as never before. Those sometime core certainties were less available than ever to sustain the self-confidence of the European élites among whom they had originated. Unhappily, it was the self-confidence of the well-inclined, not that of the bully and barbarian, which was being sapped. It was liberal civilization that was the loser.

THE OPTIMISTIC YEARS

In spite of their important long-term effects, most of these changes consciously troubled only a minority that was especially conscious of them, and it was a western, and predominantly conservative, minority. Most of the human race, after all, are creatures of habit and heard or saw little that went on outside the ambit of their daily lives. What is more, a mood of optimism was nourished in the western world by the return of prosperity in the 1920s, and its later spread to other parts of the world. The harsh immediately post-war years, bad as they had been, proved to have been a prelude to a gradual recovery shared in some degree by most of humanity outside the Soviet Union. The years from 1925 to 1929 were particularly encouraging. This was especially notable in the United States, but Europeans, too, who remembered the old days as normal, had some excuse for thinking things were getting back to what they had been before 1914.

Those who sought to revive that normality (or 'normalcy' as Americans liked to call it) accepted that there would be cyclical fluctuations in the economy, persistent poverty and continuing high rates of unemployment. The upturn in mood is nevertheless understandable. The worst physical damage of the war was repaired by 1925, transport was running normally again (and in a new dimension, for the first regular airline schedules were in place), harvests were back to normal levels, currencies had been stabilized after bad bouts of inflation (money prices in Germany had at one time risen by a multiple of 1,000 million). Not all European countries had been equally successful in tackling their problems, but economic well-being at last seemed again in sight for many of them. A big international loan to Germany in 1925 was a landmark; by that year, though the old great industrial powers, Great Britain and Germany, had still not reached their 1913 levels of manufacturing output, Europe's aggregate food and raw material production passed pre-war levels. True, in 1926 world commodity prices began to fall, but this was a harbinger of higher purchasing power in the pockets of the wage earners of the developed world, whatever it meant to primary producers.

For the next four years things continued to go well. World output of manufactures rose by over a quarter, world trade by nearly a fifth. Major currencies were again steady and could be exchanged for gold at fixed prices. The industrial laggards caught up; Great Britain's manufacturing production was back to the 1913 level by 1929, and Germany's was by then well ahead of it. The main facts behind this recovery were the change in the political climate in Europe as Germany came back into the community of states, the repair of the damage done by the war and, above all, a long boom in the United States, the biggest national economy in the world. This prosperity sustained, among other things, optimism about the political future of the new democracies. It was not to last. 1929, though no one knew it, was in fact to be the best year for European trade until 1954. Economic recovery had been built on insecure foundations. Nevertheless, economic improvement had provided the background for what looked at the time a long-awaited and major advance in settling festering problems left over from the Great War and the peace settlement.

LOCARNO AND AFTER

Outstanding among these problems was that of Germany, a new one or an old one re-emergent, as you wished. It had not taken long after 1919 for it to appear that the role of Germany had not been settled, after all. She had been defeated, disarmed, had undergone political revolution and had lost much territory. But she had not been destroyed; it was logical to recognize that, for good or ill, she would one day again exercise the weight assured her by geography, population and industrial power. This was bound to be the most important issue in post-war European international relations. It was certain that one way or another a united and economically rebuilt Germany would one day again overshadow central Europe and be likely to threaten France. The French wondered how long this could be put off and whether it could happen without war; for them the problem long remained purely one of national security. They at first put their faith in military sanctions (the British garrison stayed in the Rhineland until 1929 and the French until 1930) and in fortification of their frontier. But French diplomacy also sought allies and treaties of mutual support between France and the new states of central and eastern Europe.

For the most part, the diplomats of other countries approached the problem accepting the fact that in dealing with Germany an attempt would have to be made to make the terms of the peace treaty work by agreement. It took some time for the difficulties of this to become apparent, and the German government, continually under pressure from right-wing nationalists, soon began to seek revision of the Versailles settlement. In the 1920s its demands began to be listened to abroad and the problems of realizing them slowly came to be tackled in a more hopeful spirit. The reparation burden was identified as the key area for action. The Commission set up to supervise German reparation payments declared in March 1921 that the payments Germany was due to make under the Treaty (they amounted to the vast sum of 132 billion gold marks) were in default. The German government borrowed enough to make a down payment of 1 billion, but the mark began to fall faster and in the following year it was granted a year's moratorium on further payments. The French nonetheless remained obdurate over full exaction of what they regarded as due.

Urgency seemed suddenly to be given to a search for a new basis for settlement, when the German and Russian government startled Europe in 1922 by unexpectedly coming to an agreement with one another at Rapallo. Both powers had a strong revisionist interest;

each was seeking to emerge from diplomatic isolation in Europe.[12] The sensation in other countries was immense, especially in France (and would have been even greater there had it been known that the Rapallo agreement provided for training and experimental facilities in the Soviet Union for the German army). Meanwhile, Great Britain and France had drifted apart. French efforts to enforce fulfilment of the treaty on Germany came to a violent climax in January 1923 with a Franco-Belgian military occupation of the Rühr, to assure coal deliveries by way of reparation. The virtual closing down of Germany's greatest industrial region and the complete collapse of the mark as the German government turned to the printing press to meet its obligations to its citizens followed; by November four million million marks were needed to buy one United States dollar. With the currency in ruins, the savings and reserves of millions of Germans were obliterated and their lives were devastated. This was the worst moment of tension Europe experienced in the whole decade. It lasted until the French government realized that its policy could not be made to work. Military action could not give France what she wanted, and soon French financial stability, too, was endangered. The Rühr's mines could not be made to deliver on a scale which met the cost of running them. A change of government in France led to a gradual rapprochement with Germany, and American financial action helped to ease the reparation problem by releasing a new flow of American investment to Germany. Statesmen began to talk of the need of reconciliation with Germany and of the desirability of 'appeasing' her. Yet the best guarantee of general peace in Europe had been the preoccupation of Germans (and Russians, too) with their domestic problems and the sheer exhaustion of the aftermath of defeat.

Gradually the way was opened to agreements at Locarno in 1925 that ended the distinction of 'enemy' and 'Allied' powers and formally reconciled France and Germany in guarantees of the Franco-German and German-Belgian frontiers against attack from either side. Significantly, nothing was said about Germany's eastern frontiers; it was

[12] There had already been the Soviet–Turkish treaty of 1921, of course, as a step towards this by the USSR.

clear that the British would undertake no commitments over them.[13] When Germany was admitted to the League of Nations in the following year, it seemed that the way was opening at last to a new world of peaceful diplomacy and understanding. Germany had acquiesced in the Versailles territorial settlement in the west, while France was reassured by guarantees given to her frontiers by Great Britain and Italy.

Locarno was, nonetheless, another illusory solution. It had given one part of the Versailles settlement (its frontiers in the west), a privileged position. That very fact weakened by implication the eastern settlement and made the eventual fate of former German territory and German people now under Polish or Czech rule look uncertain again. It did not settle the question of how a country potentially as strong as Germany could be related to its neighbours in a balanced, peaceful way, given its particular historical and cultural experience. Many people hoped that the danger of a Germany once again asserting itself would prove to have been settled by the creation of a democratic German republic whose institutions would gently and benevolently re-educate German society and once more allow the many and widely admired qualities of German culture to flourish. Yet while it was true that the constitution of the Weimar Republic was liberal and democratic, too many Germans were out of sympathy with it from the start. That Weimar had not solved the German problem was revealed when another widely-shared assumption was dissipated – the illusion that prosperity could be taken for granted.

Nonetheless, after Locarno a certain diplomatic euphoria hung over the rest of the decade. The background of growing material prosperity was soothing and the League chalked up a number of minor successes that improved its image (though none involved a great power). In 1928, when a much-praised and virtually meaningless pact (eventually of sixty-five nations) was signed renouncing aggressive war, optimism was at its height. In the following year Germany's reparation burdens

---

[13] 'For the Polish corridor,' said the British foreign secretary, 'no British Government ever will or ever can risk the bones of a British grenadier.' Q. in F. P. Walters, *A History of the League of Nations* (London, 1952), p.284. It was a conscious echo of a remark made by Bismarck about risking the bones of a Pomeranian grenadier over the Balkans.

were further lightened and in 1930 the last Allied occupation forces were withdrawn from the Rhineland.

AN EASTERN ENIGMA

At Rapallo in 1922 Germany and the USSR had agreed to exchange ambassadors, and a few years later there were signs that the Bolsheviks' relations with other countries were beginning to look more promising, too. Though there remained a deep division of belief between them and the rulers of all other countries about the way history was moving – still towards revolution, said the Comintern – improvement in economic conditions in the Soviet Union and the ending of civil war gave them (or should have given them) less cause to fear the outside world. The failure of revolutions in the west in the aftermath of the war also suggested that the USSR might have to live side by side with capitalist countries for a long time before they crumbled. Meanwhile, the Soviet Union needed to trade with the outside world. Slowly, therefore, normal diplomatic contacts were opened with other countries. Though Rapallo had caused alarm, it turned out to have begun the process of bringing Soviet diplomatic isolation in Europe to an end (as well as founding a secret special relationship which was to bear further fruit in military cooperation which was to last until 1933). Soviet policy remained suspect even in Germany, though, as local communists made attempts to seize power in 1923 in Saxony, Thuringia and, most seriously, Hamburg. Yet in 1924 came British diplomatic recognition of the USSR. There followed the establishment of Soviet diplomatic relations also with France and Norway, Austria, Greece, Sweden, Canada, Denmark, China and Mexico, all in all a substantial normalization of Soviet relations with the non-communist world. In the remainder of the decade a number of non-aggression treaties were made between the USSR and nearby countries, one of them with Germany in 1926.

Such steps made no difference, of course, to the distrust with which the Soviet Union was viewed in some western circles, or to its promotion of communist activity abroad and frequent and enthusiastic assertions of confidence about the coming overthrow of the capitalist world. The Locarno agreements, too, were denounced by the USSR as an attempt to form an anti-Soviet coalition by the British. Still, what looked like more normal relations with the outside world fitted a mood of optimism about international affairs in the late 1920s. A new official Soviet slogan, 'Socialism in one country', was taken to mean that the country's rulers saw themselves as committed first to building a solid socialist society at home before getting involved in the process of exporting revolution abroad.

This did not, though, alter the fact that there had been a revolutionary change in international affairs since 1917. After the Bolshevik revolution there were people in every country who were devoted to the idea of revolution which would overthrow the existing order, and they were able to look to a foreign government for encouragement, inspiration and sometimes practical help. In theory and principle, the world was already divided into two fundamentally opposed and irreconcilable camps, even if they seemed to be getting on with one another on a day-to-day basis. Between 1927 and 1929, too, there appears to have been an actual fear in Soviet ruling circles that an imperialist war against the USSR was imminent, under the leadership of Great Britain (which for a time broke off diplomatic relations with the USSR in 1927 after evidence of Soviet espionage activities in London had been given publicity).

THE UNITED STATES

It would be a misrepresentation to say that none of the affairs that preoccupied European statesmen in the 1920s interested Americans. The government of the United States, the officials of the State Department and the admirals who thought about ratios of battlefleets and cruisers all paid sometimes close if sporadic attention to developments in Europe. There was continuing concern over financial questions, above all the war debts of the Allies, and German reparations payments. Yet it hardly seems that most Americans cared much about any of these things. A tradition of abstention from world affairs outside the hemisphere was reinforced by new circumstances turning them back into isolation after briefly playing a world role. In 1918, the United States had been the strongest of the victor nations. Her citizens had suffered less and prospered more than those of her allies and her territory was untouched. Soon after the fighting was over, though, American politicians seemed to resist overseas involvement again, almost as if they were fed up with the outside world. The Senate (one of whose tasks is the approval of treaties made by the government) turned down the treaty that Wilson had signed at Versailles. Besides abandoning America's commitments to uphold the peace settlement, this also meant staying outside the League of Nations. Against the wishes of the sick and dying Wilson, his fellow-citizens retreated into psychological isolation. Broadly speaking, they were to remain remarkably uninterested in world affairs for twenty years.

A little-known Republican senator, Warren G. Harding, won the presidential election of 1920. Republican presidents were elected again in 1924 and 1928 with large majorities.[14] Americans were casting their votes for 'normalcy' – getting on with business at home behind the protection of tariffs, and not worrying much about the outside world. It seemed to work. The 1920s brought greater prosperity to Americans than ever before. Their average income per head rose by over a quarter between 1921 and 1929. There was a huge building boom. There were 8 million American motor cars in 1920 and 23 million ten years later. Radios were few in 1920; in 1930 American households had 13 million of them. Like refrigerators, gas and electric cookers and other domestic 'gadgets', they were still luxuries, but luxuries more widely and rapidly spread than any in the past. Prices fell; those with jobs in the towns had more to spend than ever before. The other side of the economic coin was seen by the unemployed, the small farmer, and the rural poor who were worst off and forgotten. The annual income per head in the mid-1920s of the non-farm population of South Carolina, a poor and backward state, was $412. That was not much – but that of its farm population was $129. To confront such facts the United States could deploy nothing like the social welfare arrangements already achieved and taken for granted in many European countries.

With hindsight, it is easy to be wise about the shaky foundation of

[14] Calvin Coolidge (who, as vice-president, had succeeded on Harding's death in 1923) and Herbert Hoover.

American prosperity and the huge overseas lending of the United States, and to regard sceptically the optimism and the self-absorption of Americans convinced that (as one president put it) 'the business of the United States is business'. As for politics, the Republicans seemed solidly entrenched in office, buttressed by the general sense of well-being. A Democrat recovery seemed unlikely, partly because the party was associated with 'Prohibition'; a problem left over by one of the last changes of the Progressive era that ended with Wilson. Millions of Americans had always deplored the use of alcohol and in 1920 they had at last succeeded in persuading Congress to prohibit the making and selling of alcoholic drinks. The effects astonished advocates and opponents of the ban alike. Among them was the appearance and rapid growth of an enormous criminal industry devoted to smuggling, bootlegging, illicit distilling and, subsequently, to the crimes of violence that flowed from them. Even hitherto once normally law-abiding citizens took to breaking the law without scruple. Fifteen thousand legal 'saloons' or bars had sold alcohol in New York City before Prohibition; when they were closed under the new law, 35,000 'speak-easies' or illegal drinking establishments sprang up to take their place. Corruption was rife; gangsters became famous (and sometimes admired) figures and Chicago a place notorious for violent crime (there were 227 gang murders there between 1927 and 1931 and not one conviction for them in the courts).[15]

For all the tragedy that came with it there still seems something slightly comic about an idea that backfired so badly. But the 'dries' who favoured Prohibition did not falter in their beliefs. They were especially strong in southern states where they made up much of the Democratic party's electoral support. The party's other strongholds were in the north-eastern cities; there, well-established and Democratic-voting Irish and Italian communities were overwhelmingly 'wet'. When the Democrats tried to cash in on the unpopularity of Prohibition by running a 'wet' presidential candidate in 1928 he won the cities, but lost heavily in the South.

One marker of a new American inward-lookingness and of the end

---

[15] In 1925, Chicago had 16,000 arrests for drunkenness: this was more than the whole of England and Wales.

of an era of American history came with new limits on immigration. The old generous acceptance of immigrants almost without restriction (the main one had been on grounds of infectious disease), though it had served the country well, was given up. A literacy test had already been introduced in 1917 over Wilson's presidential veto. After 1921 quotas finally brought down the total number of immigrants allowed each year until 1929, when it was stabilized at 150,000 – fewer than the annual arrivals from Italy alone had been between 1900 and 1914. The United States could no longer claim to be a refuge and opportunity for all humanity, but drawing up the ladder fitted the national mood of the 1920s. The rejection of the idea of assimilation was first promoted by conservatives, by exclusion. A half-century later it was being rejected by discontented radicals, in the name of cultural pluralism.

BOOK 4

WORLD REVOLUTION

I I

An Emerging Global History

THE WORLD DEPRESSION

The economic depression of the early 1930s was unprecedentedly worldwide and more severe than any earlier slump. No continent was untouched and most nations and peoples were badly damaged by its specificity, its extent and the suddenness of its onset. Great plagues and folk-movements in the past had slowly rolled across the Euro-Asian landmass and North Africa, but there had never been such simultaneity about them, nor had they so ravaged every continent. Perhaps the world depression was the first truly world-historical event ever. Fighting and diplomacy had tangled the political fates of peoples round the world, but never so as to involve every known part of it at once. The blight that settled on economic life all over the world in the 1930s was a truly universal fact. It may be reckoned the single most influential historical development between two world wars, because it was so general in its effects. It made much possible, and some things inevitable. Without the damage it did there would have been less intense frustration needing release, fewer challenges for politicians with good intentions and inadequate understanding, and fewer opportunities for wicked men or even simple adventurers.

This was to be particularly evident in Europe. If judgement is made worldwide and in purely material terms, her leading industrial countries were by no means those worst blighted by slump. Nonetheless, Europe's political situation and her still great (if already reduced) importance in the international system of great power relationships gave the damage done to them greater consequence than elsewhere. It dislocated the conduct of international relations much more than, say, the collapse of Chilean nitrate and copper mining, or the fall in demand for Malayan or Indo-Chinese rubber, dreadful for their peoples though those disasters were. Europe's troubles enhanced those of other continents, too, and at every level, politically and culturally, as well as economically. For three centuries, she had grown in importance as a consumer of raw materials from the rest of the world and a provider of goods and capital for non-European countries. Though she did not account for so large a share of world manufacturing output or world trade between 1919 and 1939 as before 1914, she still provided a huge part of both. What happened to Europe was bound to have major world repercussions.

In spite of the ups and downs of the trade cycle and the disruption brought to some industrial countries in the aftermath of the Great War and its destruction, the long-term trend of the world economy down to 1929 had looked benevolent. All food-producing countries had enjoyed twenty years or so of advantageous terms of trade from the 1890s onwards. After the post-war years of reconstruction and stabilization, there had then come five years of growing prosperity. Yet by 1929, farming was already moving into crisis in some countries, for world prices were already falling. But there was worse to come.

The United States had become a determining factor on world prosperity. Her role in international finance had been transformed by the Great War, which made her a capital-exporting nation. She produced nearly 40 per cent of the world's coal and over half the world's manufactures, too. This abundance, enhanced by the demands of war, made her people in the 1920s the first in the world millions of whom could take for granted, for example, the ownership of a family car. Their domestic prosperity had consequences abroad. It lubricated world trade and generated the capital America exported in loans and investment. Between 1925 and 1929 Europeans borrowed nearly $3,000 million in the United States in addition to the big debts they still owed that country from the war years. In 1928, though, short-term money began to cost more in the United States. There were other signs that the end of the long domestic boom might be approaching, too, though it looked at first only as if the old business cycle was again at work. Soon, though, it led to the calling back of American loans from Europe. Soon, there were European borrowers in difficulties. Meanwhile, demand slackened in the United States as people began to think a severe slump might be on the way. Almost incidentally, this detonated a particularly sudden and spectacular stock market collapse in October 1929. Great bankers bought heavily to support the stock market, but though a temporary rally followed, confidence disappeared. It was the end of a prosperous phase. After a last brief rally in 1930 American money for investment abroad dried up.

It took another year or so for the full weight of economic depression that followed to be felt worldwide as purchasing power fell away. In Europe it came only after a major financial crisis in which politics played a part. As governments cast about for ways of protecting their domestic marketing and industry, and sought to manage problems of debt suddenly grown more intense, the Austrians began to consider the possibility of a Customs Union with Germany. Almost at once, France denounced any such step as a contravention of the treaty of Versailles, which had forbidden the union of the two countries. By way of driving home the point, the Bank of France refused to come to the help of an Austrian bank that was in difficulties. The collapse of the *Kredit-Anstalt* into bankruptcy started a run on other Central European banks. As they looked to collect their deposits and debts from German banks, the run spread further, first to Germany, and then to London. In September the United Kingdom ceased to make payments in gold. By the end of 1932 twelve countries had followed suit in going off the gold standard. The USA did so in the following year. Soon, among major currencies only the French franc was any longer convertible to gold. This dethronement of the gold standard, one old idol of liberal economics, was an overt financial symbol of a tragedy that was by then facing millions.

The collapse of investment went with deflation as countries struggled unsuccessfully to keep the value of their currencies steady in relation to gold and to balance their books. But the struggle to maintain currencies made things worse. Falling demand was now joined by tariffs and quotas (with the aim of reducing imports) in driving down world prices. As their earnings fell, countries producing primary goods found themselves unable to earn enough to buy manufactures from abroad. Export markets for the industrial world withered; there were soon 30 million or so people unemployed in the leading manufacturing countries. In 1932 (the worst year) the index of industrial production for the United States and Germany was in each case only just above half of what it had been in 1929; taking that year's level of industrial production as 100, in 1932 that of the United States had fallen to 52.7, that of Germany to 53.3. (That of the United Kingdom stood at 83.5, which was bad enough.)

Dramatic changes like these were the simplest markers of what happened as manufacturing countries cut back production. As workers lost their jobs, and their wages became unavailable to buy goods, other manufacturing trades, food suppliers and service industries sold less. As the demand for imports of raw materials fell back, the non-industrialized countries had less foreign earnings than ever with which to buy manufactured exports. As world trade crumbled further, so less business was done by shipping firms, insurance and banking, less money was available to lend to people who might start up new businesses or invest in improving their existing ones (not that a slump was likely to encourage many to do that) – and so on, and on, and on. The national income of the richest nation in the world, the United States, fell by 38 per cent in these years. Had that been equally shared among her citizens, each would have had less than two-thirds of the income they had enjoyed in 1929. But there was no such equality of suffering. Millions of Americans, like other millions all over the world, did much worse than the average.

Worldwide, too, the depression was by no means uniform in its effects, except in so far as it was everywhere very grave. For most people, any social and economic gains made in the 1920s were wiped out. This was most obvious in the industrial world. Steel-workers in Germany, ship-builders in Great Britain, coal-miners in the USA all suffered – and with them their families and the great majority of their countrymen, whatever their occupations. But so, much more, did nitrate-workers in Chile, cowboys in Argentina, jute-growers in India and farmers in the USA. No country had a monopoly of misery but it was worst for those who already started at a low level. Unemployment, though most conspicuous in the United States and Germany, shot up all round the world; though vividly present in the streets of silent industrial cities, it was disguised or hidden in the villages and farmlands of primary producer countries. As world prices of manufactured goods fell, those of raw materials and foodstuffs fell faster still (by 56 and 48 per cent respectively, between 1929 and 1932).[1] In spite of appearances, it was the poorer nations and the poorer sectors of the mature economies that suffered most.

This was not always recognized. The poorest of all lived far away from the industrial areas that got most notice and had less far to fall in the first place. Transylvanian or Indian peasants, Bolivian and African miners, might have always lived in misery, comparatively speaking, but the newly unemployed German or Belgian clerk or factory hand was suddenly and surprisingly plunged into it after years of slow improvement in his life and that of his family. Even between developed nations, too, the disaster of unemployment was unequally shared. In Europe, Germany suffered most, Sweden least; France felt the depression later than other countries (she went off the gold standard only in 1936) and the United Kingdom felt it less than many countries. The USSR was preoccupied with miseries and upheavals of her own making and, somewhat insulated by her own political and economic system, she was not so exposed to world trends; international depression affected her less than her neighbours. Soviet government could present the hardships of its people as necessary sacrifice to future strength, too.[2] Among the industrial countries the relatively worst affected were the United States and Japan, vastly different in scale and nature though their problems were.

When it came, recovery, like recession before it, came at a different pace and in different ways in different countries. World agricultural prices remained low right through the 1930s, so that the later part of the decade was relatively good for those who still had jobs or who had them again; the cost of living had gone down in real terms since 1929, and if you had money in your pocket it cost less to eat. But overall recovery was very slow. International trade in 1939 was still running at less than half of its level ten years earlier. The United States then still had 10 million unemployed. Many countries were still seeking

---

[1] That of rubber fell from 22 to 3 American cents a pound between 1928 and 1932.
[2] As Stalin had put it in 1931, 'Do you want our socialist fatherland to be beaten and to lose its independence? If you do not want this you must put an end to its backwardness in the shortest possible time . . .' *Problems of Leninism* (Moscow, 1953), p.456.

'protection' behind high tariffs, or even a kind of autarky, and governments were interfering with the economy as they had not done since the heyday of mercantilism. It was natural for countries with democratic electorates to please to adopt what looked like protectionist solutions in the short term, but this held up recovery for the export-dependent. With vivid memories of the colossal inflations of the early 1920s, though, few governments were likely to try to spend their way out of depression.

Yet as people clamoured for something to be done about the slump, governments in the United States, Great Britain and Germany turned, by different routes, to capital investment in what would now be called 'infrastructure'.[3] Hard times increased the demand for the provision of relief for poverty; countries already moving down the road to the 'welfare state' (such as the Scandinavian nations and Great Britain) now went further. Thanks also to price-changes, the unemployed British worker was better off on the dole paid him in the 1930s than the average British wage-earner had been while in work at the beginning of the century. But such relief did little to offset resentment everywhere of an economic culture that could produce such upheaval and distress. In the end the biggest fact helping to take the edge off economic depression was the approach of another war; rearmament and the stockpiling of raw materials gave economic life almost everywhere a new stimulus as the end of the decade drew nearer. Attempts to meet economic disaster by international action (there were meetings of statesmen, of which the most ambitious in scope was a World Monetary and Economic Conference in London in 1933) all failed. Some individual countries (Great Britain, Sweden, Germany, for example) were showing signs of industrial recovery even by 1936. There was to be no world recovery, though, before 1940.

Economic disaster looked a promising setting for those who expected, advocated or strove to achieve the collapse of liberal civilization. Birds of prey began to flap expectantly about the enfeebled carcass of the international economy. For revolutionaries everywhere

---

[3] And so did other countries that imitated them. Interestingly, the policies of Argentina won the approval of the economist J. M. Keynes, whose fame is associated with the ideas of public investment and maintenance of consumer demand as techniques for throwing off the depression.

the world depression had been a godsend. New and violent political demands were heard for solutions to poverty and unemployment. Some were successful in winning popular support. Marxists found fresh and compelling empirical support for the argument that capitalism was doomed to self-destruction. The millions of unemployed, the end of the gold standard and belief in a self-regulating, self-correcting economy indeed marked the collapse of a world order in its economic dimension. That liberal civilization had demonstrably and frighteningly lost its power to control events was also to be made clear in other ways, above all in the rise of totalitarian regimes and of nationalism to a new climax of destructiveness. Yet many Europeans still dreamed of the restoration of an age when that civilization enjoyed unquestioned supremacy, though its values had rested on a political and economic hegemony in fact in decay all round the world.

ASIA IN THE ERA OF EUROPEAN CIVIL WAR

Some of the first symptoms of that decay had appeared long before, in the appearance of challenges and challengers to European supremacy in Asia and the advances they had made before 1914. Then had come the Great War, a catalyst in Asia's history. This was not because of the scale of Asian participation in the fighting. Important though they had been and though some of them involved sizeable armies, the Asian campaigns of the Great War were very much 'sideshows', secondary in importance to the great battles in Europe. In the Far East, the isolated German port of Tsingtau was besieged and taken by the Japanese with some British support before 1914 was over and in the Pacific the Marianas and Carolines were seized by the Japanese without bloodshed. Thereafter the Great War had only an indirect impact on Asia beyond the Near East until the Bolshevik revolution and its opening of the way to Japanese intervention in Siberia. The most important fighting in Asia was done by the Russians and Turks in the Caucasus and eastern Anatolia, by the Anglo-Indian expeditionary force that eventually drove the Turks out of Mesopotamia (and went on later to operate in the Caspian region against the Bolsheviks) and by the British and Dominions army that conquered

Palestine. The Arab revolt that won British logistical and financial support mattered politically because of its implications, but did not involve large resources or deploy large numbers. In contrast, German efforts to exploit subversive activity in India, or to achieve the diplomatic seduction of Japan away from the Allied cause, hardly mattered at all.

The war's indirect impact nonetheless was crucial. When the war had begun, the peak of European domination in the Far East was already past, yet the European Asian empires were still swept up into it at their rulers' behest. India had gone to war from the start. Her resources proved very important to the British imperial war effort. Although there was some initial uncertainty about the loyalty of Muslims in a struggle against the Ottoman empire whose ruler was Caliph, most of the subjects of the Raj either took it for granted that they should support it or that they had no say or interest in the matter. Princes gave of their wealth, members of Congress demonstrated their loyalty, and an Indian lawyer named Gandhi threw himself into supporting the war effort as enthusiastically as he had organized ambulance services for the British in the Boer war. The Indian army at once demonstrated its value as an imperial strategic reserve; within a few months an Indian army corps of two infantry and two cavalry divisions was serving in France. Its infantry was withdrawn during 1915 to serve elsewhere (leaving behind an Indian cavalry division awaiting the opportunity of an Allied 'breakthrough' for another two years). More important still, sufficient confidence was felt about India's own security for over fifty British regular battalions to be withdrawn from the sub-continent in the first months of the war to make up new divisions for service in France. At one time there were only eight white battalions left in India (and committed to the North West Frontier); the regular units already withdrawn were gradually replaced by territorials who could complete their training in India while serving as a garrison there.

Meanwhile, Indian manufacturing industry was stimulated by the demands of the imperial war effort. Indian recruiting shot up.[4] Even

---

[4] Over the duration of the war, 800,000 Indian combatants and 400,000 non-combatants were enlisted.

the Dalai Lama of Tibet offered 1,000 men to the Indian army. By 1917, the British government appeared to want to recognize the contribution India was making to the Allied cause. It was announced in that year that London envisaged a policy of steady advance towards responsible government for India within the empire – which seemed to mean some sort of Home Rule. This fell short of the full Dominion status that some Indians hoped for, but showed that the war had already begun to shape politics in Asia.

THE SEQUEL TO THE CHINESE REVOLUTION

The impact of war was even more striking, and much more complex, in non-colonial Asia. Both China and Japan underwent and were affected by it in very fundamental ways, slight though their actual military or naval participation was to be. The war's effects were inseparable from the story of their relations with one another, entwined as their destinies were, thanks to China's prolonged weakness and ineffectiveness and Japan's continuing dynamism. That effect also fell upon a situation which, at least in the case of China, was evolving and fluid.

Though potentially the greatest of Asian (and even of world) powers, China did not emerge from an era of eclipse and humiliation in 1911. Marking an epoch even more fundamentally than had done the French Revolution of 1789, the Chinese revolution nonetheless had limited immediate effect though, in the longest perspective, its importance was vast. 1911 was the end of more than 2,000 years of history during which the Confucian state had held China together and Confucian ideals had dominated Chinese culture and society. Inseparably intertwined, Confucianism and the imperial order went under together when the revolution brought down the political structure within which traditional China lived. Yet the revolution was, in the first place, destructive rather than constructive.

The empire had ruled a vast country, virtually a continent, of widely different regions. Its collapse meant that the centrifugal regionalism that so often expressed itself in Chinese history could once again have scope. Secret societies, the gentry and military commanders all stepped forward to exploit central government's weakness to their own advantage. Many revolutionaries, too, nourished deep envy and distrust of Peking. Somewhat masked while Yuan Shih-kai (the former imperial general who had become president of the republic) remained at the head of affairs, these divisive tendencies had still burst out very plainly. The revolutionaries themselves had quickly split between Sun Yat-sen's Chinese National People's Party, or Kuomintang (KMT), established in 1912, and those who upheld the central government based on the parliamentary structure at Peking. Sun's support was drawn mainly from Canton businessmen and some of the soldiers in the south. Against this background of division, warlords, soldiers who happened to dispose of substantial forces and arms, thrived. Between 1912 and 1928 some 1,300 of them controlled important and often large areas of China. Some carried out needed reform, some were simply bandits. Some looked like plausible pretenders to government power. Nothing took the place of the old scholar-bureaucrats, though, and most of the warlords could simply enjoy themselves exploiting the void. Yuan Shih-kai can indeed be regarded as the forerunner of the type; he proclaimed himself emperor in 1915. Republicans forced his abdication but with his death in the following year the warlord era was under way.

Yuan Shih-kai's high-handedness with opposition (he had at one time suppressed the KMT) reflected a fundamental limitation of the revolution of 1911: it had revealed no general will in China on which to base agreement for further positive progress. Sun Yat-sen had said that the solution of the national question would have to precede that of the social, but even about what a nationalist future might mean there was much disagreement. Meanwhile, the removal of the dynasty removed also the common enemy of revolutionaries and reformers alike. Their intellectual confrontations were deeply divisive. In 1915 a journal called *New Youth* which strove to focus debate was founded. Chen Tu-hsiu, a cultural reformer, preached to Chinese youth, in whose hands he believed the revolution's destiny to lie, a total rejection of the old Chinese cultural tradition. Like other intellectuals who talked of Huxley and Dewey and introduced to their wondering compatriots the works of Ibsen, his followers still thought the key to progress lay in western culture; its Darwinian sense of struggle, its individualism and utilitarianism, seemed to them to point to the way ahead. But important though such leadership was and enthusiastic though its disciples might be, a western emphasis in re-educating China was a handicap. Many educated and patriotic Chinese were sincerely attached to the traditional culture; western ideas were only sure of a welcome among untypical elements of Chinese society, the seaboard city-dwelling merchants and their student offspring, often educated abroad. The mass of Chinese could hardly be touched by such ideas and appeals at all (and the demand of some reformers for a vernacular literature was one symptom of this).

Nationalist enthusiasm in China, whether among the élite or at a more popular level, had been energized by anti-western feeling and dislike of western-inspired capitalism. For many Chinese, capitalism, an authentic expression of the civilization some modernizers urged them to adopt, was another name for foreign exploitation. As for the masses, the peasantry seemed after 1911 relapsed in passivity, apparently unmoved by events and oblivious to the agitation of angry and westernized young men. It is not easy to generalize about economic conditions. China was too big and too varied. But while the population steadily increased, nothing was done to meet the peasants' hunger for land; instead, the number of the indebted and landless grew, their wretched lives often made even more intolerable by warlord ambitions and the destruction, robbery, exploitation, famine and disease that went with them. The Chinese Revolution would only be assured success when it could activate the Chinese masses. The cultural emphasis of literate and middle-class reformers sometimes masked their unwillingness to envisage the practical political steps necessary for this. It was therefore still against a background not only of political confusion and disorder, but of ideological division and incoherence that the Chinese republic entered the Great War on the Allied side in August 1917. It did so largely in the hope of winning goodwill and support that would give China an independent voice at the peace. A Chinese labour force was sent to France, and Japanese help in the form of loans and military instructors was also sought by Peking. But this was feeding the appetite of an already very predatory tiger.

JAPAN

In 1912 the Meiji emperor had died, and was succeeded by his third son, whose reign (1912–26, with a regency after 1921) took the era name of Taisho. There was a sense of real change: the end of Meiji announced, too, the passing of the oligarchy of elder statesmen – the *Genro* – who had provided Japan with its rulers during its crucial period of evolution into a modern state. Parties were now to matter more and populist and imperialist forces began to exploit new possibilities. The Great War provided some of the first of them.

A European war was above all an opportunity for Japan to exploit the situation on the mainland of Asia at a moment when western powers were distracted. When the Japanese decided to open operations against Tsingtau, the German enclave on the Shantung peninsula, they had presented an ultimatum to Germany on 16 August. Yet although thus entering the war at the outset, Japan's rulers prudently sidestepped later British and French requests for a Japanese army to serve in France, and confined their support in the European theatre to the provision of escorts for Allied troopships in the Mediterranean.[5] For her, a world war meant she could push forward again in China without European interference. Japan's allies could hardly object to her seizure of the German Pacific colonies, and if they did, they could do little about it while they needed Japanese ships and manufactures. Japanese ammunition went to the Russian armies via Vladivostok and Siberia and Japanese beer via Bombay to the British expeditionary force in Mesopotamia. But though the Allies never gave up the hope that the Japanese might in the end provide an army to fight in Europe, they were always to be disappointed. Instead, irritatingly, the Japanese finessed, arousing fears that they might make a separate peace with the Germans while exploiting their indispensability to the Allies to press ahead in China, profiting from the new distraction of western diplomatic pressure and power from that country's affairs.

At the beginning of 1915 the Japanese government presented to the

---

[5] Among Asia's non-colonial countries, only Siam sent a small expeditionary force to Europe to join the Allies after declaring war on the Central Powers in July 1917.

Chinese government a document that was to become notorious under the name of 'the Twenty-one Demands', following it up with an ultimatum which amounted to a proposal for a Japanese protectorate over China. The United Kingdom and United States did what diplomacy could do to have these demands reduced but, in the end, the Japanese got much of what they asked for from the Chinese, including further confirmation of Japan's special commercial position and leasehold rights in Manchuria. Chinese patriots were enraged, but there was nothing they could do, given China's internal disorder and weakness. They were divided and confused; indeed, Sun Yat-sen himself had at one moment sought Japanese support against Yuan Shih-kai.

The next intervention came in 1916, when Japanese pressure was brought to bear on the British to dissuade them from approving Yuan Shih-kai's attempt to restore stability by styling himself emperor. In the following year came another exploitative treaty, this time extending the recognition of Japan's special interests as far as Inner Mongolia. Even after the Chinese government entered the war with Germany, the United States formally recognized the special interests of Japan in China in return for endorsement of the principle of the 'Open Door' and a Japanese promise to maintain Chinese integrity and independence. All that the Chinese got from the Allies in reward for the labour contingents they sent to France was the ending of German and Austrian extra-territoriality and agreement for the payment of Boxer indemnities to the Allies to be delayed. The Japanese, though, secured still further concessions from China in more secret agreements in 1918. Moreover, they had greatly prospered by then from the war. The economic growth it released rescued Japan from the financial morass in which the Russo-Japanese war had left her and from the current account deficits in international payments that had dogged her down to 1914. During the war her GNP rose by 40 per cent.

THE PEACE SETTLEMENTS AND ASIA

India, Japan and China all sent representatives to Paris for the peace conference. Patriots in all these countries were deeply disappointed by the result, though. Japan and China had hoped for improvements in their international position and standing, and Indian nationalists had hoped for further progress towards self-government as a reward for wartime loyalty. The constitutional reforms introduced in India in 1918 before the war ended had won only a limited gratitude. Much more had been hoped for by Congress. As for Japan, now indisputably a world power (by 1918 she had the third largest navy in the world), she won solid gains at the peace, retaining the former German rights in Shantung promised to her by the British and French in 1917, and being granted a mandate over some of the former German Pacific islands and a permanent seat on the Council of the League of Nations. Yet the gain in 'face' implied in such recognition was offset in Japanese eyes by a failure to have a declaration in favour of racial equality written into the Covenant of the League.

The Chinese had much more to feel aggrieved about. In spite of widespread expressions of sympathy over the Twenty-one Demands (notably in the United States) they were unable to obtain a reversal of the Shantung decision. Disappointed at western diplomatic support and crippled by the divisions within their own delegation between the representatives of the Peking government and those of the Kuomintang, the Chinese refused to sign the treaty. This was followed by a movement to which some commentators have given an importance in Chinese history as great as that of the 1911 revolution itself.

The 'May 4th Movement' of 1919 stemmed from a student demonstration in Peking against the peace and the cession of former German rights in Shantung to the Japanese. Originally planned for 7 May, the anniversary of China's acceptance of the 1915 demands, the demonstration was brought forward to anticipate action by the authorities.[6] It escalated, at first into a riot and the resignation of the head of the

---

[6] Among the students demonstrating was the seventeen-year-old Deng Xiao-ping, later to be leader of the Chinese communist republic.

university, then into nationwide student disturbances (one of the first political consequences of a vigorous spread in China of new colleges and universities after 1911). These in turn grew to embrace others than students, stimulating strikes and a boycott of Japanese goods. A movement that had begun with intellectuals and their pupils swept up other city-dwellers, notably industrial workers and the new Chinese capitalists who had benefited from the war. For the first time a modernizing industrial China entered the political scene.

Parts of China, like Japan, had enjoyed an economic boom during the war. Though a decline in European imports to China had been partly offset by increased Japanese and American sales, Chinese entrepreneurs found they could make money by producing for the home market and new industrial areas had begun to appear in the treaty ports. They bred progressive capitalists who sympathized with revolutionary ideas all the more when the return of peace and the collapse of the wartime boom brought renewed western economic competition and evidence that China was not, after all, free from tutelage to the foreigner. Workers shared their resentments for a different reason, as their jobs were threatened. Many of them were first-generation town-dwellers, drawn from the countryside by the promise of employment. Any uprooting from the tenacious soil of peasant tradition was itself a personal revolution in China, where family and village ties were especially strong. The migrant to the town broke with patriarchal authority and the reciprocal obligations of the independent producing unit, the household: this was a weakening of the age-old structure which had survived the revolution and still tied China to the past.

The May 4th Movement first showed what could be made of such facts as these by creating the first broadly based Chinese revolutionary coalition. Progressive western liberalism had not been enough; implicit in the movement's success was the disappointment of the hopes of many reformers. Capitalist western democracy had been shown up by the Chinese government's helplessness before Japan. Now, that government faced humiliation from its own subjects: the boycott and demonstration forced it to release arrested students and dismiss its pro-Japanese ministers. But this was not the only consequence of the May 4th Movement. For all their limited political influence, reformers had for the first time, thanks to the students, broken through into the world of social action. This aroused enormous optimism and popular political awareness. It provides a case for saying that the Chinese twentieth century begins in 1919 rather than 1911.

Yet ultimately the movement had been caused by another Asian force, Japanese ambition, and it was in 1919 operating on a China that seemed as weak as ever. The warlords could provide no legitimating authority. Nor could they restore or sustain orthodoxy. The ending of the examination system, the return of the westernized exiles and literary and cultural debate during the war years had all pushed things too far for any reversion to the old stagnation. And now even western liberalism, the great solvent of tradition, was itself under attack because of its association with the exploiting foreigner. In China, Western liberalism had never had mass appeal but now it had been discredited just as another ideological rival was appearing on the scene.

CHINESE COMMUNISM

Soon after the Bolshevik revolution, Soviet agents had begun to seek political influence in Asia by propaganda and the encouragement of Asian communist parties both within the colonial empires and in independent countries. Russia had long been an Asian power; it is often forgotten that in Soviet as in tsarist times most of its territory lay in Asia, where it occupied an area four times as big as the Indian sub-continent, and nearly twice that of China. The length of its frontiers was by itself bound to give any government in St Petersburg or Moscow a close interest in the affairs of its Asian neighbours. The Bolshevik revolution had thus directly settled the fate of a huge part of the Asian land mass, but, almost as importantly, one of the first acts of the Bolsheviks had been to renounce formally all extra-territorial rights and jurisdiction enjoyed by the old tsarist regime. Chinese patriots therefore credited them with cleaner hands than other governments. Finally, the establishment of the USSR had created a centre and place of arms for anti-imperialism; rebels against colonial governments and those resisting western interference alike could look to it for inspiration, encouragement, guidance, and sometimes material support.

In China, the February 1917 revolution and the Bolshevik victory had much excited one of the contributors to *New Youth* who was later to be a leader in the May 4th Movement, Li Ta-chao. In 1918 he became librarian at Peking University. At a moment of disillusion with western capitalism, the new Russia was very popular among Chinese students. The Soviet revolution – a revolution in a great peasant society with a relatively small but already rapidly growing industrial sector – claimed to be built upon a doctrine whose applicability to China seemed especially plausible. Li Ta-chao came to see Marxism as the harbinger of world revolution and under his encouragement there began to meet at Peking University a Marxist study society. One of its members was an assistant in the university library named Mao Tse-tung;[7] others were, like Li Ta-chao, prominent in the May 4th Movement. By 1920 Marxist ideas were finding outlets in the student magazines that expressed the aspirations of that movement.

Yet Marxism brought further division to the reform movement. The liberals began to be left behind, as intellectuals turned to communism. The Comintern observed its opportunities and had sent its first agent to China in 1919. The effects were not entirely happy: there were quarrels. Nevertheless, in circumstances still obscure – we know precisely neither names nor dates – a Chinese communist party was formed in Shanghai in 1921 by delegates from different parts of China, Mao Tse-tung among them. At almost the same time, the Comintern opened negotiations with Sun Yat-sen through a Dutch communist from Indonesia. These led Moscow to select the KMT as the agency through which it should operate in China. In the following year it was agreed that members of the Chinese communist party should be allowed to join the KMT on an individual basis.

So began the last stage of the Chinese revolution and yet another twist of the curious dialectic that has run through Europe's relations with Asia. Another alien western idea, Marxism, born and shaped in

---

[7] In 1953 a new system of romanizing Chinese characters was officially adopted, after which Mao's full name was increasingly rendered as 'Mao Zedong' and Peking as 'Beijing'.

a society totally unlike any in Asia, embodying a background of assumptions whose origins were rooted in Judaeo-Christian culture, was now being taken up among an Asian people. It was to be deployed not merely against the traditional sources of inertia in China, in the name of the western goals of modernization, efficiency and universal human dignity and equality, but even against the source from which it, too, came – the European world. What was called 'capitalism' now became a more plausible scapegoat than ever in China for a wide range of different problems and troubles.

JAPANESE DYNAMISM

The major source of the continuing revolutionizing of Asia, nevertheless, was still to be Japan. For over twenty years after 1919 her dynamism broke out again and again in both economic and territorial aggression. For a long time the first seemed part and parcel of an overall process of what was still seen by outsiders as the 'westernizing' of Japan. That process in the 1920s still masked somewhat in foreign eyes the persistent and deeply entrenched expansionist and imperialist drive of many in Japan's ruling circles and, indeed, among the populace at large. There was no evidence of sympathy in Japan for another Asian people when a 'Declaration of Korean Independence' on 1 March 1919 was followed by a revolt in which thousands of Koreans were killed by the Japanese forces. Yet this complicity with aggression flourished at the same time as the tendency to what was called 'Taisho democracy', which had been much in evidence during the Great War,[8] and what appeared to be clear advances in constitutional liberalism. In 1920, it is true, the electorate was limited by a franchise based on property, and extended to only about one in twenty of the whole population; in 1925, though, universal suffrage for males over twenty-five was introduced. For all the evidence from other countries that this had no necessary connexion with liberalism or moderation, and in spite of much to emphasize the authoritarian tone of Japanese

[8] The Taisho emperor who occupied the throne at the time was succeeded by the Showa emperor in 1926, who became familiar in western countries under the name Hirohito, which he had used as crown prince.

government, it still seemed to many of their admirers abroad that the Japanese were continuing along a line of steady constitutional progress they had entered upon in the nineteenth century.

The economic opportunities presented by the Great War also encouraged a mood of expansive optimism because markets (especially in Asia) in which Japan had formerly been faced by heavy western competition were abandoned to her. Former exporters found they could not meet the demands of the war in their own countries, let alone provide exports. Allied governments moreover had ordered great quantities of munitions and other supplies from Japanese factories: a world shipping shortage had given her new shipyards the work they needed. Though interrupted in 1920, economic expansion was to be resumed later in the decade. By 1929 the Japanese had an industrial base that had in twenty years seen steel production rise almost tenfold, textile production triple, and coal output double. Still small though her manufacturing industry was by comparison with that of the western powers and though it coexisted with an enduring and substantial small-scale and artisan sector, Japan's new industrial strength was beginning to affect both domestic politics and foreign relations in the 1920s. She was, though, still predominantly an agricultural country: when the decade began less than 15 per cent of the population lived in cities of more than 150,000 inhabitants. In 1929 manufacturing industry still employed only one in five of the workforce.

Japan imported iron ore from China and Malaya, coal from Manchuria. That province of the old Chinese empire was still strategically a crucial theatre. A Japanese military presence there went back to 1905 and heavy Japanese investment had followed the peace with Russia of that year. At first the Chinese acquiesced in the development of Japanese interests in Manchuria, but in the 1920s began to question it, with support from the USSR which foresaw danger as Japanese influence pushed towards Inner Mongolia. In 1918, too, a Japanese had taken command of the inter-allied intervention forces in Siberia. Nor until 1922 did the Japanese withdraw their troops (who at one moment numbered 70,000).[9] In 1929 the Chinese also came into conflict

[9] The last American soldiers had left Vladivostok in April 1920, the last British in May and the last Czechs in December that year.

with the Soviet Union over control of the railway across Manchuria which was the most direct route to Vladivostok. There was fighting and what appeared to have been a Soviet plan to exploit the Chinese Eastern Railway as a means of penetration of Manchuria was successfully resisted. This impressed the Japanese. If the nationalist KMT was going to be able to reassert itself in the territories of the old empire that might not only threaten Japanese ambitions in Manchuria, but also, perhaps, in Korea, where anti-Japanese feeling persisted.

At this moment, the terms of international trade turned against Japan. Even before the onset of the great depression, economic conditions were hard in Japan. By 1932, they were catastrophic. The price of silk had collapsed. Half Japan's factories were idle and working-class standards of living had fallen dramatically. But the worst effects were felt in the countryside. To millions of city-dwellers, the country's economic plight was vividly brought home by the spectacle of ruined peasant farmers tramping their streets and country girls sold by their families into prostitution in order to obtain money for food.

CIVIL WAR IN CHINA

In the 1920s the KMT gradually mastered many of the warlords and appeared to win control of all save a few border areas from its new capital, Nanking. It whittled away further at the treaties of inferiority, helped by the fact that the western powers began to see in Chinese nationalism a means of opposing communism in Asia and were willing to be somewhat more accommodating. Yet these achievements, significant though they were, nonetheless masked continuing domestic weaknesses. The crux was that though the political revolution might continue, social revolution had hardly even begun before it came to a stop. Intellectuals were in the 1920s already withdrawing their moral support from a regime that was not providing needed reforms – of which to do something about peasant poverty was the most obvious.

Furthermore, even what looked like helpful international developments could not conceal the fact that China still counted for little in world affairs. When, under the agreements made in Washington in

1922, nine powers with Asiatic interests were got to guarantee Chinese territorial integrity and Japan agreed to hand back to her former German territories which she had taken in the Great War, this was only a subsidiary part of a complicated set of agreements which were really about restraining Japan and imposing limitations on the size of her fleet. The old 'unequal' treaties were still recognized as binding on China, and Japan's special position in Manchuria was left unchallenged. The core of the deal was a set of international limitations on naval strength (there was great uneasiness about the cost of armaments), which in the end still left Japan relatively stronger than in 1914. The four major powers had guaranteed one another's possessions, and thus provided a decent burial for the Anglo-Japanese alliance, whose ending had long been sought by the Americans. But any guarantee to China now depended for its effectiveness on whether the Americans would fight to support one; the British had been obliged by the Washington treaties *not* to build a naval base at Hong Kong and would thus be unable to come to China's aid to resist aggression even if they wanted to. Meanwhile, foreigners continued to administer the customs and tax revenues on which the government of China depended while foreign agents and businessmen went on dealing directly with the warlords as they needed.

It was against this disappointing background that the new rival to the KMT, the Chinese Communist Party (CCP), grew in strength. The apparently continuing grip of the 'foreign devils' on Chinese life was one reason why Marxism's appeal to Chinese intellectuals went far beyond the boundaries of the party itself. Sun Yat-sen stressed his doctrinal disagreement with it but adopted views that helped to carry the KMT away from conventional liberalism and in the direction of Marxism. In 1923 he had agreed to admit CCP members as individuals to the KMT and had nominated three of them to its Central Executive Committee. In his view of the world, Russia, Germany and China had a common interest as exploited nations. They shared oppressors and the same enemies, the old imperialist powers (Germany was well regarded after she had undertaken in 1921 to place her relations with China on a completely equal footing). Sun coined a new expression, 'hypo-colony', for the state of affairs in which China was exploited without formal subordination as a dependency. At least for the immediate future, his conclusion was collectivist: 'On no account must we give more liberty to the individual,' he wrote. 'Let us secure liberty instead for the nation.' This was an endorsement of a traditional emphasis of Chinese civilization. The claims of family, clan and state on the individual had always been paramount. Paradoxically, for all his enthusiasm for 'westernization' Sun Yat-sen's vision of a period of one-party rule in order to make possible mass indoctrination was likely to reconfirm Chinese attitudes which might be in danger of corruption by western ideas. It was much assisted by the help he received from Comintern advisers in turning the KMT into a centralized, disciplined and ultimately dictatorial party.

At the outset, then, there was cooperation between the CCP and KMT. As for the USSR, friendship with the anti-imperialist power with which China had her longest land frontier was at the very least prudent and potentially very advantageous in KMT eyes. For its part, the Soviet government favoured cooperation with the Chinese nationalists to safeguard its interests in Mongolia and as some kind of step towards holding off Japan. The USSR had been left out of the Washington conferences, though no power had greater territorial interests in the Far East. For her, cooperation with the likely winners in China was an obvious objective. It helped, too, that Marxist doctrine fitted such a policy; orthodox Marxism as interpreted by Lenin argued that bourgeois nationalist revolution had to precede the victory of the proletariat. From 1924 onwards the CCP was advised by its Comintern counsellors therefore to work with the KMT in spite of the doubts of some of its members. The behaviour of the western powers and of the warlords provided common enemies and Soviet encouragement helped to keep them together. As individuals, many communists joined the KMT, and Sun Yat-sen's ablest young soldier, Chiang Kai-shek, was sent to Moscow for training. A military academy founded by Sun Yat-sen with Soviet support provided ideological as well as military instruction for a new national officer corps.

When Sun Yat-sen died in 1925 the united front still endured. His will (which Chinese schoolchildren were meant to learn by heart) had truly said that the Revolution was not yet complete. CCP and KMT alike were now contributing to its advance. While the communists in certain provinces won peasant support for it, the new revolutionary army led by idealistic young KMT officers made useful headway against the warlords. By 1927 something of a semblance of unity had been restored to the country under KMT leadership. Anti-imperialist feeling supported a successful boycott of British goods, and led the British government to surrender its concessions at Hankow and Kiukian. Alarmed by the evidence of growing Russian influence in China, it had already returned Wei-hai-wei to China, while the United States had renounced its share of the Boxer indemnity. Such successes once again helped to give credence to the idea that China was on the move at last.

One important aspect of this revolution long received less notice abroad. Theoretical Marxism stressed the indispensable revolutionary role of the industrial proletariat. But though Chinese communists were proud of the progress they had made in politicizing the new urban workers, the mass of Chinese were peasants. Trapped in a Malthusian vice of rising numbers and land shortage, their centuries-old sufferings had often been intensified in the warlord years. The basic need of the Chinese economy was to increase their purchasing power, but that would imply a revolutionary social change to ensure that any gains generated by their efforts went to the peasant and not to the landowner or moneylender. Some Chinese communists now began to see in the peasants a revolutionary potential which, if not easy to reconcile with contemporary Marxist orthodoxy (as retailed by the Moscow theorists who stressed the necessity, in every sense, of social evolution through a capitalist phase as the basis of the class formation which could sustain revolution), none the less embodied Chinese reality. The young Mao Tse-tung and others who agreed with him turned their attention away from the cities to the countryside in the early 1920s and began an unprecedented effort to win over the rural masses to communism. Paradoxically, Mao seems to have gone on cooperating with the Kuomintang longer than some Chinese communists; it was more sympathetic to the organization of the peasants than was his own party.

Success followed, especially marked in Hunan. By 1927 some 10 million or so Chinese peasants and their families had been persuaded by the communists to give them their allegiance. 'In a few months,' wrote Mao in a report on the Hunan peasant movement, 'the peasants have accomplished what Dr Sun Yat-sen wanted, but failed, to accomplish in the forty years he devoted to the national revolution.'[10] Communist reorganization began the removal of many of the ills that beset the peasants. Landlords were not at once always dispossessed, but they were harried and tormented, rents were often reduced and usurious rates of interest brought down to reasonable levels. More important, cooperative enterprises were set up that pointed to new possibilities for rural industry. Yet true revolution in the countryside had eluded all previous reformers; Mao identified this as the great failure of 1911. Communist success was based on the discovery that it could be brought about by tapping the revolutionary potential of the peasants themselves. Mao revalued urban revolution accordingly. 'If we allot ten points to the democratic revolution,' he wrote, 'then the achievements of the urban dwellers and the military units rate only three points, while the remaining seven points should go to the peasants in their rural revolution.' In an image twice repeated in his report Mao compared the peasants to an elemental force: 'the attack is just like a tempest or hurricane; those who submit to it survive, those who resist perish'. Even the image is significant; here was something rooted deeply in Chinese tradition and ages of struggle against landlords and bandits. The communists tried hard to eradicate superstition and break up family authority, but they drew upon tradition, too. What they did in the countryside seemed to indicate new possibilities in other parts of Asia, too.

Communism's entrenchment in the countryside was to prove the key to survival when its alliance with the KMT broke down. A rift had opened among the nationalists between a 'left' and a 'right' wing after Sun Yat-sen's death. The young Chiang, who had been seen as a progressive when he was commandant of the Whampoa military academy, now emerged as the military representative of the 'right', which reflected mainly the interests of capitalists and, indirectly, landlords. Within the KMT, he began to undermine the communists who had previously been admitted to the party. Differences over strategy were resolved when Chiang, confident of his control of his troops, committed them to destroying the Left factions in the KMT

---

[10] *Mao's Selected Works* (Peking, 1964), vol. I, p.27.

and the Communist party's urban cadres. This was accomplished with much bloodshed in Shanghai and Nanking in April 1927, under the eyes of contingents of European and American soldiers who had been sent to China to protect the foreign concessions from the nationalists.

The CCP was proscribed, but this was not the end of Soviet cooperation with the KMT. It continued in a few places for some months, because of Moscow's unwillingness to break with Chiang. Soviet direction had made easier the destruction of the city communists; the Comintern in China, as elsewhere, myopically pursued what were believed to be Soviet interests refracted through the lens of dogmatic Marxism. These interests were for Stalin in the first place domestic; in external affairs, he wanted someone in China who could stand up to the British, the greatest imperialist power, and the KMT seemed the best bet for that. After the triumph of the KMT was clear, the USSR withdrew its advisers from the CCP, which now became a subversive, underground organization. Chinese nationalism had in fact done well out of Soviet help even if Chinese communism had not.

THE TURNING TIDE IN INDIA

The disappointment of Indian nationalist leaders with the coming of the peace in 1918 was exacerbated by popular distress as the wartime boom of Indian industry collapsed. In the 1920s the Indian government itself was trying to bring to an end commercial and financial arrangements favouring the United Kingdom. It soon insisted on the imperial government paying a proper share of India's contribution to imperial defence. London was no longer to be allowed to settle Indian tariff policy so as to suit the interests (or believed interests) of British industry, and India set up tariff protection of her own. To this important extent, the government of India was evidently responsive to the interests and representations of Indians. Yet in spite of it, Indian opinion at this juncture was notably inflamed against the British.

One reason lay in the suspension in 1919 of normal legal safeguards in order to deal with what was perceived as a growing threat of conspiracy. This was against the wishes of all the Indian members of the legislative council but in accordance with those of administrators over-impressed by the spectacle of the Bolshevik Revolution (though an Indian Communist party was not founded until 1923). The atmosphere was further heated by the ostentatious intransigence and isolation of the British community in India and by one particularly appalling event. Convinced that Indian nationalism was only a matter of a few ambitious and noisy intellectuals, British residents continually pressed for strong measures to impress the masses. One outcome of the imposition of stricter security arrangements was the first wave of strikes and a new pacifist civil disobedience campaign mounted by Gandhi. He now moved to the forefront of Indian politics, becoming the first Indian politician of sub-continental significance. In spite of his efforts to avoid violence there were riots. In 1919, attacks, some fatal, were made on English people in the Punjab. At this dangerous moment, a British officer in Amritsar, the holy city of the Sikhs, decided to show his countrymen's determination by dispersing a crowd by force. When the firing (by Indian troops) stopped nearly 400 Indians had been killed and over 1,000 wounded. Brigadier Dyer was officially reprimanded for his folly and his career came to an end, but an irreparable blow had been dealt to British prestige by what he had done. The effect was even worse when British residents in India and members of parliament in London loudly applauded him.

Gandhi's leadership and strategy were accepted by Congress and a period of boycott and civil disturbance followed. Although Gandhi himself continued to emphasize that his campaign was non-violent, India was (and remains) a violent country. After much more disorder he was arrested and imprisoned for the first time in 1922 (though soon released because of the danger that he might die in prison). This was the end of significant agitation in India for a few years and British policy began to move slowly forward again towards constitutional concession. A commission was sent out from London in 1927 to look into the working of the last series of constitutional changes, though it awoke fresh resentment because no Indians were appointed to it. Much of the enthusiasm that held the nationalists' cause together just after the war had by now evaporated, though. There was a danger of a rift, bridged only by Gandhi's efforts and prestige, between those who stuck to the demand for complete independence and those who wanted to work for Dominion status. Congress, less a political party than a coalition of local bigwigs and interests, was not so solid a structure as its rhetoric suggested. Furthermore it was embarrassed by the deepening division between Hindu and Muslim. The leaders of the two communities had watched the relations between their respective followers deteriorate rapidly in the 1920s into communal rioting and bloodshed. By 1930 the president of the Muslim political league was proposing that the future constitutional development of India should include the establishment of a separate Muslim state in the north-west.

That year was again a violent one. The British viceroy had announced that a conference was to take place which should aim to achieve Dominion status for India, but this undertaking was made meaningless by conservative opposition in Great Britain to this course; Gandhi would not take part. Civil disobedience was resumed after a second conference foundered on the question of minorities' representation, and it intensified as distress deepened with the world economic depression. The rural masses were now more ready for mobilization by nationalist appeals. Although this alienated some elements in Congress, who saw their movement changing in unwelcome ways to take account of mass interests, it made Gandhi the first politician to be able to claim an India-wide following.

In spite of the firm response of the Raj to public disorder, though, the wheels of the India Office had already begun to turn. Its officials absorbed the lessons of the discussions and the 1927 commission. As a result, a major devolution of power and patronage came in 1935, in a Government of India Act. It was passed after strong opposition from Conservative MPs (among them, one Winston Churchill, who squandered in the process much of his power to influence the government on other matters) and it took the establishment of representative and responsible government much further. It left provincial government wholly in Indian hands. The viceroy retained sole control only over such matters as defence and foreign affairs. The transfer of national power that the Act also foreshadowed was never to be wholly implemented because of the coming of war in 1939, but, significantly, work began on a building for a future national parliament. This was the culmination of pre-war concessionary legislation by the British.

They had by now effectively provided a framework for all-India politics, and it now looked as if at all levels the decisive struggles between Indians would be fought out within the Congress party.

That organization was in fact under grave strain. The 1935 Act once more affirmed the principle of separate communal representation and almost immediately its operation provoked further hostility between Hindu and Muslim. Congress was by now to all intents and purposes a Hindu organization (though it refused to concede that the Muslim League should correspondingly be the sole agency representative of Muslims). But Congress was also divided between those who still wished to press forward to independence and those – some of them beginning to be alarmed by Japanese aggressiveness – who for at least the immediate future were willing to work the new institutions in cooperation with the imperial government. The evidence that the British were in fact devolving power had been bound to be a divisive force. It drove different interests to seek to insure themselves against an uncertain future.

With hindsight it now seems clear that well before 1939 the tide was set irreversibly towards Indian independence. Congress had been able to ride the wave of discontent in the 1930s caused by worldwide depression and was the governing party in seven of India's eleven provinces. Yet to the rage of many Indians, the viceroy committed the country to war in 1939 without any pretence of consulting Indian leaders, among whom Congress Party politicians were the most important. Angry, they at once resigned from their ministerial posts in local government. Yet nearly twenty years' actual working of representative institutions in local government and the steady Indianization of the Indian Civil Service already meant that the sub-continent was now governable only with the consent and help of native élites. Education and experience had begun to prepare them for future self-rule. War would show that the Raj could still maintain its grip, but India had been revolutionized by British rule; there as elsewhere empire had nurtured the germs of its own overthrow.

THE UNITED STATES

North and South, the two American continents were deeply traumatized by the great depression, but in very different ways and with very different results. A couple of months after President Hoover had taken office in 1929, the prices of shares on the New York stock exchange had begun to rise. They reached a peak in September. Then came the break. After a misleading rally prices plummeted downwards; hundreds of thousands of investors lost what they had paid for their investments. The blow given to confidence by this stock market crash ended the investment boom, which was already faltering. As demand fell off, labour was discharged, factories closed. Wage income shrank; as there was less money to spend, retail and service trades suffered. Mortgages were foreclosed as payments on them ceased; but banks could not collect on many of the loans they had made. When they collapsed, bankrupt, those who had placed money on deposit with them often lost it. In 1932, at the height of the Depression, 13 or 14 million Americans, a quarter of the workforce and mainly men, were out of work. Industrial output was down by 60 per cent. The banking machinery appeared to have broken down; 10,000 banks in due course went under. Farmers looked out on crops and livestock they could never sell, because the price they could get would not pay for taking them to market; they ploughed in their corn and slaughtered their livestock. Some people thought the United States might be heading for revolution.

Nineteen thirty-two was the year for another presidential election and the Republicans were now stuck with the reputation of being responsible for the Depression. Hoover, though able, had not been able enough to deal with the economic collapse. The Democrats, instead, found the candidate for the moment in the governor of New York State, Franklin Roosevelt, a master politician, skilled in creating an impression of what he might do rather than in setting out specific policies. He won overwhelmingly – forty-two out of forty-eight states voted for him – after a campaign which forged a new electoral coalition of those who had done badly out of Republican America and revived some of the enthusiasms of the Progressive era. For the next two decades, the poor (more specifically, the trade unionists, the South, the farmers, the Catholic immigrants of the eastern cities and the blacks) and the liberal intelligentsia were to give the Democrats five successive terms in the presidency.

Roosevelt was to win the next three presidential elections. To stand on four successive occasions as an American presidential candidate remains almost unprecedented; to have won each time is astonishing.[11] To do so with at each election an absolute majority of the popular vote (and since the Civil War no Democratic candidate for the presidency had ever had a majority of it at all) was something like a revolution. It was another paradox that Roosevelt, a rich, patrician figure, should have emerged as a popular leader in an electoral contest that was basically one of hope versus despair among the insecure. Roosevelt's greatest triumph came in his first term; he changed America's mood, turning the tide of despair. This was a true victory for personal leadership. He did it by making people believe he cared and had the will to tackle America's problems. 'Let me assert my firm belief that the only thing we have to fear is fear itself,' he said in his inaugural address; within a week half a million letters arrived at the White House (the president's residence) thanking him for giving his fellow-citizens back their hope. He galvanized Congress into passing a mass of new legislation to revitalize the economy and provide relief for those in need; he also ended Prohibition.[12] 'I think this would be a good time for beer,' he said (though the states of the Union still continued to have a local power to ban the sale of alcohol if they wished). Roosevelt used the powers of the presidency as they had never been used since Lincoln's day. This was the foundation of the 'New Deal' for the American people which he had said he would provide.

The New Deal did not do all that its supporters hoped, but it changed American history. It introduced Americans to the welfare state. Federal grants-in-aid were made for the first time to support unemployment insurance (introduced in the United Kingdom in 1911) and old age pensions (first legislated for in Germany in 1863). Federal

---

[11] And, to some, frightening: the Constitution was amended in 1951 to prevent ever again the election of a president for more than two successive terms.

[12] Whose rural supporters had always distrusted the eastern cities where so many of the recently immigrant Democratic voters were to be found.

legislation also rebuilt the banking system and rescued agriculture. It brought to part of the poverty-stricken South a great scheme of regional development under a new federally funded 'Tennessee Valley Authority'. Yet it could not prevent another, though less fierce, slump in 1937 or get unemployment down below 10 per cent before 1941. But it saved American democracy and gave American capitalism a new stimulus. It was also a demonstration to the world, as well as to Americans, that democracy could still solve its problems. Finally, it provided the most important extension of the power of the federal authorities over American society and the states that had ever occurred in peacetime and one that was to prove irreversible. The New Deal changed the course of American constitutional and political history as nothing had done since the Civil War.

In the Roosevelt era American politics thus began to reflect the same pressures towards collectivism which affected other countries after 1918. Some saw Roosevelt's achievement as an offer to the world of an alternative to fascism and communism, a liberal and democratic version of large-scale governmental intervention in the economy. It indeed rested almost entirely on the interested choices of politicians committed to the democratic process and not on the arguments of economists (some of whom were already advocating greater central management of the economy in capitalist nations). It was a remarkable demonstration of the ability of the American political system to deliver what people felt they wanted. The same machinery, of course, could also only deliver a foreign policy the American democracy would tolerate. Roosevelt was much more aware than the majority of his fellow-citizens of the dangers of ignoring Europe's problems. But though he began to comprehend the dangers of what was happening in Europe long before most of his electors did, he could reveal his own views about it only slowly. On Latin America he could change things faster, but less was at stake there.

LATIN AMERICA

Though the social and political history of Latin American countries had long been of little but marginal political or diplomatic significance to outsiders (including, even, the United States, the predominant hemisphere power), a few Latin American countries participated in the First World War on the Allied side. It had nonetheless required of them no such military exertions as those of the major combatants. The economic impact of the war was another matter, and has to be put in the context both of the long view and of one great internal upheaval, the revolution that began in Mexico in 1911.

For most of this century, the central thread to the story of Latin America has often been that of an uneven, often inadequate and still somewhat incomplete encounter with a modernity presenting itself, above all, in the form of economic growth. Capital had for years flowed steadily into Latin America (preponderantly from the United Kingdom), attracted by higher rates of return than in Europe and only occasionally checked by crises, disasters and disillusionment brought on by the difficulties of recovering debt or the vagaries of xenophobic politicians. It helped to finance infrastructure and develop markets for import, and profited both sides (when the interest was paid).

At the end of the nineteenth century, some Latin American countries already looked forward to comfortable futures based on continuing primary exporting. Though extractive industry was another matter, Latin America's manufacturing sectors were little developed before 1914, and for a long time its republics seemed little troubled by such social and political problems as those which haunted contemporary Europe; Latin American socialists did not look to the rural masses. They had less success (and perhaps interest) in organizing support in the continent's vast agricultural spaces than they had in the rural slums of Europe. But even if there was class conflict aplenty in rural areas, Latin American cities, too, showed less of the class conflict already familiar in industrialized Europe in 1901. Yet labour organization had made some headway in the Argentinian, Mexican and Chilean capitals in the 1890s.

This was the continental background to the only social revolution

Latin America could claim to have had in the first half of this century (as opposed to countless and often violent coups and changes in government personnel). It began with the overthrow of the Mexican dictator Porfirio Diaz in 1911. He had ruled Mexico almost continuously since 1876 with apparently great success, combining, it seemed, steady economic development with civil order, after a long period of violence and instability, and some show of upholding native as against foreign interests.[13] He revealingly termed his political methods as '*pan y palo*', 'bread and stick'. Its major beneficiaries had been the oligarchy of major landowning families and the foreign investors whom 'Don Porfirio' had drawn into the development of Mexico with valuable mining and other concessions. Though himself a *mestizo*, a fact that tended to be obscured in his later years, the Mexican peasantry gained little from Diaz's regime; it had begun to move Mexico towards modernization, but the material benefits that provided were monopolized largely by the hangers-on of government. They were paid off with government jobs and favours. As for the landowners, they found the government's rural police helpful in keeping their peasants in order. Both these categories of beneficiaries were likely to be *creoles*, the 'white' Mexicans. A growing urban and middle-class population outside this system nonetheless sought to break in to share its favours.

Surprisingly, in 1910 a rich cotton-grower and landowner, Madero, stood in the presidential election as a reform candidate against Diaz; he was credited with 196 votes in all and Diaz with several million. But this outcome detonated a soldiers' rebellion in the north. There followed a peasant insurrection led by a charismatic and soon-to-be-legendary popular figure, Emilio Zapata, in the south, where village lands had been lost to encroaching plantations. Madero returned from the exile into which he had fled and this gave the Mexican revolution a political leader and a political goal, constitutional and honest government. It was to transcend this, to become a phenomenon far more complex and uncontrollable, a chaos in which middle-class city-dwellers, land-hungry peasants, local grandees, bandits, nationalists and ideologues all bubbled to the top at different times.

---

[13] Most of the railway system, formerly in American hands, had been nationalized by 1907.

It was not hard to drive out Diaz. But then it appeared that Madero could not satisfy the forces the revolution released. The land-hunger of the countryside and the indiscipline of self-appointed generals and improvised armies were too much for him. There followed his own murder, ten years of fighting, a million deaths and a virtual breakdown in many parts of any government except that of bandits before civilian legalism again prevailed. It was also true that there were areas virtually undisturbed by revolutionary activity in all these years. At one moment, one revolutionary general crossed the northern frontier and sacked the little town of Columbus, New Mexico; this led to the dispatch of a United States expeditionary force to hunt him down. This was not the only instance of foreign intervention, though the most direct; British, German and American diplomats all sought to influence the outcome in Mexico.

At last in 1917 a new president, Venustiano Carranza (assured of support by the United States since 1915), felt able to promulgate a new constitution based on universal male suffrage, envisaging land reform, asserting the overriding claim of the nation to mineral rights in the subsoil – a warning to foreign investors – and introducing a right to strike. President Carranza was killed in a military rebellion in 1920 but a turning point had been reached with his constitutional inauguration and the new constitution was not abandoned. There began a period of consolidation and recovery that was to take up most of the 1920s and established a viable regime in the end. For the next half-century the Mexican republic was to be governed by something like a Latin American version of the English eighteenth-century Whig oligarchy, a party monopoly of power and jobs; it was a one-party state, but one that was non-totalitarian and in many ways liberal and disposed to reform. It began to provide mass-education in the 1920s for the first time, introduced (in theory) an eight-hour working day and undertook a land distribution programme sufficient to draw the sting of rural discontent.[14] Successive presidents encouraged nationalist feeling (particularly against the United States) and took powers to safeguard national resources from exploitation by

[14] By 1939, indeed, some 45 million acres had been redistributed by successive governments – nearly a tenth of the total area of the republic.

foreigners at the Mexicans' expense. In the mid-1920s, a clash with the Church led to an anti-clerical phase provoking another widespread insurrection by peasants loyal to their faith, but the risings were ruthlessly suppressed until agreement was reached at last with the Vatican. The political grip of the regime remained firm and it provided something of a model of progressiveness for other Latin American countries. In spite of its slogans and language, though, it was hardly a very revolutionary state. The victors in its struggles were the commercial and professional classes and those liberal-minded Mexicans who could now believe that the days of brute force and the overt looting of the public purse were over at last.[15]

Though Mexico had been far from settled as the First World War came to an end, the prospects of Latin America were for the most part promising-looking as the 1920s began. Specific ups and downs apart (rubber, which provided a quarter of Brazil's export earnings in 1910, was a notable instance of rapid boom and slump), the current of the century had been in the long term favourable. Argentina's exports of 1901 increased in value ten times by 1928. The world war had enhanced demand for almost everything the continent could produce, though it had some specifically damaging effects (Chile lost her best market for nitrates, Germany, and was never to recover it). Oil had established itself as a major industry in Venezuela and Mexico. The war had implied, too, important changes in the continent's relations with Europe and North America. Before 1914, while remaining politically predominant in the Caribbean, the United States had hardly shown her potential economic weight in South America's affairs except in Mexico. In 1914 she supplied only 17 per cent of all foreign investment south of the Rio Grande; Great Britain held far more of it. But the liquidation of British holdings in the Great War changed this. By 1929, at the end of a prosperous decade, the United States was the largest single source of foreign investment in South America, providing about 40 per cent of its foreign capital. Foreign investors, those from the United States in the lead, had continued readily to

[15] The domestic and regional aspects of the Mexican revolution are far from exhausting its historical interest. For the impact on Anglo-American relations, for instance, see P. Calvert, *The Mexican Revolution, 1910–1914: the Diplomacy of Anglo-American conflict* (Cambridge, 1968).

lend money to Latin American borrowers, buying both government bonds and shares in local companies. One United States concern alone acquired holdings in utilities and transport enterprises in no fewer than eleven different countries. This was not welcome to all local élites, who found Americans cutting into markets and activities they had previously reserved to themselves, and strengthened a dislike of 'gringo' intervention going back to the high-handedness of the days of Panama and the Roosevelt 'corollary'. Yet yields on bonds soared on upwards, sometimes to over 10 per cent, tempting in more investment.

Then came the world economic crash. The bottom dropped out of the export markets within a year and for Latin America the twentieth century truly began at last. The price of integration in the world economy came home sharply as exports fell by 40 per cent on average – and went on falling. At the same time the lifeline of recent prosperity, foreign investment, was cut. Many Latin American governments defaulted on their interest payments; there was no possibility of foreigners enforcing payment in the old nineteenth-century imperial style by bullying and sending in the creditor's accountants to manage national revenues over the heads of the natives. The collapse of credit-worthiness would have intensified the difficulties of governments even had there been foreigners with money to lend. These difficulties soon included mounting unrest and violence at home. Three decades of mounting prosperity had brought increasing urbanization, industrialization and technical modernization of the major cities. Social differentiation had increased since 1914, let alone 1901. The pace of change was, inevitably, uneven, hardly visible in the plantation economies of the Caribbean or southern Brazil, but substantial in states where new mining (Chile and Peru) and oil (Venezuela) interests had prospered. It had created new and vulnerable, and now vociferous, bodies of workers and producers. But there were others. Government employment had grown with prosperity; by 1931, though, half those Brazilians employed in public services were out of work.

One response to economic collapse was a growing and xenophobic assertiveness directed against the foreigners, above all North American; *gringo* banks and companies were blamed by demagogues for the plight in which Latin American countries found themselves. Some of them took over foreign companies' property (in 1938 Mexico expropriated all the foreign oil companies – about 60 per cent were British and 40 per cent American). But governments had to face political upheaval and violence at home, too. The traditional Euro-peanized political classes and the leaders they supported were compromised by their failure to meet the problems posed by falling national incomes. There were more coups, risings and aborted risings between 1930 and 1933 than at any time since the wars of independence. The result was a virtually continent-wide transformation of politics. The world depression compromised liberal constitutional government as much in Latin America as in Europe.

Two patterns of Latin American government had more or less prevailed in the continent hitherto. One was that of the constitutional, semi-parliamentary regimes, however qualified (Argentina and Uruguay were outstanding examples). The other, obtaining in most of the republics, had been a matter of dictators holding power with the support of the armed forces and the narrow oligarchies of landowners. Both were now seen to have failed, and failed badly. Along with the hated foreigners they were in some countries blamed for the disasters of depression and, indeed, they notably could not deal with the ills it had presented. Now, for almost the first time, the urban masses entered Latin American politics. But this force was not to be marshalled by socialists or communists in their own support. Instead, it provided the sustaining power for a new generation of 'strong men', leaders of a new kind who grasped the possibilities of exploiting social discontent and the importance of keeping it from being channelled to serve the Left. They seemed to pick up ideas from a wide range of sources – Stalin's social engineering, Roosevelt's New Deal and the new 'Nazi' regime that emerged in Germany after 1933 – and expressed them in demagogic, somewhat incoherent programmes offering a variety of nostrums to their supporters. Land reform, labour legislation to the benefit of unions, unemployment relief were all given a run in different countries. These programmes combined with police brutality and aggressive and xenophobic condemnation of outsiders to enable new dictators to ride out the storms of the early 1930s and reach the comparative calm of the last years of the decade; commodity prices were then beginning to rise again as war approached. They also substantially increased the power of the state and its acceptance of new functions.

The depression was thus a qualified setback to the advance of democracy in Latin America. Yet distinctions must be made between states; in Mexico, there was a substantial realization under president Cardenas of goals still unachieved until then by the ruling party.[16] Yet social and economic power were in most countries still in much the same hands at the end of the decade as at its beginning; the old oligarchies found they could support the new regimes once they had stabilized the situation and shown that they would not permit any real slide to the Left. Nor, in the longer run, was the story one of stagnation. The main instruments with which Latin American governments had fought the depression had been protection and industrialization, both in pursuit of import substitution. This had encouraged some fragile and artificially dependent new enterprises, but also had carried forward further the process of industrialization and the social consequences that went with it. Broadly speaking, it was the countries with already large internal markets – notably Argentina, Chile, Brazil and Mexico – which did best in meeting the depression's challenges. This, of course, exaggerated existing regional contrasts between countries.

The 1930s had also brought new contentions between American states themselves. In one of them, futile attempts were made by the League of Nations to play a part in the affairs of the continent when it tried to restore peace as a nineteenth-century border quarrel between Bolivia and Paraguay erupted into what was called (after the area in dispute) 'the Chaco War'. This struggle went on bloodily, from 1932 to 1935, costing the combatant countries over 200,000 lives, but was of little interest to the outside world. A truce was at last made at the insistence of a group of American governments led by the United States (though a final peace was not signed until 1938). The treaty that ended the struggle embodied the principle that boundary disputes between South American states should in future be the subject of arbitration.

[16] It changed its name before 1939, always continuing to emphasize its claim to democratic and revolutionary origins: the National Revolutionary Party set up in 1928 becoming the Revolutionary Party of Mexico ten years later. In 1946 it became the Institutional Revolutionary Party and retains that paradoxical name today.

In spite of efforts to do so, the United States had not contributed much to the process of inter-regional cooperation until the 1930s. By 1939, though, a significant change was observable in the way the United States exercised its preponderant power towards its southern neighbours. This was most striking in a negative sense in the Caribbean and Central America. Twenty times in the first two decades of the century American armed forces had intervened directly in that area's republics, twice going so far as to establish protectorates. Between 1920 and 1939, though, there were only two such interventions (in Honduras in 1924 and in Nicaragua two years later). Indirect pressure on Latin American governments also declined. In large measure this was a sensible recognition of changed circumstances. There was nothing to be gained by direct intervention in the 1930s nor any danger to be averted by it. President Roosevelt made a virtue of this by proclaiming a 'Good Neighbour' policy that stressed non-intervention by all American states in one another's affairs.[17] This policy, combined with discreet pressure, helped to assure hemisphere security between 1941 and 1945, when a number of the Latin American republics entered the war on the side of the United States.

[17] Roosevelt was the only United States president before 1945 actually to visit South America officially, when he attended a conference in Buenos Aires in 1936, though in 1909 Taft had crossed the border to go to Mexico.

12

The Path to World War

THE APPROACH TO THE ABYSS

Some have said that the Second World War started in 1937, when Japanese and Chinese soldiers exchanged shots at the Marco Polo Bridge outside Peking. But if specific acts of violence are candidates for the notoriety of detonating a world disaster, there are other times and places worth thinking about. If we stick to the Far East, some would prefer 1931, six years earlier and the year of Japanese aggression in Manchuria. Others choose Europe in 1934, when Croats murdered the king of Yugoslavia in the streets of Marseilles. Yet others would pick 1936, when a civil war broke out in Spain, or because in that year German troops reoccupied without meeting any resistance the Rhineland from which the treaty of Versailles had excluded them. All such dates can be identified as the beginnings of chains of events leading to greater and greater violence in international affairs. The fact that they spread over years – and over continents – emphasizes the increasingly violent and crisis-laden nature of the decade. The optimism of the later 1920s had disappeared long before Germany attacked Poland in 1939.

The turbulence of the 1930s does not mean, of course, that we should not look for beginnings back into the optimistic years or even to the settlement of 1919 to discern when the die was actually cast, if it ever was. Overall, too, the crumbling away of the European peace settlement – and, for that matter, the successful aggrandizement of Japan – can be given a deceptively simple general explanation: no great power was prepared to fight to prevent either until it was too late to avoid disaster. At the crucial moment the victors of 1918 always drew back. First France and then Great Britain did so at Chanak on the Dardanelles as early as 1921 when their governments decided they could not risk a war to uphold the peace imposed on the Ottoman empire only a year earlier. Yet that really says very little. Great powers have to make their decision in contexts of changing circumstance and the most damaging of all the changes in the context of world politics between the world wars had come right at the beginning of the 1930s, in the form of unprecedented general economic disaster. Perhaps, then, Manchuria as the decade opens is a sensible place at which to begin the story of the descent into the abyss.

THE MANCHURIAN CRISIS

The depression expressed itself politically in Japan not only in conflicts of rich and poor such as were seen in other industrial nations but also in a new surge of sympathy for the nationalist extremists who already attracted much popular support. They pointed abroad to solutions and scapegoats. Japan's remaining Asian markets now seemed crucial, and anything that seemed to threaten them provoked alarm. It looked as if circumstances were propitious for strong action to secure them. European colonialism was clearly on the defensive, if not in retreat. The Dutch had faced rebellions in Java and Sumatra in the 1920s, the French a Vietnamese revolt in 1930; these countries were already supplying evidence of the sinister novelty of communist help to nationalist rebels. In China, the British wanted only a quiet accommodation with the nationalist government. Besides enfeebling the European powers with Far Eastern interests, too, economic depression had knocked the stuffing out of the likelihood of decisive American opposition to Japan.

In the end, the hand of the Japanese government was forced by extremists. There had been armed conflict with China in 1928 when the Japanese had tried to prevent KMT soldiers from operating against warlords in the north whom they found it convenient to patronize, and the Japanese government itself was by no means unambiguously in control of the forces it had on the mainland. Effective power in Manchuria rested with the Japanese commanders there. When in 1931

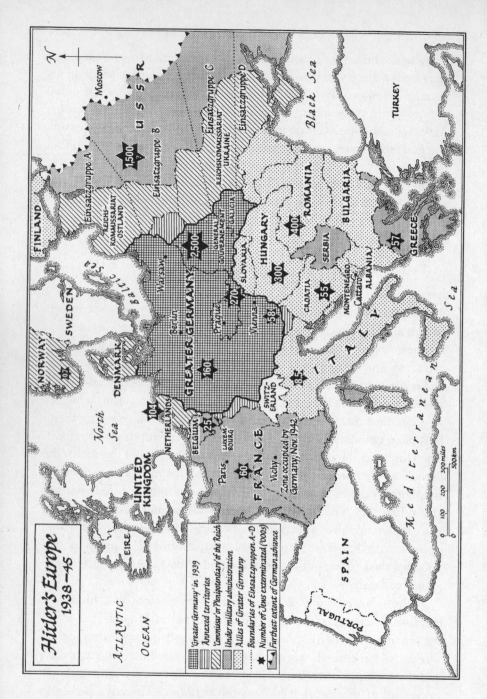

Hitler's Europe, 1938–45
(from *Dark Continent*, Mark Mazower, Allen Lane, 1998)

they organized an incident near Mukden and used it as an excuse for taking over the whole province, those in Tokyo who wished to restrain them could not do so.

From this, there emerged in Manchuria a new Japanese puppet state, Manchukuo (soon to be ruled by the Manchu emperor who had as a child abdicated the imperial Chinese throne in 1911). At the League of Nations there was an outcry against Japanese aggression, assassinations of liberal and peaceably-minded politicians took place in Tokyo where a government much more under military influence than hitherto took office, and the quarrel with China was further expanded. In 1932 a Chinese boycott of goods was answered by landing Japanese troops at Shanghai; in the following year others came south across the Great Wall. The peace settlement they then imposed left Japan occupying a part of historic China itself. The prospects seemed hopeful for further aggression.

The KMT faced problems after establishing its new capital at Nanking. At a time when the Chinese revolution needed to satisfy mass demands if it was to survive, the split within the revolution was a grave setback. It made it impossible to dispose finally of the warlord problem. More seriously still, it weakened the anti-foreign and anti-Japanese front. As for the peasants, they had never given the KMT their allegiance and many of them were turning to the communists. Unfortunately for loyalty to his government, Chiang fell back more and more upon direct government through his officers and showed himself more and more conservative at a time when the traditional culture had decayed beyond repair. The regime was tainted with financial corruption, often at the highest level. The foundations of KMT China were therefore insecure at a moment when it was danger-ously exposed to renewed Japanese aggression, and there was a real rival waiting in the wings.

THE CHINA 'INCIDENT'

The central leadership of the CCP for some time continued to hope for urban insurrection; in the provinces, though, local communist leaders continued to work along the lines indicated by Mao in Hunan.

They dispossessed absentee landlords and organized local soviets as a way of harnessing traditional peasant hostility to central government. By 1930 they had organized an army in Kiangsi. A 'provisional government', with Mao as its chairman, presided over the Chinese Soviet Republic founded in 1931, ruling 50 million people, or claiming to. In 1932 the CCP leadership abandoned Shanghai to join Mao in this sanctuary. KMT efforts were directed towards destroying it but without success; it required a second front at a time when Japanese pressure was strongest. The last great KMT effort had a partial success, it is true, in forcing 100,000 or so communists to embark on the 'Long March' to Shensi which began in 1934, furnishing the greatest epic of the Chinese Revolution and an inspiration ever since. Once there, the 7,000 survivors found local communist support and a degree of safety, since it was a region hard to blockade, but only the need to hold off the Japanese prevented the KMT from doing more to harass them.

Consciousness of external threats to China explains further occasional and tentative essays in cooperation between CCP and KMT that took place later in the decade. They owed something, too, to another change in the policies of the Comintern; it was an era of 'Popular Fronts' elsewhere which allied communists with other parties of the Left. The KMT was also obliged to mute its anti-western line and this won it a certain amount of easy sympathy especially in the United States. But neither the cooperation of communists nor the sympathies of western powers proved safeguards. Japan never ceased to keep China under pressure and in 1937, the decisive (but perhaps unintended) exchange of fire took place between Chinese and Japanese soldiers at the Marco Polo bridge. It opened eight years of fighting.

The Japanese were always to call what followed 'the China Incident', though the scuffle with which it began can be seen as the beginning of the Second World War, for, inexorably or not, it led eventually to Japanese–American confrontation. It was a struggle which did China enormous damage. Within a year the Nanking government had been forced to flee for safety to Chungking, in the far west, leaving virtually all the important northern ports and coastal areas to Japanese occupation. The USSR helped the KMT by sending aircraft and the League again condemned Japan, but neither affected the struggle's outcome. The only bonus drawn by the Chinese in the first black years was the achievement of an unprecedented level of patriotic unity. From 1937 to 1941 political and military cooperation between CCP and KMT was a reality. Communists and KMT alike could see that the national revolution was at stake, and each had an interest in rallying to it. This was the view of the Japanese, too; significantly, in the area they occupied, they encouraged the re-establishment of Confucianism.

The Japanese overreached themselves by invading Soviet territory in August 1939 and suffered a shattering defeat in consequence. Prudently, they therefore sought to do nothing further to antagonize the USSR. Meanwhile, the western powers felt helpless to intervene in China. Their commercial interests were no longer what they had been; by 1936 most of the treaty-port economy was Chinese-owned. Their protests, even on behalf of their own citizens, were brushed aside. By 1939 the Japanese made it clear that they were prepared to blockade the foreign settlements in China, above all in Shanghai, if recognition of the Japanese new order in Asia was not forthcoming. The British and French had troubles enough elsewhere, and could not spare strength for the Far East. American ineffectiveness had deeper roots; it went back to a long-established fact that however the United States might talk about mainland Asia, Americans would not fight for it. When the Japanese bombed and sank an American gunboat near Nanking the State Department huffed and puffed but eventually swallowed Japanese 'explanations'.[1] It was all very different from what had happened after the USS *Maine* blew up in Havana harbour forty years previously.

By 1941, the republic of China was all but cut off from the outside world. Yet she was at that moment on the eve of rescue; at the end of that year her struggle was merged in a world war, and she acknowledged the fact by formal declarations of war on Germany and (somewhat belatedly) Japan. By then, though, grave damage had been done to her. Up to that point Japan had clearly been the winner, even if not yet decisively. Though the economic cost of the struggle

[1] The attack on the USS *Panay* was the first instance of Americans and Japanese in action against one another to be recorded on film. On the same day, Japanese artillery fired also on two British gunboats, killing a British rating.

had been high, and Japan's occupying forces were in fact facing increasing difficulties in China, the Japanese international position had never appeared stronger. She had shown it by ostentatiously humiliating western powers, harassing their residents in China and forcing the British in 1940 to close, for a time, the Burma Road by which supplies reached China and the French to admit an occupying army to Indo-China. The prestige of the Japanese military and their power in government remained high, in consequence. What has been called a 'home-brewed ultranationalistic military socialism'[2] enjoyed a practical ascendancy in government. Its success was a temptation to further adventure. Yet there was also a negative side to apparent triumph. Campaigning in China made it at first desirable and then imperative for Japan to secure access to the economic resources of south-east Asia and Indonesia, above all, their oil supplies, more and more urgently needed as her military commitments grew. But Japanese aggression was also at the same time slowly preparing the Americans psychologically for armed defence of their interests. By 1941 it was clear that the United States would have to decide before long whether its voice was to count in Asia at all; the 'Open Door' had been left to the care and maintenance of the European powers and now this was obviously not enough.

In the background lay something even more important. For all her aggression against China, it was with the window-dressing slogan of 'Asia for the Asians' that Japan had first advanced on the crumbling western empires in Asia. Just as her defeat of Russia in 1905 marked an epoch in the psychological relations of Europe and Asia, so did the independence and power which she showed in 1938–41. When followed by overthrow of the European empires, as it was to be, it would signal the opening of the era of Asian decolonialization, fittingly inaugurated by the one Asian power at that time successful in its 'westernization'.

[2] R. J. C. Butow, *Tojo and the Coming of the War* (Princeton, 1961), p.16.

INDO-CHINA AND INDONESIA BETWEEN
THE WARS

In 1927 a Vietnamese National party had been founded with support
and encouragement from the Chinese Kuomintang. Its frustration in
the absence of a freely working Indo-Chinese political system soon
turned its leaders towards revolutionary violence and terrorism. It
was to be joined only three years later by a new organization, the
Communist Party of Vietnam, enjoying the even more effective help
of the Comintern. The communists' guiding figure was Ho Chi Minh,
a Vietnamese who had gone to France before the First World War as
a student. There he turned away from the influence of Sun Yat-sen which
had originally inspired him and had taken up Marxism. He had been in
1920 one of the founders of the French Communist Party in the disruption that followed the collapse of the Second International and the foundation of the Comintern. Next, after spending a couple of years in
Moscow (at a new 'University for Toilers of the East') he had made
his way to China, where he gathered about him a number of young
Vietnamese exiles. When there followed the split between the KMT
and CCP, he organized the exiles and others in the new Vietnamese
communist party. At the beginning of what was to be a turbulent decade,
a new factor thus began to operate in Indo-Chinese politics.

By 1930, the economy of Indo-China had already suffered badly
from falling world prices. Growing distress provided new support for
anti-colonialist feeling. The Vietnam National party in that year
attempted a coup in Tonkin followed by a rising in Annam. The
outcome was immediately disastrous; the French deployed overwhelming military counter-measures with air support against the rebellion
and it was ruthlessly crushed. Paris, firmly supportive of the resident
French population in Indo-China, was determined not to show weakness in defence of the plantation economy that they had created there.
In addition, though, to the economic problems caused by the world
economic crisis, the French also faced growing population pressure
(thanks in no small measure to what the regime had done to improve
public health) and in a context of growing impoverishment, the balance
of population and food supply remained fragile.

More fighting followed when the Communist party attempted in 1931 to exploit the colonial government's difficulties in a wave of strikes and demonstrations but this, too, was unsuccessful. The Communist party structure was for the time being smashed in the French counter-action. But this led in turn to a more united front approach between nationalists and communists. Both could find a common enemy in French imperialism, but the communists came more and more to take the lead from the nationalists in their own movement and drew to themselves more and more of the support of young educated Vietnamese. Social and anti-colonial revolution cohered more obviously in Indo-China than even in China. The logical outcome of this was the creation on Chinese territory in 1941 of a new united front movement of which much was soon to be heard, the Viet Minh, or league for the independence of Vietnam. It was dominated and led by the communists, but also had the support of the KMT.

Communism also quickly established itself in Indonesia in the aftermath of the Great War. Though Indonesia's history in the next twenty years was to be much less violent that that of the French colonies, a variety of forces (of which population growth was the most fundamental and continuous) was sapping the likelihood of successful multiracial nationalism such as had been envisaged by the original 'Indian Society'. In the early 1920s, it became solely a native Indonesian organization and a greater degree of alienation between the white and native communities was perceptible. Troubled economic conditions in the immediate aftermath of 1918 and the collapse of wartime markets, the beginnings of communist agitation and disappointment with measures to open the civil service to more native Indonesians, all contributed to a hardening of attitudes. It was on a nationalist movement already much radicalized by comparison with the hopes of 1916 that there then fell the blows of the depression at the end of the decade.

World prices had, in fact, been falling before the depression itself broke.[3] On the eve of the worst, Indonesia was already much less prosperous than she had been. The index value of her exports fell by

[3] Between 1926 and 1929 the price of two important Indonesian exports, sugar and tin, both fell by about a third (Furnivall, p.429).

almost a half between 1928 and 1931 and efforts to offset the resulting imbalance were virtually unavailing after the devaluation of the Japanese yen in 1931 brought a flood of Japanese imports.[4] Nationalists and communists made much of the distress and strains that followed, the Islamic organization *Sarikat Islam* (founded in 1916) making most of the running. Nevertheless, it was still possible in 1937 for all the members of the multinational legislative council (the *Volksraad*) to unite in a unanimous petition to the Dutch government for a grant of independence on the lines of British Dominion status within the next ten years.

THE GERMAN PROBLEM

During most of the 1930s there appeared to be almost daily news of the dissolving of the old framework of international relations and colonial structure in the Far East. Meanwhile, in Europe, the even more recently created structures of 1919 were also crumbling away. Contrary to what many might have expected in the aftermath of the depression, this did not come about through the agency of international communism. The main revolutionary force at work was the much older one of German nationalism. By 1935 the German problem was clearly once more the dominating fact of the European political scene.

It had been hoped that republican and democratic government would gently and benevolently re-educate the German people to the acceptance of a new role in international life and a milder and, as some put it, less 'Prussian' regime (by which was meant one less overtly military and nationalist in tone and psychology). Unfortunately, inflation and unemployment helped to destroy the Weimar democracy and to promote a revolution. The illusion that Weimar had solved the German problem was revealed when economic collapse shattered its shallow foundations. The republic had masked destructive forces in German society and had not eradicated them; they survived to challenge and in the end overthrow it. Their historical

[4] Of the islands' total imports, Japan had provided 1.2 per cent in 1905, 10.9 per cent in 1929, but 31.8 per cent in 1934 (Furnivall, table on p.431).

roots went deep and were refreshed and nourished by the very circumstances of Weimar's birth. The terms of the Versailles treaty were almost universally seen by Germans as unjust; reparation payments were visible irritants when they appeared to hinder the recovery of German industry and public finance. As for the treaty's military terms, even democratic German politicians felt justified in turning a blind eye to the dogged experimental and training effort carried out in Sweden and the USSR with Soviet cooperation by the new republic's supposedly crippled armed services.

The economic terms of the treaty, too, had been blamed for the appalling inflation that had twice devastated Germany – first, just after the war ended and then, even more damagingly, during the French invasion of the Ruhr. Money then lost its value overnight; when notes of the high values required were unavailable because not yet printed, wheelbarrows were taken to collect weekly pay packets. Soon, people became unwilling to work except for payment in kind, gold or a foreign currency. The saving classes found it easy to turn against the republic that they blamed for accepting the '*Diktat*' of Versailles. They complained that it was dominated by Marxists (which, of course, the socialists who dominated the immediately post-war government officially claimed to be). A continuing drizzle of insurrections and attempted coups, Left and Right, showed that there were plenty of people about anxious to benefit from these facts.

To outsiders, nevertheless, a turning point in Germany's fortunes seemed eventually to come when it was realized abroad that the exaction of reparations on the scale and at the rate envisaged at Versailles was madness. The stabilization of her currency and a spectacular economic recovery followed concessions over reparations and the provision of American loans. Once again, it seemed, Germany, with her large population, huge reserves of skill, ingenuity, organizing capacity, natural resources, industrial plant and high level of culture, was beginning to show her potential. This, of course, resurrected a fundamental question: with so many strengths to build on, together with a strategic position at the heart of Europe, a matchless military tradition and strong national feeling, was not Germany bound also to play a big and perhaps a dominating role as a great power? If she did, what was to be the outcome for her neighbours, above all, a

France determined, if possible, never to find herself facing German invasion for a third time? This was the German problem at the heart of European statesmen's concerns between 1918 and 1939. In the end, they failed to solve it. Perhaps, though, it looked a little nearer solution in the second half of the 1920s than at any other time.

With the recovery of prosperity, the dangers so marked in the years immediately after the war somewhat faded away, or seemed to do so. In spite of its difficulties, Weimar Germany looked viable in the mid-1920s. It was a free, democratic republic, admired abroad because of its vigorous artistic, scientific and scholarly life; it had a constitution which guaranteed fundamental rights and a supreme court to uphold them. Its elections gave support to coalition governments anxious to uphold this constitution. Yet its very cultural vigour often expressed itself in denigration of liberal, bourgeois values, and its political opponents were never eliminated. Many Germans remained unreconciled either to the peace or to the republic. The communists steadily and bitterly attacked those who upheld it. A variety of nationalist groups appealed not only to old-fashioned conservatives who looked back with regret to the great days of Bismarck when Germany bossed Europe (or had seemed to) and old hierarchies kept their power, but also to a new kind of mass emotion that sought to submerge internal differences in a more or less tribal belief in the German people (*Volk*). Though the restraints laid on Germany by the treaty of Versailles were whittled away by concessions as the 1920s went on, and though Germany's free accession to the decisions taken at Locarno seemed to mean an end of quarrels in the west, there was an enduring psychological grudge over the lands lost to Slavs by Germany in the east (to Poles in west Prussia and Poznan, to Czechs in Bohemia and Moravia). The imagined fate of people of German blood in the new states of central Europe (fed by news of acts of petty hostility always exaggerated by propaganda) kept nationalist anger simmering.

ADOLF HITLER

These forces and circumstances were to be exploited successfully by one of the few men of whom it can realistically be said that they changed twentieth-century history by their conscious acts. Adolf Hitler did so overwhelmingly for ill. Little in his early life could have led anyone to predict his role for him. By birth an Austrian, he had led an unsuccessful and thwarted youth as a frustrated artist and drifter before he found a sense of direction in the Great War. No admirer of the Habsburgs, he had avoided military service to them by migrating to Munich in 1911. In 1914 he was able to join a Bavarian regiment in the confused opening days of the war. For the first time, he seemed to find a role he enjoyed. He proved a good soldier; he was soon promoted corporal and was twice decorated, once with the highest class of the Iron Cross, an unusual decoration for so junior an NCO. For Hitler, it has been rightly said, 'the war was a godsend'.[5]

This made Germany's defeat a pill all the more bitter to swallow; the rest of Hitler's life was above all to be dedicated to undoing the verdict of 1918. He began to meditate bitterly upon it. After a period of training as a political agent (and much-needed support) by the army, he discovered his greatest talent, an astonishing ability to captivate mass audiences. Hitler entered politics as a nationalist agitator, denouncing Versailles with hypnotically effective oratory. As a political vehicle he joined one of many *völkisch* extremist factions, the National Socialist German Workers' Party (Nazis for short), a name usefully blending class and national feeling. Backed by valuable patronage and funding from the army and important figures in *völkisch* politics, he became leader of the Nazis in 1921. Over-confident, he joined in an attempt to overthrow the government of Bavaria in November 1923, as a prelude to marching on Berlin (as Mussolini was supposed to have done on Rome). This failed, and he was locked up for a time. In prison he began to write a rambling political bible, *Mein Kampf*, a mish-mash of often imaginary autobiography, Dar-

---

[5] The verdict of Professor Ian Kershaw on p.87 of his *Hitler, 1889–1936: Hubris* (London, 1998), the best biographical study now available.

winian notions of selection by struggle, antisemitism, admiration for a medieval German empire which had never existed, fear and hatred of Slavs and continuing violent denunciation of Versailles.

The appeal of this was complex, but such messages were effectively simple and were grateful to many German ears. Hitler identified clear sources of the country's ills – the Treaty of Versailles and its upholders, and the anti-national activities of the Marxists and Jews whom he denounced as the traitors and agents of national collapse in 1918. He said that the righting of Germany's wrongs demanded a renovation of German life and culture, and that this was a matter of purifying the racial stock, by excising 'non-Aryan' elements. Much of this was opportunistic; Hitler spoke to Germans already familiar with such messages and in a political atmosphere soaked in antisemitism. But he exploited them better than others. In the 1924 elections the Nazis won fourteen seats in parliament. Yet Hitler was still only a minor politician and the return of more settled times did not help him. He could do little but consolidate his grip on his followers, continuing to condemn Versailles and advocate that all Germans should be united in a nation-state which would acquire new lands for the Germans – 'living-space', as he put it – in the east. He also said the Nazis wished to end the struggle of parties, rewrite the law so as to give expression in it only to the will of the leader (*Führer*), and terrorize the enemies of the state and race, after coming to power by constitutional means. For a long time many people did not take him at his word. It was still fairly easy not to do so when times were good, as they were until the end of the decade. Then came the crash. In 1929, as the economic weather turned sour, the German republic began to run into choppy water. Businesses began to fail; unemployment rose. By 1932, the economic storm had reached hurricane force; Germany had 6 million unemployed and people feared another inflation like that which had wiped out savings ten years earlier. In attempting to grapple with these threats, Weimar's rulers increasingly sidestepped parliament and sought to govern through emergency presidential decrees.

Hitler and the Nazis reaped the political benefits of the hour. In 1928 they had won less than 3 per cent of the votes cast in the Reichstag elections, and only twelve seats; in 1930 they won 107 seats and became the second largest party in the Reichstag (the socialists were the largest, with the communists running third). There was no chance of forming a majority coalition committed to the defence of the republic. Nazism appealed to the wish of many Germans to solve their political problems through strong measures made possible by a national unity overriding private interest. Many were impatient with the parliamentary politicians who had failed to prevent economic collapse. Others who sought scapegoats were happy to identify enemies of the German people in capitalists, Marxists and Jews. Antisemitism was a powerful and traditional draw. Unlike Marxist explanations of Germany's troubles in terms of class war (which, naturally, antagonized some Germans while attracting others), Nazism's racialism cut across social divisions; all Germans could accept it. Resentment against the Versailles settlement was universal. Another important reason for the Nazi success was the division of their opponents; throughout the 1920s the communists had spent much of their time and energy fighting the socialists and were still doing so. On the streets, the semi-military 'Storm Troops' of the Nazi movement (the SA organization) presented a useful and very apparent alternative to both. They grew rapidly in numbers as the economic crisis got worse, recruits joining them for the uniform and rations. Justified as a means of protecting Nazi meetings from interruption, they quickly evolved into bands of thugs who (like the early Italian Fascists) broke up their political opponents' meetings unchecked by the police.

Nineteen-thirty was also the year when the last Allied occupation forces withdrew from Germany. Although the German government became more right-wing and nationalist under a Centre Party chancellor after the socialists had been forced out of a coalition government, few conservative politicians at first much sympathized with the Nazis. Yet they sometimes agreed with their identification of Germany's enemies at home and liked what they heard of the Nazi's patriotic messages about rearmament and the revision of the Versailles treaty. They knew, too, that antisemitism was a popular draw and saw in the street-fighting SA gangs an insurance against communism. Some among them began to think that Hitler – whom they took to be a party leader like any other – might be useful in their own game. Then, in July 1932, new elections made the Nazis the biggest party in parliament, with 230 seats, though this was still not a majority. When they lost some seats later that year it was argued that their impetus was failing. The president of the republic, Field Marshal Hindenburg, long distrustful of Hitler, was at last persuaded by right-wing advisers that the Nazis must be given a chance to show whether they could deal with Germany's problems. He may have thought that office alongside right-wing parties in a coalition would show them up as politicians like the rest, good at barracking and opposition but not at providing answers to the country's needs. He may have thought that they could be tamed by conservative colleagues, but would help in turning Germany's back on the republic he (like so many other Germans) associated with defeat and national shame. He asked Hitler to be chancellor and in so doing made what must be reckoned one of the momentous political decisions of the century.[6]

THE GERMAN REVOLUTION

Hitler took office on 30 January. Just over a year earlier he had told the then chancellor, Brüning, that 'when a constitution proves itself to be useless, the nation does not die – the constitution is altered'.[7] He now asked the president to authorize new elections (as he was entitled to do) and promised to govern in a coalition with other conservative and right-wing groups. Hindenburg had himself been overwhelmingly confirmed as president the year before (when he got more votes then than the Nazi and Communist candidates combined) and no one could object on legal grounds to his support for his chancellor; he had acted constitutionally, and the Nazis' takeover was to continue along formally legal channels. Their party newspaper warned Germany that if they had their way the forthcoming elections would be Germany's last. They set about winning them with no scruples about methods. Now a governing party, they controlled the radio and used it to promote their campaign. The police, which Nazis

[6] There is an excellent discussion of the 'miscalculation of a political class' and its responsibility for bringing Nazism to power in Kershaw, pp.423–7.
[7] Q. in A. Bullock, *Hitler and Stalin: Parallel Lives* (London, 1991), p.284.

now directed, often looked the other way while opponents were terrorized and beaten up. Almost on the eve of polling, a huge round-up of political opponents took place on the pretext that a communist rising was planned in the aftermath of the mysterious burning of the Reichstag building. Yet at the end of the campaign (with 17 million votes – nearly 44 per cent of the electorate), the Nazis still had not won a majority, though a majority of voters had voted for the coalition of which they were the main part.

Hitler now asked parliament (where, with his coalition allies, he had a majority) for special legislation giving the government extraordinary powers to rule by decree. This was done. Armed with these exceptional powers, the Nazis could follow the Fascist and Soviet models of changing state and society from the top downwards. So began the revolutionizing of Germany, its redirection on a course of aggression which would in the end destroy both it, and Europe, and end by making possible the creation of a new world order. The communist deputies were imprisoned and their party, like that of the socialists, disappeared. The Nazi party was soon the only permitted one. Strikes were forbidden, trade unions were dissolved. The old Centre party dissolved itself, and the Nazis soon squeezed their conservative allies out of government. Thousands of arrests were made and hundreds of political murders took place (including some in 1934 of Nazis who were too radical or independent for Hitler's taste). German life was transformed, at least in appearance, from top to bottom; the churches were harried, the professions dragooned, the universities purged – even freemasonry and the Boy Scouts were banned (as in the Soviet Union). The one conservative force that Hitler had really respected was the German professional army; it alone had the power to stand up to the SA. Yet it soon caved in, too, transferring its loyalty to Hitler and taking a special oath to him when he added the office of president to that of chancellor after Hindenburg died in 1934.

The Nazis' new power soon seemed to be used effectively in dealing with unemployment. This must explain much of the docility of the German working class under Hitler. Over 5 million had been out of work when he took office. By 1939, there was virtually full employment in Germany. Yet in other ways, and in spite of a huge propaganda success in depicting the new Germany as a transformed, dynamic, united nation, Nazi successes were qualified; it is hard to see what real benefit the German people enjoyed in the next twelve years (and they were, of course, to end in disaster). The recovery in the economy put many men back to work by 1936,[8] though after that real earnings did not go up and the leverage workers might have exercised through independent trade unions had gone. Welfare provision in industry improved, but otherwise rearmament, a priority for Hitler, soaked up benefits that might have gone to the consumer. Food prices rose, and supplies (notably of fats) were reduced. Yet the Nazis stayed in power, continuing to govern under the emergency measures of 1933 without significant opposition.

The regime's survival and success, startling though they seemed against the background of other countries' seeming failures to grapple with their problems, do not seem hard to explain. Hitler's driving, obsessive sincerity and his personal magnetism gave voice to what many, perhaps most, Germans hid in their hearts, a mixture of hatreds, resentments, ambitions and ill-disciplined idealism. Well-established myths and scapegoats of German history were continuously exploited by Nazi propaganda. The quickly established monopoly of communication through press and radio skilfully blended these with emphasis on the more spectacular and visual possibilities of the cinema and mass rallies to generate admiration or at least awe. The German public, too, became more and more silently aware as time went by of a ruthless readiness to deploy police powers; an atmosphere of uncertainty and fear mattered more in Germany than terror itself (though there was plenty of that) in silencing opposition. Psychologically, the party and its associated organizations (the Labour Front, the Hitler Youth) gave its many members a sense of status and of going somewhere (even if its leaders were often second-rate) which they probably would not have had without it. Hitler made millions of Germans feel better. Above all, for years, he provided indisputable and spectacular successes in foreign affairs (which meant, usually, the destruction of some part of the Versailles settlement), while presenting

[8] The qualification by sex is important. One continuing strain in Nazi policy was to attempt to deal with unemployment by replacing women employees by men.

a well-managed, flashy and up-to-date looking image of a revitalized
nation at home. Both helped quickly to reconcile waverers to a regime
that had deprived them of the free press, free speech, and free parliament they had known under the Weimar constitution, and kept
workers in line, holding down real wages. Any irksomeness in its
restrictions and demands seems to have been balanced in Germans'
eyes by its successes abroad. That the containment of Germany quickly
became once more an international problem could be reckoned
achievement enough by German patriots who wished to overturn
Versailles – and perhaps have revenge for it – and does much to
explain the absence of resistance to the regime.

THE CRUMBLING BALANCE OF POWER

France had always hoped to find insurance in the east against German
revival. She had accordingly made agreements there (starting with a
treaty with Poland in 1920, and later ones with the 'Little Entente'
partners, Romania, Yugoslavia and Czechoslovakia). But in the 1930s
the largely agricultural economies of eastern Europe had been terribly
devastated by the world depression and the politics of the national
states there were more than ever rent by internal dissension. Their
very existence, too, actually made it more difficult, if not impossible,
to bring to bear the uncertain power of the USSR, ideologically
indisposed as it was to easy cooperation with capitalist democracies.
No Soviet forces, moreover, could reach Germany without crossing
one or more of the east European countries whose histories were
haunted by memories of Russian domination or aggressiveness under
tsarism (the Baltic states and much of Poland and Romania had,
after all, once actually belonged to the old Russian empire) and of
communist expansionism (as it had seemed) in 1919, which had only
been halted by Polish victory in 1920.

 If the United States and the USSR were unavailable, Great Britain
and France were ill-placed to act as the policemen of Europe. They
remembered all too well how difficult it had been to deal with Germany
even with Russian numbers on their side, and they had often been at
odds with one another since 1918. They were militarily weak, too.

France, conscious of her inferiority in manpower should Germany ever rearm, invested in a programme of strategic defence by fortification; it looked impressive but was incomplete and effectively deprived her of the power to act offensively.[9] The Royal Navy was no longer without a rival, nor, as in 1914, able safely to concentrate its resources in European waters; the growing aggressiveness of Japan was an important distraction. British governments had long cut down their expenditure on armaments and economic depression reinforced this tendency. It was feared that the costs of rearmament would cripple recovery by causing inflation. Many British politicians, too, believed that Germany's grievances were just, and were for a long time sympathetic to the claims of German self-determination. They even talked of handing back German colonies and the British voter did not seem likely to disapprove.

Both Great Britain and France were also troubled by a joker in the European pack, Italy. Under Mussolini, she looked like a great power. Hopes that she might be enlisted against Germany disappeared, though, in the mid-1930s. In 1935, Italian forces invaded Ethiopia in a belated attempt to participate in the 'Scramble for Africa'. Like earlier sallies in Italian imperialism, this was to prove only briefly successful.[10] Still, it was a clear breach of the Covenant of the League of Nations that one member should attack another, and the question was posed of what the League should do; hopes were not high as the ineffectiveness of League condemnation of Japan over Manchuria was recalled. France and Great Britain were in an awkward position. As great powers, Mediterranean powers and African colonial powers, they were bound to take the lead against Italy at the League. But they did so feebly and half-heartedly; the French especially did not want to alienate a country they would like to have with them if they quarrelled with Germany. The result was as bad as it could be. The

---

[9] This was the celebrated 'Maginot Line' of works eventually running from the Swiss to the Belgian frontiers. It was never breached, but in 1940 was outflanked.

[10] After the brief post-war adventure in Cilicia, Italy had been able to retain formerly Ottoman Libya and Tripolitania (at the cost of reducing the indigenous population by a third in a couple of decades; see Iliffe, *Africans*, p.208) but without establishing significant settler communities. Nor did she do so in Ethiopia: see H. M. Larebo, *The Building of an Empire* (Oxford, 1994).

League failed to check aggression but imposed limited and half-hearted 'sanctions' on Italy, which was thus alienated from France and Great Britain. Ethiopia lost its independence (though, it later proved, only for a few years). It was to all intents and purposes the end of any faith in the League as a regulator of international life and one of several moments at which it later looked as if fatal errors had been committed. But it is still hard to say at what stage the international situation which developed from these facts became unmanageable. Certainly the emergence of a much more radical and ferociously opportunist regime in Germany had been a major turning point. But the Depression had preceded this and made it possible.

IDEOLOGY'S CONTAMINATION OF INTERNATIONAL AFFAIRS

Economic collapse made easier an ideological interpretation of events in the 1930s which further embittered them. The intensification of class conflict by economic collapse led interested politicians to interpret international relations in the 1930s in terms of fascism versus communism, or of (by no means the same thing) Right versus Left, or Dictatorship versus Democracy. This was all the easier after Mussolini, angered by British and French reactions to his invasion of Ethiopia, came to ally with Hitler and talked of an anti-communist crusade. But Soviet propaganda was important, too, in bringing this about.

In the early 1930s the internal situation of the USSR must have seemed precarious to such of its rulers as were in possession of the facts. Collectivization and industrialization were imposing grave strains and sacrifices, often made worse by incompetence, technical inadequacies and sheer inefficiency. Industrial and transport breakdowns and accidents – some trivial, but some leaving many dead and wounded – were all damned as sabotage and 'wrecking'. They were mastered – though sometimes also magnified – by a savage intensification of dictatorship expressing itself not only in the virtual war unleashed against the peasants, but in the turning of terror against the cadres of the regime itself from 1934 onwards. Millions of Russians were executed, imprisoned or exiled, often to forced labour, in the next four years.[11] The world looked on amazed as a great series of show trials took place and batches of defendants grovelled with grotesque 'confessions' before their accusers. The purges helped to consolidate for good Stalin's grip on the party and the whole administrative and police machinery of the state. Old comrades of his own, or of Lenin, were paraded in court, made to confess to improbable crimes, and then shot or lost to sight in the prisons and labour camps of the secret police. But trials of the well-known were only the tip of the iceberg. Hundreds of thousands of state and party bureaucrats were made away with. Nine out of ten generals in the army were purged, and, it was alleged, half the officer corps, though a smaller figure now seems likely.[12] A new party élite replaced the old one; by 1939 over half the delegates who had attended the party Congress of 1934 had been arrested.

It was very difficult for outsiders to be sure what was happening. Reasonably, policy-makers in the western democracies doubted that the Soviet Union was a very strong potential ally, let alone a civilized or liberal state. The country could hardly be believed to have been strengthened by Stalin's outpouring of the blood of men and women loyal to the regime, and the wasting of their help and talents that he imposed. Yet the Terror was truly revolutionary, too: the Soviet Union now passed effectively into the hands of Stalin's creatures. By 1939, 70 per cent of CPSU members had joined the party since 1929. A

[11] Current estimates of Soviet population in 1933 indicate losses running from 5 to 11 million (C. Merridale, 'The 1937 Census', *Historical Journal* 39, 1996, p.236). Yet another figure of some significance was noted in an article by Professor Norman Davies (in *the Independent* newspaper for 29 December 1987) which showed that a gap existed between projections and census figures from 1929 to 1937 of some 17 million. He also noted that the director of the census and his staff disappeared in the purges. Recent official estimates suggest that between 1 million and 1.5 million were killed in the 1937–8 purge, but some claim a higher figure, some a lower. R. W. Davies has suggested that 1937 brought the highest number of executions (over 350,000) and that nearly 800,000 took place between 1921 and 1952 ('Forced Labour under Stalin', *New Left Review*, no. 214, 1995, pp.62–80).

[12] R. W. Davies says about 15 per cent of the officer corps was purged 1937–8 (ibid., p.71).

generation of Soviet citizens had grown up since 1917 which took the new regime for granted and admired it. They learnt about the past only through the official history; doubts were set aside by the material achievements visible since the Bolshevik revolution, and by well-orchestrated and incessant indoctrination. The result was a state whose subjects appeared more aware of the benefits given to them than of the handicaps they suffered and one in which politics effectively came to an end for the mass of the population. The party provided the élite where the only debate that mattered took place, and even there it was muted. The USSR governed one-sixth of the land area of the world. A respected and feared great power, it had enormously diminished illiteracy, tapped new sources of intelligence, talent and skill, done much to emancipate women in some of the most backward societies in the world and had created a huge educational and scientific system to supply the technicians and teachers it needed. Stalin put Russia back on the high road towards modernization and world power first pointed out by Peter the Great. Whether she needed his methods to get there remains an open question.

The Soviet Union shaped the international situation directly through the propaganda that it put out, as well as through its diplomatic behaviour. There was a deliberate promotion within the country of a siege mentality; far from being relaxed, the habit of thinking of the world in terms of Us versus Them which had been born in Lenin's personal predilections, Marxist dogma and the interventions of 1918–22 was encouraged even more by Stalin in the 1930s. Meanwhile, the Comintern went on preaching class struggle abroad. The reciprocal effect was predictable. Conservatives everywhere found it easier than ever to think that any concession to left-wing or even mildly progressive forces must be a victory for the Bolsheviks. But any hardening of attitudes on the Right gave communists new ammunition for their thesis of inevitable class-conflict and revolution.

Yet nowhere was there a successful left-wing revolution. Revolutionary dangers in the west had subsided rapidly once the immediate years of post-war hardship were over. Labour governments had peacefully and undramatically presided over Great Britain for part of the 1920s. When the second of them ended in financial collapse in 1931, it was replaced by a conservative-dominated coalition that, with

overwhelming electoral support,[13] proceeded to govern with remarkable fidelity to the tradition of progressive and piecemeal social and
administrative reform which had marked the advance of the British
welfare state. This course had already been shaped even more firmly
in the Scandinavian countries, often held up for admiration in the
inter-war years for their combination of political democracy and
practical socialism, and as a contrast to communism. Even in France
and after the Depression, a large and active communist party remained
unable to win over a majority of the electorate, though it helped to
sustain a left-wing 'Popular Front' government in 1936. In Germany
before 1933 the communist party had been able to get more votes
than the Social Democrats, but had never displaced them at the head
of the working-class movement, and had no chance of doing so after
the Nazi revolution. Elsewhere, communism's revolutionary success
was smaller still. In Spain it had to compete with anarchists as well
as socialists; Spanish conservatives certainly feared it and may have
been right to fear also a tendency to slide towards social revolution
felt under the republic which appeared in 1931, but Spanish communism was far from the only enemy they faced.

Yet the ideological interpretation of politics had great appeal, even
to non-communists, and was much strengthened by Hitler's accession
to power. Though the Nazis denounced plutocracy, capitalists, banks,
and big stores on their way to power it was not hard for many people
to see their party as fundamentally 'capitalist', given its violent and
consistent anti-Marxist rhetoric and fairly obvious right-wing support.
Yet this was an inadequate understanding of it and of its ideological
distinction. Nazism is better understood, negatively perhaps, by
emphasizing its freedom from any restraint, humanitarian or Christian
alike, and by its nihilism.

When the Nazis unleashed persecution against the Jews, liberal
Europe found itself to its astonishment witnessing revivals in one of
its most advanced societies of the pogroms of medieval Europe or
tsarist Russia. Many foreigners found it hard to believe what they

---

[13] It is rarely now recalled that the 'National' (really Conservative) governments
which emerged from 1931 and 1935 are, together with the Liberal government of
1906, the only British governments in the entire century whose support in the House
of Commons has rested on absolute majorities of the votes cast in general elections.

were told was going on. But by September 1939 more than a quarter of the 525,000 German Jews of 1933 had already emigrated.[14] To think merely in terms of traditional antisemitism in explaining the persecution of German Jews is inadequate; there was conscious exploitation of many different strands of envy and dislike, and even of a mad pseudo-science. Since 1919 Germany had seen many expressions of a special antisemitism rooted in counter-revolutionary propaganda about a Bolshevik–Jewish danger from the east, too, which cohered with Nazi racist ideology. Civil disabilities were imposed on Jews in the 'Nuremberg laws' of 1935 which removed rights which European Jews had won in all civilized countries since the French Revolution. Even in 1939 and later it was to many people outside and inside Germany still incredible that Nazi rhetoric was to be taken at its face value and that deeds would follow words, though Hitler's personal and pathological detestation of Jews, whom he believed to threaten Germany's 'Aryan' racial purity, should have been evident enough from his writings and speeches alone.

Confusion (which such barbarism helped to deepen) over the fundamental nature of the Nazi regime made it very difficult to deal with. Some misinterpretations saw Hitler simply as a nationalist saviour bent, like an Atatürk, upon the regeneration of his country and the assertion of its rightful claims, though none too scrupulous about his methods. Others saw him as a crusader against Bolshevism (and even when people only thought he might be a useful barrier against it, that increased the likelihood that their opponents on the Left would correspondingly underrate him as a mere tool of capitalism). No simple formula, though, contains Hitler or his aims. He expressed Germany's resentments and exasperations in their most negative and destructive forms and embodied them to a monstrous degree. Obsessed and haunted as he was by the fanatical animosities shaped in his youth, he was given scope by economic disaster, political cynicism and a favourable arrangement of international forces to release these negative qualities at the expense of all Europeans, Germans included. In doing so, he felt no internal restraints and the outcome was a barbaric regime and international disaster.

[14] S. Friedländer, *Nazi Germany and the Jews*, vol. 1 (London, 1997), pp.388, 393.

It is now even more difficult to sense – let alone explain – the extraordinary fact of the positive admiration and attraction excited abroad by both Hitler's Germany and Stalin's Soviet Union. Sheer ignorance and the deployment by both regimes of skilful propaganda[15] no doubt went a long way in shaping reactions among those who did not have to live under these regimes, but the willingness of foreign intellectuals and opinion-formers to be deceived remains almost incomprehensible. A few doubtless identified their personal interests and, in the case of communism, perhaps their peace of mind, with adherence to what looked like defenders of values they held dear. But both countries were reasonably accessible to foreigners in the 1930s (though the USSR less than in the previous decade) and visitors might have been expected to use their own eyes and ask their own questions. Though Hitlerian Germany had not revealed all its horrors by 1939, its pogroms and denunciations of enemies of the *Volk* were blatant enough, while the rhetoric of the great purges should have made sympathizers with communism wary, given the implausibility of charges levelled against old Bolsheviks and party stalwarts.

As there were always some independent and respectable witnesses vocal in their criticisms of Germany and the USSR, it is also difficult to understand why what they said did not have more effect, and why these appalling regimes should have been so widely admired. One reason must have been that the corruption of politics by ideology had made too many Europeans ready to hate what they feared and to idealize what they wished to defend. The fact that Nazis and Communists alike were enemies of the old liberal values and the primacy of the individual and private was in itself enough for some misguided idealists; they could see both extremes as healthy-minded opponents of the selfishness, special interests and privileges that seemed to undermine the common good in constitutional countries grappling with difficult problems. Bourgeois society and constitutional politics both appeared to stand in the way of successful achievement of collective goals – whether those of the *Volk* or of the international working class. Weight must also be given to the reciprocal effect of the propaganda of both sides; there was a closing of minds in some circles, Left and

---

[15] Particularly, that of the cinema.

Right alike, which derived from the antagonism of the two systems. Only when they at last came together to cooperate did the eyes of earlier believers begin to open. Until then, support for either the Nazi defenders of civilization against Bolshevism or for the only true opponents of fascism (according to your point of view) meant that the silencing of well-grounded criticism of the one to which you inclined was acceptable even to those who should have known better. As a British left-wing publisher put it in 1937, in words that might just as well have been used by any of those wealthy people in France and England who saw in Hitler a potential ally against communism, 'anything that could be quoted by the other side should not be said'.[16]

TOWARDS A NEW GERMAN WAR: THE SPANISH CIVIL WAR

While a logical progression towards war seems with hindsight to have been clearer before 1939 than before 1914, argument goes on about when, and if ever, there was a chance of avoiding the final outcome. Hitler would always have sought war in the end. One possible milestone was passed, too, when Mussolini, in spite of German ambitions in central Europe, formally became his ally. Mussolini had always liked the idea of playing off Germany against France. Before Hitler came to power he had secretly encouraged German rearmament. He was temperamentally sympathetic to revisionism over Versailles and, like many people, underrated Hitler's ambitions. Flattered by him, Mussolini had sent him money to fight elections. In 1933 he said that 'the victory of Hitler is also our victory'.[17] The *Duce* then hoped he might find in the junior dictator an ideological partner. Nevertheless he always had other irons in the fire and took a decisive step only after he had been alienated by the British and French over his Ethiopian adventure.

British and French governments had by then already had plenty of experience of the difficulties of dealing with the new Germany. Hitler

[16] The words of Victor Gollancz, quoted by M. Mazower, *Dark Continent: Europe's Twentieth Century* (London, 1998), p.127.
[17] Q. in D. Mack Smith, *Mussolini* (London, 1981), p.181.

had withdrawn it from the League of Nations in 1933 in protest against the League's pursuit of disarmament. He then announced in 1935 that Germany's rearmament (forbidden at Versailles) had begun, and reintroduced conscription. Until they too could rearm, the western democracies were in a very weak position. The first consequence of this was shown to the world in March 1936 when German troops re-entered the 'demilitarized' zone of the Rhineland from which they had been excluded by the Treaty of Versailles. France and Great Britain were distracted by the Ethiopian crisis and in neither country did public opinion show any willingness to support sanctions against Germany, if that meant a possible risk of war. Evidence later available suggests that a positively hostile reaction would have been effective but no attempt was made to retaliate or to counter this move except by denouncing it, though it was a violation of the Versailles treaty. Significantly, it was also accompanied by Hitler's denunciation of the Locarno guarantees to Germany's western frontiers.

In July that year, a group of generals mutinied against Spain's left-wing republic in a more or less traditional *pronunciamiento*, but with new technical efficiency as soldiers were flown from North Africa to reinforce the rebels. Civil war followed. Hitler and Mussolini both sent contingents to support the man who emerged as the rebel leader, General Franco. His efforts to overthrow the republic did more than any other single event to give an ideological plausibility to Europe's divisions. Hitler, Mussolini and Franco were all now lumped together as 'fascist' by the European Left. Soviet diplomacy began to coordinate support for Spain within western countries by directing local communist parties to abandon their attacks on other left-wing parties and encourage 'Popular Fronts'. Spain came to be seen as a conflict between Right and Left in its purest form; this was a distortion, but one which helped people to think of Europe as divided into two camps, a notion given further substance by the announcement in October 1936 of a German–Italian 'axis'. Earlier that year, a Japanese delegation had walked out of a naval disarmament conference in London, announcing it would not renew old agreements. Not only the Versailles system, but also its Far Eastern counterpart settled at Washington in 1922, was now collapsing.

Events in Spain meanwhile kept opinion in Great Britain and France in disarray. The 'axis' understandings having removed Mussolini's former misgivings about the fate of Austria, Hitler annexed that country in March 1938. Once again, the terms of Versailles (which forbade the fusion of Germany and Austria) seemed to the French and British electorates hard to uphold by force; the *Anschluss* (as the union was called) could be presented as a satisfaction of legitimately aggrieved nationalism. The Austrian republic had long had internal troubles and a strong native Nazi movement; its citizens turned out to cheer the arriving German soldiers. In the autumn came the next German aggression, the seizure of part of Czechoslovakia. The acquiescence of France and Great Britain in this was glossed over by the specious invocation of self-determination (for the Sudeten Germans who lived in Bohemia and Moravia). The Czech lands involved were so important that their loss crippled any prospect of successful Czechoslovak self-defence, but they were areas many of whose inhabitants were of German blood. Hitler was gradually fulfilling the old dream that had been set aside when Prussia drove Austria out of Germany in the nineteenth century – the dream of a united Great Germany, defined as the lands inhabited by those of German blood.

The dismemberment of Czechoslovakia, though, proved within a few months to have been a turning point. It had been embodied in agreements made at Munich in September 1938 in which Great Britain and Germany took the leading roles. These were the outcome of a British initiative which was aimed at satisfying Hitler in order to get him to behave in a civilized manner. The British prime minister, Neville Chamberlain, still unwilling to appeal to force, and temperamentally disinclined to support the Czech government, hoped that the transference of the last substantial group of Germans (about 3 million of them) under alien rule to that of their fellow-countrymen might deprive Hitler of the motive for further revision of Versailles – a settlement which was now looking very tattered, in any case. He had misjudged the situation. Munich had certainly removed the danger of war over the Sudetenland and had given the French a face-saving way out of a guarantee they had given to Czechoslovakia. Yet it dismembered the one democratic state in central Europe and eliminated the one serious ally the British and French might find in the area. It also offended Stalin; he had not been consulted. At home, Hitler's success convinced even sceptical Germans (among whom had been some of his generals) that he was a wonder-worker who could be followed with blind confidence. He himself now believed that the British and French democracies would always give way to a threat of war. That Poland and Hungary had both also picked up a few crumbs of Czechoslovak territory at the table hardly mattered in such a perspective.

HITLER MOVES BEYOND THE GERMAN LANDS

Yet Munich was to turn out to have been the high-water mark of 'appeasement', a notion that had hung about in British thinking on Germany almost since Versailles itself. Originally a blend of hope (that Germany could be satisfied if the right concessions were made) and guilt (that Germany had been harshly treated), it was later to be justified in terms of *Realpolitik* (that it gave time for Britain to rearm). British public opinion, for all the hysteria with which it acclaimed Chamberlain at the time of Munich, soon began to hint at sombre reflexions. It was particularly shocked in November by a sudden pogrom mounted by the Nazis against Jews all over Germany, the *Kristallnacht* (so called because of the broken glass it generated). Then, early in 1939, it became clear that Hitler saw Munich not as a settlement, but as a point of departure. In March he seized most of what remained of Czechoslovakia on the pretext that the republic (hyphenated after Munich as Czecho-Slovakia, a new federal state) had broken down. Bohemia and Moravia now became German protectorates, while Slovakia retained its nominal independence. This was an extension (the first) of German aggression into areas where it could not be speciously defended as a resumption of ethnic German lands. It brought about a revulsion of British feeling. The government accelerated the preparation of the country for war (conscription was introduced in peacetime for the first time in its history) and, with France, gave guarantees against aggression to Poland and Romania. It was clear that the question of Germany's frontiers with Poland would next be opened, and Chamberlain had by now concluded that there could be no negotiation with Hitler and that only the prospect of force would deter him. He hoped that it would.

Many Germans had long wanted to get back what had been German Poland. They fretted particularly over the 'Polish Corridor', a strip of territory connecting Poland with the sea and cutting off Germany from direct land communication with East Prussia and the historic German city of Danzig, since 1919 a 'Free City' under League of Nations authority. The Poles were alarmed in March when Hitler went on from the destruction of Czecho-Slovakia to seize Memel, another historic German city, from Lithuania, thus setting right what was in German eyes another Versailles injustice. They therefore welcomed the British guarantee. But they remained adamant about not letting Soviet forces on to their soil; perhaps they were only prudent, but it was an insuperable obstacle to military cooperation with the USSR by the British and French. Only when Hitler, alleging Anglo-Polish 'encirclement', denounced his own agreements with Poland did the Polish government at last agree that the British and French should try to enlist the support of the USSR against Hitler.

It seems that Stalin had been keeping the Spanish Civil War going with support to the republic as long as it seemed likely to tie up German attention, but then turned to seeking other ways of buying time against the attack from the west which he always (and correctly) feared. To him, it no doubt seemed likely that Great Britain and France would willingly encourage any German assault on the USSR as a diversion towards the workers' state of the menace they had so long faced. No doubt many Britons and French would have done. For a long time, too, there had been little practical possibility of working with the British or French to oppose Hitler, even if they were willing to do so, because the Poles so long feared the prospect of a Soviet army on Polish soil.

The British government's guarantees of March and April 1939 had not been, on the face of it, the wisest choice. At the time they were made, they appeared to imply that the strategic and political interests of the United Kingdom were better served by alliance with Poland than with the USSR. The initiative, meanwhile, remained with Hitler. Within a few days he directed his generals to be ready to attack Poland on 1 September. It is scarcely surprising that there followed arrangements for a fourth partition of Poland (as a Soviet diplomat had remarked to a French colleague would be the case at the time of

THE PATH TO WORLD WAR

the Munich decisions).[18] German–Soviet negotiation bore fruit in written agreement on 23 August. After years of bitter propaganda about, respectively, Bolshevik–Slav barbarism and fascist–capitalist exploitation of the workers, Germany and the USSR came to terms to carve up Poland between them and to cooperate in other ways, notably in exchanging political refugees each had harboured from the other. Authoritarian states enjoy great flexibility in the conduct of diplomacy. Hitler could now go ahead confidently with the obliteration of Poland.

[18] He had in mind the eighteenth-century partitions of 1772, 1793 and 1795, the last of which had removed Poland from the map until 1918.

13

The Second World War

FROM BLITZKRIEG TO BARBAROSSA

In Europe the Second World War began at last in the small hours of
1 September 1939 with German aircraft bombing Polish cities and
airfields and the bombardment of a Polish fort outside Danzig by a
German training ship on a 'goodwill' visit. Soon after, the German
army crossed the frontier in several places and in overwhelming
strength. Two days later the British and French honoured their guarantee to Poland and declared war on Germany. Almost to the last their
governments had not been keen to do so. It was obvious that they
could not offer practical and immediate help to Poland. That unhappy
nation soon collapsed, to disappear once again from history, divided
between Soviet and German occupations about a month after the
outbreak of war. But for the British and French not to have gone to
war would have meant acquiescing to the German domination of
Europe, for no other nation would have thought their support worth
having. So, uneasily and without the popular excitement and buoyancy
of 1914, the balance of power was to be fought for again.

It was an almost incidental political fact that the only two constitutional great powers left in Europe now at last found themselves
facing a totalitarian regime in battle. This was a largely fortuitous
outcome; it had not been an ideological necessity. Neither the British
and French peoples nor their governments had much enthusiasm for
their roles, and the decline of liberal and democratic forces since 1918
put them in a position much inferior to that of their predecessors in
1914. Nonetheless, exasperation with Hitler's long series of aggressions and broken promises made it hard to see what sort of peace

could be made with him which would be sufficiently reassuring. The basic cause of the war was, therefore, as in 1914, German national ambition. But whereas then Germany had gone to war because her rulers felt threatened, now Great Britain and France responded to the danger presented by Germany's expansion. *They* felt threatened this time and went to war because of it.

Yet the war was to transcend the issue over which it broke out, and this, in retrospect, seems to have been almost inevitable from the start. Nineteen thirty-nine – or perhaps 1941 – can now be seen to have marked a break in European and world history like no earlier one. Those years register the final, no longer deniable fact that the history of Europe had come to an end as a self-contained, coherent, self-explanatory entity. Soon, the capitals of Europe would count for little in determining even the continent's own affairs; there would be difficulty for decades in discerning a purely domestic European history; even the internal business of Europe's governments would show a loss of control to outsiders. When a purely European history came again to be discernible, it would be in a world setting totally unlike that of 1939.

Nothing so portentous, though, was at once obvious. To the surprise of many observers, and the relief of French and Britons, the first six months of the war were almost uneventful once the short Polish campaign was over. Vestiges of Polish resistance were prolonged for just over a month, but the country's fate was settled even before the Soviet army invaded the country from the east on 17 September and the new Polish partition followed. Those few weeks of fighting made it plain that mechanized forces and air power were likely to play a much more important part than between 1914 and 1918, and set a pattern for future German victories, the *Blitzkrieg* ('lightning war') of sudden assault and quick overthrow of the opponent in a fast-moving campaign based on superior mobility. Apart from this, a German submarine campaign at once began against Allied shipping, but it was on a small scale. Not much else could be predicted. The memory of the slaughter on the Somme and at Verdun was too vivid for the British and French to plan anything but an economic offensive; the weapon of blockade, they hoped, would in the end be effective, though the prospects were much less promising than twenty-five years earlier

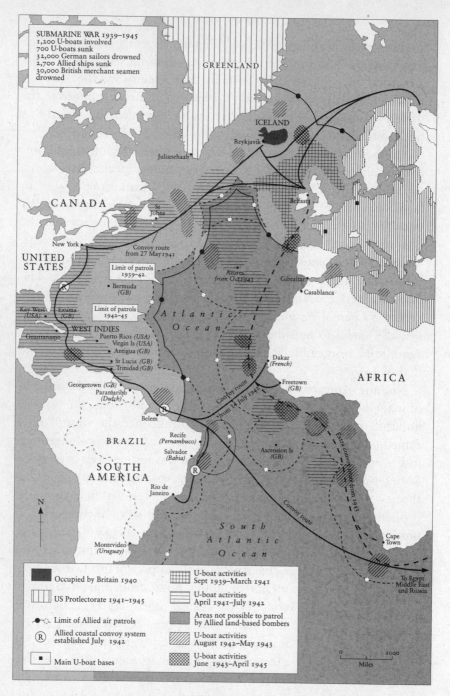

SUBMARINE WAR 1939–1945
1,200 U-boats involved
700 U-boats sunk
32,000 German sailors drowned
2,700 Allied ships sunk
30,000 British merchant seamen
drowned

GREENLAND

ICELAND

Reykjavik

Julianehaab

Belfast

CANADA

St
Johns

New York

UNITED
STATES

Convoy route
from 27 May 1941

Azores
from Oct 1943

Gibraltar

Casablanca

Limit of patrols
1939–42

Bermuda
(GB)

Atlantic
Ocean

Key West
(USA)

Exuma
(GB)

Limit of patrols
1942–45

Guantanamo

WEST INDIES

Puerto Rico (USA)
Virgin Is (USA)
Antigua (GB)
St Lucia (GB)
Trinidad (GB)

Dakar
(French)

AFRICA

Georgetown (GB)
Paramaribo
(Dutch)

Belem

Freetown
(GB)

Convoy route
from 14 July 1941

BRAZIL

Recife
(Pernambuco)

Salvador
(Bahia)

Ascension Is
(GB)

Extra convoy route from 1943

SOUTH
AMERICA

Rio de
Janeiro

Convoy route

N

South
Atlantic
Ocean

Cape
Town

Montevideo
(Uruguay)

To Egypt
Middle East
and Russia

Occupied by Britain 1940

US Protlectorate 1941–1945

Limit of Allied air patrols

Allied coastal convoy system
established July 1942

Main U-boat bases

U-boat activities
Sept 1939–March 1941

U-boat activities
April 1941–July 1942

Areas not possible to patrol
by Allied land-based bombers

U-boat activities
August 1942–May 1943

U-boat activities
June 1943–April 1945

Miles

1000

The Second World War: the Atlantic theatre

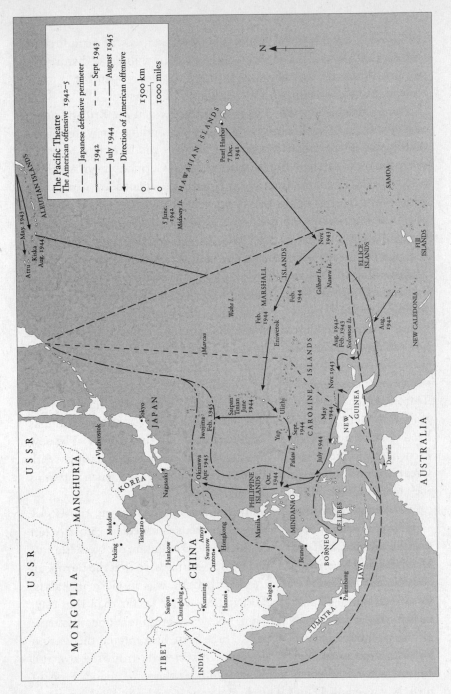

The Pacific Theatre
The American offensive 1942–5

- - - - Japanese defensive perimeter
⸺ 1942
- - - Sept 1943
-·-·- July 1944
-··-··- August 1945
⟶ Direction of American offensive

1 500 km
1000 miles

N ⟵

USSR

ALEUTIAN ISLANDS
Attu May 1943
Kiska Aug. 1944

HAWAIIAN ISLANDS
Pearl Harbor 7 Dec. 1941

5 June 1942. Midway Is.

SAMOA

Wake I.

Marcus

MARSHALL ISLANDS
Feb. 1944
Eniwetok
Feb. 1944

Gilbert Is. Nov 1943
Nauru Is.

ELLICE ISLANDS

FIJI ISLANDS

NEW CALEDONIA

USSR

MANCHURIA
Vladivostok

Tokyo
JAPAN
Nagasaki

KOREA

Mukden
Peking
Tsingtao
Hankow
Swatow Amoy
Canton Hongkong
CHINA
Kunming
Chungking
Saigon
Hanoi

MONGOLIA

TIBET

INDIA

SUMATRA
Palembang
JAVA

BORNEO
Brunei
CELEBES
MINDANAO
Manila
PHILIPPINE ISLANDS
Oct. 1944
Okinawa Apr. 1945
Iwojima Feb. 1945
Saipan Tinian June 1944
Ulithi
Yap
Palau I. Sept. 1944

CAROLINE ISLANDS

Nov 1943
May 1944
July 1944

NEW GUINEA

Aug. 1942–Feb. 1943
Solomon Is.
Aug. 1942

Darwin

AUSTRALIA

The Second World War: the Pacific theatre

because of Germany's easy access to the resources of Scandinavia, eastern Europe and the USSR. Hitler was unwilling to disturb the western Allies; he was anxious to leave the door open for a peace which would leave him with a free hand in the east.

The resulting stalemate was only broken when the British sought to intensify the blockade by laying mines in Scandinavian waters. This coincided with a German invasion of Norway and Denmark to secure the route by which iron ore supplies reached Germany from northern Sweden. The German attack on 9 April 1940 opened an astonishing period of successful fighting by the German army and airforce. Only a month later, came another demonstration of *Blitzkrieg*, with a German invasion first of the Low Countries and then of France. A powerful mechanized attack through the Ardennes bypassed the Maginot line and opened the way to the division of the Allied armies and the capture of Paris. On 19 June, German forces reached the Atlantic port of Brest. Three days later the Third Republic signed an armistice with the Germans. Italy had joined in on the German side just ten days earlier; Mussolini, who had been planning to enter the war only much later, had been surprised by the speedy German successes and wished to assure himself a place at the peace-table. The Third Republic came to an end on 10 July with the installation of the hero of the ferocious Great War battle of Verdun, Marshal Pétain, as head of state, and a German occupation of half the country. The new French government (established at Vichy) broke off relations with Great Britain after the British had seized or destroyed French warships they feared might fall into German hands.

With only a handful of neutral states left in Europe, the USSR supplying Germany with the war materials it asked for, no ally left on the continent, half of France, the whole of Belgium, the Netherlands, Denmark and Norway occupied by the Germans, so that the European coast from the Pyrenees to the North Cape was in German hands, Great Britain faced a strategic situation worse by far than that even of her struggle against Napoleon. She was not quite alone, it is true; all the Dominions except the Irish Free State had entered the war on her side, and a number of governments in exile from the overrun continent had still some small forces under their command. Frenchmen, Norwegians, Danes, Dutch, Belgians, Czechs and Poles were to fight gallantly, and often to outstanding effect, in the years ahead. The allegiance of some Frenchmen was especially important because of the potential for exploitation of the French overseas empire, whose fate was in many places uncertain, but their leader, a junior general who had left France before the armistice (and had been condemned to death *in absentia*), Charles de Gaulle, represented only a faction within France, not its legal government, and was distrusted by many Frenchmen. He saw himself nevertheless as constitutional legatee of the Third Republic and the custodian of France's interests and honour and began almost at once to show an independence which was in the end to make him the greatest servant of France since Clemençeau. He was soon recognized by the British as 'leader of the Free French'.

One reason why the British found de Gaulle important was that in some parts of the French empire he believed he might find sympathizers who would join him in continuing the fight. Earlier imperial history determined much of the way in which the geographical extent of the war was now beginning to spread outside Europe. Above all, Italy's entry into the war meant that her east African empire and the Libyan and Tripolitanian coasts south of the Mediterranean sea lanes had become operational areas. On the German side, the new availability of Atlantic and Scandinavian ports meant that what was later called the 'Battle of the Atlantic', the struggle to sever British sea communications by submarine, surface, and air attack, would now become much fiercer, and further extended than before.

Immediately, though, the British braced themselves to face direct attack. The hour had already found the man to rally the nation. Winston Churchill, a politician with a long and chequered political career behind him, had become prime minister when the Anglo-French Norwegian campaign collapsed, because no other man commanded support in all parties in the House of Commons. To the coalition government which he immediately formed he gave vigorous leadership, something hitherto felt to be lacking. But to the surprise of some (given his record), his leadership soon proved able to reach well beyond the political and administrative élite. Churchill called forth in his fellow-countrymen, whom he could address and exhort by radio, qualities they had forgotten they possessed. It was not long before it was clear that only defeat after direct assault was going to get the British out of the war.

This was all the more certain after a great air battle over southern England in August and September had been won by British science and the Royal Air Force. It is remembered as the 'Battle of Britain' – the right name for the conflict, for the survival of the country was at stake. For a moment, classically minded Englishmen felt they knew the pride and relief of the Greeks after Marathon. It was precisely true, as Churchill said in a much-quoted speech when the battle had scarcely begun, that 'never in the field of human conflict was so much owed by so many to so few'.[1] Victory in the Battle of Britain made a German seaborne invasion impossible (though a successful one had always been unlikely). It also established that Great Britain could not be defeated by bombing alone. The islanders had a bleak winter of rationing and night-bombing ahead and years of further discouraging setbacks, but the direction of the war now changed: the decision in the air in the west opened a period in which German attention turned elsewhere.

In December 1940 detailed German planning began for an invasion of Russia in the following May. Until then, the Soviet Union appeared to have done well out of its agreement with Hitler, notably making important gains on its western frontiers, apparently with an eye to securing a glacis against a future German attack. The Soviet occupation of Poland had been the first step (and it had been one not entirely unwelcomed by Ukrainians and Jews in the formerly Polish Ukraine). A war against Finland in the winter months then provided an improved strategic frontier in Karelia. Then in 1940 the Baltic republics of Latvia, Lithuania and Estonia (which Soviet forces had occupied the previous year) were formally swallowed in the USSR. Bessarabia, which Romania had taken from Russia in 1918, was the next acquisition, together with the northern Bukovina. At this point, Stalin was beginning to go beyond the old tsarist frontiers.

Hitler never doubted that he would in the end fight the USSR and almost always envisaged this as a result of a deliberate German attack on it. He had spoken in June 1940 of turning to his 'great and true

---

[1] 18 June 1940. It was delivered first to the House of Commons and then broadcast.

task: the conflict with Bolshevism' as soon as peace had been made
with the British.[2] His precise decision and its timing were influenced
by concern about further Soviet expansion: he wished to keep Soviet
power away from the historic European foci of Russian imperialism,
the Balkans and the Straits. He wanted also to show, by a quick
overthrow of the USSR, that further British war-making was pointless,
and thus to anticipate the effect of increasing American help to the
United Kingdom. But the deepest roots of Hitler's decision to attack
the Soviet Union were probably personal; he had long sincerely and
fanatically detested Bolshevism and had also long believed that the
Slavs, in his view an inferior race, should provide Germans with living
space, labour and raw materials in the east. He cherished a last,
perverted and racialist vision of the old struggle of the Teuton to
impose western civilization on the Slav east. Many Germans responded
to such a theme, and it was to justify greater atrocity than any earlier
crusading myth.

While Hitler's generals began to prepare for the invasion of the
Soviet Union, they first fought a brief spring campaign in 1941. In
this overture to the coming clash of titans, the Germans attacked
Yugoslavia (where a revolution had just overthrown a government
that had aligned itself with the Axis powers) and Greece on 6 April.
Italian forces had been unsuccessfully and unhappily engaged with
the Greeks since October 1940 in pursuit of Mussolini's Adriatic
ambitions. Once again, committed to a disastrous campaign in support
of the Greeks in inadequate strength, British arms were driven from
the mainland of Europe. Crete, too, was lost to a spectacular German
airborne assault. Now all was ready for 'Barbarossa', the great
onslaught on the USSR, named after a crusading German emperor
of the Middle Ages.

The attack was launched, by the largest force (of over 3.5 million
men) ever assembled in European history, early in the morning of 22
June 1941. There were immediate and remarkable German successes;
the Soviet forces proved woefully unprepared. The German army took
vast numbers of prisoners, inflicted huge casualties and drove hundreds

[2] Q. in R. A. C. Parker, *Struggle for Survival. The History of the Second World War*
(Oxford, 1989), p.60.

of miles into the Soviet Union in what looked briefly as if it might be another victorious *Blitzkrieg*. Its advance guard came within eighteen miles of entering Moscow. Yet that margin was not quite eliminated, and the German army was by then exhausted. At the beginning of December, the first successful Soviet counter-attacks announced that Germany was pinned down; the Soviet government, which had left Moscow for Kiubyshev, 500 miles to the east, was back in the capital ten days before Christmas. German strategy had lost the initiative, as well as nearly a million men. If the British and Russians could hold on, and if they could keep together, then failing some radical technical modification of the war by the discovery of new weapons of great power, their access to American production would inexorably increase their strength. This did not, of course, mean that they would inevitably defeat Germany, only that they might force her to terms.

GERMAN EUROPE

Once Barbarossa was under way, though, the slim chance that there might be a negotiated peace virtually disappeared, even if Stalin seems to have always feared that his western allies might seek to make one behind his back and cast at least one fly of his own in that direction. At the end of 1941, even allowing for the recent setbacks on the eastern front, the German grip on continental Europe seemed likely to be unbreakable except by military defeat (for a long time a somewhat remote prospect). Europe's remaining neutrals had to tread carefully to avoid awakening German hostility. In the occupied territories (which were to be extended further still in the next two years) collaboration, exploitation and bullying were at first sufficient to contain the few feeble shoots of resistance that had as yet appeared, although the British government had soon tried to encourage them with arms and advice. This was to continue to be the case until Germany suffered major defeats in the east, and had antagonized many of its conquered subjects by the behaviour of its forces, and when there was some real likelihood of the physical re-entry of allied forces to western Europe.

In every country there were collaborators with the German occupying forces. Not all of them acted from wicked or even self-interested

motives. Some simply wished to win better treatment for their compatriots or to shelter them from punitive barbarity. There were of
course also those who sincerely and even idealistically believed German
propaganda about the dangers of communism, the perfidy of Albion,
and Jewish–Masonic plots, or who were taken in by the specious
glamour of a vision of a rationally reordered Europe. Others were
glad to reject the institutions of a corrupt and decrepit democracy
that they believed to have betrayed them. Everywhere the Germans
were able to find volunteers of some sort, too, for national contingents
in their military formations, or for local police and paramilitary units,
even if in some countries only very few came forward. Among the
collaborators there were also criminals and self-seekers with an eye
to the main chance. Finally, there were always sadists and thugs
available who could give rein to their own perverted tastes in the
context of occupation.

Undoubtedly, though, it was a major German error to fail to
conciliate positive support and take advantage of what were at first
favourable circumstances in many occupied territories. From the start,
German treatment of occupied Poland and its peoples was atrocious.
Poles and Jews were turned out of the western lands and deported,
with little warning, to the 'General Government' area in the east, in
order to make room for *Volksdeutsche* recalled from abroad. Polish
universities were closed, their teachers deported or shot. One result
was the early emergence of an underground Polish Home Army that
was to mount in Warsaw in August 1944 one of the most gallant,
though tragically unsuccessful, risings against the occupying power.
As the war went on, too, the systematic looting of occupied countries
drove down standards of living and in some areas (Greece, for example)
produced famine conditions that further alienated subject peoples.
Next came the conscription and deportation of labourers to work in
German industry under conditions that often resembled slavery. The
French resistance movement became numerically significant when
large numbers of young men began to go into hiding to escape labour
service in Germany.

Such policies now seem unwise not merely because of the antagonism they created but also because they did not always serve German
interests directly. By the last year of the war, for example, there were

in the east competing industrial empires run by the SS and local commanders squandering their human resources through inefficiency and their callous neglect of the slave-labourers themselves. Often no attempt was made even to make illegal use of prisoners; 2 million Soviet prisoners of war are said to have died in captivity in the first six months of the war in the east, for the most part from sheer neglect.

The darkest brutalities of the German ascendancy in Europe were to be revealed only after the war, and must be placed in the context of Nazi racial policy. But even while it was in progress the effects of racial antagonism that might have been avoided by more rational approaches were apparent. It is now sometimes forgotten that in 1941 German advance-guards in the Ukraine had been welcomed by a local population glad to have shaken off Soviet rule; the potential value of the support of Ukrainian nationalism was nonetheless ignored by Hitler. An independent Ukrainian state that was proclaimed in Lvov on 30 June 1941 was almost at once swept aside and a campaign was launched by the Germans against Ukrainian nationalism. Those Ukrainian patriots who survived it were driven into a partisan movement against the German army.[3] Meanwhile, 3 million Ukrainians were moved west by the Germans as conscript workers.

The always distracting and sometimes militarily significant activities of resistance movements were, understandably, often to be exaggerated in retrospect. Yet above all in the Balkans, they much preoccupied Hitler himself and were highly effective in some countries in utilizing the alienation of the local population from the German occupation authorities. Yugoslavia provided the outstanding example. But they also bred divisions within those populations, notably after the participation of communist parties in resistance activity after the German attack on the USSR. In France, these were largely overcome in a unified resistance organization, but in Italy, they led to something like civil war once the allied liberation had begun, and in Greece they produced outright fighting of Greeks against Greeks well before liberation was achieved. They also provoked ferocious German reprisals;

---

[3] After the return of Soviet forces in 1943, the Ukrainian partisans turned their weapons against the USSR, too; it was only in early 1948 that Soviet, Polish and Czech forces together finally wiped out the Ukrainian nationalist resistance.

the murder of 335 Italians in the Ardeatine caves after a partisan attack at Rome was a vivid example.

WORLD WAR

In 1939, legislation had been passed by the United States Congress allowing foreign governments to buy arms if they paid for them in cash and took them away in their own ships or towed them across an American border. That was as far as American public opinion would go at that point; it was a step away from complete isolation, but a long way from intervention in Europe's quarrels. A straw in the wind that may in retrospect be thought just as significant, though, was the beginning of a privileged confidential correspondence between the American president and Winston Churchill (then only First Lord of the Admiralty) in October the same year. At least from that winter, when he won his third presidential election, Franklin Roosevelt believed that in the interests of the United States, Great Britain had to be supported both up to the limits his own public support and the law of neutrality would permit and a little beyond them both at times. A crucial step was an American 'Lend-Lease' Act in March 1941 which authorized the president to lend or lease defence materials to any country whose security in his judgement appeared to be in the interest of the national defence of the United States. In effect, this meant that goods and services were to be provided to the Allies without immediate payment. By the end of the war something between 40 and 50 billion dollars in aid went to Great Britain, the USSR, and the European governments in exile.[4] Soon afterwards, the American government extended naval patrols and the protection of its shipping further eastward into the Atlantic. After the invasion of the Soviet Union came a meeting on a British battleship between Churchill and Roosevelt which resulted in a statement of shared principles termed the Atlantic Charter. In it, one nation at war and another formally at peace spoke of the needs of a post-war world 'after the final destruction

---

[4] About $8 billion 'reverse' lend-lease went to the USA from allies who supplied US forces with goods and services.

of the Nazi tyranny'. Such language was far from what American opinion would have tolerated eighteen months earlier. By the summer of 1941, Hitler knew that to all intents and purposes the United States was an undeclared enemy.

This was the background to his second fateful and catastrophic decision of the year, a declaration of war on the United States on 11 December. It followed a Japanese attack on British, Dutch and American territories. The war thus became global. Hitler had earlier promised the Japanese his support, but if he had not kept his promise British and American declarations of war on Japan might have left two separate wars to rage, with only the British and the Dutch engaged in both: Hitler's action threw away the chance that American power might be kept out of Europe and concentrated in the Pacific. Few single acts, therefore, have so marked the end of an epoch. It announced the eclipse of European affairs. Europe's future was now to be settled not by her own efforts but by the two great powers on her flanks, the United States and Soviet Russia.

THE CONFLATION OF WARS

The Japanese decision had been a rash one, too, though the logic of Japanese policy had long pointed towards conflict with the United States. Japan's ties with Germany and Italy, formalized in a 'Tripartite Pact' in September 1940, though they had some propaganda value for both sides, did not amount to much in practice. The Japanese appear to have valued them chiefly so long as it seemed it might be possible to get the USSR, too, to join the three powers in an attack on Great Britain, the greatest of the European imperialists in Asia. What mattered most in the timing of Japanese policy was the resolution of debates in Tokyo about the danger, or lack of it, in a challenge to the United States that would be bound to lead to war. The crux of the matter was Japan's need for oil in order to conclude the war in China successfully. She could only obtain it with the open or tacit consent of the United States. In 1937, when the 'China Incident' began, Japan still imported more than two-thirds of her oil and petroleum from the USA. No American government, though, could give Japan a licence to destroy China. Instead, the American stance hardened. The Japanese occupation and announcement of a protectorate over Indo-China was followed by the prohibition of the export of scrap metal to Japan by Americans, and a freezing of Japanese assets in the United States.[5] Finally the American government imposed an embargo on all trade by United States citizens with Japan.

There then followed the last stages of the process which had its origins in the ascendancy established in Japanese government by reactionary and expansionist forces in the 1930s. Determination to uphold Japanese interests on the mainland of Asia by physical intervention had been demonstrated in 1904 by war with Russia, in 1910 by the annexation of Korea, in 1931 in Manchuria, and in 1937 in the beginning of the 'China Incident'. The question had by the autumn of 1941 become for the Japanese military planners purely strategic and technical; since they would have to take by force the resources in south-east Asia which they needed to maintain their position in China (a view the navy had resisted, while the army supported it), all that had to be settled was the timing and nature of the inevitable outbreak of war with the United States. The basic decision was fundamentally irrational, for the chances of ultimate success in such a war, unless a complete American overthrow was achieved at the outset, were very small; once the arguments of national honour had won, though, the final calculations about the best point and moment of attack were carefully made.

It was decided to strike as hard a blow as possible against American sea power at the outset in order to gain the maximum freedom of movement in the Pacific and South China Sea. The result was the onslaught of 7 December 1941, whose centrepiece was an air attack on the American fleet at Pearl Harbor in Hawaii that remains one of the most brilliantly conceived and executed operations in the history of warfare. In a couple of hours the Japanese all but wiped out the American air units there and sank their battleships and several other vessels. By mischance, though, they fell short of complete success. The attack did not destroy American naval air power, because the

[5] American scrap and iron ore met about half the needs of Japanese industry, the rest being supplied by Manchurian ore.

American aircraft carriers were at sea and not in harbour. A few hours later an even more crippling attack followed on the main US airbase in the Philippines that broke the back of the American air forces in the Far East.

These operations gave the Japanese for months the strategic freedom they sought. Exploiting their initiative, they wrought terrible destruction on the colonial empires of the Far East. Almost at once they sank the two capital ships intended to be the core of the British Far Eastern fleet and went on to conquer Malaya and the fortress of Singapore, the Philippines and Indonesia within a few months. They pressed through Burma towards the frontiers of India and China. On 19 February they bombed the north Australian port of Darwin for the first time from bases in New Guinea. By mid-1942 European rule in east and south-east Asia had come to an end everywhere beyond Burma except in the tiny Portuguese colony of Macao and (Japanese-occupied) French Indo-China. The initial failure to inflict a decisive defeat on the United States, though, remained; after it the Japanese faced a prolonged war they were bound to lose. Pearl Harbor had united Americans as little else could have done. Isolationist sentiment could be ignored after 8 December and Hitler's subsequent folly in declaring war on the United States. Roosevelt had a nation behind him.

GLOBAL CONFLICT 1941–5

After Pearl Harbor the war was now a world war as the first had never been; even the American mainland received a few Japanese shells and balloon-carried bombs. German operations had already by then left only five neutral countries in Europe – Spain, Portugal, Sweden, Switzerland and Ireland. In North Africa, fighting had raged back and forth in the deserts between Italian Libya and Egypt, and had been extended to Syria earlier in 1941 by the arrival there of a German mission, and to Iraq when a nationalist government supported by German air units was removed by a British force. Iran had been occupied by British and Soviet forces while Ethiopia was liberated and the Italian east African colonial empire destroyed, all in the same year. Meanwhile, a much-intensified naval war was being fought by German submarine forces, aircraft and surface raiders over much of the Atlantic, Arctic and Indian Oceans and the Mediterranean. Only a tiny minority of countries was left outside this vast conflict.

The demands of such a war were colossal. They carried the mobilization of whole societies much further than even the First World War had done, though Germany's was more slowly achieved than that of either the United Kingdom or the USSR. The appalling Soviet losses of economic resources in the first year of fighting were followed by a dramatic mobilization which revealed what had been done to overcome the mismanagement which had dogged the tsarist state in the Great War. In the end, though, the role of the United States was decisive. Her huge manufacturing power made the material preponderance of the 'United Nations' (as the coalition of states fighting the Germans, the Italians and Japanese came to be called) incontestable.[6]

Nonetheless, the first part of 1942 was very bleak for the United Nations. The turning-point only came in four great and very different battles. In June a Japanese fleet attacking Midway Island was broken in a battle fought for the most part by aircraft and in which the Americans from the outset possessed superior signals intelligence. Japan's losses in carriers and aircrews were such that she could never regain the strategic initiative, though her yards made vigorous efforts to build more carriers. Other defeats at sea followed as a long American counter-attack in the Pacific now began to unroll with the aim of destroying Japanese resources and acquiring the island bases from which Japan itself could be attacked. Next, at the beginning of November, the British army in western Egypt decisively defeated the Germans and Italians at El Alamein and began an advance that was to end in Tunisia. The victory had coincided with landings by Anglo-American forces in French North Africa. By May 1943 German and Italian resistance, reduced at last to Tunisia, came to an end and the long struggle for control of

[6] The term 'United Nations' was first officially employed in the United Nations Declaration, a war alliance signed on 1 January 1942 by China, the UK, the USA and the USSR. Other nations later signed up to terms of which the most important was an undertaking not to make any separate peace with the Axis powers. It was the first alliance for war made by the USA since 1778.

the Mediterranean was over. Six months earlier, at the end of 1942, the Red Army had bottled up a German army rashly exposed by Hitler at Stalingrad on the Volga. Its remnants surrendered in February 1943 in the most demoralizing and costly defeat yet suffered by the Germans on the eastern front, but one that was only part of three splendid months of Soviet winter advance which marked the turning-point of the war on the eastern front.

The other great Allied victory was in the battle of the Atlantic. It has no specific date and the struggle went on until the end of the war, but was just as important as the Pacific, African and Russian victories, and even more so than any one of them. Its climax came in the early months of 1942 and victory in it in 1943. In March 1942 nearly 850,000 tons of allied shipping were lost and six U-boats were sunk; in September that year, the figures were 560,000 tons and eleven U-boats. The tide had turned, though there was still hard fighting ahead. At the end of the year over 8 million tons of shipping had been lost for eighty-seven U-boats sunk. In 1943 the figures were 3.25 million tons and 237 U-boats. The Battle of the Atlantic was crucial for the United Nations, for on it depended British and, to some extent, Soviet ability to draw on American production; victory in it was especially attributable to the penetration of German signals intelligence by the British and the provision of long-range aircraft by American production.

Command of the sea and clearance of German and Italian armies from North Africa made re-entry to Europe possible from the west. In July 1943 Anglo-American forces landed in Sicily and six weeks later on the Italian mainland. Soon afterwards Mussolini was overthrown by a monarchical coup. Roosevelt had agreed to give priority to the defeat of Germany, but an invasion of northern France to take the strain off the Russian armies could not in the end be mounted before 1944. The delay angered Stalin, but when it came, the Anglo-American invasion of northern France in June 1944 was the greatest seaborne expedition in history. Now Germany had to fight major land battles on three fronts, while still maintaining major commitments in the Balkans. Soon after the landings in Normandy, Soviet armies entered Poland. Going faster than their allies, it still took them another nine months to reach Berlin in April 1945. Allied forces had by then broken out of Italy into central Europe and from the Low Countries into northern Germany. Almost incidentally, terrible destruction was inflicted on German cities in a great air offensive that, nonetheless, exercised no decisive strategic effect until the last few months of the war.

That the end was bound to be an Allied victory had long been clear. It was now confirmed by the entry to the war of previously neutral states anxious to have a say at the peace and to become members of the new international organization, the United Nations, which was in process of evolution.[7] Hitler, who had ignited this conflagration, can no longer by this stage be deemed to have been sane, however we define true madness. He had no wish to spare his fellow-Germans, let alone his enemies, and when on 30 April 1945 he killed himself in a bunker in the ruins of Berlin, historic Germany as well as historic Europe were both literally and figuratively in ruins about him. His death was not quite the end, but the formalities of the next few days were soon over; the Soviet army took the surrender of the German forces in Berlin on 2 May, and the final German capitulation came five days later at Rheims.

The war in the Far East took a little longer. At the beginning of August 1945 the Japanese government knew it was lost. Many of Japan's former conquests in the Pacific and much of south-east Asia had already been retrieved, though her forces had given little ground in China, which had remained a huge military and strategic irrelevance except in so far as Japanese forces were tied up in large numbers in occupation duties in that country. At home, her cities were devastated by American bombing and her sea power, on which communications and safety from invasion had rested, was in ruins.[8] At this moment two weapons of a destructive power hitherto unknown were dropped by the Americans with terrible effect on the Japanese cities of Hiroshima and Nagasaki. As the scientists had predicted, the power of these two 'atomic' bombs, released by tapping the energy of the atomic nucleus, far outstripped anything to be obtained by chemical

---

[7] Turkey, which declared war on Germany in February 1945, was the outstanding example.

[8] Two-thirds of the Japanese merchant marine, and two-thirds of the Japanese navy, had been sunk before the end of the war by US submarines alone.

explosives. Between the explosions, the Russians declared war on Japan. On 2 September the Japanese government abandoned its plan for a suicidal last-ditch stand and signed an instrument of surrender. The Second World War was over.

THE MEANING OF VICTORY

In its immediate aftermath it was difficult to measure the colossal extent of what had happened. Only one clear and unambiguous good was at once visible, the overthrow of the Nazi regime, and the delivery of Europe from an appalling terror. No regime so systematically vile had ever before dominated so much of the civilized world. As the Allied armies advanced into Europe, the deepest evils of a system of terror and torture were revealed by the opening of the prison camps and the revelations of what went on in them. It was suddenly apparent that Churchill had spoken to no more than the bare truth when he told his countrymen in 1940 that 'if we fail, then the whole world, including the United States, including all that we have known and cared for, will sink into the abyss of a new Dark Age made more sinister, and perhaps more protracted, by the lights of perverted science'.[9] The reality of this danger could be seen at once at Bergen-Belsen and Buchenwald, the sites of the first two camps of victims of the regime to provide horrifying films of the Nazis' treatment of their prisoners. They were soon being shown in the cinemas of the victors, and awoke strong feelings against Germans.[10] As more horrors were uncovered, distinctions ceased to be meaningful between the degrees of cruelty inflicted on political prisoners, on slave labourers from other countries (of whom millions had been brought to work in German factories or on military construction projects like the 'West Wall' fortification of the French coast), or on some of Germany's prisoners of war. Even all these, though, were eclipsed as the evidence became available of a systematic Nazi attempt to wipe out European

[9] In the speech of 18 June.
[10] The appalling images from Bergen-Belsen in fact testified as strongly to neglect as to cruelty; huge numbers of unburied dead that confronted the British liberators were the victims of unchecked disease and starvation.

Jewry in a so-called 'Final Solution' of an irrational problem: the pursuit of racial purity.

The ultimate origins of what came to be called the 'Holocaust' lay back well before 1901, in deep-rooted antisemitism, crackpot theories about international Jewish conspiracy, mistaken eugenic ideas. After 1933, inadequate men and women and even psychopaths were easily found to be enlisted for official persecution of the Jews, a sinister enough piece of evidence about Nazi society, but many ordinary Germans were, sometimes from fear, sometimes from indifference, also willing to go along passively with what they knew and saw of persecution and, later, of extermination policy. The notion that Germany might actually itself be cleansed of Jews had surfaced (in the offices of the Nazi security service) as a practical proposition as early as 1934, but the exact process by which it developed into a scheme for total extermination was complicated, cloaked in secrecy, and is still debated. In it, the Nazi élite, the SS organization, played a major part. The outcome was a transformation of the demographic map. Overall, though complete figures may never be available, it is probable that between 5 and 6 million Jews were killed, whether in the gas-chambers and crematoria of the extermination camps, by shootings and extermination on the spot in east and south-east Europe, or by overwork and hunger. Polish Jews were almost wiped out, and Dutch Jews, too, suffered terribly in proportion to their numbers. But distinctions at such a level of atrocity hardly mean much.

No nation had engaged in the war because it saw it as a struggle against such wickedness, though no doubt many people were heartened as it went on by the sense (assisted by intelligent propaganda) that the conflict had a moral dimension. Even while Great Britain was the only nation in Europe still on her feet and fighting for her survival, many of her people had sought and had begun to see in the struggle positive ends going beyond mere survival and even beyond the destruction of Nazism. Hopes of a new world of good relations between great powers and of social and economic reconstruction were embodied in the Atlantic Charter and the organization of the United Nations for peaceful cooperation. They were encouraged by sentimental but wholly understandable goodwill and gratitude towards allies and a tragic blurring of differences of interest and social ideals that would re-emerge only too quickly when fighting ended. Much wartime rhetoric then boomeranged badly; disillusionment often followed inspection of the world soon after the guns were silent. Yet for all this, the war of 1939–45 in Europe remains a moral struggle in a way, perhaps, in which no other great war has ever been and without any of the combatant governments intending it to be when they entered it (except, pervertedly, the German). It is important never to forget this. Too much has been heard of the regrettable consequences of Allied victory; it also brought to an end the worst challenge to liberal civilization and human goodness that has ever arisen.

There was a deep irony in that. Germany had for so long been one of the most progressive countries in Europe, the embodiment of much that was best in its culture. Germany was a major contributor to the civilization which had gone round and, indeed, had made, the modern world. That she should fall prey to collective derangement on the scale implied by the Holocaust (to say nothing of other atrocities) suggested something rotten at the root of that civilization itself. The crimes of Nazism had been carried out not in a fit of barbaric intoxication with conquest, but in a systematic, scientific, controlled, bureaucratic (though often inefficient) way about which there was little that was irrational except the appalling end that it sought and the lunatic mythologies which fed it. In this respect the Asian war was different, for all its brutalities. Japanese imperialism replaced the old western imperialisms for a time, but the subject peoples did not always wholly regret the change, even if they were often ruthlessly exploited and cruelly treated. Allied propaganda during the war attempted to give currency to the notion of a 'fascist' Japan, but this was a distortion of so traditional a society's character. When all the atrocities of Japanese occupation have been weighed, it remains hard to believe that such appalling consequences as faced European nations under German rule were in Asia bound to follow a Japanese victory.

Glib comparisons are, of course, useless and perhaps dangerous. When we say that Nazi behaviour in Europe and the Holocaust were 'worse' than earlier atrocities, and that therefore the men who carried them out were 'worse' than the villains of the past, we speak truly, but must be clear about what that means. It is not just a matter of the scale and intensity of brutality and destructiveness made possible by the capacities of industrial societies. Great atrocities have taken place in the past whose precise extent we can never measure, and the subjective and relative impact of which we cannot imagine, because the mental and cultural context is so hard to understand. Doubtless, too, innumerable acts of appalling cruelty have been lost in oblivion. The most exquisite deliberate tortures, physical and mental, have been inflicted by human beings on one another (and were repeated between 1939 and 1945; many who did not themselves suffer in the evil of the Holocaust died under them). Terrible things, too, would be done after 1945. The overall record of the Nazis, nonetheless, strikes us still as uniquely dreadful because its perpetrators had no excuse for not knowing better. The torturers and exterminators were born of cultures that had centuries of moral reflexion and argument behind them, all the progressive thought of the last three centuries of European civilization, all the slowly refined, humanized teaching of Christianity. They had no excuse of ignorance or tradition. They had deliberately turned their back on the good.

Distinctions can of course be made among villains and certainly between perpetrators of brutal acts of war. There is a line that can be drawn between the evil and perverted Hitler and the bombastic, bullying but less corrupted Mussolini, between the doctrinal, lunatic cruelty of the SS and the often revengeful, embittered but still rationally defensible planners of the Allied strategic bombing offensive. However it felt to be its victim, there is a distinction to be drawn between Nazi tyranny and the fanatical, devoted ruthlessness of the Japanese, or even between Nazism and the brutal defensiveness expressed in Stalin's near-paranoia with possible opposition. It was above all in Germany that the twentieth century revealed itself as an age when men in power in a civilized country deliberately chose to turn their backs on civilization.

The most immediately obvious further result of the war was its unprecedented physical destructiveness. Hiroshima and Nagasaki, the first victims of nuclear warfare, were not, in fact, the best evidence of this. It was most visible in the German and Japanese cities devastated by bombing. One of the major features of the Second World War, this proved much more costly to life and buildings than had been the bombing of Spanish cities in the Spanish Civil War (though those early essays in terror had been enough in their day to convince many observers that bombing alone could bring a country to its knees). In its effects, although bombing was often invaluable in combination with other forms of fighting, the huge strategic offensive against Germany built up by the British Royal Air Force from tiny beginnings in 1940, and steadily supplemented by the United States Air Force from 1942 onwards up to the point at which their combined forces could provide a target with continuous day and night bombing, achieved very little of decisive importance until the last few months of the war. Nor was the fiery destruction of Japan's cities strategically so important as the elimination of her sea power.

The cost of victory in lives had been very great. The numbers will never be exactly known; it seems as if more than 50 million people must have perished round the world in military and naval operations. Battle casualties, above all on the eastern European fronts, far surpassed those of the Great War; Germany suffered more dead than in 1914–18 (about 3 million on the eastern front alone) and Russia the staggering possible loss of more than 20 million people, though not all on the battlefield. About half that number of Chinese, military and civilians together, died in all. Famine and disease helped to send up the overall total even as the fighting was drawing to a close – in Greece, for example – and in India a great famine in 1942 had carried off 2 million dead. As for individual acts of violence, bombing had killed hundreds of thousands of Germans and Japanese, while the deaths at Hiroshima and Nagasaki showed that similar holocausts could be even more easily achieved by the enormous power of nuclear weapons, of which those used in 1945 were only early and relatively feeble examples. It was probably true that no one before 1939, however fearful of war, would have guessed that human society could endure such bloodshed and survive.

BOOK 5

A NEW WORLD

14

Appearance and Reality

EUROPE: AMID THE RUINS

Appearance and reality were less far apart in 1945 than they had been in 1918. In the aftermath of the Second World War, it should at once have been clear to anyone seriously concerned with public affairs that the age of European hegemony was over (though that need not mean they would feel able to say so). Like its predecessor, that war had as its heart a European struggle, a second German War. It, too, had grown from that into a combination of wars, but in an even more spectacular and all-embracing way than the conflicts of 1914–18. Making ever greater and more unprecedented demands, in the end it left little of the world untouched, undisturbed, unmobilized, untainted. People spoke, realistically, of 'total war'. The enormous destruction it wrought, materially and institutionally, was the clearest sign that the post-war world would have to be built anew – in some places, literally, from the ground up – and on new lines. Behind the damage done by the war, moreover, there was the psychological legacy of the bitter experiences of the 1930s, above all of economic depression. The economic foundations of western preponderance had already then been shaken to their roots. There was psychological as well as material repair work to be undertaken. As for Europe's reach beyond her shores, although six European nations still had significant overseas possessions in 1945 (Great Britain, France, Belgium, the Netherlands, Portugal and – just – Spain), the policies of the greatest of them, Great Britain, had already shown that European empire was in retreat.

Within Europe, only the neutral states of Ireland, Portugal, Sweden and Switzerland had escaped serious damage. Spain, though neutral

Reykjavik
ICELAND

N

NORWAY

SWEDEN

FINLAND
Helsinki

Oslo

Stockholm

GREAT
BRITAIN

NORTH
SEA

DENMARK

RUSSIA

London

Elbe

Stettin

NETH.

Berlin

Oder

Warsaw

BEL.

Bonn

EAST
GERMANY

POLAND

LUX.

Paris

WEST
GERMANY

CZECHOSLOVAKIA

FRANCE

SWITZ.

Vienna

Budapest

AUSTRIA

Trieste

HUNGARY

ROMANIA

PORTUGAL

Belgrade

Bucharest

Lisbon

Madrid

ITALY

YUGOSLAVIA

SPAIN

Rome

Sofia
BULGARIA

GREECE

Athens

	Founding members of NATO
	Later members of NATO
	Warsaw Pact countries
*	Treaty of Rome members

Cold War Europe

during the war, had been deprived by it of the possibility of economic recovery from her own civil war (which had ended in 1939). She was a poverty-stricken country. The formerly combatant nations, though, faced the most obvious material problems in 1945. Of Europe's farmers, only those of the United Kingdom, Sweden and Switzerland were producing more in 1945 than in 1939. Coal output everywhere – above all in Germany – was far below even the averages of the depression years of the 1930s. Europe had suffered more physical damage than any other continent, and the cost of the war's direct destruction there has never been accurately measured. One estimate is that 7.5 million dwellings had been destroyed in Germany and the USSR alone. Of the unhappy peoples of those two countries it is likely that some 25 million died, half, perhaps, as a direct consequence of fighting or as prisoners of war. The non-Russian populations of the republics of the USSR that had been occupied longest by the German forces had suffered most; Soviet estimates were that 5.4 million civilian deaths took place in the Ukraine alone.[1] In stricken countries those who survived camped amid ruins, while 11 million people wandered among them as refugees – now termed 'displaced persons'. The United Nations Relief and Rehabilitation Administration (UNRRA, set up in 1943) was looking after 50,000 abandoned children in Germany alone. Disease was a threat and often a reality for months after the fighting ended; it was fortunate that DDT was available to delouse possible typhus carriers and there was no such epidemic of that disease as there had been in the aftermath of 1918. Starvation and lack of shelter had nonetheless left their own grim residues; a majority of Greek children were said to be tubercular after the liberation.

Something of a demographic revolution had occurred, too, as a consequence of the war and its aftermath. It was shaped by movements of peoples as much as by absolute loss. Whereas after 1918 it had been assumed that it should be possible to make arrangements for ethnic minorities to live contentedly among majorities alien to them

[1] Even within large approximations, Soviet figures published after 1945 continued to be misleading. Only in 1959, when the census revealed a huge gap between earlier projections from 1939 figures and actuality, did the figure of approximately 20 million Soviet war dead emerge.

in blood, language, culture, Europe seemed almost without thinking to have rejected such confidence in 1945. Already before the fighting was over, Germans were pouring westward to escape the fate they feared at the hands of the Soviet army. Poles and Czechs were determined to expel those Germans who remained on their territories, not merely as an act of vengeance but also to ensure that the question of their 'protection' by a strong Germany could never arise again. Within a decade of 1945, something like 10 million Germans left the east to look for homes and jobs in a new, diminished Germany. As an example of ethnic cleansing it was another of the sad triumphs of nationalism.

It was often the case that the infrastructure on which the relief organizations[2] could rely was non-existent. Communications in the zone between the Rhine and the Vistula had been shattered. There was nothing with which to pay for the imports Europe needed except dollars provided by American aid or expenditure in Europe. In the defeated countries currencies had collapsed; Allied occupation forces found that cigarettes, spam and bully beef were better than money. Civilized society had given way not only under the horrors of Nazi warfare, but also because Nazi occupation had transformed lying, swindling, cheating and stealing into acts of virtue; even when they were not necessary to survival, they had been for years legitimized and even celebrated as acts of 'resistance'. Arms in private hands presented in many places the danger of private vendetta supplanting law.

As the Allied armies advanced, the firing squads of those with grudges or fears to work off got to work in their wake. In some places they anticipated the arrival of the victors: brutal civil wars had been going on in Yugoslavia and Greece well before their liberation. Old scores were wiped out and new ones run up. It was alleged that in France more perished in the 'purification' of liberation than in the great Terror of 1793, but any such comparison, true or false, is dwarfed by the vengeances taken in Yugoslavia. There, old community hatreds had been opened up again by wartime decisions to cooperate with or fight the Germans. Three million Serbs, it was alleged, had been

---

[2] Of which the most important was UNRRA. It spent over $4 billion on refugees and other needs between then and 1947, when it closed.

murdered by the Croat *Ustaša* in Bosnia and Croatia. Such massacres had driven old hatreds even deeper into the subsoil. Albanians, annexed to Italy in 1939, did not ignore their opportunities as the war went on, notably when, two years later, the formerly Yugoslav district of Kosovo was transferred to Italian administration. Albanians recruited to the German SS had joined in terrorizing the Serbian partisans' supporters, so creating further bitterness in an already ethnically troubled region.[3] In other countries, too, revolution seemed a danger, and on better evidence than in 1918.

Germany had once been the flywheel of industrial Europe: she should have been the engine of continental recovery. But even if her communications and productive capacity had been intact – and they were in ruins – the Allies were at first bent on holding down German industrial production; their aim was to prevent, not to encourage, Germany's resumption of a leading economic role in Europe. They all at first conceived her government as a unity, although she was temporarily split up between four occupation forces. From the start the Soviet occupation forces had been carrying off capital equipment from their zone of occupation as 'reparations' to aid the recovery of their own ravaged lands (as well they might after what the USSR had suffered; the Germans had destroyed 39,000 miles of railway track alone in their retreat).

THE FRAMEWORK OF RECOVERY

Even before the war ended, when Europe's immediate post-war shape had been debated at a conference at Yalta in February 1945, a new set of divisions within the continent was settled. Yet though Yalta produced the nearest thing to a formal peace settlement which Europe was to have for decades, it did so because Roosevelt, Stalin and Churchill accepted the realities that lay behind it: as Stalin put it, 'whoever occupies a territory also imposes on it his own social system'.[4]

[3] Although the 'Skanderbeg' SS division, named after a fifteenth-century Albanian hero, never mustered more than 6,500 and proved of little use to the Germans except during their retreat in 1944.
[4] Djilas, *Conversations with Stalin* (London, 1962), p.105.

Yalta's effect was to divide the old central Europe, and, indeed, Europe as a whole into eastern and western halves. A winding line from the Adriatic to the Baltic defined the way in which occupation zones now layered new differences on top of old. By Christmas 1945 all countries east of it except for Greece had communist governments or coalition governments in which communists shared power with others. The Soviet armies had proved far better instruments for the extension of international communism than revolution had ever been.

Bismarck's Germany was now partitioned into zones occupied by the Russians, Americans, British and French. Germany did not exist as a political entity. Austria had been separated from it again and was also divided between occupying forces, though re-established as an independent republic. The other major political units of pre-war Europe, though, had reconstituted themselves after occupation and defeat; all the nation-states of 1919 reappeared except for the three pre-war Baltic republics, which did not re-emerge from the Soviet Union. That country now absorbed parts of pre-war Poland and Romania, too. Most countries outside the Soviet sphere were much enfeebled; Italy, which had changed sides after Mussolini had been overthrown in 1943, had, like France, a much strengthened and enlarged communist party which still said it was committed to the revolutionary overthrow of capitalism. In France that seemed a real possibility when the communist party emerged as the strongest party in the constituent assembly set up in October 1945. This seemed even more likely when de Gaulle (elected head of government in November) resigned in January 1946 because of left-wing opposition.

Among the former European great powers other than the USSR, only Great Britain retained her pre-war stature in the world's eyes. For a little while she was recognized still as an equal of the USSR and the United States (formally, France and China were victorious former great powers, too, but the fiction was more obvious in their case). Yet Great Britain's moment was past; her eminence was illusory and temporary, though morally enhanced by recollection of her stand almost alone in 1940 and 1941. She was a nation-state that had not given way under the strain of the war like many others, and by a mobilizing of her resources and people in a way unparalleled outside the USSR, she had been able to survive. But she had been let out of strategic impasse only by the German attack on Russia, and kept afloat only by American Lend-Lease. That had not been without its costs: the Americans had driven hard bargains, insisting on the sale of British overseas assets to meet the bills before it was forthcoming. The sterling area was now dislocated. It now consisted, too, overwhelmingly of countries where the British had huge debts (tactfully renamed as 'sterling balances'). American capital was about to move on a large scale into the old Dominions, and they had learnt new lessons, some from their new wartime strength and some, paradoxically, from their weakness. Australia and New Zealand, in particular, had looked to the mother country for their defence, and found it not to be forthcoming when needed, whereas American help had been. From 1945, the Dominions more and more acted with full as well as formal independence, though not without regard to old ties (Canada, notably, made a loan of $1,250 million in 1946 to the United Kingdom to help it through post-war balance of payments difficulties).

In the event, it did not take long for the change in the position of the greatest of the old imperial powers to become clear. Symbolically, even Great Britain's last great military effort in Europe in 1944 had been under overall American command. Though British numbers in Europe for a few months afterwards matched the American, they were by the end of the war fewer. In the Far East, too, though the Indian army and imperial forces from Africa under British command reconquered Burma, the defeat of Japan had been the work of American naval and air power. For all Churchill's efforts, Roosevelt was by the end of the war negotiating over his head with Stalin, with an eye to dismantling the British empire. Great Britain, for all her prestige at the moment of victory, had not escaped the war's shattering impact. In some ways she was the former great power which, together with Germany, best illustrated the revolution in international affairs brought about by it. Subtly and suddenly, the kaleidoscope of world authority had shifted, and it was still shifting as the war came to an end, even if many Europeans still had to make the painful psychological discovery that the European age was over.

RECONSTRUCTION

That reflexion on history can sometimes be useful was shown by some steps taken while the war was in progress to prepare for the world after it. The results of nations seeking their own economic salvation in the 1930s seemed to many influential persons on the United Nations side to have been so awful that they had begun to discuss the likely economic problems of the post-war years. From the urge to make arrangements which would keep the world economy on a more even keel than in the past had come a major conference at Bretton Woods in July 1944. Although the USSR refused to agree to the conference's decisions, it agreed a system of more or less fixed exchange rates in terms of the US dollar, which thus became, in a measure, a new gold standard.[5] This was part of an attempt to tackle the illiquidity problems that had so hampered recovery in the 1930s, when would-be buyers lacked the appropriate currency to buy from would-be suppliers. It led also to the setting-up of the International Monetary Fund (IMF) and the World Bank, which were to channel investment by capital-exporting countries into what came to be called the 'developing' world. The IMF was to hold 'deposits' made by participating countries that could then be made available, at fixed parities, to any other participants needing another currency in exchange for its own at fixed rates. Member states bound themselves not to devalue. In 1947 the major victorious nations went on to sign a General Agreement on Tariffs and Trade (GATT). These arrangements were to prove able to work pretty well until the 1970s.

Like the great shifts in power relationships between countries, such facts further emphasize that while after the First World War it had still been easy to embrace the illusion that an old order might be revived, no one could believe that restoration pure and simple was possible in 1945. This was healthy, and in strong contrast with the circumstances in which inter-war attempts to reorder twentieth-century international life had been made. The victors could not start with a clean sheet, of course. Events had closed off too many

[5] Haiti, Liberia and New Zealand also stood out.

possibilities. Among the far-sighted decisions already taken during the war, moreover, some by agreement, some not, one of the most important had been to set up an international organization to maintain international peace. The fact that the two greatest powers saw such a step in different ways, the Americans as a beginning to the regulation of international life by law and the rulers of the USSR as a means of maintaining the Grand Alliance of the victors, did not hinder their cooperation.

Thus the United Nations Organization (UNO) came to birth at San Francisco in 1945. Much thought had been given to the reasons why the League of Nations had failed. One of its most obvious defects was to be avoided by the United States and USSR belonging to the UNO from the start. Apart from this, its basic structure in outline somewhat resembled that of the League. Its two essential organs were a small Security Council and a large General Assembly. Permanent representatives of all member states (at the outset, fifty-one nations) were to sit in the General Assembly. The Security Council started with eleven members, five of them permanent: the United States, the USSR, Great Britain, France (included at the insistence of Winston Churchill) and China. Other member nations filled the other places in turn. That the Security Council was given greater power than the old League Council was largely at the insistence of the USSR, whose representatives thought that there was a strong likelihood that they would always be outvoted in the General Assembly because the United States would call not only on the votes of its allies, but also on those of what Moscow regarded as its satellites in Latin America. Naturally, not all the smaller powers liked this. They were uneasy about a body on which at any moment any one of them was unlikely to sit, which would have the last word, and in which the great powers would carry the main weight. Nevertheless, the structure the great powers wanted had to be adopted if any organization was to work at all.

The other constitutional issue much disputed was a veto power given to the permanent members of the Security Council. This, too, was a necessary feature if the great powers were to accept the organization. Its starkness was in the end somewhat qualified, in that a permanent member was not allowed to prevent investigation and discussion of matters which especially affected it unless they were likely to lead to action inimical to its interests. In theory the Security Council possessed very great powers, but, of course, their use and operation were bound to reflect political reality at any moment. For a long time (and, some might say, still, over a half-century after its foundation) the importance of the United Nations proved to lie less in its power to act than in the forum it provided for discussion. For the first time, a world public linked as never before by radio and film – and later to be linked by television – would hear the cases made at the General Assembly for what sovereign states did. This was something quite new. If the United Nations at once gave a new dimension to international politics, though, it took much longer to provide effective new management of its problems. Sometimes, the new publicity of international argument led to feelings of sterility, as increasingly bitter and unyielding views were set out in debates which changed no one's mind. But even this must have had an educational force outside the UN. It was important, too, that it was soon decided that the permanent seat of the General Assembly should be in New York; this drew the attention of Americans to it and helped to offset historic American ignorance of the rest of the world and to make isolationism a little less likely.

The first ordinary meeting of the United Nations General Assembly none the less took place in London in 1946. Bitter debates at once followed; complaints were made about the continued presence of Soviet soldiers in Iranian Azerbaijan, which had been occupied during the war. The USSR representatives promptly replied by attacking that of British forces in Greece. Within a few days the Soviet delegation cast the first veto in the Security Council. Many more were to follow. The instrument which the Americans and British had regarded and continued to use as an extraordinary measure for the protection of special interests became almost a regular and certainly an unexpectedly frequent piece of Soviet diplomatic technique. From the start the USSR contended in the United Nations with a still inchoate western bloc that its policies were soon doing much to solidify.

Though the origins of conflict between the United States and the Soviet Union are sometimes traced back a very long way, in the later years of the war the British government had begun to feel that the Americans were too willing to make concessions to Stalin and were over-friendly to him. Of course, the fundamental ideological division between the USSR and her western allies had never gone away; if the Soviet leaders had not always had a deep, crudely Marxist preconception about the roots of behaviour of capitalist societies, they would certainly have behaved differently after 1945. It is also true that some Americans had never ceased to distrust the USSR and always saw her as a revolutionary threat. But this did not mean that they had much impact on the making of American foreign policy. In 1945, as the war ended, American distrust of Russian intentions was much less than it later became. Of the two states the more suspicious and wary was the Soviet Union.

GREAT POWER REALITIES

In 1945 thoughtful (and well-read) Europeans might have contemplated with admiration the prescience of the French political philosopher and historian, Alexis de Tocqueville, over a century earlier, about the American and Russian peoples. Each, he noted, seemed marked out 'to sway the destinies of half the globe'.[6] At the end of a second world war the destinies of the world did, indeed, appear dominated by them, and therefore by two great and very differing political systems, one based in what had been Russia, one in the United States of America, and even by two different cultures. The fate of Europe, the old master of the globe, was for a long time to come to be irresistibly shaped in the last resort by decisions taken in Moscow or Washington. Hitler's decisions of 1941 to go to war with the USSR and USA had been the last taken by a European ruler for many years that can be said to have changed the history of the continent. Whatever the USSR and the USA owed to Europe or reflected of it in their behaviour (and both were at least grounded in ideologies European in origin and shaped by European culture), their concerns were different from those of the old continent. Geography alone settled that. Much of their behaviour towards Europe in the

[6] The quotation comes at the end of the first part of de Tocqueville's *Democracy in America*, published in 1835.

next few years can only be understood in a global setting; this is yet another reason why European history becomes inseparable from world history in the years after 1945, besides the entanglements arising from old colonial and economic connexions.

In that year, there were really no other great powers left, for all the legal fictions expressed in the composition of the Security Council. Great Britain was gravely overstrained and breathless; France, barely risen from the living death of occupation, was rent by internal division. Germany was in ruins. Under occupation Italy had discovered new quarrels to add to old; her change of sides during the war still left uncertainties about her treatment in the peace negotiations. Japan was ruined and occupied, and China, never a great power in this century for all her indulgence by her allies, was about to engage in civil war anew. The USA and USSR, immensely stronger than any possible rival, had provided the means of victory. They alone, moreover, had made positive gains from the war. The other victorious states had, at best, won only survival or resurrection, while to the two greatest powers, the war brought new ascendancies.

Though that of the USSR had been won at huge cost, it was stronger than the tsarist empire had ever been. Soviet armies dominated a vast European glacis beyond the USSR of 1939. Much of it was now sovereign Soviet territory; the rest was organized into states that were soon in every sense satellites. One of them, East Germany, contained major industrial resources. All of them were primarily related to Moscow, rather than to one another. Some of them, indeed, would continue to show suspicion of their communist neighbours, even well into the 1980s. Beyond this glacis lay Yugoslavia and Albania, the only communist states to emerge since the war without the help of Soviet occupation;[7] in 1945 both seemed assured allies of Moscow, but were regarded by it as suspiciously and carefully as all the others. This advantageous Soviet position had been won by the fighting of the Red Army, but also reflected strategic decisions taken by western governments and their commander in Europe from 1943 to the closing

---

[7] Though the Red Army had entered Belgrade briefly, they had subsequently withdrawn, leaving the field to Tito's partisans (by then enjoying the formal support of the Yugoslav monarchy-in-exile).

stages of the war, when General Eisenhower had resisted political pressure to get to Prague and Berlin before the Soviet armies.

The Soviet occupation forces (carefully segregated from the local populations) gave the USSR a strategic preponderance in central and eastern Europe which looked all the more menacing to those west of it because the barriers to Russian power which had existed in 1914 – the Habsburg empire and a united Germany – had both now gone. An overtaxed Great Britain and an only slowly reviving and divided France could not be expected to stand up to the Soviet armies, and no other conceivable counterweight on land existed if the Americans went home. Soviet soldiers also stood in 1945 on the borders of Turkey and Greece – where a civil war between communists and monarchists was going on – and occupied northern Iran. In the Far East Soviet power held much of Sinkiang, Mongolia, northern Korea and the old tsarist base of Port Arthur as well as having 'liberated' the rest of Manchuria, though the only territory taken by the USSR from Japan itself was the southern half of the island of Sakhalin and the Kuriles. The rest of Soviet gains had been effectively at China's expense. All this looked very alarming not only to those who feared communism, but to those less ideologically sensitive who read Soviet policy primarily as a continuing steady pursuit of a view of Russian strategic advantage with a long tradition behind it. Another alarming fact soon to add to the misgivings of those worried about the USSR's hegemonic position was that the end of the war in China left communists who could be expected to be friendly to Moscow already in control of much of the country. Stalin might have backed the wrong horse there in the past, but the Chinese communists could not hope for moral and material help from anyone else. It seemed likely, then, that in Asia, too, a Soviet satellite was in the making.

The new world power of the United States rested far less on territorial occupation than did that of the USSR. At the end of the war there was indeed an American garrison in the heart of Europe, in Germany, but American electors wanted it brought home as soon as possible. It was quickly run down. By the beginning of 1948, the United States army's strategic reserve consisted of just over two divisions (at that moment the USSR had 185 divisions in the field). There was reluctance among those electors, too, to spend on defence other than that provided by air power and the atom bomb. But there were American naval and air bases round much of the Eurasian land mass and although the USSR was a far greater Asian power than ever, the elimination of Japanese naval power, the acquisition of island airfields and technological changes had together turned the Pacific Ocean into something like an American lake. Hiroshima and Nagasaki had demonstrated the power of the atomic bomb which the United States alone appeared to possess (though in fact she had for some time no further available examples of this weapon once the only two which existed had been dropped on Japan). But the deepest roots of American empire lay in industrial and financial strength.

Along with the land-power of the USSR, the industrial might of the United States had been decisive in achieving Allied victory. America equipped both her own huge forces and many of those of her allies in both the European and Pacific wars. Moreover, by comparison with them, victory had cost her little. American casualties were fewer than theirs; even those of the United Kingdom had been heavier, and those of the Soviet Union colossally so. The home base of the United States had been immune to enemy attack in any but the most trivial sense. It was undamaged; America's fixed capital was intact, her resources greater than ever. Her citizens' standards of living had actually risen during the war; the armament programme ended a depression still left unmastered by Roosevelt's New Deal. She was a great creditor country, with capital to invest abroad in a world where no one else could supply it. Finally, America's old commercial and political rivals were staggering under the troubles of recovery in the post-war years. Their economies drifted into the ambit of the American because of their own lack of resources. The result was a worldwide surge of indirect American power, its beginnings visible even before the war ended. Effectively, the United States dollar had already by then become the indispensable source of international liquidity. Through lend-lease, relief channelled through UNRRA, and direct expenditure on services overseas by the American armed services and other governmental agencies, Europe was by 1945 relying on a dangerously contingent source to fund its imports. The United States had become Europe's sole banker, but that went unnoticed by millions of Europeans, however uneasy some of its officials might be.

Something of the future implicit in a great power polarization could thus dimly be seen even before the fighting stopped in Europe. It was by then obvious that Soviet forces would not be allowed to participate in the occupation of Italy or the dismantling of her colonial empire, and that the British and Americans could not impose any Polish settlement unacceptable to Stalin. On the other hand, the British were to have a free hand in Greece, Stalin had agreed, while he had one in Romania. Somewhat oddly (in view of their record in their own hemisphere), the Americans were not happy about explicit spheres of influence as a way round potential conflict; the USSR was readier to accept them as a working basis. There is no need to read back into such divergences assumptions which became current a few years later, when conflict between the two powers was presumed to have been sought from the start by one or other of them. Appearances can be deceptive. For all the power of the United States in 1945, there was little political will to use it; the first concern of the American military after victory was to bring the boys home and achieve as rapid a demobilization as possible. Lend-lease arrangements with allies were cut off even before the Japanese surrender, a step which actually reduced America's international leverage; it weakened friends she would soon be needing, by imposing graver recovery problems upon them at a time when they could not provide a new security system to replace American strength. Nor (even when more of them at last became available) could the use of atomic bombs be envisaged except as a last resort; they were too powerful for use except in extremity.

It is much harder to know what was shaping Stalin's policy or, even now, quite what was going on in the USSR. Her peoples had clearly suffered appallingly from the war, more even than the Germans. With the colossal Soviet losses in the war, Stalin may well in 1945 have been less aware of Soviet strength than of Soviet weakness. True, his governmental methods relieved him of any need, such as faced western countries, to demobilize the armies which gave him supremacy on the spot in Europe. But the USSR had no atomic bomb nor a significant strategic bomber force, while the decision to develop nuclear weapons put a further grave strain on the Soviet economy at a time when economic reconstruction was desperately needed. The years immediately after the war were to prove for Soviet citizens as grim as had been those of the industrialization race of the 1930s. Yet in September 1949 a nuclear explosion was achieved and in the following March it was officially announced that the USSR had an atomic weapon. By then, though, much else had changed.

FRICTION

Piecemeal, relations between the two major world powers deteriorated badly by 1948. This was largely the result of events in Europe, an area obviously in need of imaginative and coordinated reconstruction. The division between eastern and western Europe established by Soviet victories had soon deepened. The British, in particular, had from the first been alarmed by the fate of Poland, which seemed to show that Stalin would only tolerate subservient governments in eastern Europe, although this was hardly what the Americans had envisaged as freedom for eastern Europeans to choose their own rulers. Until the war was over, though, neither government nor private persons in the United States had expressed much doubt in public that reasonable agreement with the USSR was possible. Broadly speaking, Roosevelt had been sure, even after his last inter-allied conference (at Yalta, in February 1945), that America could get on in peacetime with its wartime ally; they had common ground, he thought, in resisting a revival of German power and supporting anti-colonialism; he showed no awareness of the historic tendencies of Russian policy. Americans disapproved strongly, too, of British action in Greece against the communist revolutionaries seeking to overthrow the monarchy there, and Roosevelt had deep suspicions of anything looking like the restoration of colonial rule in Asia.

President Truman (who had succeeded Roosevelt on his death in April 1945) and his advisers came to change American policies partly as a result of their experience in Germany. At the outset, the three major powers were wholly in agreement that in due course, and under proper safeguards, a disarmed but still united Germany should be their ultimate aim, though the French did not agree with this and opposed from the outset any attempt at a central administration of Germany. The Soviet authorities had been punctilious in carrying out their agreement to admit British and American (and later French) armed forces to Berlin though they had not fought their way to it as the Red Army had done, and to share the administration of the city they had conquered with their allies. It was clearly a Soviet interest that Germany should be governed as a unit (as envisaged by a meeting of the victorious heads of the American, British and Soviet governments – but not the French – at Potsdam in July 1945), for this would give them a hand in controlling the Ruhr, potentially a treasure house of reparations. Yet the German economy soon bred trouble between West and East. Russian efforts to ensure security against German recovery led in practice to the increasing separation of her zone of occupation from those of the three other occupying powers. Probably this was at first intended to provide a solid and reliable (that is, communist) core for a united Germany, but it led in the end to a *de facto* solution by partition to the German problem which no one had envisaged and which was to last for most of the rest of the century.

The problems of the management of the western zones of occupation soon faced the British, Americans and French with a social crisis. Mass starvation appeared to be in the offing. In May 1946 the reparations delivered to the Soviet Union from the west were halted (as were those previously delivered from the American to the British and French occupation zones), pending new agreement on the economic management of Germany as a whole. This was not something Soviet policy could accept without protest. Meanwhile the social and administrative entrenchment of communism in eastern Germany was going forward and a new 'Socialist Unity Party' was set up to fuse the communists in the old socialist party – whose leaders violently rejected it. This seemed to repeat patterns seen elsewhere. In 1945 there had been communist majorities in elections only in Bulgaria and Yugoslavia; in other east European countries at that moment the communists only shared power in coalition governments. Nonetheless, it increasingly looked as if those governments could, in fact, do little more than behave as Soviet puppets. Something like a communist bloc was already appearing in 1946. In the following year Hungary, Romania and Poland all dropped non-communists from their government. Meanwhile the votes and propaganda of the communist parties of western Europe were evidently being deployed in Soviet interests.

Stalin's calculations remain in doubt; perhaps he was waiting, expecting or even relying upon economic collapse in the capitalist world. There was also always a strong element of opportunism in his undertakings. At bottom, though, Stalin could not accept any reunited Germany except under a government he could control. An independent Germany would always have a potential for aggression which a satellite could not have. Russia had too many experiences and memories of attacks from the west to trust a united Germany. This was likely to have been true whatever the ideology dominant in Moscow; it only made things a little worse that a united Germany might be capitalist. Unsurprisingly, when the foreign ministers of the victorious powers gathered in Moscow in March 1947 they found themselves unable to agree on any basis for a German peace treaty.

Outside Europe, the USSR showed more flexibility. While anxiously organizing eastern Germany safely on the Soviet side of the line slowly hardening across Europe, in China she still formally and officially recognized the KMT government. In Iran, on the other hand, there was an obvious reluctance to withdraw Soviet forces as had been agreed and even when they finally departed they left behind a satellite communist republic in Azerbaijan – to be later obliterated by the Iranians, to whom the Americans were soon giving military aid. In the Security Council the Soviet veto was more and more employed to frustrate her former allies. Yet, there had been and still was much goodwill for the USSR among her former allies for years after the war. When Winston Churchill drew attention to the increasing division of Europe by an 'Iron Curtain' he by no means spoke either for all his countrymen or for the American audience that he was addressing;[8] some, indeed, strongly condemned him. Yet though a British Labour government that had been elected in 1945 was at first hopeful that 'Left could speak to Left,' it had quickly become more sceptical. British and American policy began to converge during 1946, as it became clear that the British intervention in Greece had in fact made free elections possible there and as American officials had more experience of the tendency of Soviet policy. Nor did President Truman have prejudices in favour of the USSR to shed. The British, moreover, were

[8] At Westminster College, Fulton, Missouri, 5 March 1946.

by then clearly committed to leaving India; that, too, counted with American official opinion.

THE TRUMAN DOCTRINE AND THE MARSHALL PLAN

Europe was facing a hard winter as 1947 began. Weather conditions were unusually severe. In Great Britain electricity supplies were at times cut off. Meat became unobtainable in France except on the black market (and in April the bread ration was to be further reduced). It was against this background that in February the American president took a momentous decision to change American policy in a radical way. It followed messages from the British government which, perhaps more than any other step it had taken since the end of the war, conceded the long-resisted admission that Great Britain was no longer a world power. The Labour government had inherited a British economy gravely damaged by the effort made during the war; there was an urgent need for investment at home. It wished to reward its supporters by extending the 'welfare state', a costly business. The first stages of decolonization, too, were expensive. A part of this expense reflected imperial defence commitments, but there were others in non-colonial areas which were very burdensome.[9] A big American loan made in 1945 had soon been used up. Grain had to be paid for in hard currency and bread rationing (not found necessary in Great Britain during the war) had been introduced in the previous July to keep imports down.

By 1947 the British balance of payments could no longer support British forces in Greece, or the cost of aiding Turkey and the American government was told so. Yet if such efforts were not maintained, the security of Greece would be threatened; civil war against a communist

[9] Military expenditure abroad in 1947 was £209 million; the annual average of *all* British government expenditure abroad 1934–8, including administrative and diplomatic as well as military costs, had been £6 million. A. S. Milward, *The Reconstruction of Western Europe 1945–51* (London, 1984), p.41. In spite of relief received in the next two years, the British government was forced into a devaluation in 1949 (which was, of course, a breach of its IMF undertakings).

rebellion was still going on there. The country might fall to the communists. The case of Turkey, under diplomatic pressure by the USSR, was less urgent but still dangerous if deprived of foreign aid. President Truman at once decided that the United States must fill the gap. Financial aid was to be given to Greece and to Turkey. In his personal appearance before Congress, though, the President went further by drawing attention to the implication that much more than propping up two countries was involved. 'No government is perfect', he said, (and went on to acknowledge that the Greek, in particular, was not), but nevertheless, he pointed out, it was a virtue of democracy 'that its defects are always visible and under democratic processes can be pointed out and corrected'.[10] The ideological challenge was explicit. 'It must be the policy of the United States,' he said, 'to support free peoples who are resisting attempted subjugation by armed minorities or by outside pressures.' Although only Turkey and Greece were to receive aid, Truman was offering the 'free peoples' of the world American leadership to resist threats to their independence, with American help, though 'primarily through economic and financial aid'.

This was more than merely a reversal of that turning away from Europe which many Americans had seemed to hanker after in 1945; it was a break with the historic traditions of American foreign policy. The decision to 'contain' Soviet power, as it was soon termed, was possibly the most influential in American diplomacy since the Louisiana Purchase. Behind it lay Soviet behaviour and the growing fears Stalin's policy had aroused over the previous eighteen months, moreover; the British *démarche* had only been a detonator for the new policy. Ultimately, it was to lead to unrealistic assessments of the effective limits of American power (and, critics were to say, to a new American imperialism) as the policy was extended outside Europe, but this could hardly have been envisaged at the time.

Republican though Congress was, its leaders persuaded it to support the president's request for $400 million, though some congressmen

---

[10] The President's message was delivered on 12 March (the British had warned that they would shut down their Greek commitment on 31 March). See *Public Papers of the Presidents of the United States – Harry S. Truman, 1 January to 31 December 1947* (Washington, 1963), pp.176–80, for the full text.

expressed alarm at the potential for dissipating American strength that the 'Truman doctrine' might imply. The next step, though, went further still in its demands for resources. This was the 'Marshall Plan' to assist European economic recovery, named after the American Secretary of State who announced it. It was the product of fierce debate in the United States about the politics of European reconstruction. The continent appeared in 1947 to be heading towards an exchange crisis (in part because of the vigour of its recovery). Many American officials had by now come to see the survival of democratic and friendly regimes in Europe as an American interest. They may have exaggerated the political dangers facing France and Italy, but theirs was a new perception. The way to secure that interest, it now appeared, was to relieve Europe's chronic balance of payments problems, thus assuring its economic recovery and health, and so help to achieve a non-military, non-aggressive form of containment of the USSR.[11]

The British Foreign Secretary, Ernest Bevin, appears to have been the first European statesman to grasp the possibilities of the Marshall Plan. With the French, he pressed for the acceptance of the offer by western European nations. It was made to all Europe, but the USSR neither wished to participate, nor would it allow its satellites to do so; the plan was instead bitterly attacked in Moscow. The French communists, who had at first welcomed Marshall's proposal, had to eat their words. Soon (though with obvious regret) the Czechoslovakian coalition government also declined to join up; the Czechs, the only people in eastern Europe still left without a fully communist government and one not yet regarded as a Russian satellite, were obviously having to toe the Soviet line. Any residual belief in Czechoslovakia's independence was then removed by a communist *coup* in February 1948 and the installation of a puppet regime in Prague.

An important signal of a move towards a more intransigent Soviet stance had been the revival of the Comintern under the name of 'Cominform' in October 1947. It at once began the denunciation of what it termed 'the imperialist and anti-democratic camp' whose aim (it said) was 'the world domination of American imperialism and the

[11] See Milward, *Reconstruction of Western Europe*, for the origins and launch of the Marshall Plan.

smashing of democracy'.[12] Once the Cominform had been set up the Italian and French communist parties at once disowned their own earlier participation in coalition governments in their countries and the 'fetish of coalitionism' was condemned in Moscow.[13] Finally, when in 1948 western Europe set up an Organization for European Economic Cooperation (OEEC) to handle the Marshall Plan, the Russians replied by organizing their own half of Europe in a Council for Mutual Economic Assistance (Comecon), which was window-dressing for the Soviet domination of the command economies of the east. The first phase of Europe's post-war history can with this step be considered at an end. The next was to be a phase in global history, too. What came to be called 'the Cold War' – an expression whose first recorded use came little more than a month after Truman's message to Congress on Greece and Turkey[14] – had begun. One of the fundamental lines of the history of the next forty years was drawn.

[12] From the 'Declaration on the Formation of the Cominform', 5 October 1947, printed *AR 1947*, pp.522–5.
[13] The French communists had left the government a month before General Marshall's speech, in order not to continue sharing responsibility for the privations and rationing that the French people were undergoing; the Italian party had been ejected from government when a new coalition government was formed by the Christian democrat leader Alcide de Gasperi in 1947.
[14] By the American financier, Bernard Baruch, in addressing the legislature of South Carolina, 17 April 1947.

15

The Cold War Unrolls

ROOTS OF CONFLICT

Perhaps too often, the story has been told that the Chinese communist leader Chou-en-Lai, on being asked what he thought was the historical significance of the French Revolution, replied, 'It is too soon to say.' Truly reported or not, it is hard to see why such a prudent response should be thought (as it has been) funny, strange, or as evidence of an extraordinary and exotic viewpoint. What happened in France in 1789 when certain ideas were first launched on a world career is in fact still influencing many countries as the twentieth century draws to a close, even if it is not much invoked by name, or very obvious. It seems sensible not to lose sight of that. It is a long time since the Bastille fell, but the French Revolution is one of those historical facts (like others, older still, such as the establishment of Confucianism in China, the Spanish conquest of South America, or the Ottoman conquest of south-eastern Europe) with whose consequences we live today. All of which is merely preliminary, but suggests that for all the dramatic changes that followed 1945, we ought not to treat that year (nor of course, any other) as a sudden amputation or severance of history. Although long-term trends and forces alone do not explain everything that happens and (as in all previous ages) much of the second half of the twentieth century arises from accident, circumstance, or personality, its explanation must take account of long-term and historical forces, many of which go back far before that year.[1]

[1] The whole British cabinet formed by Attlee in August 1945 had been born while Queen Victoria was on the throne, a majority of its members before 1889, and one twenty years earlier than that. One could make not dissimilar observations about contemporary ruling élites in most of the world.

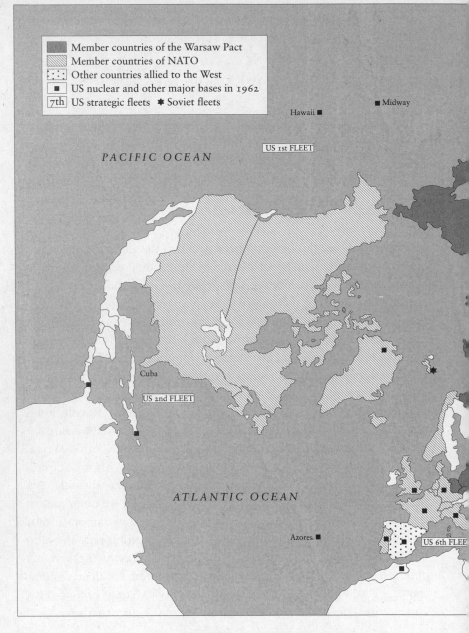

The Cold War World in 1962

Legend:
- Member countries of the Warsaw Pact
- Member countries of NATO
- Other countries allied to the West
- US nuclear and other major bases in 1962
- 7th US strategic fleets ✹ Soviet fleets

Midway ■

Hawaii ■

PACIFIC OCEAN

US 1st FLEET

Cuba

US 2nd FLEET

ATLANTIC OCEAN

Azores ■

US 6th FLEET

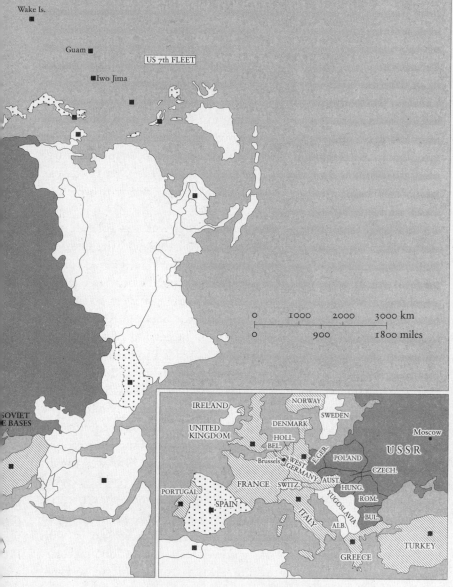

Wake Is.

Guam ■

US 7th FLEET

■Iwo Jima

0   1000   2000   3000 km
0   900   1800 miles

SOVIET
E BASES

IRELAND   NORWAY
                      SWEDEN
UNITED   DENMARK
KINGDOM   HOLL.
              BEL.   Moscow
        Brussels ● WEST   POL'AND   USSR
              GERMANY   CZECH.
PORTUGAL   FRANCE   SWITZ.   AUST.
        SPAIN   HUNG.   ROM.
                        YUGOSLAVIA
                    ITALY   BUL.
                        ALB.
                    GREECE   TURKEY

By the year 1950, there had begun a period of two and a half decades during which the central characteristics of the world political order seemed to be frozen and irremovable, even if revolutionary developments were going on elsewhere. Then came a renewed quickening of the pace of change, reaching its climax in the 1980s. By 1990, landmarks taken for granted for thirty years and more would disappear (sometimes almost overnight) and others were already called in question. But this was after a long time during most of which a prolonged and bitter Soviet–American antagonism overshadowed almost every other part of international life. It was far from the only force shaping history, and perhaps not the most fundamental in those years, but Cold War is a central theme running through them and the one with which to begin.

The first phase of Europe's post-war history was very brief. It may be thought ended, and a phase in global history with it, with the communist takeover of government in Czechoslovakia. The next phase saw most of the world divided into two groups of states, one led by the United States and one by the USSR, each striving to achieve their own security by all means short of war between the principal contenders. Its history was marked by a succession of crises. The contest, and the process of forwarding it, tended to be talked about mainly in ideological terms as one of communism and capitalism, Marxism and liberal democracy. This was always somewhat misleading. In some countries (Yugoslavia and Greece, for example), the Cold War appeared first masked as civil war. In other countries it broke out in moral and political debate about values such as freedom, social justice and individualism. Much of the Cold War was fought in marginal theatres by propaganda and subversion or by guerrilla movements, political parties, governments and armies sponsored by the two great states. Fortunately, the USA and USSR always stopped short of fighting one another, for they would have to do so with nuclear weapons whose increasing power made the notion of a tolerable outcome more and more unrealistic. During this tense time, there was also an economic competition between them, conducted by example and by offers of aid to satellites and uncommitted nations. Inevitably, in so complicated a process on so wide a geographical scale much opportunism got mixed up with doctrinaire rigidity. So

THE COLD WAR UNROLLS

did much human inadequacy. The Cold War was a blight that left little of the world untouched, a seeping source of crime, corruption and suffering for more than thirty years.

For all the brutal simplicities of the language the Cold War employed and generated, it nonetheless now looks in retrospect somewhat like the complex struggles of religion in sixteenth- and seventeenth-century Europe, when ideology provoked violence, passion, and even, at times, conviction, but could never wholly accommodate the complexities and cross-currents of the day. Above all, it could not contain national interest. As in religious struggles of the past, too, though there were soon signs that its specific quarrels might die down and disaster be avoided, the rhetoric and mythology of Cold War went rolling on, embittering attitudes long after they ceased to reflect reality.

The exact origins of antagonism between the USA and USSR have been much debated, and not only by propagandists. In part, identifying them depends on definitions of 'Cold War'. In the most abstract sense, after all, it was only a late and spectacular manifestation of a rupture in ideological and diplomatic history that had opened in 1917. That was what Lenin and his colleagues on the one hand would have said, and perhaps what Woodrow Wilson and his successors could have agreed, on the other. That rupture would have mattered much less, though, if history had not so unrolled as to produce by 1945 a new world power, the long-awaited modernized Russia, far better placed than any previous Russian regime to have its own way in eastern Europe, and to advance its ambitions in other parts of the world. Soviet diplomacy after Stalin's accession to power often reflected historic Russian great power ambitions, and was almost bound to do so; it is difficult to imagine how it could have pursued pure ideological objectives. Russian national interest, shaped by geography and history, was to be inseparable from ideological struggle; communists and those who sympathized with them everywhere believed that it was their first duty to safeguard the Soviet Union, the champion of the international working class and, indeed (true believers affirmed), the guardian of the destinies of the whole human race. Its survival appeared to them self-evidently crucial for world history. 'Socialism in one country' might for a time be a plausible and necessary slogan, but however qualified in practice frankness about their revolutionary goals might be, Bolsheviks had said their aim was to overthrow the social institutions of non-communist societies, and they meant it, so far as the long run was concerned. Soviet diplomacy could never have been merely a part of the technique of managing international relations but nor could it ever forget Russian national interest.

Once much of the world appeared to have divided into two camps, each proclaimed itself anti-imperialist and each often behaved (if effective domination is the test) in imperialist ways. Even if the Cold War stopped short of actual armed conflict between the two principals, subversion, bribery, murder, espionage, propaganda and diplomatic quarrelling long gave fresh colour to the basic premise, that it was impossible for communist and non-communist societies to cooperate and relate to one another in the way civilized societies had once believed to be normal.

THE BERLIN CRISIS AND NATO

Within a few months of the coup in Czechoslovakia, which completed the communizing of the governments of Eastern Europe, there followed what was to prove to be the first battle of the Cold War, over the fate of Berlin. It was decisive in that it defined a point at which, in Europe, the United States was prepared to fight. It does not seem that this outcome had been anticipated by the Soviet authorities. Yet they had helped to provoke it by their efforts to avoid the re-emergence of a reunited and economically powerful Germany which would not be under their control. This was a not unreasonable policy goal, given the deep historical background to Teuton–Slav relations. The western powers had a different interest. Having already come round to the view that they should reanimate the German economy, at the very least in their own occupation zones, and that they should get on with this before Germany's future political shape was settled, because it was vital for the recovery of western Europe as a whole, the western powers in 1948 then introduced a currency reform in their own zones with a view to removing restraints on trade between them. It had a galvanic effect, releasing the process of economic recovery in western Germany, which now began to become an economic entity. Following on Marshall Aid, though available (thanks to Soviet decisions) only to the western-occupied zones, this reform cut Germany in two; the recovery of the eastern half could not now be integrated with that of western Europe. A strong western Germany might now emerge by itself. That the western powers should get on with the business of putting German industry on its feet undoubtedly made economic sense, but eastern Germany was thenceforth decisively on the other side of the Iron Curtain.

The western currency reform had been carried out without Soviet agreement and quickly provoked a Soviet response. The city of Berlin, too, isolated though it was in the Soviet occupation zone, was divided by the currency change, and this prejudiced communist chances of staging a popular putsch there. There had already been Soviet interference with communications between the western zones of occupation and the city and some western officials had already had it in mind that a complete isolation of western Berlin might be attempted; the word 'blockade' had been used. When, at the end of June, the Soviet authorities cut road and rail links with Berlin their action was so interpreted; the rights of the western allies to have access to their own forces in their own sectors of Berlin were not questioned but the Soviet aim was now to demonstrate to the people of Berlin that the western powers could not assure their supply. They hoped thus to remove the obstacle which the presence of elected non-communist municipal authorities presented to secure Soviet control of Berlin.

To supply West Berlin, the British and Americans organized an airlift to the city. With that, a trial of strength was under way. The western powers, in spite of the enormous cost of maintaining such a flow of food, fuel and medicine as would just keep West Berlin going, announced they were prepared to keep it up indefinitely. The implication was that they could be stopped only by force. For the first time since the war American strategic bombers moved back to bases in England. Neither side wanted to fight, but all hope of cooperation over Germany on the basis of wartime agreement was dead. The blockade lasted nearly a year and breaking it was a remarkable technical achievement.[2] Berlin's airfields (and a lake on which flying

---

[2] It lasted from 24 June 1948 to 12 May 1949.

boats could land) handled over 1,000 British and American aircraft a day for most of the time, with an average daily delivery of 5,000 tons of coal alone. Because Allied supply was not interrupted, the West Berliners were not intimidated. This was a major political victory for the western powers. Psychologically, they ceased to be conquerors and became protectors. The Soviet authorities made the best of defeat by deliberately splitting the city (among other things, refusing the mayor access to his office, which was in their zone).

By that time, the western powers had in April 1949 signed a treaty setting up a new alliance, the North Atlantic Treaty Organization (NATO). The Berlin blockade had crystallized a western alliance that was the first Cold War creation to transcend Europe. The United States and Canada were members, as well as most European states outside the eastern bloc (only Ireland, Sweden, Switzerland, Portugal and Spain had not joined). It was a recognition that Europe could not expect to defend itself if war with the USSR broke out. As its first secretary-general allegedly put it, it was 'to keep the Americans in, the Russians out, and the Germans down'.[3] The New World was to be drawn back militarily as well as economically into the balance to offset the disarray of the Old. It was explicitly a defensive alliance, providing for the mutual defence of any member attacked and thus marked yet another retreat from the now almost-vanished isolationist traditions of American foreign policy. The foundation of NATO suggested that as well as two Europes perhaps there might also be two worlds, for events in other continents were already suggesting the likelihood of the spread of Cold War. The maintenance of an American garrison in Germany – and, notably, in Berlin – provided a tripwire guaranteeing that the United States would at once be involved in the event of war in Europe.

In 1949, the Greek civil war ended, with the elimination of the communist threat in that country; those communists who had survived the Greek army's assaults fled across the frontiers to Albania and Yugoslavia, and the last British forces were withdrawn from Athens. Before that, a new German national state, the Federal Republic, had

---

[3] Q. in T. Garton Ash, *In Europe's Name. Germany and the Divided Continent* (London, 1994), p.389.

emerged in May 1949 from the three western zones of occupation and in the following October a German Democratic Republic (the GDR) was set up in the east. Communists controlled its government, officially that of the 'Socialist Unity party'. Henceforth, there were to be two Germanys; the Cold War now ran along an Iron Curtain dividing them (and not, as Churchill had suggested in 1946, further east, from Trieste to Stettin). The first, somewhat dangerous, phase of the Cold War in Europe was over.

Some contribution to that was made also, ironically enough, by a further uncertainty introduced into the continent's affairs by an event which followed only a few days after the initiation of the Berlin blockade, the expulsion of the Yugoslav communist party from the Cominform on 28 June 1948. Until that moment, few western officials and politicians had seen Tito as anything but a loyal member of the eastern camp. While some still held this view (even to the extent of thinking that the expulsion was a Soviet ruse), the event complicated the emerging simplicities of east–west confrontation. Within twelve months the Cominform was vilifying Tito for 'betraying the Greek democratic cause for dollars'.[4] Within a few years, Stalin was meditating a Hungarian-led attack on Yugoslavia, and the Americans, British and French were considering how best to come to that country's assistance if one took place. Meanwhile, the example set by Tito so alarmed Stalin that a wave of purges and show trials was now mounted (and went on for years after 1948) throughout the other countries of the Soviet bloc. The aim was to remove any further danger of what was beginning to be called 'national communism'.[5]

NEW NATIONS: THE BEGINNINGS OF DECOLONIZATION

The emergence of a growing number of states which either did not feel committed, or did not find it convenient to say they were committed, to one side or the other in it, was an important complication of the stark

[4] *AR 1949*, p.291.
[5] The tightening of the Soviet grip implied in these events was also expressed in an intensification in all the east European states of industrialization in these years.

simplicities of Cold War. Several of these emerged out of what was called 'decolonization', a great and worldwide change in international relations. It transcended even the Cold War, though often exploited by Cold Warriors in a way that obscured that. The United Nations General Assembly became just as important as a platform for anti-colonial as for Cold War propaganda. It was not, though, where the empires were brought to an end, but merely the place where their demise was made evident.

The Second World War had been the death-knell of imperialism. Though, as Great Britain went to war, her future leader announced that the struggle was one for the rights of the individual,[6] it had not begun as an ideological conflict. It nonetheless picked up an increasingly ideological flavour as it proceeded, rolling up in itself and sometimes exacerbating a number of ideological issues of which anti-colonialism was one. Anti-colonialism was implicit, for example, in the declarations first of the Atlantic Charter and later of the Charter of the United Nations about the rights of nations to choose their own governments and the ultimate goal of independence for colonial territories. Such statements owed more to the accidents of great power involvement in the war (above all that of the United States) than to successful independence movements among imperial subject populations themselves; Indian nationalism, for example, was still manageable enough on the spot; it became much more important than hitherto, though, in aggravating the difficulties of British policy when it attracted patronage by Americans. Only a few months after Pearl Harbor (and less than a year after the meeting that produced the Atlantic Charter), an American under-secretary of state had announced that the 'age of imperialism is over'.

This was hardly a statement which the British, French, Dutch and Australian allies of the United States would at that moment have endorsed. The United States, though, was resuming an old national tradition. American policy had accepted in the 1930s that it was necessary to concede a major degree of autonomy to the Philippines

[6] Winston Churchill, 3 September 1939, in the House of Commons. He described the war as one, 'in its inherent quality, to establish, on impregnable rocks, the rights of the individual, and it is a war to establish and revive the stature of man'. See *Parliamentary Debates*, Commons, 5th series, 351, col. 295.

(though full independence would have to wait until 1946) and had never been willing to concede that the Monroe doctrine might be a cover for imperialism in indirect forms. Before the end of the war, missionary and business interests, too, were both excited and pressing on American government the hopes aroused in them by an anti-colonial stance that would offer advantages in commercial access to the empires in Africa and Asia.

It was not likely, though, that the other colonial nations would willingly acquiesce in American policy except in so far as the one defeated colonial power, Italy, was concerned.[7] Her African empire had finally been lost in 1942–3, and at the end of the war the Greeks were given the Dodecanese (which they had long claimed were really Greek). Elsewhere, although the costs of military action in recovering or maintaining empire might sway them, the colonial powers were not psychologically prepared before 1945 (except, perhaps, in a measure, the British) to go with an anti-colonial tide. Even the British, too, though they might talk of colonial independence as an ultimate goal, made distinctions. India might be well on the road to it but in 1938 a British official had still felt able to speak of independence for Africa as a matter of 'generations, or even centuries'.[8] When the French began to think about their post-war empire, the conference of African colonies and Madagascar that they summoned in early 1944 at Brazzaville was solely one of governor-generals and governors. No elected representatives of subject populations were present. After a speech at the opening session by General de Gaulle, the conference concluded that even though some participation in government by indigenous elected representatives might lie ahead, such an evolution would still take place firmly within the French imperial structure. Any idea of local autonomy was specifically excluded from consideration. This was, of course, wholly consistent with the old concept of a French *mission civilisatrice* which would turn France's subjects into her citizens, after turning them first into dark-skinned Frenchmen. What was perhaps to be surprising in the next decade was the degree to

[7] Defeated, of course, in 1943, but by the end of the war a 'co-belligerent' of the United Nations.
[8] See H. S. Wilson, *The Imperial Experience in Sub-Saharan Africa since 1870* (Minneapolis, 1977), p.290.

which metropolitan populations in the imperial countries showed far less concern than their politicians about the fate of their foreign colonies. Where there were not substantial white colonial populations, most concessions of independence were greeted by many Britons and Frenchmen with profound indifference.

Although there were great differences of circumstance and timing, it was the Asian nationalist movements that were most confident and hopeful in 1945. The card castle of European imperialism began to tremble in the defeats suffered in 1940 by imperialist powers in Europe. This had eased the extension of Japanese power by diplomacy and intimidation which had forced the closure for a short time of the Burma Road along which western aid could reach the KMT government in Chungking. Even more important was French acquiescence in the occupation by Japanese forces of Indo-China in 1941 and an effective Japanese domination of Siam. Then had followed the outright destruction of European empire in south-east Asia and Indonesia early in 1942. The repercussions of this were colossal even in areas (such as the Indian sub-continent) where the imperial power was not actually displaced by the Japanese. The surrender of 60,000 British, Indian and Dominion troops at Singapore had been a signal that European rule in Asia was doomed. No efforts could retrieve a disaster far worse than Yorktown 165 years earlier for the moral ascendancy of British imperial power. When there followed the Japanese occupations of the Dutch East Indies, the Philippines, Malaysia and Burma, they compromised the prestige and undermined the confidence of every white person in the Far East. It did not matter that the Japanese often behaved badly to their new subjects. In any case, and at least at first, they did not always do so and found plenty of collaborators (those of the Burma Independence Army for instance) who sought to fight for them against the British. By comparison with the upheavals caused by bombing, fighting, labour conscription, starvation and disease in Europe life went on in most Asian villages little disturbed. Parachuting arms to former colonial subjects to encourage them to resist their conquerors achieved little, save to create the possibility that they would be used in due course against their former rulers in London, Paris or The Hague. There were notable side-effects of the disappearance of western rule in economic life and culture, too. By 1945 a big potential for change existed in the Asian empires. Nor was territorial rule all that was now in question. Though Russian and American spheres of influence in Europe were clearly enough demarcated in 1948 to remain unchanged in practice for forty years, the settlement of great power relationships in the Far East would remain in doubt much longer.

INDIAN INDEPENDENCE

Even before the Second World War, after all, it had seemed likely that India would one day become an independent and perhaps a dominant Asian power. The restoration of imperial rule in India as it had existed in 1901 was already inconceivable. The timetable and form of its replacement was already being discussed before 1939. Englishmen who favoured Indian independence had hoped to keep it linked to the British Commonwealth of Nations, the name officially given to the empire since the Imperial Conference of 1926, which had produced an official definition of 'Dominion Status' as independent association to the Commonwealth in allegiance to the Crown, with complete control of internal and external affairs. This was a conceivable goal for India, though not one which British governments conceded as the next, immediate aim until 1940. Much progress towards self-government in practice had been made by then, though, and in part that explains the absence in India of a revulsion of anti-western feeling so complete as had occurred in China.

The war brought further change. Once again, a huge volunteer army was raised in India to fight for the Raj; as ever, India was the largest single source of first-class mercenaries in the world. Though the approach of war made the British increasingly aware of their need of the Indian army, they had already given up trying to make India pay for it; by 1941 the British tax-payer was financing its modernization. Indian formations fought to great effect in Africa, Italy, Syria, Iraq and Burma. Huge numbers of other Indians received training as never before in technical skills, some in the armed forces, some in the Indian industries that benefited from wartime demand. Changes long under way in other spheres were further advanced, too. Nearly four decades of introducing representative institutions in government up to provincial level and the progressive Indianization of the higher civil service (by 1939, of its administrative class of 1,000 or so officials the majority was Indian) had already produced a country which could not be governed except with the substantial consent of its élites and the practical collaboration of huge numbers of its people. Its nationalist leaders had undergone a preparatory education in self-government, if not in democracy. Moreover, many of them were men who in both formal and in very broad and informal senses, had grown up shaped by a British education in western political assumptions.

By taking India into the struggle with Germany without even a pretence of consultation in 1939, the government of India had to fight without the support (which, with tact, it might have engineered) of the men who could sway the Indian masses, notably, Gandhi. Under the surface, by 1941 the tide was running fast towards independence. The Japanese onslaught forced the hand of the British government. The first positive reaction by the British government came in 1942 in the form of an offer of autonomy for India after the war, with a right of secession from the Commonwealth. This was too little and too late. The Indian nationalists were now demanding complete and immediate independence. With a Japanese army at the gates of India some Indian politicians welcomed the idea of a Japanese victory. A nationalist army of liberation was mustered from Indian prisoners of war and sent into action by the Japanese in Burma, though to no military effect. After launching a 'Quit India' campaign (of which they quickly lost control), Congress leaders were imprisoned. The campaign was within weeks crushed rapidly and easily; it caused some material damage, principally to communications, but in what was potentially the gravest crisis since the Mutiny, a death-roll of 800 Indians in a population of 350 million as a result of police action was hardly very worrying, while only ten government servants had been killed.[9] Control was never lost; thanks to the war, the British forces available in India were much stronger than they had been in 1939, and even while fighting off the Japanese in Burma could deploy over

---

[9] See the table in J. M. Brown, *Modern India: The Origins of an Asian Democracy*, 2nd edn (Oxford, 1994), pp.322–3.

fifty battalions to suppress unrest. As one authority has put it, 'Quit India' was pathetically like a flotilla of rafts colliding with a battleship.[10]

Paradoxically, too, the German invasion of the Soviet Union had marginally improved the British position; it brought round the Indian communists to support the war and break with Gandhi's Freedom Movement. On their release from jail the communists' leaders were condemned by Indian patriots as the agents of British imperialism. In the following year the Raj faced another crisis, although one which, paradoxically, helped to quieten things on the political front; the occupation of Burma by the Japanese cut off Bengal's supply of rice and there followed a famine which cost 2 million lives. The army enforced rationing and organized food supplies in the big cities. Nonetheless, the sands were running out. Indian opinion was evolving even more rapidly as the war went on. The shock given to British prestige by defeat particularly sapped the foundations of British power in the sub-continent. Once it was clear, too, that the British, whatever the circumstances, were going to leave after the war, whether sooner or later (and for the Indian politicians the crucial moment seems to have come with the offer of dominion status by a British ministerial mission of 1942), new assessments of possibilities and dangers for individuals and groups began to be made. There were two dangerous aspects to this.

The more serious, ultimately, was the growth of conflict among those who would inherit – they hoped – imperial patronage and power. All of them sought to protect the interests of particular groups and communities. As more and more Indian politicians became confident that the British would have to quit India soon after the war was over, their own ranks became more divided; the division between Hindu and Moslem had grown wider and Moslem leaders spoke of a future separate Islamic state after independence – a 'Pakistan'. The second outcome of changed expectations was a subtle oozing of power away from the administrative armature of the Raj as its servants began to look to the future, uncertain about what the detail of their future might turn out to be. Whatever they might feel, industrialists, land-

[10] Ibid., p.321.

owners and members of the ICS who had looked to the Raj to provide the order in which they could prosper had to look to the rising star of Congress, to which, it became clearer than ever by 1945, the power of the British would in due course devolve.

American opinion was also counting for more in British policy. The involvement of the United States in other people's wars foreshadowed revolutionary change just as it had done in 1917. President Roosevelt had discussed confidentially with Stalin his hopes for Indian independence (as well as that of other parts of Asia, and the need for trusteeship for French Indo-China). Yet when in 1945 the Labour party came to power at Westminster it felt it had far more urgent issues to attend to than India, though the independence of the sub-continent and of Burma had long been part of its programme. Only realities forced its hand. On 14 March 1946, while India was torn with Hindu–Muslim rioting and its politicians were squabbling over the future, the Labour government offered India full independence. By this time, there was looming up the question whether the viceroy could retain control of the situation at all. The problem was not one of resistance to the British but of the violence increasingly evident between communities fearful about their future after the Raj had gone. In 1946 the governor of Bengal reported his view that his police had disintegrated into an unreliable rabble and that within twelve months he would have no province left to administer; only his British troops, he said, made it possible to avoid a complete collapse. In that year 40,000 Muslims, it was claimed, were killed in Bihar, and in August there were 4,000 dead in a week in what is remembered as the 'Great Calcutta killing' but which was only the worst of many inter-communal atrocities. 'Our time in India is limited and our power to control events almost gone,' wrote the viceroy in his journal.[11]

The viceroy had often asked an unresponsive government in London for a fixed date by which power should be transferred. In February 1947, the British government finally acted and put a pistol to the head of India's politicians by announcing that it would hand over power not later than June 1948. A new viceroy, Lord Mountbatten, was appointed to oversee the process. He was distrusted by Jinnah, the

[11] *Wavell: The Viceroy's Journal*, ed. P. Moon (London, 1973), p.368.

Muslim leader, and won the confidence of Nehru, the leader of Congress. The tangle of communal rivalries was then cut through by the partition of the sub-continent and the end of the only governmental unity it had ever enjoyed. At midnight on 15 August 1947 two new Dominions appeared, Pakistan and India. The first was Muslim and was itself divided into two slabs of land at opposite ends of northern India; the second was officially secular but was overwhelmingly Hindu in composition and inspiration and contained very large Muslim minorities. Mountbatten's achievement was the maintenance of as much administrative continuity as was possible in the circumstances.

A little before the actual declaration of Indian independence, British soldiers took down the Union flag that had flown ever since 1857 in the grounds of the residency at Lucknow, site of the most famous siege of the Mutiny. Empire was nearly over. Partition, in the event, actually came only just in time, for in the crucial border areas the security forces were by the summer of 1947 powerless and Indian army units were breaking up on communal lines. Nor were the nationalist politicians able to control the local forces released by fear and ambition. Even the British had never ruled all India directly, and Hindu and Muslim had been dividing since the Mutiny. Nevertheless, the cost of partition was enormous. The psychic wound to many nationalists was symbolized by Gandhi's murder by a Hindu fanatic, who killed him for his part in achieving a maimed independence he had in fact deplored. There were huge massacres in areas where there were significant communal minorities. Something like 2 million people fled to places where their co-religionists were in control. Almost the only clear political gain on the morrow of independence was that for the immediate future the communal problem had been solved, though bloodily and far (it was to appear) from finally. Apart from this, the assets of the new states were much goodwill (arising from very mixed motives) shown to them by great powers, the inheritance of a well-trained civil service already largely native-born before independence, and an important infrastructure of institutions and services. These inheritances were not, however, equally shared; India enjoyed more of them than Pakistan.

Nor could these advantages by themselves provide the means to deal with the grave problems of the sub-continent's economic and social backwardness. The worst was demographic. A steady rise in population had gone on under British rule, only occasionally and briefly mitigated (if that is a permissible word) by Malthusian disasters like the great influenza epidemic at the end of the First World War which struck down 5 million Indians, or by famines like that in Bengal during the Second World War. In 1951 there was once more famine in India, and in 1953 in Pakistan. The spectre of it lingered into the 1970s before it seemed at last to have been driven away. Industrialization, which had made important progress in the Second World War, hardly offset population pressure. It could not provide new jobs and earnings fast enough. The new India had most of what industry there was in the sub-continent, but her problems were grave. Outside the cities, most Indians lived as peasants in villages where, for all the egalitarian aspirations of some of the leaders of the new republic, inequality was as great as ever, and the great majority was landless. The landlords who provided the funds for the ruling Congress party and dominated its councils stood in the way of land reform. In many ways, the past lay more heavily than ever on a new state proclaiming the western ideals of democracy, nationalism, secularism and material progress, but now lacking an alien ruler to blame. History continued to encumber India's road to democracy.[12]

THE LAST THROES OF THE CHINESE REVOLUTION

China had for a long time been engaged in fighting off Japanese imperialism; western imperialism in that country, dwindling since 1918, effectively disappeared in the Second World War when signifi-

---

[12] As it did that of Burma. The country was proclaimed an independent republic in January 1948 but was already plunged into political violence. Ethnic conflict, civil war and rebellion continued until the imposition of military rule ten years later. There are grounds for believing that the troubles of the new state owe something to the destabilizing efforts of some Britons (though not of the British government) in Burmese politics. See Fergal Keane, 'Save us from our friends', in the *Guardian*, 19 July 1997.

cantly, the last vestiges of the 'unequal treaties' with Great Britain, France and the United States were swept away. Survival of Japanese aggression and completion of the Chinese revolution was made possible by that conflict too. In 1941, when the Sino-Japanese war merged in a world conflict, China's diplomatic position at once improved. She now had powerful allies and a new international standing. Symbolic and moral support was for some time as important as any military help the Allies could then give; they were too busy extricating themselves from the disasters of early 1942 to do much for China, though the Americans operated air force units from Chinese airfields against the Japanese. A Chinese army, too, came to help to defend northern India and the Burma Road from the Japanese. For the rest, still hemmed in as a government to the west of their country, the Chinese had for a long time to hold out as best they could, only just in touch with their allies by land and air. Nonetheless a decisive change was under way.

For all the continuing friction and sometimes open conflict between communists and nationalists, a measure of national unity and cooperation endured between KMT and CPC, broadly speaking, until 1941. Paradoxically, the appearance of a real prospect of victory then began to weaken their ties. The new fact that the United States was now Japan's major enemy, and was almost certain to defeat her in the long run, began subtly to transform the attitude of the Chungking government. It came to feel that as that outcome was assured, there was no point in using up men and resources in fighting the Japanese when they might be husbanded for the struggle against the communists after the peace. Some KMT supporters went further and were soon fighting the communists again.

The other, communist, China was nonetheless solidifying as the war went on. Chungking increasingly displayed the lethargy, self-seeking and corruption which had from the early 1930s tainted and divided the KMT because of the nature of the vested interests on which it drew for support. Though vigorous in the promotion of national feeling against the western powers, the regime was repressive and stifled criticism. It alienated the intellectuals. Its soldiers, often badly officered and undisciplined, terrorized the peasants as much as did the Japanese. Communist China was different. In the large areas the communists controlled (often behind the Japanese lines, but much of China had never been effectively occupied by the Japanese), there were often violent and brutal attacks on 'enemies of the people', though deliberate attempts were also made to retain the support of interests won over by moderate but unambiguous reform and disciplined behaviour. Peasant goodwill was culti- vated by enforcing lower rents and abolishing usury. Meanwhile, Mao set out the theoretical framework needed to prepare the new communist cadres for the task that lay ahead. When Japan collapsed in 1945 there were about a million Chinese communist soldiers. Their commanders responded quickly to the new opportunities that then appeared.

The suddenness of Japan's surrender was thus the second major factor shaping the last stage of the Chinese revolution. Huge areas of China had to be reoccupied and reincorporated in the Chinese state. Often this could not immediately or easily be done by the KMT government. Many areas under communist control could not be reached by nationalist forces before the communists dug themselves in there. The Americans sent their own soldiers to hold some of the ports until the nationalists could take them over, and flew nationalist units to other crucial spots. In some places the Japanese were told to hold on until the KMT government could re-establish its authority. But by the end of the year the communists held more territory than they had ever held before and held it in the main with the support of people who had found that communist rule was by no means as bad as they had heard. The KMT supported the landlords and oppressed the peasants in order to squeeze taxes out of them in the areas it controlled. But in 1937 it had still been able to draw heavily on patriotic goodwill; many Chinese then believed that it was the authentic carrier of the Chinese revolution. The war, though, destroyed the chance of exploiting this, if it were true. It made poss- ible the completion of the Chinese revolution the Japanese had long feared and which, in 1937, they declared it their intention to crush. Terrible though it had been for millions of Chinese, the war had also enabled China to resume by another route the long march back towards the world power from which she had been deflected first by Europeans and then by fellow-Asians. The frustration of Chinese nationalism was about to end, and the beneficiary would be the CCP.

The civil war went on for three years after the Japanese collapse. Though Japanese units usually sought to surrender to nationalist or American troops, the communists often acquired from them large new stocks of arms. Soviet forces, invading Manchuria in the last days before the Japanese surrender, handed over to their communist allies weapons taken from the Japanese there. Mao made deliberately moderate policy pronouncements and continued to push forward with land reform. His own sense of identification with the fate of China strengthened his leadership and broadened his appeal beyond the CCP. This conferred a further great advantage on the communists in the civil war; victory in that war was essentially a victory of the countryside over a city-based regime. There were some KMT successes but, in the end, division within the KMT and erosion of its support were the other decisive factors.

American officials became increasingly disillusioned by the all-too-apparent inadequacy and corruption of the KMT government presided over by Chiang-Kai-shek. In 1947 American forces were withdrawn from the country and the United States abandoned its efforts to mediate between the two Chinas. In the following year, with most of the north in communist hands, the Americans began to cut down the financial and military aid they were still giving to the KMT. From this time, the nationalist government ran militarily and politically into the sands; as this became obvious, more and more employees of government and local authorities sought to make terms with the communists while they might still do so. The conviction spread that a new era was dawning: the Mandate of Heaven was passing. By the beginning of December 1948, no important nationalist military force remained intact on the mainland and Chiang withdrew to Taiwan (formerly Formosa, and Japanese from 1895 until the end of the war). The Americans, increasingly fed up with their former allies, cut off their aid while this withdrawal was under way, denouncing the inadequacies of the nationalists and blaming them for the débâcle. Finally, on 1 October 1949, the People's Republic of China was officially inaugurated at Peking. The most populous communist state in the world had come into existence. Its government faced as its first task the actual establishment of its authority throughout the whole country – something no Chinese government had achieved for over 100 years.

IMPERIAL REALITIES IN 1945

Europeans did not get their empires back in 1945 in the form they had left them three or four years earlier. In the first place, they could not overcome the psychological impression produced by defeat. Though the British sent forces to Indonesia and Indo-China quickly in 1945 to take over from the Japanese and hold them until the Dutch and French could resume control, the returning colonial rulers often met with armed resistance from former subjects armed with weapons parachuted to them by the British and Americans so that they could harass the Japanese occupying forces during the war, or taken from the surrendering Japanese in the first moments of liberation in 1945. It is not surprising that there opened a new era of colonial rebellions. Unlike earlier movements they were because of the Cold War soon able to look for support from the outside by Soviet (and some Chinese communist) advice, arms and money. Every instance of colonial unrest provided an opportunity and a temptation for the promotion of superpower interests. Furthermore, the numbers of countries in the United Nations who were sympathetic to the movements of liberation steadily grew, as former colonies won independence. The United States always tended to be against restoring old colonial rulers; Americans had begun their own history with a colonial rebellion, they thought, and saw no reason to deny their own roots by sticking up for imperialism. Franklin Roosevelt had dreamed of returning Hong Kong to China at the peace. Besides, it suited American business to win friends in new nations, and American diplomacy not to have Asian nationalists depending only on communist support. The coming of Cold War was only the final addition to a rich stew. Altogether, it is hardly surprising that by 1960 the Asian colonial empires had all but disappeared.

In south-east Asia and Indonesia the Second World War had undermined colonial rule more decisively than anywhere else, and the pace of actual decolonization was faster and more violent in Dutch and

French colonies than in the British. The grant of representative institutions by the Dutch in Indonesia before 1939 had encouraged the
further growth of an existing nationalist party. A flourishing communist movement also existed by then. Some nationalist leaders, among
them one Achmed Sukarno, collaborated with the Japanese when they
occupied the islands in 1942. They were favourably placed to seize
power when the Japanese surrendered, and an independent Indonesian
republic was proclaimed before the Dutch could return; though British
troops were quickly sent to take control of the major centres, there
was a crucial interval in which the Japanese encouraged the Indonesian
nationalists and gave them arms. When the Dutch arrived, it was
already too late to remedy this, and fighting and negotiation followed
for nearly two years. The presence of large numbers of Dutch expatriates in the islands, some of them dangerously isolated, and the belief
of Dutch officials and politicians that Indonesia was of crucial importance to the post-war economic recovery of the Netherlands, meant
that there was to be no swift recognition that the days of empire were
over. At first, an agreement was reached for an Indonesian republic
still under the Dutch crown but this settlement did not work. Fighting
began again, the Dutch pressing forward vainly with 'police operations' in one of the first campaigns by a former colonial power to
attract the full blast of communist and anti-colonial stricture at the
United Nations. Both India and Australia (which had concluded that
she would be wise to conciliate the independent Indonesia that must
eventually emerge) took the matter to the Security Council. Finally
the Dutch gave in. Thus, a story launched by a handful of Amsterdam
merchants three and a half centuries earlier came to an end in 1949
with the creation of a new state, the United States of Indonesia. It
brought together more than 100 million people scattered over hundreds
of islands, and divided into scores of races and religions. A vague and
formal union with the Netherlands under the Dutch crown survived,
but was dissolved five years later.

INDO-CHINA

The French in Indo-China for a time seemed to hold on better than the Dutch. The wartime experience of that country – or, rather, group of countries – had been somewhat different from those of Malaysia and Indonesia. Although the Japanese exercised complete military control there from 1941 onwards, French sovereignty was not formally displaced until March 1945. The Japanese then set aside the French governor-general, and amalgamated Annam, Cochin China and Tongking in a new state of Vietnam under the emperor of Annam. Until that moment, the colonial government had never actually gone away, though much discredited locally by its seemingly supine acceptance of Japanese rule *de facto*. Conditions in Indo-China had deteriorated during the war. There had been famine in 1944. In that year, too, the Americans had begun to give material support to the guerrilla activities of the Viet Minh against the Japanese. When the Japanese surrendered, Ho Chi Minh was sure he had the sympathy of nationalist China (with whom British forces divided the country in the immediate aftermath of Japanese occupation) and probably believed he would also have the support of the United States in anticipating the return of French rule. He installed himself in the government palace at Hanoi, the emperor abdicated and the Vietnam republic was proclaimed. Within a few weeks, though, the British had gone and (Free) French authority had returned in the south. French soldiers promptly overturned the Viet Minh government.

It was soon evident, though, that it would not be easy for the French to re-establish themselves. It was not merely a matter of sniping at French soldiers and attacks on their convoys that went on through the winter of 1945. Increasing forces had to be sent to Indo-China, a costly burden for liberated France. Well into the spring of 1946, the position of the Viet Minh in Hanoi, in the north, too, was safeguarded by the protection of the Chinese occupying forces. This gave the Vietnamese nationalists (among whose leaders the communists were predominant) a solid base. In March the French appeared to come to terms; they recognized the existence of a 'Democratic Republic of Vietnam' as an autonomous state within the French 'Union' (a word that had replaced 'Empire' under de Gaulle). Yet the presence of a large expatriate population in Indo-China,[13] coupled with the work in Paris of well-organized colonial lobbies and the preoccupation of Gaullists with national prestige, much limited the freedom of action of any French government to make real concessions.

The formal compromise of the March agreement quickly broke down over, above all, the question of giving Cochin (that is, Southern Vietnam) special status. At the end of 1946, the French attempted a coup, proclaiming a special regime for Cochin China. A bombardment by them of the port of Hanoi, reputedly killing over 6,000 people, opened what was to be the longest and bloodiest of post-colonial wars. Attacks on French residents in Hanoi quickly followed. The capital was seized by French troops. Ho Chi Minh again fled abroad.

A major war had begun that was to go on for the better part of thirty years. It was essentially a nationalist, anti-colonial and peasant war, in which the nationalists, led by the Viet Minh and, increasingly, the communists, fought to achieve a united, independent country while at first the French struggled to retain a diminished Vietnam that, with the other Indo-Chinese states, would remain inside the French Union. But by 1949 outsiders were becoming interested. There had come to power the communist regime in China. The government of Ho Chi Minh was recognized in Moscow and Peking, that of the French-sponsored Annamese emperor by the British and Americans. The latter began to supply the French with material aid in the summer of 1950. The Cold War was well under way and it turned the French war of colonial restoration (or, the Vietnamese war of national independence) into a war against international communism.

Asia's decolonialization had thus quickly burst out of the simplicities of Roosevelt's vision. This was apparent, too, though in a lesser degree, as the British began to liquidate their own recovered empire. Burma and Ceylon (which was to become the first post-war self-governing Dominion within the Commonwealth) followed India into independence in 1947. In the following year, a communist-supported

[13] In 1942 there were over 5,000 French resident officials governing Indo-China; the Indian Civil Service at that moment had less than a tenth as many British in post to run a sub-continent.

guerrilla campaign began in Malaya, though it was to be unsuccessful. It did not impede steady progress towards eventual independence in 1957, but was one of the first of several post-colonial problems which were to complicate and torment American policy-makers who wished to appear as good anti-colonialists. Growing antagonism with the communist world soon muddied the clear waters of policy in Washington. It became clearer and clearer there that the collapse of empires might create conditions on the Asian mainland, Indonesia – and in the Philippines – which would require more active American involvement in the region, not less. The decolonization experience – to use a glib phrase – had turned out to be a much more diversified and locally varied matter than American policy anticipated, and its consequences followed suit.

THE RUNNING SORE OF THE OTTOMAN SUCCESSION

In 1922 the question of the Ottoman succession in the Middle East had been settled with regard to Turkey by the foundation of a new national state. The arrangements put together to deal with the former Arab lands of the Ottoman empire had far less solidity. The Arab states that emerged nonetheless survived the Second World War. In May 1948, though, the fragility of the pre-war settlement was once more revealed when another new national state, Israel, came into existence in Palestine. Its creation marked the end of nearly thirty years during which only France and Great Britain among the great powers had been much concerned with the Near and Middle East. They had not found agreement too difficult. In 1939 the French still held mandates in Syria and the Lebanon (their original mandate had been divided into two), and the British retained theirs in Palestine, but had renounced their protectorate of Egypt. Elsewhere in the Arabic-speaking lands they had unloaded their other responsibilities under the mandate system as soon as possible and exercised varying degrees of influence or power after negotiation with the new rulers of individual states. The most important were Iraq, where a small British garrison, mainly of air force units, was maintained, and Egypt, where a larger British land force still protected the Suez Canal. The latter had come to look even more important in the 1930s as Italy became increasingly hostile.[14]

The war of 1939 turned out in due course to have released change in the Middle East as elsewhere. After Italy's entry to the war, the vital importance of the Canal Zone in British strategy meant that Egypt suddenly found herself with a battlefront on her western border with Italian Cyrenaica. Egypt remained formally neutral almost to the end of the war, but was in effect a British base and little else, exercising little of the independence she had formally acquired in 1922. The war also led the British to armed intervention to assure the supply of oil from the Gulf in 1941 when Iraq threatened to move in a pro-German direction after another nationalist *coup*. A British and Free French invasion of Syria to keep it out of German hands led in 1941 to an independent Syria after the defeat of the Vichy forces, and soon afterwards the Lebanon followed suit. The French tried to re-establish their authority at the end of the war, but unsuccessfully, and during 1946 these two countries saw the last foreign garrisons leave. The French by then also faced difficulties in the Maghreb. Fighting had broken out in Algeria in 1945, though at that moment nationalists were asking only for autonomy in federation with France. The French made some concessions in 1947, but this was to be far from the end of the story.

Where British influence was paramount, anti-British sentiment was still a splendid rallying cry for dissidents. In both Egypt and Iraq there was much hostility to British occupation forces in the post-war years, even though the British announced in 1946 that they were prepared to withdraw altogether from Egypt. Negotiations for the basis of a new treaty which would ensure the safety of Suez broke down so badly, though, that Egypt referred the matter (unsuccessfully) to the United Nations. By this time the whole question of the future of the Near East had been transformed by the Zionist decision to establish a national state in Palestine, if need be, by force.

The Palestine question has been with us ever since, but the catalyst

[14] It is an interesting sidelight on this looming hostility that the BBC's first essay in broadcasting in a foreign language was to begin to transmit in Arabic in 1937. A. Briggs, *The BBC. The First Fifty Years* (Oxford, 1985), pp.141–3.

had come years before, with the Nazi revolution in Germany. At the time of the Balfour Declaration 600,000 Arabs lived in Palestine beside 85,000 Jews – a number already felt by Arabs to be threateningly large. In some years after this, though, Jewish emigration from the country actually exceeded immigration. The British went on hoping that the problem of reconciling the promise of a 'national home' for Jews with respect for 'the civil and religious rights of the existing non-Jewish communities in Palestine' (as the Balfour Declaration had put it) might be resolved. Hitler changed this. From the beginning of the Nazi persecution the numbers of those who wished to come to Palestine rose rapidly. So, in synchrony, did Palestinian Arab hostility to Jewish immigration. As the war of 1939 approached, a British army had been striving to contain a full-scale Arab rising. The Nazi extermination policies which began to unroll in the war years then made demographic and political nonsense of the British attempts to provide a balanced solution in Palestine. From 1945 onwards, the Holocaust hung over the Palestine question. Jewish history had been changed. A new diaspora was under way and Zionism's demand for a national home would not now be detached from its location in biblical Israel recast as a national state.

While the restriction of immigration was the side of British policy repugnant to the Zionists, the other side – the partitioning of Palestine between Jew and Arab – had been rejected by the Arabs when first proposed in the less tense circumstances of 1936. The issue was dramatized as soon as the war was over when a World Zionist Congress demanded that a million Jews should be admitted at once to Palestine. Other new factors now began to come into play. It did not help that the British had looked on benevolently in 1945 when an 'Arab League' of Egypt, Syria, Lebanon, Iraq, Saudi Arabia, the Yemen and Transjordan was formed; it was always a temptation of British diplomacy to believe that pan-Arabism might prove the way in which the Middle East could be persuaded to settle down, and that the coordination of the policies of Arab states would open the way to the solution of its problems. This will-o'-the-wisp hung about for some years. In fact, the Arab League was soon preoccupied with Palestine to the virtual exclusion of anything else.

The other new factor was the Cold War. In the immediate post-war era, Stalin seems to have stuck to the old communist view that Great Britain was the main imperialist prop of the international capitalist system and to have sponsored attacks on her position and influence accordingly. In the Middle East, of course, this also favoured more traditional Russian geo-political views, though the Soviet government in fact had shown little interest in the area between 1919 and 1939. With the war, pressure was brought to bear on Turkey at the Straits, and ostentatious Soviet support was given to Zionism, the most disruptive element in the situation. It did not need extraordinary political insight to recognize the implications of a resumption of Russian interference in the area of the Ottoman legacy. Yet as the Second World War came to an end American policy in the Middle East, too, was turning anti-British, or, rather, pro-Zionist. This could hardly have been avoided. Since the Roosevelt revolution in domestic politics, a Democratic president could hardly envisage an anti-Zionist position and mid-term congressional elections were held in 1946 in which Jewish votes might be important.

From 1945 the British faced both Jewish and Arab terrorism and guerrilla warfare in Palestine. Much beset, they sought only to disentangle themselves from the Holy Land. Unhappy Arab, Jewish and British policemen struggled to hold the ring there while the British government cast about for a way of bringing the mandate to an end that would be acceptable to both sides. American help was sought, but to no avail; Truman wanted a pro-Zionist outcome. In the end the British took the matter to the United Nations. It recommended partition, but this was still a non-starter for the Arabs. Fighting between the two communities grew fiercer and the British decided to withdraw without more ado. On the day that they did so, 14 May 1948, the state of Israel was proclaimed. A few minutes after the act of foundation, it was recognized by the United States. The USSR followed suit. They were to agree in little else in the Middle East for the next quarter-century.

Almost immediately, Egyptian armies invaded part of Palestine that the United Nations proposal had designated for Jews. Jordanian and Iraqi forces joined in, but limited their actions to the support of Palestinian Arabs in the territory it had been proposed to give them. But Israel fought off her enemies, and a truce, supervised by the United

Nations, followed (during which a Zionist terrorist murdered the United Nations mediator). In 1949 the Israeli government moved to Jerusalem, which became a Jewish capital city again for the first time since the days of imperial Rome. Half of the city was still occupied by Jordanian forces, but this was only one of many problems left to the future. With steady consolidation of the gains of the Mandate years, American and Russian diplomatic support and American private money, Jewish energy and initiative had successfully established a new national state where no basis for one had existed at the end of the Ottoman regime.

Yet the cost was to prove enormous. The disappointment and humiliation of the Arab states assured their continuing hostility to Israel and therefore opportunities (or dangers, according to your point of view) of great power intervention in the future. Moreover, the action of Zionist extremists and the far from conciliatory behaviour of Israeli forces in 1948–9 led to an exodus of Arab refugees. Soon there were 750,000 of them in camps in Egypt and Jordan, a social and economic problem, a burden on the world's conscience, and a military and diplomatic weapon for Arab nationalists who, while neglecting their material plight, exploited the propaganda opportunities they presented and encouraged the recruitment of guerrilla forces from among their young men. It would hardly be surprising were it true (as some believe) that the first president of Israel quickly began to encourage his country's scientists to work on a nuclear weapons programme.

Thus, many currents swirled together in confusion in an area that had often been a focus of world history. Victims for centuries, the Jews were in their turn now seen by Arabs as persecutors. The problems with which the peoples of the area had to grapple were poisoned by forces flowing from the dissolution of centuries of Ottoman power, from the rivalries of successor imperialisms, from the rise of two new world powers which dwarfed these in their turn, from the interplay of nineteenth-century European nationalism and ancient religion, from the ambitions of princes, and from the first effects of the new dependence of developed nations on oil. There are few moments in the twentieth century so sodden with history as the establishment of Israel.

COLD AND HOT WAR IN ASIA: KOREA

In 1945 liberation from the Japanese had left Korea divided along the 38th Parallel. The predominantly industrial north of that country was occupied by Soviet forces, the more agriculturally based south by the Americans. The problem of putting these pieces of an ancient polity together again was soon complicated by the polarization of interests within Korea as each occupying power patronized those it thought most promising. The issue was in due course referred to the United Nations. After abortive efforts to obtain elections for the whole country, and major American diplomatic efforts among its members, the UN recognized a government set up in the south as the only lawful government of the new Republic of Korea. By then, the northern zone also had a government claiming sovereignty over the whole country. As each regime represented deep-rooted historic factions in Korean politics there was plenty of dangerous local tinder in this situation.

Even while the Second World War was going on the US State Department had been uneasy about the possible consequences of a revival of the old Russian interest in Korea once that country was liberated from the Japanese. In the last weeks of fighting, President Truman considered the possibility that the USSR might be entirely excluded from Korea after the peace, but nothing was done beyond agreeing that the 38th Parallel should divide Soviet and American zones of occupation. The result was that Korea became the only country in the post-war world where the United States and the USSR faced one another directly and alone, without the presence of any other Allied power or, at first, of any internationally recognized Korean government to complicate matters. Soon, experience and, above all, the emergence of a communist China deepened American concern.

After Soviet and American forces had both withdrawn from the peninsula, North Korean forces invaded the south on 25 June 1950, with Stalin's fore-knowledge and approval, and with some material Soviet support. Possibly he hoped indirectly to further his aims elsewhere, whether in China, a possible rival for leadership of the communist world, or in Europe. However this may be, the attack was at once interpreted in Washington as a confirmation that the Soviet Union was ready to go beyond subversion of its non-communist neighbours and would mount overt attacks on them if not checked. It must therefore be accounted a decisive moment in the Cold War. Within two days, acting in the name of the United Nations, President Truman sent American forces to fight them. The Security Council voted to resist aggression and restore peace to the area, and as the Russians were at that moment boycotting it (as a protest, they said, over the failure to give Communist China a seat on the Council), they could not veto United Nations action.[15]

Given the Cold War setting, it was hardly surprising that, after South Koreans themselves, Americans always made up the bulk of the UN forces in Korea though sixteen other nations also in due course sent forces in support, the British as part of a Commonwealth division, with naval and air units. Within a few months the UN forces had advanced well north of the 38th Parallel and it looked as if the North Korean regime would be overthrown. The United States government sought to keep its military commanders on a close rein, and the USSR only allowed its pilots to operate in the extreme north and in the support of their nominal allies' ground forces. When the fighting approached the Yalu River (the border with Manchuria), though, Chinese communist forces intervened and drove back the UN army. China was the second largest communist state in the world, and North Korean units had taken part with the communists in her civil war. Behind her stood the USSR; a man could (in theory, at least) walk from Erfurt to Shanghai without once leaving communist territory. The confrontation of two worlds was palpable. As the United Nations fell back, the danger of a much bigger conflict seemed to arise, one fought, possibly with nuclear weapons, by the United States against China.

In the end, China committed several hundred thousand troops to Korea but Truman prudently insisted that the United States must not become involved in a greater war beyond the Yalu. It was made clear that American nuclear weapons would only be used if Moscow or

[15] The United States resolution on 27 June passed by the smallest possible majority on the Security Council, but won by 3 July approval by 41 of the 59 members of the UN. See the excellent study by W. Stueck, *The Korean War: an International History* (Princeton, 1995) p.12 – and as a whole.

Peking widened the war. That much established, further fighting
showed that although the Chinese might be able to keep the North
Koreans in the field, they could not overturn South Korea against
American wishes. The Americans might have to put up with the
Chinese drawing the line and even with a Soviet air force presence in
the North, but the war ended on American terms. A new American
administration which came into office at the beginning of 1953 was
Republican and fiercely anti-communist, and knew its predecessor
had sufficiently demonstrated the will and capacity of the United
States to uphold an independent South Korea. A psychological corner
had been turned: after 1950 there was never again any question of
American disarmament or of a slackening of efforts to build up Allied
strength in Europe (President Eisenhower's administration maintained
its predecessor's view that the real centre of the Cold War was still
to be found there rather than in Asia). A Korean armistice was signed
in July 1953. Subsequent efforts to turn this into a formal peace have
as yet failed; forty-five years later, political tension remained high
between the two Koreas. Yet, in the Far East as well as in Europe the
Americans had won the first battles of the Cold War. In Europe they
had not been real battles. Things were different in Korea; estimates
suggest the war cost that country over 3 million dead, wounded and
missing in all, civilians included, and there were 5 million homeless
refugees to be dealt with when it was over.

STALIN'S LEGACY

In March 1953, shortly before the Korean armistice, Stalin had died.
His former colleagues were terrified. They dared not announce the
news for some hours; it was indeed very difficult to guess what might
follow. In due course, there would seem to have been something of a
break in the continuity of Soviet policy, though not at once. Eisenhower
remained distrustful of Russian intentions and in the middle of the
1950s, the Cold War was as intense as ever. It was evident that Korea
had revealed a popular will in the United States to resist what it saw
as communist 'aggression' anywhere in the world. NATO forces were
rapidly increased. By 1953 its total military manpower was 7 million

and six NATO divisions in Germany (as against two in 1950) were American.[16] Yugoslavia was courted by diplomacy and aid (which may well have discouraged Soviet intentions to overthrow Tito) and defence treaties were made in the Far East and Pacific that eventually led to a South East Asia Treaty Organization (SEATO). It seems very probable that Stalin had been taken aback by the extent of American success in the Korean crisis and the subsequent rearmament of western Europe. Somewhat offsetting this, shortly after his death his successors revealed that they too had the improved nuclear weapon known as the hydrogen bomb. That was hardly an emollient element in the situation. It can stand, though, as Stalin's final memorial. It underwrote and guaranteed the USSR's status in the post-war world as one of two superpowers.

Stalin had carried forward logically and just as unscrupulously Lenin's repressive policies, though he was a much more creative figure than his predecessor. He had rebuilt most of the tsarist empire and had given the USSR the strength to survive (though only just, and only with the help of powerful allies) her gravest hour of trial. What is not clear is that this could only have been achieved at its heavy cost in human suffering, unless (as may well be thought) to have escaped the domination of a Nazi Germany was justification enough. The Soviet Union was a great power, but Russia was always likely to have become one again even without communism, and its peoples had been rewarded with precious little but survival. Domestic life after the war was as harsh as ever; consumption was for years still held down and both the propaganda to which Soviet citizens were subjected and the brutalities of the police system seemed, if anything, to have been intensified after some relaxation during the war.

A DIVIDED EUROPE IN A DIVIDING WORLD

The division of Europe was another of Stalin's memorials. Its western half was by 1953 substantially rebuilt. American economic support had been crucial; above all the Marshall Plan had made available the

---

[16] Stueck, p.349. NATO had fifteen formed divisions in all in that year.

dollars to assure enough liquidity to revive international trade. Positive efforts by western Europe's own governments and peoples had done the rest and the result was obvious in 1953. In that year they were carrying without difficulty a much heavier burden of armaments than five years earlier.[17] This had more than military importance. It was also a sign of Europeans' self-redefinition, a response to new challenges. Ideological and political facts had helped to promote mental change.

The two Germanys, in particular, had moved further and further apart, a process much advanced by a period of superfast economic growth in the western republic in the early 1950s. On two successive days in March 1954 the Soviet authorities announced that the German Democratic Republic (GDR) now possessed full sovereignty and the West German president signed a constitutional amendment permitting the rearmament of his country. The first chancellor of the Federal Republic, Konrad Adenauer, had by this time successfully built up a Christian Democrat domination of the parties of the Right in the federal parliament, and under its supervision the constitutional and economic development of the country seemed assured. Soon, the federal Constitutional Court authorized a ban on the communist party under an article of the constitutional Basic Law that said that parties rejecting 'a free democratic basic order' were unconstitutional.[18] Perhaps most important, under Adenauer's guidance, the country had successfully absorbed over 7 million German refugees from eastern Europe; many of them brought valuable energies and skills to the west, but it mattered just as much that he had adroitly drawn off the potential for a poisoning of German politics that they presented by absorbing them into his moderate right coalition.

In 1955 the Federal Republic entered NATO; the Soviet riposte was the Warsaw Pact, an alliance of its satellites. Berlin's future was still in doubt, but it was clear that the NATO powers would fight to resist changes in its status except by agreement. In the east, the GDR agreed to settle with old enemies: the line of the Oder-Neisse was to be its frontier with Poland. This was a final registration of the fact

---

[17] NATO included the USA and Canada, of course, but its defence expenditure went up during 1949–53 from 5.5 per cent to 12 per cent of total GNP of its members. Stueck, p.349.

[18] In 1956.

that Hitler's dream of realizing the greater Germany of the nineteenth-century nationalists had ended in destroying the Germany Bismarck had built. So the problem of containing the German power that had twice devastated Europe by war was settled for thirty-five years, and without a peace treaty.[19] Also in 1955 came the final definition of the line between the two European blocs, when Austria re-emerged as a fully independent state, the occupying Allied forces being withdrawn, as were American and British troops from Trieste after a settlement of the Italo-Yugoslav border dispute there.

Few European countries did not find themselves on one side or other of the Cold War alignment, but Yugoslavia managed to do so. In 1948, her Soviet advisers had been recalled when she was expelled from the Cominform, and her treaties with the USSR and other communist countries were denounced. There had opened five years of vitriolic Soviet attacks on 'Titoism'. There were hopes in 1952 that Tito might be got to join NATO. In 1953 he paid a state visit to London. Yugoslavia, though, survived without commitment to the West. She had frontiers with other communist countries but none with the Soviet Union. Albania was another odd man out. For a long time violently loyal to Moscow's leadership and a bitter opponent of Tito, who had taken the province of Kosovo back to Yugoslavia in the closing phase of the war, she was also a founder member of the Warsaw Pact. Nonetheless, Albania fell out with the USSR in 1961, while keeping up her old hostility to Yugoslavia.

We cannot, of course, attribute to Stalin or any one person another division which was already spread worldwide after the establishment of communism in China, that between what we may call capitalist and command (or would-be command) economies. Yet his policies helped to deepen it. Commercial relations between Soviet Russia and other countries had always been encumbered by politics from the October Revolution onwards. Trade had never flowed unconstrained between the USSR and world markets. After 1945, though, all earlier distinctions within the world economy were transcended; two methods of organizing the distribution of scarce resources increasingly divided

---

[19] Peace treaties had been signed between the victorious powers and Italy, Romania, Bulgaria, Hungary and Finland, in February 1947.

first the developed world and then some other areas, of which the most important was east Asia. The essential determinant of one system was the market – though a market very different from that envisaged by the old liberal Free Trade ideology and in many ways a very imperfect one, tolerating a substantial degree of intervention through international agencies and agreement; in the communist-controlled group of nations (and some others) political authority was intended to be the decisive economic factor. Trade between these two systems went on, but on a closely policed basis.

Neither system remained unchanged and intercourse between them did not cease as the years passed. Neither was monolithic or watertight. Nonetheless, they long offered antithetical and alternative models for economic growth. Their competition was inflamed by the political struggles of the Cold War and actually helped to spread its antagonisms. This could not be a static situation. Before long one system was much less completely dominated by the United States and the other somewhat less completely dominated by the Soviet Union than was still the case in the 1950s. Both experienced (though in far different degree) a continuing economic growth, but continued to diverge, the market economies moving ahead much more rapidly. The existence of two rival economic systems remained a fundamental of world economic history from 1945 to the 1980s, shutting off some possibilities even while suggesting others which were new.

16

East Asia Reshaped

AFTER EMPIRE

Neither the shapes nor the identities of many former colonial territories in Asia long survived imperial rule. At the very birth of independence, the sub-continent of India lost the brief political unity that had held it together for ninety years and split into two republics. When the French gave up Indo-China, that country disunited again into its former Cambodia and Laos, and then two Vietnams. Nor was this to be the end of the story. The formerly British federated Malay states were even by 1950 beginning to show signs of dislocation. Several of the new nations were left with enduring internal tensions, too. India had her large Muslim and Sikh communities, while the Chinese in Indonesia conspicuously exercised disproportionate economic power and weight; anything that happened in the new China was likely to affect them. Whatever their political circumstances, moreover, all Asian countries had fast-growing populations, and at independence most of them were poor. In the history of many of them, therefore, the end of European domination now seems more of a punctuation mark and less of a turning-point than once thought. As was once said of 1789 in France, decolonization was a high jump rather than a long jump, for Europe's control of Asian destinies had been brief and fitful. Europeans had for centuries increasingly shaped the lives and settled the fate of millions of Asians but their civilization had touched the hearts and minds of comparatively few of them; even if those few were important, moreover, they were to be found almost solely within ruling élites or new élites they helped to create.

In Asia, European culture had confronted deeper-rooted and more powerful traditions than anywhere else in the world. Asian civilization had not been swept aside like that of pre-Colombian America; it could not be. As in the Arab lands of the Islamic world, both the direct efforts of Europeans and the indirect diffusion of European culture through self-imposed modernization came up against formidable obstacles. The deepest layers of thought and behaviour often remained undisturbed even in those most emancipated from their past; Nehru, old Harrovian socialist and first prime minister of independent India, once remarked of himself, 'I have become a queer mixture of the East and West, out of place everywhere, at home nowhere.'[1] In India, nativities continued to be cast by astrologers in educated Hindu families when marriages were contracted and children born. China's rulers still draw on an unassailable sense of moral superiority evidently grounded less in dialectical materialism than in age-old Chinese attitudes to the non-Chinese world.

One consequence of this is the need to remember the importance to recent world history of the fact that two culturally distinctive zones of east Asian civilization remain distinct and significant, even if no longer quite so sharply contrasted as in the past. There is a western zone bounded by the mountain ranges of northern India, the Burmese and Siamese highlands and the huge archipelago of which Indonesia is the major component; its centre is the Indian Ocean. In its history the major cultural influences have been three: Hindu civilization spreading from India to the south-east, Islam, originally spread eastward across the seas in the ships of Arab traders, and the European impact, felt for a long time only through commercial and religious enterprise, and then for a much shorter era through political domination. To the east lies a second zone where China was for centuries the most important single cultural force. In large measure this was a function of the simple geographical fact of that country's huge mass, but the numbers and sometimes, the migration of her people, and, more indirectly and variably, China's early cultural prestige and influence in the east Asian periphery – above all, in Japan, Korea and Indo-China – all form part of the explanation. As for direct European political

[1] Jawaharlal Nehru, *An Autobiography*, abridged edn (Delhi, 1991), p.248. He went on to say: 'India clings to me . . . behind me lie, somewhere in the subconscious, racial memories of a hundred . . . generations of Brahmans.'

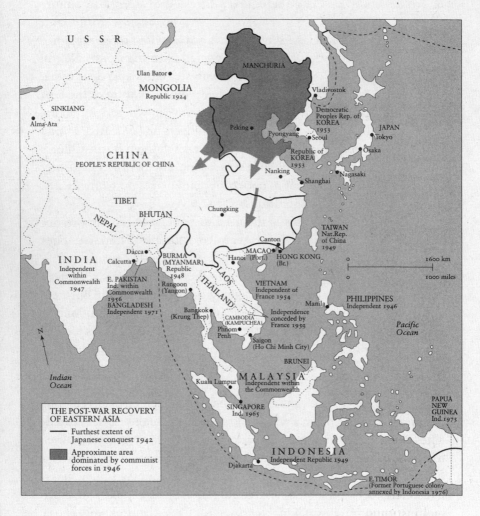

Ulan Bator •

MONGOLIA
Republic 1924

MANCHURIA

Vladivostok •

SINKIANG

Alma-Ata •

Peking •

Democratic
Peoples Rep. of
KOREA
1953
Pyongyang •
Seoul •

JAPAN

Tokyo •

Osaka •

CHINA
PEOPLE'S REPUBLIC OF CHINA

Republic of
KOREA
1953

Nanking •

Nagasaki •

Shanghai •

TIBET

Chungking •

BHUTAN

NEPAL

TAIWAN
Nat.Rep.
of China
1949

Canton •

Dacca •

MACAO •

Hanoi (Port.) •

HONG KONG
(Br.)

INDIA
Independent
within
Commonwealth
1947

Calcutta •

BURMA
(MYANMAR)
Republic
1948

LAOS

1600 km

1000 miles

E. PAKISTAN
Ind. within
Commonwealth
1956
BANGLADESH
Independent 1971

Rangoon
(Yangon) •

THAILAND

VIETNAM
Independent of
France 1954

PHILIPPINES
Independent 1946

Bangkok
(Krung Thep) •

CAMBODIA
(KAMPUCHEA)

Independence
conceded by
France 1955

Manila •

Pacific
Ocean

Phnom
Penh •

Saigon
(Ho Chi Minh City) •

N

BRUNEI

Indian
Ocean

Kuala Lumpur •

MALAYSIA
Independent within
the Commonwealth

PAPUA
NEW
GUINEA
Ind. 1975

THE POST-WAR RECOVERY
OF EASTERN ASIA

SINGAPORE
Ind. 1965

Furthest extent of
Japanese conquest 1942

Approximate area
dominated by communist
forces in 1946

INDONESIA
Independent Republic 1949

Djakarta •

E. TIMOR
(Former Portuguese colony
annexed by Indonesia 1976)

The Post-war Recovery of Eastern Asia

domination or even interference, it had never matched in this zone that in the Indian Ocean sphere, either in its extent or its duration.

THE INDIAN SUB-CONTINENT

It was too easy to lose sight of such important differences, as of much else imposed by history, in the troubled years after 1945. In both zones there were countries which for some time appeared to follow the same road: angry rejection of the West expressed in western language and appealing to world opinion on long-familiar lines with arguments based on western values of self-determination, freedom and the Rights of Man. In India's case there was also an urgent attention to the task of nation-building. Within a few years of the achievement of independence the republic absorbed the princely states which had survived the Raj and the sub-continent's remaining French and Portuguese enclaves in the name of a truculent nationalism which owed little to Indian native tradition and much to the assessment by Congress of its electoral interests.[2] Soon, the Indian security forces were energetically suppressing any danger of separatism or regional autonomy. Perhaps this should not have been surprising. Indian independence was, on the Indian side, the work of a western-educated élite which had adopted the idea of nationalism – like those of equality and liberty – from its European masters, even if at first only seeking equality and partnership with the Raj itself. A more popular, communal style of nationalism, at its extreme sometimes identified as fascist, would take decades to emerge. Any threat to the position of the educated Indian élites could easily and sincerely be interpreted as a threat to an Indian nationhood that had in fact still to be created.

This was all the more true because the rulers of independent India had inherited, to a degree soon to be forgotten, many of the aspirations and institutions, and perhaps a few of the delusions, of the British Raj. Ministerial structures, constitutional conventions, division of powers between central and provincial authorities, the apparatus of

[2] The French enclaves passed to India by agreement in 1954. Goa fell to Indian invasion in 1961, Nehru reassuring his countrymen that the non-violent Gandhi would have approved this use of force.

public order and security were all taken over, stamped with republican insignia, and then operated much as before 1947. The dominant and explicit ideology of government was a moderate and bureaucratic socialism in the current British fashion; it was not far removed in spirit from the public-works-and-enlightened-despotism-by-delegation mode of the Raj in its last decades. The Indian republic had also inherited many of the shortcomings of the Raj. Modernization in the British era had been largely confined to the administration, the higher education system, communications and hydraulic engineering, and the consequences that had flowed from the security of peace. The fiscal system of the Raj had been overwhelmingly dependent on land taxes. The realities which faced India's new rulers included a deep conservative reluctance among local notables who controlled votes to change a system of taxation whose weight mainly fell on the tenant farmer, to remove or even question privilege (except in the case of the former independent princes), or to touch traditional social practice. Yet awesome problems faced India – population growth, economic backwardness, poverty (the average annual per capita income of Indians in 1950 was $55 at current values), illiteracy, social, tribal, religious division, and (not least) great expectations of what independence ought to bring. It was clear to outsiders and many Indians that major change was needed to confront the dynamics these imposed, but it rarely figured in the politicians' electoral programmes and campaigns.

The acquisition in 1950 of a new constitution (over 200 of its clauses were taken straight out of the Government of India Act of 1935) did nothing to change facts of life, some of which would not begin to exercise their full weight until a couple of decades had gone by. Much of rural India's life still went on much as it had done even in the pre-British past when undisturbed by war, natural disaster, and the banditry of exploiting rulers. This continued to mean gross poverty for many. In 1960, over a third of India's rural poor were living on less than a dollar a week (and, at the same time, half the urban population earned less than was required to obtain what the World Health Organization deemed the minimum daily calorie intake required for health). Economic progress, though achieved, was always in danger of being swallowed by population growth. Scores of languages, many religions, and many cultures divided the Indian peoples. In the circumstances it is hardly surprising that the rulers of India should have incorporated in the constitution provisions for emergency powers as drastic as any ever enjoyed by a British viceroy, providing as they did for preventive detention, the suspension of state government and the submission of states to Delhi's control under what was called 'President's Rule'.

Uneasiness and awareness of the internal difficulties of a 'new nation' made things worse, too, when India quarrelled with her neighbour, Pakistan. This happened almost at once over Kashmir, where in 1947 a Hindu prince ruled some 4 million inhabitants, three-quarters of whom were Muslim.[3] Fighting began there in October 1947 when the maharajah decided to join India. The last British viceroy had by this time become the first governor-general of the new Indian dominion; there is evidence suggesting that he personally assisted in the organization of landings by Indian troop-carrying aircraft in Kashmir during the crisis that followed. The Muslim Kashmiris tried to bring about union with Pakistan, whose forces invaded the province; the maharajah asked for Indian help and Indian forces occupied eastern Kashmir and his capital. To complicate things further, the Muslims were themselves divided. After India refused to hold the plebiscite recommended by the United Nations Security Council, two-thirds of Kashmir remained *de facto* in her hands. So was opened a running sore in Indo-Pakistan relations. Fighting stopped in 1949, only to break out again in 1964–6 and 1969–70. The issue had by then been further complicated by demarcation disputes involving China and quarrels over the use of the Indus waters. In 1971 there was more fighting between the two republics when East Pakistan, a Muslim, Bengali-speaking region, broke away from Pakistan to form a new state, Bangladesh, under Indian patronage (thus showing that confessional unity was not in itself enough to bind together a viable nation). It soon faced economic problems even greater than those of India or Pakistan. By that time, though, it was clear that India regarded Kashmir as an issue that potentially called in question both the unity

[3] The 1941 census suggested 77 per cent were Muslim, 20 per cent Hindu, 2 per cent Sikhs, Buddhists and others.

of the republic, and the viability of its claim to manage its communal differences in a democratic and peaceful manner.

In these troubled passages, India's leaders showed great ambitions (at times seeming to extend so far as a wish to reunite the sub-continent) and often a blatant disregard of the interests of minority peoples (such as the Nagas). The irritation aroused by their acts and gestures was intensified in western capitals by the continuation of the Cold War. Nehru had quickly insisted that India would not take sides in it, and then, almost as quickly, showed signs of doing so. In the 1950s, this meant that India had warmer relations with the USSR and communist China than with the United States; indeed, Nehru appeared to relish opportunities of criticizing American action, which helped to convince some of his admirers of India's credentials as a progressive, peaceful, 'non-aligned' democracy. It came as all the greater a shock, therefore, to them and to the Indian public to learn in 1959 that Nehru's government had been quarrelling with the Chinese about the northern borders for the previous three years without saying so. By the end of 1962, large-scale fighting was going on there. Nehru took the improbable step of asking the Americans for military aid and, even more improbably, he received it at the same time as he also took help (in the form of aeroplane engines) from the Soviet Union.

Logically, the young Pakistan had not courted the same friends as India. She was in 1947 much weaker than her neighbour, with only a tiny trained civil service (Hindus had always joined the old Indian Civil Service in much larger numbers than Muslims). She was also divided geographically east and west from the outset, and almost at once had lost her ablest leader, Jinnah. Even under the Raj, Muslim leaders had (perhaps realistically) shown less confidence in democratic forms than Congress; since then, Pakistan has often been ruled by authoritarian soldiers whose announced aims have been military parity with India, economic development, including land reform, and the safeguarding of an Islamic society. This was for a long time not a grave cause of concern to the outside world; whereas India's friends in the West were sometimes disappointed by India's policies after independence, and deplored signs of illiberalism and infringements of democracy, somehow less had been expected of Pakistan. It had from the outset distanced her from India that she was formally Muslim while her neighbour was constitutionally secular and non-confessional (India's seemingly 'western' flavour at the highest level of government seemed for a long time not hard to reconcile with her predominantly Hindu and syncretic cultural tradition). Meanwhile, Pakistan tended towards increasing Islamic regulation of its domestic affairs.

THE 'THIRD WORLD'

A new association of professedly neutralist or 'non-aligned' nations emerged following a meeting in April 1955 of representatives of twenty-nine African and Asian states at Bandung in Indonesia. Most of them came from lands which had been part of the colonial empires; of the others represented, China was the most important. From Europe, Yugoslavia was soon to join them. The Bandung nations saw themselves as poor and needy, were more suspicious of the United States than of the USSR, and were more attracted to China than to either. They came to be called the 'Third World' nations.[4] The implication was that such nations were disregarded by the great powers, and excluded from the economic privileges of the developed countries. Plausible though this might sound, the expression 'Third World' actually masked important differences both between the members of that group and in their individual relations with the developed world, and the coherence of the Third World politics was not to prove very enduring. More people were to be killed in wars and civil wars within that world than in conflicts external to it in the decades after Bandung. But there were to be future gatherings of Third World countries which continued to harp on their 'non-alignment' in the Cold War.[5]

Immediately, Bandung obliged the great powers to recognize that the weak had power if they could mobilize it and they increasingly showed they could; the State Department and Soviet foreign ministry both bore this in mind as they looked for allies in the Cold War. By

[4] A term coined by a French journalist, and a conscious echo of the term 'Third Estate', the legally unprivileged mass of Frenchmen who provided much of the revolutionary dynamic of 1789.
[5] Meetings were held in Belgrade (1961), Cairo (1964), Lusaka (1970) and Algiers (1973).

1960 there were already clear signs that Russian and Chinese interests might diverge, though each was seeking the leadership of the under-developed and uncommitted. At first this had emerged obliquely, in the disguise of differing attitudes towards Tito, long in disgrace in Soviet eyes. It was in the end to be a worldwide contest. One early outcome was the paradox (in spite of her treaty with the United States) that Pakistan drew politically and diplomatically closer to China as time passed and the USSR closer to India. When the United States declined to supply arms during her 1965 war with India, Pakistan asked for Chinese help. She got less than she hoped, but this was early evidence of a new fluidity that began to emerge in international affairs in the 1960s. No more than the USSR or China could the United States ignore it. Indeed, the Cold War was slowly producing an ironical change in the Americans' role in Asia. From being the patrons of the anti-colonialism which had done so much to dismantle their allies' empires they began in some areas almost to look like their successors, though in the Chinese rather than in the Indian Ocean sphere, where long and unrewarded American efforts were made to placate a waspish and ungrateful India (before 1960 she had received more economic aid from the United States than any other country).

INDONESIA

Another example of the new difficulties facing great powers was provided by Indonesia. Its vast sprawl encompassed many peoples, often with widely diverging interests. The departure of the Dutch released communal tensions from the discipline an alien ruler had imposed just as the usual post-colonial problems – over-population, poverty, inflation – began to be felt. Buddhist and Hindu phases of Indonesian history had left little trace except in a small Buddhist minority and Hindu Bali, but, at least formally, Indonesia has the largest Muslim population under one government in the world. More than four-fifths of the Indonesian population is reckoned now to be Muslim, although traditional animism perhaps matters as much as Islam in determining their behaviour. Indonesia also had a much smaller, but long and well-entrenched Chinese community. In the colonial period it had enjoyed a preponderant share of wealth and administrative jobs and, although its economic position had been weakened by the 'Ethical Policy', it was still very visible and powerful in 1945. True, its distinctiveness was to be diluted somewhat as an increasing number of new Chinese immigrants arrived from Malaysia, where they had been established for many years. These new arrivals brought with them modernizing ideas and practices which divided the Chinese community, already under pressure from the forces of modernization.

By the mid-1950s the central government of the new republic was increasingly resented: by 1957 it had already faced armed rebellion in Sumatra and unrest elsewhere. The time-honoured device of distracting opposition with xenophobic nationalism (directed, for want of a better target, against a continuing Dutch presence in west New Guinea) did not work any more; popular support for Sukarno was not rebuilt. His government had already moved away from the liberal forms adopted at the birth of the new state and he leant more and more on Soviet support. In 1960 parliament was dismissed, and in 1963 Sukarno assumed the presidency for life. Yet the United States, fearing he might turn to China for help, long stood by him. To the irritation of the Dutch this enabled him to swallow up (with the connivance of Washington and the formal mediation of the United Nations) a would-be independent state in West New Guinea. Sukarno then turned on the new federation of Malaysia, put together in 1957 from fragments of British empire in south-east Asia. With help from their former colonial ruler, Malaysians fended off Indonesian attacks on Borneo, Sarawak and the Malaysian mainland. Although still enjoying American patronage (at one moment, President Kennedy's brother appeared in London to support his cause), this setback seems to have been the turning-point for Sukarno. American support for him had reflected the belief that strong, prosperous national states were the best bulwarks against communism. The history of Far Eastern Asia in the last forty years can indeed be read so as to support that view, but there was always difficulty in its practical application in policy, for it drifted easily into the support of cronyism, corruption and authoritarianism. In Surkarno's case, it also meant, as in Indo-China, reinforcing failure.

Exactly what happened is still obscure, but when food shortages and inflation went out of control, a coup was attempted and failed behind which, said the leaders of the army, were the communists. It is at least possible that Indonesia was intended by Mao to play a major part in the export of revolution; the Indonesian communist party which Sukarno had tried to balance against other politicians was at one time alleged to be the third largest in the world. Whether or not a communist takeover was intended, though, the economic crisis was exploited by those who feared one. The popular and traditional Indonesian shadow theatres had been for months seasoning the old Hindu epics which were their staple material with plentiful political allusions and overtones of coming change. When the storm broke, in 1965, the army stood back ostentatiously while popular massacre removed the communists to whom Sukarno might have turned. Estimates of the number killed vary between a quarter and a half a million. Sukarno himself was duly set aside the following year. A solidly anti-communist regime then took power which broke off diplomatic relations with China (they were not to be renewed until 1990). Some of the losers of 1965 are still in jail.

THE NEW CHINA

The appearance of communist China on the international stage was at first seen in western countries not in anti-colonialist but almost entirely in Cold War terms, as perhaps a sign that Smuts's prophecy was now being realized.[6] Yet though the first demonstration by conflict that the centre of gravity might again be on the move had come in Korea, a former Chinese dependency, war in that country was seen above all in the context of a worldwide ideological struggle. The Korean war, though, had important local effects in Asian countries' perceptions of their own interests. By 1960, the dominant strategic fact everywhere east of Singapore was the re-creation of Chinese state power. South Korea and Japan had successfully resisted communism not least because of the leverage the fear of China gave them with the

[6] See page 209.

Americans and they also showed after the war an ability to buttress their independence and not to succumb to direct Chinese manipulation. It is difficult not to link this, ironically, to the deep, many-faceted conservatism of societies which had for centuries drawn on Chinese example. This has often expressed itself in a discipline, capacity for constructive social effort, disregard for the individual, respect for authority and hierarchy, and (sometimes) self-awareness as members of civilizations proudly distinct from the West. Some in the West were sometimes tempted to sum up such characteristics as a body of 'Asian values' to be admired and probably impossible to emulate. Certainly east Asians, as their modernization gathered pace, seemed to draw on something much deeper than even the example of the Chinese Revolution.

We may nevertheless begin with that revolution's final victory in October 1949. Peking was once again the capital of China. Some thought this showed that China's leaders were more aware of pressure from her land frontiers in the north than of the threats from the sea that had faced her under the old empire. However this may be, the Soviet Union was the first state to recognize the new China, closely followed by India, Burma and the United Kingdom. The old Russian threat seemed in abeyance, formally discountenanced as traditional ambitions were by Soviet official policy, and, no doubt, because of Stalin's preoccupations elsewhere. Given Cold War preoccupations and the circumstances of the nationalist collapse, the Chinese People's Republic, as it was termed, actually faced at that moment no political or military threat from the outside at all. Any taste of western nations for fresh predation in the Far East had long since vanished; the Second World War had shattered any possible basis for it; the nationalists, cooped up in Taiwan, could be disregarded for the moment, though irremovable at least for the time being. When a major external threat actually appeared, as the United Nations forces approached the Yalu River frontier of Manchuria in 1950, the Chinese reaction was strong and immediate. But the main preoccupation of China's new rulers as they took up their task had to be the country's internal state. It was relatively easy, and popular, to launch a process of squeezing western-owned businesses which virtually eliminated them in the next few years, and to harass western missionaries. Real problems were more intimidating. Poverty was universal. Disease and malnutrition were widespread. Material and physical construction and reconstruction were overdue, population pressure on land was as serious as ever, and the moral and ideological void presented by the collapse of the *ancien régime* over the preceeding century waited to be filled.

The ascendancy of Mao, the victorious leader in the civil war, within the CCP and government makes it hardly surprising that the peasants were the starting-point. Since the 1920s land reform (usually meaning the expropriation of landlords) had been carried out largely by the peasants themselves in areas the communists dominated. Now China's farms were collectivized in a way that apparently gave control of the new units to their inhabitants, but actually placed them under the control of the party. There was, nonetheless, a real overthrow of local village élites, an operation often violent and brutal. Landlords and moneylenders must have made up a large number of the 800,000 Chinese later acknowledged by Mao to have been 'liquidated' in the first five years of the People's Republic. Meanwhile industrialization was also pressed forward, with Soviet help, the only external source from which China could draw. The model chosen was the Soviet one; a Five-Year Plan was soon announced and launched in 1953. This opened a brief period during which Stalinist ideas were dominant in China; it was soon announced that the Plan had been a remarkable success. Unfortunately, after the beneficial release of energy that marked the early 1950s, rural China was subjected in 1955 to a further upheaval as an emphasis was once more laid on rural development rather than heavy industry. Hundreds of millions of country-dwellers were reorganized into 'communes' which swallowed up private property; agriculture was collectivized, new goals for production were set centrally and new methods were imposed. Some of them did positive damage (campaigns for the extermination of birds which fed on crops, for example, released population explosions of insect predators which the birds had kept in check), while others merely concealed inefficiency. The cadres which ran the communes became more and more concerned with window-dressing to show that targets had been achieved than with production. The output of food fell catastrophically. When, in 1958, yet another surge of endeavour, the 'Great Leap Forward', was proclaimed and an intensification of pressure on the communes followed, matters worsened again. Within the CPC, a hunt for 'Right opportunist' scapegoats began.

By 1960, large areas of China were undergoing famine or near-famine conditions. The facts were suppressed; many even of the ruling clique appear to have remained ignorant of them. Some later estimates say that as many as 40 million Chinese may have died in a few years, though Mao stubbornly refused to acknowledge the failure of the Great Leap Forward, a policy with which he was closely and personally identified. In 1961, senior officials began, nonetheless, to gather irrefutable evidence of what had occurred. A hidden power struggle began within the party and government, and Mao's standing suffered. His rivals slowly put back the economy on the road to modernization without letting the true facts emerge.

CHINA'S RE-EMERGENCE AS A WORLD POWER

By the 1960s, though, whatever the difficulties still hampering her government at home, China had already fundamentally changed the balance and nature of international affairs. She was once again, after a century and a half, a world power, and very evidently so in Asia where the weight of the past was clear in her behaviour. Though China came to patronize revolution all over the world, her main concern remained the Far East and, in particular, her relations with former tributary countries. In Korea, Russian and Chinese policy had soon diverged. After the Korean war the Chinese had begun to supply arms to the communist guerrilla forces in Indo-China for what was by then less a struggle against colonialism than about what should follow it – a Vietnamese civil war, in fact. This now turned into an ideological war by proxy. In 1953 the French had given up both Cambodia and Laos but were still fighting to defend an unreliable puppet regime in Vietnam. They were, though, discredited in the eyes of the Vietnamese and no longer solidly sustained by opinion in France. In 1954 they lost at Dien Bien Phu a battle decisive both for their prestige and for the French electorate's will to fight. The preservation of a French ascendancy in the Red River delta was now impossible. A conference at Geneva (attended by representatives of

China, which thus formally re-entered the international diplomatic arena) agreed to partition Vietnam between a seemingly democratic government in South Vietnam and the communists who had come to dominate the North, pending elections which might reunite the country. The elections never took place. Instead, there soon opened in Indo-China what was to become the fiercest phase since 1945 of the Asian Hundred Years War against the West begun in the Opium Wars of the nineteenth century.

On one side fought a mixture of Indo-Chinese communists, patriots and reformers supported by China and the USSR, though they were rivals for influence in Indo-China rather than allies. The western contenders were no longer the old colonial powers; the French had gone home and the British had problems enough elsewhere. Anti-colonialism, Cold War preoccupations, poor intelligence, and the belief that they should support indigenous governments led the Americans to back the South Vietnamese, as they had already backed South Koreans and Filipinos. Unfortunately, Indo-China had its own complex politics. Neither in Laos nor South Vietnam, nor, in the end, in Cambodia, did there emerge regimes of unquestioned legitimacy in the eyes of those they ruled. American patronage merely identified existing ruling cliques with the western enemy so disliked in East Asia. American support also removed any incentive to carry out reforms which would have united people behind these regimes, above all in Vietnam, where *de facto* partition produced neither good nor stable government in the south.

While Buddhists and Roman Catholics quarrelled bitterly and the peasants were more and more alienated from the regime by the failure of land reform and the disciplines imposed by the southern Vietnamese government in its attempt to master a guerrilla campaign, an apparently corrupt ruling class seemed irremovable. This benefited the communists. They sought reunification on their own terms and maintained from northern Vietnam support for the communist underground movement in the south, the Vietcong. By 1960 the Vietcong had won control of much of the South. Against this background the American president, John Kennedy, took a momentous decision in 1962 to send American 'advisers' to help the South Vietnam government put its military house in order.

It was inevitable that this should have been seen in Washington as a step in the necessary struggle to contain the communist threat in Asia. But Chinese support for North Vietnam was a more complex matter than a logical move in the Cold War. True, China's motives and, indeed, her independence of action had been blurred from the outset of the People's Republic by the superficial unity of the communist bloc (stridently promoted by Soviet propaganda) and her continued exclusion from the United Nations at the insistence of the United States. A Sino-Soviet treaty in 1950 (when Stalin acknowledged past mistakes in interpreting China's internal struggle) had simply been taken – especially in the United States – to be evidence that China was entering the Cold War as a solid member of a communist alliance. Korea confirmed that notion. Certainly, the new China was Marxist, talked revolution and anti-colonialism, and had to make choices in a context restrained by the parameters of the Cold War. Yet in a longer perspective more traditional concerns now seem discernible in Chinese policy even at an early date. Above all, it quickly began to seek to re-establish Chinese power within the regions that it had tended to dominate in imperial times. Socialist internationalism was not to find much support from communist China except when it helped to advance Chinese interests. It might therefore be argued that the establishment and growing strength of the new China had more serious implications for the USSR than for the Americans. From being one pole of a bipolarized system, the USSR now became the corner of a triangle. She lost, too, her implicit pre-eminence as the sole country to which revolutionary movements in other countries could look for help and guidance.

This, though, was not all. There was a lot of history which contained the potential for friction between China and the Soviet Union. In the long perspective of China's rejection of western domination, historic Russia had been the first and most predatory of all those who preyed upon the Middle Kingdom. A new awareness of other old dangers also appeared. The security of Manchuria might by itself have been enough to explain Chinese military intervention in Korea, but the peninsula was the old object of dispute between imperial China and Japan. A Chinese invasion of Tibet in 1950 was a conscious return to an area which had for centuries been under Chinese suzerainty, and which should in Chinese eyes, be recovered. And from the start the noisiest and most vociferous demand made for regaining control of the Chinese periphery was for the eviction of the KMT government from Taiwan. Only briefly restored in 1945 to Chinese control (it had been in Japanese hands for fifty years), the island assumed such symbolic importance to the United States government that the president announced that not merely the island itself and its KMT regime but the smaller islands near the Chinese coast which were thought essential to its defence would be given American protection. About this issue and against a psychological background provided by a sense of inexplicable rebuff from a China long patronized by American philanthropy and missionary effort, the interest of Americans in Chinese affairs tended to crystallize for over a decade. So obsessively did it do so, that the KMT tail seemed at times to be wagging the American dog. Conversely, during the 1950s, both India and the USSR supported Beijing over Taiwan, insisting that the matter was one of Chinese internal affairs; it cost them nothing to do so, of course.

It was against this background that it was revealed in the next decade to almost universal astonishment that Chinese forces were actually engaged in fighting both Indian troops and Soviet forces. One quarrel had grown out of the earlier Chinese occupation of Tibet. The Indian government had not reacted when the Chinese invaded that country in 1950, nor had it shown any concern over the harshness with which the Tibetan people were repressed, nor when the Chinese further tightened their grasp there in 1959 after an unsuccessful rebellion and the Dalai Lama had fled to India. Indian policy was at that time basically sympathetic to China. An attempt by Tibetan exiles to set up a government on Indian soil was stifled. But by then territorial disputes had already begun. They soon led to clashes of arms. The Chinese refused to recognize a border with India along lines drawn by British–Tibetan negotiation in 1914 but never formally accepted by any Chinese government. Forty-odd years' usage was hardly significant against China's millennial historical memory. In the autumn of 1962 there was much heavier fighting, when Nehru demanded a Chinese withdrawal from the disputed zone. At the end of the year, it stopped on the initiative of the Chinese who had, clearly, won.

Surprise was probably even greater when earlier in 1963 a startled world had suddenly heard the Soviet Union bitterly denounced by its allies, the Chinese communists, and that shots were being exchanged on the Sino-Soviet border. What was more, said the Chinese, the USSR had given help to India and, in a hostile gesture, had cut off economic and military aid to China three years earlier. This, though, by no means went to the root of the complex origins to this quarrel. It is said that Beijing never forgave a Soviet refusal to cancel a $2 billion debt for assistance in Korea.[7] Many Chinese communists (Mao among them) had memories which went even further back. They could remember what had happened when Chinese interests had been disastrously subordinated to the allegedly superior interest of international communism, as interpreted by Moscow, in the 1920s. Since that time there had always been a tension in the leadership of the Chinese party between Soviet and native impulses, and Mao himself embodied it.

Such complexities and subtleties were all the more difficult to disentangle because even Chinese resentment of Soviet policy had to be presented to the rest of the world in Marxist jargon. It now seems that Stalin had soon started to be uneasy about Mao as a potential Asian Tito, though once the new Soviet leadership engaged itself in dismantling the Stalin myth, the Chinese were almost inevitably led to sound more Stalinist than Stalin in their public pronouncements, even when they were not pursuing Stalinist policies at home. The quarrel was from the start, too, inflamed by tactlessness in Moscow. The Soviet leaders who followed Stalin seem to have been as careless as any western imperialists of Asiatic feelings: one of them once revealingly remarked that when touring in China, he and other Russians 'used to laugh at their primitive forms of organization'.[8] One reason for the Chinese industrialization efforts of the 1950s had been the wish to reduce dependence on the USSR, but the sudden withdrawal of Soviet economic and technical help in 1960 had been a grave affront, and one felt all the more because of the moment at which it came, when China was in the middle of the first major domestic crisis of the communist regime, the outcome of the mismanagement

[7] Stueck, p.363.
[8] *Khrushchev Remembers. The Last Testament* (London, 1974), p.272.

of agriculture (officially described as 'natural disasters' caused by flooding). Nevertheless, though some in the outside world who felt positively unfriendly to the communist regime were heartened by such information as they had been able to obtain about what was really going on in China (Chiang Kai-shek is said to have wished to have launched an invasion from Taiwan but to have been restrained by the Americans), the damage was for the most part successfully concealed by censorship and propaganda.

In any case, immediate circumstances may well have mattered less than more distant historical perspectives. Long before the foundation of the CCP, the Chinese Revolution had been a movement of national regeneration. One of its primary aims had been the recovery from the foreigners of China's control over her own destiny and, above all, territory. Among those predatory foreigners, the Russians had a record of territorial encroachment on China begun under Peter the Great. Vast tracts of inner Asia had been acquired by Russia in the nineteenth century. New acquisitions continued right through from the tsarist to the Soviet era. A Russian protectorate over Tannu Tuva had been established in 1914, but when the area was finally annexed it was by the Soviet Union in 1944. In 1945 Russian armies entered Manchuria and north China and reconstituted the tsarist Far East of 1900; they remained in Sinkiang until 1949, in Port Arthur until 1955. In Mongolia they left behind a satellite Mongolian People's Republic they had set up in the 1920s. With something like 4,150 miles of shared frontier, divided into two (partly by Mongolia) the potential for dispute was immense.

Clashes over the exact demarcation of this long border had in fact begun in 1960. Soviet officials asserted that there had been some 5,000 frontier violations by the Chinese in that year. Shortly after the public announcement of the Sino-Soviet quarrel, the Chinese were laying counter-claims to some 600,000 square miles of Soviet territory – an area about a fifth of the size of Canada – and violent incidents were increasing in number. At the core of the dispute lay disagreement over the renunciation of tsarist aggressions in 1920 by the young USSR; the Soviet authorities insisted that this only applied to the nineteenth-century 'unequal' treaties and not to boundary questions in Sinkiang, Mongolia and the old Russian Far Eastern province. By 1969 the situation would be so inflamed that the Chinese could talk of a 'fascist' dictatorship in Moscow, and were making ostentatious preparation for war.[9]

China presented the world with a striking symbol of technological success and her new status as a power with the explosion in 1964 of her first nuclear weapon.[10] Thus she acquired the expensive admission card to a very exclusive club at a very important moment. The ultimate basis of her international power, nonetheless, was bound to be her huge population. Even after the setbacks of the famine, it continued to rise to even greater totals. Five hundred and ninety million has been thought a reasonable estimate for the year 1950; twenty-five years later, there were 835 million Chinese. Even if China's share of world population may have been larger in the past than at that time, she was stronger than ever before. Her leaders talked as if they were unmoved by the possibility of nuclear war; Chinese would survive in greater numbers than the peoples of other countries. Signs that the Soviet government was alarmed by the presence of such a demographic mass on the border of the USSR's most thinly populated regions were hardly to be unexpected.

THE GREAT STEERSMAN

The recovery of China's international standing outweighed for Mao's colleagues any misgivings that had been felt about his handling of domestic difficulties, misgivings that reached their peak among the ruling hierarchy with the disasters of the Great Leap Forward, the Chairman's first serious setback for decades. His vision of the role of the peasantry in the revolution had provided the way ahead after disaster had overtaken urban communism in 1929 and from about 1935 he had been virtually supreme within the party. Victory in the civil war had buttressed his prestige. In the 1950s a new way also seemed to be opening for Mao to sway international events; it looked as if his notion of a protracted revolutionary war, waged from the countryside and carried into the towns, might be promising in other

[9] AR 1969, p.360.
[10] The first Chinese hydrogen bomb was let off in 1969.

parts of the world where the orthodox Marxist belief that industrial development was needed to create a revolutionary proletariat was not persuasive. Yet although his intellectual formation had been Marxist and although he had found Marxist categories helpful in understanding his country's predicament, Mao appears always to have been ready to dilute them with pragmatism.[11] He was a ruthless power-seeker; his judgement of political possibilities appears to have begun to weaken only after years of success, when megalomania, vanity and eventually age were taking their toll. Early in his career, he had come to advocate a sinicized Marxism, rejecting the Soviet dogma that had cost the CCP so dear in the 1920s. Rather than the bloodless categories of the dialectic, the basis of Mao's world view seems to have been a vision of society and politics as an arena of contending forces in which human willpower and brute force could be deployed to bring about morally desirable and creative change – defined, of course, by an all-knowing leader, an approach sympathetic to Chinese tradition, but one that ran headlong into difficulty when confronted by economic problems requiring for their solution not only a correct identification of goals, but also a prudent assessment of the time needed to create new institutions and habits.

Mao's relations with his party colleagues had not always been untroubled, in any case. The failure of the Great Leap Forward provided new fuel for his critics. He blamed many of them for having thwarted his intentions, and thus betraying him. One weapon he was soon able to deploy against them was the uneasiness of many communists over events in the USSR since Stalin's death, when a loosening of the iron grip of dictatorship appeared to be visible. Many feared, in the aftermath of the Great Leap Forward, that any relaxation, modest though it might be, might open the door to corruption and compromise in bureaucracy and party alike. The fear of what might happen if discipline slipped in China was paradoxically just what helped Mao to promote an upheaval that was to tear the country asunder at the end of the 1960s and paralyse the party.

[11] 'What's wrong with a little capitalism? Life would be very dull without it!' he once said, irritated by colleagues demanding the suppression of peasant plots and markets (q. in Jack Gray, 'Rethinking Chinese Economic Reform', *Journal of Communist Studies and Transition Studies*, vol. 14, 1998, p.149).

RESURGENT JAPAN

One of Washington's responses to Cold War in Asia had been to safeguard as long as possible the special position arising from the American occupation of Japan. This was virtually a monopoly, with only token participation by British Commonwealth units. Soviet delay in declaring war on Japan and the speed of Japan's surrender had made it possible. Stalin had been taken by surprise. The Americans firmly rejected later Soviet requests for a share in an occupation Soviet power had done nothing to bring about. The results of this exclusion were to be startling. The United States provided the last great example of western paternalism in Asia by imposing constitutional reform and the Japanese once more demonstrated their astonishing gift for appropriating from alien culture only what they wished to learn while safeguarding their own society against unsettling change.

The Imperial Rescript on Ending the War which was published in the Emperor's name on 15 August 1945 referred to his obligation to 'report dutifully to the godly spirit of our ancestors'. But whatever forms were preserved, defeat was to force Japan spiritually to confront a twentieth century she had already entered economically and technologically. The Japanese faced deep and troubling problems of national identity and purpose. The westernization of the Meiji era had led to the dreams of 'Asia for the Asians' and the 'Greater Asia Co-prosperity Sphere', a kind of Japanese Monroe doctrine, underpinned by the anti-western sentiment so widespread in the Far East and cloaking imperial exploitation of Japan's neighbours. Such ideas were blown away by defeat. Even had she not been humbled and devastated, the rolling back of colonialism left Japan with no obvious and creditable Asian role. True, she seemed unlikely for a long time to have the power for one. The war's demonstration of Japan's vulnerability had been a great shock; like the United Kingdom she had depended on control of the surface of the sea, and the loss of it had doomed her. Then there were the other painful consequences of defeat; the end of Manchurian and Korean ambitions, the loss of Sakhalin to the USSR, together with the Kurile Islands, and an American occupation. Finally, there was vast material and human destruction to repair.

On the asset side, Japan in 1945 still had the unshaken central institution of her monarchy, whose prestige was virtually undimmed for most Japanese and, indeed, had made the surrender possible (the emperor had overridden the enthusiasm of a few fanatical soldiers who wished to fight to the end). Many Japanese saw the emperor as the man who had saved them from annihilation. The first post-war government, which took office two days after the Imperial Rescript, set about arresting anyone who advocated abolition of the emperor system.[12] The American commander in the Pacific, General Mac-Arthur, too, was anxious to maintain the emperor's prestige in the eyes of his people and the mysterious symbolic authority of his office as instruments of a peaceful occupation. Almost single-handed at first, he used his power to have the monarchical basis of a constitution in place before republican enthusiasts in the United States could interfere. He also argued effectively that Japan should be helped economically in order to get it more quickly off the back of the American taxpayer. Japanese social cohesiveness and discipline was another huge advantage, though many Japanese were soon feeling that the Americans might undermine them by the determination with which they pressed democratic institutions upon the country.

MacArthur's place in the history of Japan (as, to all intents and purposes, an American viceroy) would have been assured by what he did to preserve the monarchy, but his contribution did not end there. Soon enjoying the advantage of the growing preoccupation of the Truman administration with Europe, his staff had a remarkably free hand for a couple of years. Before a new constitution was drafted he endeavoured to set Japanese political culture on a new course, among other things by directing the Japanese prime minister towards the introduction of such specific reforms as women's suffrage, the promotion of trade unions, the liberalizing of education, abolition of the secret police and democratizing the economic system. Soon, the 1890 Imperial Edict on education that had formed generations of Japanese minds was pronounced to be no longer valid. The new constitution was to embody provision for the protection of political rights and women's legal status (and led to

---

[12] It also decided to double the size of Japan's police forces.

much agitated debate over what was seen as the destructive tendency of some of its clauses towards the male-dominated Japanese family). Economic reform led to legislation making possible the transfer of about a third of the cultivated area of Japan by compulsory purchase from the ownership of landlords into the hands of its actual cultivators, who bought it, an attack on an old problem of rural poverty. Although the initiative was American, there was a substantial native input into the scheme and its implications went far beyond the merely economic; agriculture was, of course, still Japan's biggest industry. It helped to change old psychological and social attitudes, and to weaken the authority of family and community. It also, in the next two or three decades, provided steady electoral support for a succession of conservative governments, supported by the farm lobby it made possible and organized through agricultural cooperatives. Meanwhile, in the cities the organization of trade unions under the new, democratic order proceeded apace; already by May Day 1946, 2.7 million workers belonged to them.

By then the Emperor had announced his own support for the new constitution which the Americans were drafting. It was eventually a graft on the Meiji constitution and came into effect on 3 May 1947. The electorate was more than doubled, women being given the vote for the first time and the age of voting being reduced from twenty-five to twenty. With time, the implications of the American occupation were to change. One of the first overt signs of this was the refusal, in 1947, of the occupation authorities to permit a general strike. Encouragement of trade unions had awoken second thoughts once it became clear that communists were using them to promote political goals. There was a perceptible waning of the reforming impulse among the occupation authorities. The Cold War had come to Japan; some historians have even spoken of a reversal of course in American policy, away from the demilitarizing and democratizing thrust given it by the Supreme Commander and his team, towards the promotion of economic recovery in a potential ally.

Though the Chinese mainland was some 400 miles away, Japan was, of course, separated from Soviet territory (in the Kuriles) by less than five miles of water. Korea, the old arena of imperial rivalry, was only 150 miles away. The spread of the Cold War to Asia won Japan even better treatment from the Americans, now anxious to see her working convincingly as an example of democracy and capitalism. It also gave her the protection of the United States nuclear 'umbrella'. The Korean war was a kick-start for her economy, perhaps, too, an escape from a deflationary policy in domestic affairs imposed by new influences from Washington. The war made her important as a base, and galvanized her industries. The index of industrial production was soon going up at a rate of more than 10 per cent per year while the war continued; even by 1951 economic activity had again reached its pre-war level. The United States meanwhile promoted Japanese interests abroad through diplomacy. Finally, Japan long had no defence costs to burden her economy; she was until 1951 forbidden to have any armed forces.

By then, the basis for much that had been seen by the Americans as undesirable in old Japan had gone. The old security services had been disbanded. Shintoism no longer had official support. Democratic education and careful demilitarization were deemed to have provided a base reassuring enough for a peace treaty between Japan and most of her former enemies other than the Russians and nationalist Chinese (terms with them followed within a few years). Japan regained her full sovereignty, including a right to arms for defensive purposes, but gave up virtually all her former overseas possessions. Thus the Japanese emerged from the post-war era to resume control of their own affairs still a unified nation (as Germany was not). An agreement with the United States provided for the continued presence of American forces on her soil. In 1956 she would enter the United Nations. Confined to her own islands and unable to contemplate foreign policy adventures, Japan's position was by no means disadvantageous, even if she faced a China stronger and much better consolidated than for a century. In less than twenty years this much-reduced status was, as it turned out, to be transformed again, like much else, by the Cold War, as well as by unforeseen economic development.

Japan's close connexion with the United States, her proximity to the communist world and her advanced and stable economy and society all made it natural that she should in due course formally take her place in the security system built up by the United States in Asia and the Pacific. Its foundations were American treaties with Australia,

New Zealand and the Philippines (which had become independent in 1946). Others with Pakistan and Thailand followed. In this way the United States acquired the Asian allies other than Taiwan that she needed. Indonesia and (more important) India remained aloof. These alliances reflected, in part, the new conditions of Pacific and Asian international relations after the British withdrawal from India. For a few years longer there would still be British forces east of Suez, but for Australia and New Zealand the fall of Singapore in 1942 had been decisive; it had shown that the United Kingdom could not defend them and that the United States would. Though British forces still sustained the Malaysians against the Indonesians in the 1950s and 1960s, the important colony of Hong Kong survived, it was clear, only because it suited the Chinese that it should do so until the lease that covered part of it ran out in 1997. On the other hand, there was no question of sorting out the complexities of the new Pacific by simply lining up states in the teams of the Cold War. The peace treaty with Japan itself caused great difficulty because United States policy always saw Japan as a potential anti-communist force while others – notably in Australia and New Zealand – remembered 1941 and feared a revival of Japanese power.

Thus American Asian policy was not made merely by Cold War ideology. Nonetheless, it was long bent by what was believed to be the disaster of the communist success in China and by ostentatious Chinese patronage of revolutionaries as far away as Africa and even South America. Of course, China's international position had been transformed. She had re-emerged as a great power in her own right. The first crack in the policy of adamantine American opposition to the People's Republic had been revealed as early as the Korean war, when China's strength had forced the United States to admit her to the negotiating table. But China's new power had not further stiffened the dualist, Cold War system; in some lights, it made nonsense of it. There was the wider significance of the Chinese Revolution to consider. Overwhelmingly the most important though it might be, the Chinese Revolution was only the outstanding instance of a rejection of western domination which was Asia-wide, and Russia, whether tsarist or Soviet, had been the most voracious western predator in the far East. Ironically, that rejection, explicit or implicit, in all Asian countries was most obviously expressed in forms, language and mythology borrowed from the west itself, whether they were those of industrial capitalism, nationalism, or Marxism.

17

Africa and the Near East:
Old and New Problems

PAST HISTORY, NEW FACTS

Colonial empire all but disappeared in Africa only slightly later than in Asia, but even more dramatically. This was not because the process was more violent than in Asia; with the horrific exceptions of Algeria and perhaps Portuguese Africa, the 'struggle' for independence did not entail rebellion on anything like the scale of the fighting needed to break the will of the Dutch in Indonesia, or the long wars of Indo-China. Faced with the loss of the legitimacy of colonial empire in 1945, the greatest imperial power, Great Britain, was never prepared to envisage simple military domination of its African territories: the domestic electorate would not have permitted it. True, as the war ended, no such restraint appeared to operate on the government of France, Africa's second great colonial power (1945 was a year when French forces bombarded two colonial capitals in other continents, too: Hanoi and Damascus, killing thousands of people in the process of rebuilding the empire). In North Africa, the murder of over 100 European subjects in disturbances on VE day itself led to bombing, vigilante and police reprisals which left thousands of Muslim dead.[1] But Algeria was to remain a special case, like Portuguese Africa even after independence, when a war between revolutionary peasant nationalism and the colonial state turned into one against the

---

[1] Estimates of the killing in the first post-war days in the Constantine region run from approximately 1,000 (French) to 45,000 (Algerian). For an admirable brief account of this seminal event, see A. Horne, *A Savage War of Peace. Algeria 1954–62* (London, 1977), pp.23–8.

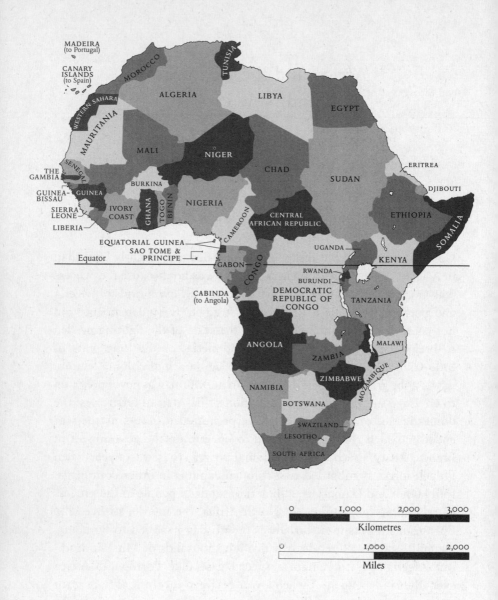

MADEIRA
(to Portugal)

CANARY
ISLANDS
(to Spain)

TUNISIA

MOROCCO

ALGERIA

LIBYA

EGYPT

WESTERN SAHARA

MAURITANIA

MALI

NIGER

CHAD

SUDAN

ERITREA

DJIBOUTI

THE
GAMBIA

SENEGAL

GUINEA-
BISSAU

GUINEA

BURKINA

NIGERIA

CENTRAL
AFRICAN REPUBLIC

ETHIOPIA

SOMALIA

SIERRA
LEONE

IVORY
COAST

GHANA

TOGO

BENIN

LIBERIA

CAMEROON

UGANDA

KENYA

EQUATORIAL GUINEA

SAO TOME &
PRINCIPE

Equator

GABON

CONGO

RWANDA

BURUNDI

CABINDA
(to Angola)

DEMOCRATIC
REPUBLIC
OF
CONGO

TANZANIA

ANGOLA

ZAMBIA

MALAWI

ZIMBABWE

MOZAMBIQUE

NAMIBIA

BOTSWANA

SWAZILAND

LESOTHO

SOUTH AFRICA

| 0 | 1,000 | 2,000 | 3,000 |

Kilometres

| 0 | 1,000 | 2,000 |

Miles

Africa in 1999
(from *Africa: A Biography of the Continent*, John Reader,
Hamish Hamilton, 1997)

post-colonial state (as it did in Indo-China). Elsewhere in Africa, armed rebellion is not a large part of the story of independence, which was usually one of swift, sometimes unexpected and largely peaceful transfer of power. The continent's worst twentieth-century holocausts were to take place after independence, by and large, when African could set about African.

The relative unexpectedness and suddenness of change in a continent where the retreat of empire had hardly been envisaged ten years earlier was much more startling than its violence. The map was transformed in barely twenty years. France, Great Britain, Portugal and Belgium were the colonial powers concerned (Germany had lost her African colonies in the Great War and Italy hers in 1943).[2] Portugal fought a long campaign against rebels and had no government willing to give in until after a domestic revolution in 1974, but long before that colonialism elsewhere in Africa had all but vanished. There had been something of a 'Scramble' in reverse and most of a new African order – or disorder – was in place by the mid-1960s. This was a special political and psychological shock in those places on the African continent where there were large and well-established white populations. Both French and British politicians sought to retain, if they could, some sort of influence by taking ostentatiously benevolent interest in their former black subjects. European settlers, rather than imperial ambitions, were to prove the main brake on withdrawal from colonial possessions. The suddenness of the change brought to birth some very fragile 'new nations'. Black Africa owes its present structure largely to decisions by nineteenth-century Europeans, for its building blocks have largely been defined by the boundaries of former colonies. They often enclose peoples of many stocks, languages and customs, for whom colonial rule had provided little but a formal identification and unification. All things considered and the vastness of the context allowed for, the enduring respect still enjoyed by territorial arrangements whose integrity is based on these boundaries seems remarkable.

[2] The UN made Eritrea an autonomous territory federated with Ethiopia in 1951, after nine years of British military rule.

PRE-INDEPENDENCE AFRICA

Twentieth-century African history, nonetheless, cannot be understood to begin with decolonization – or, for that matter, with colonization. Many things which weigh heavily in that history are negative, the implication of changes that did not happen, of dogs that did not bark in the night, of inheritances from a much more ancient and deeply-rooted past. For all the blame heaped on colonial 'exploitation' and post-colonial 'dependence' as an explanation of Africa's poverty and lopsided economic development, for example, it can still be argued that geography itself always made significant indigenous economic growth difficult if not impossible in at least some parts of Africa.[3] Nor, except along the northern and eastern coasts and their hinterland, where Islam established itself during Europe's Middle Ages, was there any integrating cultural influence among the continent's peoples such as ancient civilizations had provided to hundreds of millions of Asians. More positively, African history had long been paced by population change; for centuries it pushed people about and set limits to their achievements and, since the early years of this century, it has been by far the most important single dynamic factor at work, above all south of the Sahara.[4] As the century began, there were about 93 million Africans in all; by 1975, 385 million. The balance of the continent's peoples has now firmly tipped towards Black Africa. The numbers still continue to surge upwards, seemingly unchecked by the Malthusian disasters of war, epidemic and famine which continue to afflict much of the continent. It seems likely that Africa's total population will be nearing 700 million by the year 2000.

In 1945 there was still only a handful of sovereign African states: Morocco, Egypt, Liberia, Ethiopia and South Africa, the last being then an independent Dominion of the British Commonwealth. Most of the continent was still, as in 1901, ruled from European capitals. Africa's history, though, had already been much changed since the

[3] See the judgement of a recent survey by a leading scholar that the chief contribution of Africans to history has been that they 'have colonised an especially hostile region of the world' (J. Iliffe, *Africans. The History of a Continent*, Cambridge, 1995, p.1).
[4] See Iliffe, and J. Reader, *Africa. A Biography of the Continent* (London, 1998).

beginning of the century. In 1901 there had been little modern African industry except on the Rand, in South Africa. Since then, South Africa had become a major industrial country, and Rhodesia, Zaïre and Zambia important mining economies (raising copper, coal, manganese, iron, uranium). Today, Algeria, Nigeria and Libya are major producers of oil and gas. This is one way in which the roles of African countries in world affairs have been changed by more than the achievement of independence. They are still an object of interference and exploitation from outside – much African history has gone on being made by outsiders, rather than by Africans – but for different reasons as time passed, in new ways and with new motives. Because non-Africans seek to court the favour of African states, moreover, those states and their rulers have often enjoyed greater freedom of manoeuvre than their intrinsic strengths might suggest.

The ending of imperial rule in Africa came about, as elsewhere, against different local backgrounds with different histories. Black Africa tends, nonetheless, to have a sadly negative unity. The absence (except in a small degree in Ethiopia) of literate indigenous civilization such as could be found in India or China, or in Islamic Africa, meant that white skills and direction counted for much more in changing this part of the continent than elsewhere. Anti-western resentment and resistance to cultural subversion had roots much less deep in Black Africa than in the Islamic Maghreb and Egypt.[5] Where the climate was suitable – South Africa, Rhodesia, Kenya and Angola were the main instances – white communities were well established and complicated the politics of Africa's modernization. But white ideas had influences in other ways, too. The nationalism that appealed to the westernized African élites confirmed the continent's fragmentation, often ignoring realities which colonialism had contained or manipulated. The sometimes strident authoritarianism and demagoguery of new rulers was often a response to the dangers of centrifugal forces. For good or ill, it was a tribute to the most successful of the

[5] Though the first nationalist movement in Black Africa emerged in 1936 in Nigeria, seeking autonomy 'within the British Empire' (sic); Iliffe, p.233. This was not long after the founding of the Tunisian neo-Destour policy, and seven years before Morocco's first Independence Party.

institutions implanted by the colonialists, the sovereign state. West Africans combed the historical record – such as it was – of ancient Mali and Ghana, and east Africans brooded over the past which might be hidden in relics such as the ruins of Zimbabwe in order to forge national mythologies like those of earlier nation-makers in Europe and to find in them unifying and rallying influences.

Black Africa's geographical layout was also important in shaping its post-colonial history. Though the continent was always of great interest to outsiders, for a long time few of them could easily get at it. Whereas many Asian countries found the USSR meddling in their affairs, that country was, after all, a major Asian power; it was hardly involved in sub-Saharan Africa outside the white industrial cities of South Africa (where most communists were white) until the movement towards independence had all but run its course, and communist advisers and soldiers (from Cuba) arrived in the 1960s and 1970s.

Two world wars helped to stir up Black Africa. In prolonged if not large-scale fighting in the former German colonies African soldiers played a major role. African countries prospered economically as suppliers of goods and commodities. But in the formation of the first Black African political leaders who would take up the nationalist cause, this was less important than European education (often provided by white missionaries) and the stimulus of contact, for good or ill, with the colonial governments. Between 1918 and 1939, the colonial structure was remarkably stable. The former German colonies had been replaced by Mandates in 1919: the British held one for Tanganyika, the British and French shared others for Togoland and the Cameroons, and Belgium had one for part of German East Africa which had bordered on the Congo. South Africa was given the mandate for German South West Africa (and clung to it after 1945). Until the war of 1939–45, the rest of Black Africa and the Horn of Africa remained effectively in the hands of these outsiders, together with the Belgians, Portuguese and Italians (who had added Ethiopia to their possessions in 1936). During the war the emperor of Ethiopia was restored to his throne and Italian Somalia, Eritrea and Libya were conquered by the British. In the north, Tunisia emerged from the war still under French tutelage, and French government in Algeria had never been interrupted, though both countries had been theatres of fighting between Axis and Anglo-American forces. South of the Sudan and Sahara the map of Africa in 1945 looked hardly changed since 1919. The large area shaded pink because it belonged to the British Commonwealth (a name the British had begun to use more as they lost the taste and the nerve for empire) included two areas which were effectively independent. Though Southern Rhodesia was legally a colony, her white settlers had since the 1920s got used to governing themselves, and no longer expected interference from London. The Union of South Africa, steadily pushed by its Afrikaner voters towards complete independence, had been a fully self-governing Dominion since 1926. There was even before the war substantial agreement among its white citizens that some forms of segregation were a necessary part of governing black South Africans (the South African Native National Congress, later the African National Congress, had been formed as long ago as 1912). Given the comparative feebleness of African nationalist movements even in 1945 and the seemingly unchanged nature of colonial rule, there seemed little chance things would change for a long time, if ever, in the other, true, colonies.

Territorial changes were not all that mattered, though, between 1939 and 1945. After the disaster of the world depression of the 1930s, African economies had undergone wartime disruption and diversion because of external needs and external interests. Agriculture in some of them had shifted towards the growing of cash crops on a large scale for export. Whether this was or was not in the long-term interests of peasants who had previously raised crops and livestock only for local consumption is debatable, but the consequences were rapid and profound. So were those following the exploitation of other primary products with industrial uses – copper, for example. One was an inflow of cash in payment for produce the British and Americans needed. Some of this came through in higher wages, and the spread of a cash economy often had disturbing local effects. Unanticipated urban growth and new regional development followed; the reconstruction of Africa by the colonial system continued at a quickened pace as new towns, airfields, harbours and agricultural estates provided new social and economic foci.

Many African countries were tied to a particular pattern of development that was soon to show its vulnerabilities and limitations in the post-war world. Even seemingly benevolent intentions, expressed in programmes like the British Colonial Development and Welfare Fund, or much international aid, in fact helped to shackle African producers to a world market. Above all, population growth drove and was driven by the forces of economic change. While, we are told,[6] there 'was certainly no single pattern' of general population increase between the 1880s and the 1920s, and it is even uncertain whether the continent's *total* population then grew at all, colonialism released demographic growth in several places from the 1930s onwards. This gave new urgency to problems the colonial regimes did not tackle effectively in the 1940s and 1950s and helped to discredit them. After independence, as populations rose faster still and disappointment with the reality of 'freedom' from the colonial powers set in, discontent and disturbance were inevitable. It remains a moot point whether this was inseparable from the whole modernizing process, from the imposition of peace and creation of larger territorial units that began under colonial rule, and all the administrative and technological shock accompanying them.

THE INDEPENDENCE PROCESS IN BLACK AFRICA

Once started, the process of decolonization was hardly interrupted and drove forward with revolutionary speed. The first new and independent nation to appear in sub-Saharan Africa was the former Gold Coast, reincarnated as Ghana in 1957. This followed five years or so of quasi-autonomy and nearly a decade of constitutional change in the former British West African colonies. The British Colonial Office had soon after the war abandoned its old preference for 'indirect' rule through chiefs and had set up and encouraged local elected councils with restricted powers. By 1948, these were dominated by unofficial majorities. This made possible the formation of the first mass political parties of colonial Africa and opened the way to Ghana's independence

[6] Iliffe, p.211.

(1957), followed by that of Nigeria and Sierra Leone (1960) and of the Gambia (1965).[7]

British East Africa presented a greater variety of starting-points for the decolonizing process than the western British colonies. Kenya was a true 'crown' colony, governed ultimately by the Colonial office; it had a significant white settler population. Tangyanika had been a British mandate since 1919, while Uganda and Zanzibar were protectorates. In 1952 Kenya was distracted by a rebellion in the form of a secret society, the 'Mau-Mau' movement, which gave expression to the long-run grievances of the Kikuyu people over white land holding. It was contained; its leader was captured and imprisoned, to emerge nearly a decade later to become prime minister of a new, independent Kenya set up in 1963. By then, Tangyanika and Uganda were already independent republics. In 1964, all three of these states came to call for British help and the return of British troops in order to quell mutinies in their own armed forces – a fact which the president of Tangyanika called a 'national humiliation'. Zanzibar, which had attained national independence within the Commonwealth at the same time as Kenya, joined itself to Tangyanika soon after this episode in a new united republic, Tanzania.

The French had from the start taken a different tack. They had sought to assure in their colonies that any liberalization that might have to be conceded should be contained within the armature of the French imperial order. The first African to take his seat in the French National Assembly had done so in 1914; in pursuit of the same goal of integration with the constitutional relations of the metropolitan power, elections held in 1945 sent twenty-nine black African representatives to the constituent assembly in Paris that was at that moment founding the Fourth Republic. In French western and central Africa no fewer than thirteen new internally autonomous units were set up in 1958 as 'overseas territories' of a new 'French Community'. This was a recognition of the way the wind was blowing, as well as of an increasing French preoccupation with Europe and dislike of overseas military effort after Indo-China and during an increasingly costly war

---

[7] The Gambia subsequently disappeared for a time on amalgamation with Senegal – one of many changes in the status of the components of the new Africa, most of which cannot be registered in this book.

in Algeria. The cost of aid to Black Africa was high, too. France could no longer afford an empire but the 'Community', it was hoped, would retain some of its prestige and influence. Even in 1958, though, one former French colony, Guinea, opted (as all were allowed – though not expected – to do) for complete independence; its subsequent treatment by the government in Paris was, to say the least, cool (it is said that the departing French even took with them the local administration's typewriters), but this did not deter others from quickly following its example. During 1959 all those ex-colonies in the region which had at first chosen continued association with France renounced it. At the end of the year French Somaliland was the only remaining French colonial territory left in Africa (Algeria, of course, was at that moment still administratively a part of metropolitan France).

As for Belgium, ruler of the Congo since 1908, when it ceased to be the personal possession of the Belgian king, her governor promised independence after riots at the beginning of 1959 showed the contagion of anti-Europeanism. Elections in the following year for a national assembly brought to birth a new independent Congo Republic on 1 July 1960.[8] The worst signs of troubles still to come broke out in the Portuguese colonies of Angola, Portuguese Guinea and Mozambique in 1961, a year in which more than 200 Portuguese settlers were killed there. This opened a period of heavy demands on the colonial power's resources of manpower and wealth; by 1970, Portugal would have nearly 150,000 soldiers deployed in Africa. The commitment threw a lurid light on what might have been had the British and French decided to fight for Black Africa in an era of Cold War.

In 1960, a visiting British prime minister felt able to draw the attention of the South African parliament to a 'Wind of Change' sweeping the continent. When, in the following year, South Africa left the Commonwealth to become an independent republic, there were already twenty-four African new nations that had come into being since 1945. In 1965, a white-dominated Southern Rhodesia seceded from the Commonwealth, too, and was soon engaged in a bitter internal struggle over who its future rulers should be. Fifteen

[8] Renamed Zaïre in 1971.

years later, not one European possession would remain on the continent except for a couple of Spanish enclaves. The Portuguese, the Iberians who had led Europe into its adventure of world domination five centuries earlier, would be, fittingly, the last to abandon their African colonies.

Though in some cases (notably in the former Belgian Congo) bloodshed soon followed the ending of colonial rule, violence was no more than a supplementary stimulus for the great colonial withdrawal. Even in Portugal, it was in the end domestic revolution that was decisive. It brought to power in 1974 a left-wing junta that almost at once granted independence to Portuguese Guinea and opened negotiations with nationalists in Mozambique and Angola. The special case of Algeria always excepted, the other major colonial powers seemed even anxious to rid themselves of responsibility, once certain special interests could be secured. In the case of Great Britain, this was most evident and caused most difficulty in relations with its white settler colonies. Events there were much shaped by what was going on in South Africa.

SOUTH AFRICA AND RHODESIA

Afrikaner voters cherished their historical grievances as much as did any black nationalist. They had warmly approved a weakening of ties with the British Commonwealth after the First World War, and it was made easier by the concentration of voters of Anglo-Saxon origin in the provinces of Cape Town and Natal; the Afrikaners were entrenched in the Transvaal and the major industrial areas as well as the rural hinterland. The Union of South Africa, it is true, entered the war in 1939 on the British side and supplied important forces to fight in it; this was better than having to face Afrikaner rebellion as had been the case in 1914, but nonetheless some intransigent Afrikaners supported a movement favouring cooperation with Nazi Germany. Its leader became prime minister in 1948. By then Afrikaners dominated South African politics.

As they had steadily engrossed power inside the Union, and built up their economic position in the industrial and financial sectors, the intolerable prospect of having imposed on them a policy towards the Black African untainted by their own deep prejudices was soon inconceivable. The eventual outcome was the construction of a formal system of separation of black and white. *Apartheid* expressed Afrikaner ideology and guaranteed the dominant position of the whites in a land where industrialism and market economies had done much to break down the regulation and location of the growing black population inherent in the old tribal divisions. It meant a legal and physical separation of races that left the Black African always in an exploited and inferior position. In its completed form it not only prevented white and black from living in the same areas, but from eating in the same restaurants, going to the same hotels, using the same theatres and cinemas, sitting on the same park benches and doing a hundred and one other things together, among them having sexual intercourse or inter-marrying. It made South Africa the only country in the world where (whatever the practice elsewhere) the government argued openly that people should be deprived of legal rights, humiliated socially and oppressed economically solely because of biological origin. No such claim had been made in a civilized country since the collapse of Nazi Germany.

Apartheid had an appeal – on even less excusable grounds than the primitive superstitions or supposed economic necessities of the Afrikaners – to white people elsewhere, notably in Central Africa. The only country where in 1945 a similar balance of black and white population to that of South Africa and a similar concentration of mineral wealth existed was Southern Rhodesia, though there were important, but less numerous, white communities in the neighbouring protectorates of Northern Rhodesia and Nyasaland. In 1953 these two countries were united by the British with an already self-governing Southern Rhodesia in a federation. It was assumed that this would be the first stage in the evolution of a new self-governing Dominion, with its capital at Salisbury (as was that of the federal government). With the support of the British government, the dominating white political party of Southern Rhodesia strove to keep the federation alive, while Black Nationalist opposition to it mounted in Nyasaland and Northern Rhodesia, where it was seen as a device for extending Southern Rhodesia's white supremacy policies to those countries.

Nineteen sixty-two was a crucial year. The federation staggered as a black majority appeared in the Northern Rhodesian legislature, home rule was granted to Nyasaland by London, and a white supremacy government was formed in Southern Rhodesia. Federation formally came to an end in 1964, when Northern Rhodesia gained independence as Zambia, and Nyasaland as Malawi.

In the following year, to the great embarrassment of the British government, Southern Rhodesia seceded from the Commonwealth. The aim of the secessionists, it was feared, was to move towards a society more and more like South Africa's. The British government dithered and missed its chance. There was nothing that Black African states could immediately do about Rhodesia, and not much that the United Nations could do either. 'Sanctions' were invoked in the restriction of trade with the former colony; many black African states ignored them and the British government winked at the steps taken by major oil companies to ensure their product reached the rebels. In one of the most shameful episodes in the history of a feeble government, Great Britain's stock sank dramatically in the eyes of Africans who, understandably, did not see why a British government could not intervene militarily to suppress a colonial rebellion as flagrant as that of the North Americans in 1776 (many British, of course, reflected that it was precisely that precedent which made the outlook for intervention by a remote and militarily weak imperial sovereign so discouraging).

Though South Africa (the richest and strongest state in Africa, and growing richer and stronger all the time) seemed secure, she was, together with Rhodesia and Portugal, the object of increasingly threatening Black African anger as the 1970s began. The drawing of the racial battle lines continued there, hardly offset by minor concessions to South Africa's blacks and growing economic ties with some black states. There was soon a danger, too, that outside powers might be involved. In 1975, after the Portuguese withdrawal from Angola, a Marxist regime took power there. When civil war followed and Cuban soldiers arrived to support the government, South African support was soon being given to the rebels against it.

DISAPPOINTMENT AND DISILLUSION

By 1970 the United Nations had forty-two African states as members. But as the continent shook off colonialism, new dangers had come to the surface, especially in Black Africa. The continent was in fact one of nationalists – and not many of them, outside the political élites – rather than of nations. In part, this was a matter of poor preparation and inadequate information. In practical terms, the speed of decolonization in Africa had often meant that there was little chance of finding native Africans in sufficient numbers to provide administrators and technicians for the new regimes, some of which therefore continued for a time to rely upon white personnel. Similarly, the supporting structures of colonial rule in higher education, communications and armed forces were often nothing like so evolved as those in, say, India; this, too, made new African nations even more dependent on foreign help – soon to include that offered by Soviet and Chinese agencies – than newly independent Asian countries.

In the twenty-seven years after Ghana came to independence twelve wars were to be fought in sub-Saharan Africa between Africans and thirteen heads of state would be assassinated. There were two especially bad outbreaks of strife. The former Belgian Congo was not only woefully short of trained personnel (it had been the Belgians' calculation that this would mean they could retain much of their influence after withdrawal) but was ethnically and provincially deeply divided. When in 1960 the mineral-rich region of Katanga tried to break away on its own with the support of European mining companies, this provoked a civil war in which rival Soviet and American influences quickly became tangled, while the United Nations strove to restore peace; this was the moment at which the Cold War most obviously entered African politics. The Congo police and military apparatus at once collapsed. After complex negotiation, much intrigue, many secessions, coups and bursts of fighting, a united Congo eventually emerged in 1965 under a general who thereafter clung to power for over thirty years. The Congo episode had been of peculiar importance. It came to exemplify to other African states the dangers of dissension, of involving white settlers in the fighting, of, even, seeking to exploit

Cold War potentials (though, ironically, both the USA and USSR had sought to maintain the Congo's unity).

Then, at the end of the 1960s, came a brutal civil war in Nigeria which may have cost half a million lives. Nigeria had been seen before that as one of the most stable and promising of the new African states, perhaps as an African Saudi Arabia, but once again non-Africans were irresistibly drawn to dabble in the bloodbath (this was one cost of Nigeria's entry to the ranks of the major oil producers). In other countries, there were many somewhat less bloody but still fierce struggles between factions, regions and tribes which distracted and divided the small westernized élites and quickly led them to abandon democratic and liberal principles much advertised in the heady days when colonialism was in retreat. Coups, rebellions and ethnic wars continue to this day. Black Africa has consequently looked at times much like the nineteenth-century Balkans in the wake of the Ottoman withdrawal (or as Yugoslavia has done in the 1990s). In its new countries, some politicians struggled to make democracy work amid peoples with no training in it and old, traditional loyalties and animosities to fight about, while their less honest colleagues sought to feather their own nests and those of their families, and happily indulged old ethnic hatreds in doing so.

In many of the new nations, the wish to prevent disintegration, suppress open dissent and strengthen central authority had produced by the 1970s one-party, authoritarian government or rule by soldiers (much as had done the history of South America after the Wars of Liberation). Even an older independent Africa did not escape this trend. Impatience with a monarchy seemingly incapable of providing peaceful political and social change led in 1974 to revolution in Ethiopia. The setting aside of Haile Selassie, the 'Lion of Judah', was almost incidentally the end of the oldest Christian monarchy in the world (supposed by some to run back to the son of Solomon and the Queen of Sheba). A year later, the soldiers who had taken power there seemed just as discredited as their predecessors. From such changes elsewhere in Africa there sometimes emerged tyrant-like political leaders who reminded Europeans of earlier dictators of their own, but this comparison may be misleading. Africanists have gently suggested that many of the 'strong men' of the new nations are best seen as the inheritors of the mantle of pre-colonial African kingship, rather than in western terms. Some have looked more like simple bandits.

Their own troubles no doubt increased the irritation with which African intellectuals frequently reacted to the outside world. Encouraged by American influences, a great mythological drama was built on the old Atlantic slave trade, which Africans were encouraged to see as a supreme example of racial exploitation. Other roots of frustration lay in the sense of political inferiority that was always near the surface in a continent of, for the most part, powerless states (some with populations of less than a million). A disunited Africa could not expect to pull much weight in international affairs. Attempts were made to overcome the weakness which arose from division and an abortive attempt in 1958 to found a United States of Africa opened an era of alliances, partial unions, and essays in federation which culminated in the emergence in 1963 of the Organization for African Unity of thirty states (the OAU), largely thanks to the Ethiopian emperor, Haile Selassie, who was later so unceremoniously set aside.

Politically, the OAU affirmed as its goals the protection of the independence of its members, non-engagement with the rival blocs of the Cold War, and support for the emancipation of the remaining non-independent African countries. It was hard pressed, though, even to secure its own survival, though it successfully concluded in 1975 a beneficial trade negotiation with Europe in defence of African producers.[9] The disappointment of much of the early political history of independent Africa inevitably directed thoughtful politicians towards cooperation in economic development, above all with Europe, where former colonial powers remained Africa's most important source of capital, technology, skill and counsel. But the economic record of Black Africa has been dreadful. In this context, too, it is necessary to balance pre-conditioning facts against bad policies and simple corruption in order to explain failure. Almost all the ex-colonial territories, for example, inherited revenue systems based on agricul-

[9] As early as November 1965, OAU member states' foreign ministers voted unanimously to break off relations with Great Britain over her Rhodesian policy: only nine states eventually did so.

tural products and raw materials, whose prices were at the mercy of a fluctuating international market; this was an advantage in the 1950s and 1960s, a disaster later. Unsuitable monocultural schemes have increased agricultural vulnerability. Political concern with urban voters, corruption and investment in supposedly 'prestigious' projects, have played havoc with commercial and industrial policy. Meanwhile, populations have inexorably risen.

Nonetheless, the general trend of economics was favourable to the newly independent Black African states until the end of the 1960s. In the early 1950s the price of cocoa, for instance, rose threefold. But then came an era of falling commodity prices and economic recession after the 1973 revolution in oil prices. The shattering effect on Africa was worsened within a few years by the impact of repeated drought. In Black Africa annual per capita growth in GDP turned downward after the 1960s; in the 1970s it became a negative figure and then, after 1980, fell further at an annual average drop of 2.6 per cent until 1987. Coupled with a series of bad famines, this produced new horrors. It widened still further the gap between rural and urban populations and encouraged environmental degradation. The weight of the loans eagerly sought from the developed world in the years of high commodity prices now became intolerable: interest and capital repayment became impossible. By 1989 no fewer than thirty sub-Saharan countries were the subject of what the International Monetary Fund and World Bank called 'structural adjustment' programmes; this meant further restriction of demand.[10]

Given this background, it is hardly surprising that political cynicism and popular resentment flourished. The leaders of the independence era often lost their way, but showed little capacity for self-criticism. Their frustration found release in the encouragement of new resentments, sometimes exacerbated by external attempts to entangle Africans in the Cold War. These could be disappointing, too. Marxist revolution had little success. In the 1980s most Soviet aid was going to Vietnam, Afghanistan or Cuba, not Africa. Only in Ethiopia, most feudally backward of independent African states, and the former Portuguese colonies, the least-developed former colonial territories,

[10] T. Glaser, *The Courier*, 120, March–April 1990, p.27.

did formally Marxist regimes emerge. The sometime French and British colonies were much less responsive to Marxism.

Scapegoats were sought. Though African politicians often found it very difficult to cooperate with one another, so far as there was any will to go in the same direction, they found it in denouncing anything that smacked of white interference. Increasingly, but perhaps explicably, given the completeness and rapidity of decolonization in Africa and the geographical remoteness of much of it, plausible villains were to be found at hand; resentments came to focus particularly on the racial division of black and white in Africa itself, flagrant in the new republic of Rhodesia and the most powerful of African states, the Republic of South Africa. Both soon came to play a major role in the demonology of African politics.

Yet the South African government was slowly coming round to taking thought about the future. In the 1970s it began to seek to detach itself from the embarrassment of association with Rhodesia, whose prospects had much worsened when Portuguese rule came to an end in Mozambique. A guerrilla campaign against Rhodesia was possible (and was soon launched) from across the border. The American government contemplated with some alarm the outcome if Rhodesia collapsed at the hands of black nationalists depending on communist support. It applied pressure to the South Africans, who, in turn, applied it to the Rhodesians. In September 1976 the Rhodesian prime minister sadly told his countrymen that they had, after all their efforts, to accept the principle of black majority rule. It was another small but significant landmark in the dissolution of the world order with which the century had begun, and one of the last. Another milestone in the recession of European power had been passed. The last initiative by whites to found an African country they would dominate had failed. Yet a guerrilla war continued, worsening as nationalists sought to achieve unconditional white surrender. At last, in 1980 black and white intransigence gave way before the combined efforts of the British, Zambian and Mozambique governments. Rhodesia briefly returned to British rule before re-emerging into independence, this time as the new nation of Zimbabwe, with a prime minister known to his white compatriots mainly as a terrorist, and a Marxist one to boot. Now only South Africa survived as the sole white-dominated country on the continent. Yet it was already clear to many of its citizens that it could not do so for much longer.

ARAB AND JEW

Events in northern Africa require to be placed in a wider context than that of the rest of the continent for their full understanding. Islam tied the Maghreb and Egypt to events further east, whose own context must be understood both broadly in space and deeply in time. Fundamental to the history of the Near and Middle East has been their long and disappointing experience of modernization. Between the wars, and in the aftermath of 1945, western ideas and institutions – the national state and nationalism, socialism and communism, liberal democracy, capitalism – had indeed attracted more vigorous advocacy and promotion in Arab countries than ever before. Yet they notably failed to produce the moral and political independence, cultural self-respect and improvement in material conditions hoped for (and which was soon visible, for example, in Israel). Far less did they give reality to the constitutional and parliamentary forms some of these countries formally enjoyed. Viable states emerged in some places from the ruins of the Ottoman empire, but in the end prosperity and a Europeanized and liberal society survived only in the Lebanon, one of the oldest points of contact between the Arab world and advanced western ideas (and there too, that society would be destroyed in the 1970s and 1980s by the careless, the unscrupulous, the exasperated and the disappointed).

Soon, a more complicated and drawn-out change in many of the Arab states began to be manifest and for a time it lessened the likelihood of a speedy return to the battlefield by Israel's enemies. Widespread political upheavals removed all but the last vestiges of the old imperial hegemony in the Arab world and also replaced several rulers of the major Islamic states with much more radical and sometimes self-proclaimed regimes. By 1970, the Saudi king, the sultan of Morocco, the king of Jordan, and the shah of Iran alone among the more important monarchies still kept their thrones even if the rulers of lesser, small states were not very much troubled. Even by

1952, moreover, the French had already recognized the full sovereignty of Morocco and Tunisia; soon, they were to face the beginnings of a full-scale rebellion in Algeria which was to win it independence within a few years.

Another slowly maturing factor in the politics of the region, the transformation of its economies by oil, had also been at work. The industry had come a long way since its foundation before 1914 in Persia. By 1939, it was already beginning to bring a flow of new revenues to the area. They were to become vast, but without obvious benefit to most of its peoples. Modernization, and therefore westernization, showed little of its constructive potential, but plenty of its disruptive and corrosive effect, most evidently in non-Arab and economically well-developed Iran. There (as in Kemalist Turkey) a conservative Islamic clerisy was gradually antagonized into seeking to exploit a confluence of discontents. They tapped not only resentment of their ruler's misdeeds and errors, but decades of popular frustration, which was in part released in 1951 when a nationalist and radical government precipitated the country into the forefront of international affairs by nationalizing the country's oil industry. Since mainly British property was involved, this detonated a violent quarrel with the United Kingdom and caused much embarrassment to the United States (the Americans had been much less concerned by an earlier Iranian unilateral nullification of an oil concession to the USSR). The issue was soon tangled with domestic politics. At one moment the Shah fled the country, returning only after loyalist soldiers had overthrown the elected government. Further bloodshed followed, until in 1954 the situation was stabilized by the achievement of a successful election result by the monarchy's supporters. Thereafter, though, Iran was increasingly obviously an American client state. This, like the slowly unrolling consequences of economic development, exacerbated internal political dissent, though it was successfully contained for the next couple of decades by a strongly authoritarian regime. Iran prefigured some of the problems of other Islamic lands, too, where modernization was to chip away at deeply entrenched custom, outraging millions of the poor, and supplying them with motives to look to religious traditions for guidance and inspiration.

It was in this setting that the consequences of the establishment of

Israel in 1948 had to be worked out. Three or four thousand years earlier, Jews and Arabs had shared common origins; Hebrew and Arabic are both Semitic languages, part of a family of tongues spread over much of the Near East in ancient times, and later spread further by the coming of Islam. The teaching of Muhammad, too, had meant that most Arabs and Jews believed in the same God, though their cult practices were very different. Such historical ties, though, have long since lost any contemporary significance. The national principle now defines Israel and the quarrel between Jew and Arab is now talked about by many on both sides of it as irreconcilable. The problem of dealing with their relations has proved all the more intractable because it embodies an artificial antithesis: in common parlance 'Jew' has come to be taken to mean 'citizen of Israel' and 'Arab' to lump together meaningfully all of a highly diverse collection of peoples spread from the Tigris to the Nile, from the Yemen to Cilicia, many of whom attach more importance to Islam as a tie between them than they do to any national identity.

At moments in the recent past, Israeli–Arab quarrels have even seemed to threaten world war and the intensification of the Cold War, while a huge demand for oil in industrialized countries made them yet harder to solve. Such external influences created new interested parties, and revolutionized the region's politics. Not just because of her victorious survival of the crisis of 1948, Israel became in the next few years the focus of the hostility of Arab nationalism and pan-Arabism as even Great Britain had never been. The Arab masses could brood bitterly, and Arab rulers agree on the injustice of what was seen as the seizure of Arab lands, the plight of the Palestinian refugees from them in the camps where they turned from peasants into landless labourers, and the seeming neglect of their obligations by great powers, and the United Nations' inability to do anything.

After the defeat of 1948–9, though, Arab states had been for some time indisposed again to commit their forces openly. A formal state of war persisted between them and Israel, but a series of armistices established *de facto* borders for Jordan, Syria and Egypt solid enough to last until 1967. There were numerous troubles on those boundaries in the early 1950s, though, and many raids on Israel from Egyptian and Syrian territory by bands of young guerrilla soldiers recruited from the Palestinian refugee camps established in the Gaza Strip and in the sprawling 'West Bank' (of the river Jordan) which jutted out into Israeli territory and was part of Jordan. Immigration, hard work and money from the United States meanwhile steadily consolidated the new Israel. A siege psychology helped to stabilize its internal politics; the prestige of the party that had brought about the very existence of the new state was scarcely troubled while the Jews cultivated their new land and nurtured their nationhood. Within a few years they could show massive progress; desert was blossoming as the proverbial rose as new enterprises and settlements were established. The gap between Israel's per capita income and that of the more populous among the Arab states widened continually. It was a strategic help, too, that Jordan shared the Zionist interest in preventing the emergence of a Palestinian Arab state.

Arab resentments mounted. Foreign aid to their countries produced nothing like such dramatic change. Egyptians had suffered badly from inflation and the consequent fall in real wages during the Second World War, and now their country faced particularly grave problems of population growth. Even when the oil-producing Arab states began to benefit from growing revenue and a higher GDP, this, too, led to further strains and divisions. Contrasts between (and within) Arab states deepened. Small, wealthy, sometimes traditionally minded and conservative, sometimes nationalist and westernized, élites, usually uninterested in poverty-stricken peasants and slum-dwellers, ruled many of these countries. A new Arab political movement, the Ba'ath party, sought to exploit such contrasts, and attempted to synthesize Marxism and pan-Arabism. The Syrian and Iraqi wings of the movement (it was always strongest in those two countries) had fallen out with one another almost from the start, though.

Pan-Arabism had many divisive forces to overcome, for all the impulse to united action stemming from anti-Israeli and anti-western feeling. The Hashemite kingdoms, the Arabian and Gulf sheikdoms, and the Europeanized and urban countries of North Africa and the Levant all had widely divergent interests and very different historical traditions. Some of these states (Iraq, Jordan) were artificial creations whose shape had been dictated by the needs and wishes of European powers after 1918; some (Oman or the Yemen) were social and political fossils. Arabic was in many places a common language only within the mosque, and not all Arabic-speakers were Muslims. Nor were all Muslims united in belief: most of the Arab states contained substantial minorities of Shi'ites (the main body of that persuasion, of course, being found in non-Arab Iran). Though Islam was a shared heritage, therefore, it for a long time seemed to mean little in political terms; in 1950 few Muslims talked of Islam as a militant, aggressive faith. Israel provided the strongest tie between them: that of a common enemy.

THE EGYPTIAN REVOLUTION AND AFTER

Hopes were awoken among radical-minded Arabs in many countries by a revolution in Egypt. From it there eventually emerged in 1954 a young soldier, Gamal Abdel Nasser, as leader of a military junta that had overthrown the Egyptian monarchy two years before. For a time he looked to many to be a man who might both unite the Arab world against Israel and open the way to social change.

Egyptian nationalist feeling was at this time still finding its main focus and scapegoat in the British garrison in the Suez Canal Zone. To old grievances, too, was now added resentment against Great Britain for not thwarting the establishment of Israel. The British government, for its part, did its best to get along with Egypt's rulers, as with others in the region. It feared Soviet influence in an area still thought crucial to British communications and oil supplies. As the tankers passing through Suez increased in number, the Near and Middle East seemed no less important to British foreign policy than they had been before imperial withdrawal from India. Elsewhere in the Arab world, too, there were strong anti-western currents. In 1951 the king of Jordan had been assassinated; in order to survive, his successor had to show that he had severed an old special tie with Great Britain.

Further west, the Algerian problem had by this time turned into a revolutionary war against the French. The problems of the Maghreb had been brewing for a long time. As long ago as the 1870s and 1880s, Algerian insurrections had been crushed with great brutality by the

French army. In the 1930s, Tunisia had thrown up a true nationalist party, the Neo-Destour, and Morocco had an independence party in 1943. By 1945, there were several Algerian nationalist factions, too. But Algeria was different. No French government could easily abandon a country where there were a million residents of European stock, and whose government was technically and formally as much a part of metropolitan France as the Pas-de-Calais. Most of these European Algerians lived in the cities; 30,000 of them were farmers, producing a third of Algeria's agricultural output.[11] Meanwhile, something like a quarter of the Muslim population of the Maghreb was landless and this was both a root and symptom of the long-running land problem and the poverty associated with it. To complicate matters and excite appetites, oil and natural gas were being discovered in the Sahara in the 1950s. Nasser's rhetoric of social reform and nationalism had in this context an appeal well beyond Egypt. As the French began to be aware that they were fighting what soon looked like another full-scale colonial war in Algeria, they identified him as a danger.[12]

Nasser added to his popularity by negotiating a successful agreement with Great Britain for the evacuation of the Suez base. The Americans, increasingly aware of Soviet menace in the Middle East, inclined for a while to look on him with favour as an anti-colonialist and potential client (as they were to do on Sukarno in the 1960s).[13] Yet Nasser's appeal to them soon waned. The guerrilla raids on Israel from the Gaza Strip (the Egyptian territory where the most important Palestinian refugee camps lay) provoked irritation and the American administration were inevitably sensitive to pressure from Jewish supporters of Israel in the USA. When Nasser carried off an arms deal with Czechoslovakia on the security of the cotton crop and Egypt recognized communist China, second thoughts about him further hardened; perhaps he was taking sides in the Cold War. In 1950, the British, French and Americans had agreed to limit their supplies of arms to Middle

[11] S. Amin, *The Maghreb in the Modern World* (Harmondsworth, 1970), pp.84–5.
[12] In 1956 the French conceded independence to both Morocco and Tunisia, in the case of Morocco after considerable violence, while in Tunisia fighting went on sporadically until 1961. In both the French retained military bases after formal independence.
[13] And, somewhat more cynically, Saddam Hussein in the 1980s.

East states and to provide them only on such terms as would keep a balance between Israel and the Arabs. By way of showing their displeasure over the Czech deal, an American and British offer to finance a cherished internal development project, a high dam on the Nile, was now withdrawn. As a riposte, Nasser seized the assets of the private company that owned and ran the Suez Canal, saying its profits should finance the dam.

Nasser's act touched an old nerve of British imperial sensibility. Instincts only half-disciplined by imperial withdrawal seemed for once to be in step both with anti-communism and with friendship towards more traditional Arab states whose rulers were beginning to look askance at Nasser as a revolutionary radical. The British prime minister, too, was obsessed with a false analogy which led him to see Nasser as a new Hitler, as a dictator to be checked before he embarked upon a career of successful aggression (and he was not alone in this).[14] As for the French, they were aggrieved by Nasser's support for the Algerian rebels (though it was remarkably unproductive of material support) and happy to join in punitive action against him. Both nations formally protested over the Canal's seizure. In collusion with that of Israel, their governments began to plot Nasser's overthrow.

The outcome was an Israeli invasion of Egypt in October 1956; its aim, the Israeli government announced, was to destroy the bases from which Arab terrorists harassed their settlements. The British and French governments at once said freedom of movement through the Canal was in danger and called for a ceasefire. When Nasser rejected this they launched (on Guy Fawkes' Day) first an air attack and then a sea-borne assault on Egypt. Collusion with Israel was denied, but the denial was preposterous; it was a lie, and, worse still, an incredible one from the outset. Soon, the Americans were thoroughly alarmed; they feared the USSR would draw the dividends on what looked like a renewal of imperialist adventure. Their financial pressure forced a British acceptance of a ceasefire negotiated by the United Nations. The Anglo-French adventure thus collapsed in withdrawal and humiliation. Before long, the British prime minister resigned; his French

[14] As late as 1 November 1956, *after* the Israeli attack on Egypt, the *New York Times* was still drawing the parallel between Nasser's action and Hitler's militarization of the Rhineland only twenty years earlier.

equivalent remained in office without difficulty, but with a further diminution of confidence among French soldiers that the politicians had the nerve to back them up in the end.

Suez looked (and was) a western political disaster, but it was far from an unqualified triumph for Nasser. He had not won a victory, but had been saved. In the long run its main importance was psychological and presentational. The British suffered most; it cost them much goodwill, particularly within the Commonwealth, and squandered confidence in the sincerity of their retreat from empire. It shook their faith in American goodwill and inflicted a financial and economic crisis on them. As for the Arab peoples, the operation merely confirmed their hatred of Israel; the conviction that she was indissolubly linked to the West made some of them yet more receptive to Soviet blandishment. Some in western Europe and the USA thought, too, that Suez had distracted western attention at a crucial moment in the Cold War from eastern Europe (where a popular revolution in Hungary against its Soviet satellite government had been crushed by the Soviet army as the western powers bickered amongst themselves). Nasser's prestige benefited, too. As those in the Maghreb saw it, Egyptians had effectively thrown off the imperialist yoke and could (and would) now help the Algerian rebels more. Nevertheless, the region was actually left by the crisis much as before, re-embittered though its quarrels might be. Suez changed nothing in the Middle East balance, or in the Cold War.

The Arabic-speaking world changed much more in 1958. Syria and Egypt then joined one another in a new United Arab Republic of the two countries. This was not to last and proved of little more than symbolic and inspirational effect, though it led to a meeting of Moroccan, Tunisian and Algerian nationalists at Tangier to air hopes of a united Maghreb (though nothing came of them). In the end, one session of a Syrian–Egyptian parliament was eventually held in 1960 but a coup in Syria followed which dissolved the union. Syria then entered upon three years of disaster and paralysis in which soldiers, pro-Nasser agitators and Ba'ath party supporters intrigued and sometimes fought for power. Nineteen fifty-eight, though, had brought other more important changes to Arab countries. In July the Iraqi monarchy was swept away by revolution in which the king and his prime minister were both murdered. A few days later British forces were summoned to Jordan to sustain its government against pro-Nasser elements. At the end of the year, even the Sudan underwent a military coup that overthrew the existing constitutional regime. Sporadically, fighting had meanwhile continued on the Syrian–Israeli border, where the Jews were holding Palestinian guerrilla forces in check.

ALGERIAN INDEPENDENCE

Overwhelmingly the most important development of 1958 in the Arab world was, for all that, none of these, but came in Algeria, where the revolutionary war, led since 1954 by the Front de Libération Nationale (FLN), had developed into a bloody and unrelenting struggle not only with the French garrison and its Muslim supporters, but with virtually the whole European population. FLN forces committed appalling atrocities in the field; French soldiers tortured prisoners in their interrogation centres. Increasing violence and savagery further irritated the frustrated *pieds-noirs* (as the European Algerians were called) who more and more inclined to believing that their government was unwilling to act effectively to suppress the rebellion. Feeling was polarized and Muslims who still wished to remain loyal to France were frightened into disloyalty. The detonator for a crisis came with the murder of three French prisoners by the FLN on 9 May 1958. It was scarcely one of the more terrible atrocities of a war abundant in horrors, but there followed a rising on 13 May against the authorities in Algiers. With the collaboration of discontented generals, an evocatively named 'Committee of Public Safety'[15] was set up to coordinate repression of the nationalists. The governor-general had already left for Paris bearing a barely disguised ultimatum from the soldiers threatening insurrection if parliament would not clearly endorse a policy of *Algérie Française*. His residency was sacked in his absence by the angry *pieds-noirs*.

[15] The most celebrated 'Committee of Safety' had been set up during the French Revolution in April 1793. Legendarily, it had saved the first republic from extinction in 1793–4.

This was the beginning of the end of the Fourth French Republic which had been set up at the end of the Second World War after liberation of the home territory. Its politicians were bitterly divided over North Africa. France had already lost Indo-China; the prospect that she might also lose Algeria, where more than a million French citizens of European stock lived, had been too much for the *pieds-noirs*. They were happy to cast off the authority of Paris in order to work with the soldiers, many of whom were bitter at being asked to do what they already felt was an impossible job if they were not supported whole-heartedly in Paris.

Two days after the Algiers rising, General de Gaulle broke a long political silence by announcing from his retirement that he held himself ready to assume the powers of the state; there had already been shouts of '*Vive de Gaulle*' in Algiers. The last throes of the Fourth Republic now began. On 29 May the president of the Republic called on the general to form a government of national safety, saying that the country was in danger of civil war. To few people's surprise, the invitation was accepted. A few months later, in October, the constitution of a new (Fifth) Republic was promulgated and in December de Gaulle was elected its first president, winning nearly four-fifths of the votes cast.

The war in Algeria continued. In September 1958 the FLN announced in Cairo the formation of a provisional Algerian government whose aim was the restoration (as they put it) of Algerian independence. In Algiers the early faith in de Gaulle's commitment to maintaining the integrity of France's possessions in North Africa soon faded. Dismay and bitter hatred began to replace the enthusiasm that had greeted his carefully misleading pronouncements to the settlers.[16] Soldiers began to turn against him, too. But he was already by then taking effective steps to restore control over and discipline in the army. In April 1961 control of Algiers was lost by Paris for a couple of days, but an attempted coup by *pieds-noirs* and soldiers then collapsed. The French government finally opened secret negotiations with the Algerian rebels and from a much less advantageous

[16] The most famous and ambiguous was his first: 'Je vous ai compris' – words received with wild enthusiasm by the *pieds-noirs*.

position than when de Gaulle had come to power. In July 1962, after a referendum, and the deaths, over eight years, of perhaps a million people, France formally granted independence to a new Algeria. As Libya had emerged from United Nations trusteeship to independence in 1951, the entire North African coast outside the tiny Spanish enclaves of Ceuta and Melilla was now clear of European overlordship.[17]

Yet external influences continued to bedevil the history of Arabic-speaking Islam as they had done ever since the Ottoman conquests centuries before. Now, though, they often did so in covert fashion, as the United States and Russia sought to buy friends. In this competition, the United States laboured under a handicap; no American president or Congress could abandon Israel, though President Eisenhower had been brave enough to face down the Jewish vote over Suez.[18] American policy-making was nonetheless increasingly to cling to its only ally in a region from which the old stabilizing influence of the imperial powers had so evidently been driven. In spite of America's clean hands at Suez, therefore, Egyptian and Syrian policy continued to sound anti-American and prove irritating. The USSR, on the other hand, had dropped Israel as soon as supporting it ceased to be an anti-British stance. Soviet policy swung round to take a steady pro-Arab line, assiduously fanning Arab resentment. Marginally, too, the Kremlin was to earn a cheap bonus of Arab approval in the later 1960s by resuming old Russian traditions and harrying its own Jews.

[17] Since 1961, when she appealed to the United Nations to recognize them, Morocco has asserted her rights to the Spanish enclaves, so far without effect, but with insistence that Morocco would enter and occupy them, resuming sovereignty, in the event of any Spanish recovery of Gibraltar from British sovereignty.
[18] In an election year, too.

BOOK 6

SHIFTING FOUNDATIONS

18

Changing Minds

When the canvas is that of world history, it is tempting to say that very little can be usefully said about broad patterns of mentality, intellectual and cultural change and to leave it there. There is too much relevant evidence and the possible scope of inquiry is too vast to support easy generalization. Whose minds, after all, are changing? About those of the vast majority of our fellow human beings we know nothing. Even their behaviour is only sporadically observed or recorded in ways that easily reveal the thinking behind it. About the articulate minorities who record and publish their thoughts – not only writers and publicists, but also artists and scientists of all kinds, politicians, ministers of religion and mere obsessives – we know much more, but even that, taken alone, can for all its volume give us only a lopsided perspective on the history of ideas in this century. It can tell us only about the changing minds of small segments of different societies – and usually segments confined to our own western world, too.

Just a little firmer ground can be sought in long-term historical shifts even if they cannot be accurately measured. For the last few centuries at least it is apparent that the ideas of small minorities within western civilization have exercised a disproportionate influence on world history. In recognizing that, it does not matter that only a very small proportion of the human race knows what, let us say, the laws of thermodynamics may be; all the science now done in the world is western science that incorporates and takes account of those laws. Nor is any country unaffected by that fact, for science is practised in some measure in all of them. To take a different example, not all, but overwhelmingly most of the government going on in the world today is conducted in a way that pays at least lip-service to some of the major political and social ideas – democracy, nationality, sovereignty – thrashed out in western societies over the last three centuries. Great traditional religions and cultures are visibly under challenge in our own day by modes of thinking once confined only to those parts of the world dominated by cultures of European origin. They have now spread more widely than ever, being adopted and acclimatized in very different and once alien cultural settings. If there is a salient fact about the history of ideas in the twentieth century, this is surely it. There has been an always-hastening onrush of modernity rolling outwards from western civilization, whether for good or ill is irrelevant. Western ideas have been at the heart of it.

It has been one notable and paradoxical consequence that even the colossal disasters of this century appear to have left more people than ever before believing that human life and the condition of the world can be improved. Moreover, their behaviour suggests, they believe they should be. People everywhere seem to be less willing to accept that unavoidable, irredeemable pain and tragedy are part of human destiny. Yet until quite recently such a new, optimistic idea was confined to cultures of European origins, and it still remains unfamiliar to many of the human race, and in most parts of the globe. Few could yet formulate it clearly or consciously, even if asked; yet if it is true it must affect behaviour everywhere. It has almost certainly been spread less by conscious philosophical, moral or even political preaching (though there has been plenty of that) than by material changes. They have everywhere broken up the cake of custom because they suggest the astonishing proposition that change is possible, that things need not always be what they have been.

Perhaps the paradox can be pressed further, for such a fundamentally optimistic orientation has established itself just when there is more evidence available than there ever was in the days of gods and magic to suggest that human beings have less power than they thought to control their own destinies. We now often hear that our actions are powerfully shaped by genetic endowment or by childhood experience, for example; both sides of the 'nature versus nurture' argument thus can be used to diminish confidence in the autonomous personality. No doubt most people in the world are unaware of the very specific and technical grounds that exist for holding such views. They have seeped in crude form into some areas of popular culture in developed societies, though, and coexist there with unexamined, sometimes contradictory perceptions suggesting, quite in contrast, that something ought to be done about the ills of our existence because something always can be done about them. It should not worry us that such incoherence exists in the way the world is seen by millions of people. It is interesting that it does. It may at least be possible that it is in a search for the origins of such ideas that the best clues to the history of the changing consciousness of growing numbers of men and women in this century lie, and that change in them makes up most of what we may call the history of ideas – or should do.

THE MANAGEMENT OF THE NATURAL WORLD

A truly decisive change in the human mind, one of those identifying the modern era, thus came about with the vulgarization (first in developed societies of the West, and to some extent the world round) of the idea that humanity could in principle control and manipulate the rest of nature at least on this planet in its own interests. The instrument that demonstrated this proposition was science and especially science expressed in technology. In that way its power strikes laymen even when they do not understand it – and hundreds of millions of them do not even know that nuclear fission is used to generate energy, that computers can control machine tools, or that biochemical research produces better medicine. Yet already by 1950 modern industry was dependent on science, directly or indirectly, consciously so or not, and so was much of the shape of daily life – the overcoming of darkness, for instance – in many societies. Moreover, the transformation of fundamental science into an end product is now often very rapid, so that its impact is now almost immediate. The generalization of the use of the motor car after the principle of the internal combustion engine had been grasped took about half a century; the gap between the discovery of penicillin in 1928 and its large-scale manufacture was less than twenty years. But it has to be recalled that such acceleration is not apparent in all branches of science; they do not necessarily move abreast. The advance from nuclear fission to nuclear fusion as a source of usable energy seemed nearer a half-century ago than it does today.

Once we go beyond the immediate awe awakened by the technology scientists and engineers provide, even educated people find it much more difficult than in the past to weigh the true importance of what scientists do. Nor does the popular understanding of science appear to spread so rapidly as does impatience with it when problems prove recalcitrant. The growing complexity of scientific work, and the way it has evolved both make lay understanding more difficult. Already before 1914 boundaries between individual sciences, some of them intelligible and usefully distinct fields of study for two or three centuries, were tending to blur and even to disappear. The impact of electromagnetic research in physics was one hint of what was to come. The full implications, though, have only begun to appear very lately. Most of the early twentieth-century revolution in physics (for example) remains not only unintelligible to all but a few, but is unknown to the vast majority of mankind. Even that majority, though, was to have by mid-century, in the appearance of nuclear weapons and nuclear power, first-hand evidence that drove home more decisively than ever the crude notion that science was a matter of mastering nature through technology. That suggests that what is usually thought of as the 'history of ideas' – the evolution of high culture and landmarks in philosophical, scientific and aesthetic development – may not be the best way to approach its recent history. Great names such as are customarily associated with such a history of ideas in western cultures seem to have become harder to identify. Late twentieth-century successors to Marx, Darwin, Freud do not readily spring to mind; there seem to be fewer system-makers and redefiners of fundamental philosophical orientation about nowadays. Yet ideas matter as much in history as they ever did, though perhaps at a different level. In particular, science has continued its advance so as to have become, with its technology, the most important single force directly or indirectly changing the world since 1950.

The idolizing of science, of course, was well under way by 1901.

To many people then alive it already seemed to be the most efficient and productive way of understanding and managing nature yet discovered. For them it had shown it could out-perform religion and magic in that task. This belief has now spread much more widely, but in a paradoxical way. A century ago, even well-educated persons in western societies were still hardly disturbed by the transformation of physics already under way. Yet their views of science, too, were soon to be dislocated beyond repair by the exploration of thermodynamics and the discovery of radio waves: radioactivity, relativity, fluid and quantum mechanics were all to make it even more difficult for the educated lay mind in the early twentieth century to arrive at an understanding of the contemporary state of science comparable to, say, an eighteenth-century amateur's capacity to understand Newton's universe. Since 1950, any such widely-shared lay understanding is virtually impossible.

Nor is this all. While mass communications have helped to spread (notably, outside the western world) an unprecedented awareness of what science can do, fundamental research has changed the landscape of the sciences themselves so as to make them more difficult to approach. Distinctions between once-autonomous fields or activities – physics, chemistry, biology, mathematics – have crumbled. Some sciences have blurred into one another, wholly new sciences have appeared, and problems that were previously kept apart have been consciously rolled together. Even by 1950, much more had disappeared than just a long dominant set of general laws. The content and the idea of science changed, too. Any one of its great traditional divisions was by then beyond the mastery of a single mind. The conflations required by, say, importing physical theory into neurology or of mathematics into biology put new barriers in the way of attaining that synthesis of knowledge that had been one of the long-cherished visions of the nineteenth century. The rate of acquisition of new knowledge became faster than ever and it could not be easily ordered in a comprehensive picture.

The consequence has been that while the science originally conceived in Europe and later practised in all western countries has now spread and is the dominant model worldwide, this success has been accompanied by no similar spread of understanding. That understanding was always a matter for minorities; now it is one for minorities of specialists, too. Awareness of the importance of science, though, is a different matter. That is more widespread than ever, simply because of the visibility of what science has been able to do, its provision of wonders and benefits. In most countries, millions more than ever before are actually taught some science at school, which should encourage such recognition. Yet for most people in the world it may well be true that what science does or can do forms only, at best, a quasi-magical background to their lives.

POWER

Some of science's most impressive achievements in this century have been devoted to the provision of power. Sometimes this has been shown in the crudest sense, through destruction. The importance of the revolution in physics first came home to many people in this way. Three years after Rutherford had said that nuclear physics would never have any practical usefulness, Einstein wrote to the president of the United States to warn him that in the near future it was likely that a bomb of unprecedented power could be made by releasing the energy contained in a mass of uranium. Six years and four days later, the first 'atom bomb', as it was then called, was exploded over Hiroshima. Nuclear weapons of still greater power were soon to be produced. The first practical employment of a new form of energy, that of the atomic nucleus, was, therefore, tragic and sinister. The knowledge acquired in building the bomb was nonetheless soon utilized to provide power for peaceful uses. Energy was taken in the form of heat from a nuclear reaction to make steam to drive turbines that would generate electricity. This new source of energy was tapped for its first peaceful public use when a large nuclear power station for the supply of electricity was opened in England in 1956. Not much later, reactors were at work generating power in many countries. Soon the first nuclear-powered ships were at sea.

The share of the world's energy needs met at present by nuclear sources is small, but the amount of power thus generated is already vast. This has been the work of the second twentieth-century energy revolution; the first was the full exploitation of electricity, already in use well before 1901, but most widely available as a source of power only after that date. To coal-burning and oil-burning plants, and to hydro-electric developments, we owe large-scale and cheap production of electricity, but its revolutionary effect was not only a matter of scientific and technological, but of administrative and organizational innovation, notably the building of great national distribution systems. Nuclear energy has now added to the supply (roughly a quarter of French electricity is now derived from nuclear power); it is an attractive resource to countries seeking to reduce their reliance on non-renewable fossil fuels. To coal and oil, though, has also been added natural gas, which has since 1950 become the source for about one-fifth of world electrical generation. The even greater attractiveness – in theory – of deriving energy not from nuclear fission, but from fusion has, however, continued to excite scientists and to draw investment though a usable technology remains elusive. Meanwhile, the use of other sources of energy has become more feasible. In some countries substantial wind-farms have been built to 'harvest' the energy of the winds. Solar power has been tapped sufficiently to provide motive power for a few ingenious cars, and is in reasonably wide domestic use – where the sun shines – to provide heating and lighting. Perhaps the most striking use of solar energy, though, has been in furthering scientific investigation itself, by providing power for instruments in the exploration of space.

COMMUNICATIONS AND INFORMATION TECHNOLOGY

The interaction of events and trends in all parts of the globe as never before suggests another way into the history of mentality. Such interaction would not have been possible without the communications that have tied humanity together in this century with unprecedented rapidity and a wholly new intimacy and immediacy. Hard as it is to be sure of what are the most influential messages among all those now spread so widely, it is at least possible to sense the revolutionary way in which their number, speed of transmission and immediacy have all increased in this century. Much of that story is one of continuing technological advance, but the communications revolution embodies far more than that. It has been a major determinant of the spread of new ways of thinking. For a jump of comparable importance, we have to go back to the transformation of European culture by printing.

Unsurprisingly, the military needs of a violent century were a major stimulus to innovations in radio and telecommunications. In 1935, near Daventry, the first successful experiment was carried out with an apparatus built to detect the position of an aircraft, through the deflection of a radio beam. From this came 'Radio-location', later better known as Radar (from 'Radio Detection And Ranging'), a system of locating aircraft before they were in sight, which helped the Royal Air Force to defeat the German Luftwaffe in 1940 and thus made a decisive contribution to world history only a few years after its invention. But in the 1930s there were at least eight nations working on such devices. The great Marconi demonstrated a system to Mussolini and his generals in 1935 and experiments with large airships carrying special equipment may well have provided Germany with better radar sets than the British had when the war broke out. War itself then vastly extended the use of the technique beyond aircraft location and gun ranging and in due course the peace released its enormous potential for other applications. Virtually all navigation at sea and in the air now incorporates radar 'fixing'; it provides safe navigation in bad weather, and safe handling of air traffic in crowded air lanes, to take only two examples.

Most of the important later advances in radar can be traced back to the British invention, in 1940, of a new small source of short waves of great power, the cavity magnetron, which gave the country a decisive lead in airborne radar for the next two years. Television was to be a future beneficiary of this device. More and more sophisticated electrical and radio equipment has been made possible by smaller and smaller sources of power. The ordinary valve was displaced by the production of the transistor in 1948 in the American Bell laboratories. Since then, the microcircuit and the silicon chip have successively opened vast new technological horizons because of the progressive 'miniaturization' (a post-war word) which they made possible. This was the key to the rapid commercial development of a new world, that of information technology.

The nineteenth century had produced mechanical calculating and sorting machines, relatively crude devices that could nonetheless speed up simple operations of information handling by a large factor. A real qualitative and quantitative leap only took place, though, when the science of 'electronics' was applied to such tasks.[1] The computers that it made possible so speeded up calculation and information retrieval that scientific advances could be made which would without them have required decades of work by thousands of highly trained personnel to arrive at the same result. By 1961, there were 4,000 computers at work in the world; ten years later the figure was about 150,000. Millions are now used in government, industry, transport, business, academic life, and the home (at least in the developed world); much of the daily life we now take for granted would be impossible without them. Modern information technology has already brought about a social change comparable to the coming of literacy itself.

For all its importance, though, this huge topic still resists historical comprehension. It has too many aspects. Familiar technology had begun at a very early date its slow liberation from dependence on humans with high levels of motor skills. The application of feedback and servo-mechanisms to more and more machinery was hugely accelerated in the Second World War. Information systems based on storage of punched tape or cards that could be automatically sorted were already familiar by 1939. The coming of the information technology age, though, dwarfed all such earlier changes. If there is a single step crucial to its rapid diffusion it was the discovery of the properties

---

[1] The first lecturer in electronics in the British university system was appointed in 1941 at Southampton, where the first British department with the word in its title ('Electronics, Telecommunication and Radio Engineering') was opened six years later. A proto-computer ('Colossus') was built for Bletchley Park's decoding operations in 1941 and what the United States Institute of Electrical and Electronics Engineers terms the 'first true computer', 'Baby', at Manchester in 1945. By then, Harvard had in 1944 put into operation the IBM Automatic Sequence Control Calculator that was driven by instructions on paper tape, though carrying them out electromechanically. Another machine for which claims of priority are made was ENIAC, which ran at Philadelphia in 1946, but does not in its early form meet the strict definition of a 'stored program' machine (like 'Baby').

of single-crystal silicon and the creation of the silicon 'chip' carrying electronic circuitry. Computer programs can now be left to interact with sensing devices, to receive and store data, to detect and compare patterns, to discriminate among stored data, to search memories past and present, and to make decisions about action. The impact of this on human work – indeed, on all sorts of human activity – has been immense and is already immeasurable.

We can still only sense the scale of the revolution in the provision of information, one of the greatest cultural changes in history. It has already displayed abundant paradoxes. A social historian might reflect, for example, that although our new powers of communication and information appear to militate so powerfully against the weight of cultural tradition and the historical past, among the earliest evident beneficiaries of the spread of television were the most conservative and traditional forms of religious faith in the United States. The introduction of electronics-based information technology to western culture (it can be approximately dated from the 1940s) announced the latest of those waves of innovation provoking 'industrial revolutions' since the eighteenth century. Since then, it has swept through societies worldwide. Information technology has made anything that requires the understanding of large and complex systems vulnerable to exploration as never before. It is not only a matter of natural science, engineering, economics; all of them had long been accessible to numerical exploration, if on a limited scale. The computer (to speak loosely) has opened up to our gaze biological systems (notably those explored by genetics), medical processes, the understanding of traffic flows, telecommunication networks, governments, industrial companies and ecological systems.[2] All these can be 'modelled' and simulated as never before, while other programs invent ways to overcome the difficulties they pose, and even make it possible to create 'natural' facts (new molecules, new species). Meanwhile, the demand for information technology remains a dynamic force for growth in its own development and manufacturing industries. The potential historical impact of information technology is surely far from exhausted.

As an exemplary instance of the accelerating pace of technological

---

[2] The Human Genome project (see below) is a good example.

change in the unrolling twentieth century, too, information technology can hardly be bettered. In 1965 one of the founders[3] of what is now the world's largest maker of microprocessor chips used in personal computers formulated what came to be called (after him) Moore's law. This 'law' stated, originally, that the processing power of a chip would double every eighteen months, since technological advance would make it possible to double every eighteen months the number of transistors that could be packed on to a given wafer of silicon. This prediction was then revised to cover periods of two years, but on that basis it was borne out over the next twenty. No other technology has ever improved so rapidly for so long. Between 1970 and 1990 the transistor density on a chip went up from 1,000 to 1,000,000 per chip; if aeroplanes had improved so much in the same time, it has been pointed out, a London to New York flight would now take five minutes or so and would cost only a few pence.

Its author has himself predicted the eventual breakdown of Moore's law: exponential growth is usually curtailed in the end. Yet that does not mean that there is not life in it yet. Nor does it mean that information technology will now remain in the channels already explored. The most important innovation of recent years already shows this: the Internet. This is a method of allowing computer users to share data – which includes text, images and music, as well as numbers – over telephone networks. It provides both a carrier and personal mail system, whereby messages can be sent from one individual to another, and a library of data or messages for anyone who wishes to make them available broadcast, whether a great national or university library, or an obsessive individual. Curiously, this system grew for a long time in a quite informal way, originating in a network of amateurs in the 1960s. Then, in 1988, the Internet began to double in size annually. The World Wide Web came into existence in 1993. Given the colossal accretion of communication it offers, an effort is needed to remember that something like half the world's present population may as yet still never have made an ordinary telephone call in their lives.

Unfortunately, any selection of instances of the way in which new

[3] Mr Gordon Moore, of the company Intel.

technology has had deeper and more remote effects than might have been anticipated has to leave out others that some people might think just as important. If the speed with which the change has descended on us can be easily recognized, the ramifications of its effects, above all in communications and information technology, have now gone far beyond what was envisaged at mid-century by any except a few visionary experts. By the 1980s, they were changing politics and international relations. They did not merely offer new opportunities to politicians in democracies to enlarge their audiences by presenting policies for debate, or to non-democratic regimes to pump out propaganda; both had been already made possible by radio broadcasting in the 1930s. What may have been more important was the way in which better communication undermined what had been in some countries near-monopolies of information by their governments.

In the 1980s this was to be shown dramatically by the influence of western European and satellite television in eastern Europe, especially in the GDR, from which its signals could not be excluded as radio signals had formerly been. Satellite transmission proved particularly important. That the outcome of greater 'transparency' could be embarrassing even in what was proclaimed to be a democracy was vividly shown when the Indian government found, to its dismay, that it could not prevent knowledge of inter-communal troubles reaching its people. Before satellite transmission, Indian television had been totally controlled by government and operated only through terrestrial channels. Its supply of information had therefore been manageable, and the dangers of inflaming communal feeling had been confinable. In the early 1990s, though, a huge diffusion of satellite discs and television sets in semi-public places had already been achieved. When a Muslim mosque of especial sanctity was destroyed by Hindu zealots in the northern city of Ayodhya in December 1992, pictures of the riot were quickly available to millions. There followed a wave of rioting often hundreds of miles away from the original seat of disorder and in great cities such as Calcutta and Bombay. In a month or so, well over 1,000 people were reported killed. Better access to information thus proved an explosive and ambiguous benefit to Indian democracy. Nor did greater transparency affect only the domestic management of news by governments. There are also new possibilities of international publicity. An outstanding instance came in China in 1989. A situation of growing tenseness in Beijing was then monitored for weeks by foreign news-gatherers who were able to transmit immediate images of what was going on, right up to its tragic culmination in Tiananmen Square.[4]

THE LIFE SCIENCES

For all the money that continued to be poured into high-energy physics by governments, and into computer software by businessmen, an impressionistic judgement might be that the intellectual baton passed after 1950 to what were increasingly termed the 'life' sciences. New specialities blossomed within them – cybernetic physiology, electron microscopy, biochemical genetics, molecular biology and, at last, genetic engineering. Like earlier work in physics, much rested on nineteenth-century foundations. It had then been discovered that cells could divide and that they developed individually. By 1901 the idea that individual cells provided a good approach to the study of life was familiar. This now became a major theme of biological research. Nineteenth-century biological science had also created a new discipline, genetics (not yet named in 1901), the study of the inheritance by offspring of characteristics from parents. Darwin had invoked the principle of inheritance as the means of propagation of traits favoured by natural selection. The first steps towards under-standing the mechanism underlying this were those of an Austrian monk, Gregor Mendel. His breeding experiments on pea plants led him to conclude that there existed hereditary units controlling the expression of traits passed from parents to offspring. In 1909 a Dane gave them the name 'genes'.[5]

Experiments next revealed a visible location for genes in chromo-somes. In the 1940s it was shown that genes controlled the chemical

---

[4] See below, p.797.
[5] Johannsen. The name 'genetics' had already been given in 1902 to this whole branch of study by the Englishman William Bateson.

structure of protein, the most important constituent of cells. In 1944 the first step was taken towards locating the specific effective agent in bringing about changes in certain bacteria, and therefore in controlling protein structure. In the 1950s it was confirmed that the agent was deoxyribonucleic acid, or DNA. Its physical structure (which became widely known as the 'double helix') was established in 1953. This is the carrier of the genetic information which determines the pattern of life itself, the particular synthesis of protein molecules which lies at its basis. The chemical mechanisms underlying the diversity of biological phenomena and of mankind itself were at last accessible and the era of molecular genetics began. It would imply a transformation of human self-perception unprecedented since the onset of Darwinian ideas a century earlier.

The identification and analysis of DNA has been the most conspicuous single step taken so far towards the understanding of nature at the level of the shaping of life-forms, and therefore of their effective human manipulation. Once again, new definitions of fields of study and new applications followed. 'Molecular biology', 'biotechnology' and 'genetic engineering' have become familiar terms in the last quarter of the century. The genes of some organisms could, it was soon shown, be altered so as to give those organisms new and desirable characteristics. By manipulating their growth processes, yeast and other micro-organisms could be made to produce novel substances. This was one of the first extensions of the new science; the empirical biotechnology which had been accumulated informally by millennia of experience in the making of bread, wine and cheese could at last be overtaken and often dispensed with.[6] Genetic modification of bacteria can now be carried out so as to grow enzymes, hormones or other chemicals. By the end of the 1980s a worldwide collaborative investigation, the Human Genome Project, was under way whose almost unimaginable aim was the mapping of the human genetic apparatus so as to identify the position, structure and function of every human gene. There are up to 100,000 of them in each human

[6] With varying results. Readers interested in the calculus of human happiness may like to reflect on the effects this has already shown in wine-making, those (apparently beneficial) in cheese-making, and the spreading prevalence of mediocre mass-produced bread.

cell, each of which has up to 30,000 pairs of the four basic chemical units that form the genetic code. To deal with these numbers would not have been practical without the computer. Yet screening for the presence of certain defective genes, and even the replacement of some of them, is now commonplace.

The medical implications of such work are enormous. We can at least speculate that, within two or three decades, there may exist techniques making it possible to avoid the infliction on unborn children of congenital blindness or deafness. Less obvious in its implications, but perhaps of even greater immediate medical importance was the sequencing in 1995 of the genomes of two bacteria that are disease-carriers. Much smaller than the human genome (the smallest bacterial genomes have as few as half a million 'letters' in their genetic makeup, while the human genome has 3 billion) the work now being addressed to the sequencing of other bacteria – that of tuberculosis among them – could throw unprecedented light on the resistance of microbes to the human immune system. At a more obvious level, that of day-to-day police work, what is called DNA 'fingerprinting' has been used (inter-estingly, in the case of two American presidents) to identify individuals from blood or semen samples. Somewhat more eerily, a patent has been registered for a laboratory mouse genetically prone to cancer. Then, in 1996 British scientists achieved the successful 'cloning' (that is, genetically exact reproduction) of a sheep, a much larger mammal. Progress in these matters has thus in some ways been startlingly rapid – and disconcerting: it has seemed conceivable to some that work now under way could realize the old Enlightenment dream of a totally predictable humanity.

Such immense progress has been dependent on advances in other sciences than the biological. It owes as much to the availability of computers to handle very large quantities of data as did physiology's first golden age, in the seventeenth century, to the then new microscope. It is a good instance of the way scientific advance accelerates by incorporating new technology, by applying existing techniques and by rescrutinizing settled assumptions and landmarks. Beyond saying that what is being done has potentially enormous effects, though, it is sensible not to try to predict what cultural, social, or political effects will follow. For all the recent fundamental work in the 'life sciences', it is unlikely that even their approximate ultimate importance can at present be assessed by any of us.

MEDICAL SCIENCE

Yet while it seems overwhelmingly likely that in developed societies there is greater public awareness of what scientists are doing than in any earlier century, it is not easy to form any picture of the way science is seen by most human beings or if, indeed, they have any picture of it all as an entity. No doubt, though, many people the world round are aware of this century's continuing applications of science to medical problems. Scientific medicine has in the second half of the twentieth century advanced on every front to which it has addressed itself and in so doing has indirectly contributed to the power of another great radical force transforming world history, population pressure. Some problems have proved harder to tackle than others – cancer, for example, and mental illness still await any great advance such as those obtained in the last century in dealing with the old infectious killers. Hitherto unknown diseases, on the other hand, have been identified for the first time. Acquired immunodeficiency syndrome (AIDS), caused by the human immunodeficiency virus (HIV) was first reported only in 1981 (though it has been argued that earlier instances can now be identified) and work is already well advanced in evolving appropriate prophylaxis, though there is as yet no remedy for the disease. In surgery and therapeutic treatment, technology has now brought to bear resources inconceivable in 1901, when the first 'x-rays' represented the best scientific medicine available.

Many of the most important medical victories of this century, though, have not been won in contests with individual maladies. A vast body of research work in nutrition (for which the identification of the vitamins by chemists was crucial) has probably done almost as much, though indirectly, to cut into mortality rates as the creation of specific drugs. So have better nursing practice, better child-rearing education and midwifery, and better organization and management. Statistically, the most important medical change of the century may well have been the slow advance of the public provision of medical care and its input into social engineering in both developed and under-developed countries. Concern for public health has increasingly led to action by public authorities which has produced comprehensive systems of medical provision by the state, something hardly conceivable a century ago. This has had major – and perhaps its greatest – effects in increasing life expectancy.

Important advances in the use of vaccination came about as a result of the identification of virus diseases and, as a result, the control of some diseases in places where they have long been endemic became at last a practical proposition. The World Health Organization has been able to record the worldwide disappearance of smallpox. Polio, in spite of sporadic recurrence, has been largely eliminated in Europe. Tuberculosis, on the other hand, which appeared to be in terminal retreat in the 1960s, has surged back as a threat to city-dwellers in some countries. Further progress in dealing with infectious disease was not only achieved by better medication of those who suffered from them and the development of effective vaccines, but by attacks on the vectors of disease. One of the most important developments out of wartime need was DDT, available in quantity by 1944 and first used on a large scale to deal with an epidemic of typhus (carried by the louse) at Naples. Its biggest impact, though, was on malaria, a disease from which it was calculated that 700 million people were suffering in 1939. Over large areas of the world it has been virtually eliminated by the employment of DDT on the breeding-grounds of the mosquitoes which carry the disease.

What can be sensed in recent medical advances is the continuing provision of new solutions to many long-standing problems, many of them (certain forms of childlessness, for example) going beyond the traditional preventative and therapeutic concerns of doctors. In 1978 the first so-called 'test-tube baby' was born in England. At first sight, the cumulative effect of such progress appears to reinforce the assumption that human problems are all, in principle, susceptible to solution by the application to them of science and its methods. In turn, this strengthens the further assumption that a natural world that includes humanity is best approached with a limitless aspiration to improve it. On the other hand, like fundamental work in the life sciences, medical progress generates new moral and political problems, at present obvious and debated only in the rich countries where such startling innovations as sperm banks and frozen embryos first came to public notice, and where decisions about huge public expenditures on health have to be made.

SPACE AND THE PUBLIC IMAGINATION

The discovery of space has as a general fact (like many other technological and scientific advances) only a limited relevance to conventional and political chronologies and periodization. Yet it has provided examples of the most exciting technological achievements in the second half of the twentieth century and has done as much as anything else to reinforce belief in human capacity to rise to meet unprecedented challenges. It changed the awareness of millions. The space age can be said to have begun for most people, at least in the northern hemisphere, only in 1957, when an unmanned satellite, launched from the USSR, went into orbit around the earth. Sputnik I, as it was called, marked a break in historical continuity as momentous as the European discovery of America. Like that discovery, too, it had historical roots of some depth.

Visions of what might be on its way had been set out in the late nineteenth and early twentieth centuries in the stories of Jules Verne and H. G. Wells, and the technology of space exploration goes back almost as far. A Russian scientist, K. E. Tsiolkovsky (he too had written fiction to popularize his obsession), was designing multi-staged rockets and devising many of the basic principles of space travel well before 1914. The first Soviet liquid-fuelled rocket went up (three miles) in 1933 and a two-stage rocket six years later. The Second World War led to a major German rocket weapon programme, which the United States drew on when setting up its own in 1955. Then came Sputnik I. The race that ensued was both psychologically and politically important. The Americans started with more modest hardware than the Russians, who had a commanding lead when Sputnik I made the first dramatic comparisons possible. The first American satellite weighed only three pounds and a launch attempt was made at the end of December 1957, but the rocket caught fire instead of taking off.

The Americans would soon do much better, but within a month of Sputnik I the USSR had already put up Sputnik II, an astonishingly successful machine for its day, weighing half a ton and carrying the first passenger from the earth in space, a black and white mongrel called Laika; sadly, she was not to return, alive or dead. By then, the era when it was still possible to doubt the feasibility of human beings exploring space was over.

The Soviet and American space programmes somewhat diverged. The USSR put much emphasis on the power and size of its rockets, which could lift big loads, and for some time this continued to be its great strength. It had military implications more obvious than those (more profound but less spectacular) which flowed from an early American concentration on data-gathering and on instrumentation. A competition for prestige was soon under way, but although the 'space race' soon became a familiar idea the contestants were often running towards different goals. With one great exception (the wish to be first to put a man in space) their exploratory strategies were probably not much influenced by one another's performance, though progress speeded up as each registered new achievements. At the end of 1958 the first satellite for communications purposes was successfully launched and it was American. In 1960 the USA scored another 'first' – the recovery of a capsule after re-entry. The USSR followed this by orbiting and retrieving Sputnik V, a four-and-a-half ton satellite, carrying two dogs, which thus became the first living mammals to enter space and return to earth safely. Then, in the spring of 1961, on 12 April, a Soviet rocket took off carrying a man, Yuri Gagarin. He landed 108 minutes later after making one orbit around the earth.

The American president proposed in May 1961 that his countrymen should try to land a man on the moon and return him safely to earth before the end of the decade. His reasons for doing so, at least as he set them out to his fellow Americans, were mixed. One was that such a project provided a good national goal, and thus, presumably, a sense of purpose and direction. Another was that it would be (in Kennedy's words) 'impressive to mankind'. A third was that it was of great importance for the exploration of space; and the fourth (somewhat oddly) was that it was of unparalleled difficulty and expense. He said nothing of the advancement of science, or of commercial or military advantage. Given public alarm over the well-publicized success of Soviet rocketry, it is understandable that the project awoke virtually no political opposition. Congress was willing to fund what was to prove the most expensive technological adventure in history. Meanwhile, the Russians continued to make spectacular progress. The world was duly impressed when they sent a woman into space in 1963, but Soviet technical competence continued to be best shown by the size of their vehicles – a three-man machine was launched in 1964 – and in the achievement the following year of the first 'space walk' when one of the crew emerged from his vehicle, reassuringly attached to it by a lifeline, and moved about outside while in orbit. The USSR was to have other successes in bringing vehicles together in space and docking them, but after 1967 (the year in which the first death through space travel occurred when a Russian was killed during re-entry), the glamour passed to the Americans. In 1968, they created a sensation by sending a three-man vehicle into orbit around the moon and transmitting the first pictures of its surface on television. It was by now clear that 'Apollo', the American moon-landing project, was going to succeed.

In May 1969 Apollo X, a vehicle put into orbit with the tenth rocket of the project, approached to within six miles of the moon to assess the techniques of the final stage of landing. A few weeks later, on 16 July, a three-man crew was launched. Their lunar module landed on the moon's surface four days later. On the following morning, 21 July, the first human being to set foot on the moon was Neil Armstrong, the commander of the mission. President Kennedy's goal had been achieved with time in hand. Other landings were to follow. In a decade that had proved humiliating and divisive for them in other ways, it was a triumphant reassertion of what Americans could do.

What it might mean in a larger sense remains harder to say. It was certainly a sign of the latest and greatest extension by *Homo sapiens* of his environment, the beginning of a new phase of his history, that of exploring other celestial bodies. To be able to contemplate that future as a feasible goal was the most dramatic evidence yet available that civilization was now led by science. But after the event, the historical importance of what had happened was hard to weigh up. The only obviously comparable achievement was that of Columbus, but it had been easier thirty years after 1492 to understand what an enormous difference Columbus had made to the world, than to judge the implications of Apollo as the century wound to a close. Even at the time this achievement prompted some derision. Among its critics were those who felt that the mobilization of resources the programme needed was unjustified, because irrelevant to so many problems on earth. The technology of space travel seemed to some to be modern western civilization's version of the Pyramids, a huge investment in the wrong things in a world crying out for money for education, nutrition, medical research – to name only a few pressing needs. A moment's reflexion, though, suggests things are a little more complex than that. Much of the scientific and economic effect of the space effort is hardly quantifiable but its benefits have already been very far-reaching; the techniques of miniaturization needed to make control systems, for example, rapidly spilt over into applications of obvious social and economic value. Such knowledge would not necessarily have been available without the investment in space first. Nor can we be sure that the resources lavished on space exploration would have been available for any other great scientific or social goals, had they not been used in this way. Regrettable though it may be, modern societies have not shown much sign of being able to generate much excitement and enthusiasm among their members for collective purposes except for brief periods or in war, whose 'moral equivalent' (as one American philosopher put it well before 1914) is still to seek. The imagination of large numbers of people is not much spoken to by the prospect of adding marginally to the GDP or introducing one more refinement to a system of social services, however intrinsically desirable these things may be, or attractive to voters because of the personal betterment they promise. Kennedy's identification of a national goal was psychologically shrewd; in the 1960s, Americans were troubled, agitated and divided on many issues, but they did not turn up to frustrate the launchings of space missions.

American funding of space exploration declined dramatically after the Apollo success. An Asian war was already imposing a heavy burden on even the resources of the United States. Furthermore a great stage was passed; a giant step had been taken but the next one was likely to require the manned exploration of Mars, a far more difficult and distant objective than had been the moon. Nonetheless, space exploration continued at a still costly level and it became notably more international and cooperative. Before the 1970s the lack of trust between the two greatest nations concerned had inevitably meant wasteful duplication of effort and inefficiencies. There had been a basic national rivalry in the technological race. Nationalism had even looked at times as if it might provoke a scramble for space; ten years before the Americans planted an American flag on the moon, a Soviet mission had dropped a Lenin pennant on it. But in the end the dangers of competition were avoided; it was soon agreed that celestial objects should not be subject to appropriation by any one state. After both the USSR and USA had planted 'space stations' in orbit where humans could live in an artificial environment in space, cooperation became in 1975 a startling reality in a remarkable experiment some 150 miles above earth, in which Soviet and American machines connected themselves so that their crews could move from one to the other. This opened twenty years of cooperative activity in which several other nations eventually took part. In spite of doubts and reduced expenditure space exploration continued in a relatively benign international setting.

Soon, the visual exploration of further space was carried beyond Jupiter by unmanned satellite. In 1976, too, an unmanned American exploration vehicle made the first landing on the surface of the planet Mars. In 1977 the American Space Shuttle, the first reusable space vehicle, made its maiden voyage, and in 1984 the first 'space walk' of an astronaut untethered to a capsule was made, but such amazing achievements were soon hardly noticed, so jaded had become the human imagination. So rapidly did there grow up a new familiarity with the idea of space travel that in the 1980s it seemed only mildly risible that people should have begun to make commercial bookings for it and even for space burials (if that is the word), too. Meanwhile, cooperation continued, though it was not until 1994 that a Russian cosmonaut joined the crew of an American craft for take-off. By then all the planets except Pluto had undergone investigation by unmanned vehicles. The last big Russian enterprise in space came in 1998 when a satellite was launched to prepare for a manned visit to Mars. It followed into space the first section for the building of a new international space station.

PROMISE AND MISGIVING

To extend the idea of what is possible is to change the way people think as well as the way they act. The technical changes in the world since 1950 have huge implications; almost anything that now occurs anywhere in the world is potentially at once of great interest (and able to influence public opinion) elsewhere. The Cold War itself depended, amid other things, on the presentation of its issues as of universal significance. At least some of the world's leaders seem now to have grasped that no human being (not even a head of state) is an island. In 1997 there was a striking and bizarre example of what communications can do to provide common experience when over 2 billion people (it was estimated) watched the funeral ceremonies of the former wife of the heir apparent to the British throne. Even at the most superficial level such a number implies at least widely shared notions about what is interesting. At a certain intensity, too, wide interest implies importance. Having diverged for thousands of years into increasingly different ways of life, human experiences had started slowly to become more widely shared again in the process of modernization, thanks to material and technical changes, even before this century. Since 1945, long divergent paths have more than ever converged as increasing numbers of people have begun to live lives shaped by the same commodities, the same ease of access to information and the same assumptions about the manipulation of the natural world.

Of course it is not always easy to see exactly what this means in practice. But it is a plausible thought that, more than any other single force or idea, the abundance of commodities has shattered for millions a world of hitherto stable expectations, both for good and ill. The idea that things will always just go on as before has retreated worldwide, and is still retreating. The possibility of change, long accepted in developed countries, is now a reality even in very poor countries. The coming of cheap consumer goods – transistor radios, for example – advances it both indirectly and directly. The possession of such goods confers status; this is an incentive to work for higher wages to buy them (a spread of a cash economy is another aspect of the process), often a spur also to leaving the villages in which so many still live and, in the process, to the severing of ties with tradition and with ordered, stable communities. Meanwhile, the actual commodity may itself carry messages – literally, in the case of the transistor radio – which change people's minds.

Thus, as the last traces of the political predominance of European civilization faded away, so, ironically, there almost daily emerged new evidence of its cultural and ideological powers. Of course no such absolute and general statements are prudent. We must not exaggerate the extent of change in many parts of the world, or lose sight of how far it may still have to go in them. Great cultures and traditions still cling to their own values and ways of life. Some people see threats in the individualism and hedonism that comes from the West even when it comes cloaked in otherwise desirable change. They strive, often successfully, to preserve social disciplines which, though harsh in the eyes of outsiders, they nonetheless find acceptable. Yet, when all this is said, and much done to search for other ways to the future, it remains true that the political supremacy Europeans established in the eighteenth and nineteenth centuries, and the technological advances which followed, are the main reasons why more common experiences and assumptions are now shared by more people more widely than ever before.

The usual appeal of and argument for modernization is its promise of power and wealth. Optimism about material progress and the possibility of improvement has spread worldwide from its origins in eighteenth-century Europe, during a golden age of wealth creation which has unrolled over the last couple of centuries. As the end of the twentieth century approaches, an immense increase in the consumption of resources still seems to many to be unambiguous evidence of humanity's material betterment. There are more human beings alive, and more of them are living longer, than ever before. For all the notorious sinks of degradation and poverty that remain (or are being created), the human race looks as if it is making a greater success than ever before of living on this planet. For the first time in history most human beings do not die before their fiftieth birthdays – a change that has come about very quickly, in the last fifty years. Only in the last couple of decades has anyone begun to worry much about the costs of such success and what it might portend.

This has, paradoxically, led to a renewal in rich countries of old distrust of material progress and its basic source, science. Within only a few years of Sputnik I misgivings were beginning to be uttered more frequently about humanity's masterful interference with the natural world. As time passed, even space exploration itself tended to be somewhat overshadowed by uneasiness in western countries about manipulating nature. Such uneasiness was increasingly expressed with a new precision, based on new observed facts. Here was irony. The new facts were known, of course, thanks to science; it had begun to supply much better instrumentation and the data which led first to better measurement of what was going on and then to dismay about it. The phenomenon itself was not new, but there was a new recognition of the danger of possibly irreparable damage to the environment. Centuries before, migrations and the adoption of dryland crops had devastated the great forests of south-west China, bringing soil erosion and the consequential silting of the Yangtse drainage system in its train, and so centuries of repeated flooding over wide areas. In the early Middle Ages, Islamic conquest had brought goat-herding and tree-felling to the North African littoral and destroyed a fertility which had once filled the granaries of Rome. But such great changes, though they could not have been wholly unnoticed, were not then understood. The unprecedented rapidity of ecological interference initiated from the seventeenth century onwards by Europeans, however unconsciously, brought things to a head. The burgeoning impact of a technological culture forced it on the attention of mankind in the second half of this century. People began to reckon up damage, as well as achievement. By the middle of the 1970s it seemed to some of them that even if the story of growing human mastery of the environment was an epic, it might well turn out to be a tragic one.

Uneasiness about interference with Nature has for most of history usually rested on non-rational grounds, such as terror of provoking divine anger or nemesis. Superstitious fear and suspicion of science has never wholly disappeared, of course, even in western societies, let alone non-western. In developed countries, though, it has tended to be confined to a few surviving primitive or reactionary enclaves as the majesty of what the scientific revolution of the seventeenth century implied gradually unrolled. Yet at least from the eighteenth century, such primitive fear was easily contained and somewhat eroded by the palpable advantages and improvements which successful interference with Nature brought about. It was only in the 1970s that a new scepticism about science became very evident in western countries. These were, of course, the countries where so many of the dividends on science had already been drawn. In the 1980s there were signs that uneasiness was spreading as what were called 'Green' political parties sought political action to protect the environment.[7] They were slow to achieve much, but they proliferated; established political parties and perceptive politicians therefore took up and toyed with green themes, too. Environmentalists, as the concerned came to be called, made good use of modern communications, and of the increasing transparency of public life that came with them.

In 1957 a reactor fire at a British nuclear power plant had soon been followed by evidence of contamination of the atmosphere from fall-out in Belgium and the Netherlands, France and Denmark.[8] Over an area of 500 square kilometres, milk from farms was declared unfit for human consumption. In the following year Soviet security was unable to prevent detection of an explosion at a nuclear waste plant in the Urals, which contaminated an area inhabited by tens of thousands. In 1979 came a leakage of radiation from a nuclear power station at Three Mile Island in the USA, which not only led to the closure of sixteen further stations for safety checks in the ensuing weeks, but was followed by further (less serious) accidents and shutdowns at other plants later in the year. A presidential commission was appointed to investigate the original incident but, as the president himself said, Americans did 'not have the luxury of abandoning nuclear power or imposing a lengthy moratorium' on its further use.[9] Then, in 1986, an accident occurred at a Ukrainian nuclear power station

[7] In 1989, Belgium, the Netherlands, France, Germany, Denmark and Spain all elected some 'Green' candidates to the European parliament, and the United Kingdom recorded a 15 per cent share of its parliamentary elections vote for them though none of its Green candidates won a seat. Greens had been represented in the German federal parliament since 1983. They took seats in the German cabinet in 1998.
[8] The accident occurred at Windscale (later called Sellafield) on the north-west coast of England.
[9] AR 1979, p.58.

that made humanity's interconnexions and interdependence suddenly and horribly visible. The greatest manmade technological disaster in Europe's history was brought home to millions by television. Tests were soon showing that grass eaten by lambs in Wales, milk drunk by Poles and Yugoslavs, and air breathed by Swedes were all contaminated by radiation. Unknown numbers of Soviet citizens were clearly going to die from its slow effects; by the 1990s the estimates of fatalities ranged from the forty-eight that were directly consequential to half a million. Only a few weeks before, other millions had watched on their screens an American rocket blowing up with the loss of all on board. The disasters of Chernobyl and *Challenger*, different though they were in scale (seven died in the latter), awoke large numbers of people for the first time to the limitations and possible dangers of advanced technological civilization. In the circumstances, it seems prescient that a British scientific weekly had ten years earlier, in 1976, recruited its first 'Disasters Editor'.[10]

FACING NEW ISSUES

A new awareness of the environmental problem remains a complex phenomenon. It goes far beyond technological excess or failure and it is rapidly and easily entangled with other issues. Some of the doubts which have recently arisen accept that our civilization has been good at creating material wealth, but note that by itself that does not necessarily make men happy. This is certainly no new idea. Yet its application to society as a whole instead of to individuals was nonetheless a new emphasis.

Far from removing all human dissatisfactions, the improvement of social conditions actually seems to irritate some of them more acutely. It increases awareness of what is not possessed but is known to be available to others. The oppressive anonymity of crowded cities and the nervous stress and strain of modern work conditions easily erase the satisfactions provided by material gain (which, in any case, quickly come to be taken for granted as new necessities, not new benefits).

---

[10] This was the *New Scientist*.

Pollution can do the same. Even if, in the 1960s, British Clean Air legislation of the previous decade had eliminated London's legendary pea-soup fog, it could be agreed that things had come to a pretty pass when the noise level in the Place de l'Opéra in Paris was found to be greater than that at the Niagara Falls, and the Seine carried more sewer water than its natural flow. Startlingly, by the 1990s Parisians accepted that the air in their city was so fouled as to make them accept restrictions even on their freedom to use their cars.[11]

Scale has become a problem in its own right. Some problems of modern cities may have grown to the point at which they are at present insoluble on any conceivable basis. It appears to be impossible, for example, even to count the inhabitants of Mexico City or Calcutta. Renewed misgivings have begun to be felt in developed countries about the threat of over-population, increasing pressure on diminishing resources, and the possibility of intensified competition for them in a world politically unstable. Finally, in a world where change had everywhere become more rapid there are now worries about psychological costs, insecurity, loss of bearings and unease about the future. Yet though misgivings and questionings are spectres haunting the rich world from time to time, poor and backward countries tend to find them insignificant when compared with the benefits to national income and GDP which rapid industrialization and further technological advance might bring.

One result has been that new and subtly different visions of Malthusian holocausts have begun to attract interest. We may well have by no means reached the end (or anything like it) of our capacity to produce food, but it is reasonable to fear that other things than food may run out first. An impossible situation must arise if the whole world were to seek (as it looks as if it does at present) to consume goods other than food at the rate developed countries do today. There is a limit to what any one human being can eat, but virtually no limit to what he or she can consume in terms of comfort, freedom of movement, medicine, social services and the like. Not only does the supply of such goods depend on energy and material resources that

[11] On 1 October 1987, all cars whose number-plates ended in even numbers were banned from entering Paris (unless they were small cars carrying at least three people).

are (so far as we know) ultimately finite, but contemporaneously the extravagant use of them is actually changing the terms of the problem. A compounding of consumption goes forward, assuring that (for instance) changing environmental conditions leads to the further generation of new needs, for cleaner air, for example. The social and political changes that must follow from such facts have hardly begun to be grasped. Nor, in spite of limited essays in wind and solar energy, have the requirements for the development of new energy resources. In the case of the nuclear alternative that once and so recently looked to be the answer, the solution is now cluttered up with fears of contamination either by reactors or by nuclear waste. Mankind has to face the hard task that to deal with such problems nothing like the knowledge or political and social skill exists that was available to put men on the moon. Above all, to deal with them also requires confrontation with the problems proposed by differential development, by the contrast of rich and poor.

Perhaps the idea of environmental damage has not yet reached the limits of its influence. Certainly, the spectrum of concerns that it fastens upon expands almost continually. It runs from alarm at the misuse and waste of natural resources at one end, their short-sighted and unwise exploitation, damage consequential upon what are in other ways evident benefits, to the outright destruction of a tolerable environment, both in its terrestrial and atmospheric forms at the other. It can be caused by the emergence of unanticipated problems in the course of what is undoubted scientific advance, too: that of the disposal of nuclear waste, for example, or the moral questions that seem to proliferate with every advance in genetic engineering.[12] As the century ends, for instance, it seems at last to be authoritatively conceded that whether or not it can be quantified, human agency has contributed to 'global warming'.[13] But

[12] See the speculations of L. M. Silver (in *Remaking Eden: Cloning and Beyond in a Brave New World*, London, 1999) on such possibilities as the genetic division of the human race between intelligent and less-intelligent, or on whether a widower or widow might be allowed to remarry a clone of a deceased spouse.
[13] A report of 1995 from the Intergovernmental Panel on Climate Change thought that the balance of the evidence suggested this, but that view was almost at once challenged. By December 1997, though, when a conference was held at Kyoto on Climate Change, the conclusion was generally accepted.

there are other causes of alarm, for example, the irreversible effects by now already produced by interfering with nature, whether deliberately or unintentionally. They occur both at the microscopic and the macroscopic level; the smallpox virus has been eradicated in this century, but so have many species of flora and fauna – and thousands of them in the more distant past. Such change leads some to postulate a gloomy future. It is at least a possible qualification of the triumphant assurance of the last few centuries that the way to a better future lay through growing scientific control over nature.

As the century approached its close, too, a new spectre began to be talked about, the possibility of irreversible climatic change. The year 1990 had hardly ended before it was pointed out that it had been the hottest since climatic records began to be kept. Was this, some asked, a sign of what some scientists had identified as a 'greenhouse effect' produced by the release into the atmosphere of the immense quantities of carbon dioxide produced by a huge population burning fossil fuels as never before? Not that this was likely to be the only reason for the phenomenon of accumulating gases whose presence in the atmosphere prevents the planet from dissipating heat. Methane, nitrous oxides and chlorofluorocarbons, all of them produced in larger quantity than ever because of human activity, all contribute to it. And if global warming were not enough to worry about, then acid rain, ozone depletion leading to 'holes' in the ozone layer, and deforestation at unprecedented rates all provided major grounds for a new environmental concern. To take only a single problem: there is said now to be some 25 per cent more carbon dioxide in the atmosphere than in pre-industrial times. It may be so (and as global output of the stuff is now said to be 6,000 *million* tons a year, it is hardly for a non-scientist to dispute exact magnitudes).

The consequences, if the trend suggested by such figures proved to be established and no effective counter-measures were forthcoming, could be enormous. They would express themselves in climatic change (average surface temperature on the earth might rise by between one and four degrees Celsius over the next century), new agricultural revolutions, rising sea-levels (six centimetres a year has been suggested as possible and plausible) and vast human migrations. It is easier to sense the scale of such problems, and so their danger, than to envisage feasible solutions. Uneasiness about interference with Nature therefore rightly persists. People began to speak of threats to bio-diversity in the 1990s. It was already clear by then that there were plenty of interests common to mankind to cooperate about. Agreement on what had to be done, though, seemed likely to be hard for the envisageable future. In February 1991, the officials from newly created environment ministries met in Washington to begin to try to work out a treaty on global climatic change. In 1992 an 'Earth Summit' was held in Rio de Janeiro at which the industrialized nations' representatives agreed that the emission of what had come to be called 'greenhouse gases' should be reduced to 1990 levels by 2000. Unhappily, in 1997 a world conference in Kyoto on the industrial pollution more and more thought to be associated with such change got nowhere in its search for generally and practically workable limits on energy use, except to agree that some were necessary; some countries subsequently announced they would seek to restrict their own emission of green-house gases. Democracy stood in the way of self-discipline by the most greedy of all consumers, the United States, and so did envious agitation by the potentially increasing consumers of the undeveloped world, led by China. It is fair to say, too, that the Kyoto conference also brought about some clarification of technical problems still unsolved in assessing the phenomenon of climate change. This must be helpful if some measurement of global regulation of energy is ever to be brought about, but it hardly seems to presage a response to existing dangers comparable with their scale.

19

New Economic and Social Worlds

IN THE LONG RUN

As 1901 began, India was in the grip of a two-year famine. A few photographs and drawings of its effects appeared in western newspapers and magazines. A relief fund was opened with some success in London. Yet the facts of 2 million deaths, of the tragedies of cannibalism and cholera, the fate of the starvation victims cluttering India's roads, can hardly have made much impact on many people in England, let alone on the rest of Europe or the United States.

Nowadays such a lack of awareness is hardly imaginable. We are bombarded with television pictures of the harrowing details of disaster and deprivation, and continually reminded of the fact of persistent, generalized misery in poor countries. This has not necessarily meant more effective and generous response. There is now talk of 'compassion fatigue' in rich countries; charitable impulses are said to be over-taxed. The contrast in available publicity for the facts, though, is a great change in nearly a century. There has also been a new differentiation of human experience. Some parts of Europe suffered from famine as late as the 1940s (Greece at the end of the war, the USSR when it was over), but even then that was unusual, an outcome of special circumstances. Only a half-century earlier, though, when many more Europeans lived in extreme poverty than today, they would have found the contrasts between their own lives and those of contemporary Africans and Asians less sharp than would their modern descendants. Starvation was for them a real possibility, too. The most significant change in life experiences that has come about since then in the developed world is one of expectations and therefore of perceptions of what is tolerable.

Like our longer lives, economic growth has now come to be taken for granted. It has become the 'norm', in spite of hiccups and interruptions along the way or our awareness of what looks like hopeless management in some countries; even a slowing-down in it now occasions alarm, and its absence requires special explanation.

Paradoxically, the assumption that growth is normal in already rich countries and a perception of widening inequalities because of that has also been accompanied by a real increase in gross consumption per capita in most of the underdeveloped world, too. A rough comparison of population figures at the beginning and end of the twentieth century is revealing. In the mid-1990s, a world population of something over 5,500 million was divided between the inhabited continents roughly as follows:

	Million	Approximate share of total world population (to nearest 0.25 per cent)
Europe	745	13.5
Asia	3,424	62
Africa	701	13
South America and the Caribbean	308	5.5
North America	294	5.25
Australasia and Oceania	47	0.75

This suggests a total increase of some three and a half times in the century, and in the instances of some continents, greater growth still.[1]

[1] The table sets out rounded numbers, and (by way of further qualification) they are not strictly comparable to the similar figures set out for 1901 on p.43. The figures in this table should be marginally closer to reality than those for that date, and are taken from variously dated UN estimates 1990–98; although the UN Population Fund produced different figures in 1998, they do not much distort the overall distribution. The dissolution of the USSR also makes direct comparison harder; I have allocated six of the republics of the CIS to Asia, and seven (of which Russia is the biggest, and includes 'Russia in Asia') to Europe. South America and the Caribbean begin for this table on the Rio Grande, the border between the USA and Mexico (which is sometimes counted as part of 'North America'). Antarctica has now a few longish-term human residents as it did not in 1901, but can be ignored in the magnitudes considered here.

The changing shares in these totals are also interesting, the comparative decline in Europe's position being the most remarkable. They reflect, above all, striking changes in life expectancy, particularly, and however qualified, in the less developed parts of the world. Wherever people are living longer, more food, the most basic form of wealth, is being consumed.

Another outcome of a century's population growth has been change in the relative strength and importance of individual countries. Mere numbers do not by themselves, of course, indicate power rankings. Other material resources come into the matter and power for one purpose is not always power for another. Nonetheless, population matters in any computation of it. In the mid-1990s, the ten most populous countries in the world were thought to be:[2]

		Million
China	..	1,209
India	..	919
USA	..	265
Indonesia	..	192
Brazil	..	153
Russia	..	148
Japan	..	125
Pakistan	..	127
Bangladesh	..	118
Nigeria	..	108

In that list, China and India stand out, seemingly destined to be great powers on grounds of numbers alone. China is indeed almost militarily invulnerable thanks to them, and perhaps India is, too. China's social revolution has visibly begun to increase her wealth per capita, though, whereas the obstacle to India and some other highly populated countries becoming very powerful is a poverty that until now has remained crippling. It lies like a dead weight on efforts to generate improvement in the lot of the masses, in part because rising production has barely

[2] Most of these figures are set out to the nearest million and are taken from 1994 UN estimates; that of Russia is for 1997 (i.e. post-USSR). Germany, with over 81 million, is now the most populous European country, after Russia.

kept pace with rising numbers. To the unreflective observer, the position of, say, most Indians or Africans may not seem much improved since this century began. Yet it has been, for in that time life expectancy has risen everywhere. This is for many countries the major break with the past that this century has brought them, whether they are countries where natural resources are poor (Bangladesh is an example), or relatively rich.

Yet the growth of wealth has not always brought an obvious increase in well-being. In the early 1970s India was thought to be about to enter a period of self-sufficiency in food. Her agricultural output doubled between 1948 and 1973. Yet this new wealth only just succeeded in holding the line for a population growing by a million a month and on the average, surviving for longer. Potentially sufficient resources can be swallowed up by population growth that is too fast (as has been the case in India, Bangladesh and, until recently, Indonesia). Newly generated wealth often has simply been consumed and it then becomes hard to see increased life expectancy as a contribution to greater human happiness; often it turns out to mean a prolongation of misery. On the horizon, too, lies another problem; that of those societies with low fertility rates and high life expectancy, when the number of non-working elderly is increasing much faster than the labour force of the young.

The story of how such long-term demographic changes came about, of course, is another that should not be picked up suddenly in 1945. The appropriate 'long run' in which to understand both such spectacular population growth and the unprecedented generation of wealth that has so far successfully carried the burden of it is at least the whole century. In spite of brief and localized, though sometimes terrible, interruptions by two world wars and the worldwide setback of economic depression in the 1930s, positive wealth creation has gone on since 1901. It slowed in the 1970s and again in the 1990s, but even allowing for notable contrasts between different economies in the developed world, and between different regions and even continents in the undeveloped, the trend for a hundred years has been upward, and for fifty years continuously so. Recent calculations provide the following selected examples of estimated change in the Gross Domestic Product per capita (in terms of 1988 dollars).

	1900	*1988*
Brazil	436	2,451
Italy	1,343	14,432
Sweden	1,482	21,155
France	1,600	17,004
Japan	677	23,325
UK	2,798	14,477
USA	2,911	19,815

Any such selected figures obviously require cautious interpretation. They show nonetheless that although the world has become much richer its new wealth has been created, distributed and saved or consumed at widely differing rates and in many different ways. All the countries in the table, with the possible exception of Brazil (in some ways best seen as a mixture of developed and undeveloped economic sectors), were rich countries in 1988, parts of the developed world. There are others that remain woefully poor. In the same year, Afghanistan, Madagascar, Laos, Tanzania, Ethiopia, Cambodia and Mozambique still all had an annual GDP per capita of less than $150. It has been alleged (by no less an authority than an archbishop of Canterbury) that over a billion human beings still live on less than one US dollar a day. The major fact of twentieth-century economic history nonetheless remains that of wealth creation, reflected most obviously in population growth and increased longevity, and unevenly shared.[3]

Another observation that jumps to the eye in the long run is that for all the discontinuities along the way, many of the fundamental processes promoting (and often used as measures of) economic growth were under way a long time ago. A vast and steadily mounting increase in the international exchange of commodities was already taking place in the nineteenth century thanks largely to technological innovation.

[3] It was pointed out in 1984 by *The Economist* (14 April) that '2% of the world's farmers – the 24 millions in the rich countries . . . are providing nearly a quarter of all the world's food, and nearly three quarters of its food exports. The other 98% of farmers – the 1.2 billion in the poor countries where up to two thirds of the people are on the land – grow three quarters of the world's food but still do not have enough to eat.'

Both absolute growth and its dependence on technology continued and intensified in the twentieth century. National economic independence diminished except in the terrible 1930s and the Second World War and, especially after 1950, most countries have come to rely on imports to satisfy many of their needs. The management of national economies slowly changed in its nature. Instead of occasionally being propelled by war or crisis towards measures to assure the supply and distribution of essential foodstuffs, raw materials or fuel, the task of economic policy became one of assuring the continuing availability of commodities of all kinds and the promotion of wealth that could be taxed to provide for spending on welfare goals.

Such changes, over such long periods, were very unevenly paced. Important distinctions can be drawn in tracing them, and of these the one most obvious is that between the two halves of the century, crude though it is. Clearly, the first half saw much more interruption of wealth creation than the second and much slower growth over its whole extent. The first half was characterized, too, by growing governmental interference with national economies, the second by a new respect for the market as a regulator. Furthermore, any general explanation of a growing abundance visible since 1945 must surely reflect its special feature, a long peace between major powers. For all the bloody and destructive conflicts that have taken place, and for all the sufferings of the surrogates who have done the great powers' fighting for them, and long periods of international tension, the absence of major power conflict has been of enormous importance. There has been no such widespread destruction of human and material capital as that which took place in Europe in two world wars, and, just as important, no such collapse of international exchange and commerce as that of the 1930s. International political rivalry has, on the contrary, sustained economic activity in many countries and provoked it in others, has provided much technological transfer and advance, and has encouraged major capital investments and transfers. Thus political and military considerations have often helped to increase real wealth.

EUROPE'S 'GOLDEN AGE'

The first such investments and transfers came about when the United States aid underwrote and subsidised the recovery of western Europe in the later 1940s and 1950s. The enormous wartime expansion of the American economy had pulled it out of its pre-war depression. Together with the immunity of the American home base from physical damage by war, this made the financing of European recovery possible. American economic strength, rebuilt in the war, embodied the potential for a post-war American economic hegemony somewhat like that the United Kingdom had exercised before 1914, but far transcending it in scale. Much more has to be taken into account, though, to explain how American strength came to be tapped to international advantage. The explanations must include international circumstances (of which the Cold War was overwhelmingly the most important) which made it seem in America's interest to behave as she did, the imaginative grasp of opportunities shown by some of her statesmen and businessmen, the absence for a long time of any alternative source of capital on such a scale anywhere in the world, and the efforts of many men of different nations who, even before the end of the war, had tried to set in place institutions which could prevent any return to the economic anarchy of the 1930s.

What was done at Bretton Woods in 1944 made possible an unprecedented degree of sensible international economic management instead of the simple reliance on 'natural' economic harmony which had been the basis of the pre-1914 economic order and had been disrupted by the virtual absence of order between 1914 and 1945. The International Monetary Fund and the World Bank were fundamental to post-war cooperation, even if they had less immediate impact than the post-war flow of dollars to Europe that culminated in the Marshall Plan. They promoted stability and cooperation after 1947, when a General Agreement on Tariffs and Trade (GATT) was signed by the representatives of twenty-three nations. For some twenty-five years, the restraints laid upon the USA by international agreement effectively limited the power of its markets to disrupt the international economy as domestic political pressures had done in the 1920s and 1930s. The economic stability which these arrangements and institutions provided underpinned two decades of growth in world trade at nearly 7 per cent per annum in real terms. Between 1945 and the 1980s the average level of tariffs on manufactured goods traded between the major national economies fell from 40 per cent to 5 per cent, and world trade multiplied more than fivefold. Tariffs were not all that stood in the way of trade, nevertheless, this was a huge step forward.

Second only to the United States itself, western Europe was, and for a quarter-century stood out as, the major beneficiary of this long surge of prosperity. Marshall Aid had assured a high level of imports that enabled Europeans to sustain higher rates of capital formation than they could have achieved by themselves. In the summer of 1947 industrial output in France, Belgium, the Netherlands, Italy and Germany was still below that of 1938. Thanks to the combination of American economic support and the Europeans' own efforts, the economies of the western European countries were substantially rebuilt by 1953. It was an era of remarkable achievement. The settling down of old rivalries in western Europe, the stabilization of liberal-minded governments there, and increasingly effective provision of welfare were all very positive steps. Western Europe was embarked on what has been called a 'golden age' of economic growth lasting until the early 1970s. Unemployment had fallen to rates of a quarter or so of those of the 1930s and what had been indulged as dreams of security and comfort in the dark days of 1945 were realities ten years later. Figures drawn from twelve 'western' European countries (they include Finland) show an average annual growth rate of 4.6 per cent in real GDP and of 0.7 per cent in population between 1950 and 1972 (the comparable figures for 1913–50 had been 1.4 and 0.5, respectively).[4] But historians are still arguing about the specific reasons for this improvement and their comparative weight, to say nothing of disagreeing over the variations from it shown by individual countries. Economists, too, disagree about why it happened, and the unexciting conclusion of the historian must be that a multiplicity of causes made it possible.

[4] See N. F. R. Crofts, 'The golden age of economic growth in Western Europe, 1950–1973', *Economic History Review*, xlviii (1995), pp.429–47. These figures are slightly different from those compiled by G. Toniolo for his study (see above, p.121).

Some of them were political. Even before the Marshall Plan, politics had begun to make available to Europe the American dollars needed for her reconstruction. As the Cold War went on, but especially in its early years, international rivalry brought European rearmament and larger American garrisons in Europe, both of which helped to sustain economic activity and provoke more than simple recovery. Huge sums were involved. In 1948 and 1949 no less than 3 per cent of the United States' GDP came to Europe. In 1951 the life of the Marshall Plan was extended; in the end, $17 billion in all was given under it outright to its recipients, who also absorbed some $3 billion of World Bank loans. Such transfers provided major capital investments that increased Europe's real wealth, making easier a series of agreed devaluations of European currencies in 1949 that gave a huge boost to European competitiveness for two decades or so. Above all, they assured a supply of hard currency to support international trade. The pre-condition of Europe's return to economic health thus lay outside Europe. The recovery of Europe as a major world centre of industrial production predicated the existence of the American dynamo. But that source of energy was not the sole explanation either of economic recovery or of the movement towards greater economic integration in western Europe that so assisted it. They also owed much to the European businessmen who rose to the challenges of opportunity that faced them, and to the statesmen who, almost unwittingly, helped indirectly to maintain demand by putting up 'welfare' expenditure of all kinds.

EASTERN EUROPE

By the mid-1950s it was clear that the benefits western Europeans were drawing from that recovery were outstanding, particularly when they considered a notable contrast that was to hand. Eastern Europe was a zone weighed down by historic handicaps. Ever since the October Revolution, commercial relations that might seem natural between the USSR and her neighbours had been sporadically encumbered by politics. In the huge disruption and net decrease of world trade after 1931 as the capitalist economies plunged into recession and sought salvation in protection or autarky, and the USSR grappled with other disasters of its own making, any hope of overcoming economic fragmentation there (and in central Europe, too) had disappeared. Then came the destruction of the war years; eastern Europe and European Russia were the scene of the fiercest fighting and Germany (of which the eastern half was to go the Soviet way after 1945) of the heaviest bombing. Eastern Europe's recovery from the war also showed notable economic growth. It was registered not only in the rebuilding of social capital destroyed in the war (housing, hospitals and schools and their support), but in new departures, the reduction of infant mortality and a spread of better nutrition levels. Many parts of eastern Europe had been sinks of rural poverty before 1939. Beggars now began to disappear from their villages as peasants moved to the cities again and industry provided new jobs. Yet most of the east's economic progress 1945–50 was a matter of remedying pre-war backwardness. The contrast with the recent past was striking, but eastern European countries remained relatively poor by comparison with western countries.

The exigencies of the Cold War undoubtedly made things worse in the east. All earlier divisions of the world market were transcended as two methods of organizing the distribution of scarce resources divided Europe (and later the world) with increasing sharpness. This can hardly have been helpful to the wealth-creating process. There was trade between the market and 'command' (or would-be command) economies, but it was restricted and difficult, and, as the years passed, did little to bring them much closer to one another. Comecon remained very much an instrument of Soviet policy, and national interests were subordinated to those of the USSR. The competition of two systems as models for economic growth was inflamed by the propaganda of the Cold War and probably helped to spread its antagonisms. Each had its missionaries who strove to win over the uncommitted. Yet it became clearer and clearer, as time passed, that whereas western Europe's superpower patron poured positive benefits into it, eastern Europe was milked of capital by the USSR.

This could not be a completely static situation. Even by 1960 one system was much less completely dominated by the United States and the other somewhat less completely dominated by the Soviet Union than had been the case ten years earlier. Both shared (though in very differing degree) in a surge of economic growth in the 1950s and the 1960s. Soviet-style development, stressing the establishment of heavy industry, was the general rule in these decades. Comecon expanded outside Europe (Mongolia, Cuba and Vietnam all came to belong to it), yet it proved comparatively ineffective in increasing the trade between its member states, in spite of attempts to encourage national economic specialization. Western and eastern Europe's standards of living diverged as the market economies moved ahead more rapidly. By 1970, there could clearly be discerned in the west a Europe that looked like a new continent, whose member states enjoyed the motorways, supermarkets, television advertising and mass tourism of a new international style. The east presented an altogether shabbier and less inviting prospect. Its showpiece was the GDR, but that country, the richest in the communist zone, increasingly fell behind in its ability to service its foreign debt, in spite of cheap energy supplies from the USSR, an assured market for its manufactures elsewhere in Comecon, and help from the Federal German Republic. Loans made by western countries only exacerbated the need for hard (western) currency it needed to pay its interest charges. East German technology fell steadily behind, too; the GDR was, for example, by 1980 producing far fewer computers than Austria, and they were, by comparison, poorly made and obsolete in design.[5] The West Germans were by then effectively underwriting the GDR. By 1989 it would be bankrupt. The East Germans, like the Czechs, had for a long time congratulated themselves that they were at least doing better than the Hungarians or Poles, who had begun trying to provide a larger role for market influences in their economies even in the 1960s. By the 1980s, though, there were signs that other eastern European countries might overtake them.

The whole of eastern Europe was by then displaying a more vivid contrast with western Europe than ever, and not just because of the ever-advancing standard of living of the latter. Eastern countries all had their black markets, their environmental pollution, their antique

[5] C. Maier, *Dissolution: the Crisis of Communism and the end of East Germany* (Princeton, 1997), pp.74–5, though *prima facie* the figures cited for Austria seem surprising.

massive heavy-industrial plants operating at low productivity and low levels of capacity, their creeping inflation, their shops barren of decent consumer goods, their formidable labour disciplines, their housing shortages and, above all, their own visible inequalities of reward. Nor could the regime turn to the harsh discipline of unemployment as a way out. This was the reality that lay behind a decade moving towards revolution.

WORLD CONTRASTS

Given the divergences of east and west, to seek to identify and summarize the economic position of Europe as a whole, and to compare the result to that of other parts of the world, is unrealistic and artificial. Nonetheless, in the eyes of the have-not countries of the developing or undeveloped world, Europeans west and east could both be counted among the rich. The western economies showed it more obviously, but even those of the USSR and eastern Europe, where mismanagement and political priorities held back growth, seemed opulent to many Asians and Africans in the 1950s and 1960s. Many western Europeans lived in countries most of whose citizens had already enjoyed high standards of living in the world before the war, when all European countries had some well-developed urban sectors. This had helped to give Europe a privileged place among the continents as a consumer, and she had not entirely lost it through her self-destruction from 1939 to 1945. In 1970 the three greatest agglomerations of industrial capacity in the world were still to be found, as they had been thirty years earlier, in North America, Europe and Russia, though they had by then been joined by Japan as a fourth.

There was, of course, disappointment. New wealth did not obviously bring about a global prosperity. Setting aside the special cases of the command economies of the communist world, which supported, for most of this period, about one third of the world's population, the disparity between rich and poor nations has not only grown more obvious but has actually increased since 1945. This has been for the most part not a matter of the poor becoming poorer, but of the rich getting richer faster. Spectacularly, some Asian countries, for example,

pushed up their agricultural outputs between 1952 and 1970 proportionately more than did Europe and much more than North
America but could not succeed in offsetting the disparity, because of
their rising populations. Though their ranking in relation to one
another may have changed and their numbers have grown, the major
industrial countries that were in the group enjoying the highest standards of living in 1950 still enjoy them today, though they have been
joined by others. That fact spurred many poorer countries to seek
their own betterment in industrialization.

In 1980 it was pointed out in a document awaking much attention
and concern in the developed world that the world could be divided
'North' and 'South' into rich and poor countries. Together, the 'North'
contained a quarter of the world's population and consumed four-fifths
of the world's income.[6] The other three-quarters of the world lived
on the remaining fifth. Over 90 per cent of the world's manufacturing
capacity lay in a privileged minority of countries. In the light of
history, of course, this was a novel phenomenon. In earlier centuries
the technological basis for such violent disparity in the distribution
of the world's resources did not exist. Whether or not such comparisons
could be made accurately, it was an unhappy fact that the late twentieth
century appeared to face ever-widening economic inequality as a
concomitant of its unprecedented success in creating an abundance
that had improved the material lot of more people more rapidly than
any earlier burst of economic expansion.

There had always been hopes – and they were expressed again in
the Brandt report[7] – that aid from developed to undeveloped countries
would erode and perhaps eliminate the vast gap in world incomes
between rich and poor countries. Aid certainly helped the poor. It is

[6] The 'Brandt report', or Report of the Independent Commission on International
Development Issues (London, 1980), North–South: a programme for survival, p.32.
The commission drawing it up, under the nominal chairmanship of Willy Brandt,
was one of individuals independent of governments, but owed its formation to the
then president of the World Bank, Robert McNamara, and perhaps its power to
produce a report at all to others. See Sir Edward Heath's memoirs, The Course of
My Life. My Autobiography (London, 1998), pp.608–10.
[7] It recommended that by 1985 developed countries should be allocating 0.7 per cent
of their GNP to development assistance. In the event only the Dutch and Scandinavians
achieved this.

doubtful, for instance, if Bangladesh could actually have survived as a country without it. There were notably successful progressions to record, too – South Korea, Thailand, Brazil and Colombia were instances – where countries were much helped by development aid before 1980. Even the USSR had its own overseas aid programmes, focused though they were on such important strategic targets as Cuba and Vietnam. Major institutional and bureaucratic growth, too, was observable around the IMF and World Bank and some took that for an index of advance. Yet the real inequalities remained, as striking and troubling as ever.

CHANGING LIFESTYLES

Not everyone, of course, found progress pleasant, even in prospering societies. Here, again, a glance at the long term is helpful. This century has produced for hundreds of millions of people unexpected changes in what sociologists call their 'life courses', which took no account at all of the wishes of those millions themselves. It has brought about sometimes startling disruptions of long-established patterns in which people could grow up, enter work, create families, experience old age and die. Some such changes jump vividly to the eye when they are a matter of individual fortune, when, say, the child of the first literate generation of a Russian family makes his or her way up the hierarchy of the Party apparatus to secure a bourgeois lifestyle, or another adolescent English girl is singled out from thousands of contemporaries by some accident of physique to embark upon the highly specialized life course of the international fashion model. Such startling transformations are well publicized but in the context of general history insignificant. Of changes in the lives of hundreds of thousands of Africans who moved within a decade or two from the village life of herdsmen to become wage-earners in mine or factory, living in cities, we are less likely to be aware, but they are surely more revealing as historical facts. Still other changes, even more important, because they have affected even larger numbers of people, have taken place as this century has unrolled, though often gradually and almost unnoticed.

To risk yet another generalization about the long run, most of the last two centuries have meant more specific choices to more individuals in societies where economic and technological change was fastest. They brought increasing freedom in mobility and location, for example, and the enjoyment of a new heterogeneity and variety, not only in the consumption of goods, but also through the slackening of earlier social restraints. Among these are those of the family. All round the world, in pre-industrial societies, the typical life course was once likely to be narrowly focused on it. It is still an institution of huge importance and many, in many different societies, even today never leave its comforting or stifling embrace. Training and education were for most of human existence a matter of learning from parents what life required; work was a matter of contributing to the family's well-being, either through its own land or animals, or by working with another's. Few institutions other than the family existed anywhere to cushion individuals against the sudden disasters of illness, death in childbed, accident, drought and flood, except in marginal ways. Such misfortunes intensified the pressures of interdependence and mutual support. Outside the developed world millions still live in this kind of society today, but within it many more than in the past do not.

The displacement or at least disturbance of the family has now gone a long way. Everywhere, it has come under new pressure. Patterns first observable in western countries are now tending to be replicated elsewhere. Industrialism was from its start, a century and a half ago, a huge force driving disruptive wedges into many constricting but also comforting institutions of the *ancien régime*, the family among them. Mass industrial employment for the first time offered young and strong workers (men and women alike) not only a modest economic benefit but also some new measure of independence until they acquired their own families and the responsibilities that went with them. In due time, industrialization appeared also to indicate that a modicum of schooling could enhance the value of the workforce; typically, elementary education was one of the first services widely provided by governments. After a brief period of education and another of youthful employment, there then usually followed for the individual a marriage, parenthood, a period of fairly assured employment, until declining physical vigour and health, the threat of unemployment and eventual old age and sickness had to be faced. For a long time and still in many countries, the family was the central institution to which men and women could turn for help in facing them.

Very roughly, this might be said to have been the way life went for most people even in the developed world at the beginning of this century, though one or two qualifications were even then beginning to creep into the picture. More governments began over the next three or four decades to provide greater support against the risks of unemployment and sickness, and to meet the difficulties of old age.[8] As the process of industrialization matured and grew more complex, education, too, came to be valued more highly still and to be provided more generously, by public authorities. One way in which societies grew more distinct was in the levels of ability and technical sophistication to be found in their workforces.

While earlier and more traditional patterns still persisted over much of the world, the expectations of those who lived in the developed world were thus gradually transformed in the next three-quarters of a century. This was in part because of political change, in part because of the slow implicit educational power of better and more available technology. By 1939 the outlines of a new order of life courses, resting on industrial mass production and the high real wages that made it possible, were already emerging as the characteristic pattern in many countries. Not only the schooling and welfare support provided by the state, but also (in spite of interruptions, and notably after 1950) the long-run tendency of real wages to rise gave more people access to material benefits. Those rewards seemed more secure, too, provided as they more and more tended to be by long working lives in the same occupation, and even in the same organization. More married women

___

[8] By the end of the century, this was even happening in the Far East, though as the danger of unemployment loomed up there again in the mid-1990s, it became obvious that wide differences existed between its own vigorous economies (while Singapore had a well-developed old-age pension structure already in place, Hong Kong had little such provision), to say nothing of differences between them and older developed economies. Retirement pensions today represent the largest single item of social expenditure in every EU country.

felt able to stay at home without paid employment. Old age began to be better provided for by private savings as well as by public funding in developed societies.

Nor was the expectation that the benefits that states provided should go beyond order and defence much disrupted by the world economic collapse of the 1930s. North and South America, Australasia and Europe all saw extensions during it of social welfare provision to meet both long-term needs and the emergencies and hazards presented by ill-health and cyclical unemployment. The first person in the United States to draw a social security (old age) pension did so in 1940. After 1945, structures that provided social support and protection and the standardization of the levels of consumption that they implied became major preoccupations of all western governments. For twenty-five years rising prosperity allowed more employment in manufacturing and service industries to be accompanied by rising real wages and extension of public welfare provision. It became a cliché of British popular journalism in the 1960s to describe the outcome as the conversion of the working class to middle-class values.

In the 1970s, though, came signs of further and less benevolent change. Not only did a dramatic rise in the price of oil send tremors through political life everywhere in the developed world and inflation become a major preoccupation of governments, but also it began to be recognized that bills for welfare provision were growing uncontrollably – and electorates were against reducing them. Technical changes in industry – above all in the application of information technology – were also beginning to change work and employment prospects in fundamental ways. So did geographical shifts in the location of production, as new labour forces became available in developing countries. Mass production still looms large within the industrial world, but it is significant as well as symbolic that it is frequently (to speak somewhat figuratively) now in the hands of robots; the diversity of forces that are now at work shaping society through employment has led some sociologists to talk of a 'post-Fordist' industrial era, in which assembly line mass production operated by specialized workmen carrying out repetitive tasks no longer sets the pattern. Outside the factory, this qualified for many people in developed countries the homogenizing and standardizing of experience that had paradoxically gone with increasing consumer choice in the first two-thirds of this century.

These forces have everywhere begun to increase differentials of reward and to change expectations. Entry into employment in developed societies continues, as it has done for over a century, to be later than in the past, both for those joining the workforce from higher education and for those who have undergone full-time education only to the end of secondary schooling, and who now find on joining the labour market that there are fewer jobs available. Qualification has come to count for more in creating career choices. Changing sexual behaviour has meant that in developed societies there are more people who never become parents, and more women who do without the support of a married partner (or often, of any continuing partner at all). What is more, even within the same societies, distinctions in such matters have further sharpened existing distinctions between groups. The collapse of family life among black urban North Americans is a case in point.

Employment in industrial society has again become more intermittent, possibly benignly interrupted by periods of renewed training, but more by a new precariousness. The typical life course embedded in lifelong employment is no longer the rule. 'Downward career mobility' (to adopt a British euphemism of the 1990s) and the experience of unemployment are now much more widely and often quite rapidly shared: West Germany's unemployment rate of 1 per cent in 1980 had risen to 12 per cent a decade later in a united Germany. Of course, structural social change like this might still well not seem very startling to the Cambodian peasant or the Cairo slum-dweller. Even in developed countries, though, comparative standards and the widening of differentials in pay put more people into the category of the poor.[9] For many of their individual citizens the golden age was coming to a close in the last quarter of the century.

[9] Poverty is only a helpful term when set in a specific context so that it can draw attention to relativities. In OECD countries, it is defined as having an income of less than half the national average, and in the EU the proportion falling below this line has grown in every country since 1975.

THE OIL CRISIS AND AFTER

Thus by the time the Brandt report was published its message seemed ironic; some developed economies had already begun to experience high unemployment again. Though the welfare state continued to advance, there was growing concern both over its expense and over evidence that it was not reducing inequalities inside the rich countries themselves. In the 1980s, there was worse still to come. Young people began to discover the very different prospects waiting for them when they left school to join the workforce, and officials began to worry about the implications of ageing populations. Politicians, naturally, lagged behind them, but would in due course catch up. Almost incidentally, and certainly in an unanticipated way, employment for men began to appear challenged for the first time by the entry into labour forces of substantial numbers of educated women. Finally, technological progress and information technology exercised a steady encroachment on employment in traditional manufacturing, and widened pay differentials.

Much of the new distress felt in many countries after 1970 can be traced back to the catastrophic blow that affected rich and (much more) poor countries alike, if they were oil-importing and oil-dependent, the substantial increases in oil prices in a decade. They came in two spurts, the first as a consequence of the Yom Kippur war, and the second at the end of the decade, thanks to the Iranian revolution. The inflation in oil prices soon spread to other costs. It was, moreover, made the more significant by the years during which the United States accumulated huge budgetary deficits and had printed money to pay for the Vietnam war, while not earning sufficient trade income. For this reason, Nixon's abandonment in 1971 of a fixed-rate exchange for the dollar has been identified by some as the detonator of a global economic turndown even before the Yom Kippur war. It was the end of the era of stable exchange rates stemming from Bretton Woods.

The picture of a divided world of haves and have-nots, rich and poor, developed and undeveloped, was to be complicated much further in the 1980s as a group of what came to be designated 'Newly Industrializing Countries' (NICs) began to draw ahead rapidly. In what is called the 'Pacific Rim', autonomous growth that escaped the supposedly fatal restraints of dependence and ex-colonial status seemed at last to have been shown to be possible. By the mid-1980s, Singapore, Taiwan and South Korea already provided notable examples, and Hong Kong the outstanding instance. The exports of these four countries (or, rather, in two instances, cities) accounted for 1.4 per cent of world trade in 1964 and 8.4 per cent twenty-five years later. A different comparison is further revealing: in 1960 the seven leading Arab economies had national per capita incomes higher than the seven east Asian economies (Taiwan, South Korea, Hong Kong, Singapore, Thailand, Malaysia and Indonesia). Thirty years later not only had these two groups reversed their positions, but east Asian figures were well ahead of those of the Arab countries. More and more, the tenacious poverty of countries (notably those of Africa) which seemed unable to shake off handicaps (variously attributed to different causes) looked less and less easy to remedy as time passed. Growth in world food production and a general decline in agricultural prices were among those reasons for this that were easiest to agree about.

Meanwhile, the rich went on getting richer, although more slowly and although the old predominance of the four major industrial regions was notably changed by 1990. The USSR was then still one of the big four, but had fallen far behind the others. It could not even match a single nation within the western European industrial agglomeration, West Germany. Japan had replaced the United States as the largest source of overseas investment. As for the Pacific Rim NICs, they had continued to achieve astonishing levels of growth and a much greater share of world trade. Because of this the peoples of Taiwan and South Korea enjoyed in 1988 a per capita GDP of, in the first instance, nearly eighteen times that of India, and, in the second, more than fifteen times.

The blow of the first oil crisis had struck at the heart of the arrangements that had provided fairly stable exchange rates for nearly a quarter-century and had inaugurated a period of greater currency instability. Some attempts were made to cope with it by new formal agreements (a European Monetary System was set up in 1979 between some European Community countries), but it had its most obvious effect in much greater volatility in currencies. At the same time there was a great and continuing increase in flows of capital from one country to another, partly under the influence of an increasing use of information technology. Money could be moved more easily than ever before, and in instant and round-the-clock response to price movement.

Yet a widespread slowing-down in the developed world at the end of the 1980s proved endurable. In no sense did it approach in gravity the cyclical recessions of the early 1920s and certainly not the great depression of the 1930s. The world economy continued to grow overall, though at a slower annual rate. The bulk of world trade continued to be generated by the developed world, its numbers now augmented in the Far East and by the larger South American nations. Meanwhile, the ability of governments to pursue effective national policies seemed to be on the wane: the impact of the oil price rise and the new rapid surges of currency flows between markets at short notice undermined confidence in economic *dirigisme* more than ever. Signs of this were to be seen in reluctance to restore old barriers to trade (such as tariffs) in developed countries, and the new success of developing countries in attracting foreign investment in search of cheap labour.

STRUCTURAL CHANGES

Short-term fluctuations can be very important but can also mask deeper change. Developed industrial powers now no longer much resemble their nineteenth-century predecessors. The old heavy and manufacturing industries, dependent on large numbers of low-skilled employees, which long provided the backbone of economic strength, were even by 1960 no longer a good measure of it. Industries that had once been the staples of leading countries were declining in importance. Of the three major steel-making countries of 1901, the first two (the USA and Germany) were still among the first five world producers eighty years later, but by then in third and fifth places respectively; the United Kingdom (third in 1900) was by 1980 tenth in the same world table – with Spain, Romania and Brazil, all of them insignificant as steel-producers in 1901, close on her heels. In 1982, Poland made more steel than had the USA in 1901. Newer industries, too, which had not existed as the century began, sometimes found a better environment for rapid growth in developing countries than in the mature economies. Much of the economic growth of rich countries has been in industries – electronics and plastics are obvious examples – which had far less importance before 1945.

Modern developed societies are therefore by no means simple extrapolations of the technology and structure of past industrial giants. Coal, which replaced running water and wood in the nineteenth century, had long before 1939 been joined, and in most places overtaken, by hydro-electricity, oil and natural gas as a major source of industrial energy and, very recently, by power generated by nuclear fission.[10] Service industries, too, provide much more employment nowadays. But the most visible outcome of the growth of industrialization in the second half of this century has been an enormous surge in the number and volume of commodities now available directly for the use and pleasure of the consumer.

The ramifications of an increased consumption of manufactured goods were enormous. By the 1980s, for example, Ford would not have recognized the shape of the car manufacturing industry he had pioneered; it was in several countries the most important part of the manufacturing sector, but it was also highly integrated internationally. Eight large producers made three out of four of the world's automobiles, and did not make these always in those producers' countries of origin. New techniques had stimulated major investment in many new places and in many other industries; by 1990 half the robots employed in the world's industry were welders in car factories (another quarter did the painting in them). What is more, change on a huge scale was still going forward. Japan, which could attribute a major part of its rise to economic ascendancy in the 1960s and 1970s to its car industry, was already by 1990 consciously running it down in anticipation of new challengers from abroad. The popularization of

[10] In 1966, for the first time, electricity generated by nuclear power cost less on the basis of contemporary accounting, than that made by burning fossil fuels. This was of some psychological importance, though it appears not to have taken account of decommissioning and fuel disposal costs.

the car contributed also to transport's rising demand for oil (this had first begun to be apparent even before 1914, as more ships became oil-powered). Large numbers of people came to be employed in the supply of fuel and services to car-owners, though transport is now no longer oil's only major consumer. Investment in road building – and later in arrangements for temporary storage (that is, parking: the sign 'P' became a significant and well-understood international message in the 1980s) – became a major local and national concern of governments and profoundly affected the construction industry.

Far back in the nineteenth century, Americans had promoted the idea of producing interchangeable, standardized parts for machinery. Henry Ford had also shown more dramatically than other manufacturers of the early twentieth century what could be done with mass-production. Like many great revolutionaries, Ford brought other men's ideas to bear on his own. The result had been the assembly line, along which the article under manufacture moved steadily forward from worker to worker, each one of them carrying out in the minimum necessary time the precisely delimited and, if possible, simple task in which he or she was skilled. Mass-production's psychological effect on the worker soon came to be deplored, but the technique was fundamental both to the production of weapons on the new scale demanded by two world wars and then to a wider sharing of the wealth of the industrial economy.[11] The assembly line became a universal device, used in the manufacture of many consumer products. It was a cultural force of incalculable significance. But Henry Ford had also been among the first to see that such work would be very boring and this made him an innovator in the sociology of production, too. He had paid good wages to compensate for boredom (thereby incidentally contributing to another revolutionary economic change, the fuelling of economic prosperity by increasing purchasing power and, consequently, raising demand).

Better management practice has now begun to generate other solutions to the psychological problems of mass-production; the drudgery of the assembly line is often now carried out by robots. The single

[11] The Ford company built a factory at Willow Run outside Detroit in 1941 that, in its final, perfected form, turned out one four-engined bomber every 103 minutes, 8,685 of them in all before the end of the war.

greatest technological change since 1945 in the major industrial economies has been the application of information technology, the complex
science of handling, managing, and devising electronically powered
machines to process information. Few innovative waves have swept
so fast through industry and economic life as a whole. Applications
first worked out in the 1940s were diffused in a couple of decades
over a huge range of services and industrial processes. Rapid increases
in the power and speed, reduction in the size, and improvement
in the visual display capacity of computers meant that much more
information could be sorted and processed more quickly than hitherto.
Commercial and industrial advance, in the handling of numerical and
logical data, had never been so suddenly accelerated. At the same
time, there was revolutionary growth in the capacity and power of
computers and technology made it possible to pack their potential
into smaller and smaller machines. Within thirty years, a silicon 'chip'
the size of a credit card was doing the job which had at first required
a machine the size of a room. Miniaturization has gone even further
since then.

The transforming effects have been felt in every service – and, indeed,
almost every human activity, from money-making to war-making.
Notably, though, they have contributed to decline in the absolute size
of industrial workforces in developed societies: some have thought
their industrial working classes might be following their peasantries
into history, as numbers in service employment rose correspondingly.[12]
In these changes, though, many other forces than the introduction of
better IT have also been at work. Taking a broad and speculative
view, as no doubt the student of history should not, it may be that
the computer, like the typewriter in the nineteenth century, will
actually increase, rather than diminish (as some have feared or hoped)
the need to employ people as it comes to have more and more
non-industrial applications.

[12] The phenomenon to be studied is larger, but perhaps it is an interesting straw in
the wind that in the proposals for the topics for discussion at the Twelfth International
Economic History Congress, held at Seville in 1998, the 'disindustrialization' of
Europe in the last two centuries was included as a subject now worthy of the
professional concern of economic historians.

CULTURAL CONSEQUENCES IN A
WEALTHIER WORLD

It grows more difficult, as this century proceeds, to fit global history to the traditional chronologies and categories of state, nationality and religion. Of none of its changes is this more true than of one of the more sweeping (but almost silent) changes of all, the global retreat of peasant society. Most of the world's population in 1901 were peasants. This was so because they lived by direct labour on the land, consuming and satisfying their needs from their own production however exact arrangements varied from country to country, district to district. By the century's end some of the greatest peasant societies of 1901 – Russia and China, for instance – had ceased to be describable in such terms: they had huge manufacturing sectors, a much greater proportion of their population living in towns and cities. Latin American cities and manufacturing sectors have grown, too, while the continent's peasants are even more locked into 'agro-industry' and international commodity markets than in 1901. Communications and education had everywhere cut into the old isolation of the countryside from the ideas and tastes of city-dwellers. Great wars have been fought often basically around the issue of the oppression and disruption of traditional peasant societies by colonial governments, but the outcome has been the 'liberation' of those societies to embark on further and more rapid modernization and adaptation of the traditional economy by indigenous rulers. Everywhere, the twentieth century has seen a huge retreat of the traditional peasant world. In Europe it has virtually disappeared, and for all its huge resilience in Africa, south-east Asia and India, it is giving ground there, too.

It would be virtually impossible to describe so varied a process in anything less than a book to itself. Even in a long study, too, niceties of timing and detail would be blurred. The same is true of other generalizations that might be set up about cultural change – for instance, the proposition (which appears broadly to be true) that since 1950 important cultural trends as well as the new economic abundance have tended first to be observable in the United States, then in Europe and later to spread to other continents. This has provided one of the basic rhythms of something often stigmatized as an 'Americanization' of everyday European culture and now beginning to awaken concern in other continents. A growing flow of material goods and an improving standard of life implied and promoted other changes, also to be shared among developed societies round the globe. Such changes went beyond the superficialities of taste and fashion that reflected the more obvious impact of American culture and more easily caught the eye.

For all the surviving cultural variety of European countries, virtually all of them have since 1950, for instance, shown notable changes of a similar tendency in the attitudes and behaviour of their young people. American examples and leadership have increasingly influenced their amusements and style. Specially targeted merchandising, surely the supreme accolade of respect, has now been directed to the young. Together with special entertainment and journalism it shows how commercially important 'youth' has become. In the second half of the century, for the first time in history, something like an international youth culture has appeared. In some places (mainly the cities of western Europe) and for a time in the 1960s this helped to produce a certain turbulence which, though attention-catching, was largely froth, the least profound manifestation of a great change. The new inter-nationalizing of taste, values and assumptions among young people was much more important, and it was to go on manifesting itself for the rest of the century, spreading into non-western countries as it did. It was based on the new prosperity of developed economies and the wealth to which it gave access (even to survive without gainful employment was becoming easier than in earlier times, thanks to the increasing readiness of democratic electorates to vote for social welfare). Wealth brought privileges in leisure and movement, as well as cheaper and more material goods.

The much-noted stirrings of youth were another reflexion of new communications. So was what conservatives saw as a growing corrup-tion of the young. Uneasiness, one may guess, ran highest in the most traditional non-western societies, but, with a slightly different emphasis, it was also voiced in communist eastern Europe. Radio and television were steadily making increasingly available to its young people the dangerous temptations of what was called 'capitalism'. There were already signs in the 1960s that the ruling élites of communist countries were worried. They could no longer feel confident of the loyalty, far less the enthusiasm, of the young. As more and better information about life in the West became available to them, and a rising tide of visitors from the non-communist world encountered them, young East Germans, Poles, Czechs and Hungarians no longer gratefully compared their own standards of material life with those of the previous generation – as many of their parents could still do – but with what was available to their peers in the West. This was a much graver cause of alarm to their elders and rulers than the specific content of the froth and fizz of youth culture on the other side of the Iron Curtain.

GLOBALIZATION

Computers transacting business with one another are part of two centuries' improvement in the physical and mechanical movement of messages, goods and people. Eighty years after the first flight by a man-carrying, powered, heavier-than-air machine, the value of goods imported and exported through Heathrow, London's biggest airport, was greater than that through any seaport in the country. Aeroplanes are now the normal form of long-distance travel. They offer a mobility to the individual hardly imaginable at the start of this century. Such advances in communication accelerate economic, cultural and social change. They have contributed to (among other things) the phenomenon that began to be commented on in the 1990s as 'globalization'.

The roots of this lay in the liberalization of trade, sometimes willingly embraced by, sometimes forced upon, almost all developed and many developing countries after 1970. Its essence was a new degree of international integration of economic life at virtually all levels. It was vividly expressed in a new internationalization of financial markets. A new scale of capital flows between countries first manifested itself after the oil crisis, though its origins could be traced back by those minded to do so as far as the emergence of New York as a rival and alternative financial centre to London after 1918, qualified though that was for a long time. In the 1970s and 1980s, the balance between them shifted notably in the Americans' favour; London and New

York were then joined, first by Tokyo, and then by a flowering of new major financial markets, not only in Europe, but in the Far East. This owed much, too, to technological innovation. But so did other aspects of the process, as transfers of knowledge and skills multiplied, and transport and communication costs fell. As they fell, the economic integration of the globe grew.

Globalization also owed – and contributed – much to the self-feeding process of growing world trade. For twenty years world trade grew faster than world output. Primarily expressed in the growing volume of trade in manufactured goods between the advanced industrial countries which were one another's best customers, this was itself a symptom of another structural change, the development of truly international companies. More importance may have been given to this than is warranted, but it led some of them to organize their production in several countries. They could no longer be said to have a single home base and their organization came to reflect this. Some such companies are sometimes little more than holders of investments, with little real control over an anthology of national or regional production and marketing organizations they formally 'own'. Because of the variety of real situations covered when the word 'globalization' is used of them, the extent and distinctive nature of the economic impact of 'multinationals', for all their visibility, is still debatable. Paradoxically, one of the impulses for the growth of capital investment in many countries has been a wish to share in the prosperity of the NICs by assisting import substitution even behind tariff protection and some of them seized such opportunities. Many multinationals can be best regarded as part-owners of joint enterprises shared with emerging national economies. Their activities have further speeded up the technological diffusion which is still changing the world so rapidly.

Another characteristic of the closing decades of the century has been the formation of new supranational economic regions and trading blocks. The first of these had been the European Common Market. By the end of the century there were NAFTA and Mercosur in the Americas, ASEAN in the Far East. This world of potentially wider free trade markets than ever before was, of course, given further extension when Chinese markets became more accessible in the 1980s and a series of astonishing political changes in the former communist sphere in Europe followed. Though part of the story of globalization, this suggests it is unwise to rush too rapidly to judgement about a phenomenon that no doubt displays connexions between many economic activities, but can still hardly be defined as a clear-cut structural fact. That, of course, is not likely to inhibit users of the word, which is just as useful and confusing as another overused in talking about this century: capitalism.

20

Authority and Its New Challengers

A LIBERATING CENTURY

It may seem at first sight almost wilfully paradoxical to suggest that the century of Stalin, Hitler, Pol Pot and the Ayatollah Khomeni has been one of growing personal freedom.[1] Even in democratic countries, there are good grounds to share de Tocqueville's pessimism that the triumph of public opinion must bring oppression of the individual. Moreover, even if we could agree about a way to measure freedom, it is very easy to disagree about what the data tells us when we think we have found the object we need to measure; one person can view a particular concrete example of a restriction of human freedom of choice as a reasonable and proper expression of demands society can justifiably make, while the same facts are seen by others as outright stifling of individuality. Most judgements about the extent of human

---

[1] Three of these names (and the vast differences in their aims and moral status) find sufficient explanation elsewhere in these pages. Pol Pot does not and it may be worth explaining here that he became the general secretary of the Cambodian communist party in 1963, as leader of the 'Khmer Rouge' faction was prime minister of Democratic Kampuchea in 1976, and presided over the killing of as many as 2 million (out of 7 million) of his countrymen and countrywomen in the name of a radical Maoist and fanatically xenophobic (and anti-Vietnamese) ideology. Such are the cross-currents of Cold War history that when, a few years later, he and his supporters were driven back into the jungle by the Vietnamese, he received support from the Chinese, US and Thai governments. When, in the 1990s, the Chinese cut off aid to the Khmer Rouge, it was divided by faction and mutiny and Pol Pot died in April 1998, apparently of a heart attack, a prisoner of his former comrades. His death had been preceded by reports that the Americans had initiated steps to catch him and bring him to trial on charges of crimes against humanity.

freedom are likely to start from so subjective a viewpoint as to be unacceptable *a priori* by many of those to whom they are addressed.

Yet if we contrast our own day with the world of 1901, it is simply evident that many more people are now alive who enjoy access to more and better information, that more people have better control of their personal timetables, more power to shape their personal environment, to dispose of their income, to choose how to spend 'spare' time and even what clothes they wear, more freely than in the past, and that this is not only true of the richest parts of the world. On the other hand, if we use different criteria, we can reflect that when, in the late 1940s, a British foreign secretary said that he wished to see a state of affairs in which someone could set off for a trip abroad with no need to do anything except buy a ticket, without passport, visa or any other required documentation, he was virtually asking for a return to conditions that had been taken for granted eighty years before and had disappeared since.

Given such apparent complexity, it seems best to try to look again at a few more things that stand out as changes since the century began. Among them are the powers and influence exercised by certain traditional sources of authority to shape behaviour. Many of them did so 100 years ago to an extent they no longer can hope for. True, much of humanity appears to rest still undisturbed in traditional pieties. Western, metropolitan-based intellectuals can be surprised to discover Christians, Muslims, Hindus, Marxists, Jews – and many others less numerous – who every day faithfully observe and sometimes vociferously defend the demands made by the teachings and practices of their faiths. Yet there are also many others raised in those same observances, whose parents and grandparents behaved unquestioningly, but who now find it impossible, or at least inconvenient, to obey in the same way. Science, technology and material improvement, however diluted their influence, have all made it harder to believe, and harder to conform to patterns of behaviour arising from specific beliefs. For millions in the sphere of western civilization, modernity has meant learning to do without the idea of God.

DISSOLVING CERTAINTY

Because change like this is most obvious among the intellectual élites who are disproportionately prominent in histories of thought and culture, we can easily exaggerate its extent. In the past, their ideas, or changes in them have only slowly tended to affect the climates of opinion in which most of mankind live. Nonetheless, in recent history, growing literacy and increasing rapidity of communication have pushed new ideas further into mass culture in the developing world than ever before (and this seems likely to continue). The impact of new ideas on élites, though, still remains easier to trace than that on the masses. In the eighteenth century, Newtonian cosmology settled down into coexistence with theocentric modes of thought without much disturbing the social and moral beliefs tied to them in many western countries. In this century, things have gone differently. Science has seemed harder and harder to reconcile with any fixed belief at all. It has encouraged relativism and appeared to deny that there are unchallengeable assumptions or viewpoints. It has undermined the status of the observer even of physical phenomena. This has spilled out through our communications networks to reach, in crude and often misapprehended forms, larger numbers of men and women than were in any sense aware of a new cosmogony fifty years after Newton's death. It is another of those changes which remains more true, though, of the western than of the non-western world.

One example can be found in psychology. The systematic investigation of the mind evolved in the nineteenth century away from the traditional limitations of 'mental philosophy' into a subject with reasonable claims to be a science, largely under the influence of medical men. Freud (to return again to that example) began his own career as a neurologist and an investigator of the clinical use of hypnosis. His later, most famous views had been first stimulated by the clinical observation of mental disorder, or what was said to be such. One outcome was Freud's own therapeutic technique; it was based on the belief that relevant data could be assembled and therapy pursued by interrogating subjects about their wishes, feelings and thoughts, and interpreting this data in accordance with an appropriate body of theory. This was the foundation of the activities that may conveniently be grouped under the name Freud gave to his work, 'psychoanalysis', though not all of them sprang directly from his ideas. Psychoanalysis in non-Freudian as well as Freudian versions quickly had effects beyond therapy, exciting and influencing artists, novelists, teachers and advertising specialists in many western countries.

Another important early twentieth-century approach to psychology was more mechanistic. Though the word is often used imprecisely, 'Behaviourism', as it has been termed, appeared to generate a body of data much more impressive than psychoanalysis, because truly experimental. Theoretically and conceptually, it was soon under fire from the philosophers, but this did not seem to matter; it went on to win much applause and achieve apparent practical success. The outstanding name associated with it is that of the Russian scientist I. P. Pavlov who, in a series of celebrated experiments in the first decade of this century, established generalizations which, with due qualification, were taken to be applicable to human beings. His most influential single discovery was the 'conditioned reflex'. Essentially this relied upon the manipulation of one of a pair of variables in an experiment in order to produce a predicted piece of behaviour by a 'conditioned stimulus'. The classic experiment provided for a bell to be sounded before food was given to dogs. After a time, the sounding of the bell produced in the dog the salivation that had earlier been produced by the presentation of food. Refinements and developments of similar procedures followed, providing new insights into human psychology which were exploited in many ways (one of the most depressing features of our age, perhaps, is the use made of them by torturers, though without successes which conclusively demonstrated superiority to earlier methods). Some beneficent results were observed, notably in the treatment of mental illness and the improvement of teaching techniques.

If an attempt is to be made to grasp so shapeless a subject, the diffused effect of Behaviourism, though confined consciously to a relatively few countries and centres, seems curiously like that of Freudianism in one important respect: it, too, now seems as striking a cultural, as a scientific, phenomenon. Both undermined the idea of the autonomous, rational mind, and therefore the sense of responsibility and individualism that has lain at the heart of European moral tradition. They made it easier, and perhaps more tempting, for people to find excuses for what they had previously been told was their own bad behaviour and weakness. The same process was also likely to be advanced by more empirical and experimental approaches to understanding the mind, notably through the treatment of mental disorder by chemical, electrical and other physical intervention. These methods (particularly the psycho-pharmacological) have been employed more and more widely in medical practice in recent years, with, it would appear to laymen, growing success. But they have not left the autonomy of the rational individual mind its old mythological status as the unquestioned central datum of human life and society. Their implications, like those of the teachings of Freud and the behaviourists, though they may not be widely grasped, are influential and inevitably came in the end to colour even widely-held views.[2] In spreading a relativistic view of human life and destiny, they may be thought ultimately of even greater significance than the science which in the previous century already had done so much to sap the vigour of theocentric world-outlooks.

RELIGION IN THE LATER TWENTIETH CENTURY

What this means for organized religion, except that it means something, is almost impossible to say. A new psychological and moral relativism no doubt suggested new explanations of what were previously taken by many people to be matters falling clearly within the province of religion. They were bound to suggest that things hitherto thought mysterious and inexplicable could now be made more manageable by human effort. Surely this was likely to further undermine the age-old magical authority of religious institutions, in however qualified a way? The answer must be yes – but by no means everywhere and

---

[2] Perhaps one of the most general and easily observable effects has been in the effect of ideas of diminished responsibility in judicial and penal processes in the western world.

not in the same ways. As one might say, it all depends on what you mean by 'religious belief'. In some formerly Christian societies there now live side-by-side men and women who still defend accounts of Creation and Redemption set out in the Bible in a quite literal sense, with others so content with the evaporation of any transcendent element in their faith that it is for them quite satisfactorily reducible to the observation of certain moral principles and standards derived from the Christian tradition. Comparison between different religions, of course, reveals even starker contrasts.

Yet, paradoxically, it may well also be true of our age that there are now more people who respect religious authority than ever before. This is in part a consequence of world population growth. Numbers more than trebling since 1901 have indeed led to huge consequential growth of adherence to established Christian churches in Latin America, or to other religions in Africa and the sub-continent of India. But other facts – modern communications, for instance – are part of the story, too. No pope had stepped outside the Vatican for over thirty years when this century began: in all history, none had gone further than Constantinople. Religious newspapers existed then, but no religious radio or television stations such as have now proliferated and support new evangelical action by American missionaries, for example. Any diminution of respect for religious authority, let alone belief in the supernatural such as is often alleged to be characteristic of the contemporary era, needs careful qualification, and continued recollection of the degree to which we may be over-impressed by a few western countries.

Indeed, when people talk about the waning power of religion, it tends to be countries of Christian tradition that they have in mind. Often, too, they are talking about the waning authority of Christian churches, not about the influence of Christian religious belief the world round. It would be a bold presumption that religion in many parts of the United States was less influential in the age of television than in 1901. What people believe, too, is often better shown by what they do than what they say, and many people still behave superstitiously. The last English monarch who took the precaution of consulting an astrologer about an auspicious day for her coronation was Elizabeth I; in the 1980s, though, the world was surprised (and perhaps just a little alarmed) to hear that the wife of the president of the United States was in the habit of seeking astrological advice. More symptomatically, in 1947 the timing of the ceremony marking the achievement of Indian independence was only settled after appropriate consultation of astrologers. Indian politicians cared about what the heavens said because millions of other Indians did. In 1962 in Delhi 250 holy men carried out three weeks of chanting and other ceremonies to mark the conjunction of eight planets in Capricorn; in Burma, the prime minister released animals, birds and fishes to mark the same event.

India, though, is now a republic that is formally and constitutionally non-confessional and secular. The constitutional provisions that are intended to secure this reflect the adoption of western ideas about the boundaries of religious practice, if not belief. Pakistan, in contrast, is a confessional state. Its founders were secular-minded, westernized men who might well have seemed likely, before independence, to accept a religious settlement after it not dissimilar to the one adopted in India. In a struggle with the conservative *ulema* after independence, though, they lost. Pakistan became an orthodox Islamic state. Its rulers now go well beyond mere respect for Islam as the religion of the majority of its people, and have intensified the degree to which Pakistani law is shaped by Islamic tradition.

Nor, if established religions are now less usual than they were (most examples are in Muslim countries), need this mean that their real power over their adherents has everywhere declined. The voices of large numbers often drown those of the modernizing few. It was a surprise to *bien-pensant* British in the 1980s when Iranian Muslims denounced an admired novelist as a traitor to Islam and put a price on his head; intellectual London suddenly discovered, as it were, that the Middle Ages were still in full swing in other parts of the world, a fact that had previously escaped it. Some Britons were even more startled when large numbers of their own Muslim fellow-citizens appeared to sympathize with the *fatwa*. It is possible to continue to believe that in such matters (as in others) western society has indicated a path that other societies will follow, and that conventional western liberalism will prevail. It may be so, but, also, it may not be; it may be prudent to be cautious. As long ago as 1963, after all, Jewish zealots were demonstrating against Christian missions in Jerusalem.

It seems unlikely, in looking at the record, that even Islamic societies can altogether avoid cultural corruption by the technology and materialism of the European tradition, though they appear to have been able to resist the missionary version of that tradition expressed in atheistic communism. When a gathering of heads and representatives of Islamic states took place in Teheran at the end of 1997, it heard the Muslim prime minister of the Islamic republic of Iran acknowledge publicly that Islamic society should take account of and utilize the positive achievements of western civilization: a few years earlier this would have been a message too unacceptable to the religious authorities to be set out in public by any Iranian. Elsewhere, though, Islam is still an expanding and vigorous missionary faith. Nor is the notion of Islamic unity by any means dead in Islamic lands. Appalling events in Algeria and in Afghanistan have shown only too well what political action and atrocity it can still spawn. Religion as an identifier of community produced terrifying massacres in the Indian sub-continent both during the months before and after partition in 1947 and in the struggles which led to the establishment of the new state of Bangladesh as a breakaway from Pakistan in 1971. In Ulster and Glasgow, there are still those who prefer to set out their hatreds and dispute the future of their country in images and words forged in Europe's seventeenth-century religious conflicts rather than in secular terms. This should encourage us to be more ready to consider religious influences as matters of social and cultural institutions, rather than intellectual belief. Whatever is left of the supernatural content of belief in the country, in what used to be Yugoslavia religion is as important today as a badge of group membership as ever. Though the hierarchies and leaders of different religions find it appropriate on the world stage to moderate their language, exchange public courtesies, and even to cooperate in practical matters, and though the major Christian churches have lost (for the most part) their old triumphant aggressiveness, it cannot be said that religion ceases to be a divisive force when doctrine becomes more amorphous.

Within the world that could no longer be called Christian but that was still unmistakably one of Christian origins, 1950 had been proclaimed a Holy Year by the Roman Catholic Church.[3] A million foreign pilgrims came to Rome, and the year was in due course marked by the publication of the papal encyclical *Munificentissimus Deus*, which defined the dogma of the assumption, body and soul, of the Blessed Virgin Mary into heavenly glory; this was, among other things, an assertion that her corporeal remains underwent none of the natural processes of decay and, indeed, were miraculously removed from the earth. This dogma was one of the last major expressions of what was in origin very much the stance of a Church still consciously facing the challenges of 100 years earlier. Yet it came at the opening of decades of striking challenge and change in the most widespread and numerous of the Christian communions.

For most of the century, a decline of dogmatic rigour and sectarian strife has in fact gone along with a fading and loss of definition of belief in the Christian revelation and, often, with a loss of ecclesiastic nerve. Ecumenism, the movement within Christianity whose most conspicuous expression was the setting up of a World Council of Churches in 1948, has complex roots.[4] It owes much to Christians' growing sense in the developed countries of Christian tradition that they are living in increasingly hostile environments, but something also to greater uncertainty about what Christianity is, and what it ought to claim. Unsurprisingly, the Roman Catholic Church has never joined the Council, though it has now given it a measure of recognition. In the USSR the Council was pronounced an American-influenced anti-communist development and the Moscow Synod condemned its foundation. It is hard to see ecumenism, though, as an unequivocally hopeful sign of an unexhausted vigour in Christianity. For those looking for such signs, a more promising one has been the growth – largely by natural increase outside Europe – of the Roman Catholic Church. Most Roman Catholics are now non-Europeans (although

---

[3] There have been twenty-three such 'Jubilee' years since the first in 1300, the last in 1975.
[4] The definitive moment is usually agreed to have been at an International Missionary Conference held at Edinburgh in 1910.

the first two African bishops were only consecrated by Rome in 1939).[5] This change was dramatized by the spectacular and popular successes of the first papal visits to South America and Asia in the 1960s. By 1980, 40 per cent of the world's Roman Catholics lived in South America and a majority of the College of Cardinals came from non-European countries.

A certain numerical confidence and assertiveness was curiously accompanied in the 1960s by what seemed a measure of softening in the historic stance of the Roman papacy and its claim to authority within the Church. This owed much to a pope already elderly (he was seventy-seven) at the moment of his election in 1958. John XXIII then won within a few years respect and even popularity within and outside the Roman Catholic Church. Thanks to modern communications, this probably made him the most widely loved pope there had ever been. In October 1962 he inaugurated an ecumenical council at the Vatican attended by almost 3,000 Catholic prelates, and, strikingly, by invited observers from other Christian churches and organizations. Its purpose was to interpret the message of the Church to the age and it proved to be radically innovative in helping to bring about what was soon being called the 'aggiornamento', or 'bringing-up-to-date', of the Roman Church. Liturgically, it took one very visible step towards discarding tradition where it no longer seemed helpful as a guide, by authorizing the use of local, vernacular languages in the Mass. Later decried as divisive by many vociferous European Catholics though it was, only nineteen of those prelates attending the Council voted against this measure, while 2,158 voted for it. But the next two years (the Council only concluded its work in 1964) brought a more fundamental reorientation than this. John died in 1963, but his successor, Paul VI, immediately showed that he was as willing to contemplate new approaches as had been his predecessor. Having almost at once asked on behalf of the Church for divine forgiveness for the injuries it had inflicted in the past on other Christians whose representatives were present, he issued in 1964 an encyclical (his first) that, though unequivocally asserting the unique truthfulness of the Christian

---

[5] The first black Anglican bishop was ordained priest in 1843 and consecrated bishop of the Niger territory in 1864.

revelation, spoke also of recognizing and respecting 'the moral and spiritual values of the various non-Christian religions' and of his desire to join them in promoting and sustaining shared social and ethical ideals.[6]

Nineteen seventy-eight was a year of three popes in rapid succession. The last of them to ascend the throne of St Peter was also the first Polish pope (and, indeed, the first non-Italian for four and a half centuries). He was, too, the first whose investiture was attended by an Anglican archbishop of Canterbury. John Paul II soon showed a vigorous determination to exploit to the full the historic possibilities of his office; his pronouncements were to be much attacked as over-conservative. It is hazardous to project trends in the history of an institution whose fortunes have so obviously fluctuated across the centuries. But it can be acknowledged that contraceptive practice – an issue sharpened by science and technology – had by the end of the century confronted the Papacy with a grave threat to its hitherto unquestioned authority in the eyes of millions of Catholics and one which, in spite of the pope's own unbending leadership, seemed likely to bring into question even the prudent concessions of the Second Vatican Council.

GOVERNMENT, DEMOCRACY AND NATIONALISM

Over most of the world, and since time immemorial, organized religion and the notion of unchanging moral law often linked to it have usually underpinned the management of any society regarded as legitimate. Both have been much weakened in recent times. The sovereign state, another great historic agent of social order, has at first sight kept its end up much better. At the beginning of this century, it was already at a peak of prestige and acceptability in the western world. It went

---

[6] The Council's decisions and the pronouncements of Paul VI affected public law in some countries: the Spanish Organic Law of 1966 which launched the cautious transformation of the Spanish state once again into a constitutional monarchy provided, *inter alia*, for lifting the ban maintained hitherto on non-Catholic religious ceremonies and other manifestations in public.

on to success round the globe. No form of political organization has ever been so widely taken for granted. There exist today more sovereign states – that is, recognized and geographically defined political units claiming legislative independence and a monopoly of the use of force within their own borders – than ever before. What is more, expectations of what states can and ought to do have greatly risen while, as a matter of fact, their coercive puissance has grown out of recognition since the days when even the greatest monarchy could not carry out an effective census or demolish the obstacles in the way of unified internal markets.

The state's virtual monopoly of the main instruments of physical control is only a part of this story, but it is an important one. Even in 1901, police and armed forces unshaken by war and uncorrupted by sedition provided almost certain assurance of survival for any regime. Improved technology only increased this near-certainty (recently, and not least, through better information systems). New repressive techniques and weapons, though, are now only a small part of the story of state power. State intervention in the economy, as consumer, investor or planner, and the improvement of mass-communications are also political facts of great importance. Demands are made everywhere that governments indirectly promote the material welfare of their subjects and undertake the provision of services impossible or inconceivable hitherto, or left in the past to individuals or such 'natural' units as families and communities. This has been most obvious in the economically developed world. In western Europe, for example, spending by governments on 'welfare' (including education and housing) rose from roughly 25 per cent of GNP in 1950 to some 45 per cent in the middle 1970s.[7] More people than ever before now expect government to try to maintain a favourable economic climate. They have acquiesced in governments being given new powers to do this and expect them to use them. Whatever evasive steps individuals may take to avoid taxation, the ability of modern governments to raise money by it would have amazed any politician in the western world of 1901; even in 1914, only one of the great powers that went to war that year had so far been able to levy an income tax.

[7] A. S. Milward, *The European Rescue of the Nation-State* (London, 1992), p.33.

No doubt this helps to explain why politics – conceived as the struggle to take hold of state power – has in some countries apparently replaced religion (and sometimes even economics) as the focus of faith that can move mountains. The welfare state was a reality in Germany and Great Britain before 1914, and attempts to regulate the economics of demand and supply are as old as government itself. These, however, seemed only pale prefigurings of the Leviathan which came to terrorize imagination in the 1940s in countries where people still remembered life in a more liberal climate. Institutions specifically designed to protect individuals remain notoriously absent in many countries; something like the Chinese communist *dang'an* system of a file on everybody in employment, containing details going back to school-days, can hardly work perfectly, but must be an instrument of enormous power over individuals.[8] For a long time the United States was the outstanding example of a rich country where there prevailed 'minimalist' views of the role of government in national life, but it can also provide some of the most striking examples of the actual extension of central authority (notably under the New Deal and in the Second World War), within a federal system. This century's great wars and peacetime tensions have helped such evolution worldwide. Both required huge mobilization of resources and led to unprecedented extensions of governmental power.

Another force favouring the accretion of state power in some countries has been the urge to modernize. Russia and China, two great agrarian societies, appeared to provide outstanding examples of successful modernization through state power. The role played by the urge to modernize in strengthening the state – something prefigured by a Kemal or a Reza Shah before 1939 and even more observable in the era of political revolution which has followed – also illustrates the change in the sources from which the state has increasingly drawn its moral authority. Instead of relying on personal obligation to a group, a dynasty or a supernatural sanction, it has come to rest increasingly on its claim to satisfy collective desires. Not all these desires have been material. It would be very difficult to say that material benefits came first among the *desiderata* of, say, the brutal

---

[8] 'The X-Files', *The Economist*, 14 February 1998, p.72.

regime that took power in Cambodia in 1975, but perhaps that never achieved legitimacy in the eyes of the majority. Elsewhere, though (in Serbia, perhaps), people also can see the state still as the supreme expression of national spirit and consciousness, the psychic force still driving much of world politics.

Nationalism's tenacity has been remarked on page after page of this book; it has been successful in mobilizing allegiance to (and sometimes against) the state as no other force has been able to do. Against it, other ideologies have proved largely ineffective; economics, communications and technology rather than comparably powerful moral ideas or mythologies have been the main forces working the other way, and helping to spread beliefs and attitudes across frontiers instead of entrenching them behind them. In spite of much specious talk about majority rule, democracy – or at least liberal democracy – has been an ideology much compromised or weakened by triumphant nationalism. It is fair to make the point, of course, that, thanks to two out of three of the victorious great powers of 1945 being democracies, a victory for that system was actually won in western Europe. There was no such false dawn of constitutionalism and liberal democracy after 1945 as there had been in 1919, but within a few years that victory was stabilized, entrenched and broadened until finally even dictatorships that had survived the war (those of Spain and Portugal) and one that had come into existence since (a military regime in Greece) disappeared. With slightly less plausibility, it could be argued, too, that many formally liberal and democratic regimes had been left behind in non-European countries by the retreat of imperial power (and even that some of them had survived). Even the dictatorial and despotic politics of some Latin American countries seemed to have taken a turn for the better by the 1990s. Above all, there was to come after 1980 a virtual wiping of the slate of communism in eastern Europe.

Nonetheless, scrutiny of actual political behaviour in some of the countries into which formal democracy has extended itself presents a less reassuring picture. There are many corrupt, brutal, intimidatory regimes talking the language of rights and constitutionalism. Very often, too, the force that corrupts the working of democratic politics has been nationalism. All successful states in this century have been

nation-states (though obviously not all nation-states have been continuously successful). Western Europe's efforts to integrate its
component nations in larger organizations can be seen as the
expression of wishes to safeguard national aims and interests.[9] When
it has been in conflict with nationalism, even the democratic state
has often been gravely disadvantaged, for all its physical power. As
formerly non-democratic and formally multinational regimes, shaped
by the traditions of communist centralization though they had been,
both the USSR and Yugoslavia disintegrated into national units in
the 1990s. Basques still agitate for autonomy within Spain or for
separation from it, Scotchmen for a reversal of the Union of 1707.
The Quebecois seek self-government. If speculation were pursued, it
would be possible to cite many other instances of even more alarming
potential; the Kurds, after all, seek to escape from the grasp of no
fewer than three states (Turkey, Syria, Iraq) in which they live and
between which they are divided.[10] In each instance, tribalism writ large
– nationalism – is the explanation. Once it has found an expression
in a state-form, too, nationalism tends to reinforce the power of
government and extend its real scope. This is one reason why politicians usually set to work to foster new nationalisms in countries
where they do not exist in order to bolster the shaky state structures
that emerge from decolonization.

When nationalism and the state work together, people tend usually
to feel that government is stronger and less resistible than ever, even
in countries where government has traditionally been distrusted and
where institutions exist that can rein it in. The strongest checks on
the abuse of power remain those of habit and assumption; so long as
electorates in liberal states can assume that governments are not likely
to fall back quickly or automatically on the use of force, they do not
feel very alarmed. But there are now more dictators, bandit rulers and
authoritarian political regimes in the world than in 1939 (though none
remain in the European union, many uncertainties hang over eastern

[9] E.g. in Milward, *The European Rescue of the Nation-State*, as its title suggests.
[10] Though there are between 25 and 30 million Kurds, they face a future that seems
as unpromising as that of the Armenians in the first decades of this century; not only
scattered over different countries, they are divided, are unloved by their host states,
while the Great Powers remain unwilling to commit themselves in their defence.

European countries and the republics of former Yugoslavia). Like the undermining of other liberal assumptions, its disarray in many parts of the world has revealed the essential contingency of the liberalism which was once thought the cause of the future. It depended historically on a few progressive societies which opened the way to it in the nineteenth century. Yet the forms of liberal politics, at least, have survived. Everyone now uses the cant phrases of democracy and the rhetoric of constitutionalism has never been more widely prostituted. That is a testimony to its importance.

The century has in fact brought much export of formally liberal institutions to contexts inimical to them. To deplore what has sometimes followed is unhistorical and unrealistic; as Burke pointed out long ago, political principles take their colour from circumstances. Too often in the last half-century it has been shown that representative institutions and democratic forms can hardly work properly in societies lacking habits coherent with them, or where there are powerful divisive influences. In such circumstances – for example, in many post-colonial territories – authoritarian styles of government have sometimes seemed the best way to resist fragmentation once the discipline imposed by an outside power is withdrawn. Only too obviously, this has not led to greater democracy, let alone happiness.

CHALLENGES TO THE STATE

Yet the sovereign state is not as powerful as once it was, in principle, at least. Since 1945, new supranational factors have come into play that may indicate the start of a turn in the tide that began to run in its favour in sixteenth-century Europe, and has so run ever since. One is the appearance of more effective international organization than has existed hitherto. Although the United Nations is made up of sovereign states it has been able to undertake positive action in support of international peacekeeping under its charter, and has sometimes organized collective action as the League of Nations never could. On a smaller stage, but still impressive scale, the nations of western Europe have moved a long way towards a shared institutional framework restricting and encroaching upon their freedom of action. Nor are formal organizations the whole story. Many supranational problems today are the subject of lengthy examination and negotiation *ad hoc* (over, for example, concerns about the environment).

The old idea of state sovereignty which lay at the heart of international relations for most of this century has also been compromised recently in other ways. Since the 1960s at least, willingness has grown to approve coercion of sovereign states and interference in their internal affairs (through the imposition of sanctions, for example) which would have been unthinkable in 1901. This has more than one root. As long ago as 1948, a majority of the United Nations undertook to uphold human rights and prevent genocide (this was a notable reflexion of wide agreement that nothing like the Holocaust should ever again be allowed to occur).[11] Sometimes, too, flows of refugees across international frontiers have excited a new awareness of the dangers presented to states neighbouring those where bad (or the lack of) government drove people to flight and has therefore encouraged coercive action. In 1999, though, a further step was taken when an armed assault was made on a sovereign state, Serbia, with the aim of changing its internal behaviour towards its own subjects.[12]

The doctrine that statesmen should seek something more than order in their dealings with one another, and should try to change the internal regimes of sovereign states, is a new radicalization of international relations, implicitly discarding the old notion of sovereignty. Intervention on ethical or ideological grounds was only attempted under very specific occasions in the past and in particular places (by, for instance, the Holy Alliance in Europe for a few years after 1815). United States actions in the western hemisphere under 'corollaries' to the Monroe doctrine, or Soviet policy in eastern Europe during the Cold War were unabashedly defended on grounds of security and interest. Nor had anyone, of course, ever seriously contested (at least until 1935 and the Italian invasion of Abyssinia) the right of imperial powers to interfere by force in the affairs of ramshackle and decaying 'uncivilized' polities adjacent to their own colonial possessions. In all

---

[11] The convention on genocide so defined the offence as to cover acts intended to destroy, in whole or in part, national, racial and religious groups. It was approved unanimously in the General Assembly.

[12] See Chapter 27.

such cases, the international community had only had to recognize that the facts of the situation and the established interests at stake would make it prudent to allow *de facto* what it could not prevent except at unacceptable cost. But what happened in Serbia in 1999 went much further than this.

Some would also identify cultural and, in a sense, non-political influences as from time to time cramping the freedom of action of sovereign states. Religion has sometimes seemed to do so in a way perhaps faintly reminiscent of medieval Europe. Certainly the modern state has not established itself so successfully in, for example, the Islamic Middle East as elsewhere. Other examples might be the evocation of pan-Africanism, a phenomenon virtually unrooted in objective reality, or a loyalty to what has been labelled *négritude*. There was a time, too, when people thought a Third World might be a reality. Another check, or determinant – words are not easy to choose at so general a level – on state power has been the growing integration of the world economy. Institutionalized by international agreement or by the simple organic growth of the interests of large organizations, and driven by rising expectations, this has more and more dashed the hopes of statesmen seeking effective unilateral management of domestic economies. It has sometimes been expressed in regional groupings of nations that require the observance of common disciplines. Some, like the South American or the North American free trade areas, have as yet only modest scope, but may yet take on other tasks.

Such reflexions anticipate much that follows. It is still, obviously, too soon to predict the disappearance of the state as the characteristic and central political institution of modern history. But it seems likely that the way of working and the effective sphere of action of the state power may continue to change, leaving forms largely intact, and perhaps while power flowers and accumulates in other institutions. This at least looks more likely than that revolutionary forces will succeed in destroying state power as some feared only a few years ago. Less menacing opponents of the state also from time to time draw strength and appear to prosper by espousing new causes: ecologists, feminists and anti-nuclear and 'peace' movements have all patronized them. What are sometimes inelegantly called 'transnational advocacy networks' have sometimes been effective. But in forty years of activity such causes have only been successful when they have been able to influence and shape state policy itself, changing laws, and setting up new institutions. The idea that major amelioration can be achieved either by overthrowing or wholly bypassing so historically dominant an institution still seems as unrealistic as it was in the days of the anarchistic and Utopian movements of the nineteenth century.

WOMEN

Few as they were in western societies in 1901 (and almost invisible in non-western), it also seems very unlikely that any of those women who were then trying to bring about change in the status and roles of their sex would have been able to foresee the actual changes ahead. Yet in some developed societies in 1950 much that was sought by earlier feminists had already been achieved, most notably, perhaps, in the public and formal sphere. One key and symbolic struggle had been for political suffrage, and it had been widely, though somewhat unevenly, successful. In 1920 the United States constitution was amended to give women the vote. By then, women over thirty already had it in the United Kingdom and in 1928 British women got it on the same terms as men. Weimar Germany, Belgium, Denmark, Canada, Holland and Sweden all also introduced female suffrage soon after the Great War. In 1919 the Pope had already said he was in favour of giving women the vote and among European Catholic countries it was important that the Spanish republic did so in 1934. In Latin America, Ecuador, Brazil, Uruguay and Cuba had all done so by 1939. Argentina was only to follow suit in 1951, but by 1980, female suffrage was usual in most member-states of the UN. The sequence of its appearances had some interesting features; Japanese women were only a little behind Frenchwomen (1944) and Italians (1945) in winning the vote, and well ahead of the Swiss in national elections. Yet in 1991, France installed her first female prime minister, though well after several other countries, including India.

Less changed before mid-century were the ways men and women behaved towards one another in society. Working men in developed countries at mid-century still assumed that the breadwinner ought to have the last word in such matters as the allocation of the household's resources or the discipline of children. Some of the economic changes that had offered women new roles in the first three decades of the twentieth century were eaten into by the depression years, too, while in one or two places – fascist Italy and Nazi Germany, in particular – there were conscious efforts to draw back from what were seen as dangerous instances of female emancipation. This qualifies such examples of relative advance for women as were achieved as a result of the general overcoming of backwardness and illiteracy in the Soviet Union. There still also remained huge and unquestioned formal and legal inequalities even between the countries most advanced in these matters. Nevertheless, in western countries such inequalities were under almost continuous legislative attack and moral questioning in the post-war years, especially in what would once have been called Catholic Europe. Marriage law everywhere came to take account of women's demands for equitable treatment, even if it was only in 1977 that German law removed the requirement that a husband give permission for his wife to work, and only in 1980 that the right to civil marriage (an important issue in most European countries in the nineteenth century, and usually settled then) was finally won in Greece.

Such advances – made under European Community, as well as national, law – left many questions still open and inevitably threw up new areas of contention (for instance about the recognition of the effects on women's economic lives of the natural restriction of their childbearing years, and the allowances that should be made and adjustments that were required in law and custom in order to recognize the mother's role). Nonetheless, so sweeping have been changes (broadly speaking) in the 'western' countries, or among westernized élites elsewhere, that they have thrown into relief everywhere else in the world the persistence of the exploitation of women's labour, or of the compulsion to bear children who will survive to look after parents in old age, or of respect for traditions that say that women shall not enjoy the same educational opportunities as men.

Many indicators now suggest that examples set by western countries in the treatment of women are more and more influential around the world, as other western influences have been in other matters. This was observable early in this century, though at first only in occasional facts. A campaign for women's suffrage was mounted in the Philippines before 1914; well before that, though, a handful of women delegates had attended the 1889 meeting of the Indian National Congress, and in 1917 a women's deputation called on the viceroy to ask for the vote and Congress endorsed their request the following year. The Chinese communist party almost from the start advocated female suffrage. Such scattered evidence might be taken as signs of a change in the wind, closely linked to modernization and the expanding success of the western model of civilization in this century.

In most of the developed world, too, the forces pre-eminent in changing the condition of women are still, though much intensified and reinforced, ones already at work in 1901. The influence of economic and technological change on women's roles through the provision of new employment opportunities has gone on growing. As the end of the century approaches, a dual-career family is thought normal in the Nordic European countries, and to a large extent in Great Britain and the USA. Meanwhile, new forces have also come to bear in developed countries that have made for greater equality of treatment for women in the labour force.[13] Together with more widely available professional education this has led to the emergence in western and even some non-western countries of significantly larger numbers of women in employment in managerial and professional roles which they would not have occupied a century ago. Female doctors and lawyers no longer seem remarkable and at least in western countries significant numbers of women now serve as bank managers, sit on boards of directors or are executives of major industrial and commercial concerns. At lower levels, millions more women have now come to benefit both from the spread of educational provision and from greater access to information about opportunity resulting from the huge development of modern communication. In some countries – Spain and Greece, for example – changes in their political circum-

---

[13] Though not without difficulties arising from the failure of male-dominated European and North American trade unions to welcome women into their ranks in the first half of this century.

stances encouraged autonomous women's organization after years of official disfavour by authoritarian regimes.

THE PILL

While some of the legal and political advances secured by women before 1950 conceivably might have been read in the sands of the future by an intelligent observer even in 1901, it would have been less likely that another advance of vast consequence for women could have been anticipated, the rapid and wide diffusion in the 1960s of a new contraceptive device, quickly and widely known as, simply, 'the Pill'.[14]

The crucial research had been done in the previous decade. In the 1930s a female sex hormone called 'progesterone' had been isolated and noted as possibly a useful agent in fertility control because it modified cycles of ovulation and menstruation in women. Research then began to be directed towards compounds containing this that might be administered orally. Towards the end of 1951, an American, Dr Carl Djerassi, who had been working for a small pharmaceutical company in Mexico on the extraction of useful substances from yams, filed a patent for such a compound that was orally effective. By 1958 other scientists had carried out biological tests and clinical trials for both his compound (norethindrone[15]) and a similar compound that had been made for a Chicago company. The United States Food and Drug Administration had already authorized the marketing of norethindrone as a treatment for menstrual disorders and certain fertility problems; in 1962 it permitted its use for contraception. The manufacturer of the drug was nonetheless not at that time willing to risk what was felt likely to be overwhelming Roman Catholic hostility if its preparation was sold as a contraceptive, and another company had in 1960 already put the first contraceptive pill on the market with

[14] This colloquialism was, oddly enough, coined before the device itself was actually available. ' "The Pill" has not yet been invented,' noted Aldous Huxley, a well-known man of letters, in his *Brave New World Revisited* (London, 1959).
[15] The name it bears in the USA, also called norethisterone.

FDA approval ('norethynodrel'). Very rapidly, though, the world began to change for millions of women.

The Pill is a very characteristic product of modern science, and the story of its development has its own interest in that light. Nevertheless, it is the larger context in which it appeared that concerns us here. For more than a century and a half, women in western societies had been slowly acquiring more and better access to contraceptive information and advice. They had also experienced changes in social attitudes that made the use of that knowledge more widespread. The Pill, thanks to its convenience and the way it worked, though, was the greatest single fact transferring power in these matters to women. The decision to use contraception henceforth rested with them, if they wished it to do so. In 1960, it is true, there were still several developed countries – the Republic of Ireland, for example – where contraceptives might not be sold or made available. There are still now some – Japan for example – where the full range of what is available is not permitted, and abortion is the officially preferred option for birth control.[16] The current, nonetheless, in most developed societies is firmly set towards a greater readiness to use all such convenient means as are available for the limitation of family size and the removal of the risk of conception. The rapidity with which the Pill was taken up in those countries where it was available showed that women indeed wished to exploit this new freedom. It opened a new phase in the history of sexual culture, though there was no uniform worldwide spread in its use (and the 1960s were still a decade in which hesitation was properly felt among doctors about side-effects). Forty years after its introduction, the Pill has still not been taken up by women in the non-western world as by their western sisters. Governments striving to promote family limitation (in India, for example), have been more likely to advocate irreversible but voluntary surgical sterilization (usually of men), or the supply of mechanical contraceptive devices, than the Pill. In some parts of the world opposition also remained fierce to any promotion of family limitation at all. The Roman Catholic Church found it easier in the non-western world than the western to maintain its own opposition to what it continued to denounce as artificial forms

[16] See 'The Pill in Japan', *The Economist*, 8 November 1997.

of family limitation. In developed countries, though, debate over the control of women's reproductive lives has tended to shift to a sometimes intense concentration on the rights and wrongs of abortion, its availability and non-availability, and on its regulation by law. Such issues were much exacerbated by continuing scientific and technological advance that enlarged both the knowledge and the management of pre-natal life.

NEW WAVES

The coming of the Pill accompanied in the second half of the century a new multinational feminist agitation. Like early feminism, it stemmed from Europe and North America. The contrasts in its national manifestations were striking. In some western countries, there were changes that merely brought their institutions into line with those familiar before 1939, notably in winning women the vote. Yet divorce was only approved by the Italian parliament in 1970 and even then it required a referendum four years later before it was put into law. Virtually everywhere, though, the new feminism embraced a wider range of specific causes than before and particularly laid stress on sexual freedom and on psychological, implicit and covertly institutionalized forms of male oppression (as they were seen).

The noisiest attempts to change attitudes and to dissolve complacency came in the USA. This could be thought to argue either that attitudes in that country had changed so much already that a higher level of stridency on the part of feminists was found more tolerable there than elsewhere, or, on the other hand, that there was greater need to change things there. So large a subjective element is involved in deciding such matters that it is hardly appropriate to try to settle them here. The freedom of women (to use a very sweeping idea) in western society has always been and remains a cause embodied in a larger context; it has been a logical derivative of more freedom for everybody. Greater freedom in sexual behaviour, for example (or, at least, the retreat of traditional restraints upon it) has affected men, too. Even if, historically, greater tolerance in these matters has been shown to men than to women, improved contraceptive technique changed their life possibilities, too. Their obligations have been redefined in many countries by laws affecting parental and marital responsibility under the influence of feminist pressure.

WOMEN IN THE NON-WESTERN WORLD

Changing patterns make more visible the endurance of conservative attitudes outside the western countries (where they had continued to crumble after 1945). Once more, the picture is very varied: Egypt gave women the vote, but banned feminist organizations in 1956. The status of women, if judged by western measures, remains lowest outside the lands of the European tradition and among the world's poor. In matters of sexual culture and politics, a new emphasis on the conservative treatment of women has in recent years sometimes been a sign of a search to assure communal identity. This seems to have been especially marked among some non-western communities (particularly if they were Muslim in religion) of immigrants who came to find work in the European economies in the 1960s and 1970s. The disciplining of Asian children in the ways of their parents by seeking to segregate them from social intercourse with their white peers while at school (at first, when school years were over, too) was soon marked in the United Kingdom and has not disappeared. Insistence on traditional dress caused uproar when attempts were made in France, unsuccessfully, to prohibit the wearing of headscarves at school by Muslim girls. British law on the wearing of safety helmets has had to take account of the headgear of Sikhs. These things may well appear specifically as minor matters, capable of evolution towards agreement in practice under the pressure of growing commercialism, fashion and the large tolerances of western liberal values. More striking is the persistence of much deeper special attitudes towards women across whole cultures.

On such attitudes, the impact of change has been very uneven. In one particular institutional setting in this century it has been very great, nonetheless. Probably the most indisputable sign of the impact of western ideas about women on other cultures in this century has been the recession of polygamy. Though still prevalent worldwide, there are few societies that still officially support it, though it is tolerated in practice in several. It has often been the subject of hostile legal action and public denunciation. Despotism, benevolent or otherwise, has helped to contest it (communist regimes were often a decisive agency of change), in others, colonialism. In Africa, one of the most lasting achievements of missionaries and the old colonial officials may well prove to have been the grafting of monogamy on native societies. Even in Muslim countries, where Islamic law authorizes under defined conditions the practice of taking up to four wives, governments like those of Turkey (where polygamy was abolished in 1926 as part of the Kemalist revolution) or of Tunisia (where the change came in 1956) have been willing to act against it.

The status of women in many Muslim countries, though, is still striking enough to bring home to western observers more sharply than any other fact a sense of the degree to which the culture of Islam is alien to them. It is a topic formidably difficult to weigh up, notoriously open to subjective judgements and almost inaccessible to generalization. Custom is infringed by law and politics to different degrees in different societies. Islamic societies are not the same as Arab societies. City and countryside are notoriously different: Istanbul is not Anatolia, nor is Casablanca the Rif. Within a few miles of one another, women of the Omani coastal towns go about without the veil while their sisters from the interior still wear it in the markets both share. Western observers are easily shocked (and often find it tempting to say so) at what they regard as a humiliating and lopsided difference of power between Muslim women and men in the Islamic regulation of divorce; from the other side of the cultural divide, Muslims are just as repelled by the fragility and insecurity (as they see it) of western marriage and the lack of institutional support for the individual's responsibilities that it seems to imply.

Specification is as hard as generalization, and just as likely to be misleading in these matters. The Islamic world evidently retains to a formidable degree institutions and practices which, often very blatantly, protect and buttress an ultimate male dominance, and the Muslim male ego often seems easily affronted. Many formal changes in the position of women attempted in Muslim countries have been thwarted or aborted. When, as long ago as 1927, the Uzbek communist party decided that 'International Women's Day' should be the occasion for the abolition of the veil, 100,000 women supposedly conformed, most of them to resume it the next day (some outraged husbands having by then already murdered their liberated spouses in protest). Yet not all Muslim societies impose the veil and in the Iranian Islamic Republic, both secular feminists and devout Muslim women have found that wearing the *chador* is not incompatible with seeking – and sometimes winning – the support of Islamic scholars in defending central personal and economic rights.[17] Turkish schoolgirls who have taken part in demonstrations to win the right to wear headscarves in secular schools as a mark of their religious allegiance still demand and take up training in the professional skills of modern society. Such instances sometimes suggest an uneasy equilibrium, sometimes an easy compromise.

It was as long ago as 1962 that the ancient institution of Al Azhar in Cairo admitted its first female students, and though much attention has been given to the fierce opposition of the Afghan Taliban to female education in any form, Saudi Arabia and several of the Gulf States have done much to provide for it. Selected Omani women have been allowed to study abroad in the dangerously unregulated society of a western university such as Oxford, while even those who remained at home have been able in recent years to attend the country's mixed-sex new university. The latter are, nonetheless, obliged to sit apart from their male fellow-students and to enter lecture rooms by separately demarcated doors; even a returning western graduate, too, encouraged to pursue a successful professional career, can nonetheless face strong disapproval in the highest official quarters of Oman if found driving in a car alone after nightfall. Pakistan has had a female prime minister, and the difficulties and failures of her tenure of office did not arise primarily from her sex, but the same country forbids mixed hockey.

Given varieties of behaviour, it may be helpful to recall that it is not so long since startling contrasts would have appeared within Europe itself in the way in which its peoples treated women. It could still cause something of a sensation when a few years ago a young

---

[17] See the interesting study by H. Afshar, *Islam and Feminisms. An Iranian case study* (London, 1998).

Sicilian woman refused to meet the demands of a traditional code of behaviour by marrying her abductor. Strong cultural contrasts within close distance of one another are not new, as twentieth-century North America amply illustrates. In the early years of this century, some Chinese found Confucian safeguards of the rights of widows preferable to the insecurities they felt such women might suffer in the individualism of western societies. For all China's traditions of concubinage, Sun Yat-sen and his young follower Chiang Kai-shek both shocked Chinese conservatives when they dismissed their wives in order to marry younger, more sophisticated women.

Perhaps all that can usefully and legitimately be done is to note that all traditional societies are now under challenge in trying to define women's roles. In some degree all are beginning to show signs of strain, and some express it in the adoption of a ferociously conservative stance. Within the countries of western tradition such challenges have long been familiar, and appropriate change is now usually the outcome of what is regarded as legitimate propaganda and campaigning, combined with the economic pressures bound to arise in societies firmly oriented towards consumption. In other traditions, different pressures make the running for change or the lack of it. Some are formal and deliberate, promoted by governments, international organizations and specific women's groups. But even they operate more effectively because they are seconded by powerful forces that cannot be kept out of even very remote areas. The insidious pressure of the images and messages conveyed by the global communications networks and the impossibility of any longer preventing the spread of knowledge of what must at times seem the vast tolerances of western liberalism operate today as never before. Questions about women's status and treatment are inevitably raised for those regimes that seek to make only a selective choice among the dangerous gifts of the West that they wish to accept. It may follow that, enormous though this century's changes have been in the institutional and material lives of women in the West, they are not, in the end, so important as the moral and psychological examples they have provided.

Three tempting propositions, needing much qualification, may be hazarded. One is that in many western and developed societies there are now positive grounds for thinking that the 'women's movement' has wholly broken out of its old confining bias towards the concerns of middle-class women. It now influences every level of society through its impact on activity, employment, religion and ideology; there is now almost no political movement, for example, which has not taken account of feminism. Any particular and local 'treatment' of women has now to be specifically justified. The second is that the steadily growing enrichment of the spectrum of issues and groups involved in the assertion of justice for women has revealed new problems and raised new moral difficulties that were scarcely envisaged by early feminists. It now seems woefully out-dated to assume that all that is necessary is to give women world over the same opportunities and legal rights in every walk of life as men. The third proposition, somewhat depressingly, is that over many countries and peoples the women's movement still has yet to exercise any significant influence outside a narrow élite. One further comment may perhaps be made: in the last few years it has for the first time become clear that one repercussion of changes in the roles of women in developed societies has been that the old question of the way we should treat women is being overtaken by a new one. How should society treat men, whose self-images are now under threat the world over?

YOUTH

It may well be that young people have never anywhere wholly satisfied the vast appetite for deference and duty that their elders felt, but that question need not be considered here. It is a simple fact that in the twentieth century a quite new freedom from established disciplines and authority has come to be enjoyed by young people. By 1990 it was observable almost universally. Once again, the forces making for a very widespread change appeared first in western societies. From them, currents then flowed outward. They were multifarious and complex. Technology and science played their part in removing restraints on movement and communication; educational provision had made knowledge and critical attitudes more widely available; politicians and businessmen sought support and markets among the young. All these forces and yet others contributed to a major change in self-consciousness among the young and in the view their elders took of them.

That young people had special needs had already been grasped by few nineteenth-century enthusiasts; the twentieth century discovered adolescence. In 1904 an American published a study with that word as its title. Only fifty-five years later, though, came another book revealingly entitled *The Vanishing Adolescent*, a symptom of the rapidity with which twentieth-century awareness of young people could change in developed societies.[18] That there were youthful age-groups in society with identifiable characteristics had been already recognized and had underlain the success of such innocent manifes-tations as the international Boy Scout movement and its derivatives. Like other organizations, Baden-Powell's brainchild came also to take account of the needs of children, too, and in this they were followed by the much more sinister and deliberately exploitative youth organiza-tions of totalitarian states in the 1920s and 1930s.[19] Only after 1945 did commerce and industry begin to recognize the special needs and tastes of the young in developed countries as a potentially lucrative market.

This was a reflexion of the growing wealth of such societies. Whether because they could find well-paid employment or because of greater parental indulgence than in the past, their young people had more money to spend. This had two effects: a major expansion in the provision of goods and services especially intended for purchase by young people, and (perhaps more important in the long run) the cultivation through advertising and entertainment of something that came to be recognized as a specific 'youth culture'. Chicken and egg are hard to separate: the belief of industrialists and merchants that a

---

[18] G. S. Hall, *Adolescence: its psychology and its relations to physiology, anthropo-logy, sociology, sex, crime, religion and education* (New York, 1904); E. Z. Frieden-berg, *The Vanishing Adolescent* (Boston, 1959). Another word, 'teenager' (or 'teen-ager'), seems to have become current in American speech in the 1940s, though the adjective 'teenage' was in use perhaps twenty years earlier.

[19] Young Pioneers in the USSR, the Hitler Youth in Germany, the *balilla, Piccoli Italiani* and *Figli della Lupa* in Italy. In all these states (and in other authoritarian regimes) positive action – amounting to a total ban in the USSR and Germany – was taken against the Boy Scouts.

youth culture existed led them to action helping to create one. It became an international fact, shaping the behaviour of young people through its promotion of specific style and fashion in any country where they had access to the mass media. The first indications that this might have political implications came in grumblings in the communist countries of eastern Europe about the dangerous temptations of 'corrupting' and 'capitalist' music and fashion.

Communist officialdom was perceptive; in the 1960s there was an observable drift towards standardization of appearance, dress and demeanour between young people who were abreast of the currents of the time in all countries. This was one aspect of the internationalism of youth. Its most striking expression came, very briefly, with a series of 'student' disturbances that took place in institutions of higher education in European and North American countries in 1967–8. There was a pervasive element of paradox in this. By definition, students in rich countries were comparatively rich: they did not need to work for their living, being sustained at various levels ranging from the very generous to the merely adequate by the societies against which they briefly raged. A specifically American current of protest against involvement in the Vietnam war was the detonator of the wave of disturbances in that country, but a wide variety of other issues was soon raised in them. A strong feeling of international solidarity fed by television images among participants underlay their use of anti-colonial and anti-imperialist slogans (another paradox, because there was little left of the empires by 1968). The most violent troubles (other than those of the North American universities, where demonstrations over Vietnam led to deaths) took place in French and German universities, where students protested, with justification, about inadequate teaching, resources and facilities. But besides such political foci, the disturbances agitated also against traditional and institutional authority of all kinds, including that of the family, and promoted specious claims to be resisting threats to free speech and from oppressive policing. A coincidence with the now widespread availability of the Pill did much to add to the attractiveness of the large gatherings, manifestations and 'sit-ins' that were for a time fashionable. A slippage into violence – mostly of a mild character, such as the wrecking of professors' studies and laboratories – was not prolonged. Soon the 'events' (as they were sometimes called) of 1968 had passed into history as predominantly middle-class activists grew older and sought jobs. In retrospect, 1968 looked like a letting-off of steam such as only rich societies could afford.

BOOK 7

A CHANGING WORLD
BALANCE

21

The Cold War at Its Height

AFTER STALIN

The death of Stalin brought no obvious or immediate change in Soviet foreign policy, though a few domestic differences were quickly visible. A duumvirate of Malenkov and Beria, the head of the security service, which took over almost at once was soon followed by a collective reassertion of its authority by other members of the Politburo. One outcome was Beria's arrest, trial and richly deserved execution (with five accomplices) in July 1953. By the time that happened, another Politburo member, Nikita Khrushchev, had been appointed general secretary of the CPSU. There was, it seems, general support within the Soviet hierarchy for the view that the collective role of the party should be reasserted in government. After Beria's removal, a number of small relaxations led a few western Kremlin-watchers to speculate about the possibility (at least in minor matters) of 'liberalization', but it was probably more important that there were some further personnel changes. Molotov, Stalin's old henchman and veteran of Soviet diplomacy, was removed from his post as foreign minister. Bulganin, a man believed to be dominated by Khrushchev, was made prime minister. It has been argued that Khrushchev was using his powers as party secretary somewhat in the way Stalin had used his in the 1920s, to ensure a strategic placement of those loyal to him in the hierarchy and bureaucracy.

By 1956 Khrushchev seemed to have emerged as the dominant figure in the Soviet government. He was never to enjoy unrestrained power such as Stalin had done, and the bloodlessness of his advancement (after Beria and his cronies, no one else was shot) and the non-violent

G. Abaco I.
Cat I.
Bahamas
Andros Is
Turks & Caicos Is.
Havana
CUBA
1898
DOMINICAN
REP.
San Juan
HAITI
Puerto Rico
Antigua
Montserrat
Guadeloupe
Marie Galante
Dominica
BELIZE
(Former British
Honduras)
1884
Jamaica
Kingston
Caribbean Sea
Martinique
St. Lucia
St. Vincent
Barbados
Grenada
North
Atlantic
Ocean
GUATEMALA
1838
HONDURAS
1838
NICARAGUA
1838
COSTA RICA
1838
PANAMA
1903
Tobago
Trinidad
VENEZUELA
Orinoco
Georgetown
Paramaribo
Cayenne
COLUMBIA
GUYANA
SURINAM
FRENCH
GUIANA
Quito
ECUADOR
Branco
Amazon
Japura
Amazon
Jurua
Purus
Madeira
Tapajos
Xingu
Parnaiba
Tocantins
São Francisco
Pacific
Ocean
LIMA
PERU
B R A Z I L
Paraguay
Brasília
LA PAZ
BOLIVIA
PARAGUAY
ASUNCION
Parana
N
Salado
Uruguay
South
Atlantic
Ocean
SANTIAGO
URUGUAY
Montevideo
BUENOS AIRES
ARGENTINA

Falklands Is (Br.)

Land over 1000 metres
States within British
Commonwealth

0   800 miles
0   1200 k
                          m

South and Central America in 1999

consolidation of his position must be reckoned a major advance in Soviet political civility. More significant still, he felt confident enough to take a truly momentous step in that year. At a secret session of the twentieth congress of the CPSU he denounced the misdeeds of the Stalin era and declared 'coexistence' was now the goal of Russian foreign policy. This was to turn out to be one of the most influential acts by a statesman of any nationality since 1945. It shook the mono-lithic front communism had hitherto presented, and for the first time alienated many communist sympathizers in western countries – or, perhaps, allowed them to express their alienation at no cost to their consciences. In the longer run, it was to allow the emergence in some countries of independent left-wing criticism which was no longer so likely to be tarred with the brush of 'fellow-travelling' since it explicitly abjured the evils of the Stalinist era.

The sensational news of the speech was soon given wide publicity (thanks, not least, to the United States Central Intelligence Agency). Together with announcements of Soviet reductions in armaments, it might have heralded a new mood in international affairs, had not the atmosphere in 1956 quickly been fouled by the Suez invasion, severe anti-Soviet rioting in Poland and a revolution in Hungary.[1] The first led to Soviet threats to Great Britain and France; Moscow was not going to risk Arab goodwill by failing to show support for Egypt. The Polish disturbances and revolution in Hungary had a deeper background. Ever since 1948 Soviet policy had been almost morbidly sensitive to signs of deviation or dissatisfaction among its satellites. In that year, Soviet advisers had been recalled from Yugoslavia, which was then expelled from the Cominform. Yugoslavia's treaties with the USSR and other communist states were denounced and there followed five years of vitriolic attacks on 'Titoism'. In 1957 the two governments finally came to an understanding and Soviet aid to

[1] Originating in economic grievances, the Polish disturbances rapidly took on a nationalist, patriotic tone and helped to bring about the release from solitary confine-ment of a Polish communist leader, Wladislaw Gomulka, who had been dismissed from government in 1949 and fell victim to a Stalinist purge. At one moment there were even exchanges of fire between Soviet and Polish forces. The return of Gomulka to office (which he was to retain until 1973) represented something of a high-water mark of Soviet concession to 'national communism' until the 1980s.

Yugoslavia was symbolically resumed. In the end, the USSR had climbed down. The Soviet request to reopen diplomatic relations was conceded. Yugoslavia's damaging and embarrassing survival as a socialist state outside the Warsaw Pact had left Moscow even more sensitive to tremors in the eastern camp.

Like anti-Soviet riots in East Berlin in 1953, those in Poland in the summer of 1956 showed that patriotism inflamed by economic discontent could still challenge communism in Soviet Europe. They help to explain how disturbances in Budapest in October 1956 grew into a nationwide movement that led to the withdrawal of Soviet forces from the city, a new Hungarian government and a promise of free elections and the end of one-party rule. Perhaps rashly, the new regime soon went further and too far. When it announced its withdrawal from the Warsaw Pact, declared Hungary's neutrality, and asked the United Nations to take up the Hungarian question, the Soviet army returned. The Hungarian revolution was crushed. Many fled the country. The UN General Assembly twice condemned the intervention, and the episode hardened attitudes on both sides. The Russians were once more made aware of how little they were liked by the peoples of eastern Europe and therefore became even more distrustful of western talk of 'liberating' them. Western Europeans were again reminded of the real face of Soviet power.

A more important fact that was part of the context of these events was the emphatic return of China to the international stage as a great power. This was first manifest in the Korean war. If she did not at first possess the nuclear weapons of the two superpowers, she had from the start an enormous potential to absorb punishment undefeated just because of her huge population and vast territory. These facts had implications going beyond the Cold War. Almost inevitably, most observers had at first seen communist China as a clearly aligned participant in that struggle. But there was soon evidence that this might be too simple a view. China's re-emergence as a power in her own right did not intensify the dualist Cold War system, but complicated and even undermined it, though at first only in a limited sphere.

As signs multiplied that Soviet and Chinese interests might compete over leadership of the 'Third World', shadow-boxing had begun between Moscow and Peking over differing attitudes to Yugoslavia. Later in Europe, the violence with which Albania, the tiniest of the communist countries, condemned the Soviet Union and applauded China when the two fell out again showed that not all European Marxists thought alike. Moscow had to endure this pinprick; Albania had no frontier with a Warsaw Pact country and did not need to fear invasion by the Soviet army. It was more striking that Romania's leaders, also with some Chinese encouragement, successfully contested the subjection of their country's economy to Comecon, asserting their right to develop it in her own national interest. Under a ruler who imposed on his countrymen one of the most rigidly dictatorial regimes in eastern Europe, Romania even took up what sometimes sounded like a vaguely neutralist position on questions of foreign policy, though remaining within the Warsaw Pact. But Romania had no land frontier with a NATO country (Albania had one with Greece), and had one 800 kilometres long with the USSR alone; Romanian skittishness could be tolerated, for limits to it could easily be enforced if necessary.

It is worth glancing a little further ahead at this point to the next significant revelation that limits would always be imposed by the Soviet Union to any qualification of the old monolithic front of communism. Such limits were next brutally evident in 1968, when the communist government of Czechoslovakia set about liberalizing its internal structures and developing trade relations with West Germany. This was very striking: the impetus for change was coming not from outside the Party but from its members themselves (as in Hungary, twelve years earlier). After a series of threats and attempts to persuade the Czechs to come to heel, Prague was occupied in August by Warsaw Pact forces. To avoid a repetition of the 1956 bloodshed, the Czech government did not resist. A brief attempt to provide an example of a socialism that had not lost its human face, as the secretary of the Czech communist party put it,[2] was obliterated. There followed, in a speech to a Polish audience in November 1968 by the general secretary of the CPSU, Leonid Brezhnev, a warning of the dangers of 'imperialist' efforts to undermine socialist solidarity and the blunt assertion that any threat to the cause of socialism in one country was the concern

[2] Alexander Dubcek, in a newspaper article, 19 July 1968.

of them all and might properly give rise to military 'assistance' from other communist countries to meet it. This was the formulation of what came to be called the 'Brezhnev' doctrine, henceforth a datum of international affairs, and something of an indicator of the degree to which Moscow no longer felt sure of its satellites. Even those who governed them on the most Stalinist lines (for example, Ceausescu, the dictator of Romania) were capable of showing a measure of independence in defence of their countries' national interests.

By 1968, the rulers of the USSR must long since have given up any hope of revolution in Europe west of the Iron Curtain. They had been obliged to face the virtual eclipse of communism as a revolutionary force within the western democracies in the 1960s as the power of communist parties to win votes declined, above all in France and Italy. A few dissidents in western countries had broken – publicly or discreetly, according to taste – with communism because of their dismay over events in Hungary in 1956. Italian party leaders talked of a new ideological stance, 'polycentrism', which implied a liberation of national communist parties from the discipline of Moscow. Often to some effect, though, the fears and idealism of non-communist but left-wing sympathizers and those alarmed by confrontation between the superpowers could still be exploited by the Soviet Union and the western communist parties over such issues as disarmament and anti-colonialism. All such changes added up to subtle changes in the way the superpowers were regarded. But the superpowers were changing, too.

THE SECOND BERLIN CRISIS

In October 1957, Sputnik I had done much more to alarm the American people and promote a hardening of their feelings about the Cold War than any of the brutal events of the last few years in eastern Europe. The age of evident space competition between the superpowers began when the psychological unease provoked by Sputnik I's presence 'up there' shattered any confidence that Soviet technology lagged significantly behind American. Wider implications were lost to sight in alarm over what the exploration and utilization of space might mean for the military balance. The immediate beneficiaries were the American space scientists who now entered a golden era when they could draw on public money almost without question in the advancement of their art. Soldiers and industrialists also shared in the new bounty as the arms race was technologically intensified. Even American colleges and schools benefited briefly, for the immediate public panic had extended to alarm that there was something deeply wrong with the way America was teaching its children mathematics, science and even foreign languages. A public competition not merely for scientific success but for prestige was soon under way between the two superpowers. In March 1958, the Americans could with relief applaud their own first successful launch of a satellite.

Soviet foreign policy in the Khrushchev era meanwhile displayed a continuing recalcitrance and uncooperativeness, and sometimes remarkable confidence, as events in Germany soon showed. Fearing the danger of a rearmed West Germany, the Soviet leaders were anxious to strengthen their satellite, the German Democratic Republic. The all too visible success and prosperity of West Berlin – surrounded by GDR territory – was embarrassing. The city's demarcation lines between west and east were easily crossed. Its material well-being and freedom drew more and more East Germans – especially skilled workers – to the west. In 1958, the USSR moved; it denounced the arrangements under which Berlin had been run for the last ten years. It threatened to hand over the Soviet sector of the city to the GDR if better arrangements could not be found. Two years of drawn-out wrangling followed. As an atmosphere of crisis over Berlin deepened there was a huge increase in the outflow of refugees. The numbers of East Germans crossing to the west were 140,000 in 1959, 200,000 in 1960 and more than 100,000 in the first six months of 1961. Then, in August of that year, the East German authorities suddenly put up a wall (soon reinforced by land-mines and barbed wire) to cut off Berlin's Soviet sector from the western. Tension shot up in the short run, but the new wall probably eased it in the long. Its gloomy presence (and the sporadic killing of East Germans who tried to cross it) were to be for a quarter-century a gift to western Cold War propaganda. The GDR had succeeded in stopping emigration, though, and Khrushchev quietly dropped more extreme demands when it was clear that the

United States was not prepared to give way over the legal status of Berlin even at the risk of war.

This, though, was only the beginning of a period during which Soviet policy tested American resolve much harder than before. The next crisis came not in Europe but in the Caribbean, an area in which the European allies of the United States were much less interested than they had been over possible changes in Germany.

LATIN AMERICA ENTERS WORLD POLITICS

The outbreak of the Second World War was at first a new setback for Latin America. Loss of access to continental markets in Europe – and, later, Asia – was a severe blow. In the end, though, it made possible a resumption of the process of recovering prosperity. For all the sympathy Argentina's rulers showed for Nazi Germany, most of the southern republics were, under United States pressure, sympathetic enough to the Allies eventually to break off diplomatic relations with all or some of the Axis powers, though few of them actually declared war until 1945. Most of the Central American and Caribbean states had done so soon after Pearl Harbor, but without making significant military or naval contributions to the war, even if Brazil eventually sent soldiers to Europe to fight in Italy, and a Mexican air force unit took part in the Pacific war. This did not mean that the 1930s-born distrust of the outside world of great powers on whom Latin Americans blamed so many of their troubles went away. The most important effects of the war on Latin America, though, were once again economic and benevolent (and they were to be prolonged, in due course, by the Korean war). Many Latin American states were now, on balance, creditor nations.

The old dependence on the United States and Europe for manufactured goods had become apparent in shortages in many Latin American countries during the war. The drive to industrialize and provide import-substitution had gathered more speed in some of them. On the urban workforces which industrialization built up there was built sometimes the political power of authoritarian, some said semi-fascist, popular movements. Among the beneficiaries in the post-war era,

Perón in Argentina was the most famous, but Colombia in 1953 and Venezuela in 1954 had similar regimes. Sometimes they were actually called fascist by their opponents, but this was hardly an adequate description. Communist parties had no such conspicuous success among the masses as did native radical movements, though they were organized in most countries by 1939.

The European political commitments left in the hemisphere were comparatively few by 1945. The British, French and Dutch had between them still a scatter of Caribbean and Central American possessions, but the British had in September 1940 already allowed the United States to set up naval bases on long leases in some of its island colonies.[3] Such as they were, the surviving relics of imperialism were about to participate in the decolonizing era. As for Russia, neither tsarist nor Soviet governments had ever had territorial or investment interests in the area. The United States' political and military predominance in the Caribbean, as well as American economic weight in Latin America as a whole, were more evident than ever after 1945.

The 1950s brought about another change. After Korea, American policy was influenced more than before by global perceptions of a communist threat. Washington had not been unduly alarmed by noisy manifestations of Latin American nationalism (which were always likely to look for and find a scapegoat in American policy), but became increasingly concerned lest the hemisphere should provide a lodgement for Soviet influence. There followed covert American subversion operations and greater selectivity in giving support to Latin American governments. In 1954 a government in Guatemala which had communist support was overthrown with United States help, a step that seemed to confirm in the eyes of many Latin Americans a return to old, bad *gringo* ways.

It was consistent with its new nervousness that some in Washington increasingly wanted to see removed the footholds for communism provided by poverty and discontent. The United States began to deliver more economic aid to Latin America. During the 1950s the southern continent, which had hitherto received only a tiny fraction of the

[3] Denmark had ceded the Danish West Indies to the United States by treaty in 1916.

help that went to Europe and Asia, benefited much more. The State Department patronized governments that said they sought social reform and some of them indeed acted effectively (notably that of Bolivia, which carried out significant land reforms in the 1950s). But it remained true that, as for most of the previous century, the worst-off Latin Americans still could obtain virtually no hearing from either populist or conservative rulers; both listened to the cities, but most of the poorest were (as ever) peasants. Unfortunately, though, whenever the programmes of their governments moved towards the eradication of American control of capital by nationalization, American policy tended to veer away again, demanding compensation on a scale and in a way which made reform very difficult. On the whole, therefore, while it might deplore the excesses of an individual authoritarian regime (such as a brutal dictatorship installed in 1933 in Cuba by Batista), the American government tended to find itself south of the Rio Grande, as in Asia, supporting conservative interests. For all the North Americans' uneasiness about the appeal of communism, significant social change for the better in Latin America was small. The only victorious social revolution in Latin America in the post-war period was to be one that began in Cuba in 1958.

CUBA

The Cuban revolution was to produce greater political effects than any other event in Latin America in the second half of the century. Yet a crisis that broke in 1962, and led to a confrontation of the two superpowers, was a purely Cold War creation, although it came to be something of a consummation of a phase in Latin American history. Cuba was in a number of respects exceptional. Its island position in the Caribbean, within a relatively short distance of the United States, gave it special strategic significance. There had been an American naval base on the island since 1901 (with a lease running to 1999). The approaches to the Canal Zone had often been shown to matter as much in American strategic thinking as Suez did in British. Secondly, Cuba had been especially badly hit in the world economic depression; it was virtually dependent on one crop, sugar, and that crop had long had only one outlet, the United States. This economic tie, moreover, was only one of several that had given Cuba a closer and more irksome 'special relationship' with the United States than any other Latin American state. There were historic connxions that went back before 1898 and the winning of independence from Spain. Until 1934 the Cuban constitution had in consequence included special provisions restricting that country's diplomatic freedom. Americans invested heavily in urban property and utilities in an island not far from their shores (about 130 miles away), and Cuba's poverty and low prices made it an attractive holiday resort for Americans, particularly during the Prohibition era and for those with a taste for gambling and girls. All in all, it should not have been surprising that Cubans showed, as they did, particularly strong anti-American and nationalist feelings.

In the late 1950s American favour and support were withdrawn from Batista. The United States government looked on with benevolent approval when his regime was overthrown by a young and patriotic guerrilla leader, Fidel Castro. He looked like a liberal. In 1959, when he became prime minister, Castro described his regime as 'humanistic' and he was idolized by many North Americans as a romantic figure (beards now became fashionable among campus radicals). But official relationships soured rapidly. Castro began to interfere with American business interests and to denounce those Americanophile elements in Cuba that had supported the old regime. This turned out to be a rewarding theme; Cubans responded to anti-Americanism by uniting behind the revolution. The island's nationalism found a focus in Castro. There was talk of the completion of a Cuban revolution alleged to have been frustrated by United States occupation in the early years of the century, an idea some have seen as central to Castro's early thinking. One of the first acts of the new revolutionary government was an agrarian reform law that appeared to threaten United States sugar companies with the loss of over a million and a half acres of land.

Castro's original aims are nonetheless still not known. Perhaps he was himself not altogether clear what he thought or wanted, except a better life for Cubans. He had worked with a wide spectrum of people who wanted to overthrow Batista, from liberals to Marxists, and this had helped to reassure the United States, which had at first patronized him as a possible Caribbean Sukarno. When Castro turned towards the USSR for support, though, a new and much more explicit phase of the Cold War began in the western hemisphere. American public opinion now swung round against him. In January 1961 the United States broke off diplomatic relations with his government; the administration had begun to believe that Castro's increasingly obvious dependence on known communists meant that the island was about to fall into their hands. Thus, the Cold War arrived in the western hemisphere.

It did not improve matters when Khrushchev warned the United States publicly of the danger of retaliation from Soviet rocket forces if it took military action against Cuba and announced that the Monroe doctrine was dead. The State Department quickly assured the world that reports of its demise were greatly exaggerated and an embargo was imposed on exports to Cuba. By now, President Eisenhower's administration had decided to promote Castro's overthrow by financing and arming Cuban exiles to carry it out. Preparations had been under way for an invasion by them when a new president took office in 1961. Perhaps understandably, John Kennedy was neither cautious enough nor sufficiently informed at that moment to impede it. The outcome, the so-called 'Bay of Pigs' operation, was a fiasco. No one believed official denials of United States complicity, and disapproval of American support for an attack on a popularly-based government was almost worldwide, even among the United States' European allies.

Castro now turned in earnest to Moscow for support. At the end of 1961 he declared himself a 'Marxist–Leninist'. The Soviet government must have believed it faced a golden opportunity. It is not known why or when exactly it took the decision to exploit it in the way it did, by deciding to install in Cuba missiles with the range to reach any target in the United States (thus roughly doubling the number of American bases or cities which were potential targets). It was long uncertain whether the initiative came from Havana or Moscow, even though now the second seems likeliest. The outcome, whatever the origin of the decision, was the most serious confrontation of the Cold War and perhaps its major turning-point.

In October 1962 American photographic reconnaissance confirmed that launching sites for Soviet rockets were being built in Cuba. A tense period for American policy-making then ensued while President Kennedy waited until this could be incontrovertibly demonstrated. He then announced that the United States navy would stop any ship delivering further missiles to Cuba and that those already in the island would have to be withdrawn. A Lebanese ship making for the island was boarded and searched. Soviet ships were closely observed and photographed. The American nuclear striking force was made ready for war with the Soviet Union and forces were assembled in Florida for an attack on Cuba. After a few days and an exchange of personal letters between Kennedy and Khrushchev, it was agreed on 28 October that the Soviet missiles should be withdrawn, assurance being given that there would be no American invasion of Cuba once this had been done.

It is unlikely that the USSR's allies had been enthusiastic for the Cuban cause, even though Castro's regime proclaimed itself to be Marxist, but publicly they had gone along with their ally. The allies of the United States, as it were, gritted their teeth and did the same. Notably, the Organization of American States had authorized the use of armed force to impose the quarantine on further Soviet arms installations when the crisis was at its height. What had really been at stake for them, as for nations all round the world with no direct stake in the Caribbean, was Cold War solidarity. On both sides it was important that the credibility of the will and power of their own particular superpower patron should be confirmed without a nuclear war. In the end, enough face was saved on both sides. President Kennedy avoided action or language that might have been dangerously provocative. He had left retreat open to Soviet diplomacy by confining his demands to essentials (and discreetly agreeing to a reciprocal withdrawal of American missiles from Turkey after a few months). After something as near to a pure confrontation as is easily imaginable, the USSR appeared to have been forced to give way, but not to have been humiliated.

With hindsight's advantage, it is clear that the prospect of nuclear war as the price of a geographical extension of the Cold War had indeed been faced and found unacceptable by the Soviet Union. The setting-up of direct telephone communication between the heads of the two superpowers – the so-called 'hot line' – was a recognition that the danger of conflict through misunderstanding made necessary something more intimate and immediate than the usual diplomatic channels. It was also clear that in spite of Soviet boasting to the contrary, American preponderance in weapons was as great as ever. What mattered most for purposes of direct nuclear exchange between the two superpowers was the inter-continental ballistic missile (ICBM); at the end of 1962 the Americans had a superiority over their likely opponents of more than six to one in this class of weapon (the Soviet consumer was to bear the burden of the choice between rockets and butter as the USSR set to work to reduce this disparity). Meanwhile, the Cuban confrontation had probably helped to achieve the first international agreement on restricting the testing of nuclear weapons in space, the atmosphere or underwater, between Great Britain (during the crisis the only European state with its own nuclear weapons), the United States and the Soviet Union. Disarmament would still be pursued for many years without further success, but this was a positive beginning to dealing with the problems of nuclear weapons through diplomacy, and an encouragement to the pursuit of further negotiations.

THE AFTERMATH IN LATIN AMERICA

That she had emerged successfully, even victoriously, from the Cuban missile crisis did not mean that the United States faced no further problems to the south. The anti-Castro initiative that had ended at the Bay of Pigs had incurred disapproval everywhere because it was an attack on a popular regime. Henceforth, Cuba would be something of a revolutionary magnet for Latin American radicals. Even as Castro's torturers and jailers replaced Batista's, his government pressed forward with policies which, with Soviet economic help, very visibly promoted egalitarianism and social reform (in the 1970s, Cuba claimed to have the lowest child mortality rates in Latin America). Though the United States had promised not to invade the island, it went on trying to isolate it as much as possible from its neighbours because of its potential influence elsewhere, and to do as much economic damage to the new regime as possible. Unsurprisingly, the appeal of Cuba's revolution seemed just for that reason for a while to wax stronger elsewhere in Latin America. This, though, did not make other Latin American governments more sympathetic towards Castro when he tried to use Cuba as a revolutionary centre for the rest of the continent. In the event, as an unsuccessful attempt to start a guerrilla war in Bolivia showed, revolution elsewhere was not likely to be easy.

Cuban circumstances had after all been very atypical. Hopes entertained by would-be revolutionaries of mounting peasant rebellions elsewhere proved illusory; there was to be no Latin American Vietnam. There was still to be plenty of rural unrest in specific areas even in the 1990s, but the edge of peasant misery was blunted sufficiently by land reform and the improvement of rural services. Communists in other states deplored Castro's efforts, too. While there was plenty of revolutionary potential about, it turned out to be urban rather than rural. It was in the major cities that terrorist left-wing organizations were within a few years making the headlines. Though they were often spectacular and even locally threatening to the authorities, it is not clear that the radicals who advocated and turned to violence enjoyed wide popular support, though the brutalities practised in dealing with them alienated middle-class support from government in some countries. Meanwhile, anti-Americanism and a generalized distrust of the United States continued to run high.

Kennedy's hopes for a new American initiative, based on social reform, an 'Alliance for Progress' as he termed it with a revealing choice of words, made no headway against the animosity aroused by American treatment of Cuba. Johnson did no better, but he was probably in any case less interested in Latin America than in domestic reform; he tended to leave speculation about hemisphere policy to fellow-Texans with business interests there. The Alliance initiative was never recaptured after its initial flagging. Worse still, it was soon overtaken by fresh evidence of the old Adam of intervention. Four years before, American help had assisted the overthrow and assassination of a corrupt and tyrannical dictator of the Dominican Republic and his replacement by a reforming democratic government. When this was then pushed aside by soldiers acting in defence of the privileged who felt threatened by reform, the Americans cut off aid; it looked as if, after all, the Alliance for Progress might be used discriminatingly. But aid was soon restored and a rebellion against the soldiers in 1965 resulted in the arrival of 20,000 American troops to put it down.

By the end of the decade the Alliance had virtually been forgotten. There was a new wave of threats to American property by governments which did not need to fear any ultimate loss of American support while the CIA remained obsessed by a largely illusory communist threat. As in Asia and Europe, Cold War gave opportunities to the weak. Chile nationalized the largest American copper company, the Bolivians took over oil concerns and the Peruvians plantations. In 1969 there was a historic meeting of Latin American governments at which no United States representative was present and *Yanqui* behaviour was explicitly and implicitly condemned. A tour undertaken by a representative (bearing the evocative name of Rockefeller) of the president of the United States that year led to protest, riots, the blowing up of American property and requests to stay away from some countries. It was rather like the end of the previous decade, when a 'goodwill' tour by Eisenhower's vice-president (Richard Nixon) had ended in him being mobbed and spat upon. All in all, it looked by 1970 as if Latin American nationalism was entering a new and vigorous period (there was even a war between Honduras and El Salvador, beginning in riots when Honduras was defeated by her neighbour in an early qualifying round of the World Cup). If Cuba-inspired guerrillas had ever presented a danger, they appeared to do so no longer. Once the spur of fear of Castro was gone there was little reason for governments not to try to capitalize on anti-American feeling.

THE CHANGING USSR

In 1958, Khrushchev had taken over from Bulganin the premiership; together with the party secretaryship he was to hold it until 1964, when he was removed from office. He had evidently provided a great shaking-up to both government and party, though more to the first. His ascendancy had brought some real 'de-Stalinization' of personnel, a huge failure over agriculture, and a change in the emphasis of the armed services (towards the strategic rocket services that became their élite arm). Khrushchev's alarming personal initiatives in foreign policy (above all the Cuban adventure) may have been the fundamental cause of his removal. Yet though he was set aside with the connivance of the army by party colleagues he had offended and alarmed, he was not killed or sent to prison; he even succeeded in having his memoirs published abroad. Nor, momentously, could his speech at the Twentieth CPSU Congress ever be unsaid. Though much of it had been aimed at diverting criticism from those who (like Khrushchev himself) had been participants in the crimes of which Stalin was accused, it had provoked uncontainable debate on what the USSR had really been under Stalin. Symbolically, Stalin's body had been removed from Lenin's tomb, the national shrine. In the next few years there had been what some called a 'thaw'. Marginally greater freedom of expression had been allowed to writers and artists, while the regime appeared briefly to be a little more concerned about its standing in the eyes of the world over such matters as its treatment of Jews. But this was personal and sporadic: liberalization depended on who had Khrushchev's ear, and the re-emergence of the party as a much more independent factor in Soviet life did not mean that the fundamentally authoritarian nature of Soviet government changed.

It now seems odd that for a time there was a fashion to say that the United States and the USSR were growing more and more alike. The once-popular theory of 'convergence' gave undue emphasis to one undoubted truth: that the Soviet Union was a developed economy. In the 1960s many people in many other countries still thought social-ism a plausible road to modernization because of that. It was over-looked that the Soviet economy was also by many standards inefficient. Soviet industrial growth, though in the 1950s supposedly faster than that of the United States, had been most evident in heavy industry. The individual consumer in the Soviet Union remained poor by comparison with his American (or, increasingly, western European) counterpart, and would have been even more visibly so but for a costly and inefficient system of subsidies for basic commodities. Russian agriculture, which had once fed the cities of Central Europe and paid for the industrialization of the tsarist era, was a continuing failure; paradoxically, the USSR often had to buy American grain. The official CPSU programme of 1961 announced that by 1970 the USSR would outstrip the United States in industrial output. It did not happen. Over the same period, the proposal that President Kennedy had made in 1961 to put an American on the moon was carried out with time to spare.

By comparison with many undeveloped countries, though, the USSR was rich; to the poor of the Third World the USA and USSR could look quite similar. In 1961 official Soviet figures announced that the urban population of the Union now outnumbered the rural. Soviet citizens, too, were more aware of the happy contrast with their memories of their stricken and impoverished country in the 1940s than of that with the contemporary United States, about which for a long time they could know little that was true. Moreover, the contest of the two systems was not always one-sided. Soviet investment in education, for example, may well have achieved literacy rates as good as the American. Yet all such comparisons, which fall easily over the line from quantitative to qualitative judgement, could hardly obscure (except in the eyes of the faithful) the basic fact that the per capita GDP of the Soviet Union in the 1970s still lagged far behind that of the United States. There had been a long legacy of backwardness and disruption to eliminate; only in 1952 had real wages in the Soviet Union even got back to their 1928 level. If its citizens had at last been given old age pensions in 1956 (nearly half a century after the British), they also had to put up with health services which fell further and further behind those available in the western countries.

One indisputable achievement, by 1970, was the creation of a scientific and industrial base in the Soviet Union which could match in scale and challenge in quality that of the United States. It was able, too, to do some great and very visible things. The first Soviet nuclear power station had begun to operate in 1958, but the most blatant expression of what Soviet science could do, and a great source of patriotic pride to the Soviet citizen, was the exploration of space. The public imagination is so jaded by news from space nowadays that it is difficult to recapture the startling impression made by the first Soviet successes and the many other outstanding Soviet space achievements that followed. Space exploration fed the patriotic imagination of Soviet citizens and rewarded their patience with the realities of daily life in the USSR. Space technology justified the revolution; it made it clear that, technologically, the USSR could do almost anything that could be done by another nation, much that only one other could, and perhaps one or two things which, for a while, *no* other could. Mother Russia was modernized at last.

Whether this meant that the Soviet Union was in a diplomatic sense becoming a satisfied nation, with leaders more confident and less suspicious of the outside world and less prone to disturb the international scene, is a quite different matter. Their responses to Chinese resurgence were not encouraging; there was muffled talk of pre-emptive Soviet nuclear attacks on the Chinese border. Soviet society was beginning to show some new strains, too, by 1970. Dissent and criticism, particularly of restraints upon intellectual freedom, mounted, if tentatively, in the 1960s. More was heard of antisocial behaviour such as hooliganism, corruption and alcoholism, though these were neither new nor surprising in a country that had been still so backward and barbarous in 1917. But such weaknesses probably held both as much and as little potential for significant change as they did in other large countries. In the long run less spectacular changes may have turned out to be more important; looking back, one watershed was surely passed in the 1970s, when native Russian-speakers for the first time became a minority in the Soviet Union. It mattered, too, that much did not change. All Soviet citizens continued to live in a state where the limits of freedom and the rights of the individual were defined in practice by a police apparatus backed up by administrative decisions and prisons. There were still thousands of political prisoners in 1970. Foreign radio broadcasts were still jammed, at enormous cost. The real difference between the Soviet Union and the United States (or any west European nation) was still best shown by such yardsticks.

THE CHANGING UNITED STATES

The fact that change in the United States is easily observed, and by none more so or more noisily than by Americans, does not always make it easier to discern what is going on in that country. Of the sheer continuing growth of American power in the mid-century decades there can be no doubt, nor of its importance to the world. In the middle of the 1950s the United States contained about 6 per cent of the world's population but produced more than half its manufactured goods. In 1965 the state of Illinois had a larger GDP than Africa, and California's was larger than China's. More Americans than ever (of a population which passed the 200 million mark in 1968) lived in cities or their suburbs, and the likelihood that they would die of some form of malignancy had much increased since 1901 – a paradoxical but sure sign of improvement in public health, for it showed a growing mastery of other diseases. The immensely successful American industrial structure was dominated by very large corporations, some of them already commanding resources and wealth greater than those of some nations. Concern was sometimes expressed for the interests of the public and the consumer, given the power and influence of these giants. But few doubts existed in the 1960s about their ability to create wealth. American industrial strength was and has remained the great constant of the post-war world. It sustained a huge military potential, too, which encouraged illusions about limitless international power and about the inevitable tendency of other countries to follow American models.

In the 1950s, the second of President Truman's and both President Eisenhower's terms in office were marked by noisy debate and shadow-boxing about the danger of governmental interference with free enterprise; most of it was beside the point. Ever since 1945 the federal government had held and indeed increased its importance as the leading customer of the American economy, and American voters had grown fonder of the welfare state. Government spending was the primary economic stimulant and to benefit from it was the goal of hundreds of interest groups; hopes of balanced budgets and cheap, businesslike administration tended to run aground upon this fact. As for what looked like a distrust of social service provision in European eyes, the United States was a democracy and whatever the rhetoric devoted to attacking it, the welfare state inexorably advanced because voters wanted it that way. These facts made the old myths of free enterprise unchecked and uninvaded by the influence of government more unrealistic than ever in the 1950s and 1960s, even if the country was committed to market economies as was no other leading industrial power. The Democratic coalition that had been Roosevelt's political masterpiece was still in being in 1970. Though a Republican president had been elected in 1952, benefiting from war-weariness, Eisenhower had not been able to persuade Americans that they should also elect Republican congressmen. Yet by 1960 the first cracks were appearing in the Democratic bloc; that year's Republican presidential candidate appealed to many southern conservative voters.

The 1950s had nonetheless left an impression of domestic quiet in all but one very visible respect. The Truman administration's last year had witnessed the rise of an embarrassing public concern, fanned by interested politicians, over allegations of dangers presented to the United States by subversive action and disloyalty in various areas, and especially in branches of the executive government. Uproar and embarrassment mounted to come to a climax in the early Eisenhower presidency. In so far as the roots of concern were real, they lay in some well-founded revelations of Soviet espionage activity (not only in the United States, but in Canada, too), in puzzlement and unease over what many Americans regarded as the inexplicable 'loss' of China to communism, in the frustrations of a Korean war, which was won, but not obviously nor in some eyes decisively, and in uneasiness after the USSR had revealed its possession of nuclear weapons. At least one highly-placed State Department employee was revealed as a spy and the outcome was great public alarm. There followed much so-called 'witch-hunting', as a congressional inquiry sought evidence of other potentially subversive individuals (membership of the Communist party or a refusal to answer incriminating questions on that topic were taken as *prima facie* evidence of guilt). This was often led and was much exploited by a United States senator, Joseph McCarthy, who for a couple of years won much popularity – as well as notoriety and opprobrium among liberally minded Americans – by a demagogic and totally unscrupulous pursuit of the supposed guilty men and women. The investigations of the congressional committee began to damage the executive branch of government itself, and many loyal and innocent American public servants, as well as many unconnected with government, suffered obloquy, intimidation and social and professional harassment.

The McCarthy episode was in part prolonged because it was not part of Eisenhower's vision of the presidential office that he should provide a strong lead to public opinion on such a matter. Over 6,000 government employees were moved from their jobs in the eighteen months during which excitement was at its height but, in the end, the senator went several steps too far in attempting to interfere with the US army. The implausibility of his charges began to dawn on the public and, slowly, other senators began to recover their nerve. McCarthy was condemned by a formal vote of the Senate and McCarthyism at last subsided. But it had done great psychological and ideological damage to the confidence of American democracy, and its wounds took a long time to heal.

In 1960, a very narrow majority of the popular vote after an election in some respects questionable in its propriety brought to the presidency a Democratic candidate, John Kennedy. He was also, as presidents go, a youngish one. This helped to create a misleading sense of striking change. Too much was made of the more superficial aspects of this at the time, but in retrospect it can certainly be agreed that both in foreign and domestic affairs, the eight years of renewed Democratic rule from 1961 indeed brought great change to the United States, though hardly in a form that Kennedy or his vice-president, Lyndon Johnson, would have hoped for when they took office. Nor did the 1960s reverse the slow crumbling of Roosevelt's Democratic coalition of voters.

This was in part because of what could still in the 1960s be called the Negro question. Once again, the long-term dynamics were fundamental to it. A century after emancipation and sixty years after the century had begun, the black American was still likely to be poorer, more often on relief, more often unemployed, less well housed and less healthy and more often murdered than the white American. As the twentieth century ended, this would still be the case, although in the 1950s, there had been some optimism about evolutionary change.

Three new facts had then begun to make their impact. One was internal migration from south to north, which had begun during the Second World War and turned a local southern question into a national problem. Between 1940 and 1960 the black population of northern states almost trebled, as first the wartime boom and then the long surge of economic growth made their impact. Jobs – or the belief that they were available – sucked people into manufacturing areas and northern cities; New York came to have the biggest black population of any state in the Union. This brought the black problem into view in new places and in new ways. It gave prominence not only to the thwarting of the exercise of black Americans' legal rights, but also to more complex disadvantages, and to new issues of comparative economic and cultural deprivation.

The second fact pushing the question of the black American forward on to the national stage originated outside the United States, as new nations of black, brown and yellow peoples grew in numbers at the UN. It was an embarrassment – of which communist propaganda always made good use – for the United States to display at home so flagrant a contravention of the ideals she spoke up for abroad as was provided by the plight of many of her blacks. The third and final fact bringing about change was the action of black Americans themselves under their own leaders, some inspired by Gandhian principles of passive resistance to oppression. This not only frightened conservatives, it won over many liberal-minded whites.

The first and most successful phase of the campaign for black Americans' equal status was a struggle for civil rights. The most important of these was the unhindered exercise of the vote (always formally available, but often actually not in many southern communities), but access to equality of treatment in other ways was also sought. Winning battles over these issues began with decisions of the Supreme Court in 1954 and 1955, with, that is, judicial interpretation, not legislation. These important first decisions provided among other things that the segregation of different races within the public school system was unconstitutional and that where it existed it should be brought to an end within a reasonable time. President Eisenhower's decision to use federal power and to use it very visibly, in the form of soldiers – there were unlikely to be many votes lost in doing this in the solid Democratic South – to support this decision challenged the social system in many southern states. By 1963 some black and white children were attending public schools together in every state of the Union, even if all-black and all-white schools still survived in many places.

After a successful campaign of 'sit-ins' by black leaders (which itself achieved important victories in individual states), Kennedy in his turn initiated a legislative programme that addressed itself to segregation and inequality in other forms. Poverty, poor housing, bad schools in run-down urban areas were symptoms of deep dislocations inside American society, north as well as south and were inequalities made more irksome by the increasing affluence in which they were set. The Kennedy administration appealed to Americans to see their removal as one of the challenges of a 'New Frontier'. Even greater emphasis was given to legislation to remove them by Lyndon Johnson, who succeeded to the presidency when Kennedy was murdered in November 1963.

This crime struck and alarmed both his countrymen and the world far more than had done the murder of President McKinley sixty-two years before and not merely because it was seen by huge audiences on television. It caused much heart-searching about the state of the national life. Not only had a young president died with his promise unfulfilled after millions had come to believe he would become most worthy of his office had he been but put upon. Much more also seemed to depend on and was expected of the presidential office in the second half of the twentieth century than when it had begun. Not only had executive and political power been much amplified in two world wars and economic disaster, but also Americans were conscious of the dangers of navigating waters very different from and much more dangerous than those of 1901. The processes of the constitution worked in their orderly way and the vice-president, Lyndon Johnson, was at once sworn into the highest office in the aeroplane carrying Kennedy's body back to Washington for his funeral. In the tragedy of the moment, it was easy to overlook the stability and durability of such constitutional practice. President Johnson, though, was to see his presidency, too, cut short, though not by personal violence.

One of his earliest preoccupations was to win support in Congress for further attacks on the injustices of black Americans' lives. He was the first national leader to speak of giving his less fortunate fellow Americans 'a stake in society'. Unhappily, laws were to prove not to help much; the deepest roots of the American black problem appeared to lie beyond their reach in what came to be called the 'ghetto' areas of great American cities. Altering the legal and political position of black Americans for the better by no means solved all the problems tangled up with colour. Bitterness and resentment were not eliminated, and in some places they increased. More blacks than ever remained evidently poor and actually deprived and in 1965 (100 years after slaves had been emancipated throughout the whole United States) a ferocious outbreak of rioting took place in Watts, a black district of Los Angeles. It was estimated to have involved at its height as many as 75,000 people, and left thirty-four dead and over 800 injured. There were disturbances in other cities, too, though not on the same scale. It had been a hot summer, and youth unemployment, it was agreed by an investigative commission, lay at the root of the Los Angeles outbreak, but the explosion had dramatically exposed much wider social problems for black Americans.

To President Johnson this must have been deeply frustrating. His own far from affluent southern background had made him a convinced and convincing exponent of a 'Great Society' in which he discerned America's future and that seemed to hold promise for the handling of the black economic problem more effectively. Yet, for all his aspirations, experience and skill, that was not happening. Nor was it to do so, for Johnson's potentially great reforming presidency was soon to end in tragic failure. His constructive work was to be forgotten and his achievements lost in the shadows of a disastrous Asian war.

22

Vietnam and After

THE AMERICAN ENTANGLEMENT

A few years after Kennedy's assassination it became a famous quip that violence was 'as American as apple pie'. In 1968, Kennedy's brother, whom many expected to become president and who was already attorney-general of the United States, had been shot dead.[1] So, earlier in the same year, had been the most celebrated of the leaders of the struggle for civil rights, the black minister of religion Martin Luther King. Yet it was more than political murder or attempted murder that seemed to many to give plausibility to the smart-alec phrase. By the end of the decade the United States was in huge disarray because of the concomitants and consequences of a disastrous foreign war.

In the 1950s, American policy in south-east Asia had come to rest on the dogma that a non-communist South Vietnam was essential to national security. That country had to be kept in the western camp, it was believed, if others in the region – or even, perhaps, as far away as India and Australia – were not to be subverted. The policy had perhaps been influenced by the infection of the American imagination with fear of communist subversion in the McCarthy years. Thus the United States became the occasional midwife, continuing nurse and virtual prisoner of conservative and incompetent governments in Saigon.

[1] Sixteen attempts to kill US presidents have been made in this century, none successful except those on McKinley and Kennedy, though Mr Reagan was wounded and Mr Ford was the victim of two attempts in the same year (1974) – both, curiously, by women.

On taking office, Kennedy no more questioned the Asian policies he inherited than that towards Cuba. Indeed, he almost at once took them further by providing more American military aid to South Vietnam in the form of 'advisers'. At the time of his murder there were already 23,000 there, many in action in the field. President Johnson followed the same course, believing that American pledges to other countries had to be shown to be sound currency. But government after government in Saigon turned out to be broken reeds. At the beginning of 1965, just after a presidential election which he had won with a huge Democratic majority,[2] Johnson was advised that South Vietnam might collapse. Under authority to act given to him by Congress after North Vietnamese attacks on American ships the previous year, he now ordered American air attacks against targets in North Vietnam. Soon afterwards, the first officially acknowledged American combat units were sent to the South. After this, American participation quickly soared out of control. In 1968 there were over half a million American servicemen in Vietnam; by Christmas that year a heavier tonnage of bombs had been dropped on North Vietnam alone than had fallen on Germany and Japan together in the entire Second World War.

The outcome was politically disastrous, and militarily ineffective. It is now almost forgotten that the first of President Johnson's State of the Union messages had envisaged a reduction of military expenditure, and that a few weeks later he sent a bill to Congress proposing to spend $5,000 million in fighting poverty in the United States. The American balance of payments was wrecked by the war's huge cost. That money was diverted from the badly needed reform projects at home, though, was almost the least of Johnson's tragedies. Worse was the bitter domestic outcry that arose as casualties mounted and attempts to negotiate seemed to get nowhere. The young (among them a future president) sought to avoid the machinery of conscription. Rancour grew, and with it the alarm of moderate America. It was small consolation to know that Soviet costs in supplying arms to North Vietnam were heavy, too.

---

[2] He won approximately 61 per cent of the votes cast – a figure which had not been reached by any president since Franklin Roosevelt in 1936.

As domestic uproar mounted over Vietnam, more came to be involved than the agitation of young people rioting in protest and distrust of their government, or the anger of conservatives who found their ideals outraged by ritual desecration of the symbols of patriotism and the refusals of the young to carry out military service. Vietnam brought about a transformation in the way many thoughtful Americans looked at the outside world. In south-east Asia it was at last borne in on them that even the United States could not obtain any result she wanted, far less obtain it at any reasonable cost. For the first time in its history, the republic experienced a major and unqualified military defeat. The late 1960s saw the sunset not of American power but rather of the illusion that American power was limitless and irresistible. Americans had entered the 1960s confident in the knowledge that their country's strength had decided two world wars. Far back behind them there stretched a century and a half of virtually unchecked and unhindered continental expansion, of immunity from European intervention, of unthreatened hegemony in their hemisphere. Nothing in that history had been wholly disastrous or irredeemable, hardly anything in it had ended in real failure, and it presented to most Americans' consciences nothing over which most of them felt any guilt. It had been easy and natural against that background to sustain a careless assumption of limitless possibility and for optimism to be carried over from domestic to foreign concerns. It is hardly surprising that Americans should forget the special circumstances in which their success for history had been possible. Most contented peoples do forget such things; it is the circumstances of failure that linger in the mind.

The reckoning had in fact already begun to be drawn up in the 1950s though few could then acknowledge it. Some Americans had even then regretted having to accept a lesser victory in Korea than they had hoped for. There had followed twenty years of frequent frustration in dealing with nations often enjoying not a tenth of the power of the United States, yet sometimes able to thwart her, even if they were also, in specific confrontations with the USSR, years of successes. At last, in the Vietnam disaster, both the limits of power and its full costs were revealed. In March 1968 the strength of domestic opposition to the war was shown clearly in the primary elections.

Johnson had already drawn the conclusion that the United States could not win, had restricted the bombing campaign and asked the North Vietnamese to negotiate. Dramatically, he also announced that he would not stand for re-election in that year. Just as war-weariness and the casualties of Korea had helped to win Eisenhower election in 1952, so the body bags and wounded from Vietnam, the pictures on television of its battlefields and the psychic divisions they provoked at home, helped to elect another Republican president in 1968; with a third candidate in the race, Richard Nixon was able to achieve a narrow margin over his Democratic opponent. Vietnam had not been the only factor, but it was one of the most important in helping to finish off the old Democratic coalition. Among others were the shift in the allegiance of southern conservatives, the 'Dixiecrats' who had long delivered the Democratic vote of the 'Solid South'; they had been increasingly offended by policy made in Washington which favoured black Americans; many of them voted in the presidential election of 1968 for the third, diehard and segregationist candidate.

President Nixon began to withdraw American ground forces from Vietnam soon after his inauguration; of a total (at its highest) of over a half a million only 40,000 were still there at the end of 1972. Peace-making was slow, nevertheless. In 1970 secret negotiations had begun with North Vietnam, accompanied by withdrawals (but also by renewed and intensified bombing of the north) by the Americans. The diplomacy was tortuous and difficult. There were further American tactical offensives while it went on. The war was extended to Cambodia, too, a nominally neutral country, in search of Vietnamese forces and supply dumps there, with tragic results. The United States could not admit it was abandoning its ally in the south, though it became clear it would have to do so. Yet the North Vietnamese would not accept terms which did not leave them able to harass and bring down any southern regime.

Amid considerable public outcry in the United States, bombing was briefly resumed for the last time at the end of 1972. Soon afterwards, on 27 January 1973, a ceasefire was signed in Paris. The war had gravely damaged American prestige, eroded American diplomatic influence, ravaged domestic politics and had frustrated social reform. In 1971 President Nixon had been obliged to end the convertibility of the dollar to gold, and the uncertainty of unstable exchange rates had further complicated the management of the domestic economy. What had been achieved at the cost of immeasurable suffering, vast sums of money and 57,000 American dead was a brief extension of the life of a shaky South Vietnam saddled with internal problems which made its survival improbable, while terrible further destruction had been inflicted on much of Indo-China. The last tended to be overlooked, as did the deaths of, possibly, as many as 3 million Indo-Chinese. Perhaps the abandonment of the illusion of American omnipotence somewhat offsets this bill.

THE CHANGING ASIAN CONTEXT

It was a major domestic political success to disentangle the United States from the morass, and President Nixon reaped in 1972 the benefit in re-election with an absolute majority of the popular vote like Johnson's of 1964. The liquidation of the venture followed other signs that he recognized how much the world had already changed since the Cuban crisis. In 1971 the American secretary of state was sent secretly to China to meet its prime minister. Later that year, China had been admitted to the UN and Taiwan had been cast out: a step formally approved by the United States.[3] One of the first declarations of the new delegation as it took its seats was that China was part of the 'Third World'. Nixon now launched a new policy of establishing normal and direct relations with mainland China with a startling initiative, making a presidential visit to that country in February 1972, an attempt to begin to bridge what he described as '16,000 miles and twenty-two years of hostility'. As the first visit by an American president to mainland Asia, it might almost have been said to have been a step towards the bridging of 2,500 years of civilization and history, too. One of Mao's last major initiatives was to encourage

[3] The final debate on the issue took six days to complete and on the crucial proposal to recognize the representatives of Beijing as 'the only legitimate representatives of China in the United Nations' seventy-six states voted in favour, thirty-five against and seventeen abstained. The majority for the expulsion of Taiwan's representatives was smaller.

rapprochement with the United States (he later claimed to have known where he was with Nixon)[4] and the presidential visit was followed by an exchange of diplomatic representation. Formally, full diplomatic relations with the United States were not opened until 1979 when American relations with Taiwan were officially closed down but even before Mao's death in 1976 one of the greatest changes in post-war diplomacy had taken place.

When Nixon followed his Chinese trip by becoming also the first American president to visit Moscow (in May 1972) and this was followed by an interim agreement on arms limitation, it seemed that another milestone had passed. The stark polarized simplicities of the Cold War were becoming blurred, however doubtful the future might look. In achieving a Vietnam settlement, both Moscow and Peking had needed to be squared before there could be a ceasefire. China's attitude to Vietnam was, we may guess, by no means simple; it was complicated by potential danger from the USSR, by the United States' use of its power elsewhere in Asia, notably Taiwan and Japan, by Vietnamese nationalism, and by rivalry with the Soviet Union. For all the help China had given, it knew its Indo-Chinese satellite could not be trusted; the Vietnamese had centuries of struggle against Chinese imperialism behind them.

In the immediate aftermath of the American withdrawal, what happened in Vietnam (and then spread to Cambodia) had become more and more evidently an Indo-Chinese civil war. The North Vietnamese had not waited long before resuming operations. For a time the United States government had to pretend not to see this; there was too much relief at home over withdrawal from the Asian commitment for scruples to be expressed over the actual observation of the peace terms. When a political scandal forced Nixon's resignation, in August 1974, his successor (and formerly vice-president), Gerald Ford, faced a Congress now suspicious of what it saw as dangerous foreign adventures and ready to thwart them. Distrust of the executive power was in the air. Confidence in the traditional foreign policy leadership of the presidency crumbled. There could be

[4] Sir Edward Heath, *The Course of My Life, My Autobiography* (London, 1998), p.493.

no American attempt to uphold the peace terms of 1972 as any sort of guarantee of the South Vietnamese regime against overthrow. Early in 1975, American aid to Saigon came to an end. A government that had lost virtually all its other territory was now reduced to a backs-to-the-wall attempt to hold the capital city and the lower Mekong with a demoralized and defeated army. At the same time, the Cambodian communists were destroying another regime the United States had supported, but Congress prevented the sending of further military and financial help to it. The pattern of China in 1947 was being repeated; the United States cut her losses, mainly at the expense of those who had relied on her (though 117,000 Vietnamese fled with the Americans).

This outcome was doubly ironic. In the first place it suggested that the hardliners on Asian policy had been right all along – that only the knowledge that the United States was in the last resort prepared to fight for them would guarantee that post-colonial regimes would resist communism. Secondly, a swing back to isolationism in the United States was accentuated, not muffled, by defeat. Those who reflected on the American dead and missing and the huge financial cost now saw the whole Indo-China episode as a pointless and unjustifiable waste on behalf of peoples who would not fight to defend themselves. As for the allies of the United States, an alternative reading of the American position in East Asia was possible. It was arguable that better relations with China mattered much more than the loss of Vietnam, and that they could now become a reality. Yet the United States looked and Americans felt confused and worried as the 1970s drew to an end. When President Ford faced a Congress unwilling to countenance further aid to its allies in Indo-China, and Cambodia collapsed, to be quickly followed by South Vietnam, questions inevitably began to be asked at home and abroad about how far what looked like a worldwide retreat of American power might go. If the United States would no longer fight over Indo-China, would she, then, do so over Thailand? More alarmingly still, would she fight over Israel – or even Berlin? There were good reasons to think the Americans' mood of resignation and dismay would not last for ever, but while it lasted, their allies felt uneasy and all the more so in the aftermath of an oil crisis and the revival of tension in other parts of the world.

The situation was not easy to read. Objectively, there were good grounds for reassurance, though they were so familiar that they were easily overlooked. The American democratic system showed no sign of breaking down, or of not being able to meet the country's needs, even if it could not find quick answers to all its problems. The economy had astonishingly been able for years to pay for a hugely expensive war, for a space exploration programme that put men on the moon, for garrisons around the world, and for a rising standard of living. In the end the burden proved too heavy but such facts offset the continuing plight of black Americans, the urban decay visible in some of the country's greatest cities, and the deep psychological wounds felt by many who had hitherto believed unquestioningly in the traditions of American patriotism. As the presidential election of 1980 came in sight, though, a new source of alarm and confusion appeared, this time in the Middle East.

OIL AND THE ISRAEL PROBLEM

Politics and economics in the Middle East were already by 1970 being shaped by more than the Cold War and Arab–Jew antagonism. In the 1950s two important developments had owed nothing to ideology or regional rivalries. One was a much-increased rate of oil discovery, particularly on the southern shores of the Persian Gulf, in the small sheikdoms then still under British influence and in Saudi Arabia. The second was a huge acceleration of energy consumption in western countries (especially in the United States) and in Japan. The prime beneficiaries of the oil boom were Saudi Arabia, Kuwait, Libya and, some way behind, Iran and Iraq, the established major Middle Eastern producers. This had two important consequences. Industrial countries dependent upon Middle Eastern oil – the United States, Great Britain, Germany and, soon, Japan – had to give even greater weight to Arab views in their diplomacy. It also meant big changes in the relative wealth and standing of Arab states. None of the three leading oil producers was either heavily populated or traditionally of much weight in international affairs. A more remote consequence, too, was a new vigour in searching for oil in other parts of the world.

The importance of oil was still not very evident in the crisis which had followed when an extremist Ba'ath party government took power in Syria with Soviet support in 1963. It soon began to agitate for a new campaign against Israel. The king of Jordan was threatened if he did not support the Palestinian guerrillas (organized in 1964 as the Palestine Liberation Organization, or PLO) on Jordanian territory and Jordanian forces began to prepare to join Egypt and Syria in an attack on Israel. But in 1967, provoked by an Egyptian attempt to blockade their only Red Sea port, the Israelis struck first. In a brilliant campaign they destroyed the Egyptian air force and army in Sinai and hurled back the Jordanians, occupying Arab Jerusalem and winning new borders on the Suez Canal, the Golan Heights, and the Jordan in six days of fighting. For defence, these were far superior to their former boundaries and the Israelis announced that they would keep them (in the event, they later withdrew from much of the Sinai). This was not all. Defeat ensured the eclipse of the glamorous Nasser, who had briefly looked like a plausible leader of pan-Arabism, but now had a decade of sterility and failure behind him. He was now left visibly dependent on Russian power (a Soviet naval squadron arrived at Alexandria as the Israeli advance guards reached the Suez Canal) and on subsidies from the oil states. Both demanded more prudence from him, and that meant difficulties with the radical leaders of the Arab masses; he died in 1970, his charisma already much dissipated.

Yet the Six-Day War of 1967, like the Suez crisis and, for that matter, many previous wars of the Ottoman succession in the Near East, solved no problems, changed nothing that was fundamental and made some things worse (notably by the Israeli seizure of all Jersualem, duly condemned without dissent – though with some abstentions – by the UN General Assembly). It had produced new waves of Palestinian refugees and by 1973 about 1,400,000 Palestinians were said to be dispersed in Arab countries, a similar number remaining in Israel and Israeli-occupied territory (the Jewish population of Israel was then about 2.5 million). When the Israelis began to establish Jewish settlements in their newly-won conquests, Arab resentment grew even stronger. Time, oil, and birth rates might seem to be on the Arab side, but not much else was clear. Al-Fatah, the most powerful Palestinian guerrilla group, led by Yasir Arafat, gave up reliance on the Arab states and turned to terrorism outside the disputed lands and revolution within them to promote their cause. After 1969, when the king of Libya was displaced by a young soldier, the Palestinians could look to a different sort of oil-rich patron. Like the Zionists of the 1890s, they had decided that the western myth of nationality was the answer to their plight; a new state should be the expression of their nationhood, and like Zionist militants in the 1940s, they turned to assassination and indiscriminate murder as weapons. It was clear that in time there would be another war. If American and Soviet interests were identified with opposing sides, as seemed likely for a time, it could be feared that a world war might suddenly blow up out of a local conflict, as in 1914.

There was indeed a fourth Arab–Israeli war, in 1973. It produced a major crisis, too, though one whose nature had not been anticipated. It began when Egypt and Syria, exasperated by the failure of the UN to make Israel comply with its resolutions, launched a new attack on the Jewish holy day of Yom Kippur (6 October). For the first time the Israelis seemed in danger of defeat by the much improved and Soviet-armed forces of their opponents. Nonetheless, they beat off the onslaught successfully, though only after the Russians were reported to have sent nuclear weapons to Egypt and the Americans had put their forces on the alert around the world. This grim background, like the possibility that the Israelis, too, had nuclear weapons which they might use in extremity, was not fully discernible to the public, perhaps, but clearly, the Middle East retained all its alarming potential to detonate crises which went far beyond it. A ceasefire followed on 25 October; terrorist activity then continued on Israel's border with Lebanon, provoking strong Israeli counter-measures.

Israel had survived, but with heavy losses, while the war cost her economy dear. Tension was high when the UN General Assembly agreed in 1974 to receive a delegation from the PLO, and to be addressed by Arafat; subsequently a large majority voted that Israel be not allowed to present its case in a debate on the Middle East. In the following year the General Assembly denounced Zionism as a form of racism and granted the PLO 'observer' status at its meetings. That organization was henceforth a major fact of world politics, though still unrecognized by Israel as anything but a mask and cover for terrorists. Later, a 'Group of 77' supposedly non-aligned countries achieved the suspension of Israel (like South Africa) from certain international organizations and, perhaps more important, a unanimous resolution condemning the Israeli annexation of Jerusalem. Another called for Israel's withdrawal from Arab lands in exchange for recognition by her neighbours. Even the Americans accepted a resolution in 1976 criticizing Israel's behaviour in her occupied territories. Secure in the knowledge that, nonetheless, in the last resort help would always be available from the United States (which had on several occasions used its veto to protect her), Israel could survive such gestures and slights though inconvenienced and made unhappy by them.

The most immediate and obvious outcome of the 1973 war on world history had been economic: the impact of the announcement by other Arab states, led by Saudi Arabia, that they would restrict oil supplies to Europe, Japan and the United States. There had long been talk of an 'energy crisis' on the way, in the sense that demand would outrun supply. This was something different, a very large rise in the world price of oil. Now the tensions of Arab–Israeli relations were brought home to the man in the street all over the world except the communist bloc. Oil prices quadrupled in a single year. Suddenly, the implication of twenty years of a historic change largely unnoticed by most of the world was made evident. The developed world was overwhelmingly oil-dependent. Sweden and the Netherlands actually introduced petrol-rationing and the United Kingdom got ready to do so.

Throughout the 1950s and most of the 1960s the western world had enjoyed and got used to stable and cheap oil supplies. They had been assured by the informal influence of the United States and United Kingdom in the Gulf States and Saudi Arabia (and in Iraq until 1963, when the Ba'ath seized power there). In the 1970s this assurance broke down. Overnight, economic difficulties that had gone grumbling along but had still been manageable in the 1960s became acute (and among these had been lower rates of investment and exploration by the United States oil industry for a decade or so). The international monetary problems that had followed the end of dollar convertibility to gold were suddenly made far worse. Exchange problems, as the dollar fluctuated violently, drove France and Germany to seek liberation from the hitherto benevolent dollar despotism. Subsequent institutional bickering and squabbling on economic and financial matters reminded Europeans of the limits to any continental cohesion their governments had so far achieved. Dependence on oil imports played havoc with balance-of-payment issues. The United States was badly shaken and Japan suffered deeply. There was suddenly talk of a new world depression like that of the 1930s. The golden age of economic growth that had begun with post-war recovery seemed to be at an end.

THE IRANIAN REVOLUTION

Though oil prices again fell somewhat and steadied in the mid-1970s, they were to rise steeply again at the end of the decade. Egypt had fallen out with Syria, her ally of 1973. Nasser's successor had turned to the United States in the hope of making a face-saving peace with Israel, and Egypt drifted away more and more into isolation from other Arab states. Meanwhile, the PLO's activity across Israel's northern border was not only harassing Israel, but was steadily driving Lebanon, once a bastion of western values, into ruin and disintegration. In 1978 Israel invaded southern Lebanon in the hope of ending the PLO raids and inaugurated an occupation of a 'security zone' of Lebanese territory that was still to be in place twenty years later.

President Carter, who had won back the American presidency for the Democratic party in the election of 1976, threw himself vigorously into the cause of negotiating peace between Israel and Egypt. After lengthy discussion (and the commitment of a promise of large-scale American financial support for both states) he was successful. The non-Islamic world applauded when the Israeli and Egyptian prime ministers met in Washington in 1979 to sign a peace treaty providing for Israel's withdrawal from Sinai. Two years later the Egyptian was to pay the price of assassination by those who felt he had betrayed the Palestinian cause by making peace. Nonetheless, this settlement looked for a moment like a sign of recovery in the American position in the Middle East when one was badly needed by Mr Carter. American morale was by then very low, and it was not to improve during his presidency. The Asian settlements of Nixon and Ford had been real, but they had also been built on the management of American with- drawal and were soon forgotten or looked on as hollow successes. In the background a continuing fear was felt by many Americans over the alleged rising Soviet strength in ballistic missiles. All this shaped American reactions to a virtually unforeseen event.

In 1978 the Shah of Iran, long the recipient of American favour as a reliable ally, was driven from his throne by a coalition of outraged liberals and Islamic conservatives. Millions of Iranians had found their traditional ways dislocated by the modernization in which the Shah had followed – with less caution – his father Reza Khan. Western diplomacy had been notably unperceptive in gauging what this meant for the political volatility of the country. Riots began in the first weeks of January and successive attempts to pacify the religious leaders who led the masses failed until, in December, the country was virtually out of control. The Shah went into exile in January 1979. An attempt to set up constitutional government in the aftermath soon collapsed. Popular support rallied to the Islamic revolutionary faction. In April, a Shi'ite Islamic Republic led by the Ayatollah Khomeni, an elderly and intransigent cleric returned from exile abroad, was proclaimed. The United States quickly recognized the new regime, but to no avail: Americans were tarred with guilt by association, as the patrons of the former Shah (the Soviet Union had stood by him, too, in early 1978, but had thereafter smoothly disengaged itself from support for him). The United States was morally denounced by religious radicals, too, as the stronghold of capitalism and western materialism. As they unavailingly sought accommodation with the revolutionary leaders, American diplomats could draw only small consolation from the fact that the Soviet Union was soon undergoing similar Iranian vilification. Students in Teheran relieved some of their personal exasperations by storming the American embassy and seizing members of its staff and others as hostages, while demanding that the Shah be sent back from exile in the United States to face trial for his supposed misdeeds. A startled world suddenly heard that the Iranian government supported the students, had taken custody of the hostages and endorsed the demand for the return of the Shah.

President Carter could hardly have faced a more awkward situation. At that moment American policy had also to adjust itself to a sudden Soviet intervention in Afghanistan. That country, too, had been the scene of a revolution in 1978, which (unlike that in Iran) had brought to power a left-inclined, though self-proclaimedly 'non-aligned' regime. The USA recognized it, but in 1979 it turned to the USSR for help. Soon, substantial Soviet forces had entered the country. It was this that led to the denunciation of the USSR as another 'Satan' by the Iranian leaders. By then, the USA had responded to the Iranian seizure of hostages with economic sanctions and a freezing of Iranian assets in the USA. Then came a dismal failure when a botched American rescue operation cost eight lives. The unhappy hostages were in the end to be recovered by negotiation and, in effect, a ransom: the return of frozen Iranian assets in the United States. Once again the United States appeared humiliated.

It was some consolation and Americans took heart when the ferocious Ba'ath regime in Iraq, already viewed with favour in Washington for its ruthless execution and pursuit of Iraqi communists, fell out with its neighbour, the new Iran. In spite of Ba'athist secularism, this was a conflict inflamed by the traditional animosity of Mesopotamian Suni and Persian Shi'ite Muslims; ancient history was again at work. In July 1979 a secular-minded Ba'athist ruler called Saddam Hussein had taken over as president in Baghdad. To the State Department he seemed likely to offset the Iranian danger in the Gulf.

ISLAM IN INTERNATIONAL AFFAIRS

The Iranian revolution threw into relief much more than just the American loss of a client state. The seizure of the hostages and acceptance of responsibility for that by the Iranian government had been symbolic acts of major scope. They gave a shock (registered in a unanimous vote of condemnation at the UN) to the established convention that diplomatic envoys should be immune from interference, a European convention developed over more than three centuries throughout the civilized world. The Iranian government's action had announced that it was not playing by the accepted international rules. It was a blatant rejection of western assumptions and made some in the West wonder what else Islamic revolution might imply. Further cause for alarm soon appeared. A coalition of grievances had made possible the overthrow of the Shah, but speedy reversion to archaic traditions (visible to western observers most strikingly in the treatment of women) confirmed that Iran had repudiated more than a ruler. The Iranian Islamic republic soon began to be seen as an expression of a rage shared by many Muslims elsewhere.

In the Middle East, as nowhere else, western nationalism, socialism and capitalism, the great answers of Europe to the problems of modernization, had failed to solve the region's problems, let alone satisfy passions and appetites they had aroused. Nor had they assuaged long and deeply felt awareness of humiliation by western power. The fading of the promise of modernization, moreover, had not only left behind disappointments, but had also revealed threats. The onset of secular westernization challenged Islamic orthodoxy in many particulars of behaviour. Muslim rigorists proclaimed that Atatürk, Reza Khan and Nasser had all led their peoples down the wrong road. Islamic societies might have successfully resisted the rival faith of atheistic communism, but to many Muslims the material and moral contagion of the West seemed more threatening as the century drew to a close than they had done in the past. Paradoxically, western left-wing doctrines of capitalist exploitation themselves helped to feed this revulsion of feeling. The Iranian revolution expressed a deep and complex background of discontents within many Islamic societies.

It was also a background brought vividly to western attention in recent years, as Israel catalysed Islamic feeling. In 1972 a gang of terrorists from the Middle East had seized, held as hostages and then murdered eleven members of the Israeli team competing in the Olympic Games at Munich. Thanks to plentiful television coverage, this was one of the most spectacular and therefore successful acts of political terrorism in twenty years. Random acts of murder, kidnapping and violence – and not just those carried out by Muslims – had multiplied since the 1960s. There had long been a tradition of terrorism in Europe itself that continued to produce bloodshed (for example, the massacre when a bomb was set off, apparently by extreme right-wing Italian political groups, at the Bologna railway station, and the murder of the British ambassador at The Hague by the IRA). But terrorism mounted by Arabs or Islamic organizations came to exercise a growing and special fascination for the European and North American imagination and media. In the 1980s this preoccupation was reinforced further by the rhetoric of the Iranian revolution, by talk of *jihad* (holy war) by some terrorists, by dramatic events inside the Arab world itself – such as the murder in 1981 of the Egyptian prime minister who had negotiated peace with Israel (another television spectacular) – by the bizarre statements and behaviour of the Muslim dictator of Libya, and by political changes in Muslim countries.

As well as raising the international temperature over the chronic issue of Arab–Israeli conflict, the Iranian revolution thus also appeared to entangle old economic and political problems with other, vaguer but much larger confrontations. These sometimes came to be seen – and proclaimed – as conflicts between the western world as a whole and Islam. Such a view could tap the long history of friction and conflict between Islam and Christianity to nourish its enthusiasms. In the early 1990s this even led commentators in western countries to talk of a forthcoming struggle of civilizations, an exaggeration too manifest to be taken seriously, but an interesting symptom of the importance which came to be attached to a contrast, and sometimes clash, of cultures. As the Cold War ebbed, what was somewhat inadequately labelled by the blanket term 'Islamic fundamentalism' (by ill-judged analogy with conservative 'Christian fundamentalism' in the United States) even somewhat replaced the old communist nightmare as a bogey haunting western consciousness.

Nevertheless, symptoms visible across most of the Muslim world could also give western politicians occasion to recall once again that Islam is the creed of many very different lands and peoples. They stretch from Morocco in the west to China in the east. Indonesia, the largest south-east Asian country, Pakistan, Malaysia and Bangladesh between them contain more than half the world's Muslims. Outside those countries and the Arabic-speaking lands, the tsarist government of Russia had been alarmed by revolution in Persia because of its possibly disturbing effect on its own Muslim subjects, and the USSR now had more still, while Nigeria, with a majority of Muslims, was the most populous and potentially (thanks to her oil) the richest of the ex-colonial African 'new nations'. But new perceptions of the Islamic world took time to appear, and well into the 1970s the rest of the world seemed obsessed with the Arab countries of the Middle East, when it thought of Islam.

The Iranian revolution, in a non-Arab land, helped to change this, with its hard anti-western (and occasionally anti-Christian) rhetoric and its coupling with a new discipline and austerity in the imposition of Islamic law and custom on westernized élites. There soon followed, too, a successful struggle of the Afghan *muhjaheddin* ('holy warriors') against the communist government in Kabul and its supporting Soviet army, and a subsequent Islamic radicalization of Afghanistan under the influence of its Iranian neighbour. In its brief communist days that country had not undergone such modernization as had Iran under the Shah, but its religious leaders found plenty of popular support for rejection of what little social modernization there had been and for renewed emphasis on Islamic tradition. It was merely a predictable paradox that this should lead quickly in the 1980s to clandestine American support for the *muhjaheddin* (they were, after all, on the 'right' side of the Cold War). As the 1980s proceeded, electoral successes for avowedly 'Islamic' parties in several countries led to the installation of other 'Islamic' regimes, notably in the Sudan.[5] The winning of a majority of votes by an Islamic party in the Algerian election of 1990 had an immediate European repercussion, for France felt itself obliged to support the Algerian military regime's attempts to repress what it claimed to be another fundamentalist movement, although what soon appeared to be going forward was straightforward repression of political opposition.

Before long, the world began to be used to hearing reports of Pakistan's bans on mixed hockey, of Saudi Arabia's Islamic punishments of death by stoning and amputation of limbs, of the segregation of men and women students during lectures at the splendid new university built by the ruler of Oman – and much more. Even in a comparatively 'westernized' Egypt students had already in 1978 voted for those the West now called fundamentalists in their own elections. Some Egyptian girls were by then refusing to dissect male corpses in

---

[5] Some prefer the adjective 'Islamist'.

medical school and demanding a segregated, dual system of instruction. Everywhere in the Arab lands, the pressure of radical Islamicizing forces was felt in some degree; it could always find something to feed on in opposing governments which upheld privileged, sometimes overtly westernized, minorities, showed signs of growing tolerance towards Israel, or pursued programmes of social modernization.

In Europe and the United States, such varied phenomena were easy to misjudge. They seemed to form a more coherent pattern than was in fact the case, even, perhaps, a coordinated anti-western movement, aspiring to Islamic unity. Islamic rhetoric often seemed to confirm this. Yet Islamic 'fundamentalism' is full of qualifications and complexities and has obvious limitations as an explanatory term. It is not of equal weight in all Islamic countries. Indonesia and Nigeria have not shown the continuing excitement expressed in some Arab countries and Iran. Moreover, the expression of Muslim unease in political action (including terrorism) outside Muslim countries is a more limited phenomenon than is sometimes recognized. Its emergence has in fact aroused new disunity and division within Islamic societies and has brought old problems to the surface.

By 1990, it could certainly not be said to have opened an era in which the Islamic peoples of the Middle East and North Africa could feel that the tide of history had turned in their favour. In the first place, nothing had happened to qualify or remove a fundamental flaw in radical Islamic thinking, its violent but inconsistent anti-modernism. Even Islamic conservatives usually wanted to have the benefits of a selective, controlled modernization; could they combine their own cultural goals (and rejection of those of the western world) with economic, technological, scientific advance? There was no sign that this was likely. A second weakness soon became evident, too. In the 1980s division within the Islamic world erupted in one of the bloodiest wars since 1945, between Iraq and Iran. Religious difference between Suni and Shi'ite gave it a uniquely deep historic background. The struggle lasted eight years and cost a million lives. Evidently, bitter struggles could go on between Islamic countries, whatever their attitudes towards Europeans and Americans. Finally, to the dismay of Muslims all over the Middle East, no progress was made in solving what they saw as the Israel problem (which might mean at a maximum the elimination of that country, or, at its most modest, satisfaction of reasonable Palestinian demands).

Many Arabs came to feel that the western principle of nationality so often advocated since the 1880s as an organizational remedy for the instability that followed Ottoman decline had not worked. Nor, evidently, were the wars of the Ottoman succession over, although, in fact, the pattern of states that emerged from the Mandates and decolonization has proved broadly stable. A favourable conjunction of embarrassments for superpowers and above all the USA had made things look promising after the recent revelation of the potency of the oil factor (during 1979, world oil prices had again almost doubled), but pious Muslims had become increasingly aware that western commerce, communications and the simple temptations offered to those rich with oil were more dangerous to Islam than any earlier (let alone purely military) threat had been. When the descendants of Mehemet Ali sent their sons to Harvard and Oxford, they did not acquire only academic instruction there but, it was feared, bad habits as well.

Nor were such issues all that divided and infuriated Muslims. Even in the 1940s, the Ba'ath socialist movement which inspired many Muslims and which became entrenched in Iraq had become anathema to the Muslim Brotherhood, which also deplored the 'godlessness' of both sides in the Palestinian quarrel. Popular sovereignty was a goal fundamentalists rejected; they sought Islamic control of society in all its aspects. That Islamic 'radicals' should happily espouse obviously reactionary causes can partly be understood in the context of a long absence within Islam of any statist or institutional theory such as that of the West. Even in orthodox hands, and even if it delivers some desirable goods, the state as such is not self-evidently a legitimate source of authority in Islamic thought. Moreover, the very introduction of state structures in Arab lands since the nineteenth century and of the idea of legal sovereignty itself had been in imitation, conscious or unconscious, of the West. Youthful radicalism which had tried and found wanting the politics of left-wing socialism (or what was thought to be that, and was in any case another western import) felt that no intrinsic value resided in states or nations; its disappointed advocates looked elsewhere. This in part also explains efforts shown first in Libya, and then in Iran, to arrive at new ways of legitimating authority in new experiments with institutions. Whether the age-old Islamic bias towards tribalism and the brotherhood of Islam can be sustained remains to be seen, but the violence of politics in many Arab states now frequently exhibits a simple polarization between repressive authoritarianism on the one hand and the fundamentalist wave on the other. Both Morocco and Algeria were to find their domestic order thus troubled. The situation was made all the more dangerous and explosive by the demography of the Arab lands. The average age of most Islamic societies in the Mahgreb and Levant is said to be between fifteen and eighteen, and they are growing at very fast rates. There is just too much youthful energy and frustration about for the outlook to be benign.

AN UNEASY LATIN AMERICA

Though they were of a very different order and nature from those of the Middle East, it was clear also in the 1970s and 1980s that many of the problems of another continent, Latin America, were not being met. An old thesis was heard renewed, the analysis which blamed general economic backwardness or lack of development throughout Latin America, for all its variety, on an alleged economic dependency on outsiders, first the Europeans who had sucked surplus value out of basically export-oriented and monoculture economies they had imposed on the region, and then the North American investors who succeeded them. Latin American intellectuals revelled in associating themselves with the concept of a dependent 'Third World'. Their continent had not at first been associated with this, of course, for the simple reason that the American liberation from colonial imperialism had taken place about a century and a half earlier than that of the countries that had met at Bandung.

Such over-simplified thinking won some support among middle-class intellectuals as Latin America's economic troubles worsened until they seemed to be crippling steady growth. One of them was that for all its new industrialization, the continent could not keep pace with its very rapid population growth. At rates current in the 1980s, it could confidently be predicted that there would be 500 million

Latin Americans and Caribbean islanders by the year 2000 (there were about 100 million at mid-century). Such possibilities began to attract attention just as the difficulties of the Latin American economies were again beginning to look intractable. The aid programme of the Alliance for Progress had patently failed to cope with them, and did little but spawn quarrels over the use of American funds. Mismanagement in individual countries produced huge foreign debts that crippled attempts to sustain investment and achieve better trade balances. Currencies readily went out of control and very steep inflation was common. Social divisions remained menacing. Even the most advanced Latin American countries continued to display vast discrepancies of wealth, well-being and education. Constitutional and democratic process, where they existed, seemed increasingly impotent to confront such problems. In the 1960s and 1970s, Peru, Bolivia, Brazil, Argentina and Paraguay all underwent periods of prolonged authoritarian rule by soldiers. Some who sympathized with those regimes undoubtedly believed that only authoritarianism could bring about changes of which nominally democratic and civilian government had proved incapable.

In the 1970s, Latin Americans' problems began to be more vividly brought to the world's notice through reports of torture and violent repression from countries like Argentina, Brazil and Uruguay, all once regarded as civilized and constitutional states. Chile, which had a longer and more continuous history of constitutional government than most of its neighbours, had enjoyed a period of moderate and even reforming right-wing government under an administration elected by a large majority in 1964, but this collapsed when, in the 1970 election, a divided Right let in a minority socialist coalition. When the new government embarked upon measures which brought economic chaos and seemed to be slipping further leftwards, and even into a breakdown into lawlessness, the outcome was, in 1973, a military coup. Elected though the displaced regime had been, it had too little support for a programme of building socialism. The counter-revolutionary movement had United States approval and undercover support, and many Chileans went along with it, too, in the belief that the overthrown government had been under communist control. They had been frightened by what looked like a worsening revolutionary situation. Chile's new and authoritarian military government soon showed it had no qualms in mounting a brutal and wide-ranging persecution of its opponents and critics, using the most savage methods to do so. In the end it rebuilt the economy and even, in the late 1980s, began to look as if it might be able to restrain itself. But it drove ideological division deeper into Chilean society than the country had ever hitherto known, and Chile became the outstanding symbol of dangers undoubtedly latent in other Latin American countries.

It was thus on a troubled and distracted continent that there had fallen, to cap its troubles, the oil crises of the 1970s. The first finally sent the foreign debt problems of its oil-importing countries (that is, most of them other than Mexico and Venezuela) out of control. In the next two decades, many economic remedies were to be tried in one country or another, but all turned out to be unworkable or unenforceable. It seemed impossible to deal with runaway inflation, interest charges on external debt, the distortion in resource allocation arising from past bad government, and simple administrative and cultural inability to sustain good fiscal policies. Latin America still appeared to be, perhaps more than ever, an explosive, disturbed continent of nations growing less and less like one another, for all their shared roots, except in their distress. Culture itself was still a divisive force. To the layers laid down by Indian, slave, colonial and post-colonial experiences, all strongly reflected in differences of economic well-being, had now been added the differences brought by the arrival in the 1950s and 1960s of the assumptions of developed, high-technology societies, whose benefits were available to the better-off but not to the poor who envied them. Just as in Asia, though it has been less obvious, the strains of the impact of modern civilization on historically deep-rooted societies are now more visible than ever before, even if Latin America has been undergoing some of them since the sixteenth century. In the 1980s they were expressed additionally through the terrorism displayed by radical revolutionaries and reactionary soldiers alike, and they continued to threaten civilized and constitutional standards achieved earlier.

The 1990s, though, were to bring change. A major recovery of constitutional and democratic government in Latin America was at last observable. In all the major states, military government was formally set aside, though there were still dangers of attempted coups (for instance in Paraguay in 1996), and though some states (notably Colombia, where normal problems of government were exacerbated by criminal drug-dealing interests and a heavy dependency of peasant farmers on growing and selling cash crops of drug-producing raw materials) continued to experience considerable violence. Elsewhere, improvement in government was linked to economic recovery, until it was again interrupted by continent-wide financial problems in the middle of the decade. Argentina, Brazil and Peru once again suffered inflation; only Chile seemed able to navigate these troubled economic waters. One Brazilian finance minister, after building an earlier career as a sociologist on the reiteration of an anti-capitalist and anti-colonial interpretation of the continent's history, succeeded finally in mastering an inflation rate of 7,000 per cent per annum with a firm deflationary, free-market economic programme. He was in due course rewarded by being made president.

There were some hopeful continent-wide factors at work, too. Mercosur, a customs union of Brazil, Argentina and Uruguay, which aimed to achieve free movement of goods and services between its members by the end of 1994, was a sign of a growing self-confidence based on real growth in economic strength.[6] At a 'summit' meeting of American nations held at Miami in 1994, the main topic for discussion was a possible free-trade area of the Americas, including the northern continent. When the next such meeting was held, four years later in Santiago de Chile, further progress proved impossible along this line, largely thanks to the domestic politics of the United States; nonetheless, there were signs (not least over the issue of the continued isolation of Cuba so fervently sought by Washington) that Latin America was beginning to assert itself more effectively than in the past against the hemisphere's preponderant power.

---

[6] Paraguay had also signed up, but later dropped out.

23

The Reshaping of Europe

For a long time, the idea of Europe has inspired some and dismayed others. To most Europeans most of the time it has hardly mattered at all. Those who have tried to think about it have often found themselves grappling with an abstraction that eluded their grasp. It has had to be invented and reinvented. Only after 1945 did a significant number of European politicians in western countries begin to interest themselves in the nature of Europe as a whole with an eye to its future and the possibilities of shaping it. The disaster of the war had been the stimulus; in no sense could Europe be said to have benefited from it except in averting an even more barbaric fate than the one she had undergone. The roots of new thinking lay in horrified feelings of revulsion about what had occurred and fears of possible repetition, but also in idealism. Nationalism had twice demonstrated its terrible power, in 1914 and 1939; it was understandable that it should be identified as a fundamental source of European weakness. Some felt that history showed it to be a matter of life and death that the continent's old divisions should be overcome. Still others turned to Europe simply as a solution for the German problem; in 1945, though, what lay beyond occupation was impossible to say. Yet, for the second time in the century, the question had to be posed sooner or later: how was that potentially mighty nation to be contained except by reorganizing Europe?

Many other sources – some of them traceable even further back, to the aftermath of the Great War, for example – also contributed to what came to be called the 'European Movement'. But circumstances, too, were crucial, first those of 1945 and, soon, those of the Cold War. They gave a special twist to European integration; they encouraged and gave opportunities to those who sought a new way of organizing Europe. Such enthusiasts threw themselves enthusiastically into trying to do so, though within a context decisively shaped by non-Europeans. As might be expected, national governments responded in different ways. Properly and unsurprisingly, they looked to national interest for guidance. Broadly speaking, their views, in so far as they were not wholly pragmatic, tended in the late 1940s and early 1950s to take one of two directions on questions of European organization. One – fairly consistently that of British governments, usually with support from Scandinavia and Ireland – looked to inter-governmental cooperation to achieve defined and specific ends. European institutions would thus give further protection to proper national interests, rather than set them aside. In contrast, some continental European governments were more quickly and more willingly to listen to plans for further, far-reaching, supranational integration, perhaps even going so far as federal structures and a European parliament.[1] Such plans could be and were influenced by the hopes of enthusiasts prepared to override, if necessary, national state objectives in the pursuit of Europe-wide policy goals. Even by 1948, this difference had led to important divergences. In that year, the British deeply opposed the development on any but a minimal basis of what became a 'Council of Europe' (formally inaugurated early in 1949), and thwarted a Franco-Italian proposal that the new body should be called the 'European Union'.

The Marshall Plan had been followed up by a specific and local European defence arrangement, when Great Britain, France, Belgium, the Netherlands and Luxembourg signed what was known as the Brussels Treaty in March 1948, a fifty-year alliance against armed attack. It was soon to be transcended in practice by the formation of NATO. There followed the emergence of the two Germanys. The major new institutional facts confronting European statesmen in the post-war years were then in place, just as at last signs began to appear

---

[1] In the jargon of the specialists, this second tendency is sometimes called the 'competence accretion' view of integration.

that economic recovery was under way. It was soon, at least in the western half of the continent, going ahead at a notable pace, especially in western Germany. The fact of decolonization was another historical experience affecting Europe's internal arrangements, but much less important. Economic ties with former overseas dependencies proved quite durable in the era of decolonization (as they had done when Great Britain made peace with her newly independent American colonies in 1783, the historically-minded could note), and the soon to be ex-colonial powers seemed little affected. Some sociological consequences – the return (or first arrival) in a few countries of returning settlers or indigenous natives from former colonies – and some psychological effects, as familiar assumptions slowly dropped away and old ties withered, may have seemed more significant than the economic impact of decolonization.

There were obvious and persistent obstacles to political integration. Portugal and Spain, for instance (allowing for certain nuances and compromises dictated by circumstance) had remained neutral during the war and were still ruled by dictators in 1945. Spain had only broken off diplomatic relations with Germany on the very day of Hitler's suicide.[2] Some called their regimes 'fascist', and they posed psychological and political problems to other European governments. In the event, it proved easier for Salazar's Portugal than for Spain, which, under Franco, had even sent troops to help Hitler on the Russian front, to resume its full place in international life. A resolution of 1946 barring Spain from entry to the United Nations led for a time to the withdrawal of the British, Italian and Dutch ambassadors from Madrid and was not rescinded until 1950. In the early 1950s, nonetheless, both Iberian countries were clearly on the western side of the Cold War, and Spain, which had suffered particular economic hardship since 1939, began to enjoy American loans and military aid. The great divide of Cold War mattered more than constitutional orientation or past ideology. Yet, in the long run, that rapprochement with the Spanish dictator would prove to have advanced the cause of

[2] The Irish government, which had remained neutral during the war, was more punctilious in preserving diplomatic formalities; the prime minister and minister for external affairs went in person to the German embassy to express their official condolences on 3 May.

democratic and constitutional government in Spain too. Another step significant for the future had in fact been taken by Franco himself in 1947, when it was announced (and approved by referendum) that Spain was to resume her monarchical constitution.[3]

The psychological changes of perspective and psychology brought about by Cold War also very broadly (and often without acknowledgement) favoured aspirations to European unity and ideological arguments that had first surfaced at the end of the First World War. The growing sense of a Soviet threat, the need for, and then the experience of, economic reconstruction and recovery, led some to try to rediscover shared civilized values that they could identify as 'European'. They were encouraged, too, by the facts of the decline of the power of individual European states in global affairs and the loss of the nerve or taste of European peoples for colonialism. Intellectuals argued enthusiastically that nationalism's grip on the human potential for large-scale organization was loosening in the very continent where nationalism as a political doctrine had been born. Nonetheless, it was national interest itself that was to supply the main driving force of European integration in the next few years.

The Marshall Plan and NATO turned out to be only among the first of a series of milestones on a road leading to a more coherent Europe. A major simplification became possible once the emergence of two Germanys had provided in partition an institutionalized and seemingly durable solution to the German problem. Old fears in France were quietened, even if not removed, and the likelihood of another great civil war in the West over Germany's place in Europe seemed to have receded. Western European countries slowly worked out, largely through economic change and by implication, a peace settlement with West Germany (that of the USSR with her had to wait until the 1970s). Soviet policy, too, gave western European countries conscious of their individual weakness new reasons to cooperate more closely. Events in eastern Europe in the late 1940s and 1950s, large and active communist parties in France and Italy,

---

[3] The monarchy was in due course restored in 1975, on Franco's death, Juan Carlos (whose father as pretender to the throne had denounced the 1947 decision) ascending the throne on 22 December. A few months earlier, Portugal had held its first free democratic elections for a half-century.

and the propaganda of the Cominform provided warnings of what might happen if the Americans ever went home. They also made it more likely that they would not.

A month after the signing of the NATO treaty, political bodies representing ten different European states appeared under the umbrella of the new Council of Europe. Economic forces making for integration were developing more rapidly than the political, though. Customs Unions had already been set up in 1948 between the 'Benelux' countries (Belgium, the Netherlands, and Luxembourg), and (in a different form) between France and Italy ('Francital'). The most important of these early steps towards European economic (and, in due course, political) integration emerged in the end from a proposal about specific industries. A plan by the French foreign minister, Robert Schuman, for the international organization and management of Europe's main industrial resource, coal and steel production, came to fruition in 1951. France, Italy, the Benelux countries and, most significantly, West Germany, then signed a treaty agreeing to set up a European Coal and Steel Community (ECSC).[4] This was based on good principles of economic rationalization, but was also intended to provide an insuperable obstacle to future Franco-German conflict and assured access to German coal for French steel-making. Coal and steel resources in western Europe were to be administered by a new supranational authority likely to improve the market by removing tariff and technical barriers to integration and (it was hoped) to allow better management of fluctuations and mismatches in coal and steel supply. But the major significance of the treaty was political; it is not too much to say that the ECSC resolved many of western Europe's central political difficulties. It opened the way to much broader political horizons, too, bringing with it the settlement of the problem of the control of the Saar basin, an issue that had quickly begun to envenom Franco-German relations after 1918 and had popped up again with the ending of the Second World War. Jean Monnet, the mastermind of the French Planning Commission, saw the ECSC as more than this, though; it was indeed the first supranational organization embodying significant European integration.

[4] The Treaty of Paris, 18 April 1951.

The most important of the immediate diplomatic consequences was that the ECSC brought about the first formal incorporation of West Germany into a new international structure. It had provided a way of containing the strength of a country that, it was becoming increasingly clear, would be needed in a western Europe menaced by Soviet land-power. The German share in intra-western European trade had already begun to grow strikingly. To the consternation of some, moreover (above all, the French), American official opinion under the influence of events in Korea was fast coming round to the view that Germany had to be rearmed, a spectre bound to awake memories of 1871, 1914 and 1939 which had been lulled by the occupation and division of Germany and the creation of the ECSC. Franco-German cooperation anchored in economics was still the goal of French governments.

The subsidence of the political weakness symptomized by falling communist votes in both France and Italy also helped somewhat to ease the way for further European integration. Whether Stalin had ever envisaged allowing the French and Italian parties to act in a truly revolutionary role is a debatable point, but communists had ceased to sit in the governments in those two countries as early as 1947 and the danger that their democracies might go under as Czechoslovakia's had done had disappeared by 1950. By then French and Italian anti-communist opinion tended (as it did elsewhere in western Europe except the Iberian peninsula) to coalesce about parties whose integrating forces were either Roman Catholic politicians or social democrats vividly aware of the fate of their comrades at the hands of communists in eastern Europe (though this did not prevent vigorous campaigning against them by opponents who insisted that all Marxist roads led, in the end, to Moscow). Broadly speaking, these changes meant the predominance in western Europe during the 1950s of moderate right-wing governments pursuing similar aims of economic recovery, welfare service provision, and western European integration when it suited them, as it often did. Christian Democracy in its various national manifestations drew upon a hitherto somewhat overlooked current in European politics, the Catholic social ideas first set out authoritatively in the encyclicals of Leo XIII. It produced economic and social regimes comfortable with the idea of intervention in the economy in the interests of the needy and willing to provide substantial welfare benefits.

Between 1952 and 1954 efforts were made to form a European Defence Community to supersede the Brussels treaty arrangements; this seemed to be a possible way of getting round the problem of rearming West Germany by doing it within a larger whole. Although the French government had taken the lead in this, French suspicions in the end brought these initiatives to nothing. In 1955, the Federal Republic was nevertheless admitted to NATO. Arguments about European defence organization died away (together with Italy, Germany had joined the Brussels Treaty group – renamed Western European Union or WEU – already in 1954). The Federal Republic was to be denied nuclear or chemical weapons (it would appear, to the great relief of German voters), but she could now provide manpower for the NATO land forces which were the shield of western Europe (and which were bound to be stationed on German soil).

The main thrust towards greater unity, as before, remained economic. Crucial steps were taken at Rome in 1957: the signing of treaties establishing the European Atomic Community and (more importantly) the European Economic Community (EEC). France, Germany, Belgium, the Netherlands, Luxembourg and Italy joined in the latter, whose first significant outcome was the institution of a Customs Union (as had been agreed at Messina in 1955). It finally became operative in 1968, on a basis that there should be no differential duties on trade within the EEC (a goal still unachieved as the century ended), and a common external tariff with the objective of promoting economic and social progress within the signatory states. The means envisaged to the accomplishment of this goal were the establishment of the 'Common Market', as the EEC was itself soon called, the progressive removal of restrictions on the movement of labour and capital, and the availability of services, and certain common economic and social policies (notably, in agriculture and transport). These changes took up most of the early 1960s.

The 1957 Treaty was a major creator of new institutions, too. It provided for a system of Commissions presiding over a bureaucracy to monitor the treaty and promote further integration, for a Council of Ministers as a decision-making authority, for a Court of Justice and, finally, for a European parliament with advisory (and emphatically not legislative) powers. There was talk of the reconstitution of Charlemagne's heritage; a geographical correspondence of sorts could, indeed, be detected. The Treaty spurred countries that had not joined the EEC to set up their own, looser and more limited, European Free Trade association (EFTA) two and a half years later.[5] By 1986, the six countries of the original EEC (by then it had become simply the EC – the word 'Economic', significantly, had been dropped) were twelve, while EFTA had lost all but four of its members to it. Five years later still, and what was left of EFTA was envisaging a merger with the EC.

Western Europe's movement towards greater unity was slow and complicated but by 1960 it had already demonstrated clearly enough (among many other things) the determination of those of Europe's rulers who mattered that armed conflict could never again be an acceptable alternative to cooperation and negotiation between their countries. The era of war between western European powers, rooted in the beginning of the national state system, seemed to be over. Sadly, though recognizing that fact, Great Britain's government had not seized at the outset the chance to join in giving it institutional expression; when more imaginative successors came along, they were twice to be refused admission to the EEC before finally being allowed to join. Meanwhile the Community's interests were steadily cemented together by the Common Agricultural Policy (CAP) agreed in principle at Rome in 1957, but not defined until 1962. It was, to all intents and purposes, a huge bribe to the farmers and peasants who were so important a part of the German and, above all, the French electorates (one third of the French workforce was in 1945 still employed in agriculture), and, later, to those of poor countries which sought to become members. It was to prove, as the years passed, to be much more effective in assuring the prosperity of large farmers than in sustaining peasant smallholders. This was not what all those who supported it had envisaged, though hardly surprising; farmers turned out to be divisible into different interest groups, too. As time passed,

[5] The 'Outer Seven' who constituted EFTA were the United Kingdom, Denmark, Norway, Sweden, Austria, Portugal and Switzerland.

new members of the EC rapidly supplied new claimants to share in the generosity of European consumers who provided most of the taxes, and silently endured the high food prices that paid for CAP.

From the inauguration of 'Benelux' and 'Francital' in 1948 onwards, economic concerns and their technical demands had thus driven forward the generation of new institutions. Although some disappeared with time, others endured (together with some functional non-economic bodies). But the working of the Rome Treaty itself imposed a new factor, the necessities and ambitions of an administrative apparatus. This was focused at Brussels. The budgetary needs of the Community required a new treaty in 1970 to give it what were called its own budgetary resources. The outcome was somewhat confusing and was bound to create some new tensions. The life of the headquarters of the Community at Brussels, meanwhile, brought about an unprecedented surge of true transnational experience for individuals: a new 'European' self-consciousness was by 1970 beginning to be visible among some civil servants, industrialists and businessmen in several countries. Inevitably, its emergence more and more provoked hostile nationalist feelings.

The evolution of institutions, many overlapping in function and membership, complicated the notion of what 'western' Europe ought to be or in fact was. The OEEC of 1948 was in due course joined by the new Federal Republic of Germany, by Spain and by Finland before becoming in 1961 the Organization of Economic Cooperation and development (OECD) – of which the United States and Canada, too, were members. The ten members of the Council of Europe of 1949 would grow to twenty-three by 1990. The mere increase in complication in arriving at agreements on special problems and the practical and human consequences of this (for example in the integration of civil servants from so many countries) would alone have been sufficient to encumber further definition of the goals and nature of the 'Europe' which was in the making. All the time, too, any notion of how western Europe might be organized (and therefore defined) always tended to be overshadowed by American perceptions of Cold War realities. Western Europe could never be identified solely with the EEC or its successors – which disappointed some enthusiasts. On the other hand, it reflected what might be thought a beneficent trend in western

European political culture. The eventual entry of such countries as Spain, Portugal and Greece to the community after their replacement of authoritarian by liberal and democratic domestic government registered a triumph of government by consent that had eluded Europe after 1918.[6] The heart of the integration process nonetheless for a long time remained strongly pragmatic; it had been, and was to remain, essentially a process for the pursuit of economic self-interest by a predominantly prosperous small group of western states, and for the removal for ever of the danger of renewed Franco-German conflict.

THE DIVISION OF EUROPE

Europe continued well into the 1960s to be the main focus of the Cold War and the German Federal Republic and the GDR moved further and further apart. On two successive days in March 1954 Moscow announced that the eastern republic now possessed full sovereignty and the West German president signed a constitutional amendment permitting the rearmament of his country. In 1955, when the Federal Republic entered NATO, the Soviet riposte was the creation of the Warsaw Pact, an alliance of its satellites. Berlin's future was still in doubt, but it had been clear from the outset that NATO would fight to resist changes in its status except by agreement. In the east, the GDR agreed to settle with old enemies: with Soviet approval the line of the Oder-Neisse became the frontier with Poland. Paradoxically, Hitler's dream had ended not only in the obliteration of the united Germany which had been Bismarck's triumph, but historic Prussia was now ruled by revolutionary communists, while the new West Germany was federal in structure, non-militarist in sentiment, with Roman Catholic and Social Democratic politicians (Bismarck's *Reichsfeinde*, or 'enemies of the state'), the only realistic competitors for power. Though at times with the help of others' votes in parliament, the Christian Democratic Union dominated the Federal Republic and excluded the Social Democrats from power until 1969. Without a peace treaty, the problem of containing the German power that had

---

[6] Greece joined in 1981, Spain and Portugal in 1986.

twice devastated Europe by war was in the end managed with relative ease by partition for thirty-five years. The ascendancy of the moderate Catholic Right was something of a European as well as a German fact, too; everywhere in Europe it exercised an ascendancy reminiscent of that of the German socialists over the international Left before 1914.

A further settlement of land frontiers in central Europe had taken place in 1955, when occupying forces were withdrawn from Austria, which then re-emerged as an independent nation. At the same time, a long-running Italian–Yugoslav border dispute was settled, and the last American and British troops were withdrawn from Trieste. The two Europes were settling down.[7] This no doubt helped to ease the position of the two communist countries that had somehow slipped out of the Cold War alignments, Yugoslavia and Albania. Their ambivalence, together with periodic tremblings within other eastern bloc countries, gave some credibility to suggestions that the communist world was abandoning bipolarity for 'polycentrism', a word coined by an Italian communist. This qualification of Cold War simplicities was much remarked. Less interest was taken in the closing of the story of European empire in Africa, which was largely accomplished in the 1960s. Integration could now be the unobscured focus of western Europeans' political attention, though not all Europe's leaders saw it in the same way.

NATIONAL INTERESTS

All western European governments had since 1945 tended to show similar commitments to social provision by means of what had come in the United Kingdom to be labelled the 'welfare state', and to the achievement of economic well-being (which meant, above all, maintaining a high level of employment). Nonetheless, they did so against the background of different histories and psychologies. In

---

[7] Peace treaties had been signed in February 1947 between the victorious powers and Italy, Romania, Bulgaria, Hungary and Finland.

particular, two old nation-states stood somewhat apart from political integration in the 1960s.

The United Kingdom was one. Like the Russians, the British did not feel that nationalism and the nation-state had failed them in the Second World War. They had, too, the tie of language and the illusion of partnership in victory with the USA around which hopefulness was easily built to help sustain a special national psychology and some special fantasies after 1945. When Winston Churchill, no longer in office, but a figure of weight in the international scene, spoke in a much-applauded speech of 1946 at Zürich of a more integrated Europe, he was careful to distance his own country from involvement in the process of achieving it, and indicated that the first need was Franco-German *rapprochement*. There followed, as a major preoccupation of British policy, twenty years or so of largely successful, virtually bloodless and almost total decolonization. Along with other circumstance, this preoccupation meant that the British retained (and their elected representatives sometimes encouraged) some damagingly unquestioned assumptions over the fundamental direction of their foreign policy. It was too long diverted by old imperial legacies (even when decolonization was virtually complete) and distracted by old 'Atlanticist' ideas. In consequence, the United Kingdom remained too long outside the process of integration going on across the Channel.

In so far as European integration had political dimensions, though, there had also been a slowing in its pace while France was ruled by General de Gaulle, who returned to politics in 1958 with a mandate for change. The Fourth Republic was at that moment threatened with civil war over Algeria, and de Gaulle's first task after forming a government of 'national safety' was to prepare to negotiate these rapids by carrying through a constitutional revolution. By the end of the year, a new constitution, approved by referendum, initiated the Fifth Republic whose dominant feature was the allocation of much enhanced power to the executive – of which de Gaulle, as president, was the head.[8] He performed a service to France as great as any in his wartime career, by liquidating in 1962 her Algerian connexion, though on terms much less favourable than he had originally intended

---

[8] The formal proclamation of the presidency of de Gaulle came on 8 January 1959.

and sought. The legions came home, some disgruntled (there were plots and attempts against de Gaulle's life), but the general could settle down after this decisive withdrawal to giving France an independent and powerful voice in world affairs once more. A referendum almost immediately approved the further constitutional change of making the presidency directly answerable to election by universal suffrage, and armed with this he proceeded to reorganize and re-equip the army (France had acquired an atomic bomb in 1960, and was to have a hydrogen bomb in 1968).

The general's view of Europe's future was clear and not surprising to those who had studied his past. Sweeping aside the dream of those who envisaged a sovereign Europe based on a European parliament ('the Council of Europe', he once said, was 'dying on the shore where it was abandoned'), he wanted integration to be limited to political action based on agreement between independent states, or (as in his promotion of agreement on the Common Agricultural Policy) to clear satisfaction of a national interest. His foreign policy vigorously expressed this. He saw the EEC as above all a way of protecting French economic interests and was quite prepared to strain its organization to get his way. A Franco-German treaty of cooperation was ostentatiously signed in 1963 just as de Gaulle in effect vetoed British application to join the EEC. Wartime experience had left de Gaulle with a deep distrust of the 'Anglo-Saxons' and a belief, by no means ill-founded, that British statesmen still hankered after intimacy with an Atlantic community embracing the United States, rather than with continental Europe.

De Gaulle also suspected those (like Jean Monnet) whom he thought were 'Atlanticists' and, he believed, too much influenced by the United States. In 1964 he annoyed the Americans by exchanging diplomatic representatives with communist China. He insisted that France go ahead with her own nuclear weapons programme, scorning to be dependent on American weapons technology and patronage, and had refused in 1963 to sign an Anglo-American-Soviet nuclear test ban treaty (to which some ninety-six other states in the end adhered). The Treaty of Rome had anticipated moves towards the adoption of majority voting by the EEC by 1967, but in 1965 French representatives were withdrawn from EEC meetings in Brussels. What might be termed the Gaullist ascendancy in Europe reached its climax in 1966 in a 'Luxembourg compromise' which institutionalized a national right to veto within the EEC's Council of Ministers. This substantially offset the further degree of formal integration which was achieved in the following year. Finally, after causing much trouble within NATO, in 1966 he withdrew France and the use of French territory from that organization.

In 1969, though, de Gaulle resigned the day after defeat and before the count was over in a referendum he had himself sought (but which his ministers had divided over) on his proposals for further constitutional change in France. With him disappeared a force that had made for uncertainty and disarray in western Europe. Those who led France for the next couple of decades, while trying to sound like him (and perhaps sometimes feeling like him, notably in their suspicion of the British whose second application to join the EEC had been blocked by de Gaulle in 1967: six centuries of national prejudice do not easily evaporate, north or south of the Channel), were to prove much less intransigent than he, although French policy always hesitated over evolution towards a true Common Market, free from internal restraints on trade, or towards a politically united Europe on any terms that would sacrifice national independence to European cohesion. France provided an outstanding instance of the way in which the EEC was the creature of national interests and went on being shaped by them. For many Frenchmen, the construction of Europe still only meant, in the last resort, the paying of a necessary price to contain Germany. Increasingly, though, Germany's economic strength would drive up that price.

OSTPOLITIK

As the 1970s opened, though, there had already begun to appear other new forces operating upon Europe in such a way as to suggest that the old ideas of the 1940s and 1950s on integration would no longer suffice. One was technology. Some Europeans began to worry whether, without much closer political and economic integration, European nations could in fact provide the base required by (for example) effective information technology or aeronautical manufacturing industries. Such doubts easily connected with a sense of political weakness. Superpower rivalry left some Europeans feeling that perhaps the only way for them to preserve their own independence in political action was for Europe to become a superpower, too, though it was not easy to see how. More specifically and immediately, though subtly, West German policy, too, was evolving. Goals which could hardly have been dreamt of in the 1950s were becoming thinkable. Old political landmarks had begun to disappear. At their congress at Bad Godesberg in November 1959 the socialists had accepted free enterprise and competition as appropriate (they used the word 'important') features of the economy they envisaged, thus renouncing at last the old Marxist tradition which went back to the 1870s. Ten years later a coalition government of liberal and socialist politicians took power under a new chancellor, Willy Brandt; for the first time since 1930 Germany had a socialist chancellor (and, as it happened, for the first time since 1925 also a socialist president). Brandt introduced his government's programme to parliament in a statement that made special reference to the GDR; while, he said, its formal international recognition by the Federal Republic was impossible, he spoke of it as one of the 'two German states within one German nation'.[9]

This mysterious formula excited much interest. It was clear (and other facts soon confirmed this) that the German chancellor was willing to soften West Germany's tone towards her neighbour, and to extend to it a measure of informal recognition it had not earlier received. Without abandoning the goal of reunification, he sought to make sure the two Germanys did not move further apart and to bring about real contacts which might eventually help to change the GDR. In 1969, this was both idealistic and pragmatic, given a contemporaneous superpower tendency to move towards some measure of *détente* in the Cold War. It frightened some, nonetheless, that the Federal Republic might be acquiring real independence of its western allies in its relations with the eastern states and the USSR. The implications for further European integration were that its advocates would in future have to take account of the possibility of embracing German reunification

[9] *AR 1969*, p.247.

and a special role for Germany in the east. It was also certain that the new German government was less enthusiastic about any advance towards supranational European integration, were that to be confined only to western Europe, than its predecessors had been. On the other side of their common frontier, the GDR began to benefit from loans and credits from the Federal Republic that sustained a standard of living for its subjects that its economy could not itself sustain. The communist state was to become more and more dependent on this prop as a supplement to the cosseting of its economy through artificially low prices for raw material and energy from the USSR.[10]

From this time, the ill-defined notion of *Ostpolitik* became a primary theme of German politics, and a source of worry to American policy-makers. Whether or not a unity of state form could be achieved between the two German regimes (and it long seemed unlikely in any foreseeable future), a gradual process of informal association through cultural and commercial links, advocacy of reform from the western side and even a few signs of greater understanding and psychological *détente* became more apparent. *Ostpolitik* increasingly seemed to be an acceptable alternative if reunification was not available.

THE PATH TO HELSINKI

By the end of the 1960s the USSR had to face the truism proclaimed by Marxism (and overlooked by some Sovietologists) that consciousness evolves with material conditions. Soviet society had indeed given its citizens some real but limited rewards since Stalin's day, both material and institutional. The concessions made might not look very liberal in western eyes, but they were noteworthy after the ice age of the Stalinist era. One outcome was a visible dissidence, trivial in scale, a matter of individuals rather than significant groups, which nevertheless suggested a growing demand for greater spiritual freedom. Less explicitly, there could be sensed also a ground swell of opinion that further material gains should be forthcoming. The Soviet Union never-

[10] By 1989, 60 per cent of the GDR's yearly export earnings was being spent on servicing its foreign debt. C. S. Maier, *Dissolution. The crisis of Communism and the end of East Germany* (Princeton, 1997), p.60.

theless continued to spend colossal sums on armaments. Advances in western technology might well mean it would have to go on doing so into the indefinite future in order to keep up the USSR's impressive military power.

Yet, for all the harshness of their rhetorical exchanges, there were real pressures towards new accommodations between the super-powers. The deepest of them derived from the compelling tie between the USA and USSR that had been visible in the Cuban emergency and had grown more evident since. Americans, with their gift for the arresting slogan, concisely summed it up as MAD; that is to say, both countries had weapons able to bring about 'Mutually Assured Destruction' if they went to war. More precisely, each of two potential combatants had enough striking power to ensure that even a successful surprise nuclear attack by one of them would still leave its victim able to retaliate with devastating power. The outcome would be not one but two incinerated societies and, because of fall-out, perhaps a ruined globe. These facts turned out to have great cautionary and conservative force. Even if madmen (to put the matter bluntly) are occasionally to be found in seats of power, the knowledge that a blunder may be followed by extinction can be a stimulus to prudence. Here may well lie the most fundamental explanation of a new degree of cooperation that began to be shown by the United States and the Soviet Union in spite of their continuing irritation of one another on specific issues.

The two powers had, inevitably, very different notions of what *détente*, a popular word at the time, might mean. Many of the efforts to make it a reality grew out of circumstance as much as design. It had long been a Soviet aim, put forward more than once in the 1960s, to hold a European conference which would agree a settlement of European boundaries. This, it was hoped, would give international sanction to the realities established in 1945; it would be at least, in effect, a peace settlement that would leave Germany divided. In the 1970s talks began on further arms limitations, as well as about the possibility of a comprehensive security arrangement in Europe. A treaty in 1972 on missile limitation showed that not all military research made for an increase in tension: it embodied a new awareness that science could now monitor infringements of such agreements more effectively. Discussion on arms limitation continued while other talks begun at Helsinki in 1973 finally came to fruition there two years later at the conclusion of a Conference on Security and Cooperation in Europe (CSCE), in which representatives of thirty-three European states (including the Holy See) as well as the United States and Canada took part. Its conclusions were embodied in a 'Final Act' signed on 1 August 1975 and were very important. In return for agreement by the participating states to refrain from using force or the threat of force in their mutual relations and to recognize and respect the frontiers of all states in Europe (above all and implicitly, that between the two Germanys), Soviet negotiators agreed to encourage economic intercourse between eastern and western Europe, to non-intervention in one another's affairs, to recognition of the principle of self-determination and guarantees of 'human rights and fundamental freedoms', and to the promotion and effective exercise of civil, political, economic, social, cultural and other rights and freedoms. These last, of course, were unenforceable provisions. Yet in a decade when it was to become increasingly difficult and finally impossible to keep information and messages from and about the West from east Europeans and Soviet citizens (thanks to improved television broadcasting and a virtual cessation of radio jamming), Helsinki had silently set aside restraint on what had hitherto actually been deemed interference in the internal affairs of communist states. It was, indeed, to encourage publicity about what were seen as infringements of rights. Though very slowly, there began to flow more freely between East and West a generalized public criticism that eventually came to challenge long-held assumptions in the communist states.

It may not at first have been clear to the Soviet leaders that this was part of the price to be paid for Helsinki; as it became clearer, they did not like it. Yet they had secured at Helsinki the success they most wanted, the nearest thing that there was to be to a peace treaty ending the Second World War in Europe and a recognition of the territorial consequences of Soviet military victory. This could be reckoned a great foreign policy success. It could be reasonably asserted that the position of the USSR after 1975 was diplomatically stronger than ever and, indeed, in comparison with that of the United States on the global stage at the moment, a more favourable one than for some time. But there was the other side to the equation. While the

USSR saw the Final Act as an underwriting of territorial stability and non-interference in the affairs of eastern Europe, western Europeans and Americans stressed the CSCE's symbolic and practical value (there were to be a number of follow-up conferences) as the legitimator of interest in human rights and a reminder of ties which transcended a divided Europe. Significantly, they spoke of a Helsinki 'process'.

THE BRITISH CRISIS

Great Britain was the nation which, alone in Europe, long strove to behave as if the world of 1939 was still alive.[11] This was most notable in foreign policy, but was reflected in a certain economic conservatism, too. The vulnerability of the traditional British economy's commitment to old-established patterns of international trade was a handicap. Others lay in its old staple industries, starved of investment, and the deeply conservative attitudes of its people. Though the United Kingdom was undoubtedly growing richer (in 1970 virtually no British manual worker had four weeks' paid holiday a year and ten years later, after an economically disastrous decade, a third of them did), it fell further and further behind other developed countries in wealth and in its rate of creating it. Yet it was assumed that the basic structures of the country needed little change, while for a quarter-century all British governments sought and failed to combine economic growth, rising welfare provision and a high level of employment. The second depended ultimately on the first which, when difficulties arose, was always sacrificed to the other two. The United Kingdom was a democracy; its gullible voters had to be placated and for a long time lived in a dream world that only began to collapse when industrial strikes hamstrung Conservative and Labour governments alike in the 1970s, and finally provoked the acceptance of harsh terms for an IMF loan in 1976.

The British had by then one great achievement and creative acceptance of change to their credit: they had managed to dispose humanely

[11] This was allegedly once put rather more sardonically by West Germany's first chancellor, Konrad Adenauer, who is supposed to have said that the British reminded him of a millionaire who did not know he had lost all his money.

and rapidly, without violence and domestic division, of the greatest empire the world had ever seen. A decision to join Europe would have complemented that withdrawal from empire had it come earlier. It gradually became unclear, though, whether the country could shake off enough of its past to ensure itself even a modest prosperity outside Europe, and two attempts were made to join the EC in the 1960s.

The mainland electorate remained preoccupied by its material concerns. Inflation was to rise during the 1970s to unprecedented levels (the annualized rate 1970–80 was over 13 per cent) and was accompanied by a new turbulence in industrial relations as the oil crisis bit. There was speculation about whether the country was 'ungovernable'. When a miners' strike brought down one government, leaders and interpreters of opinion turned obsessively to themes of social division.

By then, though, that government had joined the EC in 1973. This was the major achievement of the Conservative party led by Sir Edward Heath and the climax, though not quite the end, of an era of uncertainty that had lasted almost since 1945. When continued membership was finally submitted to the constitutionally revolutionary device of a referendum in June 1975 the outcome was an unambiguous majority for it.[12] Many politicians were surprised. Perhaps this was the first sign for a decade or so that the views of the country at large were not necessarily represented by those who claimed to be its spokesmen.

Bad times continued; inflation (prices in mid-1975 were going up at an annual rate of 26.9 per cent and wages at 35 per cent) was at last identified by a Labour government as the major threat. Wage demands by trade unions by then habitually anticipated inflation still to come but it began to dawn on some that the era of unquestioned growth in consumption was over. There was a gleam of hope offshore; a few years earlier vast oil fields had been discovered under the seabed off the coasts of northern Europe and some were British. In 1976 the United Kingdom became an oil-exporting nation. That did not at once help much; in the same year, a loan from the IMF on terms which imposed stringent restraints on the British government was required. When Mrs Thatcher, the country's first woman leader of a major political party (the Conservatives), and Europe's first woman

[12] 17,378,581 votes for, 8,470,073 against membership.

prime minister, took office in 1979 she had, in a sense, little to lose; her opponents were discredited. So, many felt, were the ideas which had been long accepted uncritically as the determinants of British policy: full employment and rising social provision, with their implications of ever-rising public expenditure.

The British government had by then also had to face another problem in Northern Ireland, a part of the United Kingdom where Protestant and Catholic hooligans at times seemed alike bent on destroying their homeland rather than live at peace with one another. Irish nationalism had not been appeased by the 1922 settlement that set up the Irish Free state, because the northern six counties had remained part of the United Kingdom.[13] Ulstermen's fears of republican nationalism had meanwhile grown as demography slowly turned against the Protestant majority in the north. Violence in the six counties that remained under the British crown was to cost the lives of over 3,000 British citizens – soldiers, policemen and civilians, Protestant and Catholic, Irish, Scotch, and English alike – in the 1970s and 1980s. After a particularly grave error on the part of the security forces in 1972, when ill-disciplined fire killed thirteen nationalist demonstrators in a few minutes, the province slid into a state of contained disorder for the rest of the decade. The best that could be said of this situation was that in 1969 this did not poison British party politics as Irish questions had done in the previous century.

[13] The transformation of the Free State into the Republic of Eire in 1949 had encouraged republican nationalism in Ulster again.

BOOK 8

THE END OF AN ERA

24

A World in Evolution

THE LAST YEARS OF CHAIRMAN MAO

The world was deeply interested as the 1960s came to an end in China in a noisy and puzzling upheaval. The 'Cultural Revolution', as it was called, lasted ten years, from 1966 to 1976. It had its mysterious origins in an article published in a Shanghai newspaper criticizing a play about a wicked emperor. The play had been written by a deputy mayor of Beijing and it was thought to contain allusions to Mao's autocratic style of rule. In what followed, millions were killed, imprisoned, deprived of their jobs or purged as an intensely moralizing campaign revivified the sense of revolution and the cult of Mao was reasserted. Senior party members, bureaucrats and intellectuals were harried, universities were closed and physical labour was demanded of all citizens in order to change traditional attitudes. In a conscious imitation of May Fourth Movement attitudes, Chinese youth was mobilized to conduct the persecution. By 1968 the country had been turned upside down by these 'Red Guards', who were terrorizing their seniors in every walk of life. Opportunists struggled to join them before themselves being destroyed by them. Even Mao himself at last began to show signs that he thought things had gone too far. A substantial delegation and decentralization of power had taken place, probably unintentionally. The army in the end restored order, though, often at the cost of the students. New party cadres were installed and a Party Congress confirmed Mao's leadership.

The Red Guards' enthusiasm had been real, though, and the ostentatious moral preoccupations which surfaced in this in some ways still mysterious episode remain striking. Mao's motives were no doubt complex in utilizing them as he did. Besides seeking vengeance on those who had brought about the abandonment of the Great Leap Forward, he appears really to have felt a danger that the revolution might congeal and lose the moral *élan* that had carried it so far. He had been deeply troubled by what he believed to be the dangerous 'liberalization' (if so it could be termed) of Khrushchev's 'thaw'. In seeking to protect the revolution, old ideas that might resurface if allowed to do so had to go. Society, government and economy had been enmeshed and integrated with one another in old China as nowhere else. The traditional prestige China accorded to intellectuals and scholars had endured even if the examination system had been swept away fifty years earlier; now it had to be demolished. The 'demotion' of intellectuals was urged as a necessary consequence of making a new China. Deliberate attacks on family authority, too, were not merely attempts by a suspicious regime to encourage informers and delation, but attacks on the most conservative of all Chinese institutions. Similarly, the advancement of women and propaganda to discourage early marriage had dimensions going beyond 'progressive' feminist ideas or population control; they were an assault on the past such as no other revolution had ever made, for in China the past meant a role for women far inferior to those in pre-revolutionary America, France or even Russia. The attacks on party leaders accused of toying with Confucian ideas were much more than the jibes which comparable attacks would have been in Europe; they could not have been paralleled in countries where for centuries there had been no past so solidly entrenched as China's to reject, and cultural pluralism was widely accepted.

To the extent that it can be rationally understood, the Cultural Revolution was an exercise in modernization politics, therefore (and, almost unnoticed, a reaffirmation of the primacy of local initiative over Stalinist centralization). Yet rejection of the past is only half the story of the Chinese revolution, of which this was only a fleeting episode. More than 2,000 years of remarkable historical continuities lie behind that much greater upheaval, which, for all its cost and cruelty, was a heroic endeavour, matched in scale only by such gigantic upheavals as the spread of Islam, or Europe's assault on the world in early modern times. Much more than they, though, it aspired to central control and direction in pursuit of goals set out in moralizing language. It was a paradox of the Chinese revolution that it rested on popular fervour and talked the language of a western rationalist creed, yet remains unimaginable without the idea of a state inheriting all the mysterious prestige of the traditional bearers of the Mandate of Heaven. Chinese tradition respects authority and gives it a moral endorsement that has been harder and harder to find in the West in this century. No more than any other great state could China shake off its history, and as a result its communism has sometimes had a paradoxically conservative appearance. For centuries, perhaps millennia, Chinese government drove home to its peoples the lessons that the individual mattered less than the collective whole, that authority could rightfully command the services of millions at any cost in order to carry out great works for the good of the state, that authority should be unquestioned so long as it is exercised for the common good. The notion of opposition other than in extremity was distasteful to the Chinese; it suggested social disruption. The Chinese revolution, as Sun Yat-sen understood, required a rejection of the kind of revolution involved in the adoption of western individualism, and the evolution of a conception related more closely to indigenous culture.

Mao benefited from this past though he turned against much of it, because he was easily comprehensible within its idea of authority. He was presented as a ruler-sage, as much a teacher as a politician; western commentators have been amused by the status given to his thoughts by the idolization of 'the Little Red Book' of extracts from his writings and speeches (though in Europe and North America after the Protestant Reformation similar extravagant adulation was sometimes given to the Bible), but the utterances of great teachers have always commanded respect in China. Mao was the spokesman of a moral doctrine that was to provide a core for society, just as Confucianism had done. There was even something traditional in his artistic interests; he was admired by the people as a poet whose writings won the respect of qualified judges. In China power had always been sanctioned by the notion that the ruler who did good things for his people and sustained widely accepted values was justified. Mao's actions could long be presented and read in such a way, not least during the Cultural Revolution.

NEW PATTERNS

China's prime minister, Chou En-lai, died on 8 January 1976 and this opened a notable year for China. In the months that followed, uncertainties about the succession led to riots on a scale not witnessed since 1949. Then, during the summer, a succession of earthquakes (the worst for centuries) took a heavy toll of lives and did much damage. This provided a portentous background to the news of Mao's death on 9 September. Some thought that there was even a danger of civil war. But any threat that a 'Gang of Four' of his former coadjutors (one of them Mao's widow) who had promoted the policies of the Cultural Revolution and still advocated radical courses might seize power was quickly averted by their arrest. Under a leadership dominated by party veterans, it was soon clear that the excesses of the past were to continue to be corrected. In 1977 there rejoined the government as a vice-premier the twice-previously disgraced Deng Xiaoping. His son had been crippled during the Cultural Revolution by beatings from Red Guards, and Deng was notoriously associated with the causes of restoring public order and relaxation in economic policy through the encouragement of rural development, local entrepreneurship, and the retention of profit in community enterprises.

Albeit after contentious debate, change was now to begin in earnest. One early indicator that a new course was to be steered was the party's Central Committee ruling in 1978 that the new focus of work was to be 'socialist modernization', not the pursuit of class struggle. In the following year, opprobrious social designations – 'landlord', 'rich peasant' – were officially removed from those to whom they had been applied. In April, it was announced that the Sino-Soviet Friendship treaty would not be renewed. As 1981 opened, the Gang of Four and their confederates were sentenced to long terms of imprisonment (and in two cases, to death, though this penalty was suspended). Finally, in June that year the Central Committee at last committed itself to drawing an explicit line under the past. In a long 'resolution on certain questions in the history of our Party since the founding of the People's Republic of China' the history of over thirty years was given official reinterpretation.[1] Even in the 1950s, it was said, 'Comrade Mao Zedong and many leading comrades had become smug about their successes, were impatient for quick results and over-estimated the role of man's subjective will and efforts' and the result had been the disaster of the Great Leap Forward. The Cultural Revolution and 'erroneous "left" theses' were condemned as not merely wrong, but for having caused great positive damage. The resolution was, nevertheless, careful to note that in spite of his errors Mao was 'a great proletarian revolutionary . . .' whose 'contributions to the Chinese revolution far outweigh his mistakes' and that 'Mao Zedong Thought' was 'a crystallization of the collective (*sic*) wisdom of the Chinese Communist Party'.[2] It was a gentle setting-aside of what had almost been a religion.

A few weeks before Mao's death, the president of the United States had followed his predecessor in making an official visit to Beijing. The adjustment of his country's complicated and deep-seated attitudes towards the People's Democratic Republic of China had begun with the slow recognition of the lessons of the Vietnam disaster. Now a new wave of changes within China had to be grappled with. They had to be understood in a deeper perspective than that provided by a loss of a war in Vietnam. As well as in domestic revolution, China was engaged in a slow resumption of the international and regional role appropriate to her historical stature and potential. Her admission to the United Nations in 1971 had been a clear turning-point, even if the diplomatic liquidation of the Vietnam imbroglio had only opened the way to normal relations with the United States and did not at once realize them. In 1978, though, came solid and formal recognition of what had happened, a Sino-American agreement in which the United States made the crucial concession that its forces should be withdrawn from Taiwan and that official diplomatic relations with that island's KMT government should be ended.

If only because of its sheer size, whatever happened to China mattered over a wide area. The effects of changes in its economic policies were soon also to be seen in its relations with countries

[1] For the text, and other related documents, see *Resolution on CPC History (1949–81)* (Beijing, 1981).
[2] Ibid., pp.28, 33 and 56–7.

other than the USA. By 1985 the whole of east and south-east Asia constituted a single trading zone of unprecedented potential. Within a few years it seemed plausible for an informed observer to envisage the likely emergence of a 'de facto Chinese common market'.[3] The sources of its vigour, nonetheless, lay not in China, but in NICs, the new centres of industrial and commercial activity that had developed there, particularly after 1970. Some of these matured so fast as to lead some observers to take the view that the old global balance of economic power was disappearing. There was much talk of the young 'Tiger' economies of South Korea, Taiwan, Hong Kong and Singapore. They had already by 1980 shed any aura of undevelopment; in the next decade Malaysia, Thailand and Indonesia began to move up rapidly towards joining them.

As east Asia changed, what appeared did not always fit easily into western stereotypes of left or right. Much was to be heard in due course of the coherence of 'Asian values' with development based on a capitalism given its head in societies amply supplied with low-cost labour and great market potential. There was something in this, no doubt. But Confucian society is not only a matter of self-discipline and attention to social duty. It is also a matter of patrons and clients, of cautious respect for authority that meant that government could take a far more active role in promoting capitalist enterprise than western admirers of 'free' markets always conceded. Furthermore, while (in the terms of Cold War rhetoric) eschewing communist models of development even in their varied and somewhat ambiguous Asiatic forms (China, Vietnam, Cambodia, North Korea), South Korea, Singapore, the Philippines and Indonesia all looked to strongly authoritarian regimes to preserve and buttress the market institutions which they valued. 'Managed' capitalism was often the key to development, and management was sometimes a cover for cronyism and corruption. It could by no means be said as the century drew to its end that liberal democracy was the unqualified beneficiary of the new prosperity of east Asia.

[3] M. Weidenbaum, q. in S.P. Huntingdon, *The Clash of Civilizations and the Remaking of World Order* (London, 1997), p.133.

JAPAN: THE NEW WORLD POWER

Japan had been indispensable to the building of this prosperity. The rapidity with which she, like China, recovered her former status as a power (and economically surpassed it) had obvious implications for her place both in the Asian and the world balance. By 1970 the Japanese enjoyed the second highest GDP in the non-communist world. They had renewed their industrial base and had moved with great success into new areas of manufacture. Only in 1951 had a Japanese yard launched the first Japanese ship built for export, yet within twenty years Japan had the largest shipbuilding industry in the world. At the same time she had won a commanding position in consumer industries such as electronics and motor-cars, of which the Japanese came to make more than any country except the United States (to the resentment of American manufacturers who sought protection from their government, a sincere compliment). In 1979 it was agreed that Japanese cars should be made in England, a step taken with an eye to penetration of the EC market. The debit side of such advances was provided by the ample evidence of the cost of economic growth in the destruction of the Japanese environment and the wear and tear of Japanese urban life.

Japan had been specially favoured by circumstances in her advance to the status of a world economic power since the disaster of 1945. An American enforcement of a bias towards investment rather than consumption during the occupation years had helped. The war in Vietnam, like that in Korea, had been a stroke of luck for her, another boost to an already thriving economy. Yet human beings have to seize opportunities and to take advantage of favourable circumstances, and unusually positive social attitudes appear to have been crucial in Japan. Even in the immediate aftermath of defeat, her people were able to deploy their intense national pride and showed an unrivalled capacity for collective effort. In the next decades of recovery and growth, they continued to display the deep cohesiveness and readiness to subordinate the individual to collective purposes that had always marked Japanese society. Strangely, such pre-modern attitudes seemed to survive the coming of political democracy, just as old hierarchical forms and assumptions of obligation and dependence survived acceptance of market economics.

Other survivals of the past were visible in the successful careers of many politicians whose earlier successes had been won under the wartime regime (sometimes in circumstances by no means always wholly savoury). In 1955 the Liberal Democratic Party was formed, a union of conservative and bureaucratic forces which was to monopolize power for nearly forty years. In 1958 there took office as prime minister a man who had been serving a sentence of imprisonment as a war criminal ten years earlier, and who had only been officially 'purged' in 1952 of his undertakings during the war. It may be too early to judge how deeply democratic institutions are rooted in Japanese society; after 1951, though there soon appeared something like a consensus for one-party rule, there were also strong opposition campaigns over particular issues. More alarmingly, there were also disquieting signs in the emergence of more extreme groupings, some of which were anti-liberal, even quasi-fascist. Mounting uneasiness was felt, too, over what was happening to traditional values and institutions. The costs of economic growth loomed up not only in huge conurbations and pollution, but also in social problems straining even Japanese custom. Great firms still operated with success on the basis of group loyalties buttressed by traditional attitudes and institutions. At a different level, even the deeply conservative Japanese family sometimes seemed to be under strain.

Yet the material recovery was remarkable. Japan's exports reached pre-war levels again in 1959, GNP having doubled in the previous five years. In 1960 the prime minister announced a plan to double national income by 1970; the period of economic growth which followed was so successful that by 1973 straight line growth since 1960 had been at a rate of 10 per cent per year. This had been achieved by major political interventions. A deliberate policy of running down dependence on coal as a source of primary energy had been by no means unquestioningly received but in ten years it reduced the country's dependence on this relatively expensive fuel as an energy source from 31.3 per cent to 6.1 per cent of its needs. National plans in the 1960s for the rationalization of the steel industry, the development of electricity supply and the petrochemical industry were all based on the assumption that cheap oil imports would continue to be available. From such interventions flowed substantial real wage increases and benefits to Japanese consumers, which underpinned social support for them.

Economic progress helped to change the context of Japanese foreign policy, which moved more clearly away in the 1960s from the somewhat stark Cold War simplicities of the preceding decade. Economic strength had made the yen internationally important and had drawn Japan into the world's monetary diplomacy. Prosperity involved her in the affairs of almost every part of the globe. In the Pacific basin, she became a major consumer of other countries' primary produce, in the Middle East a large buyer of oil. Japan's investment in Europe was soon thought alarming by some Europeans (even though her aggregate share was not large), while imports of her manufactured goods threatened European producers. Even the eating habits of the Japanese raised international questions. In the 1960s 90 per cent of their protein requirements were met by fishing and this led to alarm lest they be over-fishing some areas.

Japan had entered the United Nations in 1956. By then, she was already evidently on the road to resuming her great power status. The heart of the conduct of her foreign relations was the maintenance of Japan as a key factor in the United States security system. The rearmament of the former enemy, which had begun with MacArthur's innocent-looking authorization of a 'national police reserve' (which enabled four American divisions to be withdrawn from garrison duties in Japan and to be sent to serve in Korea), proceeded even more rapidly after his dismissal in 1951. Ironically, he had begun the process of undermining his own dream of a neutralized, non-nationalist, democratic Japan. By 1958 Japan had a 'Land Self-defence Force' of 180,000 men, and 1,300 aircraft.

As these and other matters changed the atmosphere and content of foreign relations, so did the behaviour of other powers, especially in the Pacific area. As Japan became the world's largest importer of primary resources, she increasingly assumed in the 1960s an economic position in relation to other Pacific countries not unlike that of Germany in central and eastern Europe before 1914. New Zealand and Australia found their economies increasingly and profitably tied to

Japan rather than to the old British market; their embassies in Japan began to matter to them as much as their High Commissions in London. Both of them supplied Japan with farm produce (particularly meat) and Australia minerals, notably coal and iron ore. The Russians and the South Koreans meanwhile complained about Japanese fishing, thus adding new complications to the old story of involvement with Korea which helped to keep alive that country's distrust of Japanese motives. South Korea was Japan's second biggest market (after the United States) and Japanese investment had begun again there soon after 1951. South Korean nationalism always had a strongly anti-Japanese tone, and in 1959 the president of South Korea could be heard urging his countrymen to unite 'as one man' not against their northern communist neighbour, but against Japan. Within twenty years, too, Japanese car manufacturers were looking askance at the vigorous rival they had helped create. As in Taiwan, so in South Korea industrial growth was built on technology diffused by Japan.

Japan's dependence on imported energy meant a nasty shock when oil prices shot up in the 1970s. There was a sharp decline in manufacturing output 1973–5 and a similar, though less violent, fall in 1979 when the suspension of Iranian production during the revolutionary crisis sent up prices again.[4] Yet this was not to be the end of the Japanese success story. Growth continued overall and such valid grounds for concern as higher inflation and speculative booms in land investment for a long time seemed hardly to affect overall progress. Japanese exports to the United States grew tenfold between 1971 and 1984. In the 1980s GDP was less only than those of the USA and USSR. As her industrialists turned to advanced information technology and biotechnology, and talked of running down car manufacturing, there was no sign that she had lost her power of disciplined self-adaptation. Altogether, the Japanese economy had the potential to develop in various directions; in 1978, when the Chinese vice-president visited Tokyo, trade between China and Japan was already worth as much as China's trade with the United States and West Germany combined.

Growing strength brought greater responsibilities. The withdrawal

[4] Revealingly, in 1973 Japan abruptly shifted her support away from Israel at the UN and began to court the friendship of Arab states.

of American direction was acknowledged openly when it was agreed in 1971 that Okinawa should be handed back to Japanese administration. Though the Americans retained control of their military bases there, this was the first of Japan's former overseas possessions to be reacquired since the war ended. There remained question marks over the main three islands of the Kuriles, still in Russian hands. Taiwan, in the possession of the Chinese nationalists and claimed by the Chinese communists, posed diplomatic problems, too, but Japanese attitudes on all these matters remained – no doubt prudently – reserved and there was at least no question of the resumption of old imperial conquests there. There was also the possibility that the question of Sakhalin, the whole of which had been consigned to the USSR at Yalta, might be reopened.

All such issues began of course to look much more susceptible to revisions or at least reconsideration in the wake of other changes in the Asian scene, not all of which stemmed from Chinese and Japanese resurgence. Sino-Soviet bickering gave Japan much greater freedom for manoeuvre towards the United States, her erstwhile patron, as well as towards China and the USSR. The embarrassment that too close a tie with the Americans might bring became clearer as the Vietnam war unrolled and political opposition to it grew in Japan. Her freedom of action was ultimately limited, in the sense that the three greatest powers in the region were by 1970 equipped with nuclear weapons and Japan was not, though she of all nations had most reason to know their effect, but there was little doubt that her industry could produce them within a relatively brief time if needed. Indisputably, Japan was once more by 1990 a world power.

THE INDIAN DEMOCRACY

If the test of a world power is the habitual exercise of decisive influence, whether economic, military or political, outside a country's own geographical area, then by the 1980s India was clearly not yet one. This is perhaps one of the surprises of the second half of this century. India had moved into independence with many advantages enjoyed neither by other former European dependencies, nor by Japan in the aftermath of defeat. The new republic had in 1947 an effective administrative tradition, well-trained and (it proved) dependable armed forces, a well-educated élite, seventy or so thriving universities, and much international benevolence and goodwill to draw upon. Soon, Cold War opportunities enhanced her freedom of diplomatic manoeuvre. India of course confronted poverty on a large scale, malnutrition, illiteracy and major public health problems, but so did China. The contrast between the two countries was very great and even visible by the 1980s; the streets of Chinese cities were by then filled by serviceably (though drably) dressed and well-nourished people, while those of India still displayed horrifying examples of poverty and disease. If visitors saw less of what could be (and was) hidden in the Chinese countryside and provincial towns, such appearances were nonetheless impressive. India's problems could not be concealed, in spite of strenuous efforts by her public relations officers to discourage television reporting of her poverty. Bitterly remembered too by some Indians was the fact that China had defeated India in the fighting of the 1960s.

In considering India's poor development performance it is easy to be pessimistically selective. In some sectors growth was substantial and impressive. But achievements were overshadowed by the fact that a rising population always trod hard on the heels of economic growth; most Indians apparently remained as poor as, or only a little better off than, those who had welcomed independence in 1947, even if they lived longer lives. It can, of course, be argued that to have kept India together at all was a great achievement, given the country's fissiparous potential and ethnic, linguistic, religious and cultural variety. No doubt it helped that the Indian revolutionary left had divided sharply at the time of the Sino-Soviet quarrel of the 1960s when the Indian communist party again split in two under the strain. Somehow a democratic electoral order was maintained successfully, even if with qualifications, and peaceful changes of government occurred as a result of votes cast. In other ways, nonetheless, India's democratic record looked less encouraging, particularly after 1975 when the prime minister, Indira Gandhi (Nehru's daughter), proclaimed a state of emergency and the imposition of presidential rule akin to that of viceroys in the old days (one of the two Indian communist parties

A WORLD IN EVOLUTION

supported her). This was followed, it is true, by her loss of the elections in 1977 and her judicial exclusion from office and parliament (though only briefly) in the following year, which could be thought a healthy sign.[5] More alarming, perhaps, was the recurrent use of president's powers to suspend normal constitutional government in specific areas and the frequent reports of brutalities of the police and security forces towards minorities. Under the Raj, Congress had sought for westernized Indians the constitutional rights of Englishmen: it was not very successful in guaranteeing them after independence, far less still in extending them to the masses.

Mrs Gandhi had been defeated in 1977 by an alliance of anti-Gandhi interests around an orthodox and explicitly conservative Hindu party, Janata, which was the first plausible threat to appear to the hegemony of Congress. For three years its government gave India its first taste of non-Congress rule since independence, though it had quickly been riven with divisions of its own. The hegemony of Congress was in fact to persist longer yet. In the fourth decade after independence, Congress was more visibly than ever not so much a political party in the European sense as an India-wide coalition of interest groups, notables and controllers of patronage. Even under the leadership of Nehru, for all his socialist aspirations and rhetoric, Congress had never shaken off its intrinsically conservative character. Once the British were removed it was never its function to bring about change. It would seek, rather, to accommodate it. This was in a manner symbolized by the dynastic nature of Indian government. Nehru's daughter was to be followed by her son, Rajiv Gandhi, as prime minister, after she was assassinated.[6]

Though democracy had briefly given India a non-Congress government, Indira Gandhi had been returned to power in the elections of January 1980. Her son won another overwhelming electoral victory in 1985 and Congress returned to office until 1989 when elections produced a minority coalition (it, too, contained two members of the

[5] Her arrest was followed by that of 50,000 Indians who had demonstrated in her favour and the hijacking of an airliner by two of her supporters at Lucknow airport.
[6] When he, in turn, was blown up by an assassin (though he was not in office at the time), Congress leaders at once showed an almost automatic reflex in seeking to persuade his Italian widow to take up the leadership of the party.

Nehru family) dependent on Janata and left-wing parties for its votes. By then, though, there had been ominous signs that even the success of Congress in keeping the country united might not last much longer. Sikh particularism brought itself vividly to the world's notice when Indira Gandhi was murdered by Sikh members of her own bodyguard in October 1984. This had followed an attack by the Indian army on the foremost shrine of Sikh faith at Amritsar, the Golden Temple, causing heavy casualties and much damage in the process and followed by pogroms. In the next seven years, more than 10,000 Sikh militants, members of the security forces and bystanders were to be killed. Fighting with Pakistan over Kashmir, too, broke out again in the later part of the decade.

This issue continued to poison the relations of the two countries. Although they had been able to come to an agreement in 1960 over the distribution of the Kashmiri waters, there had been serious fighting between their forces in 1964–6 and 1971, and it began again in 1990 and 1991. Another ceasefire then held out no better prospects of final settlement than had its predecessors.

In 1990 it was officially admitted that 890 people had died in Hindu–Muslim riots that year. Once again, it is difficult not to return to banal reflexion on the heavy weight of the past in India; no dynamic force has yet emerged to throw it off. As memories of pre-independence India faded, the reassertion of Indian tradition was always likely. Symbolically, when the moment of independence had come in 1947 it had been at midnight, because the British had not consulted the astrologers to provide an auspicious day and a moment between two days had therefore to be chosen for the birth of a new nation: this was a mark of the cultural incubus whose hampering weight would hardly be diminished much in the next forty years. It was even strengthened; partition had, after all, redefined the Indian community in terms much more Hindu than had been hoped either by Indian patriots or their British friends, or than the Constitution suggested.

By 1980 the last Indian civil service officer recruited by the British had retired. India had then, and has still, not reached the point of being assured of its modernization. It lives still with a conscious disparity between an engrafted western political system and the traditional society on which that has been imposed, and a widening gap between the Indian masses and the Indian élites. For all the great achievements of many of its leaders, an entrenched past and huge economic backwardness and their consequences in privilege, injustice and inequity, still stand in India's way. Perhaps those who believed in her future in 1947 were bound to underrate the difficulty and painfulness of fundamental change. It is hardly for those who have often found it hard to accomplish much less radical redirection in their own societies to be supercilious or censorious about that.

India's neighbour Pakistan had turned with the years more consciously to the Islamic aspect of her own tradition. This was not what Jinnah had hoped, but he had died and soon Pakistan seemed to turn to share in the movement of Islamic renewal visible across most of the Muslim world. In practical effects outside Pakistan this was most visible in the support she gave to the Afghan anti-communist guerrilla forces and the sympathy she came to express towards the unattractive Taleban movement that came to dominate Afghanistan after its overthrow of the communist regime.

So far as it went – and sensitivity to the area's problems was much heightened after the oil crisis of 1974 – even limited perceptions of the complexities of Islamic reality available in the West were themselves for a long time obscured and confused in Pakistan as elsewhere by the perspectives of the Cold War. That conflict sometimes made older spectres walk again. To some British observers a traditional Russian desire for influence in the Middle East, Gulf and Central Asia seemed now nearer satisfaction than at any time in the past. The Soviet Union had built up by 1970 a worldwide naval presence rivalling that of the United States and had established itself even in the Indian Ocean. Following British withdrawal from Aden in 1967, that base had been used by the Russians with the concurrence of the South Yemen government. All this was taking place at a time when further south, too, the Americans faced strategic setbacks. The coming of the Cold War to the Horn of Africa and the former Portuguese colonies had added significance to events taking place further north. The Soviet intervention in Afghanistan when it came in 1979 could thus be seen as a new expression of an old geo-political threat.

AFRICA'S ENDURING PROBLEMS

In the 1980s great events in Europe tended to eclipse important changes elsewhere. Yet though it directly affected far fewer people, what was happening in southern Africa may have been of comparable significance. The emergence of Zimbabwe as a new black state had left the Republic of South Africa the only white-dominated country on the continent. It was also the richest African economy, a fact that had ensured its continuing denunciation as the focus of black African hostility and, indeed, of spiteful resentment elsewhere in the world. Whatever else divided them (the OAU had been riven asunder over civil war in Angola), African (and other Third World) leaders could usually find common ground against South Africa. In 1974 the General Assembly of the United Nations had forbidden representatives of the Republic to attend its sessions because of *apartheid*, and in 1977 the UN Commission of Human Rights deftly side-stepped demands for the investigation of the horrors perpetrated by blacks against blacks in Uganda, while castigating South Africa (along with Israel and Chile) for misdeeds it was easier to denounce without political embarrassment. From Pretoria, the view northwards looked more and more menacing. The arrival of Cuban troops in Angola suggested a new power of strategic action against South Africa by the USSR. Both that former Portuguese colony and Mozambique provided bases for South African dissidents who strove to foment unrest in the black townships and sustained urban terrorism in the 1980s.

These were among the facts helping to change the thinking of the South African government. They became apparent when a new prime minister took office in 1978 and, to the dismay of many Afrikaners, began slowly to make concessions. True, it was not long before Mr P. W. Botha's initiative slowed; continuing hostility to South Africa in the United Nations, urban terrorism at home, an increasingly dangerous and militarily demanding situation on the northern frontiers in Namibia (allocated to South Africa years before as a UN trusteeship territory), and increased Afrikaner distrust of Botha (shown in elections), all led him back towards repression. By the middle of the 1980s, though, the issue already seemed fundamentally changed: it was no longer a question of whether the more obnoxious features of *apartheid* should be dismantled, but whether black majority rule could be conceded by South African whites, and, if so, whether it could happen without armed conflict.

Mr Botha's furthest and last gesture of relaxation was a new constitution in 1983. This provided representation for non-white South Africans in a way that outraged black political leaders by its inadequacy, and disgusted Afrikaner conservatives by conceding the principle of non-white representation at all. Meanwhile, the pressure of economic sanctions approved by the United Nations against South Africa was growing. In 1985 even the United States had imposed them to a limited extent; by then, international confidence in the South African economy was falling, and the effects were showing. Straws before the wind of change could be discerned. The Dutch Reformed Church acknowledged that *apartheid* was at least a 'mistake' and could not (as had been claimed hitherto) be justified by Scripture.[7] There was growing division among Afrikaner politicians. It was an important symbolic event that the first legal 'mixed' marriage in the Republic was celebrated in 1985. It probably helped, too, that in spite of its deepening isolation, the South African army successfully mastered the threats on the borders of the Republic, though it could not defeat the Marxist Angolan government so long as Cuban forces remained there. Peace was made with Angola after Namibia came to independence on terms South Africa found tolerable in 1988.

This was the background when Mr Botha (president of the republic since 1984) reluctantly and grumpily stepped down the following year, to be succeeded by Mr F. W. de Klerk, who soon made it clear that the movement towards liberalization was to continue. Indeed, he said it would go much further than most whites thought possible, even if this did not mean the end of *apartheid* in all respects. Political protest and opposition were to be tolerated. Meetings and marches were permitted; imprisoned black leaders were released. Meanwhile, there was taking place an important change in the relations between the superpowers. Agreements between the United States and the Soviet

---

[7] In 1998 its conference voted overwhelmingly that *apartheid* was 'wrong and sinful not only in effects and operations but in its fundamental nature'.

Union had helped to bring to an end the struggles in Angola and Mozambique and in due course led to freedom for Namibia.

Suddenly, in 1990 the way ahead seemed to open up dramatically. In February Mr de Klerk announced that 'a new South Africa' was in the making and nine days later the highly symbolic figure of Mr Nelson Mandela, the long-imprisoned leader of the African National Congress, was released from jail. Before long he was engaged in discussion with the government about what might come next. For all the firmness of his language, there were hopeful signs of a new realism that the task of reassuring the white minority about a future under a black majority must be attempted. Just such signs, of course, prompted other, more extreme, black politicians to greater activity and more violent opposition. By the end of the year, though, Mr de Klerk had gone a long way. He had taken his followers further than Mr Mandela had taken his, even saying he would rescind the land legislation which was the keystone of *apartheid*. It was an interesting indicator of the pace with which events had moved in South Africa that the interest of the world was by then focused less on the sincerity or insincerity of white South African leaders, than on the realism (or lack of it) of their black opponents and their ability (or inability) to control their followers. There were plentiful signs of division among black South Africans. Clearly, a stony path still lay ahead, even if once unthinkable steps towards a democratic South Africa had already been taken. Yet there were also grounds for a cautious qualified optimism.

Talks began between the Afrikaner Nationalist Party and the African National Congress (ANC) in which Mr de Klerk and Mr Mandela took the lead. Yet 1993 was the most violent year in South Africa yet. The numbers of political murders and acts of terrorism shot up. The death rate of victims of political violence, already high in the first six months of the year, soared to over 100 a month in July and August alone. By the end of June 109 policemen had been killed and the majority of them (like most victims of violence in South Africa) were black. The security forces were clearly under strain. Yet in the autumn the South African parliament approved the bill that had emerged from the politicians' negotiations. For the first time it offered black South Africans a real share in political power. There followed, just before Christmas, parliamentary acceptance of a new interim constitution.

In January 1994 the militant Pan-African Congress, which had broken away from the ANC, announced it was suspending its armed struggle against the state and would take part in the multiracial elections announced for April.

As polling day approached, new divisions appeared among political leaders, both black and Afrikaner, some reflecting tribal fears, some, ideological extremism. Acts of violence continued. Yet the elections duly took place as had been planned, and in an orderly and impressive manner. On 9 May the new parliament met. Its ANC majority at once elected Mr Mandela first president of the new South Africa. His presidency was inaugurated the following day at Pretoria, in the heart of Afrikanerdom, the capital of the old Transvaal republic with which the British had been at war as the century began. Soon South Africa joined the Organization of African Unity and, perhaps even more surprisingly, re-entered the British Commonwealth of Nations.

The picture in other parts of the continent had nonetheless darkened during the 1970s and 1980s. As the end of the century approached, sub-Saharan Africa, with a tenth of the world's population, contained a quarter of the world's refugees. There were thirty-four sub-Saharan countries with a quarter of their inhabitants infected with HIV; in one of them, Botswana, life expectancy at birth dropped from sixty-one to forty-seven years in six years (1992–8). This posed a grave demographic threat. Positive economic growth in much of black Africa had virtually come to an end after the oil crisis and a notable slackening of the interest of the old colonial powers in their former territories. The economic policies of many African countries had, too, often sacrificed the interests of food-producing peasants to swelling urban populations by keeping agricultural cash crop prices low while seeking to encourage industrial development that would reduce the need for imports. Population rose while agricultural production slowed and sometimes fell. Famine became more common. Political and administrative failure meanwhile blocked the way to solution for such problems. In 1993 Africans received $36 per capita of external aid, to little obvious beneficial effect; the comparable contemporary figure for south Asia was $4, and for Latin America $8.

In 1998, ten years after Africa had seemed to turn decisively towards democracy, the legacy of *apartheid* overshadowed the South African

Republic as heavily as Boer mythology and memory had overshadowed the opening of the century there. Outside its borders the prospects for civilized government often looked as grim as ever. Sudanese still starved because food was used as a weapon in their civil war, and a cycle of genocidal horrors in Rwanda that had opened in the mid-1980s was still going on. A rising in the Congo (formerly Zaïre) was exacerbated by the interventions of neighbours, and Eritrea and Ethiopia were at war. Only in Nigeria did the death of a dictator suggest even a gleam of a possibility that one important African country might return to civilian rule, while in Angola a fragile peace looked as if it might collapse anew into outright civil war. Per capita income in sub-Saharan Africa still lagged below the level reached twenty-five years earlier. The continent's peoples seemed to have achieved nothing since independence except, remarkably, to preserve most of the boundaries they had inherited from colonialism. Mr Mandela's deputy had said in 1997 that 'the African Renaissance is upon us', but it was hard to see why he thought so as the century drew to its close. Though often kaleidoscopic change was visible inside many African countries, over much of the continent an overall stagnation seemed to prevail.

25

Crumbling Certainties

SEEDS OF DOUBT

The closer one is to events, the harder it is to be sure that the perspective is right. Yet from time to time some events so unfold that they obviously and instantly mark a special change, sometimes in the pace, sometimes in the direction of history, sometimes in both. Events in the last couple of decades have struck many people as change of that sort, immediately and obviously significant because after them the historical landscape looks different, even in the context of a whole century. The full meaning – and even some of the most relevant details – of what has happened since 1980 can still be argued about. The starting-point for understanding it is the outstanding fact that the Cold War that had dominated world history since 1945, and can be traced back as far as 1917, came to an end.

By itself that implied at least a shift in assumptions about international relations on the global scale, and one interconnected with all sorts of other changes in many countries. Nor were such changes limited merely to political and ideological matters. Yet nothing like them seemed likely in 1980, when the seeds for it, as now appears, were already germinating. On the contrary, hopes of *détente* encouraged a few years earlier seemed at that moment to be crumbling fast, the rhetoric of Cold War was heard as loudly as ever in the United States and the leaders of the USSR were before long seriously wondering whether an American nuclear attack might be on the way. Other views of the future that had recently been in vogue were also having to be set aside. The Iranian revolution had seemed to herald sweeping change in the Near and Middle East but it remained very difficult to assess in a balanced way what it had actually achieved (as was still, in fact, to be the case in the 1990s). Certainly anyone who had hoped for emergence from the Arab–Israeli impasse (in whatever form they might have wished to see it, and regardless to whom they thought the benefits would accrue) was to go on being disappointed as the 1980s unrolled. Nor had it become any easier to be sure what Islamic 'fundamentalism' really signified. What had looked for a time like a great resurgence would also within a few years look like just one more of many waves of puritanism that have from time to time across the centuries broken into the Faith, and then died away. It owed much to circumstance; Israel's occupation of Jerusalem, the third of Islam's Holy Places, had enhanced a sense of Islamic solidarity, and the oil crisis had given a new sharpness to the sword of Islam. Yet Islam had its own difficult legacies, often pulling in different directions.

The attack by Sunnite Iraq on Shi'ite Iran in 1980 began a war which was to last eight years and cost a million lives; doctrinal difference had hardly contributed to the origins of the quarrel, but not until 1997 would representatives of all the Islamic states meet (in Teheran) in a gathering that ignored it. It soon appeared to the rulers of Iran, too, that although they could irritate and alarm the superpowers (especially the USSR, with its millions of Muslim subjects), they could not easily thwart them. At the end of 1979, they had been able only to watch what looked at first like Soviet success in propping up its puppet communist regime in Afghanistan against Muslim rebels. One reason why the Iranian government backed terrorists and kidnappers was that (like the very different Libyan government) it was the best or worst it could do in an unfavourable international environment. In spite of its play with American hostages it could not get back the former Shah to face Islamic justice (he died in exile in 1980). All in all, the successful tweaking of the eagle's tail feathers had been humiliating for the United States, but now seems to have mattered much less than it did at the time. In retrospect, a declaration by President Carter in 1980 that the United States regarded the Persian Gulf as an area of vital interest looks more important. It was an early sign of the waning of a dangerously exaggerated mood of American uncertainty and defeatism.

AMERICAN MISGIVINGS

The roots of that mood can easily be understood. Eighteen years before, the Cuban crisis had been thought by Americans to show the world that the United States was top dog. They had then enjoyed a consciousness of superior military strength and the usually dependable support of allies, clients and satellites the world round. The American public will had long sustained a world diplomatic and military effort while still grappling powerfully with domestic problems. But American citizens had come to feel differently even by 1970. After that, disillusion had deepened in a bad decade. Over the first half of the 1970s there had hung the psychological disaster of defeat in Vietnam. The turmoil over Nixon's fall from office followed and overshadowed the extent of his real international achievements. Then came the setback in Iran and the country's seeming powerlessness in the hostage affair. Finally, the United States had to stand by while the USSR seemed able to extend its own reach in Asia by sending an army to Afghanistan, when there was for a moment a whiff of a Korea replay in the air. That the Soviet adventure might not in the end turn out as satisfactorily as planners in Moscow had hoped, was foreseen only by a few at the time.

Yet in 1980 the central reality of world politics was in fact about to reassert itself. For all the pace of change since the Cuban crisis, the American republic was still in that year one of only two states in the world whose might gave them unquestioned status as (to use an official Soviet definition) 'the greatest world powers, without whose participation not a single international problem can be solved'. Even of the Chinese, that could not be said. It was true only of the USA and USSR and was the fundamental and determining fact of the way the world worked. Spectacular economic challenges in the Far East, oil blackmail by Middle Eastern princes, could not change that, far less could international terrorism.

History, moreover, has no enduring favourites. Though some Americans had been frightened by the apparent growth in Soviet strength after the Cuban crisis, there were plenty of signs even in the 1970s that the USSR was already facing major difficulties. Cold War commitments in help to Cuba and Vietnam heavily taxed her resources. She continued to spend colossal sums on armaments (of the order of a quarter of her GDP in the 1980s), but they appeared hardly sufficient in an era of ever-more expensive weaponry and supporting technology. Afghanistan added to the bill, to little advantage. To carry the burden, more resources were needed. What that might mean was debatable, but that it would require some change was certain. In that setting, it could only be reassuring that between the governments of the two superpowers the compelling tie of nuclear terror had grown even stronger. Both knew that nuclear superiority was in the last resort little but notional. A new degree of cooperation in seeking arms limitation voiced in the 1970s had persisted in spite of specific quarrels, even if as the year of a presidential election approached many Americans were still very worried at the end of the decade.

Against this background, that election was, for understandable if not easily avowable domestic reasons, fought in a way that played much on the voters' sense of national weakness and on their fears of the USSR. The winner, Ronald Reagan, won a majority of the popular votes cast and, memorably for a Republican candidate, all the southern states except Georgia (his opponent's native state). Hopes of *détente* had wilted and it is unsurprising that the conservative Soviet leadership should have voiced renewed suspicion of the trend of American policy as the new president prepared to take office, for all the difficulties he inherited. The new administration was soon to engineer a remarkable recovery in American confidence that would increase Soviet anxiety.

DISORDERED ISLAM

On the day of Mr Reagan's inauguration as president in 1981, the Iranians released their American hostages. That closed a humiliating and frustrating episode (suspicious Americans who voted Democrat believed the timing of the release to have been stage-managed by the new administration's supporters to discredit the outgoing Mr Carter). But this was by no means the end of problems in the Middle East and the Gulf. The question of Israel's borders, and even of her very right to existence, had not gone away. The war between Iran and Iraq soon reminded the world of the dangers of the tinder lying about. The instability of the Lebanon was becoming more obvious. Ordered government virtually disappeared there and the country collapsed into an anarchy disputed by bands of gunmen, some patronized by the Syrians and Iranians, and others by the Israelis. This gave the revolutionary wing of the PLO a much more promising base for operation against Israel than in the past. Israel responded by mounting increasingly violent and expensive military operations on and beyond her northern borders, heightening tension still further and provoking ever more vicious conflict with the Palestinians.

The United States was not alone in bemoaning the volatilities of the Near and Middle East; there were many Muslims inside the Soviet Union to worry Moscow, too. Some observers thought this a hopeful fact, believing that what looked like growing disorder in the Islamic world might induce caution on the part of both superpowers, and perhaps would lead to less unconditional support for their satellites and allies in the region. Should this happen, it was likely to matter most to Israel. While that might please some conservative Arabs, Iran's aggressive and Shi'ite puritanism caused alarm in the oil-rich Gulf states and Saudi Arabia; their rulers feared that sympathy for the radical conservatism of the Iranian revolution could spread to other Islamic countries. The more alarming manifestations and sometimes absurd rhetorical exaggeration of Iranian revolutionaries and Arab Islamic sympathizers meanwhile continued to preoccupy western observers more than they should have done.

A swift manifestation of what the intransigence of enthusiasts might mean was the murder of the president of Egypt in 1981 as a punishment for his reconciliation with Israel. The government of Pakistan meanwhile continued covertly to help the anti-communist Islamic rebels in Afghanistan while proclaiming and imposing Islamic orthodoxy even more strongly at home (yet by the end of the decade Pakistan had a woman as prime minister, a situation unique in the Islamic world, and in 1989 rejoined the British Commonwealth). As the decade drew on, though, North Africa presented the most alarming evidence of radical Islamic feeling. It was most noisily evident in the bizarre sallies and pronouncements of the easily excited Colonel Qadaffi, dictator of Libya, who called upon other oil-producing states to stop supplying the United States (while one third of Libyan oil continued to find a market there). In 1980 he had announced, among other things, both that he was sending a large bill to Italy, the United Kingdom and West Germany for the damage done by their battles in North Africa in 1940–43, and that *all* Libyans abroad were traitors and thieves who should be 'ferreted down and physically liquidated'.[1] He also briefly 'united' his country to Ba'athist Syria.

Political developments further to the west mattered much more, though, than such gestures. The new Algeria was a depressing spectacle as the century drew to a close. Victory in the war of independence had been followed by yet further atrocious bloodletting (mainly that of those who had collaborated with, or were suspected of collaboration with, the French regime). There had been optimism for a time that life for Algerians would change for the better. Over a million of them, mainly, but not all, of European extraction, had fled to France and this had disposed of the major problem set by the *pied-noir* community, so that no further ethnic cleansing was needed. Some of the omens at the outset were good. Algeria looked forward to enjoying substantial oil and natural gas revenues; French attempts to retain control of the Sahara (whose attachment to the coastal region of the north in the first place had been the artificial creation of French colonialism) had evaporated in the peace negotiations. Though on a world scale hardly significant – she had, after all, only 16 million or so people in 1962 – Algeria had the second largest industrial base in the continent (after South Africa). There was even talk in the 1970s of her becoming Africa's 'first Japan'.[2]

But this was not to be. By 1980, the economy was flagging badly. There had been wasteful investment in the promotion of state-owned heavy industry. Manufacturing output had fallen. Population continued still to rise inexorably (it tripled between 1960 and 1995), and the country's agricultural production remained stagnant. Algeria had to face increasing import bills, dwindling oil revenues and mounting external debt. Emigration to Europe (and, above all, France) was the favoured outlet for the energies of Algeria's young men, and the

[1] *AR 1980*, pp.210–13. He appears to have begun the implementation of the last injunction.
[2] D. S. Landes, *The Wealth and Poverty of Nations* (London, 1998), p.507.

remittances they sent home became indispensable. Without them (and, paradoxically, aid and loans from French governments until expropriation of agricultural holdings and oil and gas resources put a stop to them), the country faced bankruptcy.

Earlier optimism withered in this increasingly bleak setting. Hopes of a North African Islamic union of Algeria, Libya, Morocco and Mauritania soon evaporated. At home, the political consensus that might have been forged immediately after victory was sacrificed by the intransigence of the FLN-based government, whose members soon fell out in power struggles of their own. A gap began to open between Berber and Arab interests. The broadly socialist and secular tone of the regime, meanwhile, alienated conservatives who did not share the urban and francophone background of the revolutionary leaders. This came to matter when a long-delayed democratization of Algerian politics was attempted in 1989–91, and was botched. In local elections in 1990 an overtly Islamist party for the first time in any African country won a resounding democratic victory. The candidates of the ruling FLN suffered heavily, and with them any support for their policy of IMF-inspired economic reform. There were disturbances and, for a time, a state of siege was imposed by the government but as the year ended the regime was again routed, this time in national elections, by the extremists of an 'Islamic Salvation Front'. This success was to be their last, though; in July 1991 the army struck, installing an authoritarian regime without representative sanction. It then embarked on what turned out to be an increasingly savage campaign against the Islamists – who, in turn, took to terrorism and guerrilla warfare. The army was to be for the rest of the decade the dominant force in Algerian politics, more and more openly showing itself determined to maintain a political system rather than any particular party regime, and, it seemed, increasingly careless of the ways in which it did so.

In 1989, too, a military coup had also brought a military and militant Islamic regime to power in Sudan. It at once suppressed what little civic freedom was left in that unhappy land, most of whose existence had been spent under military rule.[3] The government established close

---

[3] The republic had been proclaimed 1 January 1956. Sudan had earlier been ruled jointly by Great Britain and Egypt.

relations with Iran and pursued with renewed vigour attempts to crush a rebellion going on in the south of the country (where both Christianity and paganism resisted Islamization) since the achievement of independence. To date it is estimated that 1.4 million have died in that war.

For all the apparent advances by radical extremists in many Islamic countries, there were even by 1990 many signs that moderate and conservative Arab politicians were being antagonized by the radicals. Indigenous opposition to extremism was sometimes effective. Would-be revolutionaries had to confront other Muslims who sought goals of power and modernization which were incompatible with Islamic teaching and custom. Libya might destabilize other African countries and arm Irish terrorists, but could achieve little else. Such military support to Islamic regimes as Iran could spare from her own war with Iraq was largely confined to Afghanistan. There, with the help of Pakistan and the American CIA, Afghan forces were maintained in the field against the Soviet army of occupation successfully enough not only to bog down the USSR in support of a minority regime but also to be a major drain on Soviet resources. Afghanistan was in effect becoming a Soviet Vietnam.

As time passed, too, the decade provided growing evidence that Saddam Hussein, ruler of Iraq and American protégé, was only tactically and pragmatically a supporter of Islamic unity. Muslim by upbringing, he led what should have been a secular Ba'athist regime based in reality on patronage, family and the self-interest of soldiers. He sought power, and technological modernization as a way to it; there is no evidence that the welfare of the Iraqi people ever mattered to him. The prolongation of his war with Iran and evidence of its costs were greeted with relief by other Arab states – notably the other oil-producers of the Gulf – because it appeared at the same time to pin down both a dangerous adventurer and the Iranian revolutionaries, even if it was regrettable to them that war between Muslim countries distracted attention from the Palestinian question and strengthened Israel's hand in dealing with the PLO.

During nearly a decade of alarms and excursions in the Gulf, some of which raised in western eyes the horrid spectre of further interference with oil supplies, armed conflict between Iran and the United States seemed at times possible. Meanwhile, the international stalemate in the Levant grew more embittered. Israel's vigorous operations in Lebanon against Palestinian guerrilla bands and their patrons, her annexation of the formerly Syrian Golan Heights after the Six-Day War, and her government's encouragement of further Jewish immigration (notably from the USSR) all helped to buttress her against the day when she might once again face united Arab armies. She had to meet in the process both costs and foreign criticism, particularly when, in late 1987, the first outbreaks of mass violence among Palestinians occurred in the Israeli-occupied territories. They were to grow into a major insurrection, the *intifada*.[4] The PLO, meanwhile won further international sympathy by officially conceding Israel's right to exist, to the irritation of some of its Arab paymasters.

THE LAST PHASE OF COLD WAR

There was, in fact, to be no transformation of the international scene in the Middle East in the 1980s, but an enormous one elsewhere, unpromising though things had looked at the outset. In his election campaign of 1980 Mr Reagan had deliberately played on the public's fears of the Soviet Union and what he called America's 'weakened defence'. This was a politician's shorthand for the assertion that the United States could no longer be sure it had preponderance in intercontinental missiles sufficient to deter the USSR. Unsurprisingly, such language reawoke alarm in Moscow; the conservative Soviet leadership denounced with fresh vigour the trend of United States policy. Matters were not helped when, within a few months of Mr Reagan's inauguration, America's nuclear striking force was twice in one week activated following erroneous computer warnings that Soviet missile attacks were on the way. It seemed likely that the few but promising steps towards disarmament so far achieved might be swept aside – or even worse. In the event, Mr Reagan's administration showed more flexibility in foreign affairs than his language as a

---

[4] Between 1987 and 1994, reported *The Times*, 9 December 1997, the *intifada* cost the lives of 1,306 Palestinians killed by Israelis, 192 Israelis killed by Palestinians, and 822 Arabs who died in violence between Arabs themselves.

presidential candidate had suggested, and even a measure of pragmatism, while, on the Soviet side, internal change was about to open the way to an unexpected future.

Nonetheless, the Soviet position in the early 1980s was very different from that of ten years earlier. The USSR had to face military stalemate at great expense in Afghanistan. Her east European satellites, far from being of economic benefit to her, were costly, required expensive garrisons and therefore increased her defence bills.[5] This was the setting when in November 1982 Leonid Brezhnev, Khrushchev's successor and for eighteen years general secretary of the Party, died. The head of the KGB who replaced him soon followed him to the grave, to be succeeded by a septuagenarian whose own expiry was even more rapid. Finally, there came to the office of general secretary in 1985 the youngest member of the Politburo, Mr Mikhail Gorbachev. Fifty-four years old, he had behind him a political life lived almost entirely in the post-Stalin era. His impact upon history is still difficult to assess accurately, but of its decisiveness and scope there can be no doubt.

Mr Gorbachev's personal motivation and the conjunction of forces that propelled him to the highest office remain in many ways unclear. The KGB, presumably, did not oppose his promotion, and his first acts and speeches were orthodox enough, though he clearly saw himself as a reformer within communist parameters. Yet he soon began to articulate a new political tone. He had, in the previous year, made an impression on the British prime minister as 'a man with whom I could do business'.[6] He spoke of 'we Europeans' sharing a culture and a 'common home' (a remark potentially highly provocative in a country whose history had been agitated for nearly two centuries by the debates of 'westernizers' and 'slavophiles' over its cultural destinies).[7] The word 'communism' was heard less and less in his speeches, which reinterpreted 'socialism' to exclude egalitarianism (though from time to time he reminded his colleagues that he *was* a communist). For want of a better term, his aim was economic and

[5] In this respect, the USSR's position was like that of the USA in NATO – but the USA could afford it.
[6] M. Thatcher, *The Downing Street Years* (London, 1993), p.463.
[7] In a speech in Prague in April 1987. See also Gorbachev's *Perestroika: New Thinking for Our Country and the World* (London, 1987), pp.194–8.

political liberalization, an inadequate western gloss on two Russian words he used a great deal: *glasnost* (openness) and *perestroika* (restructuring). For all the scepticism with which it was greeted by many western sovietologists who began by seeing it as window-dressing, the full implications of his new course were to turn out to be profound and dramatic. For the rest of the decade Mr Gorbachev grappled with them. They could hardly have been what he had in mind when he set out.

It now seems clear that Mr Gorbachev took office with a reforming goal: he sought to avoid the collapse of a communist system by opening it to his own vision of Leninism, a more pluralist system, involving the intelligentsia in the political nation. Perhaps his attempt to achieve political and economic reform at the same time was a mistake that was a fatal flaw at the root of an eventual failure. His starting-point had been his recognition that without radical change the Soviet economy had not been and would not be able to provide the USSR with its former military might, sustain its commitments to allies abroad, improve (however slowly) living standards at home, and assure continuing self-generated technological innovation. Essentially, it was at last being admitted that the great experiment of arriving at socialism through modernization which had been going on for nearly seventy years had failed. Neither material well-being nor freedom had been forthcoming. And now the costs of modernization were becoming too heavy to bear.

Mr Reagan was in the end to draw great dividends on the change in Soviet leadership, but it took almost all of his two presidential terms to do so. In the early 1980s he was encumbered by a flagging economy, significant inflation and a huge budgetary deficit. Although there were further troubles to come he had by his second term apparently overcome these to the extent that he won re-election with the largest percentage of the popular vote in American history. Lower taxes produced something like enthusiasm over the administration's handling of the economy and optimism and confidence spilled over, too, into Americans' views of the international situation. Among other things they were promised wonders by their government in the shape of new defensive measures in space. Though thousands of scientists said the project was unrealistic, the Soviet government only too evidently could not face the costs of competing in order merely to demonstrate the point. Americans had been heartened, too, in 1986 when American bombers were launched from England on a punitive mission against Libya, whose eccentric and unpredictable ruler had been giving support to anti-American terrorists. The Soviet Union expressed less concern about this operation than did many west Europeans. Mr Reagan was less successful in convincing many of his countrymen that more enthusiastic assertions of American authority in Central America were truly in the national interest, and a Congressional inquiry in 1987 concluded that he should have done more to uphold the law when arms had been sold to Iran in the previous year, and the proceeds used to finance rebels against the government of Nicaragua. There were resignations and the president said in effect that he had made a mistake but had meant well, and he survived until 1988 to leave office then as an outstandingly popular president.

Meanwhile, the USSR had been showing for years signs of growing division and difficulty in reforming its affairs. The alarm and fear with which the 'evil empire' (as Mr Reagan had once memorably termed it) of the Soviet Union was regarded by many Americans in 1980 had begun to evaporate, even if the dislike they felt for it did not. The foreign policy of the administration, too, had brought solid grounds for satisfaction with the Reagan presidency once Mr Gorbachev's new course soon became clear in meetings with Mr Reagan. The first took place in 1986 at Reykjavik; it seemed a failure but discussion of arms reduction was renewed at it and in 1987 further negotiation on arms control brought about an agreement over intermediate range nuclear missiles during another 'summit' meeting in Washington. In spite of so many shocks and its partial erosion by the emergence of new foci of nuclear power, the arms balance had held long enough for the first stand-downs by the superpowers. They had shown they could still manage their conflicts and the world's crises without war, and now were doing better than that.[8] They at least, if

[8] The 'INF treaty', as the formal agreement was called, was signed on 8 December 1987 and the heart of it was provision for all land-based missiles with ranges of between 500 and 5,500 kilometres to be destroyed within three years. 3,000 Soviet and 800 American warheads were believed to be covered, and there were provisions for on-site inspection to assure compliance. For the text, see *AR 1987*, pp.558–66.

not other countries seeking to acquire nuclear weapons, appeared to have recognized that nuclear war, if it came, held out the possibility of the virtual extinction of mankind. Two years later, the Soviet forces were withdrawn from Afghanistan. In 1991 there were to be further dramatic developments as the USA and USSR agreed to major reductions in existing weapons stocks. There were further indications in Soviet policy that Mr Gorbachev the reformer was, perhaps willy-nilly, proving to be a revolutionary.

CHANGING EASTERN EUROPE

Any change in the international scene was bound to offer new prospects to others than the superpowers. Only for convenience of exposition can superpower *détente* be separated from what was going on in eastern Europe. One process could not have occurred without the other, they were not only contemporaneous but also interdependent. At the end of 1980 few western experts on the communist world could have believed that the peoples of eastern Europe and the Soviet Union were about to enter a new phase of their destiny, and engage in changes unmatched in scope and scale since the 1940s. All that then could be safely predicted was that communist countries would go on finding it more and more difficult to maintain even the modest growth rates they had so far attained (about which there were many qualifications to be made, in any case, as later examination of the official statistics of the time has shown). Not all western 'experts' would have risked going even so far as that, though it should at least have been clear that comparison with the market economies of the non-communist world had become more and more unfavourable to the command economies. Yet even if that was conceded, no possible challenge to the verdict of 1945, and those hardly less resounding of 1953, 1956 and 1968, seemed possible in 1980. Soviet power in that year still seemed to hold eastern Europe in its grip as firmly as ever.

Some social and political change had nonetheless been going on for thirty years, almost concealed inside what had looked superficially like an unchanging, monolithic Soviet bloc. The outcome of a long experiment with a particular model of development seemed much the same in each communist-ruled country. In all of them the party was supreme; careerists built their lives round it as, in earlier centuries, men on the make clustered about courts and patrons. All of them maintained formidable internal security forces and secret police surveillance.[9] In each, (and above all in the USSR) there was also an unspeakable, unavowable and unexaminable past which could not be mourned or deplored, whose weight overhung and corrupted intellectual life and political discussion, so far as there was any.

In most of the east European economies, investment in heavy industrial and capital goods had produced a surge of growth in the 1950s (in some more vigorous than in others), within a system of trading arrangements with other communist countries dominated by the USSR and rigidified by aspirations to central planning. Increasingly and obviously, these economies could not by the 1970s meet a growing desire for consumer goods; commodities taken for granted in western Europe remained luxuries in the east, cut off from the advantages of international economic specialization. Yet there were important differences among the communist countries themselves. On the land, private ownership had been much reduced in some of them by the middle of the 1950s, sometimes to be replaced by a mixture of cooperatives and state farms. Even by 1960, though, Polish peasants were already moving back into smallholdings; eventually, something like four-fifths of Polish farmland was back in private hands even under communist government. Whatever the tenure arrangements, though, output remained low in most eastern European countries. Their agricultural yields were usually only from half to three-quarters those of the European Community. By the 1980s all the countries of the eastern bloc were in some degree in a state of economic crisis. An economic transformation was clearly necessary, but seemed impossible. The supposed exception was the GDR but this was illusory; even in that much-touted instance of communist economic success, per capita GDP stood in 1988 at only $9,300 a year, against $19,500 in the Federal Republic.

[9] For the minute scale and extent of the aspirations but actually frequent ineffectiveness of such systems in their most developed form, see the book by T. Garton Ash, *The file: a personal history* (London, 1997), which considers what is revealed by the files on the surveillance of a particular individual (that author) in the GDR.

Brezhnev had said that developments within eastern bloc countries might require – as in Czechoslovakia in 1968 – direct physical intervention to safeguard the interests of the USSR and its allies against any attempts to turn socialist economies back towards capitalism. Comparisons might be and were made, though parallels were inexact, between this and the Roosevelt 'corollary' to the Monroe doctrine pronounced in 1904. Yet Brezhnev had also been interested in pursuing *détente*. His 'doctrine' was in a measure recognition of the possible dangers presented to international stability by breakaway developments in communist Europe; it could be seen as an attempt to limit such dangers by drawing clear lines. Since then, western countries, steadily growing more prosperous, and with memories of the late 1940s and the seeming possibility of subversion far behind them, had grown in confidence. Well before 1980, after all, there were no dictatorships west of the Trieste–Stettin line. Democracy had triumphed in western Europe as it had not done between 1918 and 1939. Class conflict seemed in abeyance. Even when Paris was in uproar in 1968, and student riots filled the headlines, the French working class achieved only a brief general strike when its leaders sought to exploit the situation for their own ends and the Gaullist party won a massive majority in the election a month later. The communists proclaimed that 'violence and guerrilla warfare' were not the road to socialism. For thirty years, the only risings by European industrial workers against their masters had been in East Germany, Hungary, Poland and Czechoslovakia, all of them communist countries.

After 1970, and even more after the Helsinki agreement of 1975, as awareness of contrasts with western Europe grew in the eastern bloc, dissident groups emerged, survived and even prospered, in spite of continuing repressive efforts. Gradually, too, a few officials, economic specialists, and some party members too began to show scepticism about the costs of detailed and centralized attempts to plan economic life. There was increasing discussion of the advantages of utilizing market mechanisms. The key to stability in the east, nevertheless, remained the Soviet Army. There was no reason to believe that any fundamental change was possible in the Warsaw pact countries while the Brezhnev doctrine continued to provide support to governments subservient to the USSR, and the USSR saw all internal dissent among its allies as a potential threat to its own security.

POLISH REVOLUTION

The first clear sign that an eastern European change was at hand came in Poland. To a remarkable degree the Poles had retained their patriotic integrity (not for the first time in their history) by following their priests and not their rulers. The political influence of the Roman Catholic Church had remained great, even if it had not always shown an altogether acceptable face to the non-Polish world. In 1946 the Primate of Poland had shown himself willing to pander to traditional prejudices by blaming Jews for the behaviour of Poles who had indulged in pogroms and even murders of Jewish survivors of the Holocaust.[10] Perhaps because it was truly popular in its reflexion of widely held attitudes, though, the Church had an enduring hold on the affections and minds of many Poles. Historically, they had long seen it as the embodiment of the nation. It was often to speak for them and did so all the more convincingly after 1978 when the first Polish pope was enthroned at Rome. By then the Polish hierarchy had already identified itself with the cause of workers who protested against economic policy, and it had condemned their ill-treatment. Yet economic conditions continued to worsen.

Nineteen eighty was a year of hard times, and a series of strikes came to a head in an epic struggle in the Gdansk shipyard. Significantly, the shipyard gates were decorated with a picture of the Pope and open-air masses were held there for the strikers. From this struggle emerged a new and spontaneously organized federation of trade unions, 'Solidarity'. To the originally economic goals of the strikers, it added political demands, among them one for free and independent trade unions. Solidarity's leader was a remarkable, much-imprisoned electrical worker and trade unionist, Lech Wałesa. He was also a devout Catholic, closely in touch with the clergy. The world was

[10] B. Wasserstein, in *Vanishing Diaspora: the Jews in Europe since 1945* (London, 1996), says that half the 200,000 Jews still left alive in Poland in 1945 fled the country within a year.

soon surprised to see a shaken Polish government making historic concessions to him. Above all, it recognized Solidarity as an independent, self-governing trade union. Other new, free trade unions appeared in association with Solidarity; within a few months they had 8 million members. Symbolically, regular broadcasting of the Catholic Mass on Sundays was now permitted. But disorder did not cease, and with the winter the atmosphere of crisis deepened. Threats of possible intervention were heard: forty Soviet divisions were said to be ready in the GDR and on the Russian frontier. But the dog did not bark in the night; the Soviet army did not move. Brezhnev did not unleash it, nor were his successors to do so in the turbulent years that followed. This was the first hint of changing attitudes in Moscow that were the necessary condition of what was to follow in eastern Europe in the next ten years.

In 1981, the economic situation worsened; Wałesa strove to avert provocation, but tension rose. On five occasions the Russian commander of the Warsaw Pact forces came to Warsaw. On the last, the Solidarity radicals broke away from Wałesa's control and called for a general strike if emergency powers were taken by the government. On 13 December, martial law was declared. There followed fierce repression (costing possibly hundreds of lives). But the Polish military claimed later that their action removed the implicit threat of Russian invasion, and so may have saved the Polish revolution.

Solidarity now went underground. Seven years of struggle began during which it became clear that military government could neither prevent further economic deterioration, nor enlist the support of the 'real' Poland, the society alienated from communism, for the regime. A moral revolution was taking place. As one western observer put it, Poles began to behave 'as if they lived in a free country';[11] not only clandestine organization and publication, but strikes and demonstrations, and continuing ecclesiastical condemnation of the regime sustained what was at times an atmosphere of civil war. Another aspect of this change was the growing loss of confidence within the regime itself: the party was steadily losing its younger members and by 1987 more than half of it was over fifty years old. After a few

[11] T. Garton Ash, *The Polish Revolution: Solidarity* (rev. edn, London, 1991), p.292.

months the government cautiously abandoned martial law, but still continued to deploy a varied repertoire of overt and undercover repression. Meanwhile, the economy was sagging yet further, while western countries offered no help and no sympathy to the regime.

In the end, change in Moscow produced decisive effects, though they were not swift to appear. The climax came in 1989, for Poland her most hopeful year since 1945. It opened with the regime's accepting at last that other political parties and organizations, including Solidarity, had to share in the political process. As a first step to true political pluralism, parliamentary elections were held in June in which some seats were freely contested. In them, Solidarity swept the board. Soon the new parliament embarked on a series of symbolic affronts to the old order: it denounced the German–Soviet agreement of August 1939, condemned the 1968 invasion of Czechoslovakia, and set up investigations into political murders committed since 1981. Historical truth was emerging at last from the shadows. In August, Wałesa announced that Solidarity would support a coalition government. The Polish communist diehards were told by Mr Gorbachev that this would be justifiable (and already some Soviet military units had been withdrawn). In September a coalition dominated by Solidarity and led by the first non-communist prime minister in any east European country since 1945 took office as the government of Poland. Western economic aid was soon promised. By Christmas the Polish People's Republic had disappeared and, once again, the historic Republic of Poland had risen from its grave. Through all these events, the Soviet army had kept to its barracks.

THE CRUMBLING OF THE SOVIET SYSTEM

Poland was to prove to have led eastern Europe to freedom. Thanks to her example, 1989 was a great year in neighbouring countries, too. The importance of what was happening had quickly been perceived in them and their leaders were much alarmed. In varying degree, eastern Europe was increasingly exposed to a new and faster flow of information about other countries through television (this was especially marked in the GDR). More freedom of movement, more access to foreign books and newspapers had gradually but perceptibly advanced the process of criticism elsewhere as in Poland. In spite of some ludicrous attempts to go on controlling information (Romania still required that ownership of typewriters be registered with the state authorities), a change in consciousness was under way. But an essential pre-condition of any real change had to be change in Moscow, and this had now come about.

Mr Gorbachev had come to power during the gestatory period of the east European revolution. The importance of his arrival on the scene became clear outside the USSR for perhaps the first time when he showed that he was not likely to enforce the Brezhnev doctrine. Then, in January 1987, he announced that democratization in the USSR was to be part of his programme. *Perestroika* had begun as a technique of economic reform; now, said Mr Gorbachev, democracy was its 'essence' and free elections were required. Reconstruction was proving more difficult than expected, he added, and 'elements of stagnation and other phenomena alien to socialism' had appeared. Eighteen months later he was asking the Party Conference to renounce 'everything that deformed socialism in the 1930s and led to its stagnation in the 1970s' and to delimit the authority of the party and the state. Soon he was talking of independence for courts and the separation of executive and legislative powers.[12] Though beginning to meet serious resistance from the entrenched bureaucracies of state and party, Mr Gorbachev at this stage by no means had his back to the wall. He still knew how to manipulate the *apparat*. The name of Lenin was much invoked to give legitimacy to non-Leninist policies.

Yet soon it was clear that he had released a revolution. Power had been taken from the party, and the opportunities so provided were seized by newly emerging opposition forces. This was true above all in non-Russian republics of the Union that began to claim greater or lesser degrees of autonomy. Before long, it began to look as if Mr Gorbachev might be undermining his own authority. Perhaps his whole strategy had been misconceived from the outset if he believed (as seems to have been the case) that the CPSU would, under

---

[12] See *AR 1987*, pp.101–2, for his remarks to the Central Committee of 27–8 January, and *AR 1988*, pp.103–6, for his speech to the 19th Party Conference 28 June–1 July.

perestroika, be able to maintain its ascendancy, by winning electoral support in free elections. Alarmingly, too, the economy looked worse and worse as the months passed. It became clear that a transition to a market economy, whether slow or rapid, was likely to impose far greater hardship on many – perhaps most – Soviet citizens than had been envisaged. By 1989 the Soviet economy was out of control and obviously running down. In 1990 a fundamental decision was taken to accept only hard currencies in payment for exports – a decision that was itself the death knell of Comecon.

As often before in Russian history, modernization had been launched from the centre to flow out to the periphery through authoritarian structures. But the outcome could not now be relied upon as in the past. At the outset, because of the drag imposed by the resistance of the *nomenklatura* and the administration of the command economy, reform had not been delivered quickly enough. Then by the end of the decade, the visible and rapid crumbling of the centre's power to direct events meant that public opinion left reform behind. The broad middle position on which Mr Gorbachev had relied to pursue reform after the deposing of the CPSU had no majority or popular support: socialism with a democratic face was itself threatened.

By 1990 more information was available to the rest of the world about the true state of the Soviet Union and popular attitudes inside it than at any time since 1917. Not only was plenty of overt evidence provided by behaviour, but television teams from the West were at work there, and *glasnost* had also brought to the Soviet Union cities the first public opinion polls. Some rough-and-ready judgements could be made; the discrediting of the party and *nomenklatura* was profound, even if it had not by 1990 gone so far as in some other Warsaw Pact countries. Somewhat surprisingly to western eyes, the long supine and unprotesting Orthodox Church appeared to have retained more respect and authority than other institutions of the Soviet *ancien regime*.[13] But at the end of the decade economic failure hung like a thundercloud over the liberalizing of political processes. Soviet citizens as well as foreign observers began to talk of the possibility of civil

---

[13] At the beginning of 1991 (the date is explained by the Orthodox ecclesiastical calendar) Russians were for the first time in seventy years allowed to celebrate Christmas as a public holiday.

war. The thawing of the iron grip of the past had revealed the power of nationalist and regional sentiment excited by economic collapse and opportunity. After seventy years of efforts to make Soviet citizens, it looked as if the USSR had been, after all, just another multinational empire with unsolved ethnic problems. Its peoples had been organized in a federal union of fifteen republics and some of them (above all the Baltic republics of Latvia, Estonia and Lithuania) had been quick to show dissatisfaction with their lot. They were to lead the way to further political change. Some (Azerbaijan and Soviet Armenia) posed additional problems in the shadows cast by Islamic unrest. To make matters worse, there was believed to be a danger of a military coup; commanders discontented by the Soviet failure in Afghanistan (as some American soldiers had been by withdrawal from Vietnam) were talked about as potential Bonapartes – a danger long flourished as a bogey of Bolshevik mythology.

Amid multiplying signs of disintegration and demoralization, Mr Gorbachev succeeded in clinging to office and, indeed, even obtained some formal and nominal enhancement of his powers. But this had the disadvantage of continuing to focus responsibility for failure on him too. A dramatic moment came in March 1990, when the Lithuanian parliament declared invalid the annexation of 1939 and reasserted the country's independence, followed though this was by complicated negotiations to avoid provoking its armed suppression. This was the opening of the final crisis of the Soviet Union. Latvia and Estonia almost at once also claimed their independence, though in slightly different terms. The upshot was that Mr Gorbachev did not seek to revoke the fact of their secession, but won agreement that the new Baltic republics should guarantee the continuing supply of certain practical services to the USSR and the continuing presence of Soviet forces. Unfortunately, a period of increasingly rapid manoeuvring between reforming and conservative groups while he allied himself first to one and then, to redress the balance, to the other, led by the end of 1990 to the compromise of the previous summer already looking out of date and unworkable. Then, at the beginning of 1991, Soviet troops attacked official buildings in Vilnius and killed a number of Lithuanian protesters; they did so, they claimed, not at the behest of the Soviet government, but at that of a mysterious, conservatively oriented Lithuanian 'Committee of National Salvation'. Connivance at this repressive action (replicated in Riga) made things worse. Parliaments in nine of the Soviet republics had already by then either declared they were sovereign or had asserted a substantial degree of independence from the Union government. Some of them had made local languages official; some had transferred Soviet ministries and economic agencies to local control. The Russian republic – the biggest and most important of them – set out to run its own economy separately from that of the Union. The Ukrainian republic proposed to set up its own army. In March, new elections led Mr Gorbachev once more back to the path of reform and a search for a new Union treaty that preserved some centre to the state. The world looked on, bemused.

A NEW GERMANY

As other communist countries had noted the Polish example, hopes had grown in some of them in the last years of the 1980s that an increasingly divided and paralysed USSR would not (and perhaps could not) intervene to uphold its creatures in other Warsaw Pact countries. The Hungarians had moved almost as rapidly in economic liberalization as the Poles, even before overt political change, but made their own distinctive contribution to the dissolution of communist Europe only in August 1989, when Germans from the GDR were allowed to enter Hungary freely as tourists. This apparently modest administrative concession was of much more than merely economic significance. It indeed hardly mattered at all to Hungary herself, for her German visitors' known real purpose was to present themselves to the German Federal Republic's embassy and consulates in Hungary in order to seek asylum in the west. A complete opening of Hungary's frontiers came in September. Czechoslovakia soon followed suit and a flow became a flood. In three days 12,000 East Germans crossed from these countries to the west. The Soviet authorities remarked that this was 'unusual', and the West German Social Democrats wagged a finger at their own government for 'aggravating' matters by welcoming the refugees. For the GDR, though, it was the beginning of the end.

On the eve of a carefully planned celebration of the GDR's forty years' success as a socialist country, and during a visit by Mr Gorbachev (who, to the dismay of the German communists, appeared to be urging their subjects to seize their chance), riot police found themselves battling in the streets of East German cities with anti-government demonstrators who were demanding political liberalization. The government and party threw out their leader, but this was not enough. November opened with huge demonstrations against a regime whose corruption and decay was becoming more and more evident. On 9 November came the greatest symbolic act of all, the breaching of the Berlin Wall by crowds from the eastern half of Berlin. The German Politburo caved in and the demolition of the Wall at once began. Within a few days, it was estimated, more than 9 million East Germans visited West Berlin and other parts of the Federal Republic, their enthusiasm for doing so stimulated by the Federal Republic's payment of 100 *Deutschmarks* a head to visitors from the GDR as 'welcome money'.

Even in the wealthiest of the communist countries it had thus been shown that there was a massive alienation of popular feeling from the regime. Nineteen eighty-nine had brought it to a head and provided the circumstances that let it burst out. It was a new 1848, a 'springtime of nations', this time successful. All over eastern Europe, it was soon clear that communist governments had no legitimacy in the eyes of their subjects, who either rose against them or turned their backs and let them fall down. One expression of this alienation was everywhere demands for free elections, in which opposition parties could freely campaign. The Poles had followed theirs (in which some seats were still reserved to supporters of the existing regime) with the preparation of a new constitution; in 1990, Lech Wałesa became president of the republic. A few months earlier, Hungarians had elected a parliament from which emerged a non-communist government and Soviet soldiers began to withdraw from that country. In June 1990, elections produced a non-communist government for Czechoslovakia and it was soon agreed that the country was to be evacuated of Soviet forces by May

1991. In none of these elections did the former communist politicians get more than 16 per cent of the vote.

Elections in Bulgaria were less revolutionary: there, the contest was won by communist party members turned reformers and calling themselves socialists. In two other countries, events took even more distinctive turns. Romania underwent a violent revolution (ending in the killing of its former communist dictator) after a rising in December 1989 that revealed uncertainties about the way ahead and internal divisions ominously foreshadowing further strife, some of it originating in ethnic differences. By June 1990 a government some believed still to be heavily influenced by former communists had turned on the revolutionaries of the previous winter, who were now its critics. Student protest was bloodily crushed with the aid of vigilante squads of miners and amid disapproval abroad. The other special case was the GDR.

The question of political change in the GDR was inescapably bound up with the question of German reunification, the bogey of Soviet foreign policy since 1948 (and by no means something immediately welcome to the French, either). It was, though, almost certainly unavoidable, even if Chancellor Kohl, the Christian Democrat leader of the Federal Republic, is said to have warned his advisers in the aftermath of the breaching of the Wall that unification might take another five years.[14] Yet the Wall's collapse revealed that not only was there no durable support for communist government in the east, there was hardly any for a distinct GDR either. The regime had no general will to legitimize it. By the end of 1989 Mr Kohl, whose electoral prospects could not but benefit by successful reunification, was already concerned lest the process should run away out of control. *Ostpolitik*, though, had achieved much in both Germanys since 1969. Mr Kohl had quite changed his position in the aftermath of the breaching of the Wall since the days when Brandt had begun his veiled approaches to the GDR. Before an East German general election due to be held in March 1990 the chancellor had already proposed a scheme to assist the joining of the two countries. In the election, 48 per

[14] His predecessor as chancellor, too, said in 1988 that German unification was not on the agenda. T. Judt, 'New Germany, Old Nato', *New York Review of Books*, 29 May 1997.

cent of the vote (on a 93.4 per cent turnout) and a majority of seats went to a coalition dominated by the Christian Democrats, the ruling party of western Germany. Unity was in principle no longer in doubt, given its huge popular support. But it remained to settle procedure and timetable – and to reassure foreigners, above all in Moscow. Other international reactions, too, especially from the other three former occupying powers, were still unpredictable. 'We do not want anyone to feel themselves the loser because of German unification,' said the West German foreign minister in May 1990.

Forty years earlier, currency reform had opened the process of dividing Germany in two; perhaps it was fitting, then, that in May 1990 the process of reunification (and therefore of the demolition of the formal post-war order) began with a treaty providing for a monetary and economic union of the two Germanys. A further treaty, this time of unification, was signed on 31 August, and on 3 October they were joined politically under a new constitution, the former GDR territories becoming provinces of the Federal Republic. The first elections to the enlarged Federal parliament followed in December and confirmed the ascendancy of the Christian Democrats. Mr Kohl became the first chancellor of reunited Germany.

This was momentous change. The Americans could reflect with satisfaction that if there had to be a united Germany, it would be a member of NATO and not a 'neutralized' state, with the uncertain capacity of a loose cannon to cause havoc to the stability of a fragmented eastern Europe. The western European states had in the end been brought round at least without open expression of official concern over the reconstitution of a united Germany; they could, after all, offer no alternative. France was the major loser; her standing in Europe was diminished and it was likely that she would in future have to follow Germany's lead in the affairs of the Community. It was more surprising still, though, that no serious alarm was officially expressed in Moscow. It must have been felt there. Whatever Soviet acceptance of German reunification owed to the domestic disorder that made American persuasiveness more effective, it can be accounted Mikhail Gorbachev's great service to the German nation that he acquiesced in the re-creation of a united Germany and, moreover, one belonging to NATO. It could hardly be overlooked that with a population of

71 million and the largest economy in Europe west of the USSR itself, the new Germany would be once more as capable of playing a great power role in Europe as other Germanys had done in the past.[15]

Helskinki had undergone its first major revision. Soviet power was now in eclipse as it had not been since 1918; the halcyon days of victory in 1945 were forgotten as the Soviet Union (and, to some extent, France) appeared at last as a loser of the peace settlement, forty-five years after her soldiers had stood triumphant in the streets of a ruined Berlin. Mikhail Gorbachev's compensation was a treaty promising German economic help for Soviet modernization. It might be said by way of reassurance to those Soviet citizens who remembered 1941-5 that the new German state was not an older Germany revived, but one redefined, shorn of the old East German lands (indeed, she had formally renounced them) and no longer dominated by Prussia as both Bismarck's *Reich* and the Weimar republic had been. The Federal Republic's history was reassuring, too; it was a federal and constitutional state seemingly assured of economic success, with nearly forty years' experience of democratic politics to build on, and it was safely embedded in the structures of the EC and NATO. The new Germany had achieved, after all, the revolution that had eluded her in 1918. At least for the time being, she was to be given the benefit of the doubt, even by west Europeans with long memories. Unification was also to bring dismay, though, and hardship to many of the new state's citizens as the collapse of East German industry and widespread unemployment followed in the next few years.

[15] The occupation of Germany came formally to an end, and the last occupation forces left, in 1994.

26

Post Cold War Realities

THE GULF WAR

In 1990, after making peace with Iran, Saddam Hussein, the dictator of Iraq, took up an old border dispute with the sheikdom of Kuwait, with whose ruler he had also quarrelled over oil quotas and prices. It is not easy to believe in the sincerity of his grievances, whatever they may have meant symbolically to Hussein himself. He seems to have been moved most by a simple belief that he could seize the immense oil wealth of a tiny Gulf state at no cost and hang on to it. He had some grounds for thinking so; Israel's seizures and subsequent annexations of the Golan and West Bank had survived UN condemnation unscathed, after all. Perhaps he feared, too, an Israeli attack on Iraq's installations like one ten years before which destroyed a nuclear reactor claimed to have had military potential. During the summer of 1990, his threats intensified. In August the Iraqi army invaded Kuwait and in a few hours overran it.

Iran had long been seen as the main danger to peace in the region and the United States had been the patron of Iraq. Yet when American soldiers found themselves fighting in the Gulf, it was with the Iraqis, not with the Iranians. The United States achieved a remarkable and rapid mobilization of world opinion against Iraq following the invasion. Far from coalescing Arab sentiment against western interference, the confrontation revealed once again (though less bloodily than the Iran–Iraq war had done) the stumbling-blocks that still lay in the way of Islamic cooperation. Saddam Hussein sought to play the card of Arab unity and to confuse the pursuit of his own predatory ambitions with Arab hatred for Israel, but though this provoked

THE SOVIET UNION AND ITS SUCCESSORS

·········· Territory acquired 1939–45

Border disputes with China and Mongolia after 1945

Independent republics emerging 1990–91

Arctic

PART OF
RUSSIAN
FEDERATION

Baltic Sea

Tallinn

Vilnius   Riga

ESTONIA

LITHUANIA

Minsk

LATVIA

BELARUS

• Moscow

R U S S I A N

Kishinev   Kiev

MOLDOVA

UKRAINE

Black Sea

GEORGIA   Tbilisi

ARMENIA

Yerevan   Baku

AZERBAIJAN

Caspian Sea

KAZAKHSTAN

*Aral
Sea*

UZBEKISTAN

Ashkhabad

Alma-Ata

Tashkent   Bishkek

TURKMENISTAN

Dushanbe

KYRGYZSTAN

TAJIKISTAN

The CIS in 1999

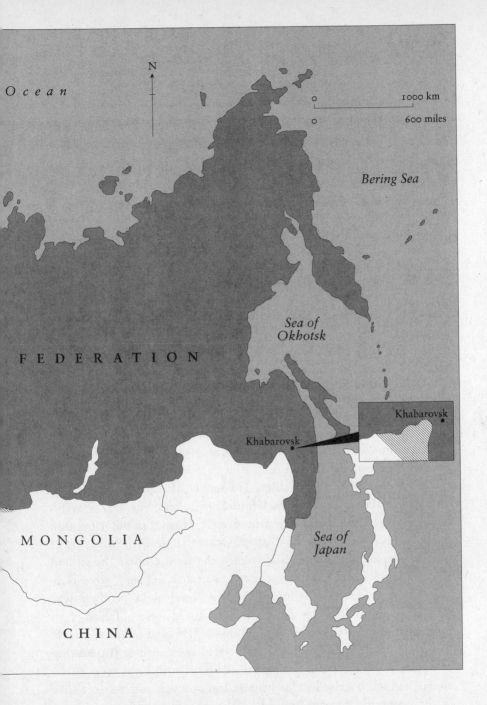

Ocean

N

1000 km
600 miles

Bering Sea

FEDERATION

Sea of
Okhotsk

Khabarovsk

Khabarovsk

MONGOLIA

Sea of
Japan

CHINA

tumultuous demonstrations in his favour in the souks in several Muslim countries, it did not work. Only the PLO and Jordan spoke up for Iraq. No doubt to his shocked surprise, Saudi Arabia, Syria and Egypt improbably joined the alliance against Saddam. British and French forces came back to the Middle East (though in a subordinate role, and under overall American command) after years in which it had been believed they had left for ever (Germany's refusal, on constitutional grounds, to send any of her troops caused dissatisfaction in Europe). Almost equally surprising to the Iraqi ruler must have been the acquiescence of the USSR. The United Nations Security Council produced overwhelming majorities for resolutions condemning Iraq's actions and authorized the use of force to liberate Kuwait.

Huge allied forces were assembled in Saudi Arabia. Iraq made rocket attacks on Israeli cities, but ineffectively; Israel prudently did not enter the war, a step that would have presented Arab countries with problems of allegiance. On 16 January 1991 the allies struck with overwhelming force. The campaign was short. Within a month, Iraq gave in and withdrew from Kuwait after suffering heavy losses (allied casualties at the time were insignificant). The humiliation of defeat did not appear to endanger Hussein's survival, or his dictatorial power; it left him disgruntled but unchastened. Another war of the Ottoman succession had ended; the liberation of Kuwait had been achieved, but without providing the turning-point in Middle Eastern politics that so many longed for.

This was true on both sides. Hussein's attempts to inspire an anti-Israel Islamic crusade had found no takers; his war was no triumph for Islamic revolutionaries even if Muslim popular opinion tended everywhere to be anti-western. Other than Iraq, the main losers were the Palestinians, who had backed the wrong horse. Israel had gained most; Arab military adventures at her expense were now inconceivable for the near future. Yet the Israel–Arab problem was still there. Formally, Hussein's prestige should have suffered from military restrictions imposed on him by the UN, and by the spectacle of UN inspectors searching the country for evidence of the making of nuclear, chemical and biological weapons; it did not seem to do so. He had in no sense lost his grip on Iraq, though as a consequence of the economic damage caused by the war and the imposition of sanctions (notably on the sale of Iraq's oil to pay for imports) the unhappy Iraqi people were poorer, hungrier, and more sickly; his propaganda soon began to emphasize the sorry state of the country's hospitals, bereft as they were of adequate medical and sanitary supplies. Meanwhile, the United States was frustratingly unable to assure itself that the threat posed by 'weapons of mass destruction' under Hussein's control had gone away. Inspections, authorized by the UN and agreed to by Saddam Hussein, were unable to overcome Iraqi evasiveness and dilatoriness and to ascertain the exact state of Iraq's bacterial and nuclear weapons.

Even before the Kuwait crisis, Syria and Iran had showed signs that, for their own reasons, they might be willing to attempt a negotiated settlement with Israel. For the United States, it became more than ever a priority to get one, and hopes sprang up with the ending of the Gulf War that Israel might, at last, show less intransigence over the territories she had occupied and the building of new settlements. The alarming spectre of a region-wide radical pan-Islamic coalition of powers had been dissipated. For all the sense of grievance in some Islamic countries, there was virtually no sign that their resentments could yet be coordinated in an effective response, nor that they could forgo the West's subtly corrosive means of modernization. Almost incidentally, too, crisis in the Gulf appeared to have revealed that the oil weapon had lost much of its power; a much-feared further oil crisis had not followed the Kuwait invasion (and, indeed, oil prices were to fall in the 1990s). Against this background American diplomacy was at last successful in 1991 in persuading Arabs and Jews to take part in a conference on the Middle East. Elsewhere, though, it remained clear that enough dangerous materials existed in the Arabic-speaking world to threaten further trouble.

PERSISTING DANGERS

With each year that passed, the inability of the Algerian government to soothe its own discontented subjects grew more and more apparent. By 1997 the evidence for this had reached horrific levels of massacre and terrorism. Acts of Islamist militant violence against the Egyptian government – and the western tourists whose spending it strove to attract – were better contained, but were telltale signs of deep discontents felt and exploited by activists. Perhaps the most alarming evidence of a potential for later trouble, though, was (and is still) to be found further east, in Saudi Arabia and the Gulf states, where it took less dramatic, but it might be thought nonetheless dangerous forms.

The long-term problems associated with modernization and economic development in the Middle East had not gone away. In 1990 the Ayatollah Khomeni (to whom puzzled western journalists had tended to refer, somewhat reductively, as an 'Islamic clergyman'), who had hitherto dominated the new Iran, had died. It was hoped that his successor might be less intransigent than he both in supporting the Palestinian cause and in encouraging what was seen as international Islamic fundamentalism. But this was marginal. Paradoxically, the very wealth – as producers of fossil fuels – of Saudi Arabia and the Gulf states is part of the seedbed of revolutionary danger. From 1930 or so, oil had emerged to rival Islam as the first linking and dominant economic factor in the modern history of the Middle East. Saudi Arabia alone possessed 25 per cent of the world's known oil resources and produced over 8 million barrels per day. In Bahrain and Oman, though the oil reserves are diminishing, discoveries of natural gas resources have been dramatic. Qatar, too, has now identified huge gas reserves. Such a wealth of fossil fuel helped to fund efforts to diversify the economies of the region in recent years, but without much success. Like the government of sixteenth-century Spain, rich with the silver of the New World, but squandering it in unproductive wars, the oil producers tended to pour away their wealth on (in their case) the appeasement of possible unrest at home. Saudi Arabia, with a population two and a half times and a land area more than five times that of the other five Gulf states combined, has the lowest income per capita of the Arab oil states. All those countries are rich enough, though, to provide their governing élites with immense personal wealth, and services to their populations at large on a scale that cannot be matched by, say, Egypt, most populous of the Arab states. Each of them employs a substantial and growing expatriate labour force. Increasingly, immigrants come to carry out tasks for which natives either could not or did not care to equip themselves. Whether in the persons of British or American technical experts, of Filipino housemaids, of Pakistani labourers on construction sites or of east European prostitutes, the oil states continued to exercise a magnetic attraction on foreigners with labour or skills to sell. Understandably, tradition-minded Muslims have found this worrying. The influx inevitably threatens an erosion of indigenous culture.

Meanwhile, Middle Eastern populations continue to grow very quickly. The average annual rate of demographic increase for countries in the area is 4 per cent – a rate doubling population every twenty years. Already two-fifths of Saudi Arabians are aged under fifteen. In twenty years' time, if present trends continue, more than half the population of the Middle East will consist of people not yet born. Population growth at such a rate is bound to create strains and needs that will deeply disturb any social and political equilibrium. At the same time, an irresistible modernization is slowly rubbing away at the structures of custom and tradition that underpin the present state of affairs.

While Islam is a culturally unifying force drawing these countries together, there remain large contrasts of view over what that tie means. In Saudi Arabia the puritanical approach of the authorities towards overt divergence from Islamic custom is notorious. It extends (for example) to the proscription of the performing and dramatic arts, a matter that may seem somewhat marginal in western eyes. Yet in 1997, considerable public excitement and incomprehension was awakened in many western countries when some alarming judicial procedures, penal codes and conditions of imprisonment were made visible in the treatment of two British nurses convicted of murder by a Saudi court. Even those disposed to take a tolerant view of cultural difference and local susceptibilities in such matters could reflect, too, that crucifixion remains punishment available under Islamic law as the twentieth century draws to a close.[1] In practice, though, even conservative states show a measure of tempering of strict Islamic law. This is not just a matter of old and traditional distinctions (such as

[1] See *The Encyclopedia of Islam* (Leiden, 1960 onwards), s.v. 'Şalb'.

the fact that women of the coastal cities of Oman rarely wear the veil, whereas those of the interior like to do so), but of the active promotion (Oman is again a convenient example) of women's education, even if in segregated forms. Yet existing cultural identities are becoming more and more difficult to preserve in an age of easy communication. This must trouble thoughtful Muslims. A more remote nightmare for them, though one no longer to be ignored as a possibility, would be a significant global shift, even if slow, towards the use of non-fossil fuel. Without speculating about such possibilities, though, it seems at the end of the century that even the most conservative of the Arab lands cannot much longer wholly escape dislocation and perhaps disorder. In the interim, every Islamic regime in the Middle East remains a despotism, in varying degree enlightened or unenlightened and usually content to divert popular dissatisfactions by welfare services, talk of *jihad* and the obliteration of Israel.

THE END OF THE SOVIET UNION

In July 1991, the USSR uttered a warning about the dangers of spreading local conflict in what had been Yugoslavia to the international level. This was the last significant diplomatic *démarche* of the Soviet Union. It was soon eclipsed by a still somewhat mysterious attempt by conservatives to set aside Mr Gorbachev. An attempted coup on 19 August failed and three days later he was again in occupation of the presidency. Nonetheless, his position was no longer what it had been; his continual shifts of position in a search for compromise had ruined his political credibility. He had clung too long to the party, never ceasing to seek to reform and modernize the communist state, not to reject it altogether. Soviet politics had now taken a further lurch forward, and to many it seemed as if it was towards disintegration. At once, while foreign observers still waited to understand what had happened, the purging of those who had supported or acquiesced in the coup was developed into a determined attempt to replace union officialdom at all levels, to redefine the role of the KGB and to share control over it between the Union and the republics. The most striking change of all came on 29 August, when the communist party of the

Soviet Union was suspended. In September the name of Leningrad was changed back to St Petersburg. The Leninist age was coming to an end. A Moscow paper was soon reporting that over two-thirds of Muscovites polled thought that Lenin's body should be taken from the mausoleum in Red Square which had been the physical focus of his cult, and buried elsewhere.

In August, Mr Gorbachev had been saved, paradoxically, by a political rival. To Mr Boris Yeltsin, the leader of the Russian republic, the largest in the Union, the coup had provided a crucial opportunity. Dominating the Russian Supreme Soviet since the previous summer, in January he had ostentatiously supported the Baltic republics in the aftermath of the violence at Vilnius, which he saw as the beginning of counter-revolution. He had firmly taken the side of radical reform, appealing to Russian troops to take no part in acts of repression there. On 19 August in Moscow, standing on a tank outside the parliament building, he called for a general strike against the 'rightists' and subsequently declared he was in charge of all Soviet security forces on Russian territory until the constitutional order was restored. The collapse of the coup followed. From this moment Mr Yeltsin appeared as a strong man of the Russian scene without whose concurrence nothing could be done in that country. He had seized the chance to consolidate his position as the defender of reform. His strength henceforth lay in the link he appeared to provide between the cause of democracy for Russians and that of self-determination for the other republics. The army, though conceivably a threat to his supporters, would not move against him after all.

Yet though the survival of reform and the steps taken after the attempted coup were enthusiastically welcomed by some, it could hardly be felt as the end of 1991 approached that the outlook was sunny. A decision to abandon price controls in the Russian republic in the near future seemed likely to release inflation unparalleled since the earliest days of the Soviet system; starvation, it was thought, might soon face millions of Russians. In one republic, Georgia, fighting had broken out between the supporters of the president and unreconciled opponents after the first free elections held there. Dwarfing all such facts, though, was the dying of the great Soviet Union itself. Suddenly and, it seemed, almost helplessly, the giant superpower which had emerged from the bloody experiments of the Bolshevik revolution to be, for nearly seventy years, the hope of revolutionaries around the world, and the generator of a military strength that had fought and won the greatest land battles in history, was dissolving.[2] A set of successor states was emerging from the old republics of the USSR. Russian, Ukrainian and Belorussian leaders met at Minsk on 8 December and announced the end of the Soviet Union and the establishment of a new 'Commonwealth of Independent States' (the CIS). On 21 December 1991, a gathering of representatives from eleven of the former republics met briefly at Alma-Ata to confirm this and agreed that the Union would end on the last day of the year. On 25 December, Mr Gorbachev resigned. He had been the last tsar of many peoples. Of what might lie ahead, no one could be sure, but the last surviving European multinational empire had gone. As the Soviet flag over the Kremlin was lowered for the last time, the world began to grasp that a second great Russian revolution had taken place.

The new Russian state ruled an area, vast as it was, which was smaller than its predecessors had ruled for two centuries or so. Not only the formal unity of a superstate disappeared, though. With the changes in the political arrangements of eastern Europe over the previous two or three years had come the crumbling of a great mythology. It was the end of an era. The faith that an international, revolutionary socialism was a real contender – some thought, the only plausible one – for the management of the future of humanity had held much of the world in thrall for seventy years. With the collapse of faith in that dream went many other claims and myths. That of Marxism to be a coherent system, the idol-like status of the great prophet himself and the apostolic succession of those who had ruled in his name, the confidence in central planning as a road to modernization, the belief that communist parties stood for more than the particular interests of pluralist political systems could ever do, were only some of them. Nineteen ninety-one was for many worldwide the

---

[2] One problem this threw into relief anew was that of the control of nuclear weapons. S. P. Keeny and W. K. H. Panofsky estimate that there were between 25,000 and 30,000 Soviet warheads in existence at the moment of the USSR's dissolution (*Arms Control Today*, Jan.–Feb. 1992, p.3). The US Congress was soon to allocate $400 million to the former Soviet republics to assist them to dismantle these weapons.

final awakening from long-dreamt dreams and for some, therefore, a tragedy, while for others it was a release from nightmare.

It was the ultimate demonstration that the Cold War was over, too, and as such a huge surprise. For nearly forty years western and especially American policy had envisaged no such end. It had been taken for granted that unless the world should blunder into nuclear war, the Soviet empire would 'always' be there, a given fact of the world order. The best professional diplomatic and academic advice available to policy-makers assumed that the Cold War might go on indefinitely, only perhaps in the very long term undergoing some softening by *détente*. Even as 1989 began, no one guessed what the European revolutions might so swiftly achieve. To that upheaval, the West had contributed virtually nothing directly – to do so would have seemed too dangerous – but had exercised positive effect indirectly, through the economic burdens imposed on the USSR by armaments and the largely unanticipated effects of mass communications. Collapse, when it finally came, had come from within.

A NEW RUSSIA

Russia was the biggest and most important of the CIS states. Mr Yeltsin, who had left the communist party of the Soviet Union in July 1990, stood on ground of more evident legitimacy than Mr Gorbachev had ever done. He had been elected in June 1991 president of the Russian republic with 57 per cent of the votes cast in the country's first free election since 1917. In November the Russian communist party was dissolved by presidential decree. In January 1992 a programme of radical economic reform was launched which led to an almost complete liberation of the economy from specific controls. Inflation in Russia had already gone far; this bold stroke appears at least to have staved off hyper-inflation. Mr Yeltsin was nonetheless faced with a huge devaluation, rapidly rising unemployment, savage falls in national income and real wages since 1990, a drop in industrial output by half, huge corruption in government organs, and widely ramifying crime. To add to these grave difficulties, a new parliament containing many of Mr Yeltsin's enemies was elected in 1993. Still other problems were posed by relations with the non-Russian republics of the CIS in which there lived 27 million Russians (there were 25 million non-Russians in Russia; 15 per cent of its citizens lived east of the Urals). In 1992 a treaty had been signed by eighteen autonomous republics within Russia itself, establishing that state, too, as a federation.

In 1993 a new constitution of a more presidential and even autocratic character had completed the formal framework of post-Soviet Russia. But it was approved by only a narrow majority in a referendum in which only slightly over half the electorate voted. When a presidential decree suspended parliament's functions tension mounted. Members of the parliament took up positions in the so-called Moscow 'White House', where the Russian Congress met and the scene of Mr Yeltsin's triumph in 1991. They, and a popular insurrection in their support, were crushed by force on 4 October. Over 100 people were killed in the bloodiest fighting in Moscow since 1917. This (like the earlier dissolution of the communist party) was seen by many as an intolerable act of presidential high-handedness. Mr Yeltsin was perhaps always unlikely to incline overmuch to concession, or to respect the parliamentary principle. His personal style and speech were rarely emollient; his impatience with opposition encouraged plausible attacks on the unconstitutionality of his actions. A constitutionally insufficient parliamentary majority had already tried to impeach him. These were dangerous weaknesses, for Mr Yeltsin could for a long time offer little positive and material return to his electors. He was not able to provide an economic recovery which the man and woman in the street could see in the form of employment and lower prices. He was increasingly opposed not only by the often hidden influence of what have been called 'clans' of political interest built around industrial and bureaucratic foci, but openly by ex-communists, fascists, and nationalists with popular appeal, as well as by disappointed ex-reformers (he had sacked many of them). He continued to enjoy, nevertheless, the ambiguous advantage of moral and diplomatic support from western Europe, notably that of Mr Kohl, who urged the priority of restoring stability in Russia upon his fellow-leaders in the West. Almost unnoticed, too, by successfully avoiding a return of Russia to militarism, other countries had been able to benefit from cuts in their defence budgets.

Russia's own security commitments, though, remained costly. In 1992 her forces intervened in the republic of Tajikstan to restore its government, overthrown by Muslim (and other) opponents with help from Afghanistan. In 1995, a Russian army was still doing garrison duty there. Meanwhile, a further unfortunate development had been an insurrection in the little land-locked republic of Chechnya in 1994 that quickly turned into a major problem.[3] In 1994 Russian forces were ordered to recover the republic. Its Muslim rebels invoked a legend of national struggle against Russian oppression going back to the conquest of the Chechens in the eighteenth century by the armies of Catherine the Great, and proclaimed their independence. A year later, thousands of Chechen civilians had been killed by Russian forces sent to restore order, the capital was in ruins after air and artillery bombardment, both sides had sunk in international esteem because of their bad behaviour (the Russian brutality in operating against civilian targets, and the Chechen practice of taking and using hostages – even on a foreign ship) but the struggle still continued and spilt over into neighbouring republics. Many Russians must have seen Chechnya as potentially a new Afghanistan and blamed Mr Yeltsin.

The Chechen rebellion was part of the background to the elections held at the end of 1995 which produced a Duma with a majority for reaction, against further reform and against Mr Yeltsin; in it, the largest of the groups of deputies was communist and the second largest ultra-nationalist. It was not a promising start on the road towards the next presidential election (in June 1996). Many Russians evidently hankered after the good old Soviet days of secure employment, cheap food and international respect. At one moment the Duma passed a motion which, though of no legal effect, declared null and void the 1991 agreement which had dissolved the USSR into the CIS. Nonetheless, Mr Yeltsin was re-elected in 1996.

As so often in Russian history, the future then looked enigmatic and mysterious. There was still little to suggest that the Russian people were inclined to accept the opening towards western traditions and ideas which had appeared to present itself in 1990. Given the major

[3] The Russian state contains twenty-one republics (of which Chechnya is one), ten autonomous areas, and two cities of federal status (St Petersburg and Moscow).

dislocations that had followed *perestroika* and *glasnost*, less and less was heard of the triumphs of liberal democracy and the market society. Further uneasiness arose as indications grew that Mr Yeltsin's health was poor and probably deteriorating. Yet there was a parliament of sorts in being, even if Russians appeared to feel as distinct as ever from other Europeans, as secluded as ever in their own zone of civilization. Unhappily, they also seemed chauvinistically responsive to demagogic suggestions that they ought again to play the international role they felt to be their due, which was usually seen as that of a countervailing power to the West. Curiously, China (with which the CIS has a frontier 6,600 kilometres long) rarely seemed to be considered in the debate this provoked. There was too much uncertainty ahead for anything but caution to be desirable.

It was a central difficulty of government to secure that even the normal functions of government were carried out, above all tax-collection and the payment of its own servants. Its wish to allow the economy to operate with the greatest possible freedom and to devolve economic power by the selling of the major state activities to private business was another weakness. A great deal of money was made by many people, but millions more suffered from the disappearance of daily necessities from the markets, inflating prices, and the irritation produced by visibly high consumption and poverty side-by-side in the streets of the great cities. When, in 1998, Russian banks began to falter in the wake of currency movements detonated by financial troubles in Asia, Mr Yeltsin's hand was forced and he had to abandon a prime minister committed to the successful introduction of the market economy and to accept one imposed upon him by his opponents in the Duma.

NEW EUROPEAN SECURITY PROBLEMS

The end of the Cold War posed questions of identity throughout eastern Europe; people everywhere looked to the past for clues to who they were. They began to see themselves and others anew in the light of a cold dawn; if some nightmares had fled, a troubled landscape was appearing. Fundamental questions began to be asked anew. Was there a distinctive zone of civilization and culture that might be called 'Central Europe', for instance, and was it the same as, or distinct from, what the Germans called *Mitteleuropa*? Was there a 'Baltic' reality? If such things did indeed exist, what could represent such regions? This was a new setting for the pursuit of older questions, too. Some in western countries considered anew how distinctive in their political arrangements ought they to be (or try to be) if Basques were to be distinguished from Spaniards – or the Scotch and Welsh from the English, or the Northern from the Southern Irish?

One half of Europe's security arrangements had disappeared with the Warsaw Pact. The other half, NATO, had meanwhile been subtly transformed, even if this tended to be for some time obscured and overlooked. The collapse of the USSR, the major possible opponent whose strengths had for so long defined NATO's tasks, had deprived the alliance of its main role. Even if, at some future date, a revived and aggressive Russia were to emerge as a new threat within that country's historic zone of influence and interest, the disappearance of the ideological struggle which had shaped NATO from its foundation forced it to consider a new role. This was slow to be recognized, though within a few years it was posing new questions. One, about the enlargement of the alliance, was raised very quickly. There were soon candidates for admission among formerly communist European countries who sought admission to a comforting and reassuring security against a possible future Russian threat such as they had known in the past. Naturally, such applications awoke much concern in Moscow. In 1999, though, Poland, Hungary and the Czech republic were all to join NATO, though no former part of the USSR (the Baltic republics were those about which the Russians showed the greatest concern) seemed likely to do so.

Another more slowly emerging consequence for NATO was the growing willingness of the American government in the 1990s to look to the alliance as a machine for dealing with problems emerging in Europe, above all, in the absence of any practical alternative. The situation throughout south-eastern Europe, indeed, was particularly hard to interpret in 1991. The facts lay under a double cloud: one was that after almost half a century of communist rule of most of it, there were many legacies of recent bitterness to grapple with, some by no means obvious. More obscure still was the emergence of the even older historical inheritances of a region whose components had no clearly defined ethnic reality. All that was clear was that for the first time in this century the fate of the peoples of south-eastern Europe was entirely and evidently in their own hands. The old dynastic empires of Habsburg and Ottoman had gone by 1919. The interference of Italian and German dictators had ended in 1945. In 1990, the Soviet scaffolding that held much of the region together had collapsed.

THE END OF YUGOSLAVIA

What followed was soon deeply discouraging. Issues re-emerged that went back beyond 1914, and even beyond the nineteenth century. Nowhere did this happen so bloodily as in Yugoslavia, where history has always weighed heavily upon the peoples who had come together in 1918 as the 'Kingdom of Serbs, Croats and Slovenes', amid hopes that the long-running sores of Macedonia and Bosnia might now be healed. The country had in 1929 changed its name to 'Yugoslavia' in an attempt to obliterate old divisions, accompanied by the establishment of a royal dictatorship. But the kingdom of Yugoslavia was always seen by too many of its subjects, Serbs and non-Serbs alike, as essentially a manifestation of an old historical dream of a 'Greater Serbia'. The new nation's greatest national festival was a Serbian one.[4] The dynasty that had seized back the Serbian throne in 1903 had assumed the throne of the new kingdom in 1918, to the irritation of the Montenegrins. Yugoslavia's second king, Alexander, was assassinated in 1934 in France, by a Macedonian aided by Croats acting with the support of the Hungarian and Italian governments. The bitterness of the country's own divisions had thus soon attracted outsiders to dabble in its affairs, and local politicians to seek outsiders' support; Croatians subsequently declared their own independence as a state once German troops arrived in 1941.

Such divisions were outstanding examples of the failures to solve

---

[4] It was, in fact, a commemoration of a fourteenth-century disaster, when (it could be argued) the Ottomans overthrew at Kosovo the medieval Serbian kingdom.

old problems. The Ottoman regime had for a long time provided conditions in which demographic and communal diversity could grow without uncontainable animosities arising between its subject peoples for it had been something of a lightning conductor, drawing off periodic outbursts of anger and rebellion against an oppressor, and thus easing the relations of peoples divided by language, ethnic origin and religion. Under Ottoman rule there had been a tendency not much resisted by its subjects to blur this diversity. They were treated as tolerated non-Muslims (or oppressed orthodox Christians, according to your point of view) and called 'Greeks', 'Bulgars', or by some other vaguely inclusive name. In the lands that made up the new Yugoslavia, though, the census of 1931 found it necessary to distinguish Serbo-Croats, Slovenes, Germans, Magyars, Romanians, Vlachs, Albanians, Turks, 'Other Slavs', Jews, Gypsies and Italians as categories for which it had to account.[5] 'Serbo-Croat' was itself a misleading label, lumping together as it did Montenegrins, Bosnians, Muslims, Macedonians and Bulgarians, as well as the Serbs and Croats who might speak the same language though Croats, being Roman Catholics, used Latin characters to write it, while the Orthodox Serbs used Cyrillic. Christian Yugoslavs, Catholic and Orthodox alike, while accounting between them for more than four-fifths of Yugoslavia's supposed believers, had at that time also to live with a substantial minority (11 per cent in 1931) of Muslims, some of them Bosnians, some Albanians.

Unsurprisingly, Yugoslavia also displayed wide disparities of custom, wealth and economic development. As late as 1950, the veil was still being worn by some of its Muslim women, nearly thirty years after Kemal abolished it in Turkey. Macedonia was one of those primitive parts of Europe where the Middle Ages had barely faded away, yet Slovenia was substantially urbanized and contained significant industry. Overall, what were mainly agricultural economies had been weighed down by fast-growing populations, though. Pressure on land had produced a proliferation of tiny holdings whose cultivators had been driven down further into poverty by economic depression in the 1930s. One of the poorest, most densely populated provinces was Kosovo. Since its acquisition by Serbia in 1913, it had been

[5] See table in A. Polonsky, *The Little Dictators* (London, 1975), p.162.

an aim of Belgrade governments to rid it of its Albanian inhabitants.

Yugoslav politics between the German wars turned out to be in the main about Croat–Serb antagonism. By 1939, government from Belgrade was detested by the Croats, who had spawned an extremist national movement already making approaches to Hitler. There was also a Croatian fascist movement, the *Ustaša*; much evil was to be heard of it during the three-sided civil war that broke out after the German invasion and occupation of 1941 between Croatians, the mainly Serb communists (themselves led by the Croatian Josef Broz, or 'Tito') and Serb royalists. This struggle began with a campaign of terror and ethnic cleansing launched by the *Ustaša* against the 2 million Serbs of the new Croatia (which included Bosnia and Herzegovina). It ended in communist victory in 1945, and there followed the containment of the nationalities by Tito's dictatorship, an effective system, somewhat reminiscent of the Ottoman model in its practical concessions to local élites. He emphasized policies of national equality within a federal structure. Forty-five years later and ten after Tito's death, old issues suddenly showed themselves still vigorously alive.

In 1990 Yugoslavia faced a tangle of troubles, economic and political alike. The federal government's attempts to deal with the first were accompanied by accelerating political fragmentation. Democratic self-determination finally undid the Tito achievement. Yugoslavs of different nationalities began to cast about to find ways of filling the political vacuum left by the collapse of communism. Parties formed representing Serb, Croat, Macedonian and Slovene interests as well as one in favour of the Yugoslav idea and the federation itself. Although by the end of 1990 all the republican governments except that of Macedonia rested on elected majorities, national minorities had even begun to make themselves heard inside the individual republics. Croatian Serbs, for instance, declared their own autonomy. There was serious bloodshed in Kosovo, four-fifths of whose inhabitants were by then Albanian. The proclamation of an independent republic there in 1990 had been a major symbolic affront to the Serbians – as well as of concern to the Greek and Bulgarian governments, whose predecessors had not ceased to cherish Macedonian ambitions since the days of the Balkan wars. Catholic Croatia and Slovenia then declared themselves independent of the Yugoslav federal republic in

June 1991 and by the end of the year Macedonia and Bosnia-Herzegovina had done the same.[6] Soon, the new republics were quarrelling with one another over the treatment of their minorities.

Slovenia had no large Serb population: Croatia and Bosnia had. In March 1991 sporadic fighting had begun in the north between Serb and Croat villages which drew in the official air and ground forces of the republics. It also broke out between Muslims and Serbs in Bosnia, foreshadowing, many feared, a further spread of ethnic conflict. Just before Christmas, to the embarrassment of other EC states, Germany gave official recognition to the new Croatia, urging its partners to follow suit; the EC did so, not all of its members contentedly, early in 1992. The prospect of outside intervention to achieve pacification, never strong, became remote after the USSR's warnings about the dangers of spreading local conflict to the international level. Meanwhile, it took little time for the Bosnian Serbs to excite wider and deeper antagonisms. They spoke of their opponents as 'Turks', and while Catholic Croatian clerics fanned the flames of conflict with the Orthodox Serbs, so there were Orthodox Serb clergy happy to set the conflict in a context of a supposed renewal of Islamic advance in Europe. Croatian and Serbian television were both soon alleging a Bosnian Muslim 'holy war' was in preparation. Anti-Muslim propaganda, though, had less resonance abroad; it even tended to rebound, as Bosnian Serb atrocities turned out to be so much more blatant and to fill headlines and television screens so much more compellingly than those also being committed by Bosnian Muslims.

The Serbian government (the only one in former Yugoslavia whose communist leaders were still in power ten years later) was in fact willing to seize the chance of settling its problems with mixed ethnic areas for good. The federal republic had been an assurance of Serbian ascendancy. The former Yugoslav army had been Serb-dominated. This gave Serbs an initial military advantage. Unlike Russia, when confronted with the wish of its former companion-republics to break away from its hegemony, Serbia chose to fight. Yet federal Yugoslavia

---

[6] Together with the division of Czechoslovakia, restored as one entity in 1945 after the Hitler era, into the two states of the Czech Republic and Slovakia on 1 June 1993, this may be counted as the final extinction of the Versailles settlement in central and eastern Europe.

was soon to be reduced merely to Serbia and Montnegro. The preservation of the federation in its old form soon ceased to be conceivable and a battle for the spoils ensued.

NATIONALITY AND ETHNICITY IN THE NEW EUROPE

Yugoslavia was by no means the only country to show potential for violence as its communist *ancien régime* came to an end. The disintegrations of 1989–91, even when they were not territorial, left millions of Europeans facing problems and difficulties set by their own histories, cultures and social and economic circumstance. Among the general facts to which they had all in a measure to submit was their need for legitimating principles and ideas. Most of eastern Europe also faced the paradox that in so far as the region had possessed 'modernizing' élites, and whether they had been effective or not, they were usually to be found in the old communist hierarchies. Unavoidably, in many countries professionals, managers and experts whose careers had been made within the communist structures continued in important roles simply because there was no one to replace them. Another problem was the fickleness of populations which, now voting freely but which, as the euphoria of political revolution ebbed, began to hark back (as Russians were to do) to the security and economic well-being, much exaggerated in retrospect, of the old days. This trend was most marked, unsurprisingly, where economic conditions deteriorated most rapidly.

As peoples cast about for a new basis for the state, it became clear that the only plausible candidate was, for good or ill, the nationalism that had so bedevilled their past politics, sometimes for centuries. Old antagonisms had quickly surfaced. In 1990, at the time of the Romanian revolution, there was evident tension between Romanians and Hungarians living in Romanian Transylvania (just over 7 per cent of the Romanian population is reckoned to be of Hungarian descent). It surfaced three years later in demands for Magyar autonomy within the Romanian state. There were other countries, too, where Hungarian minorities were substantial: proportional to its population Slovakia had a larger Hungarian component than Romania (10.8 per cent in 1998). But the most bloody evidence of the potential destructiveness of persistent national feeling in Europe continued to be provided within what had been Yugoslavia.

Other historical ethnic confrontations had been ended or reshaped years before, by the Second World War. Above all the fate of European Jewry had been determined. The Holocaust had brought to an end the story of eastern Europe as the centre of world Jewry. In 1901 three-quarters of the world's Jews had lived there, mostly in the Russian empire. In those once Yiddish-speaking areas, only a little more than 10 per cent of Jews now live; nearly half of the rest now live in English-speaking countries, and some 30 per cent of them in Israel. For thirty years after 1947 she provided a territorial focus for migrant Jews, and many of the survivors of the great persecution were drawn there. In eastern Europe communist parties anxious to exploit traditional popular antisemitism (not least in the Soviet Union) encouraged emigration by some harrying and by judicial persecution. In some countries the outcome was a virtual elimination of the Jewish population as a significant demographic element. Poland was the outstanding example; the 200,000 Polish Jews surviving in 1945 had soon found themselves again victims of traditional pogrom and harassment. Sometimes they were murdered, but most had emigrated when able to do so. By 1990 those who remained numbered a mere 6,000. This left nearly a million Jews still in the CIS republics (mainly in Russia and the Ukraine), as representatives of the centuries-old eastern European Jewish community. The heart of that community, though, had gone. Paradoxically, France in recent years has been alone among European countries in actually experiencing a significant rise in her own Jewish population as immigrants from Islamic North Africa raised its numbers to about half a million.

In some western European countries, too, nationalist recalcitrance flourished among other minorities. Basque separatists terrorized Spain. Belgians showed increasing signs of hostility between Walloons and Flemings. Northern Ireland, though, was probably the most striking instance, not least because it proved so unintelligible to outsiders. Unionist and nationalist feeling continued in the 1990s to block the road to settlement in Ulster. The roots of resistance to a solution by concession did not lie in London but in the province itself, the last place in Europe where the battles of the Reformation and counter-Reformation were still being fought in a desperate and symbolic form.[7] An Anglo-Irish agreement made by Mrs Thatcher's government in 1985 had acknowledged the Irish Republic's right to a role in discussion of the future of Ulster and set up new machinery to provide for it, but it had not reduced violence there. At last in 1994, though, there began a ceasefire respected by the terrorist organizations of both sides in the interests of peaceful discussion of Ireland's constitutional future between all the interested parties. Although it ended tragically after a little less than eighteen months, this remission of violence then appeared to have had positive psychological consequences. After the resumption of terrorism a new (Labour) government came to power at Westminster in 1997, which was willing to take the important symbolic step of opening direct negotiations with Sinn Fein, the political movement which masked the terrorists of the IRA. Before the end of the year Sinn Fein representatives had been received by the British prime minister at 10 Downing Street, something not seen since the negotiations that set up the Irish Free State over seventy-five years earlier. In cooperation with the Irish government, British initiatives succeeded, against the odds, in winning in 1998 the acquiescence of the official leaders of Sinn Fein and of the Ulster Unionists in putting to an all-Ireland referendum proposals which went further than any earlier ones in institutionalizing both safeguards for the nationalist minority in the north and the historic tie of the north with the United Kingdom. This, of course, implied a fundamental change in what the sovereignty of the Crown might in future mean (it went far further than the changes the British government was contemporaneously introducing in the government of Scotland and Wales). On both sides of the border, it achieved substantial popular support. It left the detail, still potentially very divisive, for the politicians to manage and to do so in a context in which the lunatic fringe on both sides of the old nationalist–unionist divide might still try to wreck any peace process by further atrocities. A particularly savage example in the summer

---

[7] I am told that during the 1980s there was at least one British cabinet discussion of the possibility of abandoning Ulster altogether to its own devices. It seems plausible.

in the little town of Omagh, though, seemed actually to nerve the mainstream nationalist and unionist politicians to even greater efforts to ensure a peaceful solution.

EUROPEAN INTEGRATION

On New Year's Day 1990 the president of France startled the world (and some of his countrymen too) by speaking of 'one' Europe, embracing all its nations excepting, but only for the moment, the USSR. Whether prompted by cunning, euphoria, exasperation, pious aspiration or the simple wish to fly a trial balloon, his words indicated how far the debate on Europe had come since the days of Monnet. Since 1986 new passports issued to citizens of member states of the EC had carried the words 'European Community' as well as the name of a member state. The next few years were to show how difficult it would be to sustain generous interpretations of what it might mean, but there seemed to be a reviving optimism about European integration, in marked contrast to two decades of foot-dragging. The Community had faced growing practical difficulties in giving effect to what its member states had agreed in principle. Three of its institutions, the Council of Ministers of member states, the Commission and the Court of Justice, seemed to be working; the European parliament was still finding it hard to establish a role. Common fisheries and transport policies provoked difficulties that were frequently visible on television screens. Fluctuations in exchange rates were another awkwardness; a devaluation of the French franc in 1969 and the end of dollar convertibility and the Bretton Woods system in 1971 had been followed by several inadequate attempts to restore stability as the economies of EC members reeled under the impact of the oil crisis. This contributed to the institutional bickering (particularly on economic and financial matters) which reminded people of the limits to any integration so far achieved.

In the end, though, it also helped to turn governments back towards more positive steps on the road to integration. As debate slowly continued there was solid evidence of encouraging success for the European economies. By the middle of that decade two-thirds of foreign investment in the USA (which had resumed in the 1970s its pre-1914 status as a major recipient of foreign investment) was European. From 1970 onwards, too, western Europe had accounted for the largest share of world trade. Such facts, together with a growing realization that other nations would wish to join it, encouraged further crystallization of ideas about the Community's future. The first direct elections to the European parliament, too, had been held in 1979. Some Europeans began again to think that while greater unity, a habit of cooperation, and increasing prosperity were prerequisites of political independence for the continent, such independence would always remain hollow unless Europe, too, could turn herself into a superpower. Meanwhile, there were outsiders keen to join an organization that offered such attractive bribes to the poor. Greece did so in 1981 and Spain and Portugal in 1986.

The latter turned out to be a decisive year. It was then agreed that 1992 should bring movement beyond a mere customs union to a single, integrated, border-free internal market. Capital, goods, services and people were to move freely without let or hindrance across national borders – or so the theory ran. The negotiations about this were to prove the last for a decade in which member states could be brought to agree on fundamentals. The Single European Act that came into effect in 1987 supplemented the Treaty of Rome by setting out the agreed goal of abolition in 1993 of all non-tariff barriers to intra-Community trade. Ambitious as such a policy might be thought, even on its own, the treaty also envisaged the coordination of foreign policies between member states, and defined 'social and economic cohesion' as new aims for the Community – a vague phrase covering greater uniformity in the provision of welfare, conditions of employment and standards of living – and higher expenditure on Community 'structural' policies. This by no means at once made for greater fellow-feeling as the implications sank in, but it was indisputably a sign of movement. So, many believed, was the inauguration in 1987 of a European Monetary System (EMS) agreed to be an indispensable step towards a common European currency (though the strains soon imposed on the EMS, by German reunification and the damage it did to the *Deutschmark*, quickly proved too much for some of its members). Europe's leaders finally agreed at Maastricht in December

1991 on new arrangements for the single European market and a timetable for full economic and monetary union to be achieved not later than 1999, with reservations and special arrangements (once more) for the cautious British.

QUALIFIED REORIENTATION: THE UNITED KINGDOM

That insular people had undergone in the 1980s an exciting decade, which had begun in an unpromising atmosphere of economic stagnation. There was little reason then to expect that they were soon to fight what may well prove to have been the last war in defence of overseas possessions by a European nation. Yet when in 1982 the British prime minister, Mrs Thatcher, found herself unexpectedly presiding over the reconquest of the Falkland Islands after their brief occupation by Argentinian forces, her instincts to fight for the principles of international law and territorial sovereignty and for the islanders' right to say by whom they should be governed proved to be well attuned to the British popular mood of the day. The outcome was a major feat of arms and an important psychological and diplomatic success. After an uncertain start (unsurprising, given its traditional sensitivity over Latin America), the United States had provided important practical and clandestine help.[8] Chile, too, uneasy with her restive neighbour, was not disposed to object to British covert operations from her territory on the mainland of South America. More important still, most of the EC countries joined in isolating Argentina in the UN, where resolutions condemned the Argentinian action. Notably, the British had from the start the support (not always so readily forthcoming in the past) of the French government, which knew a threat to sovereign rights when it saw one.

In the United Kingdom, the prestige of Mrs Thatcher rose with national morale; abroad, too, her standing was enhanced, and for the rest of the decade this gave her an influence with other heads of

---

[8] The North Atlantic Treaty of 1949 did not extend its protection to the Falkland Isles; it covered (Art. 6) only 'Islands under the jurisdiction of any of the Parties in the North Atlantic area north of the Tropic of Cancer'.

state (notably Mr Reagan) which British strength could scarcely have sustained by itself. A parallel with the late General de Gaulle was sometimes made; it was to the point, for not everyone agreed that her influence was always usefully deployed in international affairs and they had said the same of the general in his day. Mrs Thatcher's personal convictions, preconceptions and prejudices, like his, were always very visible. She, like him, was no European, if that meant blurring a very personal vision of national interest. Her own was by no means always exaggerated or illusory, though. Realistically, her government was the one that at last removed Rhodesia and Central Africa as issues from British politics in 1980. While sometimes violent in her language, too, she showed a sense of the limits of the possible in her negotiations with the European Community at least until her closing years in office.

Mrs Thatcher held power for eleven years, longer than any other British prime minister had done in this century. It was clear before she resigned that she had transformed British politics, and perhaps the terms of cultural and social debate, dissolving an old *bien-pensant* and too long unexamined consensus about national goals. This, together with her assertive radicalism (notably in stripping trade unions of their legal privileges and promoting 'de-nationalization' through the sale of public property) and her provocative rhetoric, awoke both unusual enthusiasm and unusual animosity at home, as well as interest and some admiration abroad. Yet she failed to achieve the aims of reducing public spending and the interference of central government in the national life that she had announced when she took up office. Central government a decade later was playing more, not less, of a role in British society, and spending more of the tax-payer's money (that allocated to health and social security had gone up in real terms by a third since 1979 though without satisfying greatly increased demands). By 1990, many of her political colleagues had come to believe that although she had won three general election victories in a row (a unique achievement in British politics), she would be a vote-loser in the next contest, which could not be far away. Faced with a collapse of loyalty and support, she resigned. Her successor as prime minister was something of an unknown quantity, without long exposure in the front rank of politics behind him.

CHANGES IN CHINA

Since 1978 China had been moving along a path of cautious and controlled modernization. As Deng Xiaoping put it, her rulers were 'crossing the river by feeling for the stones'. No other communist country was going so far, or fast, in that year, though. This approach looked to some (uneasy veterans of the heroic days of the revolution among them) like creeping liberalism; and in due course the USSR's experience alarmed them even more. Yet it implied no weakening of the party's will to power or of its grasp upon it. China's rulers determined to remain firmly in control throughout. Besides the old Chinese social disciplines they had other advantages to exploit. There was the relief felt by millions that the Cultural Revolution had been left behind, the cult of Mao's memory, however qualified, and the acumen of some among the party's leaders in deciding (contrary to what official Marxism as expounded in Moscow still said as the 1980s began) that economic rewards should flow through the system to the peasant. On the other hand, they had to face the fact that government had never in communist China been able to achieve the degree of central bureaucratic control won by Moscow in the USSR, whatever it might aspire to. True, this had also a positive economic aspect: in the 1980s and 1990s, provincial initiatives counted for much in economic development, and favoured experiment.

Deng Xiaoping continued to dominate the Chinese political scene in the 1980s, but had to work through a collective leadership which included conservatives who would have liked to follow Stalinist programmes of centralization and investment in state-owned heavy industry. Scope was nonetheless now to be given to local and community enterprise and the profit motive. Commercial connexions with non-communist countries began to be encouraged. The aim was to resume the process of technological and industrial modernization interrupted by the Cultural Revolution and to recognize and reward the success already evident in decentralized economic activity. The major public definition of the new course in appropriate language in 1981 was of the first importance. Nonetheless, no formal break with the past by the party could be expected and Deng had to wait to exploit his ascendancy until the Party Congress of 1982 had further denounced 'leftism' as an obstacle to modernization.

For all the comings and goings in CCP leadership and the coded debates and sloganizing which continued to obscure political realities, the 1980s were in fact characterized by pragmatic policies not always unlike those of Mao. The question which for thirty years had been at the heart of the party's history, and therefore at the heart of China's, too, was settled: modernization, which above all meant economic growth, was at last being given precedence and was to be led, as by now nowhere else in the communist world, by a secure and confident regime. The downgrading of dogma remained hard to acknowledge (when, startlingly, the secretary-general of the CPC incautiously committed himself in 1986 to the view that 'Marx and Lenin cannot solve our problems', he was quickly dismissed) and Marxist rhetoric still pervaded government. The language in which policy debates were cast was obscuring, though its adoption is comprehensible. There persisted in the ruling élite a solid belief in the need for positive planning of the economy in pursuit of the major goals of national economic strength, the improvement of living standards, and a broad egalitarianism. What was now dominant, though, was a new recognition of the practical limits of such planning, a willingness to try to discriminate more carefully between what was and was not within the scope of effective regulation, and a wish to use and therefore expand markets. Critics complained that China was resuming the 'capitalist road'. Tender consciences had been soothed by the adoption at the 1982 Party Congress of the mantra 'socialism with Chinese characteristics', while practical expediency assured the recognition at every step of local interests and regional differences.

New slogans – 'to get rich is glorious' – were coined to encourage the development of village industrial and commercial enterprise out of the 'communes' and 'brigades' of the era of the Great Leap. By the mid-1980s a half of rural income was drawn from industrial employment.[9] The road to development was sign-posted with 'four modernizations'. Special economic areas, enclaves for free trade with

[9] Gray points out ('Rethinking Chinese Economic Reform', p.151) the interesting fact that Taiwan and China are the only two countries where the proportion of industry located in rural areas has increased in the course of industrialization.

the capitalist world, were set up; the first was at Canton, the historic centre of Chinese trade with the West. They grew rapidly.[10] By 1986 China had become the second largest producer of coal in the world, and the fourth largest of steel. GDP had risen at a rate of more than 10 per cent a year between 1978 and 1986, while industrial output doubled in value in that time. Per capita peasant income nearly tripled and by 1988 the average peasant family was estimated to have about six months' income in the savings bank. Taking a longer perspective, the progress is even more striking. The value of foreign trade multiplied roughly twenty-five times in per capita terms between 1950 and the middle of the 1980s. The new policy was not without costs, and as higher prices encouraged farmers and gave them profits to plough back, the city dweller began to feel the effects of inflation. Foreign debt rose, too. Some blamed on the new line growing signs of crime and corruption. Yet of economic success there can be no doubt. Mainland China had begun to show that an economic 'miracle' like that of Taiwan might be within her grasp. In 1985 state investment in the planned sector of the economy was frozen and state enterprise managers were encouraged to take more entrepreneurial roles.

The social consequences of such changes were also often clearly beneficial. Urban growth followed migration to the cities from an over-stocked countryside, higher food consumption and life expectancy were registered, along with a virtual end to the worst ravages of the great killing and crippling diseases of the old regime. A huge inroad was made into mass illiteracy. China's population growth had long prompted stern measures of intervention in attempts to slow it down, and it did not, as did India's, devour the fruits of economic development (if official statistics were to be depended upon, indeed, an eventual demographic stabilization might just be in sight, thirty years away). The new line continued explicitly to link modernization to national strength, too. Thus it reflected the aspirations of China's reformers nearly a century before. China's international weight, already apparent as early as the Korean war, now showed itself more obviously in the exaction of concessions in diplomatic negotiation.

One important symbol was agreement with the British in 1984 over

---

[10] Shenzu, with 20,000 inhabitants in 1980, had 2 million ten years later.

the transfer of Hong Kong when the lease covering part of its territory ran out (in 1997). A similar agreement with the Portuguese provided for the resumption of Macao (in 1999) too. It was a blemish on the general recognition of China's due standing that Vietnam among neighbouring countries remained hostile to her; their relations at one time degenerating into open warfare when the two countries disputed control of Cambodia, anciently part of the old zone of Chinese imperial hegemony. The Taiwanese seemed for a time somewhat reassured; there were promises from Beijing that, as in the case of Hong Kong, the eventual reincorporation of the island in the territory of the republic should not endanger its economic system. Like the establishment of the special trading enclaves on the mainland where external commerce could flourish, such statements underlined the importance China's new rulers attached to commerce as a channel of modernization. It was apparent to many Chinese that China was beginning to enjoy a new respect and status abroad. One striking, if paradoxical, sign after the agreement over Hong Kong was an official state visit in 1986 by Queen Elizabeth II, the head of (in Chinese eyes) the first of the predator states of the nineteenth century. Another was that Iran and Pakistan both sought military aid from China.

As permitted rises in prices for farm produce built up rural purchasing power, they led to growing demand for capital goods for use in farming as well as consumer goods. This made for contentment in the countryside. By 1985 the family unit was back as the dominant form of rural production over much of China; without formal reintroduction of private ownership, households were allowed to enjoy the profits of higher production. The World Bank estimated that Chinese agricultural production was rising 6 per cent per annum between 1978 and 1984. Nevertheless, prosperity in the end brought difficulties. Foreign debt shot up. Farm incomes had begun to stagnate. Inflation was running at an annual rate of about 30 per cent by 1989. There was anger over evident corruption. Divisions in the leadership (some following upon the deaths and illness among the gerontocrats who dominated the Party) which led to intrigue and jockeying for position were widely known. Those believing in a reassertion of political control began to gain ground. There were signs that they were manoeuvring to win over or bypass Deng Xiaoping. Western observers and perhaps some Chinese had been led by the policy of economic liberalization to take unrealistic and over-optimistic views about political relaxation. The changes in eastern Europe stimulated further hopes of this. Perhaps some illusions were just beginning to crumble, when the Chinese government suffered a nasty shock.

TIANANMEN

Events in the USSR had naturally been followed with special interest in the second power of the communist world. Their disputed, ill-demarcated borders had brought China and the Soviet Union into limited armed conflict many times. Tension over them had reached something of a climax in the late 1960s, after which followed a decade or so of fruitless diplomatic exchange over territorial claims and counter-claims. In 1981 these flared up again into hostility when a Soviet–Afghan treaty raised the question of the status of another 20,000 or so square miles of territory that had been occupied by the tsar's soldiers and officials in the 1890s and were now claimed by China. Both nations, though, were still formally Marxist, and this was an important ideological tie. In the 1950s there had been a CCP slogan: 'the Soviet Union's today is our tomorrow': in the 1990s this might still be thought true, but in a different and uneasy sense, and it was repeated as a joke among Beijing intellectuals.[11] China's rulers had good grounds for worry about the direction in which events had appeared to be going in the USSR even in the early 1980s; by the end of the decade they were thoroughly alarmed by them.

Meanwhile, an austerity programme imposed in early 1989 to deal with acute inflation provoked a wave of new demands from students. Encouraged by the presence in the governing oligarchy of sympathizers with liberalization (notably Deng's protégé, Zhao Ziyang, the general secretary of the CCP), they sought to make the Party and government enter into a dialogue with a newly formed and unofficial Student Union about corruption and reform. Posters and rallies began to

[11] J. A. R. Miles, *The Legacy of Tiananmen. China in Disarray* (Ann Arbor, 1996), pp.41–2.

champion calls for greater 'democracy'. The leadership became alarmed. It refused to recognize the Union, fearing it might be the harbinger of a new Red Guards movement. Student demonstrations took place in several cities and, as the seventieth anniversary of the May 4th movement approached, activists invoked the memory of that heroic episode so as to give a broad patriotic colour to their campaign. They could hardly arouse the countryside and had little success in the southern cities, but, encouraged by the obvious sympathies of Zhao Ziyang, began a mass hunger strike that won some popular support, particularly in Beijing. When Mr Gorbachev arrived there on a state visit intended by the Party leadership to provide further reassuring evidence of China's international standing, his presence was bound to remind his hosts of what was going on in the USSR and eastern Europe as a result of policies of liberalization. Would-be reformers felt encouraged and conservatives frightened.

The most senior members of the government, including Deng Xiaoping, seem to have been very much frightened, as well as humiliated, by the turbulence the Gorbachev visit provoked. Given the presence of western television reporters, too, they could no longer control the information about it reaching the outside world, or even the Chinese people. Widespread disorder, even a new Cultural Revolution, might be in the offing, some feared, if things got out of control. On 20 May martial law was declared. There were signs for a moment that the government might not be able to impose its will, but the army stood behind them. The student leaders had focused their efforts in Beijing in an encampment in Tiananmen Square, where, forty years before, Mao had proclaimed the foundation of the People's Republic. From one of the gates of the old Forbidden City a huge portrait of him looked down on an exotic portent and symbol: a plaster figure of a 'Goddess of Democracy', deliberately evocative of New York's Statue of Liberty. In another gesture that also showed how much they owed to other western myths, students encamped in the square sang the Internationale, the old anthem of the Second International, as they awaited the forces brought to clear them out. That suggests both the complexity and the incoherence of the opposition movement. It may also indicate its alienation from much that more traditionally minded Chinese felt to be important.

On 2 June the first military units entered the capital's suburbs on their way to the square. The repression that followed was ruthless. There was resistance with extemporized weapons and barricades, but the soldiers forced their way through. On 4 June the students and a few sympathizers were driven out by rifle fire, tear gas, and the brutal crushing of their encampment under the tracks of the tanks which swept into the square. Killing went on for some days, and perhaps as many as 10,000 arrests followed. The world had been watching the demonstrators' encampment on its television screens for days and what television showed of the last few hours of the crisis aroused almost universal foreign disapproval. Yet, as so often in China, it is still hard to know exactly what happened. The number of those killed in the square is disputed. Estimates have run from 400 to 2,000; a figure lower than 1,000 seems likely, but there is no certainty. There was disorder, some of it serious, in over eighty cities. Perhaps the leadership had acted in a way many Chinese deplored, and perhaps the regime was less popular than a few years earlier as a consequence. Yet the masses did not rise to support the protesters; they were often against them. Nor, objectively, can it be confidently asserted that China would have been bound to benefit if the party had given way to the student movement (which, in any case, it saw as a renewal of the anarchy of the Red Guards). The experience of the USSR in combining democratization with economic reform, too, was discouraging to the Chinese who had benefited from the 1980s.[12]

In the immediate aftermath, the party and ruling hierarchy were somewhat in disarray. Vigorous attempts to impose political orthodoxy followed. Neo-Marxist slogans were heard again. Discipline was reimposed in the party. Economic liberalization was for a time reined in. China, it was soon clear, was not going to go the way of eastern Europe or the USSR. But where was she going? Perhaps the safest conclusion to be drawn at this stage is that she was once again moving to her own rhythms, stimulated by forces peculiar to her. The acts of her rulers cannot easily be interpreted in categories drawn from the western world, for all the Marxist and democratic rhetoric

[12] The comparison is developed interestingly by P. Nolan in *China's Rise, Russia's Fall: Politics, Economics and Planning in the Transition from Stalinism* (Basingstoke, 1995).

of regime and protesters alike. China after Tiananmen Square still baffled observers and futurologists by a seeming indifference to or immunity from currents outside her borders, even as she paid official lip-service to a western ideology. Two thousand years of history do not easily go away.

27

Fin-de-siècle

PROBLEMS OF PEACEKEEPING

The elimination of resident populations by means of murder, deport-ation, rape, intimidation, arson and starvation had gone on in the Ottoman empire for centuries. In 1991 such intimidatory pressures were relaunched by Serbs against their Croat neighbours in Slavonia. The victims were not slow to reply in the areas where they had the upper hand and for the next four years, the world became dismally familiar with reports of 'ethnic cleansing'.

Federal Yugoslavia had quickly been reduced merely to Serbia and Montenegro in terms of undisputed territory. Any hope of preserving the old federation had soon ceased to be conceivable. A battle for the spoils was bound to follow. Croatia and Slovenia had quickly established their own independence by throwing back the formerly Yugoslav (but preponderantly Serbian) army. Serbia attempted to seize Dubrovnik and thus achieve a port on the Adriatic. The struggle in Bosnia was bound to be especially difficult; three communities were in play there. Muslim, Croat and Serb were much mixed up in their distribution, living typically in scattered villages of one community or another or in separate quarters of shared towns (among them those of Sarajevo, the capital of Bosnia). In March 1992 a referendum that Bosnian Serbs boycotted, but in which Croats and Muslims both voted in favour, provided a majority for Bosnian independence. At this point, Bosnian Serbs took to arms to fight for Sarajevo and other areas they proclaimed to be Serb. They were soon supported by the Serbian army. This led to the imposition of sanctions on Serbian external trade by the United Nations, the last effective act of that body in the whole sorry business for nearly three years. Europe as an entity proved able to do nothing. French, Dutch and British soldiers were sent by the UN to keep the peace in Bosnia, but could not, given the limited powers allowed to them. A united political will and the machinery to deploy effective military force took a long time to appear, and had to come from Washington. Only in August 1995 were NATO forces released to undertake (under UN authorization) offensive (air) action against the Bosnian Serbs, who had consistently ignored or thwarted attempts to arrive at a settlement as well as guarantees of 'safe' areas for the civilian population of Bosnia.

In the end, the Bosnian abscess was lanced by atrocity. The air action of August 1995 was made possible by the behaviour of Serb forces in the Muslim enclave of Srebrenica in July, where, after over-running the area, they took away 4,000 Muslim prisoners and murdered them in cold blood. This was too much for the American government, which threw its weight behind authorizing the use of NATO air power and of the guns and heavy mortars of the UN peacekeeping force around Sarajevo to enforce the peace – or, rather, to make it, as opposed to merely preserving it. It also encouraged new Croat and Muslim offensives against the Serbs in northern and western Bosnia that speedily won dramatic successes.[1] This turned the tide and led to the formal desertion of the Bosnian Serbs by the Serbian government in Belgrade. The Bosnian Serbs were thus finally and reluctantly brought to accept a ceasefire, and the presidents of Serbia, Croatia and Bosnia met for peace negotiations at an air force base in Dayton, Ohio, in November 1995.

Something like 200,000 people had by then died. The International Red Cross in due course listed by name 14,000 Bosnian Muslim men who disappeared and took the view that there was little chance of ever finding out what happened to them. The destruction, in countries far from rich, was considerable. The cost of ending the war was enormous (Bosnia absorbed nearly the whole UN peacekeeping budget). Yet it was easier to fund contingents for the 60,000 strong NATO force sent to Bosnia to supervise the necessary withdrawals

---

[1] The Croats had no special sympathy for the Muslims, but were inflamed by the plight of Croats in areas claimed by Serbs.

and boundary delimitations than to devise measures and find means for reconstruction. The essentials of the agreements reached at Dayton were that Bosnia should be partitioned. Two entities were created from it, one a Muslim–Croat federation, one a Serb republic. The Croatian government had been able to secure all the territory that it wanted in the north; Serbia had been forced to abandon her hopes of territorial gain elsewhere, but was gratified to be released from the bite of the sanctions which had done her much damage. Muslim Bosnia had survived (which was more than had seemed likely at times) at a heavy cost in blood. The Bosnian Serbs, while at least at the outset complying with the terms of partition, bitterly rejected the whole settlement in spirit. They offered no grounds for hope that their old aspirations had been laid to rest. At the end of 1998 there were still, for safety's sake, 5,000 NATO troops 'keeping the peace' in Bosnia.

All too soon, it was evident that the troubles of the former Yugoslavia were not over elsewhere, either. New foci of instability continued to appear. Even after Dayton, one third of Serbia's population was non-Serbian. Magyars in the north, Muslims in the Sanjak of Novibazar, and, most evidently, an Albanian majority in Kosovo posed the question whether Serbia could survive in unmodified form, and, indeed, whether even a much reduced Yugoslavia could, given signs of Montenegrin discontent with what was left of the federal republic.

Albania was also showing alarming symptoms of strife in the mid-1990s. That small country was the creation of the treaty of Bucharest of 1913; half the Albanian people did not live within its boundaries. Its economic condition at the moment it emerged from communist rule had been, even by the standards of the Balkans, appalling. It suffered a further blow early in 1997 when a financial scandal deprived many Albanians of such savings as they had and drove many to near-desperation. One outcome was increased disorder (the first German soldier to open fire on foreign soil since 1945 did so against Albanian marauders that summer) and another was a surge of emigration. Italy, only 100 miles away, had to bear the brunt of this. The difficulties caused in that country almost brought about the fall of the Italian government when it proposed to send soldiers to Albania as part of a UN force to contain the banditry and looting of arsenals which reigned there. In the event, the proposal fell through, and Albania was left to face on its own the prospect of its first free elections with, as one Italian put it, half the electorate going to the polls carrying a Kalashnikov.[2]

Continuing and bloody disorder in Muslim Albania would have mattered less had it not been for Kosovo. Tito had made it clear in 1948 that Kosovo would never be conceded to its neighbour, Albania, although ruled as part of the Italian sector of the Axis occupation during the Second World War. From 1963, though, it had enjoyed a measure of provincial autonomy until the Serbs brutally removed it in 1989. Soon, Kosovars could reflect on the partitioning of Bosnia-Herzegovina; perhaps their problems or even those of Macedonia as a whole, might also now be solved by ethnic separation, some of them thought. By the summer of 1998, though, Serbian 'police' operations against those whom they called terrorists, the self-styled 'Kosovo Liberation Army' (such was the state of distrust in the area that this force was alleged by some to be a provocative invention of the Serbs themselves), had led to enough violence to start a flow of emigration across the border to Albania.

As reports of persecution of Kosovars multiplied, outsiders once again began hurriedly and unhappily to discuss what might be done about the latest of the problems of order in former Yugoslavia. Soon, the American Secretary of State was being denounced as an 'Islamic lobbyist' by a Yugoslav information minister.[3] A cautiously measured but, it seemed, growing American willingness to deploy air power against the Serbs had to be reconciled with the certainty of Russian disapproval. Although he had helped to bring the Bosnian Serbs to the negotiating table at Dayton, Mr Yeltsin was clearly unwilling to ignore Russians' traditional popular sympathy for their Orthodox fellow-Slav cousins in Belgrade, at a moment when he faced severe political challenges at home. Domestic political constraints – notably, mid-term congressional and gubernatorial elections – also made it difficult for Mr Clinton to envisage operations that might cost Ameri-

[2] Sergio Romano, in the *Financial Times*, 16 May 1997. Kalashnikov is a name covering a wide range of semi-automatic rifles, now used as basic infantry weapons round the world, and modelled on an originally Russian design.
[3] *The Economist*, 18 April 1998.

can lives. Nonetheless, vague menaces brought about (though with much foot-dragging) the withdrawal of some Serbian 'police' forces and their heavy equipment from Kosovo in October 1998. A draft plan for the province's future within Yugoslavia was put forward. But tension was mounting in Macedonia, whose pro-Serb government had been overthrown in November, and early in the New Year violence was renewed against the Kosovars. The threat of international intervention having by early 1999 lost its deterrent power for Serbia, Nato air forces were in March at last launched against Yugoslav targets. Belgrade was to be forced to admit a peacekeeping force to Kosovo to protect its Albanian population, which was by now, in fact, pouring in tens of thousands into their neighbours' countries. There had been no such UN authorization of military operations as had been the case in Bosnia. What was under way, too, was novel: the armed coercion of a sovereign state over its behaviour towards its own citizens.

Even before this crisis had been detonated, too, American policy had suffered a setback in the Gulf area. Attempts to carry out an effective scrutiny of Iraq's capacity to produce biological, chemical and even nuclear weapons had fizzled out with the ending of Iraqi cooperation in November 1998. The economic sanctions imposed years before by the Security Council as a way of bringing Saddam Hussein to heel were already by then undergoing increasing criticism (and some deliberate undermining) by some of its members. As before, the United States, with British support, prepared to act. Both countries got ready to mount a new bombing campaign against Iraq. Just in time, the Iraqi government stepped back. The UN inspectors were readmitted with new assurances of cooperation and the bombers were recalled. It was only a matter of days, though, before the UN team withdrew again, claiming it was unable to work effectively. This time, the United States did not hold back. Four nights of Anglo-American bombing and missile attacks were represented as another success for international law and order.

Yet long delays and now a lack of international support had shown the weaknesses of superpower. It had taken a long time for the Clinton administration to nerve itself to what seemed likely: pictures on television of Iraqi women and children wounded and dying amid the ruins of their homes, as there had been pictures of Vietnamese women and children dying twenty-five years earlier (though in 1998 there were not, in fact, many). It was not likely that an American government would long be able to resist a popular reaction of pity and a demand for cessation in such circumstances. More revealingly still, at no point was it even hinted that American ground forces might re-enter the Middle East in offensive operations. In 1992–3 they had been committed in support of a UN operation in Somalia in an attempt to bring order and an effective distribution of food to that suffering country. For a time, a majority of the 40,000-strong UN force there was American. Once, though, a number of American soldiers had been killed (and the American public had been shocked by television pictures of the maltreatment of the bodies of an American helicopter crew), the president announced that the withdrawal of most of them would shortly follow.[4]

Yet in 1998, American policy acknowledged as its revolutionary aim the overthrow of Saddam Hussein and his regime. Congress had already voted large sums of money for the support of Iraqi opposition groups. But the dictator was not removed by the December bombing, whatever damage his regime suffered. In fact, though proclaimed a technical triumph (no American or British casualties were suffered), the attack was by no means an undisputed and convincing military success, and was certainly a public relations failure. Whatever damage it may have done to Iraq's capacity to produce weapons of mass destruction, it had deeply troubled other Arab states and enraged Muslims worldwide while doing nothing to ensure the continuing security of Israel. Nor did it make it easier to see on what basis the UN inspection teams could return to Iraq. The economic sanctions (about which Iraq complained with great propaganda effect) were still in place, but had not only proved very blunt instruments but were now under criticism in the Security Council more than ever. There, and in the eyes of the world, too (especially in Muslim countries), Great Britain had to share the discredit the operation had attracted. Over the whole operation, finally, hung a nasty suspicion, justified or

[4] As it did, though American support was again made available briefly to cover a total UN withdrawal in 1995, after the Pakistan, Indian and Egyptian units left on site in the previous year had proved incapable even of assuring their own safety.

not, that its timing had not been unconnected with the American president's wish to seek domestic political support as a critical vote on his possible impeachment drew near. It was not obvious three months later that the Kosovo operation promised a better outcome.

EUROPE AFTER MAASTRICHT

Maastricht had been a step further towards a real union, opening the way to a single currency and an autonomous central bank to regulate it.[5] It required that national governments achieve certain criteria of fitness to participate in the EMU; they specified admissible levels for national debt, budget deficit and inflation. Maastricht also gave citizenship of the European Union to the nationals of all member states and laid down an obligation on its members to impose certain common standards in work practices and some social benefits. Finally, the treaty extended the area over which EU policy might be made by majority votes. All this looked like a significant accretion of centralized power, although in an effort to reassure the suspicious the treaty also set out agreement to the principle of 'subsidiarity', a word rooted in Catholic social teaching; it indicated that there should be limits to the competence of the Commission of Brussels in interfering with the details of national administration. As for European defence and security policy, this was soon all too plainly in hopeless disarray over events in Bosnia.

The Danes rejected Maastricht in a referendum the following year. A similar test in France produced only a slim majority in its favour, and the British government (even after winning carefully negotiated special safeguards) was hard-pressed to win the parliamentary vote on the issue: several 'rebels' in the governing Conservative party voted against their leader, and a split appeared which was to cripple the party when it next faced the electors. It was a difficulty in every country that so far as there was real debate about Europe's future, most people did not understand it. European voters thought for the most part only in terms of protecting or damaging traditional sectional

[5] After Maastricht, the European Community was called the European Union (EU).

and national interests, which were bound to loom larger as economic conditions worsened in the early 1990s. Such terms tended to focus debate around allegations of encroachment by the powers of the Commission at Brussels on member states, and the comparative fairness or unfairness of individual countries' use or abuse of the Union's rules. It was specially unfortunate that at a delicate moment the seemingly inevitable tactlessness and triviality of many Commission decisions on matters requiring enforcement by national governments was thrown into higher relief by the occupation of the presidency of the Commission by a Frenchman who was highly articulate and vocal about his ambitions for a Europe which would only too obviously concentrate still more power at Brussels. Two modes of European integration still in fact coexisted uneasily within the Union – one of Commission-led policy increasingly settled by majority voting, and one of government-led policy, where unanimity was the rule and the Union's own institutions were less important.

Among the practical difficulties encumbering the European road some especially affected Germany, which, under Chancellor Kohl, provided the driving force and much of the financial support of the EU. His greatest triumph, reunification, had confirmed Germany's position as Europe's major power. The apparent ideological divide of two Germanys proved after forty years not to matter; *Ostpolitik* had forged enough ties and interests for cooperation and mutual restraint to prevail at the moment of reunification. West Germany had been (unrealistically) generous, too, in providing attractive terms for currency unification. But this turned out to be only one of a number of very costly adjustments. Germany was driven into deficit on its trade account, an unfamiliar experience and one that alarmed German voters. Political dissatisfaction with the terms of reunification began to be heard as it became obvious that its financial costs would run on for years, and that the economic impact would be felt especially hard in the former GDR.[6] As time passed, more was also heard of the danger of inflation, an old nightmare for Germans, and of the load carried by the German tax-payer as a result not only of the movement

---

[6] A majority of East German enterprises quickly proved uncompetitive and went under soon after reunification, with heavy unemployment as a consequence.

of former East Germans to the west, but of very large numbers of foreign immigrants taking advantage of the country's liberal interpretation of political asylum. Unemployment, too, was rising. In 1993, there was at last agreement on constitutional change to limit political asylum, and to reduce the numbers exploiting it.

Economic recession cast long shadows in most member states of the EU in the early 1990s. It reminded their peoples of disparities and differences of economic strength between them; policies to protect special interests (or what were seen to be such) were therefore pressed more strongly. More fundamentally, in every country fiscal, budgetary and exchange problems came to undermine the confidence of governments (which had in a measure come to be taken for granted) that they could keep up employment and high levels of what may broadly be called 'welfare' spending. They not only found it harder to provide voters Europe-wide with assurance of material well-being but also were less and less certain about their ability to meet the Maastricht criteria. In such a context, specific European agreements and allocations of resources – for instance in the regulation of fishing – generated more disturbance than might have been expected.

So did the anticipation of future monetary union. Its coming would inevitably much reduce the powers of member governments to look as if they were managing their own affairs.[7] ERM had already made revaluation and devaluation to meet domestic needs more difficult; in 1992, Italy and the United Kingdom were both forced out of it by movements on the international exchanges. Ireland followed them in the next year. Currency movements even put Franco-German relations under major strain as German domestic concerns drove that country's central bank towards higher interest rates and brought about a considerable modification of its working. This cast a shadow over progress towards a common currency. Yet already in 1990, former communist countries had been knocking at the door of entry to the EC.

There were thus many cross-currents for politicians to take into account. The fundamentals dictating the position of France had in one respect changed vitally since the days of de Gaulle: Germany had

[7] As was shown, it might be remarked, by the difficulties of other countries imposed by Germany's deflationary policies to deal with the costs of unification even under existing arrangements.

been reunited. For the French, the deepest root of the European impulse had always lain in fear of Germany. French statesmen had sought to tie that reviving country firmly into first the Common Market, and then the Community. In the end, as the German economy grew stronger and stronger, they had been forced to recognize that Germany would have the preponderant share in mapping Europe's future shape. De Gaulle's ideal of a Europe of nation-states gave way to a more federal – that is, paradoxically, more centralizing – view. Making the best of this, some Frenchmen thought that a united Europe could be tolerable if it were consciously built so as to give a maximum of informal and cultural weight in it to France – through, for example, appointments at Brussels. If there had to be a European super-state, France could at least try to dominate it. Perhaps, though, the French decision in 1995 to rejoin NATO was a clearer break with the legacies of de Gaulle than the tacit acceptance that Germany would in the end have the last word in setting the pace of European integration, and perhaps its shape, too. The word *Mitteleuropa* had begun to be heard again in the 1980s. However understood, it implied a special role for Germany and special relationships deriving from it. The German government had soon sought to befriend its ex-communist neighbours. The rapidity with which German businessmen and investors got to work in those countries made this easier, though the speed and eagerness of Germany's recognition of newly independent Croatia and Slovenia was far from reassuring to other EC countries (and awakened old fears and memories – notably in Serbia – of historic Slav–Teuton, Orthodox–Catholic antagonisms).

The ending of the Cold War thus posed difficulties as well as offering new opportunities. Moreover, existing EU members were bound to be losers in cash terms if former communist countries joined the Union. Like applications being made at much the same time to join NATO, such changes would also awaken anxiety in Moscow. Nor was it clear what sort of Europe new members might join. East Germany had entered the existing fold *de facto* in 1990, but other aspirants to entry would provoke debate among existing members about what kind of Europe was desirable or possible. Expansion of the Community was bound to provoke a debate crucial for world history. One conceivable outcome might be the creation of an EU of

500 million, stretching from the Arctic Circle to the Aegean and from Portugal to the Pruth, but another was a break-up (not necessarily into its national components) of what union there was.

There was still in 1994 formally an EFTA outside the EU, but it was insignificant and disappeared the following year.[8] By 1990 there could be detected some slight cultural convergence within the EU. Increasing standardizing of consumption, though, owed much less to European policy than to shrewder marketing and growing international communication at a popular level (the outcome was often, as in the past, deplored as 'Americanization'). There may even have been some blurring of differences between national social structures. The decline in numbers of German and French farmers showed a slow but shared trend towards a more rational economic structuring. Yet even such slow convergence had been very costly and the CAP often irritated non-farming voters. Above all, the Union seemed feeble in its handling of external affairs; it blatantly failed the severe test posed by Yugoslavia's dissolution, which had been virtually taken out of its hands by the United Nations (which meant the Americans), at the end of 1995. Yet though many uncertainties thus persisted over the future of Europe as the end of the century approached, there were many more people in Europe who found the EU a comforting idea than would have done in 1945. Brussels, after all, was not likely to impose alien languages or educational systems, as national governments sometimes did. Neither the Commission nor the parliament promoted any ideology of cultural homogeneity, whatever legendary follies might be from time to time perpetrated in directives about the shape of cucumbers and the purity of cheese.

A COMMON CURRENCY

The project of a single European currency, launched at last on 1 January 1999, had always had a predominantly political flavour: it had been at the heart of Mr Kohl's vision, though purely economic

[8] Denmark, the United Kingdom, Portugal and Switzerland had all left EFTA before 1995. In 1994 it was united with the EU countries in a common 'European Economic Area'. Austria, Finland and Sweden joined the EU on 1 January 1995.

arguments for it could be and were forcefully made. It was asserted that great economic benefits would flow from its introduction, that it would remove exchange rate fluctuations damaging to trade, would reduce other costs of trade between member states, would encourage economic enterprise inhibited hitherto by currency risks. It was hoped (and sometimes confidently alleged) that lower prices and lower interest rates would be likely consequences. With equal assurance, arguments were put forward against the change. Existing differences between the economies of the participating states, it was said, must mean that some would suffer and some gain, and so promote new division. Member states would lose control over important aspects of their economic life as they subordinated their own policy to (for instance) the wishes of France and Germany to continue costly policies of concession to organized labour – both of which seemed all the more likely when socialist governments were installed in each country in 1998. Nor would participants be able to set their own interest rates to meet their own needs, but they would be effectively controlled by those who ran the central European bank which was to be part of the new system: a common currency, in fact, entailed a further loss of sovereignty. All this, and much more, was given a major airing in domestic politics in virtually every member state of the Union, as it became clear that both in countries committed to participation from the outset and those likely or wishing to participate, politics would be increasingly influenced by the need to meet the criteria.

The control of budgetary deficits, the reduction of debt, and the fiscal policies these required, could conceivably mean higher unemployment. Politicians continued to brood over what voters might think when choices had to be made which would bring home to them the consequences of monetary union. It was not hard to agree, though, that were monetary union to slip, and were enlargement not to take place, the EU could settle back into not much more than a simple customs union dominated by Germany (perhaps somewhat in the way the nineteenth-century German *Zollverein* had been dominated by Prussia, as some inclined to historical analogy pointed out). Only the firmest nationalists – or 'Eurosceptics' as they were termed in the United Kingdom – found this an attractive possibility.

After sixteen years as chancellor, Mr Kohl was defeated in the

German elections of November 1998 and the first socialist chancellor of united Germany took office. It was at once clear that his replacement as chancellor made no difference to the monetary union goal. The French government, too, though it had wobbled as it became clearer that currency union was not likely to be easily married to domestic policies, in dealing with – for example – unemployment, still remained firmly behind it. Denmark and Sweden firmly announced they would not wish to participate in the proposal, others showed uncertainty and division over it. Under the Conservative government that had held office until the summer of 1997, it was impossible to predict what the United Kingdom might do; the new Labour government, though, affirmed with fluctuating enthusiasm, as time passed, that a future British government would probably join EMU when the circumstances looked right – but would go no further. So, on 1 January 1999, Europe acquired its first common currency since the age of Charlemagne.[9]

ENLARGING EUROPE

Difficulties over enlargement of the Union remained. Among countries other than the ex-communists who wished to be admitted, the longest-standing candidate was Turkey, a particularly awkward case. Assuming the obstacle provided by intransigent Greek opposition to her application could be set aside (a very doubtful assumption), it could also reasonably be asked whether Turkey was a 'European' country at all since most of her territory lay in Asia and most of her people were Muslim. Behind that question lay a (usually silent) fear of what free movement of Turks within member states of the EU might mean. Whether non-Turks realized it or not, moreover, the Atatürk legacy was in fact at that moment under challenge inside Turkey after a sixty-year ascendancy. Islamist Turkish politicians much resented the regime's traditional secularism.

[9] It is worth remarking that the name chosen for the new currency unit – the 'Euro' – is itself testimony to the psychological divisions of Europe. Nothing but deep nationalist irrationality can explain the rejection of a whole repertoire of familiar and historical names – franc, mark, florin, livre, lira, crown, thaler, dollar, pound – in favour of a word with such an unpleasantly medical flavour.

As some Europeans had asked in 1901, Europeans were still asking in 1999 whether Turkey was part of the civilized world, even if notions of what that phrase meant had changed somewhat in 100 years. Clearly, if modernity in institutions (representative government and Atatürk's secular state, for example) and a certain level of economic development was the test of Europeanness, then Turkey stood with the European and not the rest of the Near Eastern world. Yet Turkish treatment of political opposition and minorities (particularly the Kurds) met with much disapproval abroad, and the record of the Turkish government as a guardian of human rights was often questioned. There were also geopolitical overtones. As a Near Eastern country, Turkey's military cooperation with Israel worried the Arab states. Her position, too, appeared to give her a potential control over the water supply of Iraq and Syria, as well as of the main route for Iraqi oil exports, and for the energy resources of the Caucasus and Central Asia. Turkey posed the unanswerable question of what Europe really is and revealed the likely fruitlessness of any search for essentialist answers.

When Sweden and Finland (the Norwegians rejected the idea in a referendum) had joined up, their admission, like Austria's, could hardly raise any question of their 'Europeanness'. They fitted in easily, as developed economies and countries of liberal political tradition. Greater difficulties arose, though, elsewhere, and were most vividly apparent in what had been Yugoslavia. It might be that not many problems would arise over Hungary and Czechoslovakia; the passage of time would be likely to reduce the danger of economic difficulties in these two countries if they came to join the EU, because of the progress they had made since 1990. At the end of 1997 the heads of European governments were able to agree that negotiation should begin virtually at once for the admission of the Czech Republic, Estonia, Hungary, Poland and Slovenia (at the same meeting it was decided that conditions in Turkey were not satisfactory). But some eastern countries still seemed unattractive as potential recruits, whether in terms of political culture or economic preparedness. What is more, they would almost certainly raise problems for relations between the EU states and members of the CIS, some of whom were as sensitive about political alignments on their western boundaries as had been the USSR. Finally, times seemed inauspicious for further liberalization of labour flows; the spectre of a potentially immense migration from the former USSR to the labour markets of the West was frightening.

Once more, people asked what Europe was. In a bipolar world, it had looked plausible to say that Europe was merely a geographical expression, yet the end of the Cold War had revealed that Europe had never been merely that. There seemed less point than ever in seeking in it a central European essence or spirit, far less a civilization, but the continent was (from one point of view) still the historic heart even if it was no longer the major propagator of a world civilization. From another, though, it was a collection of national cultures resonating vigorously to their own internal dynamics. Yet such ideas hardly touched most Europeans' minds and feelings. There was no sign as 1999 began of a European patriotism comparable to the old national allegiances still able to stir the emotions of the masses.

As the end of the century approached, though, much could be seen to have been achieved in the years since the Treaty of Rome. Even by 1990, what had been 'Western Europe' (and was now the EU plus Switzerland) was already in actuality one of the three identifiable major players in the new world economy shaped since 1950. She accounted by then for some 75 per cent of world trade (most of it between her own member countries) and 40 per cent of the world's Gross Domestic Product. Her own GDP was in that year larger than that of the USA (and twice as large as that of Japan). She was integrated through investment flows within the developed world as she had never been even before 1914. For all the excitement over supposed cultural challenge from across the Atlantic, two-thirds of foreign investment in the United States was held by Europeans. Yet Europeans still seemed to worry a lot about where they were going, even if they so obviously seemed to so many outsiders a team to join. As 1999 began, their ministers were turning at long last to the reform of the Common Agricultural Policy, though the attempt miscarried. A real reduction of payments to farmers still seemed as difficult to achieve as ever. Important though this issue was, too, it was quickly overtaken by a major constitutional upheaval, the resignation of the entire Commission after an adverse report on mismanagement and worse in its business. It was the first great constitutional revolution of the Union's history, and was pregnant with uncertainties and possibilities for changes in its political culture, administrative style, and the future of the European parliament's authority within it.

A TROUBLED FAR EAST

In 1989 Chinese farmers saw their incomes decline in real terms for the first time since economic reform had begun.[10] The policy of trying to balance hard-line conservatism with economic and political liberalism in the hierarchy was associated with Deng Xiaoping and it was not altogether surprising that in that year he should ask to retire (he was then eighty-five). Yet he did not do so and the question of his succession was still unsettled on the eve of the Party Congress at the end of 1991. In 1992 he appeared to have regained his ascendancy after a well-publicized trip to south China to promote further economic reforms: even if the party had decided (secretly) that entrepreneurs should not yet be allowed to be members, that year brought a further removal of price controls, the beginnings of massive investment from the western world and, soon, inflation. As the real incomes of many Chinese fell, earnings differentials widened. Though this was hardly significant by comparison with what had happened in other Asian countries, official alarm was expressed, as it was over the evident increase in corruption, organized crime, banditry and rural unrest.

As the end of the century approached, Deng's death in February 1997 reminded the world that China had not succeeded in giving any enduring protective and institutional expression to recent liberalizing tendencies. Their effects could still be thought contingent and precarious, though in the next couple of years the general trend encouraged under Deng still seemed healthily alive. In 1998 cities where state industry still predominated were urged to study the example of Wenzhou (a port that was evidently an outstanding example of entre-

[10] J. A. R. Miles, p.185 (and also p.338 for the important qualifications necessary if the growth in rural incomes derived not from agriculture but from industry is to be taken properly into account).

preneurial growth) and it was announced that subsidized housing was no longer to be made available to new entrants to the state sector workforce. The uncertainties about the future that had been intensified by the departure of the last great figure of the revolutionary generation were evidently assuaged by Deng's successor, Jiang Zemin, who soon appeared to have the skills of an accomplished political trimmer.

Technically, the collapse of the USSR had left the People's Republic the only major communist power in the world. This, though, was a less meaningful distinction than would have once been the case. Immediately, it must have transformed strategic reality; 4,000 and more miles of shared frontier with the former USSR were now replaced for about half their length by frontiers with newly independent states of the CIS.[11] But what that might portend was hard to see. Meanwhile, there was a new uncertainty evident in the later 1990s over Taiwan, one problem that had long tied together Chinese internal policy and foreign relations. The seemingly fundamental nature of the original clash between the nationalist regime which had held the island since 1947 and the People's Republic had, in fact, been slightly blurred over nearly five decades. One factor had been Beijing's hope of exploiting the South China Sea in a search for oil. The change in the policy of the United States since 1970 had led to withdrawal of American diplomatic relations with the island, and the exclusion of the nationalist regime from the United Nations. Then, in the 1990s, while Beijing still maintained its policy of reuniting Taiwan (like Hong Kong and Macao) to mainland China as a long-term goal, more began to be heard of alleged independence sentiment on the island. Beijing was evidently disturbed, alarm reaching its height when the president of the Taiwanese republic visited the United States in 1995.[12] The ambassador of the People's Republic in Washington was withdrawn and exercises were mounted in the East China Sea by units of the Chinese navy, with an obviously demonstrative purpose; 'The issue of Taiwan is as explosive as a barrel of gunpowder,' said an official Chinese newspaper.[13] It was clear that if Taiwan formally declared itself independent of the mainland an invasion of the island was likely,

[11] Specifically, with Kazakhstan, Kyrgystan and Tajikistan.
[12] President Lee Teng-Hui was the first Taiwanese to lead the KMT.
[13] The *People's Daily* of Beijing, q. in Miles, p.260.

and that it was likely too that it might command much popular support in China.

As the century drew to a close, the status of Taiwan was nonetheless far from the major problem troubling east Asia. Uncertainties about the real nature of what was going on in China and the way the cat might jump there were a continuing background to an increasing instability and volatility apparent in the region after the Cold War ended. What the closing of that relatively well-defined and therefore stabilizing struggle might mean was at first very hard to see. In Korea it changed very little, North Korea remaining obstinately locked in a confrontation with its southern neighbour and in its rulers' determination to maintain a command economy in virtual isolation. The roots of its quarrels with the south were very deep, going back beyond the Cold War itself to the political factions that had struggled with one another as well as against the Japanese before 1939. But the evaporation of Soviet economic aid and mismanagement of the economy (and, it appeared, some straightforward dynastic exploitation of power by the ruling dictator) brought North Koreans to the edge of starvation by early 1998. That country's problems thus remained unusually specific, detached somewhat from the regional trends.

South Korea could not be so detached. By the mid-1990s, she was one of several countries grappling with a growing economic malaise eventually to engulf in some degree all the former 'tiger' economies, Japan, and even to some extent to touch China through Hong Kong and the contagion of currency instability. The era of growth and prosperity had lasted through the 1980s. Its undermining had begun when the original leader of the Asian resurgence, Japan, showed in the early 1990s the first symptoms of economic disorder. Property speculation, huge investment in non-productive activity or sectors generating very small returns had encumbered her banks and financial institutions with unserviceable debts. The currency sharply weakened; speculation against it was immediate and crippling in a world of more rapid financial transactions than ever before. The prevailing business culture of Japan, firmly embedded as it was in official and financial networks that now proved unable to give decisive leadership, made solutions harder still to achieve as conditions worsened. By 1998 one estimate put the bad debts of Japanese banks at £660 billion.

The consequences of this, it soon appeared, might even become worldwide (and by mid-1998 the United States was at last seeking to engage in rescue operations). They quickly spread to other regional economies whose economic growth fell off dramatically. In many of them the same phenomena could be seen as in Japan, if on a smaller scale: investment booms had been followed by exposure to inter-national currency speculation, over-extended credit and endangered banking systems, and (more than in Japan) the migration of capital overseas. Authoritarian governments in some countries had made easy the exploitation of public resources and exercise of influence by the cronies of those in power and their families. The same governments proved inflexible and incapable of dealing with changing economic circumstances and terms of trade. In July 1997 there was something of a breaking of a dam. First Thailand lost its battle to support its currency; its devaluation was then followed rapidly by the collapse of other cur-rencies of the region, too. There was even speculation soon that the Hong Kong dollar, pegged since reunification with China to the Ameri-can dollar, was not safe. South-east Asian governments began to worry about whether they had seen the last of economic growth.

The first dramatic political consequence for a region where govern-ments had been notably stable during the Cold War years was an outburst of popular anger over economic hardship (expressed above all in rising food prices) in Indonesia. In May 1998, after the Indonesian economy had shrunk by more than 8 per cent since the beginning of the year, and the currency had lost four-fifths of its dollar value, riots drove the president from power after thirty-two assured years of a firmly controlled but formally 'democratic' system. It did not seem likely, though, that this would end Indonesia's problems. The suc-cessor government looked too much like the old one and there was much potential for inter-community strife in a country divided as Indonesia was between a large Islamic majority, and significant Hindu and Chinese communities. As the year closed, there was renewed mob violence, and reports of attacks on Christian Indonesians.

Well before the Indonesian revolt, stock markets had plunged throughout the region and national economies had been shrinking; Malaysia was soon hard hit. This was among the facts that had most vividly struck western investors and observers as perhaps presaging wider consequences than any merely confined to the region. The United States, above all, but European countries, too, had been enjoying a long stock-market advance that, it seemed, could be in danger from what was colloquially summarized as an Asian 'meltdown'. Yet it was hard to believe that world conditions would permit even an American market crash to detonate anything like the consequences of 1929. All the same, there were those who worried a lot, above all when the currency turbulence of 1998 forced the devaluation of the Russian rouble. By then, too, Latin America was beginning to be affected as, ominously, oil and commodity prices fell. Chile, as a Pacific country and one especially sensitive to a fall in the price of copper, was particularly affected.

THE INDIAN SUB-CONTINENT

It could be construed as an advantage of the Indian republic, and one possibly owing something to past policy, that in the middle of the 1990s, like China, she did not at once share the financial and economic disarray of many of the east Asian countries. Congress governments, though moving away somewhat from the socialism of the early years of independence, had remained strongly influenced by protectionist, managed, nationally self-sufficient, even autarkic ideas. The price had been paid in low rates of growth and social conservatism. But one benefit had been a lower degree of vulnerability to international capital flows than other countries, even if the rupee dipped alarmingly in 1995 and after.

In 1996 the Hindu and nationalist Bharatiya Janata party (BJP) inflicted another major defeat on Congress and became the largest single party in the lower house of parliament. Exponents of the amorphous doctrine of *Hindutva* ('Hindu-ness') began to show new vigour. BJP was not able to sustain its own government, though, and a coalition government emerged that did not survive another (very violent) general election in 1998.[14] This, too, was inconclusive in that

[14] This was the first struggle in which Rajiv Gandhi's widow was persuaded to campaign for Congress, of which she was elected president the same year.

no clear parliamentary majority emerged, but the BJP and its allies formed the biggest single group in it. Another coalition government was the outcome, whose Janata supporters soon published an ominously nationalist agenda that announced that 'India should be built by Indians'. Some found this alarming in a country where nationalism, though encouraged by Congress for a century or so, had hitherto always been offset by prudent recognition of the real fissiparousness of the sub-continent. The new government appeared, too, to offer small likelihood of accelerated social change except, possibly, in a regressive and sectarian way. Its regional allies showed no sign of any ability to restrain what many democrats and secularists saw as a looming danger of political reaction and religious demagogy.

Though it seemed consistent with a determination to win domestic kudos by playing the nationalist card, it was in the context of the running sore of the quarrel with Pakistan that the world at first strove to understand the Janata government's decision to proceed with a series of nuclear test explosions in May and June 1998. They provoked the Pakistan government to follow suit with test explosions of its own; both governments appeared, dismayingly, to enjoy wide public support in their aftermath.[15] Thus both nations joined the club of those who admitted to having nuclear weapons.[16] Much more, though, was implicit in these gestures than the exploitation of national feeling in two countries long antagonized. The correct Asian context in which to understand the tests, said the Indian prime minister, was that of Indian suspicion of China, long already a nuclear power and remembered by Indians as the victor of the Himalayan fighting of 1962. Others pondered gloomily the notion that a Pakistani bomb might also be an Islamic bomb, or, reflecting on a huge setback to the curbing of nuclear proliferation so far achieved, were simply alarmed by the evidence the test provided of the spread of nuclear weapons. Several ambassadors were withdrawn from Delhi and several countries followed the lead of the United States in cutting off or holding up aid

---

[15] Sonya Gandhi promptly said that the nuclear issue was a non-partisan matter on which every Indian stood united.

[16] Until now, restricted to the USA, USSR (and later Russia), China, the United Kingdom and France. Israel and North Korea were by 1998 believed also to possess effective nuclear weaponry.

to India (steps which did nothing to deter Pakistan from following India's example). The world, evidently, had not with the Cold War rid itself also of the danger of nuclear warfare.

THE UNITED STATES AT THE END OF THE CENTURY

Taking the broadest brush and a long (and perhaps somewhat superficial) backwards view from the mid-1990s, it is tempting to sum up the outcome of a century of change in the United States as 'more of the same'. More clearly than even at mid-century, that country is still the world's greatest power. After emerging from the heavy weather of the early 1980s and a period of cavalier piling up of debt through budgetary deficit, her gigantic economy was strong and prosperous; its dynamism was unquestionable and it had repeatedly shown huge powers of recovery from setbacks. For all its conscious political and social conservatism, America remained one of the most rapidly changing, adaptive societies in the world.[17]

Old problems remained as the decade opened, it was true, even if prosperity was already making them easier to live with for those Americans who did not have to face them in person. More was heard of the aspirations, fears and resentments of black Americans than ever, and this reflected social and economic progress they had made since the Johnson presidency, the last which had seen a determined effort to legislate black America out of its troubles. In 1990, the first black state governor in the nation's history took up office in Virginia. Yet only a couple of years later the inhabitants of Watts, notorious for its riots a quarter of a century before, again showed they saw the Los Angeles police force (who had just been authorized by their employers to add dum-dum bullets to their already formidable weaponry)[18] as members of an occupying army. Over the country as a whole, a young black male was seven times more likely than his

[17] Every year, the Board of Census figures showed, something like 7 million Americans changed the state in which they lived and nearly a fifth of the population moved house.
[18] Alexander Cockburn in *Wall Street Journal*, 4 April 1991.

white contemporary to be murdered (and probably by a fellow black, to boot) and was more likely to go to prison than to a university. If nearly a quarter of American babies were then being born to unmarried mothers, two-thirds of black babies were, an index of the breakdown of family life in black American communities. Crime, major deteriorations in health in some areas, and virtually unpoliceable inner-city areas could still leave responsible Americans believing that American problems were racing away from solution.

Yet, by the end of the century, the remarkable regenerative power of the economy had done much to make some of the statistics look better, and even if Mr Clinton had disappointed many of his supporters by the legislation he was actually able to deliver, the Republicans in Congress got the blame for that. It was noted, too, with some relief, that the at first alarming phenomenon of rapidly growing numbers of 'Hispanic' Americans, swollen by legal and illegal influx from Mexico and the Caribbean countries, seemed unlikely to present intransigent and unmanageable problems. In California, the richest state, where they provided a quarter of the population, and even in Texas, they appeared quickly to learn to use the politics of democracy to make sure their interests were not overlooked.

To use a modish contemporary figure of speech, President Clinton benefited from surfing the economic wave; even if there were disappointments in his domestic policy, they (like those in foreign policy) tended to be attributed by supporters to his opponents rather than to his own failures of leadership and excessive care for electoral considerations. If the Democrats lost control of the legislature in 1994, his re-election in 1996 was triumphant, and success for his party in the mid-term elections was to follow. Nevertheless, Congress continued to thwart many of his projects, notably putting difficulties in the way of international trade liberalization and public health reform.

It can reasonably be said in his defence that Mr Clinton had inherited an office sadly diminished in prestige and power since the Johnson presidency and the early Nixon years. The dissipation of the vast authority the presidency had accumulated under Woodrow Wilson, Franklin Roosevelt and during the early Cold War had swiftly and dramatically followed the Nixon tragedy. But Mr Clinton did nothing to stem the rot. Indeed, for many Americans he allowed it to go further when his personal indiscretions laid him open to much-publicized and prolonged investigation of alleged financial and sexual scandals. Early in 1999, this led finally to a unique historical event, the first hearings in American history of charges before the Senate against an elected president with the aim of bringing about his impeachment. Surprisingly, most Americans seemed little troubled by questions about the president's culpability or even by his admitted lies. As the hearings began, Mr Clinton's public opinion poll ratings were higher than they had been a year earlier, and the proponents of impeachment failed. Those who had voted for him were content, it seemed, with what he was believed to have tried to do, even if they were not oblivious to his defects of character.[19]

PAX AMERICANA

As the Clinton presidency unrolled, though, America's allies were more and more troubled by uncertainty about the degree to which domestic difficulties were compromising the United States' behaviour abroad and appeared to be squandering the magnificent legacy of world leadership which had been hers at the end of the Cold War. The relatively short-term changes of the 1990s, though, have to be placed in the context of more deeply rooted and long-term changes in American psychology. It is no exaggeration to say that in 1901 the average American had hardly needed, and certainly did not bother, to worry about the world outside the United States. Until President Taft briefly entered Mexico in 1909, no president had ever ventured outside the national borders while in office. Even what was going on elsewhere in the western hemisphere did not seem to matter much in those days. In 1991, whatever the average day might look like in America's local newspapers or television news bulletins, so wholly parochial a focus was impossible. They may not have been a daily

[19] In a poll taken at the beginning of 1999, when the proceedings in the Senate had not yet begun, 81 per cent of those polled thought the Clinton presidency a success, 69 per cent approved his general 'job performance', and 76 per cent said 'no' when asked if they thought the president honest (figures cited in *The Economist*, 23 January 1999).

presence in most Americans' minds, but there were now constant reminders that American interests were worldwide and inescapable; old-style isolation was no longer a plausible option. Like Great Britain when the century began, the United States had by 1999 acquired concerns requiring continuous and strenuous diplomatic effort in every part of the globe. A *pax Americana* demanded constant attention; even if much that was going on might seem to make disengagement very tempting, no swing back into isolation like that after 1919, for example, followed the collapse of the USSR. There was, though, much debate among scholars, publicists and politicians about the world role of the United States and the state of the union, about the nature and extent of the proper use of American power and the ends to which it should be applied, even about potential clashes of civilization. It was in the wildest moments of speculative euphoria that some briefly and cheerfully contemplated the possibility that history might have come benevolently to an end.

The questioning in fact reflected the truth that it had not. There were a multitude of old and new international problems to be faced. It had to be accepted, for example, that there had long ceased to be only one major potential source of nuclear danger. As alarm over North Korea's modest nuclear programme in 1993–4 showed (and the Indian and Pakistani tests of 1998 reaffirmed), the United States was now one of several and a slowly growing group of nuclear-armed states, whatever her relative superiority in delivery systems and potential weight of attack. She had no reason any longer to believe (as had sometimes been possible in the past) that all of them would make rational calculations about where their interests lay. But this was only part of the general background to policy-making. Particular moments of tension in the 1990s seemed also to suggest a pattern of American floundering in foreign policy leading not only to frustration of the country's legitimate goals, but to positively greater danger for world order.

The first obvious failure of American policy came in efforts to broker peace in the Middle East. It had looked otherwise in the early years of the decade. American financial pressure over the spread of Jewish settlement on the West Bank seemed to be helping the Israeli government, harassed by the *Intifada* and its associated acts of terrorism, to come round to the view that a merely military solution to the Palestine problem was not likely to work. Helped by the benevolent offices of the Norwegian government, secret talks between Israeli and Palestinian representatives at Oslo in 1993 led to an encouraging new departure, when the two sides declared that it was time 'to put an end to decades of confrontation and conflict, recognise . . . mutual legitimate and political rights, and strive to live in peaceful co-existence and mutual dignity and security and achieve a just, lasting and comprehensive peace settlement and historic reconciliation'.[20] More specifically, they went on to agree that an autonomous Palestine Authority (firmly defined as 'interim') should be set up, covering the West Bank and Gaza Strip, and that a definitive peace settlement should be concluded within five years. For all the issues this still left to be cleared up, it seemed a dramatic and hopeful opening to a better future for all inhabitants of Palestine, and to promise greater stability for the Middle East as a whole. For the leader of the PLO, it may have meant political salvation. Mr Arafat's political credit had been running dangerously low since the *Intifada* had begun and he was under challenge from more extreme Palestinians. He was now able to return from exile in Tunisia to take a firmer line with them.[21]

Optimism soon began to wilt. Hopes of progress in thrashing out an enduring settlement faded away when there was no cessation of terrorist attacks or of reprisals for them. Arab bombs in the streets of Israeli cities killed and maimed scores of shoppers and passers-by. A lone Jewish gunman killed thirty Palestinians in their mosque at Hebron and won the posthumous applause of many of his countrymen for doing so.[22] Even so, hope lingered on; Syria, Jordan and the Lebanon all resumed peace negotiations with Israel, and a beginning was in fact made in the withdrawal of Israeli forces from the designated

---

[20] See *AR 1993*, pp.557–63, for full text; G. E. Robinson, *Building a Palestinian State: the incomplete revolution* (Bloomington, 1997) is very helpful on background.

[21] The joint declaration with the Israeli government specified that the new Palestinian Council should set up 'a strong police force'. This was so vigorously and rapidly undertaken that it was soon reckoned that about half (60,000 or so) of the employees of the Council belonged to various police and security services.

[22] The murderer was specifically condemned in the UN, but his grave is now maintained as a shrine by his admirers.

autonomous Palestinian areas. Then, in November 1995, came the assassination of the Israeli prime minister by an Israeli fanatic. A few months later, a conservative government dependent on the parliamentary support of Jewish extremist parties took office, and its intransigence over further implementation of agreed peace terms showed that for the immediate future at least, it was unlikely that anything but an aggressive policy of further territorial settlement by Israel would be forthcoming.

Mr Clinton's administration deplored this turn to events, but he was not likely to risk inflaming Israel's supporters in his party over the failure to honour the Oslo agreements his State Department had encouraged. Soon, as so often in the past, the United States was supporting Israel virtually alone in the UN against resolutions of the Security Council and the General Assembly. The discontent of Palestinians meanwhile erupted in new acts of savage violence, especially when, in September 1997, Israel formally announced she would not hand over any more territory to the Palestine Authority as agreed at Oslo. Although assiduous American effort succeeded a year later in bringing together the Israeli prime minister and Mr Arafat for a meeting in the United States which appeared briefly to re-energize the Oslo process, the former was confronted on his return to Israel with such criticism from his supporters that it was clear that no further progress could be hoped for until new Israeli elections could be held – if then. The consequences of the creation of the Zionist programme a century earlier and of the Balfour declaration were evidently as unmanageable as ever; the embarrassment of the United States seemed likely to continue in an area now further complicated, of course, by the long frustration of American policy over Iraq.

The dangers in the Middle East had been very visible in the background to a minor success of American diplomacy early in 1996, when it had dissuaded two NATO members, Greece and Turkey, from fighting over a barren and uninhabited rock in the Aegean, but as a contribution to south-eastern European order that can hardly be treated as an episode of much significance. In the Far East, though, where major diplomatic effort had been for some time deployed towards mainland China, it was hoped that another presidential visit to that country in the summer of 1998 might bring about something of a turning-point. It did not. It must have been deeply disappointing when, in the middle of the Gulf crisis of the following December, China attacked American policy strongly in the Security Council and the *People's Daily* of Beijing ominously noted that 'the US action impels the international community to make a solemn choice: do we want a peaceful twenty-first century, or one of hegemonic menace?'[23] Clearly, something had gone badly wrong. In the background, no doubt, were irritated reflexions in Beijing on Mr Clinton's nagging about human rights, and on his 1996 dispatch of aircraft carriers to the China Sea when tension over Taiwan erased the effect of mollifying words the previous year. By 1999, too, the Chinese were confronted by what they believed to be his efforts to stop them joining the World Trade Organization. Then, suddenly, matters got far worse.

As 1999 went on, Kosovo dominated thinking about former Yugoslavia. When spring passed into summer, it was obvious that the strategic commitment to a purely air campaign was achieving little except a stiffening of the Serbian people's will to resist. The inevitable casualties which were suffered by civilians – both Serbian and Kosovar – were causing misgivings in domestic opinion within the nineteen Nato nations, while the Serbian president, Mr Milosevic, appeared to have been assured by Mr Clinton's words that he would not be the target of a land invasion. Nearly a million Kosovar refugees crossed the frontier in search of safety in Macedonia and Albania, many of them bringing horrifying stories of atrocities and intimidation by Serbs, and the imbalance of the sexes among them reminded suspicious observers of the fate of the disappeared Bosnian co-religionists of the men of Kosovo a few years before. It was now evident that it was the deliberate intention of the Belgrade government to empty the province of its non-Serb inhabitants. Then came another mishap in the bombing campaign when, on the basis of out-of-date information – and therefore by avoidable error – direct hits were made on the Chinese embassy in Belgrade and members of its staff killed. For a time, Beijing refused even to listen to the apology and explanation which President Clinton endeavoured to deliver by personal telephone call. A carefully orchestrated television campaign had already presented the Chinese people with an interpretation of the

---

[23] Reported in the *Financial Times*, 19 December 1998.

whole NATO intervention as a simple act of American aggression: well-organized student mobs now attacked the American and British embassies in Beijing (though without proceeding to the extremes experienced during the Cultural Revolution). It may have been convenient that with the ten-year anniversary of Tienanmen Square coming up soon, student steam could be let off in anti-foreigner riots.

American 'hegemony' continued to be much denounced by the Chinese, who said they would do nothing to assist the pursuit of peace in Kosovo until the bombing campaign had ceased. It seemed unlikely that this would prove an enduring position, but the sincerity of their concern about America's world role can hardly be doubted. There was no doubt, either, that the involvement of China (as well as of Russia) in the Kosovo crisis was not likely to make it easier for NATO to achieve its aims. The Chinese, strong believers in the veto system of the Security Council, saw it as protection for the sovereignty of individual nations. They were also disinclined in principle to view with sympathy would-be separatists, sensitive as they had always been to any danger of fragmentation in their own huge country. In the deep background, too, lay the theme of reassertion of their own historic world role, as well as the specific irritations of recent years. For a century after the Opium Wars, after all, China had never been without the humiliation of European troops assuring 'order' on her soil. Perhaps it crossed the minds of some Chinese that it would be a sweet reversal of nearly two centuries of history if Chinese soldiers should in the end form part of a peacekeeping force in Kosovo.

Nor was it true that popular feeling exacerbated international tension only on one side. American opinion had been stirred for months by reports of Chinese nuclear espionage in the United States and of Chinese money finding its way by clandestine routes to the influencing of American politics – which meant the Democratic party. Meanwhile NATO's strategy (thanks to the American president's wish to avoid at all costs the exposure of ground troops to danger) was imposing a heavy strain on the alliance and perhaps threatening its very existence. Just as Bosnia had destroyed the credibility of the United Nations as a device for assuring international order, it now appeared that Kosovo might destroy that of NATO.

Early in June, though, the damage done by the bombing, together with Russian mediation and British pressure for a NATO ground invasion, appeared to have weakened the Serbian government's will to resist. In the end, a land campaign was not needed. By the end of the month, Serbian military and police forces had withdrawn and Kosovo was occupied by NATO troops with the immediate task of assuring that the returning Albanians did not exact a bloody revenge on the Serbs (large numbers of whom themselves now began to flee the province). Perhaps it was at last the end of the old dream of a greater Serbia, for now nothing was left of it except the surviving federal tie with Montenegro. That did not mean, though, that the problems of the former Yugoslavia – or those of Europe – were solved.

At some moments, Kosovo had suggested a very dangerous future ahead. It had even looked for a time as if Mr Clinton might actually manage to revive the spectre of Russo-Chinese *entente* so ably kept at bay by Mr Nixon and his successors in the White House. It has been said often enough in these pages that historians should not predict nor pick and choose among probabilities, but pointing out possibilities, at least, is more allowable. One of them must be that the period of euphoria which affected some in the aftermath of 1989–90 is over. It is even conceivable that another Cold War of superpowers might be in the offing, with all the vast potential for the blighting and corruption of human life and international relations the last one displayed. But it is only one possibility, and there are others.

What remains certain is that truly global history is now a reality as it was not a century ago. The impulse to universalize values which has done so much to shape today's world was already then present at the heart of the western civilization and might be judged already to be shaping certain aspects of the future. But most of the structure of our world was not then visible, even if some of it was present in embryo. In particular, China, now a superpower interesting herself in the affairs of Europe, could not then have been recognized as a positive, let alone a significant, international fact. Even the United States, too, seemed then at best marginal to the most pressing concerns of the world's statesmen. It is something of an irony that, as the twentieth century drew to its end, those powers should have been so interested in a matter already familiar to those same statesmen of 1901 – the always intractable legacy of the Ottoman Succession.

28

Retrospect

HISTORICAL IMPORTANCE

It must surely by now be evident that to ask what is the *real* history of a century is to pose at least a hard and possibly a foolish question. This is not only because it is in large measure unanswerable. Nearly 400 years ago, in introducing his *History of the World*,[1] Sir Walter Ralegh was realistic about the dangers lying in wait even for one who, 'having been permitted to draw water as neare the Well-head as another', tried to write 'the Story of mine owne times'; he famously warned those who might have wished him to try that 'whosoever is writing a modern History, [and] shall follow truth too neare the heeles, it may haply strike out his teethe. There is no Mistresse or Guide, that hath led her followers and servants into greater miseries.' Yet one must try, for to provide no history leaves the field always to bad history.

We now know more facts about recent times, and we are more aware of the links that tie many of those facts together, than ever before. The materials of a history of the contemporary world are more accessible than ever. Yet such a history is still ultimately unattainable. Any book can only suggest or sketch the outlines of its reality, and can never describe it fully. It is not just that the history which happens to individuals always escapes the summary generalizations inherent in describing public events. When the canvas is so broad, it is hard to pick out from what happened what mattered most, what had the deepest and widest effect. That means trying to discern what has most changed the settings in which we and our contemporaries and

[1] London, 1614.

CANADA

UNITED STATES
OF AMERICA

MEXICO

Atlantic Ocean

FRANCE

SPAIN

ALGERIA

MALI   NIGER

VENEZUELA

COLUMBIA

Pacific Ocean   EQUADOR

PERU

BRAZIL

NAMIBI

BOLIVIA

PARAGUAY

N

URUGUAY

ARGENTINA

Consumption of all types of energy
(kg equivalent per person)

	8,000-20,000
	1,894-7,999
	500-1,893
	0-499
	no data

0   3000 k
                m

Energy consumption worldwide, 1998

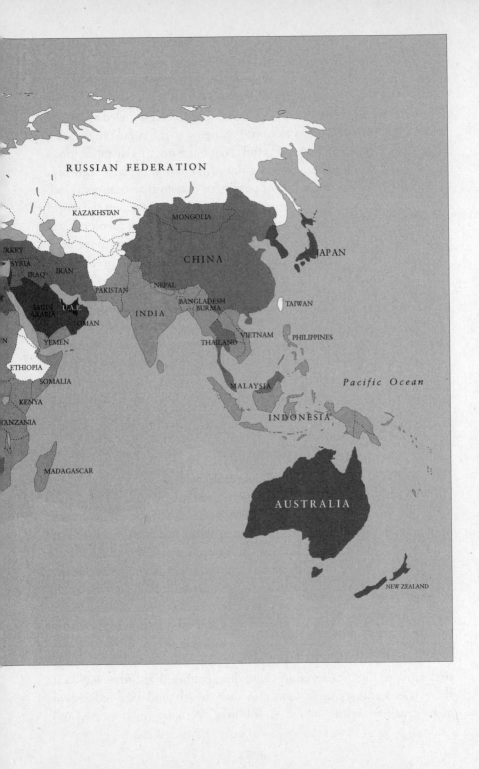

RUSSIAN FEDERATION

KAZAKHSTAN

MONGOLIA

RKEY

SYRIA

IRAQ   IRAN

CHINA

JAPAN

NEPAL

PAKISTAN

SAUDI   U.A.E.
ARABIA

BANGLADESH
BURMA

TAIWAN

OMAN

INDIA

YEMEN

VIETNAM   PHILIPPINES

THAILAND

ETHIOPIA

SOMALIA

Pacific Ocean

KENYA

MALAYSIA

TANZANIA

INDONESIA

MADAGASCAR

AUSTRALIA

NEW ZEALAND

immediate forebears could not choose but live, and the expectations aroused by direct experience encumber us with distractions and traps as we do so. One of them is the bloodshed which is a central fact of the twentieth century. For all the hopes and rhetoric that swirled about the infant UNO in 1945, many nations belonging to it have taken up arms since then. There has been no return to what from this distance looks deceptively like the comparative calm of the late nineteenth century. We have reminders every day of persistent divisions within mankind, of old scars reopening and new ones being inflicted. Much of the world still looks dangerously unstable. Nationality, culture, ideology and economics still fragment it. The bloodshed, though, might have been even worse than it has been; nuclear war, after all, did not break out.

If the bloodletting of recent history does not, on consideration, seem the most important thing about it – except to those whose blood (or the blood of whose loved ones) was shed, dates like 1939 still exercise a powerful pull. Because we know that a great European war began then (and many of us lived through its excitements) we tend to forget that there was a time when everything that happened in the next six years had not happened, that many people had believed in the years before it did that it would not happen, that many more had hoped that it would not, and that no one had anything but the crudest idea of what, if it did happen, it might actually turn out to mean. It remains enormously difficult to shake the way we see those dates and facts or to rid our minds of the cardinal roles our lives have given them. Yet a comparison of the impact of the Second World War with (for instance) that of the discovery of radio waves (whose later exploitation did so much, of course, to shape that war's course and outcome) is not easy; it is not obvious that the war, even at its widest, affected the lives of more millions than the earlier work of physicists and radio engineers has done. How, too, as an influence for change in world history, does so great a struggle, or even so radical a scientific advance, compare with major changes in human credulity? Within one limited zone of human culture alone, one of the greatest single facts shaping the lives of Europeans in the Middle Ages was surely that most of them believed in some dim, confused but firm way that there was a transcendent God and that they would face judgement after death to settle their fate for ever. Perhaps only a few, and those mainly ecclesiastics, thought about this very systematically and continuously, but many more had their behaviour shaped by such belief and sought reassurance through ritual and quasi-magical acts. Religious belief was then at the very root of most men's lives. At least in Europe, we can now guess, we confront today populations for the most part taking in their daily lives no account at all of whether there is a God or not. Religion – across all creeds and systems – seems to have lost much of the enormous advantage it once possessed as virtually the universal source of consolation, explanation and hope to men and women trapped in an unchanging order.

We have in fact no firmer ground beneath our feet for assessing where we now stand or the way in which the past has shaped it than had our parents, grandparents and great-grandparents in their day in thinking about their pasts; we merely have more information and some new ideas to bring to bear on it. Among that information is our knowledge of the extent to which guesses made 100 years ago turned out in due course to fall so far short of actuality. So we have less excuse than the men and women of 1901 for trying to prophesy and should be able to set aside the temptation to do so more easily than they. Yet because we have many more facts to take into account we are tempted to think we can and perhaps will make better judgements. It seems in principle unlikely. What cannot be denied (because it is at least crudely subject to measurement) is that this century has seen change on a scale and at a pace which has made it more difficult to assess while it went on than any earlier history. That change has been its primary characteristic. The twentieth century has been qualitatively unlike any of its predecessors in experiencing change unprecedentedly radical, intense and compound in effect. Nor has it unrolled every-where at the same pace – another complication for the historian. Wherever one looks at the human world of 1901, though, from the stone age savagery of the New Guinea forests to the decayed ancient civilization of China, change seems to have overtaken its varied societies more completely and rapidly than ever it did in the past.

THE GREAT UPHEAVALS

It remains easier to recognize such change than to explore it. Historians have traditionally seen part of their role as the weighing of the comparative influence of different facts in bringing about agreed outcomes. This is difficult at any high level of generalization, above all because of uncertainty about the appropriate criteria. If we agree that we can talk about changes in the mentalities of whole societies and of millions of men and women, then is the dwindling of even a vague belief in the supernatural more, or less, important than the slow growth of a belief among large numbers of people that there will normally be enough to eat? That simple thought is, after all, a very new thought over much of the world. How, too, is one to balance a growing assumption that it is normal for things to get better and better against the misery and pain the century has brought to millions? Conservatively estimated, our failings as a species in managing our collective affairs may have cost in the last 100 years 100 million lives in two world wars and their consequences alone. Mankind's greatest essay yet in social engineering, international communism, whose goals are still widely defended by many as benevolent, may have cost another 50 million. We can reasonably feel angry at the ingenuity and resources wasted in bringing about such holocausts. They often look qualitatively worse than the horrors of earlier times and they have stripped the idea of progress of its plausibility for many who once believed in it. With many more huge atrocities, they testify, surely, to a more damaging release of evil impulse than ever before. Out of what was once thought a buried past in much of the world, and one in at least the process of burial elsewhere, massacre, persecution and torture have spectacularly re-emerged in the last few years in Rwanda and what was Yugoslavia. What is more, even these horrors do not fill up the cup of misery and wickedness of the last half-century.

Yet there are almost four times more human beings alive than 100 years ago. The majority of them are not rich, but nor are they all living in the direst poverty, either. The dead are forever gone, and the tormented and tortured who survive can hardly be healed, but the overwhelming majority of the human race have survived the century's disasters, have lived longer than their grandparents, and long enough, too, to know somewhat better material conditions. The uncivilized and barbarous have, as ever, gone on behaving in uncivilized and barbarous ways, but what was once memorably called a 'decent respect for the opinion of mankind' has won its victories in this century, too. Great evils cannot now be launched and carried through without deliberate concealment, denial, or attempts at plausible justi-fication. At least the beginnings of a structure of international law to defend notions of human right once shared by only a tiny minority of the human race are now visible. In July 1998 representatives of 120 nations agreed (even if those of the most powerful nation on earth did not) to set up a permanent international court to try war crimes and crimes committed against humanity. In the following year, the world witnessed the unprecedented fact of the highest of British courts of justice ruling that a former head of state was liable to extradition to another country to answer there charges of crimes alleged against him.[2] Not all this century's changes have been for the worse.

Nor would there be much point in merely lamenting tragic and terrible facts, in any case. We should seek also to measure their true impact. No doubt the historians of a century hence will see that some things are important that do not now seem to be, but we should try to draw our own conclusions. They must recognize that some events have changed millions of lives for the better, even if those aware of it have been far fewer than those who were affected. Even when such changes are sometimes very recent and have not yet come to bear with their full potential weight, or have yet still to show themselves explicitly, we have to make guesses about them in order to make sense of the past.

No selection will please everybody and, like much else in historical writing, decisions about such matters are subjective and often highly personal; protestations of objectivity should be considered sceptically.

[2] This was the former dictator of Chile, General Pinochet, whose extradition from the United Kingdom for crimes committed in his country after the 1973 coup had been sought by a Spanish magistrate. The first hearing of the case granted that the general could be extradited, but was then set aside as legally flawed. A second hearing then ruled that the general was indeed liable to extradition to answer charges in Spain, but only on those arising since 1988, when the British law on extradition had changed.

That historical judgements can be challenged, though, is no reason not to make them. My own list (if that is what is expected) of the most influential changes of the twentieth century would in fact not be a long one. For all the important qualifications to be made in describing the complicated way in which it happened, first must come the simple fact of an unprecedented and revolutionary growth in the world's wealth; more people than ever before in history have had their lives materially enhanced in the last 100 years, the outstanding indicator being the rise in world population. Another distinctive change accompanying this has been a slow spreading of a dominant lifestyle, one of whose central and most paradoxical characteristics is to offer in many ways much greater choice to individuals. This has meant a new degree of shared experience. A further great change has been the huge outflowing of information which contributes to that sharing; the world is now understandable and 'transparent' (as the current jargon has it) as never before. Humanity is tied together in new ways by it. Not only is more information available more widely than ever before, it is available more swiftly. The media now transmit a greater volume of signals to larger audiences than ever, and do so with unprecedented speed. Democracy, in particular, appears to favour this as does no other political system (which does not mean, of course, that it does so in an obviously unqualified and wholly beneficial way) and the change in communications has made changes in lifestyle particularly obvious, for all the still substantial differences between even the cultures of the 'developed' world. Where the combination of a widely diffused information technology and democratic constitutional arrangements exists, it becomes more and more difficult to maintain old official and governmental practices of secrecy. But such change is not confined to well-governed countries and the implications of that are more and more difficult to weigh.[3] The century has also made a

[3] The Internet provides good examples. In 1994 a militant organization supporting the claims of peasants in the Mexican state of Chiapas attracted only minor notice until its leader, 'Subcommandante Marcos' (a faceless figure in a balaclava helmet, later revealed as a university lecturer), opened to it a whole new dimension of propaganda by issuing news bulletins and political messages in Spanish and English on the Internet from a laptop computer. Complaints have also been heard about the Internet's 'corrupting' influence in the Gulf States, where attention has been drawn

vast difference (even if much of it still remains only potential) to half the human race, to women. As for politics, the systematic relationships of the whole globe, its legal structure and institutions, have been revolutionized since 1901. Much of the machinery within which humanity long tried to solve its problems, its political instrumentation, as it were, has been swept away or radically transformed.

The final outstanding change of the century seems to be cultural and psychological: the spread of the idea that human happiness is realizable on earth and human destiny manageable. That is by no means the same – or as consciously held an idea – as the old western doctrine of progress, though it can still look somewhat like it. It is overwhelmingly the product of the incremental influence of the natural sciences which now set our main intellectual orientations.

In spite of the great transformations, though, the past, in the shape of both remembered and unremembered history, still clutters our lives. Even our exasperations are shaped by it. So much does not change that it can be difficult to measure – sometimes even to recognize – the great changes that have come about. It remains a matter for debate whether we have become a little more able to deal with the inertia of the past, so that it is consciously more managed and becomes part of the world we handle in other ways with such confidence. If that were to be true, we should perhaps reckon it to eclipse even the other great changes of this century in its importance. But at first sight it seems unlikely. Due allowance for the weight of history in our affairs, and therefore a better chance of mastering it, still often seems sadly to seek. We have all the more reason, therefore, to keep that weight in mind when trying to pin down the difference the twentieth century has made to humanity's view of its own powers.

---

to the reception of pornographic material on it. In 1998, too, there went on trial in Shanghai a prisoner charged with inciting the 'overthrow of state power', allegedly by supplying electronic addresses to the publisher of an electronic news-sheet; early in 1999 he was sentenced to two years' imprisonment.

THE MYTHOLOGY OF HUMAN HAPPINESS

A century ago, pain had still to be taken for granted. For all the small inroads made upon it by anaesthesia, it was regarded as inevitable even in the most advanced societies. Only a few optimists thought that humanity might eventually turn the corner to a painless future. Today, Utopians are even harder to find, yet it is as never before an accepted and everyday fact over much of the world that pain is more avoidable and is therefore more intolerable than 100 years ago. This is one of many paradoxical ways in which large numbers of people (and more than ever) know that things have changed, and sense that there can and probably will be still further change for the better. A spreading attitude of unquestioning, not very reflective, acceptance that human problems are in principle manageable or at least remediable is a major psychological transformation. It could hardly have been widely anticipated in 1901, even among the fortunate peoples of European origin. Yet it now seems an idea certain to outlast the European political hegemony which helped to spread it worldwide.

To weigh the importance of such a change, we have to try to set aside for a moment our knowledge of other facts. It remains true, after all, that for most of their lives millions of human beings can rarely contemplate the future except with deep unhappiness and misgiving – and that is when they can summon up the energy to consider it at all, for they are often still going hungry. In the normal course of events, though, it is also true that many other millions do not go hungry, nor do they seem in any obvious danger of doing so. Indeed, more people than ever before can now take it for granted that they will never know real need. A smaller, but still large, number can even believe that their lives will grow steadily more enjoyable and will improve in other ways, too. Unsurprisingly, they tend to look forward to such a future as in the main one of increasing consumption of material goods they already enjoy in some degree. If they raise their eyes from self-absorption, they may even come to believe that others, as time goes by, will come to share their happy lot. Even a few centuries ago, this would have been true nowhere in the world. Perhaps it might be established statistically that now more people look to the future with positive hope than used to be the case, but that could be going too far; millions of people still bow under the crushing and seemingly inescapable suffering imposed on them by bad government, poverty and disease.

A change in mass outlook is most obvious in the rich societies that now consume a far greater share of the earth's resources than the rich could do even in the recent past. In the western world, for all our comparatively deprived minorities and underclasses, we are in this sense nowadays nearly all rich. It is not so long (about 200 years) since a typical Englishman would have been unlikely in the whole of his life to have had access to the means to travel more than a few miles from the place where he was born except on his own two feet. Only 150 years ago he would not have had assured supplies of clean water. A hundred years ago, he still faced a good chance of being crippled or even killed by a casual accident, or by the onset of a disease for which no remedy was known or existed, and for which no nursing care was available to him, while he and his family ate meagre meals so lacking in balance and nourishment (to say nothing of being dull and unappetizing) that their like is now eaten only by the poorest, and they could expect in their fifties and sixties (if they survived so long) the onset of a painful and penurious old age.

Much the same could be said of other Europeans, North Americans, Australasians, Japanese and many others. The vast changes in expectations implied in such examples, though, have now spread far beyond the countries which might have been thought of as 'developed' when this century began. The enormous wealth-producing power of modern manufacture now floods the world with very visible and cheaply available benefits in the form of consumer goods. Combined with the spread of information about them, this new abundance has meant that things once sought only in the most advanced societies are increasingly available in the underdeveloped world, too. At the very least, this is true among its better-off city-dwellers. While all-too-visible differences between life in rich and poor societies now far transcend any such differences that existed in the past, this is in part because not long ago all were poor by today's standards. Millions of even the poorest now alive, though, can now glimpse possibilities of changes in their lot for the better. More important still, many of them have come to believe that such change can be sought, promoted and actually brought about. Most politicians tell them so. This has never happened before.

It may still be too much to term such a change a revolution in human hopes, but it is now more evident in their behaviour than ever before that peoples and governments implicitly believe as a matter of fact that specific problems can be solved. Many go further and feel that, therefore, they will be. We may well feel sceptical about rearranging the world to increase the sum of human happiness when we remember some of the twentieth century's attempts at social engineering, or the unassimilable cultures, intransigent moralisms and tribal loyalties which show no signs of going away. Yet we all tend to behave *as if* more of our problems are in principle soluble or remediable. If this is true, we can surely think it a revolution in human attitudes. Its ultimate origins, of course, should not be sought only in the last 100 years. This century has only brought its consummation. Its deepest roots lie far, far back in those prehistoric millennia of slowly growing capacity to manipulate nature, when pre-human beings learnt to manage fire or to put an edge on a convenient piece of flint. The abstract idea that such manipulation might be possible must have taken shape only much more recently as the insight of at first only a few in certain crucial eras and cultural zones. But the idea is now commonplace; it has triumphed worldwide. We now take it for granted that people everywhere should and will begin to ask themselves why things remain as they are when they evidently might be made better. This idea is now held, vaguely and imprecisely, more widely than ever before. Our behaviour shows it.

MASTERY OF THE MATERIAL WORLD

The exponential growth in material wealth evident in the last couple of centuries must surely have played a big part in giving humanity reasons to accept such an idea. That growth has rested on the increasing ability to manage the material world for which science provided the tools. Prophecies made a century ago about travel in space, implant surgery, nuclear power have long since become accepted realities.

Now science appears to offer even more. We stand at the edge of an era whose development may perhaps be directed and manipulated more fundamentally than ever (for instance, through genetic engineering). Some dimly glimpse a world ahead in which people will be able to commission (as it were) private futures to order, perhaps through genetic shaping of unborn offspring, perhaps through experience 'bought off the shelf' as information technology becomes available to create a 'virtual reality' more perfect than actuality. It may be that people will be able to live more of their conscious lives, if they wish to do so, in worlds constructed to their order than in those that can be provided by ordinary sense-experience.

Such perspectives may be exhilarating for some, but they are intimidating, too. They clearly have great potential for disorder and destabilization. Rather than indulging in speculation about them, it is best to reflect firmly on what we can see to have changed the inherited pasts this century once confronted. Changes in material well-being have, for instance, transformed politics by changing the circumstances in which politicians have to take decisions, the ways in which institutions operate, the distribution of power in society. In virtually no society nowadays can religion be expected to operate as it once did, as the intransigent turbulence within Islam shows. Science has accelerated and deepened such changes, not only by hugely enlarging the toolkit of knowledge humanity can use to grapple with nature, but through the direct and indirect exemplary effects it has had on the way thousands of millions think, the things they take for granted, their sense of what can be done. In this respect, whatever the century may or may not have done for political democracy, it has brought a great extension of practical freedoms.

In a new awareness of possibilities lies the seed of a transformed view of human destiny, intended or not. If many more people now think that problems ought to have solutions than did in their grandparents' day, science, directly or indirectly, has done much to make them think so, and more, probably, than any other single force. It has provided our most impressive and concentrated expression of human potential; as a historical force, two great world wars cannot compare with it. Yet a starting-point only in 1901 provides a misleadingly short perspective. Since then, millions of us have had some elementary education in science, but it is hardly that which explains its worldwide prestige and influence. Its effects on mass thinking have only in a small measure been brought about by specific and formal propagation of its ideas and methods, for all their impact on the minds of some of the educated. Opinion has been changed much more by what science has appeared to do to produce growing well-being. Overwhelmingly western in their appearance on the world stage (in spite of early sallies by Asian civilizations), the expressions of scientific knowledge in better technology swiftly became global in their effect. In this century they have directly accounted for much of its huge increase in human numbers, for fundamental changes in the relationships of nations, for the rise and decline of whole sectors of the world economy, the tying of the world together by nearly instantaneous communication, and much more of its most revolutionary change.

Much of this upheaval has excited unease, yet it has hardly dented the vague and optimistic expectancy in the minds of millions about what those who know can do to manage nature. Many relevant misgivings leave unconcerned the vast majority of mankind, which remains in blissful ignorance of them. It is only among the intellectual leadership of the richer societies that there has been some qualification of the confidence so evident in the first two-thirds or so of this century in human ability to manage the world through science and technology (rather than, say, through magic or religious ritual), and so to satisfy human wants. Perhaps such qualification will prove to have much further to go. Certainly we now face new knowledge of the fragility of our natural environment and its susceptibility to change for the worse. There is a new awareness that not all the apparent benefits derived from the manipulation of nature are without their costs, that some may even have frightening implications, and, more mundanely, that we do not yet possess the social and political skills and structures to ensure that humanity will put knowledge to good use. Discussion of public policy has only recently begun to give due weight to such concerns. Nevertheless, we can note progress. International agreements over the handling of the waste products of nuclear industry and international debate about the use of fossil fuels are now taken for granted. Attention to comparable matters could not have been expected fifty years ago; it registers an important advance in collective awareness.

It is of course crucial that faith in science has been based on real triumphs, not on illusion. If we now wish to qualify that faith, it is only because science itself has given us more knowledge to take into account. It is reasonable to say that if grave issues now face us, the human toolkit has not been shown to be exhausted in dealing with them. Even global warming, the depletion of the ozone layer, or the loss of ecological variety as the rainforest is destroyed do not imply any diminution in principle of humanity's power to rearrange the environment to suit itself.[4] History is not going to end unless the human race is extinguished, either by natural disaster independent of human agency, or as a result of indulgence of our environmental folly without reflexion. We can leave to actuaries the calculation of the danger of such possibilities as collision with an asteroid, a change in planetary orbits or any of the other cosmological scenarios sometimes proposed as ways in which the world might come to an end. Self-destruction of the human species seems improbable because the human being is a reflective, as well as a tool-making, animal. We are still some way from finishing ourselves off, even if interference with nature has already led without anyone intending it to the appearance of drug-resistant bacteria and viruses by mutation through natural selection in the changed environments we have brought into being. Problems just as great (for example, those of increasing food production to present levels) have been solved in the past. There are no grounds for believing that solutions to new problems will not in due course appear. At present the evidence remains overwhelming that human manipulative power has so far brought more good than harm to most human beings.

---

[4] For instance, an international World Ocean Circulation Experiment will soon add to our power to predict climatic change, and promote the understanding of the role of the oceans as a sink for atmospheric carbon dioxide.

THE FIRST WORLD CIVILIZATION

This does not mean, of course, that everyone finds progress (to invoke that contestable word) pleasant. Many have been sure that they do not. This century has confronted hundreds of millions of people with appalling upheavals. It has brought about sometimes cataclysmic disruptions of patterns in which people have traditionally grown up, entered work, founded families, grown old and died. Such facts continue to dramatize huge contrasts in human experience. There still exist societies and subdivisions even in rich nations, where prosperity seems unlikely for the visible future. Yet more humans than for many centuries now share similar experiences. This, too, must be central to the history of mental change in this century. Understandably, though, much of the content of this reality is so banal as to lie beneath the horizon of interest of most historians. Yet in most countries people are getting used to living in cities and over half the world's population now do so. If those cities are in developing societies they are increasingly liberated from physical differences of environment by the arrival of running water, electricity, public health provision, air-conditioning. All over the world those cities are similarly ordered (at least in aspiration) by similar traffic signals and policemen on point duty, increasingly have publicly-lit streets, studded with banks and shops, and in those shops there is a growing likelihood that much the same sort of things will be available, often, even under the same brand names; one can expect to buy many toothpastes worldwide though they were not invented very long ago. Men and women who do not share common languages use and service the same machines and derive the same or very similar advantages and disadvantages from their use. In Delhi and Djakarta, São Paulo and Paris alike the internal combustion engine has imposed its intolerable demands, inflicting similar strains and stresses. Satellite dish receivers for television programmes that are made to be broadcast internationally sprout like fungi on roofs and walls everywhere, even if those in Bombay are likely to be run up locally from recycled industrial waste, while those in Balham and Bordeaux are likely to be factory-made. There is a shared experience also of the poor, one of squalor, overcrowding, defective or absent public services, economic precariousness and comparative deprivation. For all their ethnic or cultural differences, the material essentials of life in the slums of Cairo, Calcutta, Nairobi or Mexico City often look much the same.

Material realities of such communality shape minds. They bring about a new sharing of mental signposts and assumptions. Information and popular entertainment are now increasingly produced for global consumption. Popular groups of musicians tour the world like (but much more easily and prosperously than) the troubadours who wandered about medieval Europe, presenting their songs and spectacles in different countries to audiences who turn up to hear them in large numbers. Samisen, sitar and gamelan now attract only minority (if often élite and enthusiastic) audiences; the electric guitar and drum kit draw the crowds everywhere. Young people, in particular, are losing sight of their distinctive cultural forms in the indulgence of tastes which bind them to other young people far away who have a little spare cash in their pockets – and there are millions more such than even a few years ago. The same movies are dubbed and subtitled to be shown worldwide on television to audiences that take away from them similar fantasies and dreams. At a quite different level, the language of democracy and human rights is now enlisted more widely than ever to pay at least lip-service to civilized ideals of what public life should be. Our new flood of factual information about the rest of the world is continually swollen and exploited to assure that sensibilities originally rooted in Europe, but increasingly presented as universal, are aroused to support what their promoters regard as unimpeachably reputable causes. Whatever governments do, they feel they must *say* increasingly that they believe in a version of democracy, the rule of law, human rights, equality of the sexes and much else. Only now and then is there a nasty jolt, an exposure of hypocrisies in practice, the revelation of an unacknowledged moral disagreement or a blunt rejection by a culture still resistant to contamination of its traditions and sensibilities.

Human destinies are now linked round the world not only by such impalpable forces, and by the politics of formal organizations like the UN or the IMF, but by science and technology through their complex networks, by commercial and industrial organization and by material practice. Millions of fairly primitive agriculturists can now live in a world in which most of their contemporaries take such things as vapour trails high overhead, flickering television sets in bars, and plastic fibre garments for granted, though they need understand nothing of where they come from. Nor is this incompatible with the at first sight paradoxical fact that next door to fully developed societies, there are still parts even of Europe, let alone Africa and the Middle East or yet further afield, where it can be said that the twentieth century has yet fully to arrive, let alone that anticipations of the twenty-first have come into sight. In the Balkans in recent years the full repertoire of the barbarities of the Middle Ages has erupted anew; yet those who launch pogroms, murder, mass rape and intimidation against their ethnically different neighbours also wear clothes much like those of other Europeans. When they defend what they are doing, they mouth the same rhetoric of nationalism and self-determination as Irishmen and Frenchmen have done before them. When the overwhelming majority of mankind lived very close to the land which they tilled, wealth did not much separate one people from another, although religion, costume, language might well do so. But now new contrasts have opened up, too. The gravest in the world today are between the lives of the poor in different countries; even the unemployed in Germany or Great Britain have access to wealth unimaginable to the poor of the Sudan.[5]

Generalization often seems fruitless. For all the advances of this century, their benefits are very unequally shared – and, revealingly but strangely, that makes more people unhappy than once was the case. Yet even our inequalities, and the variety still to be found in the world, have been shaped by general processes and facts. These include a central paradox: in a century that has seen the disappearance of European hegemony in all its institutional embodiments, the civilization Europe originated has made silent conquests as never before, even when its own core values seem fatally sapped by relativism and while it has been deeply traumatized by psychological shock from the revelation within itself of human capacity for evil on a horrifying

[5] For broader, but also more specific discussion of such themes, see R. Rapoport, *Families, Children, and the Quest for a Global Ethic* (Aldershot, 1997).

scale. Debates about an 'enduring' Europe, focused on certain core values and concepts unchanging and unchanged by history, are beside the point here. The continuities to be traced in the historical fact of Europe have always taken different forms at different times. Europe has always been in process, being made and remade, *reformanda*, one thing at one time, one at another, a place where important things have happened. From that place have emerged forces which changed other civilizations and created new cultures. No longer Europe-dominated, the world's politics are still organized intellectually around European ideas, however qualified and obscured in practice, just as the world's intellectual orientation is increasingly organized around the science created in Europe. On any count, these remain profoundly important facts, major determinants of human thinking and behaviour.

Europe having been from the sixteenth century increasingly the source of forces that changed the rest of the world irreversibly, most complaints about 'Eurocentrism' in modern history are beside the point. The Europe at present in the forefront of discussion and scrutiny is important, too, even if not yet, perhaps, so important as it might be. It is in a drifting phase of internal fluidity and reorganization; its cultural past is not what people think about when the politicians negotiate. Yet the historical past – what Europeans did to shape the world – is inescapably involved in explaining the world today. It is a part of world history that can only cease to be an incubus if it is consciously recognized as an influence. After all, one of Europe's most terrible gifts to the world has been the seemingly unstoppable revolution in human expectations.

This may well be why there now seem to be so many fewer plausible ways of seeing the world than there were in 1901. Quite distinctive perceptions of present and past could then exist which owed nothing to European or western culture. Without straining their credulity, Chinese could then still think of a (temporarily disrupted) world order normally centred on a universal monarchy in Peking sustained by a divine mandate. Few Muslims a century ago needed to find much place in their thinking for the abstract idea of the state and found the distinction of believer and non-believer far more significant. Hundreds of millions of Africans and Asians found no difficulty in doing without any conception of science. 'Westerners' saw the world as 'civilized' and 'uncivilized' with as much unconcern as Englishmen could distinguish in their national game between 'Gentlemen' and 'Players'.

Such sharp disparities have now been much eroded; some of these world-outlooks have disappeared altogether. Whatever remains of the emotional strength of the Chinese intellectual's sense of cultural superiority, he now talks the language of liberalism or Marxism. Even in Jeddah and Teheran, thoughtful Muslims have to confront a tension between the pull of tradition and the need to have at least some mental acquaintance with the dangerous temptations of an alien modernism. Of course, other parts of the world have their pasts to deal with. India sometimes seems schizophrenically torn between the values of the secular democracy its leaders envisaged in 1947 and its own. When the rulers of North Korea attempt to blend technological modernization and Marxism with unavowed Confucian values, their ambition testifies to the still important role of other pasts than the western in the world's memory. But the world has remembered more of what happened in Europe because, for good or ill, that settled so much of the world's fate. As the century closes, there is once again debate about what Europe may be, could be, should be, is; clearly the continent may not so obviously influence the rest of the world in a future where so much power has gravitated to Washington and Beijing. But whether it will do so or not is not the business of historians. They need not speculate about the future but should try to clarify the past. If we need a reminder, the miseries of shattered Yugoslavia alone surely should persuade us how much history can still clutter up our present.

TODAY'S POLITICAL WORLD

Except for a few metaphysically inclined persons who know the way History – often capitalized – is going, almost no one now seeks to justify government in ways still very widely accepted in 1901. Hardly anyone now appeals to indefeasible dynastic right, heredity, prescriptive authority or many other things then taken for granted in the way public life was run round the world. The greatest exception to this statement is, of course, the continuing vigour of the appeal to nationalism, not just a successful idea surviving from the nineteenth century, but one whose success has been consummated virtually worldwide since the twentieth began. Our most comprehensive international (a significant word) organization is called the United Nations. Its predecessor was a League of Nations. The units of an integrating Europe are the historic nations thrown up by its past. The old colonial empires have dissolved into scores of new nations. Many existing national states are still trying to justify their own existence to minorities which themselves claim to be nations, and therefore to have the right to break away and rule themselves. Where those minorities wish to break up the states which contain them – as do many Basques, Kurds, Quebecois, for example – they speak in the name of unachieved nationhood. The nation seems to have been supremely successful in satisfying thirsts other remedies cannot reach; it has been the great creator of modern community, sweeping aside class and religion, giving a sense of meaning and belonging to those who feel adrift in a modernizing world in which older ties are weakened and decayed. It has been the greatest of myth-makers, a mover of men and women, shaking up history and imagined history with their hopes, resentments and fears in potent cocktails of destructive excitement, the greatest single conscious force in the politics of history's most revolutionary century.

Nationalism has usually been able to underwrite a second-order argument legitimating public authority which was already articulated and familiar in 1901, but which has been much more commonly invoked since. This is the claim that the state delivers public – or at least generally desired – benefits. In a narrow sense, the moral authority of states has always in a measure rested on a claim to deliver public good, if only in the minimal form of order. Whether they can actually do so, or, indeed, actually deliver any such good at all, has, of course, by no means always been clear. Marxist orthodoxy used to argue, and in a few places still does, that the state is a machine for ensuring the domination of a class and, as such, will disappear when overtaken by the march of History. Even Marxist regimes, though, have not always behaved as if these things were true. As for the idea that a state might be a private possession of a dynasty or an individual serving private interests, it is now everywhere disavowed, whatever the actualities of government in Indonesia, the Philippines or many other places may have been at times in the last half-century. Even when there is disagreement or debate about exactly what are the benefits the state should provide in specific instances, modern justifications of government rest at least implicitly on its claim to be able to provide them, often in the form of the protection of national interests. Forms still somewhat disguise this; perhaps we should revert to oaths of allegiance like those of medieval Aragon which specified a contract between government and governed.

As for constitutional forms, there now survive few of the monarchies so prominent in 1901.[6] The sovereign state in its other forms (mainly republican, at least in name) is taken for granted, nonetheless, as it still was not in many places even a century ago. This has been largely a mechanical consequence of one great process, the breaking-up of empires. That new states had to come into being to replace them was scarcely questioned at any stage. Trusteeships under first the League of Nations mandates and then under the United Nations were seen as only interim arrangements, preparing countries for national sovereign independence. The assumption when the first mandates were set up in 1919 was not yet that such independence need be linked to democracy, though a tie between self-determination and that constitutional style tended in Europe to be taken for granted in the new nations emerging from the Great War. It was not until the collapse of the USSR, after almost a half-century of dissolving other empires, that the global generalization of the language of sovereignty of the people, representative institutions and the separation of powers reached its greatest extent.

Already by 1990, most of the world (and all major countries except the United Kingdom) had written constitutions whose very existence would have represented the limits of radical aspiration in 1901. In practice, of course, this did not always mean much. It has often been pointed out that the presence of the word 'democratic' or 'democracy' in the name of a state is almost always a warning sign that it is run as a dictatorship or oligarchy. Yet the extension of democratic

---

[6] Currently, ten in Europe (not counting either the co-principate of Andorra or the Vatican), eleven in Asia (counting Malaysia and the United Arab Emirates as collective entities), and four in Africa.

institutions during this century has been more than formal; democracy and constitutional liberty have won their victories, some comparable in extent to those of nationalism.

The chief institutional effect of the European impact on international life has nonetheless been a general reorganization of it as a system of national, sovereign and usually republican states. This began to appear likely in the nineteenth century; it has been completed in the twentieth. While Europe at home was meanwhile reconstructing its own internal arrangements, eradicating or marginalizing archaic and hybrid forms, the state machinery that it had invented – professional bureaucracies, standing armed services, police, taxation systems – began to spread overseas to its dependencies, former dependencies and imitators. This came about sometimes through adoption, more often through imposition by imperial rulers. It was soon taken to be an inevitable concomitant of modernization.

Furthermore, the states that are the result are now organized as were none of their predecessors in elaborate systems and relationships which are much more than the flimsy tissues of alliances and associations for technical matters which in 1901 barely foreshadowed what was to come. Now, 185 states belong to the United Nations Organization.[7] But there are many other groupings for specific activities or areas to impose significant restraints upon – or give new opportunities to – the states that belong to them. Even the regional examples differ greatly in their structure and the difference they make to international behaviour. The EU, ASEAN and OAU, for example, mean very different things to their members. Some (like OECD) are functional but general. Some like OPEC or the International Telecommunications Satellite Organization are highly specialized, and all, of course, vary greatly in their degree of effectiveness. Some are supra-regional, like NATO, which at times has looked as if it is evolving into more than the conventional military alliance in which it began, or the protean former British Commonwealth. There are now so many such organizations that most of us do not know what their acronyms stand for; we are puzzled and perhaps a little oppressed to be told that, for

[7] The Holy See and the Swiss Confederation also have permanent observer status in it, while the Palestine Liberation Organization was granted a special observer status.

example, SAPTA was launched by SAARC in 1995.[8] The spread of this luxuriant undergrowth to international affairs makes obsolete, nonetheless, any notion that they can form a game played by independent and autonomous players operating without restraint except that of individual interest as interpreted by *Realpolitik*.[9]

It is only at first sight a paradox that substantial inter-state structures should have emerged from a century in which more blood has been shed by states in quarrels with one another than ever before. After all, some of those structures (the League, UNO) emerged immediately and directly from such violence as responses to it, and as attempts to control it. International law now, partly in consequence, reaches further into the practical control of states' behaviour than ever before, for all the notorious examples which remain of failure to comply with it. Meanwhile, empire, another dominating feature of the regulatory landscape of international affairs in 1901, has virtually disappeared. We can ignore the relatively tiny vestiges of overseas territories still under the sovereignty of former imperial powers, and even the reassertion of the ancient claims of China over lands (such as Tibet) long regarded as dependent, and recent examples of outright aggression such as those of Indonesia in the 1960s and 1970s in East Timor (which the United Nations still reckons to be under Portuguese sovereignty). These are all manifestly eccentric to the general collapse of the great systems of territorial domination still covering so much of the world in 1901. With empire, though, went its helpfulness as a force for containing potential disorder. This is linked to other great transformations. Though the empires of, say, China, Persia and the Ottoman Sultan were still in place in 1901 and had been for many centuries, most of the imperial surface of the globe had been accumulated since 1500 in European hands. They were expressions of that

[8] Once again, the complaint of Voltaire, two and a half centuries ago, comes irresistibly to the mind of the reader of general history: 'what is it to me if one king replaces another on the banks of the Oxus and Jaxartes?' – but a little unfairly, perhaps.
[9] A recent commentator on the present plight of Africa (R. C. Kent, in *The World Today* (Vol. 55, p.9) suggests that government is actually in decline as a component of the structures of authority in that continent, and that 'governments will increasingly vie for authority with other groupings' – some functional, some merely expressive of organized violence.

largely (though not solely) white domination of history that has also disappeared as a political fact.

This disappearance is sometimes masked by the appearance in this century for the first time in history of one superpower able to deploy its strength worldwide in defence of its interests and pursuit of its goals. But there has also been renewed an old power focus in Asia (potentially, too, one of superpower if that means a worldwide potential of projection) through the revolutionary resurgence of China, as well as the slow consolidation of a much richer and potentially more powerful Europe than ever before, now virtually without territorial possession outside its own continent, and by the emergence of new centres of economic strength in the Far East, above all, in Japan. Some might claim the slowly growing political integration of Latin America with the larger world community as another positive element in a new world order which was in almost all its specifics unimaginable in 1901.

Among its negative features remain the persistent problems set by the disappearance of old empires not replaced by new ones. The Ottoman empire crumbled away finally in the Great War and its aftermath, but those who dispute the spoils have gone marching on in the new Balkan wars of Yugoslavia, and the succession struggles of the Near and Middle East which as yet show no sign of a conclusive end or of effective management of their disorder by outsiders. Russia rules today less territory than she has done for three centuries. The collapse first of her empire, even in its post-tsarist and strengthened form under the USSR until that, too, slid into dissolution, has provided another example of a part of the world where the danger of post-imperial disorder remains and may not be easily manageable. It is not only in international disorder, though, that dangers lurk in the aftermath of empire. Social breakdown may now well be what lies ahead for Algeria or Macedonia, and perhaps for Egypt. As for sub-Saharan Africa, only in the republic of South Africa have there been, so far, good grounds for hoping that ordered and effective government might follow the ending of empire.

In these circumstances, some have been much troubled by what might be called an Islamic factor in world politics, difficult though it is to assess. Premonitions of change from this quarter could be detected early in the twentieth century. They have assumed a more worrying aspect for some commentators since 1950. The numbers alone are striking. Nigeria, largest of African states, has 50 million Muslim inhabitants. Indonesia, largest of Islamic states, has nearly 200 million. All Muslim societies have burgeoning populations. Some have significant military resources. Some are still outstandingly wealthy. Yet for practical purposes Islamic unity has so far proved a mirage. Most Muslims in the world do not understand Arabic. Even in the Arabic-literate lands so often thought of as the heart of Islam they seem unable to unite either to grapple with the Palestine problem left behind by the Ottoman collapse, or with their own social and economic difficulties. It is clearer that great potential for disorder and even international danger are to be found in the Islamic world than that Islam has a role as a force in international affairs such as some Muslims have dreamed of. It cannot even be confidently alleged that some of the forces sustaining present turbulence will be with us for ever. Oil no longer looks like the resource-earner it was in the 1970s and even demographic trends will not go on indefinitely in the same way. Still more to the point, Islamic societies are far too temptingly open to misinterpretation by outsiders as culturally homogeneous. No more than the mythological 'West' of the popular sermons of the mosques can Islam be identified convincingly as a coherent, discrete, neatly-bordered civilization. Like the 'West' it is an abstraction, a useful shorthand for expository purposes, and we should not be seduced by our own choice of language. Many Muslims, including some of a devout cast of mind, seek a footing in two worlds, committed in a measure to both western and Islamic ideals. Each world represents a historical centre of dynamism, a source of energies; yet it looks as if, until now, this is more true of western civilization, however defined, than of any possible reading of Islam. Possibly the most evident contrast presently separating the two is the West's long-established cultural predilection for the display and exercise of self-criticism and its capacity to adapt, as well as its provision of men and women within its sphere with a capacity to live with a growing relativism of values as no other civilization has ever done.

CONCLUSION

The fact which runs through every one of this century's changes in the basic assumptions and structures of world politics is that they all reflect in different ways the change to a post-European phase of world history. It is now much harder than it was in 1901 to guess the sources from which future impulses to dynamic change will come. It is clear, though, that they cannot come so overwhelmingly and decisively (as they did for three or four centuries) from Europe. In that brief period, Europe wrought a world revolution. It did so not only through political, military and economic power, but through the superior cultural energy of a civilization. The result was a process interlinking all parts of the globe evident in the last 100 years. Much of its meaning is still being revealed. The contemplation of that history, it seems fair to guess, will continue to engage and fascinate people. We may like to recall for the last time in these pages, though, that the end of one of the centuries into which the Christian dating system arbitrarily divides the past has no significance, nor has any supposedly millennial year, except that of convention and convenience. The only thing we know will differentiate the year we call 2000 from that called 1999 (when this sentence is being written) is that there will then be still more to look back upon.

Once again, too it is worthwhile recalling what Burckhart said about history being what one age finds remarkable in another. The events of the twentieth century will go on acquiring new meanings as they drop below the horizon of memory and future generations start to wonder about their inheritances. There is an irreducible self-centredness about all but the most specialized and specifically academic historical enterprises. In the end, all we can do at this moment is to look back upon years virtually coterminous with the lives of the oldest amongst us, establish facts about them, analyse their connexions and disjunctions, and search them for guidance about what it is that made our lives turn out as they have done. This is a serious enough task and one all the harder because facts become so much more difficult to manage when they are so plentiful and when those that look important at first sight change and disappear at an ever-quickening rate. Personal experience, that tempting prop, vividly adds its own dangers of distortion. Moreover, the borders of that experience have changed so much in recent years that it is often hard to discern at all, let alone define exactly, what is being experienced in the first true age of mass communication. We must expect our experience, as well as our history, to be revalued.

At least it is clear, though, that the recent or contemporary historian will be wise to stay away from taking as facts things that people have put together for expository or dialectical purposes of their own (hypostatization or reification, in the fashionable jargon). History will never be fixed. It is best to be cautious of fixed claims about it, and especially of talk about irresistible trends, or of an end to history. As a cultural activity, the study of history sometimes seems best seen as a maid-of-all-work, looking after our moral and political hygiene by cleaning up our views on what has happened to humanity and what human beings have done. It can disperse illusions, open up new perspectives, reveal obstacles to our desires and aspirations which would be dangerous if left in the shadows. It is not celebration, nor indictment, enjoyable though both those activities are. That we must not expect too much of history is, in fact, one clear lesson which can be drawn from thinking even about just the twentieth century – as it can, of course, be drawn just as well from thinking about any of those that preceded it.

Appendix: The Exploration of Space

1903   Konstantin Tsiolkovsky (1857–1935) publishes paper on rocket space travel using liquid propellants.

1933   1 May: Tsiolkovsky predicts that many Soviet citizens will live to see the first space flights.

1944   German rockets bombard London and Antwerp.

1954   President Eisenhower announces a small scientific satellite, Vanguard, will be launched 1957–8.

1957   1 July: Launch of Sputnik 1 (USSR), weight 184 lb.
        3 November: Launch of Sputnik 2 (USSR), weight 1,120 lb, with the dog Laika as passenger.

1958   31 January: Launch of Explorer (USA) and discovery of Van Allen radiation belts.
        17 March: Launch of Vanguard 1 (USA), weight 3¼ lb. The first satellite with solar batteries.

1959   13 September: Luna 2 (USSR) crashes on moon, the first manmade object to arrive there.
        10 October: Luna 3 (USSR) photographs far side of moon.

1960   11 August: Discoverer 13 (USA) recovered after first successful re-entry to atmosphere.
        19 August: Sputnik 5 (USSR) orbits earth with two dogs which return unharmed.

1961   12 April: Major Yuri Gagarin (USSR) orbits the earth.
        25 May: President Kennedy commits USA to landing man on moon by 1970.

6 August: Vostok 2 (USSR) makes seventeen orbits of earth.

1962   10 July: Launch of Telstar (USA) and first television pictures transmitted across the Atlantic.
20 February: First manned orbited space flight.

1965   18 March: On Vokshod 2 mission (USSR) Alexey Leonov makes a ten-minute 'walk in space'.
2 May: Early Bird commercial communication satellite (USA) first used by television.
15 December: Launch of Gemini 6 (USA), which makes rendezvous with Gemini 7, the two craft coming within a foot of one another.

1966   July–November: Gemini missions 10, 11, 12 (USA) all achieve 'docking' with 'Agena' vehicle.

1967   27 January: First deaths in US programme.

1968   21–7 December: Apollo 8 (USA) makes first manned voyage round moon.

1969   14–27 January: Soyuz 4 and 5 (USSR) dock in space and exchange passengers.
16–21 July: Apollo 11 (USA) lands three men on the moon, Neil Armstrong, Michael Collins, and Edwin Aldrin. Armstrong and Aldrin subsequently emerge from their vehicle to walk on the moon.

1971   April: First Soviet space station put in orbit.
7 June: Three men put aboard it and remain there for three weeks.

1973   14 May: First US space station (Skylab) put in orbit.

1975   Apollo–Soyuz rendezvous successfully achieved.

1976   20 July: Viking 1 lands on Mars and transmits the first pictures of the planet's surface.

1979   5 March: Voyager I (launched 1977) and Voyager II make closest approach yet to Jupiter.
19 August: Russian cosmonauts Ryumin and Lyakhov return to earth after longest stay yet (175 days) in space.

1981   12–14 April: Maiden flight of US Space Shuttle, the first reusable manned spacecraft.
August: Voyager II reaches Saturn after four years in flight.

1984   First repair of a satellite in orbit, and rescue of others for return to earth and reuse.

1986   28 January: US Challenger explodes shortly after take-off with loss of entire crew of seven.

1990   24 April: The Hubble Space Telescope (weighing eleven tons) put into earth orbit by US Space Shuttle Discovery.

1995   22 March: Cosmonaut Polyakov returns to earth after spending 437 days in space on Mir space station.
June: US shuttle Atlantis comes close enough to Mir for crews to shake hands and exchange gifts through an airlock.

1997   4 July: Landing of Sojourner, a roving machine, on Mars and beginning of the planet's terrestrial exploration.
7 December: Galileo (US) arrives at Jupiter.

1998   20 November: Launch and successful uniting (in December) of first sections of International Space Station.

Index

Page numbers in bold denote major section/chapter devoted to subject.
t denotes table. n denotes note at bottom of page.

Aaland Islands 277
aborigines, Australian 95
abortion 112, 636
acid rain 582
Adenauer, Konrad 491
Afghanistan 82, 193
  GDP 588
  and Islam 688
  Soviet intervention and
    occupation (1979) 685, 733;
    741, 746, 748
  struggle of *muhjaheddin* against
    communist government 688,
    743
  withdrawal of Soviet forces 751
Africa 12, 734–8, 853
  agriculture 527
  aid to 737
  Christian missionaries 99
  civil wars and struggles after
    independence 534–5
  colonial rule and impact 82,
    89–90, 96–100, 524, 526,
    527–8
  conference of colonies (1944)
    (Brazzaville) 467
  decline of Ottoman empire's
    control in 231
  decolonization in 521, 523, 525,
    528–31, 534
  drought and famines 537
  economy 524, 536–7, 737
  and France 88–9, 97, 99–100,
    190, 521, 529–30
  impact on Europe of imperialism
    in 99–100
  and OAU 536, 734, 737, 851
  population growth 43t, 524, 528,
    537, 737
  and Portugal 97, 100, 523, 530,
    531, 533
  pre-independence 524–8
  problems 737
  recession of polygamy 638
  and Second World War 526–7:
    offence in North Africa 424,
    425, 426
  and structural adjustment
    programmes 537
  see also individual countries
African National Congress *see*
    ANC

Afrikaner Nationalist Party 736
Afrikaners 107, 108, 110, 531
agriculture 47, 340
    and Common Agricultural Policy
        (CAP) 702–3, 809, 813
    costs of advances in 119
    development of 117–18
    eastern Europe 752
    effect of Great War on 279,
        281
    evolution of new strains of
        cereals 118
    fall in prices in 1930s 287
    and fertilizers 118
    reforms lead to rural unrest
        287
    transformation of by machinery
        and technology 118–19
aid programmes 596–7
AIDS (acquired immunodeficiency
    syndrome) 568
aircraft 128–9
airships 128, 560
Alaska 103
Albania 705, 801–2
    creation of independent 154, 204
    economy and financial scandal
        801
    emigration of Albanians to Italy
        801–2
    and Soviet Union 446, 492, 651
Alexander II, Tsar 163
Alexander, King of Yugoslavia 780
Al-Fatah 680–81
Algeciras conference (1906) 192
Algeria 691, 744–5
    bloodletting after independence
        744
    economic decline 744
    and France 94, 483, 526–7, 530;

conquest of by (1830) 89;
    independence granted by
    (1962) 540, 549, 744; war
    against 521, 523, 540, 543–4,
    547–9, 706–7
    installation of authoritarian
        regime (1991) 745
    and Islam 688, 745
    massacres and terrorism 769–70
    oil and gas production 525
    population growth 744
    problems faced 744–5
Ali, Mehemet 65, 232
Alliance for Progress 661–2, 692
American Civil War (1861–5) 54,
    67, 246
'Americanization' 609
Amur River Society (Black Dragon
    Society) 212
anarchists 146–7, 149
Anatolia 308, 309, 345
ANC (African National Congress)
    527, 736, 737
ancien régime 8, 10, 11
Anglo-Irish agreement (1985) 786
Angola 531
    civil war 533, 734, 736, 738
    and Portugal 97, 530, 533
    and South Africa 735
Anschluss 406
Antarctica 28
apartheid 532, 734, 735
appeasement, notion of 407
Arab League 484
Arab states (Arabs) 304, 305
    and Ba'ath party 542
    and communism 307
    conflict with Israel see Israel:
        Arab/Israeli conflict
    contrasts between 542

and Jews 539–43
national *per capita* incomes 603
nationalism 232, 307–8, 484, 486,
    542
and oil 679
revolt against Ottoman empire
    during Great War 264
Arafat, Yassir 680, 681, 824, 825
Argentina 75, 373, 375, 376
    authoritarian rule by soldiers 692
    and Chile 76
    and Falklands war 789
    and Great War 252
    and Perón 655
    population growth 115
    wealth 76
    and women's vote 631
aristocracy 145
Armenia 262, 292–3, 308, 309
arms control *see* nuclear weapons
Armstrong, Neil 572
arts xviii–xix, 323–5
ASEAN 851
Asia 11–12, 345–7
    change and perceptions of
        change 207–10
    cultures 494–5
    decolonization 468–9, 478–9,
        481, 494, 522
    European imperialism in 101–2,
        236, 494
    and Great War 345, 346
    and peace settlements 352–4
    population 43, 585t
    resistance to European control
        210, 478
    see also individual countries
assembly line 606–7
astrology 618–19
Atatürk *see* Kemal, Mustafa

Atlantic Charter (1941) 421–2, 429,
    466
Australia 26, 55, 93–4, 441
    effect of white settlement on
        aborigines 95
    and Japan 518, 727–8
    and Second World War 424
Austria
    annexation of by Germany
        (1938) 406
    division of by occupied forces 440
    re-emergence as independent
        state 492, 705
Austria-Hungary (Dual Monarchy)
    161, 162, 281
    annexation of Bosnia and
        Herzegovina 184, 196–8,
        199–200, 202
    collapse 274
    and Great War 242, 260–61, 265
    industrialization 163
    and Magyars 54, 163, 183, 239
    and Russia 177, 182, 196–7, 198,
        199–200
    and Serbia 183, 198, 205, 238
    Triple Alliance with Germany
        and Italy 178, 179, 185
    war with Serbia 241–2
authoritarianism 316–18, 627
    and Latin America 317, 375,
        654–5, 692
Azerbaijan 292–3, 444, 452, 759

Ba'ath socialist movement 542, 690
Bahrain 770
Balfour Declaration (1917) 263–4,
    484, 825
Balkan wars (1912–13) 203–6
    First 203–4
    Second 204–6

Balkans 102, 182, 184, 186, 194, 243, 846
Baltic states 317, 416, 440, 759
see also Estonia; Latvia; Lithuania
Bandung meeting (1955) 501
Bangladesh
aid to 597
creation of 499, 620
population 586t
Barbarossa operation 417–18
Batista, F. 657
Battle of the Atlantic 415, 425–6
Battle of Britain 416
Bavaria 290
'Bay of Pigs' operation (1961) 658, 660
BBC (British Broadcasting Corporation) 133, 319
Becquerel, Henri 33
behaviourism 616–17
Belgium 785
and Congo 97, 100, 530, 531, 534–5
Bell, Andrew Graham 130
Bengal 228–30, 474
Bergen-Belsen concentration camp 428
Beria, Lavrenti 647
Berlin
anti-Soviet riots in East (1953) 650
blockade and airlift (1948–9) 463–4
prosperity of West 653
Berlin Wall
building of (1961) 653–4
collapse of (1989) 761, 762
Bessarabia 416
Bethmann-Hollweg, Chancellor 254

Bevin, Ernest 455
Bharatiya Janata Party (BJP) 818, 819
biology 565
biotechnology 566
birth control 112, 635 see also contraception
birth rates 112
Bismarck, Chancellor 54, 73–4, 152, 160, 177, 178
blacks, in United States see blacks
Boer War see South African War
Bolivia 376–7, 656, 661, 662
Bolsheviks 150, 257, 259, 288–9, 292, 294–5, 462
Bosnia
annexation of by Austria-Hungary (1908) 184, 196–8, 199–200, 202
crisis in (1992–95) 799–801, 827
fighting between Muslims and Serbs (1991) 783
Bosnia-Herzegovina 783
Bosnian Serbs 184, 799, 800, 801, 802
Botha, P.W. 734–5
Botswana 737
Boxer rebellion (1900) 61, 175, 207, 212, 215, 216
Boy Scout movement 642
Brandt report (1980) 596, 602
Brandt, Willy 709
Brazil 75, 374, 376
authoritarian rule by soldiers 692
economy and GDP 588t, 694
natural resources 76
population growth 115, 586t
and Second World War 654
Brest-Litovsk treaty (1918) 258, 283, 295

Bretton Woods conference (1944)
442, 590, 602
Brezhnev, Leonid 651–2, 753
death (1982) 748
doctrine 651–2, 753–4
Britain 400–401, 446, 713–15,
789–90
and Africa 97, 100, 528–9
agriculture 120
Anglo-Russian convention (1907)
193
annexation of Cyprus (1914) 304
appeasement policy towards
Germany 397, 407
aristocracy 145
and Burma 101, 220, 441
and Depression 343
economy and GDP 453–4, 588t,
714
and Egypt see Egypt
emigration from 43, 46
and Europe 714, 790: EEC 702,
707, 708, 714; ERM 807;
Maastricht 805; and monetary
union 811; view of integration
706
and Falklands war (1982) 789
falling behind other countries in
wealth 713
first women magistrate appointed
(1913) 174
and France 181, 329, 396–7:
Anglo-French agreement
(1904) 189–91
and Great War 242, 248:
blockade 253; casualties
suffered 253; conscription 250;
debts to United States 280;
declaration of war on
Germany 242; and Ottoman

empire 261, 262, 263; trade 252
and Greece 449, 450, 452, 453–4,
464
and Hong Kong 793–4
and India see India: British rule
inflation 714
invasion of Tibet (1904) 24, 101,
215
and Iran 311, 540
and Japan: alliance with (1902)
189, 191, 209, 211, 212–13,
214, 236; ending of alliance
307, 359
and Latin America 373–4
life expectancy at birth 114
and Middle East 305–6
and monarchy 57, 154
and Moroccan crisis (1905)
192–3
and Moroccan crisis (1911) 202
nationalism 153–4
and Northern Ireland 715, 786
nuclear weapons 660
and oil 714
and Palestine 263, 305, 306,
345–6, 482, 485
political crisis (1911) 155
power of in nineteenth century
180
Second World War 415–16,
440–41: and Atlantic Charter
421–2, 429, 466; and Battle of
Britain 416; casualties 432;
declaration of war on
Germany 410; guarantees to
Poland and Romania 407, 408;
preparations 408
shift of power away from in
aftermath of war 440–41
social reform 401

Britain – *cont.*
  and South African War 108–9,
    179–80, 187–8
  and Soviet Union 293, 332
  state intervention 155
  strength of 177
  and Thatcher 714–15, 789–90
  threat to naval supremacy by
    Germany 183–4, 202
  trade 50–51
  widening of electorate 284, 319
  and women's vote 631
British Broadcasting Corporation
  see BBC
British Colonial Development and
  Welfare Fund 528
British Commonwealth of Nations
  469
British empire 88–9, 101, 102
  colonies 93–4
  decline 85–6
Brüning, Chancellor 393
Brussels Treaty (1948) 696
Buddhism 17
Bulganin, Nikolai 647, 662
Bulgaria 53
  alliance with Serbia (1912) 203
  and Balkan war 204, 205
  elections (1991) 762
  and Great War 248
Burma 87
  agriculture 120
  and Britain 101, 220, 441
  and independence (1948) 474n, 481
  Japanese occupation of 424, 468,
    471
  military rule 474n

Cambodia 494, 626, 678, 794
  and France 221, 507

GDP 588
  and Pol Pot 613n
  Vietnam war extended to 675
Cameroons 526
Canada 55, 67, 93–4, 95
cancer 568
CAP *see* Common Agricultural
  Policy
capitalism 149–50
car industry 10, 127–8, 605–6
carbon dioxide, in atmosphere 582
Cardenas, President 376
Carranza, Venustiaso 372
Carter, President Jimmy 683–4,
  685, 740
Castro, Fidel 657–8, 660–61
Catholicism *see* Roman Catholic
  Church
cavity magnetron, invention of 560
CCP (Chinese Communist Party)
  359
  breakdown in relations with
    KMT 362–3, 385
  conflict with KMT in civil war
    358, 381, 382, 475–6
  cooperation with KMT 359–61,
    382, 383, 475
  and peasants 361–2, 381–2, 476
  victory in civil war 477
Ceausescu, Nicolae 651, 652
cells 565
'centuries' 3–4
Ceylon 481
Chaco War (1932–35) 376–7
Challenger 579
Chamberlain, Neville 406, 407
Charles, Emperor 265
Chechnya 777
Cheka 295
Chen Tu-hsiu 348–9

Chernobyl disaster (1986) 578–9
Chiang Kai-shek 360, 362–3, 381,
    477, 512, 640
Chile 376, 662, 818, 835n
  and Argentina 76
  and Falklands war 789
  growth in wealth 76
  military coup (1973) and
    authoritarian rule 692–3
  nitrates market 373
China 52, 54, 58–61, 214–19,
    474–8, 495, 504–7, 577,
    719–21, 791–5, 814–16, 852
  abolishment of imperial
    examination system (1905)
    217–18
  admission to United Nations
    (1971) 676, 723
  agriculture and land reform 506,
    794
  austerity programme imposed
    (1989) 795–6
  belief that emperor was ruler of
    the world 58–9
  Boxer rebellion (1900) 61, 175,
    207, 212, 215, 216
  changes in after Mao's death
    722–3
  changes under Empress Tzu Hsi
    216, 217–18
  Civil War 358–63, 446, 447,
    475–7, 519, 720–21:
    breakdown of relations
    between KMT; and
    communists 362–3, 385; KMT/
    communist conflict 358, 381,
    382, 475–6; Long March 382;
    and Second World War 476;
    and Soviet Union 363, 477; and
    United States 477; victory by
  communists 477, 505; winning
    over of peasants to
    communism 361–2, 381, 476
  communism 354–6
  Communist Party see CCP
  and Confucianism 17, 347, 383,
    640
  contrast with India 730
  and Cultural Revolution
    (1966–76) 719–20, 721, 723,
    791
  dang'an system 625
  demotion of intellectuals 720
  development of revolutionary
    movements 216–17, 218
  early cultural prestige and
    influence in east Asia 495
  earthquakes (1971) 722
  economic growth and social
    consequences 793
  economic problems 794, 814
  European imperialism in 59, 101,
    215
  famine 119
  female infanticide 112, 116
  fighting with India over Tibetan
    border 500, 510
  foot-binding 13
  formation of People's Republic
    of (1949) 477–8, 481
  Great Leap Forward 506–7, 513,
    514, 720, 723
  and Great War 347, 349, 352
  and Hong Kong 519, 793–4
  'Hundred Days of Reform'
    (1898) 60–61
  and Indo-China 507
  and Indonesia 504
  industry 506, 792–3
  and Japan see Japan

China – *cont.*
  and Korea 61, 210–11
  and Korean War 488–9, 509
  and Kosovo crisis 827
  lack of reform by Manchu
    government 218
  and Mao *see* Mao Tse-Tung
  and Marxism 355–6
  and May 4th Movement 352–4,
    355, 796
  modernization and liberalization
    under Deng Xiaoping 791–2,
    794, 814
  monarchy 58
  and nuclear weapons 513
  occupation of Tibet (1951)
    509–10
  and Pakistan 502, 794
  peasants 349, 361–2, 381–2, 793
  population growth 115, 116, 513,
    586t, 793
  problems faced by new
    communist regime 505–6
  railways 127
  re-emergence as world power
    507–13, 519, 650, 853
  resistance to western ideas by
    government in 1901 59–60
  respect and endorsement of
    authority 721
  revolution (1911) 219, 221, **347–9**
  and Russian imperialism 87, 88
  schooling for girls 26
  and Second World War 427, 475
  and Soviet Union 511–13,
    650–51, 665, 796: clashes on
    border 511, 512, 795; invasion
    of Soviet territory by (1939)
    383; origin of tensions between
    511; Sino-Soviet treaty (1950)

  509; support of KMT by 355,
    360, 363, 452; territorial
    encroachment by Soviet Union
    into 512; visit by Gorbachev
    (1989) 796; withdrawal of
    Soviet economic and technical
    help (1960) 511
  and Taiwan 815–16
  and Tiananmen Square (1989)
    565, **795–8**
  and 'unequal treaties' 359, 475
  and United States 510, 825–6:
    bombing of Chinese embassy
    in Belgrade during Kosovo
    crisis 826–7; opening of full
    diplomatic relations (1979)
    677; Sino-American agreement
    (1978) 723; visit by Nixon
    (1972) 676–7
  and Vietnam 509, 677, 794
  visit by Queen Elizabeth II 794
  women in 633, 720
Chinese Communist Party *see* CCP
Chou-en-Lai 457
Christian Democracy 700–701
Christian Democratic Union
  (Germany) 704
Christian missionaries 20, 24–5, 99,
  224
Christianity 169, 618, 621
  at start of century 15
  and Americas 44
  and Darwin's theory of evolution
    32–3
  important agency of bringing
    European civilization to rest of
    world 24–5
  lack of political influence 165
  spread to non-European
    countries 15, 24

and World Council of Churches
621
see also Roman Catholic Church
Churchill, Winston 452
and Europe 706
and India 365
and Second World War 415–16,
420, 421, 466n
CIA (Central Intelligence Agency)
662
cinema 132–3, 134, 319, 320
CIS (Commonwealth of
Independent States) 774,
812–13
cities 7, 117, 580, 844
'civilized world' 17–21
Clemenceau, Georges 277–8
Clerk Maxwell, James 33
climatic change 582, 583, 843n
Clinton, President Bill 802–3,
821–2, 825, 826
impeachment (1999) 822
cloning 567
clothing industry 124–5
coal industry 48, 605
Cochin China 480, 481
Cold War 456, 457–93, 575, 590, 698
end of 739, 775, 808
Colombia 76, 105, 655, 694
Colonial Conference (1906)
(London) 94
colonialism *see* imperialism
Columbus, Christopher 573
Cominform 455–6, 465
Comintern 291–2, 355, 400, 455
commerce 48–52
commodities, abundance of 575–6,
839
Common Agricultural Policy (CAP)
702–3, 809, 813

Common Market *see* EEC
Commonwealth of Independent
States *see* CIS
communication 28, 126–30
communications technology
559–63,564
see also information technology
Communism 291–3
and Arabs 307
decline in western Europe 652
downfall of in eastern Europe
760–62
failure of revolution in west 400
and revolution 287–9, 332
spread of in eastern Europe 451
and youth 643
Comoros Islands xvi
companies, development of
international 611
computers 561, 610
and biological advances 567
impact of 562
and Internet 563–4, 836n–37n
and miniaturization 607
and Moore's Law 563
'conditioned reflex' 616
Conference on Security and
Cooperation in Europe (CSCE)
712–13
Confucianism 17, 347, 383, 640
Congo (later named Zaire) 97, 100,
530, 531, 738
civil war 534–5
Congress of Berlin (1878) 78
Congress of Paris (1856) 78
Congress of Vienna (1815) 78
Constantinople Straits 182, 197,
203, 235, 238, 261
constitutional governments 155–8
constitutions 848

contraception 44, 116, 173
  and men 636–7
  and the Pill 634–6, 643
  and Roman Catholic Church
    623, 635–6
Coolidge, President Calvin 333n
Corfu 277
Council of Europe 696, 699, 703
Council of Ministers 701, 787
Council for Mutual Economic
    Assistance (Comecon) 456
Court of Justice 701, 787
creoles 75, 93, 371
Crimean War 79, 88, 182
Crippen, Dr 130
Croatia 780, 782–3, 799, 800, 808
CSCE (Conference on Security and
    Cooperation in Europe)
    712–13
Cuba 656–60, 660–61
  'Bay of Pigs' operation (1961)
    658, 660
  Castro's overthrow of Batista
    regime 657
  independence from Spain (1898)
    76, 104, 657
  missile crisis 658–9, 660, 711,
    741
  relationship with United States
    104, 106, 656–8, 660–61
  social reform 660
Cubism 324
Cultural Revolution (1966–76)
    719–20, 721, 723, 791
culture 320–21
  Americanization of European 609
  impact of increase in wealth on
    608–10
  roots of disintegration in western
    civilization 321

Curzon, Lord 225
Customs Unions 699, 701
Cyprus 88, 304
Czech Republic 779, 812
Czechoslovakia 273, 275, 284,
    317
  arms deal with Nasser 544–5
  communist coup (1948) 455, 460,
    462
  emergence of 262, 265
  and EU 812
  and Marshall Plan 455
  opening of frontiers to East
    Germans 760
  and Prague Spring (1968) 651
  seizure of by Germany (1938/9)
    406, 407
  withdrawal of Soviet forces
    761–2
Czechs 260, 261

Daily Mail 132
d'Annunzio, Gabriele 314
Darwin, Charles 31–3, 35, 565
Dayton agreement 801
DDT 569
de Gaulle, Charles 440
  and Algerian war 548
  elected president of Fifth
    Republic 548, 706
  and Europe 707–8, 790,
    808
  resignation (1969) 708
  in Second World War 415
de Klerk, F.W. 735–6
de Rivera, Primo 318
de Tocqueville, Alexis 445,
    613
death rate 113–14
decolonization 86, 236, 697

and Africa 521, 523, 525, **528–31**, 534

and Asia 468–9, 478–9, 481, 494

beginnings of **465–9**

and Latin America 74–5, 87, 655

deforestation 582

Delcassé, Paul 189–90

democracy 628, 836, 850

advances of after Great War 283–4

dissatisfaction with 284, 286

extension of 850–51

and nationalism 626–7

recession of 312, 316

triumph of in western Europe 753

Democratic Party (United States) 72, 334, 821

Deng Xiaoping 352n, 722, 791–2, 794, 796, 814–15

Denmark 805, 811

Depression (1930s) **339–45**, 367, 379, 398

beginnings 340–41

decline in world trade 341–2, 343

and Latin America 374, 375, 376

slowness of recovery from 343

stock market collapse (1929) 341

unemployment 241–2, 341, 342, 343

see also individual countries

détente 711, 739, 751

Diana, Princess, funeral 575

Diaz, General Porfiro 371–2

Dickens, Charles 166

disease

progress in dealing with infectious 569

divorce 636

Djerassi, Dr Carl 634

DNA (deoxyribonucleic acid) 566

DNA fingerprinting 567

Doll's House, A (Ibsen) 27

domestic appliances 124, 173, 174

Dominican Republic 76, 106, 661–2

Dreadnought, HMS (battleship) 193

Dreyfus, Alfred 156

Dual Monarchy *see* Austria-Hungary

Dunlop, John Boyd 128n

Dutch

and Indonesia 94, 222–3, 479, 502

Dyer, Brigadier 364

dynasticism **161–5**

Earth Summit (1992) 583

East Berlin *see* Berlin

East Germany 446, 463, 752, 808

building of Berlin Wall (1961) 653–4

collapse of Berlin Wall (1989) 761, 762

and communism 451

decline in technology 594

effect of western satellite television 564

foreign debt 594

opening up of Hungary and Czech frontiers to 760

outflow of refugees to West Germany 491, 653

relations with West Germany 594, 709–10, 762

riots and demonstrations (1989) 761

setting up of 465

settlement with Poland over Oder-Neisse line 704

East India Company 224
East Timor 852
eastern Europe 592–5, 751–4, 784
    agrarian unrest 146, 317
    agriculture 752
    changes in 751–2
    and dissidents 753
    downfall of communism 760–62
    economic contrast with western
        Europe 593–5
    economic crisis 752
    economic growth 593, 752
    Jews in 785
    problems faced after collapse of
        communism 784
    revolutions 286–7
    and Soviet Union 451, 592, 593,
        629, 649, 751
    youth 609–10
economy
    attempts to rectify after Great
        War 282–3
    change in management of
        national 589
    disorder in Europe after Great
        War 281–2
    eastern Europe 592–5
    effect of economic malaise in East
        Asian economies 816–17, 818
    effect of Great War on
        international 279–80
    effect of oil crisis 682–3
    Europe's 'golden age' of
        economic growth 590–92
    growing integration of world
        economies 629
    growth 340, 587–9, 604
    post Great War 279–80
    recession (1990s) 807
    recovery of in 1920s 327

state intervention 624
world contrasts 595–7
see also Depression
ECSC (European Coal and Steel
    Community) 699–700
Ecumenism 621
education 8, 598, 599
Edward VII, King 10, 154
EEC (European Economic
    Community) 611, 701, 702,
    703, 707
EFTA (European Free Trade
    Association) 702, 809
Egypt 543–7
    assassination of President Sadat
        (1981) 687, 743
    and Britain 190: ending of
        protectorate 307, 482, 483;
        garrison of Canal Zone by
        307, 483, 543; hostility towards
        occupation forces 483;
        occupation and rule of 88–9,
        233–4, 307
    drifting into isolation from other
        Arab states 683
    and end of Ottoman Africa
        231–4
    financial intervention by
        Europeans 232–3
    and Gulf War 768
    and Islam 688
    Islamist militant violence against
        western tourists 770
    and Israel 545, 681, 683
    and Nasser see Nasser, Gamal
        Abdel
    nationalism 231–2
    opening of Suez Canal 51, 232
    overthrow of monarchy (1952)
        539–60

population growth 542
revolution (1954) 543
and Second World War 483
and Six-Day War (1967) 680
and Soviet Union 680
and Suez crisis (1956) 545–6, 649
and Syria 546, 683
and United States 544–5, 549
women in 637
and Yom Kippur war 681
Ehrlich, Paul 126
Einstein, Albert 34, 558
Eisenhower, President 447, 489,
    549, 658, 666, 667, 669–70
El Alamein, battle of 425
El Salvador 662
electricity 123–4, 126, 559
electromagnetism 33
electronics 561
Elizabeth I, Queen 618
Elizabeth II, Queen 794
emigration, European 28, 43–4,
    45–6, 68, 74, 89
empires *see* imperialism, European;
    individual empires
employment
    entry into 601
    and women 172, 602, 633
    see also unemployment
EMU (European Monetary Union)
    805, 811
energy
    consumption worldwide (1998)
        830–31
    sources of 559, 581, 605
Engels, Friedrich 148
ENIAC 561n
Enlightenment 37
entente 190–91, 202
environment

damage to 577–9, 581–2
new concerns 582–3, 842
and pollution 580, 583
Eritrea 526, 738
ERM (Exchange Rate Mechanism)
    807
Estonia 266, 292, 759
    and EU 812
    independence of 283
    land redistribution 287
Ethiopia 20, 537, 738
    escapes European domination 24,
        82, 97
    GDP 588
    invasion of by Italy (1935) 397–8,
        526
    life expectancy at birth 114
    revolution and dethroning of
        Selassie (1974) 535
    and Second World War 424,
        526
'Euro' (currency) 811n
Europe 141–75, 695–715, 813,
    846–7, 848, 851, 855
    achievements 813
    after Maastricht 805–9
    alliances and entanglements
        177–82
    appearance of security before
        Great War 186–9
    cost and destruction of Second
        World War to 437
    and Depression 139–40
    disappearance of hegemony 846
    division of by Yalta conference
        440
    effect of Great War on economy
        279, 281–3
    'golden age' of economic growth
        and reasons for 590–92

Europe – *cont.*
  integration 708–9, 709–10,
    787–9: Britain's view 706;
    divisions over 805–7; driving
    force behind 698; and ECSC
    699–700; and France 707–8;
    and Maastricht Treaty (1991)
    788–9, 805–6; monetary union
    and Single Currency 789, 805,
    807, 809–11; obstacles to
    political 697; problems 787;
    seeds of 695–704; and Single
    European Act (1987) 788–9;
    Soviet threat as factor behind
    698–9; steps towards economic
    699; and Treaty of Rome
    (1957) 701–2, 703, 707
  and Marshall Plan 455
  and nationalism 152–5
  new currents in politics of
    312–18
  population 42, 43t, 44–5, 115,
    585t
  post-1945 435–9
  power and importance of 22,
    37–8, 137, 141–2
  pre-1914 tensions and strains
    169–71
  rebuilding of economies 591
  ruling class and attacks against
    144–7
  security problems 778–80
  and Soviet Union 445–6
  and United States 68, 445–6
  women in 171–4
  and world economy 813
European Coal and Steel
    Community *see* ECSC
European Commission 701, 787
  resignation of (1999) 813–14

European Community (EC) 702,
    787, 808
European Defence Community
    701
European Economic Community
    see EEC
European Free Trade Association
    see EFTA
European Monetary System (EMS)
    603, 788
European Parliament 702, 787,
    788
European Postal Union 171
European Union (EU) 629–30,
    805
  cultural convergence 809
  enlargement issue 808–9, 811–14
Europeans 17–18, 20, 21, **141–4**
  emigration of 43–4, 45–6, 68, 74,
    89
  feelings of superiority over non-
    Europeans 19, 20, 170, 171
  and imperialism *see* imperialism,
    European
  living in poverty in nineteenth
    century 144
  and religion 165–9, 833
evolution 32

Falklands war (1982) 789
family 598–9
famines 29, 119, 584
Far East **814–18**
  European empires in 220
  and Great War 345
  see also individual countries
farming *see* agriculture
fascio di'combattimento (union for
    struggle) 314
fascism 312–13, 316, 317

rise of in Italy 312–15
Federal Republic *see* West Germany
feminism 27
fertility rate 113
fertilizers, chemical 118
financial markets,
    internationalization of 610
Finland 54
    joins European Union 812
    land reform 287
    and Soviet Union 292
    and women's vote 174
First World War *see* Great War
fishing 807
Fleming, Alexander 126
FLN (Front de Libération
    Nationale) 547, 548, 745
food
    growth in supply of 47, 117–20,
    603
Ford, Henry 127, 605, 606
Ford, President Gerald 677, 678,
    723
Formosa *see* Taiwan
'Fourteen Points' 255, 261, 263
France 158, 446
    and Africa 88–9, 97, 99–100,
    190, 521, 529–30
    and Algeria 94, 483, 526–7, 530:
    conquest of (1830) 89;
    independence granted (1962)
    540, 549, 744; war 521, 523,
    540, 543–4, **547–9**, 706–7
    alliance with Russia 178, 179,
    180–81
    anti-clericalism 168
    attempt to prohibit the wearing
    of headscarves by Muslim girls
    637
    and Britain 181, 329, 396–7:

Anglo-French agreement
    (1904) 189–91
    and Communist Party 401, 440,
    456, 700
    creation (1871) 155–6
    and de Gaulle *see* de Gaulle,
    Charles
    and Depression 341, 343
    divisions within at turn of
    century 156–7
    and Dreyfus affair 156
    and Europe 707–8, 787, 807–8,
    811
    and European Defence
    Community 701
    Fourth Republic 548, 706
    Fifth Republic 548, 706
    GDP 588t
    and Germany 807–8: concern
    over future threat of revived
    328, 397, 450; Franco-German
    treaty (1963) 707; and Locarno
    treaty (1925) 329; and
    Moroccan crisis (1905) 191–2;
    and Moroccan crisis (1911)
    201–2; occupation of the Rühr
    by (1923) 329, 388; overthrow
    of by Germany (1870) 181; and
    reunification 763
    and Great War 241–2, 253, 256,
    263, 264
    and imperialism 88–9, 102, 467
    and Indo-China 101, 221–2, 385,
    480–81
    Jews in 785
    and Maastricht Treaty 805
    and Middle East 305
    and Morocco 89, 190, 544n
    and nationalism 55, 153
    and NATO 708, 808

France – *cont.*
'Popular Front' government 401
Second World War : and de
Gaulle 415; declares war on
Germany 410; invasion of by
Germany (1940) and surrender
414; invasion of northern by
Allies (D-Day) 426; resistance
movement 419, 420
student riots (1968) 753
and Suez crisis 545–6
and Syria 305, 308, 482, 483
Third Republic 156, 157, 180,
221
and Tunisia 544n
and Vietnam 507–8
and women's vote 631
Franco, General 405, 698
Franz Ferdinand, Archduke of
Austria, assassination of (1914)
239, 241
Franz Joseph, Emperor 9n, 57n,
265
Free Trade doctrine 50–51
freedom 613–14
French Revolution 457
Freud, Sigmund 321–3, 615–16
Freudianism 616–17
Front de Libération Nationale *see*
FLN

Gagarin, Yuri 571
Gambia 529
Gandhi, Indira 730–31
assassination (1984) 731, 732
Gandhi, Mahatma 109, 346, 364,
365, 470
assassination (1948) 473
Gandhi, Rajiv 731
Gaza Strip 542, 544

GDP (Gross Domestic Product)
120–21, 121–2, 587, 588t, 591
GDR *see* East Germany
General Agreement on Tariffs and
Trade (GATT) (1947) 442,
590
genetic engineering 565, 566–7, 581,
841
genetics 565–6, 566–7
genocide, UN prevention of 629
George V, King
visit to India (1911) 230
Georgia 292–3, 773
germ theory 35
German empire 53, 54, 57–8, 102,
159–61
Germans
deportation of from the east 438
Germany 45, 161, 162, 177, 205–6,
289–91, 387–9, 760–64
and Africa 97, 100
befriending of ex-communist
neighbours 808–9
and Berlin blockade and airlift
463–4
challenge to Britain's naval
supremacy 153–4, 193–4, 202
and Constantinople Straits 238
defeat of Kohl in 1998 elections
810–11
and Depression 342, 343, 391
economic recovery after Great
War 388
European concern over potential
threat 327–8, 388–9
and France *see* France
Great War 241–2, 249, 250, 253,
256, 262, 289: and Brest-
Litovsk treaty 258, 283, 295;
casualties suffered 253;

declaration of war on France 242; declaration of war on Russia 242; deployment of submarines 254, 255; final offensive 264; German/Italian axis (1936) 406; and reparations 273, 281, 282, 291, 328, 330–31, 388; and Versailles Treaty *see* Versailles Treaty
and Gulf War 768
increasing separation of Soviet zone 451
industry 327
introduction of currency reform in western occupation zone (1948) 462–3
and League of Nations 330, 405
and marriage law 632
military planning under Wilhelm II 178–9
and Moroccan crisis (1911) 201–2
and Moroccan crisis (1905) 192–3
and nationalism 55, 153
Nazi regime *see* Nazis
'New Course' foreign policy (1890s) 185
problems after reunification 807
problems with constitutional government 159–61
rearmament 405
reoccupation of the Rhineland (1936) 378, 405
reunification 762–4, 806–7, 808
Second World War: advances 418; annexation of Austria (1938) 406; attack on Poland 408–9, 410; attack on

Yugoslavia and Greece 417; brutality in treatment of occupied territories 419–20, 428; casualties 432; collaboration with 418–19; declaration of war on by Britain and France 410–11; declaration of war on United States 422, 424; invasion of France 414; invasion of Norway and Denmark 414; invasion of Soviet Union 416–18; offensive 414; pact with Soviet Union 409, 416; partitioning of into occupied zones 440, 464–5, 698; seizure of Czechoslovakia (1938/39) 406, 407; surrender 427; treatment of Poland 419
socialism in 149
and Soviet Union *see* Soviet Union
Triple Alliance with Italy and Austria-Hungary 178
Weimar republic 289–91, 330: downfall 387–8, 389; risings against 290–91
withdrawal of Allied occupation 392
see also East Germany; West Germany
Gestapo 402
Ghana 528–9
glasnost 749, 778
global warming 581, 843
globalization 610–12
'Glorious Endeavour' 223
GNP (Gross National Product) 121n
gold standard 49–50, 341, 345

Gorbachev, Mikhail 764
  attempted coup against (1991)
    772-3
  and German reunification 763
  political and economic strategy
    748-9 757-8, 777-8
  resignation 774
  and secession of Baltic states 759
  visit to China (1989) 796
government see state(s)
Government of India Act (1935)
  365-6, 498
Great Britain see Britain
Great Calcutta Killing (1946)
  472
Great Leap Forward 506-7, 513,
  514, 720, 723
'great powers', roots of idea 78
Great Trek (1835) 107
Great War (1914-18) 96, 175-6,
  238-67, 323, 411
  aerial combat 246
  and Asia 345, 346
  and assassination of Archduke
    Franz Ferdinand 239, 241
  and Austria-Hungary 242,
    260-61, 265
  and Battle of Somme 249
  beginning of 2441-2
  and Brest Litovsk treaty (1918)
    258, 283, 295
  and Britain see Britain
  and China 347, 349, 352
  cost of 266-7
  death toll and casualties 247, 249,
    253, 266
  declaration of war on Russia and
    France by Germany 242
  declaration of war on Serbia
    byAustrians 241

  effect on culture 320
  effect of technical advances
    246-7, 252-3
  effect on trade 252
  emergence of new republics 266
  end of 264-7
  enthusiasm for 244-5
  events leading up to 238-42
  exploiting of nationalism by
    Allies 259-60
  geographical spread and issues
    248-9
  and Germany see Germany
  granting of armistice to Austria-
    Hungary 265
  impact on European system of
    power 244
  and India 346-7, 352
  and Indo-Chinese 222
  and Italy 248-9, 313
  and Japan 248, 249, 347, 350,
    351, 352, 357
  launch of 'total' war 253
  military operations 249
  neutral countries 248
  and Ottoman collapse 261-4
  peace attempts 261
  peace settlement 271-5, 283, 286:
    absence of Soviet Union at
    conference 277-8; and Asia
    352-4; and League of Nations
    275-9; reasons for failure 278;
    treaties for protection of
    minorities 274-5, 284;
    Versailles Treaty see Versailles
    Treaty
  relations between Russia and
    Allies 258-9
  resources needed 250
  and Russia see Russia

seeking of new fronts 251
sickness and hunger 248
struggle at sea 246
submarine warfare 254, 255, 256
and United States 73, 249, 254–5, 263, 332
and weapons 247, 249
Greece 825
and Britain 449, 450, 452, 453–4, 464
civil war in 447, 450, 453–4
ending of civil war (1949) 464
and Great War 248
joins European Community (1981) 704, 788
and marriage law 632
and Second World War 417
and Treaty of Sèvres 308, 309
US aid to 454
war with Turks 184
Green political parties 578
greenhouse gases 582, 583
Gross Domestic Product *see* GDP
Group of 77, 682
Guam 104
Guatemala 655
Guinea 530, 531
Gulf crisis (1998) 803–4, 804–5, 824
Gulf states 770–71
Gulf War (1990–91) 765–9

Hapsburg empire *see* Austria-Hungary
Haiti 76, 106
Hamid, Sultan Abdul 195
happiness, mythology of human 838–40
Harding, Warren G. 333
Hawaii 104

Heath, Edward 714
Helsinki agreement (1975) 712, 753
Hertz, Heinrich 33
Hindenburg, Field Marshal 393, 394
Hinduism (Hindus) 17, 495
conflict with Muslims in India 229–30, 365, 366, 471, 472, 473
Hiroshima, atom bomb 427–8, 431, 432, 448, 558
Hitler, Adolf 390–93, 395, 404–5, 431
appointed as chancellor 393
becomes leader of Nazis 390–91
death 10, 427
dream of united Germany 406
early life and background 390
and Jews 391, 402
Mein Kampf 390–91
misinterpreted views of 402
and Munich 405, 406–7
and Mussolini 398, 404
reasons for popularity 395
and Second World War 416–17
HIV 568, 737
Ho Chi Minh 385, 480, 481
Holocaust 429, 430, 484, 754, 785
Honduras 377
war with El Salvador 662
Hong Kong 101, 519, 603, 724, 817
agreement between British and Chinese over terms of transfer (1984) 793–4
Hoover, President Herbert 333n, 367
Human Genome Project 566–7
human rights 14, 629, 835
'Hundred Days of Reform' (1898) 60

Hungary
  emergence of independent 265,
    266
  and EU 812
  joins NATO 779
  opening of frontiers to East
    Germans 760
  proclaimed as monarchy (1920)
    283n
  revolution and crushing of by
    Soviet Union (1956) 546, 649,
    650, 652
  withdrawal of Soviet troops 761
Hussein, Saddam 685, 746, 765,
  768–9, 803, 804
Hussein, sherif of Mecca 235,
  262–3, 305

ideas, history of 29–30, 553–4, 555,
  556
ideology
  contamination of international
    affairs 398–404
IMF (International Monetary Fund)
  442, 590, 597, 714
Imperial Conference (1926) 469
imperialism, European 82–102, 207,
  852–3
  advantage of weapons 92
  in Africa 82, 89–90, 96–100, 524,
    526, 527–8
  in Asia 101–2, 236, 494
  benefits of 83, 85
  colonial rebellions after Second
    World War 478
  criticism of 83
  dark side of 90–91
  decline and breaking up of see
    decolonization
  expansion 89–90
  and idealism 90
  impact of 83, 85, 94–5
  and Second World War 466, 468
  treatment of native populations
    by white settlers 94–6
  see also individual countries
imperialism, United States 86,
  102–6, 466–7
India 12, 228–31, 363–6, 495,
  497–501, 519, 729–33, 848
  in 1990s 818–19
  agriculture 587
  attack on Golden Temple by
    army 732
  and BJP 818, 819
  British rule 87, 88, 220, 223–7,
    236, 347, 453, 498: attitude
    towards native rulers and
    aristocracy 226–7; commission
    (1927) into 364; and
    Government of India Act
    (1935); 365–6, 498; and
    independence (1947) 469–74,
    497, 619, 729, 732; partition of
    Bengal 228–30; resentment and
    riots against 364, 365;
    separation of native Indians
    from British 226; setting up of
    own tariff protection 363–4;
    trade with 225; visit to by
    George V (1911) 230
  and Congress 228–9, 633, 731
  constitution (1950) 498–9
  contrast with China 730
  cultivation of indigo 51
  destruction of Ayodhya mosque
    by Hindu zealots (1992) 564
  divisions between Hindus and
    Muslims 229–30, 365, 366,
    471, 472, 473

economic policies 818
effect of Great War on economy
279
effect of satellite transmission
564–5
family planning programme 116
famines 119, 432, 474, 584
fighting with China over
northern borders 500, 510
Great Calcutta Killing 472
and Great War 346–7, 352
and Indira Gandhi 730–31, 732
industry 363
life expectancy at birth 114
Mutiny (1857) 224–5, 227, 473
nationalism 466, 497, 819
and Pakistan: fighting over
Kashmir issue 499–500, 502,
732; and nuclear test
explosions (1998) 819–20
partition of into Pakistan and
India (1947) 473, 494, 620, 732
poor development performance
730
population growth 474, 498,
586t, 587, 730
poverty 498, 730
problems faced after
independence 473–4, 498
'Quit India' campaign 470–71
railways 127
and religion 619
ruling of after independence
497–9
and Second World War 366,
469–70, 471
and Soviet Union 500, 502
and United States 502
Indian Census Report (1901) 207
'Indian Society' 386

Indo-China 221–2, 385–6, 480–82,
494, 508
anti-colonial revolution 386
economy 385
and French 101, 221–2, 385,
480–81
Japanese occupation (1941) 423,
468, 480
population 222
and Second World War 480
war against French 481
see also Cambodia; Laos;
Vietnam
Indonesia 222–3, 386–7, 502–4,
519, 724, 852
Chinese community 494, 502–3
communism in 386, 479
and Depression 386–7
and Dutch 94, 222–3, 479, 502
economy 386–7, 817
family planning programme 116
independence proclaimed and
new state created 478–9
and Islam 223, 502, 852
massacre of communists (1965)
504
occupation by Japanese 424, 468,
479
population growth 586t, 587
riots (1998) 817
Sukarno's regime 503
and United States 503
industrialization 22, 120–22
impact of 121
industry 327, 604–7
effect of Depression on 342
increased consumption of
manufactured goods 605
and information technology 607
INF Treaty (1987) 750

infanticide 112
information technology 131,
    559–63, 836
  and computers *see* computers
  demand for 562–3
  impact on employment 600
  impact on industry 607
  and increase in flows of capital
    604
  introduction of electronics-based
    562
  and miniaturization 560–61, 573,
    607
  in nineteenth century 129–30
inter-continental ballistic missiles
    (ICBMs) 660
International Monetary Fund *see*
    IMF
international organizations 628–9,
    851–2
International Telecommunications
    Satellite Organization 851
Internet 563–4, 836n
intifada 747, 823–4
IRA 686
Iran 311–12, 639, 794
  and Britain 311, 540
  and Iraq 685: war with 689, 740,
    742–3, 746
  and modernization 540
  nationalization of oil industry
    540
  population growth 116
  revolution (1978) 602, **683–5**,
    685–6, 687, 688, 739–40
  and Reza Khan 311–12, 620, 684,
    686
  and Second World War 424
  Shah of 539, 740: overthrow of
    684, 685

  and Turkey 312
  and United States 540, 684–5:
    hostage crisis 684–5, 685–6,
    740, 741, 742; Iran-Contra
    affair (1987) 750
  withdrawal of Soviet forces
    452
  see also Persia
Iraq 542
  assassination of king (1958)
    546–7
  attack on installations by Israel
    (1980) 765
  Ba'ath regime in 685
  bombing of by United States over
    failure of UN weapons
    inspections 803–4, 804–5
  and Britain 305–6, 482, 483
  and Gulf War 765–9
  and Hussein 685, 746, 765,
    768–9, 803, 804
  and Iran 685: war with 689, 740,
    742–3, 746
  joins League of Nations (1932)
    306
  and Second World War 424
  UN weapons inspections 768,
    769, 803
  see also Mesopotamia
Ireland
  and contraception 635
  and ERM 807
  and Home Rule 54, 153, 285
  nationalism 55, 153
  and Second World War 697n
  setting up of Irish Free State
    (1921) 285, 715
  see also Northern Ireland
Islam 495, 541, 771–2, 841, 853–4
  and Arab world 543

INDEX

attitude towards women 26, 686
contrasts between countries
771-2
divisions within 690
and divorce 638
electoral successes 688
gathering of heads of Islamic
states at Teheran (1997) 620
growing disorder 742-7
in international affairs 685-91,
853-4
and Iran/Iraq war 689
and male dominance 638-9
and modernization 689
numbers of Muslims 854
and Pakistan 619, 733
and polygamy 638
spread of 16-17, 687-8
and terrorism 686, 687
weaknesses 689
see also Muslims
Islamic empires 16-17, **64-6**
Islamic fundamentalism 687-9, 690,
740
Ismail, Khedive 232-3
Israel 769
Arab/Israeli conflict 486, 541-2,
544, 546, 740: criticism of and
call for withdrawal from Arab
lands 682, 747; invasion of
Egypt (1956) 545; murder of
Olympic Games team (1972)
686; peace conference (1991)
769; peace process 823-5;
peace treaty with Egypt (1979)
683; and Six-Day War (1967)
680, 747; and Yom Kippur war
(1973) 602, 681
assassination of prime minister
(1995) 825

attack on Iraq's installations
(1980) 765
creation of (1948) 482, 485-6,
541
exodus of Arab refugees 486
and PLO: conflict with 683, 743,
824, 825; continuation of
violence with after peace talks
824; and *intifada* 747, 823-4;
invasion of southern Lebanon
(1978) 683; peace negotiations
with 823-4
and Soviet Union 485, 549
and United Nations 681
and United States 542, 549, 682,
825
Italian Communist Party 440, 456,
700
Italian empire 102, 467
Italians, emigration of 43-4, 46
Italy 53, 177
attack on Tripoli (1911) 203, 231
dissatisfaction in (1901) 184-5
and divorce 636
emigration of Albanians to 801-2
and ERM 807
GDP 588t
German-Italian axis (1936) 405
and Great War 248-9, 313
invasion of Ethiopia (1935)
397-8, 526
and Middle East 305
and Mussolini *see* Mussolini,
Benito
and nationalism 55, 153
political problems and unrest at
turn of century 157-8
and polycentrism 652
rise of fascism 312-15
and Roman Catholic Church 168

Italy – *cont.*
and Second World War 414, 415,
417, 426, 446
seen as a great power 78
Triple Alliance with Germany
and Austria-Hungary 178, 185
and women's vote 631

Japan 19, 23, 62–4, 210–14,
350–51, 406, 515–20, 725–9,
853
admittance to United Nations
(1956) 518, 727
agriculture 517
and Amur River Society 212
assertion of independence 81, 82
and Britain: alliance with (1902)
189, 209, 211, 212–13, 214,
236; ending of alliance 307,
359
car industry 605–6, 725
and China: armed conflict (1928)
379; invasion of by (1932) 381;
retains former German rights
in Shantung 352; and 'the
Twenty-one Demands' 351,
352; trade between 728; war
against (1894–5) 60, 62, 81,
90n, 210–11, 215n; war against
(1937–45) 378, 382–4, 422–3
constitution (1947) 516–17
and contraception 635
costs and strains of economic
growth 726
dislike of 'unequal treaties' 211
economy: in 1901 62; crisis (1932)
358; disorder in 1990s 816;
effect of Great War on 279;
effect of oil crisis on 728; GDP
588t, 725, 728; growth 518,

725, 726–7, 728; reform after
war 517
expansionist and imperialist
drive 211–12, 356–8, 384, 468
features of regime in 1901 62–3
floods 218
and Great War 248, 249, 347,
350, 351, 352, 357
industrial growth 357, 725
and Korea 81, 728: annexation of
(1910) 214, 423; crushing of
revolt (1919) 356; importance
of 211, 212
and League of Nations 352
and Manchuria 351, 357, 378,
379, 359, 381, 423
and modernization 80–81, 215
monarchy 54, 58, 516
Perry's expedition to (1854) 81,
103
population 586t
railways 127
reasons for success 725–6
reform in nineteenth century 62,
63
relations with Pacific countries
727–8
rearmament 727
resistance to communism 504
schooling for girls 26
and Second World War 422–4,
430: attack on Pearl Harbor
423–4; and Battle of Midway
425; destruction of colonial
empires of Far east 424;
dropping of atomic bombs on
Hiroshima and Nagasaki
427–8, 431, 432, 488, 558;
effect of defeat 515–16;
surrender 428, 515; 'Tripartite

Pact' with Germany and Italy (1940) 422
shipbuilding industry 725
treaties and alliances made 519
and United States 422–3, 728–9: handing back of Okinawa by (1971) 729; occupation of after war 446, 515, 516–18, 725
war with Russia (1904–5) 191, 200, 213–14, 236, 351, 384, 423
and Washington agreements (1922) 359
and women's vote 631
Jews 15–16
and Arabs 539–43
in Eastern Europe 785
emigration of 46
establishment of Zionist Congress 235
and Hitler 391, 402
and Palestine 235, 263, 306, 483, 484
persecution of by Nazis 401–2, 407, 428–9, 484, 785
population 785
Jiang Zemin 815
Jinnah, M.A. 472–3, 500, 733
John Paul II, Pope 623, 754
John XXIII, Pope 622
Johnson, President Lyndon 661, 668, 670–71, 673, 675
Jordan 305, 542, 547, 680
assassination of King Abdullah (1951) 543
and Gulf War 768
population growth 115–16
and Six-Day War (1967) 680
journalism 132
Juan Carlos, King 698n
Judaism see Jews

Kashmir 499–500, 502, 732
Kemal, Mustafa (Atatürk) 308–11, 312, 811
Kennedy, President John 668
and 'Alliance for Progress' 661
assassination (1963) 670–71
and blacks 670
and Cuba 658, 659
and moon programme 571–2, 573
and Vietnam 508, 673
Kennedy, Robert 672
Kenya 529
Keynes, J.M. 344n
Khmer Rouge 613n
Khomeni, Ayatollah 684, 770
Khrushchev, Nikita 511, 647–8, 653, 658, 659, 662–3
Kijuro, Shidehara 516
King, Martin Luther 672
Kipling, Rudyard 90, 137
KMT (Kuomintang) 217, 348, 379
breakdown in relations with CCP 362–3, 385
conflict with CCP in civil war 358, 381, 382, 475–6
cooperation with CCP 359–61, 382, 383, 475
defeat by CCP in civil war 477
support of by Soviet Union 355, 360, 363, 452
and Taiwan 477, 510
Kohl, Chancellor Helmut 762, 763, 776, 806, 810–11
Korea 82, 816
annexation of by Japan (1910) 214, 423
and China 61, 210–11
crushing of revolt by Japanese (1919) 356

Korea – *cont.*
  division along 38th Parallel 487
  importance to Japan 211, 212
  see also North Korea; South
    Korea
Korean War (1950) **487–9**, 490,
    504, 507, 518, 519, 650, 674
Kosovo 439, 492, 781–2, 802
  crisis (1998/99) 802–3, 805,
    826–8
Kredit-Anstalt bank 341
Kristallnacht 407
Kronstadt 294, 295
Kruger, Paul 107, 108
Kuomintang *see* KMT
Kurds 305, 311, 627
Kurile Islands 515, 518, 729
Kuwait, invasion of by Iraq 765
Kyoto conference (1997) 583

Laos 221, 494, 507, 588
Lateran treaties (1929) 315
Latin America 74–7, 370–77, 626,
    654–6, 691–4, 818
  authoritarian regimes 317, 375,
    654–5, 692
  decolonization 74–5, 87, 655
  and Depression 374, 375, 376
  development in inequalities due
    to wealth 77
  economy 370–71, 374–5, 692,
    693, 694
  emigration of Europeans to 43
  and Great War 370, 373
  growth in prosperity 76–7, 373,
    374
  industry 370
  influence of Church 75
  integration into world
    community 853

  meeting between governments of
    (1969) 662
  and Mercosur 611, 694
  nationalism 662
  and oil crisis (1970s) 693
  population growth 43t, 585t,
    691–2
  post-independence 75–6
  recovery of democratic
    government in 1990s 693–4
  and Roman Catholic Church 74,
    622
  and Second World War 654
  terrorist organizations 661
  and United States 83: aid from
    655–6; Alliance for Progress
    initiative; 661–2, 692; anti-
    Americanism 375, 661, 662;
    'Good Neighbour' policy 377;
    and Monroe doctrine
    'corollary' 105–6
  and women's vote 631
  see also individual countries
Latvia 266, 283, 292, 759
Lausanne Treaty (1923) 309
League of Nations 275–9, 284, 305,
    376, 629, 849
  and Chaco War 376
  and Germany 330, 405
  Iraq admitted (1932) 306
  and Italy's invasion of Ethiopia
    397–8
  Japan's admittance 352
  and Manchurian crisis 381,
    397
  reasons for failure 443
  and Soviet Union 277
  successes 277, 330
  and United States 276
  weaknesses 276–7

Lebanon 234, 539
  collapse into anarchy 743
  and French 305, 482, 483
  independence 483
  invasion of southern by Israel
    (1978) 683
Lend-Lease (1941) 421, 441, 448,
  449
Lenin, V. 236, 257, 258, 291, 294,
  295, 296–7, 773
Leo XIII, Pope 168
Leopold, King (Belgium) 97, 100
Li Ta-chao 355
Liberal Democratic Party (Japan)
  726
Liberia 82, 97
Libya 526, 746
  bombing of by United States
    (1986) 750
  independence (1951) 549
  oil and gas production 525
  and Qadaffi 743–4
  replacement of king by Qadaffi
    681
life expectancy 113, 114, 586, 587
life sciences 565–8
lifestyles, changes in 597–601, 836
literacy, increase and spread of 131,
  152, 319
Lithuania 266, 283, 292, 408, 759
  Soviet attack on Vilnius (1991)
    759–60, 773
Lloyd George, David 277
Locarno Pact (1925) 329–30, 332,
  389, 405
London 49, 610–11
London Conference 205
Long March 382
Los Angeles, race riots (1965)
  671

Louisiana Purchase (1803) 67, 94,
  454

Maastricht Treaty (1991) 788–9,
  805–6
Macao 794
MacArthur, General Douglas 516,
  727
McCarthy, Joseph 667–8, 672
Macedonia 184, 781, 782, 783, 803
  and Balkan war 204
  insurrection against Ottoman
    rule (1902) 182, 186, 194
McKinley, President William 91n
  assassination (1901) 9–10, 133
Madagascar 588
Madero, President Francisco 371–2
Magyars 183, 239, 284
Major, John 790
malaria 569
Malawi (was Nyasaland) 533
Malaya 101, 424, 482
Malaysia 115, 468, 494, 503, 724,
  817
Malthus, Thomas 32, 42, 47, 112
Manchuria 216, 505, 509
  crisis (1931) 379–81, 423
  Japanese aggression in (1904) 213
  Japanese aggression in (1931) 378
  Japanese interests in 351, 357,
    359
  and Russia 181, 189, 512
Mandela, Nelson 737
  release from prison (1990) 736
Mao Tse-tung 355, 504, 513–14,
  721
  and Chinese civil war 382, 476,
    477
  and Cultural Revolution 719–20,
    723

Mao Tse-Tung – *cont.*
  death (1976) 722
  and Great Leap Forward 506,
    507, 513, 514
  and peasantry 361–2, 506, 513
  politics of 514
  and rapprochement with United
    States 676–7
  relations with party colleagues
    514
  and Stalin 511
  writings 721
Maori 95
'March on Rome' 314–15
Marconi, Guglielmo 130, 319, 560
marriage law 632
Mars 573–4
Marshall Plan 455–6, 463, 490–91,
    590, 591, 592, 696, 698
Marx, Karl 142, 147, 148
Marxism 147–9, 323, 355–6, 360,
    774, 847
Masaryk, Thomas 274
mass communications 319, 557
mass production 600, 606–7
material world, mastery of 840–43
'Mau-Mau' movement 529
May 4th Movement 352–4, 355,
    796
Mazzini 227
medical care, public provision of
    568–9
medicine 90, 125–6, 568–70
  advance of 126, 568
  at turn of century 8, 125–6
Mein Kampf (Hitler) 390–91
Mendel, Gregor 565
Mendeleyev 35
mental illness 568
Mercosur 611, 694

Mesopotamia (later called Iraq)
    234, 262, 263, 345
mestizos 75, 77
metals, production of new 125
Mexico 371–3, 376
  Diaz's regime 371
  and oil 76, 373, 375
  population growth 115
  reforms under new regime 372–3
  revolution (1911) 370, 371–2
  and Second World War 654
  and United States 94, 106, 822
Middle East 16, 304–5, 482–6, 679
  French and British interest 305
  lack of modernization and
    problems associated with 539,
    770
  and oil industry 540
  peace process 823–5
  population growth 771
  and Soviet Union 485
  see also individual countries
Midway, battle of (1942) 425
migration *see* emigration
Mill, John Stuart 227
Milosevic, Slobodan 826
minerals 48
miniaturization 560–61, 573, 607
missionaries, Christian 20, 24–5,
    91, 99, 224
modernism, notion of 324
Mohamed, Dr Mahathir 14n
molecular biology 566
Molotov, Vyacheslav 647
monarchy 8–9, 56–8, 154–5, 161–2,
    850
Mongolia 512
Monnet, Jean 699
Monroe Doctrine 74, 467
  'corollary' to 106, 374, 629

Montenegro 53, 784, 828
moon, first landing on (1969) 572–3
Moore's Law 563
Morocco 66, 544, 691
  assertion of rights to Spanish
    enclaves 549n
  crisis (1905) 191–2
  crisis (1911) 201–3
  and France 89, 190, 544n
  and Germany 192–3
  independence (1956) 540, 544n
  seen as an area of great potential
    for expansion 82
Morse, Samuel 130
mortality rates 113–14
Mountbatten, Lord 472–3
Mozambique 530, 531, 538, 588,
  734, 736
multinationals 611
Munich agreement (1938) 405,
  406–7
music 843
Muslims 14n, 486
  anti-west 686
  conflict with Hindus in India
    229–30, 365, 366, 471, 472, 473
  and divorce 638
  number of 854
  in Ottoman empire 16, 65
  and the veil 638–9
  see also Islam
Mussolini, Benito 158, 397, 406,
  431
  and Hitler 398, 404
  overthrow of 426
  rule of 314–15
  and Second World War 414

Nagasaki, atom bomb 427–8, 431,
  432, 448

Namibia 734, 735, 736
Nasser, Gamal Abdel 543, 544–5,
  546, 680, 686
nationalism 12, 53–5, 151–5, 220
  and democracy 626–7
  and monarchy 57
  in New Europe 784–7
  rise in after Depression 345
  success of 54–5, 626, 848–9
NATO (North Atlantic Treaty
  Organization) 698, 851
  and Bosnian crisis 800–801
  enlargement issue 779
  formation (1949) 464, 696
  and France 708, 808
  and Kosovo crisis 827, 828
  military power 489–90
  transformation of after Soviet
    collapse 779
  and United States 779
  West Germany's admission
    (1955) 491, 701, 704
natural gas 559, 770
nature, versus nurture 554–5
Nazis (Nazism) 390–93, 428, 430
  admiration of by foreigners 403–4
  appeal of and rise in success
    392–3
  benefits and costs of regime
    394–5
  evils and brutality of 419–20,
    428, 430, 431
  growth in power 393–4
  ideology 401–2
  persecution of Jews 401–2, 407,
    428–9, 484, 785
  racialism of 392
  reasons for success and
    popularity of regime 395–6
  see also Hitler, Adolf

négritude 630

Nehru, Jawaharlal 495, 500, 510, 731

New Deal 368–9

New Economic Policy (NEP) 295–6

New York 610–11

New York Times 132

New Youth 348

New Zealand 26, 94, 95, 441, 519, 727–8

Newly Industrializing Countries *see* NICs

newspapers 131–2, 152, 320

Newton, Isaac 33, 34, 35

Nicaragua 106, 377, 750

Nicholas II, Tsar 54, 200, 257

NICs (Newly Industrializing Countries) 602–3, 611

Nietzsche, Friedrich 166–7

Nigeria 738
  civil war 535
  independence (1960) 529
  and Islam 687–8, 854
  oil and gas production 525
  population 586t

Nixon, President Richard 602, 662, 676, 828
  election and re-election as president 675, 676
  fall from office (1974) 677, 741
  and Vietnam 675
  visit to China and Moscow (1972) 676–7

North Atlantic Treaty Organization *see* NATO

North Korea 816, 823, 848 *see also* Korea

Northern Ireland 715, 785–7

Northern Rhodesia *see* Zambia

Norway 57, 174

Novalis 15n

nuclear physics 34–5

nuclear power 137, 556, 558–9, 581, 605

nuclear power plants 558
  accidents at 578–9

nuclear waste 581, 842

nuclear weapons 460, 556, 558, 823
  control of: agreement on restricting testing of 660; and INF Treaty (1987) 750; and Reykjavik summit (1986) 750; seeking of arms limitations (1970s) 711, 742; signing of test ban treaty (1963) 707; treaty on missile limitation (1972) 711
  and Hiroshima and Nagasaki 427–8, 431, 432, 448, 558
  and ICBM 660
  India and Pakistan's test explosions (1998) 819–20

Nuremberg laws (1935) 402

nutrition 568–9

Nyasaland (now Malawi) 532

Nylon 124

OAU (Organization for African Unity) 536, 734, 737, 851

OECD (Organization of Economic Cooperation and Development) 703, 851

OEEC (Organization for European Economic Cooperation) 456, 703

oil 48, 306–7, 540, 770, 854
  fall in prices (1990s) 769
  impact of increase in prices in

INDEX

1970s 603–4, 682–3, 693, 728, 788
increase in discoveries of 679
increase in price (1970s) 600, 602, 682, 683, 690
Olympic Games
  murder of Israeli team members (1972) 686
Oman 542–3, 638, 770, 772
Omdurman, battle of (1898) (Sudan) 92
OPEC 851
Organization for African Unity *see* OAU
Organization for European Economic Cooperation *see* OEEC
Organization of American States 659
Organization of Economic Cooperation and Development *see* OECD
O'Shaughnessy, Arthur Edgar William 38n
Ostpolitik 709–10, 762, 806
Ottoman empire 23, 52–3, 64–6, 88, 152, 781
  Arab revolt against rule of 251
  characteristics 65–6
  dangers arising from weakness and decline of 183–4
  declaration of war on by Italy (1911) 202
  decline of in Africa 231–4
  decline and collapse 80, 176, 231, 261–4, 304, 309–10, 853
  east of Suez 234–6
  in Europe 54, 65
  and European imperialism 102
  parallel with Hapsburg empire 235

partition issue 188
and Young Turks 194–7, 203, 235, 261
Ottoman sultan 13, 64–5
ozone layer 582

Pacific Rim 603
pain 838
painting 324–5
Pakistan
  and Afghanistan 733, 743
  breaking away of Bangladesh 499, 620
  and China 794, 502
  famine (1953) 474
  female prime minister 639
  and India: fighting with over Kashmir 499–500, 502, 732; and nuclear test explosions (1998) 819–20
  and Islam 500–501, 619, 733
  population 586t
  separation from India after independence 473, 494, 620, 732
  treaty with Japan 519
Palestine 234, 483–4
  and Britain 263, 305, 306, 345–6, 482, 485
  and creation of Israel 485
  establishment of national home for Jews 263, 483
  and Great War 263
  immigration of Jews to 235, 306, 484
  partition proposal 484, 485
  refugees 680
  unrest between Arabs and Jews 306, 307–8, 484, 485
Palestine Liberation Organization *see* PLO

Pan-African Congress 737
Panama canal, opening of (1914)
    51, 105
Panhard 127
Paraguay 376–7, 694
Paris
    exhibition (1900) 209
    pollution in 580
Paris Commune 156
Passchendaele, battle of 256
Pasteur, Louis 35, 125
Pavlov, I.P. 616
Pax Britannica 96, 169
peace-keeping, problems of
    799–805
Pearl Harbor 423–4
peasantry, global retreat of 608
penicillin 126, 555–6
pensions 599n, 600
People's Republic of China see
    China
perestroika 749, 757, 778
Perón, Juan 655
Perry, Commodore 81, 103
Persia 66, 82, 193, 251, 311, 312 see
    also Iran
Pétain, Marshall 414
Peter the Great 37, 60, 512
Petit Parisien 132
Philippines 220
    annexation and occupation of by
        United States 91n, 104, 214,
        466–7
    independence (1946) 466–7, 519
    Japanese occupation 468
    treaty with Japan 519
    and women's suffrage 633
physics 33–5, 556, 558
Pill 634–6, 643
Pinochet, General 835n

Pius VI, Pope 622–3
Pius X, Pope 168
Planck, Max 34, 35
plastics 124
PLO (Palestine Liberation
    Organization)
    addressing of UN General
        Assembly (1974) 681–2
    conflict with Israel 683, 743, 824,
        825
    continuation of violence after
        peace talks 824
    and Gulf War 768
    and intifada 747, 823–4
    peace negotiations with Israel
        823–4
Pobedonostev, K.B. 169
Pol Pot 613n
Poland 162, 261, 283–4, 292, 317,
    396
    anti-Soviet rioting (1956) 649,
        650
    election of Wałesa as president
        (1990) 761
    elections (1989) 756
    and EU 812
    Germany's attack on and
        treatment of occupied (1939)
        408–9, 410, 419
    and Great War 261, 262, 273
    guarantees against aggression
        from Britain 407, 408
    Jews in 785
    joins NATO 779
    land redistribution 287
    peasants 752
    revolution 754–6
    and Roman Catholic Church
        754
    and Solidarity 754, 755, 756

and Soviet Union 292, 416
steel industry 605
police 624
Polish Home Army 419
political parties, development of
151–2
pollution 580
conference on industrial (1997)
583
polygamy, recession of 637–8
poor 844–5 see also poverty
population 42–3, 111–15
attempts to control 112–13, 116
by country 586t
concern over rapid growth 42
division of into continents 585t
and Europe 44–5
outcome of growth 586
rise in growth rate 39, 42,
111–12, 114–15, 115–16, 585,
618, 836
world conference on (1974) 112
populism 70–71
Portsmouth, Treaty of (1905) 214
Portugal 74, 177, 697
and Africa 97, 100, 523, 530, 531,
533
authoritarianism in 316, 318
and Great War 248
joins European Community
(1986) 788
postal services 131
Potsdam conference (1945) 451
poverty 143, 144, 584, 586–7, 601n,
603
power 558–9 see also electricity;
nuclear power
press see newspapers
Progressivism 71–2
Prohibition 334, 368

prosperity see wealth
prostitution 26–7
Prussia 78, 161–2
psychoanalysis 321, 616
psychology 615–17
public health 569
Puerto Rico 104

Qadaffi, Colonel 681, 743–4
Qatar 770
quantum physics 34, 35

Radar 560
radio 132, 133, 319, 560, 832
railways 13, 46, 120, 127
Ralegh, Sir Walter 829
Rapallo agreement (1922) 328–9,
331
Rayon 124
Reagan, Ronald 742, 747–8,
749–50
refrigerator 124
relativity, theory of 34
religion 165–9, 617–23, 630, 841
in 1901 15
decline in church going 325
decline of in Europe 166–7, 833
growth in people respecting
authority of 618
impact of psychology on 617–18
and mass communication 134,
618
and violence 620
see also Christianity; Islam
Republican Party (United States)
72–3, 334, 367
resources 48
consumption of 576
running out of 581
Revisionists 150

Reykjavik summit (1986) 750
Reza Khan (Shah of Shahs) 311–12,
  620, 684, 686
Rhodesia 97, 525, 532–3, 538
Roman Catholic Church 167–8,
  621–3
  and contraception 623, 635–6
  ecumenical Council 622
  and education 168
  growth of outside Europe 621–2
  in Latin America 74, 622
  Papacy 52, 313
  and Poland 754
  proclaiming of 1950 as Holy
    Year 621
  reorientation of 622–3
Romania 184, 265
  agricultural reforms 287
  and Balkan war 204
  and Great War 248, 251
  independence (1878) 53
  minorities in 275
  peasant rising (1907) 146
  revolution (1989) 762
  and Soviet Union 651
  and Transylvania 784
Romantics 323–4
Rome, Treaty of (1957) 701–2, 703,
  707
Röntgen, W. C. 33
Roosevelt, President Franklin D.
  367–8, 450
  achievements 368, 369
  and 'corollary' to Monroe
    Doctrine 105–6, 374
  and Europe 369–70
  and Indian independence 472
  and Latin America 377
  New Deal 368–9
  and reform 72

and Second World War 421, 426,
  441
Roosevelt, President Theodore 10
ruling class, European 145–6
Rushdie, Salman 619
Russia 102, **199–201**, 281
  advances in Far East 181–2, 189,
    211
  agrarian disorder in nineteenth
    century 146
  agriculture 164, 200
  alliance with France 178, 179,
    180–81
  Anglo-Russian convention (1907)
    193
  and Asia 354
  and Austria-Hungary 177, 182:
    and Bosnia's annexation by
    Austria-Hungary (1908) 196–7,
    198, 199–200; support of
    Serbia in tariff war with
    Austria-Hungary 198
  backwardness 79
  and Balkan Wars 203
  at beginning of century 163–4
  economic advance at beginning
    of century 163–4
  famines 119, 295
  and Great War 251, 256–7:
    absence from peace settlement
    conference 277–8; and Brest-
    Litovsk treaty 258; declaration
    of war by Germany on 241–2;
    failure of Dardanelles
    campaign 302, 303
  growth in strength 200
  handicaps to growth 164
  industry 13, 49, 79, 79–80, 164,
    295
  life expectancy 114

population 164, 586t
power of 79–80
railways 80, 127, 200, 211
revolution (1905) 146, 256
revolution (1917) 256, 257–8,
    301–2, 354 *see also* Bolsheviks
ruling houses of 162–3
war with Japan (1904–5) 191,
    200, 213–14, 236, 351, 384, 423
weaknesses 200–201
see also Soviet Union
Russia (post-Soviet) 86, 775–8, 853
and Chechen rebellion 777
crushing of parliament
    insurrection (1993) 776
devaluation of rouble (1998) 818
economic reform under Yeltsin
    775
faltering of banks (1998) 778
intervention in Tajikstan (1992)
    777
problems faced 775–6
see also Yeltsin, Boris
Russian empire 87–8, 102, 152
Rutherford, Ernest 33, 34, 558
Rwanda 738, 834

SA (*Sturmabteilung*) 392, 394, 402
Saar 277
Sadat, President Anwar
    assassination of (1981) 687, 743
Salisbury, Lord 64, 66, 179
Salvarsan, discovery of 126
Samoa 103
Sarikat Islam 387
satellite television 564–5
Saudi Arabia
abolition of slavery 19n
emergence of (1932) 305
female education 639

and Gulf War 768
and Islam 771
oil 682, 770
population growth 116, 771
Schlieffen plan 241, 253
Schrödinger, Erwin 35
Schuman, Robert 699
science 30–35, 169, 553–4, 555–8,
    615, 841–3
blurring of fields of 557
change in thinking of the
    educated by 31
difficulty in understanding 35,
    556, 557–8
distrust of 577–8
impact of 30, 135, 555–6, 567,
    841–2
increase in awareness of
    importance of 558
increase in prestige of 135
and new technology 567
in nineteenth century 30–31,
    31–4, 35, 123
and Victorians 556–7
'Scramble for Africa' 96–100, 107
sea-levels, rise in 582
Second International 149, 150,
    288
Second World War (1939–45) 243,
    378, 410–32, 832
aftermath 435–9
Allied victories and advance
    425–7
and Atlantic Charter (1941)
    421–2, 429, 466
atomic bombs dropped on
    Hiroshima and Nagasaki
    427–8, 431, 432, 448, 558
attack on Poland by Germany
    408–9, 410

Second World War – *cont.*
  attack on Yugoslavia and Greece
    by Germany 417
  Battle of the Atlantic 415, 425–6
  Battle of Britain 416
  Battle of El Alamein 425
  Battle of Midway 425
  and *Blitzkrieg* 411, 414
  blockade 411, 414
  and Britain *see* Britain
  collaborators 418–19
  concentration camps 428
  death toll 432, 437
  death-knell of imperialism 466,
    468
  declaration of war on Germany
    by Britain and France 410–11
  declaration of war on United
    States by Germany 422, 424
  demographic changes as
    consequence of 437–8
  destructiveness and damage
    caused by 431–2, 435, 437
  events leading up to 404–7
  and France *see* France
  German advances 418 *see also*
    Germany
  Holocaust 429, 430, 484, 785
  and India 366, 469–70, 471
  invasion of France by Germany
    and surrender 414
  invasion of Italy by Allies 426
  invasion of northern France by
    Allies (D-Day) (1944) 426
  invasion of Norway and
    Denmark by Germany 414
  invasion of Soviet Union by
    Germany (Barbarossa) 416–18
  Italy's entry into 415 *see also*
    Italy

  and Japan *see* Japan
  joining of Italy with Germany
    414
  as a moral struggle 429–30
  naval war 425
  North African campaign 424,
    425, 426
  Pearl Harbor attack 423–4
  resistance movements 420–21
  surrender of Germany 427
  surrender of Japan 428, 515
  treatment of occupied countries
    by Germany 419–20, 428
  and United States *see* United
    States
  use of radar 560
  and Yalta conference (1945)
    439–40
Security Council (UN) 443–4
Selassie, Haile 535, 536
Serbia 53, 239, 273, 629, 630, 783–4
  alliance with Bulgaria (1912) 203
  and Austria-Hungary 183, 198,
    205, 238
  and Balkan war 204, 205
  and Bosnian crisis 799–800, 801
  declaration of war on by
    Austrians 241
  and Great War 248
  and Kosovo 781–2, 802–3, 826,
    828
service industries 605
Sèvres, Treaty of (1920) 273n, 308,
  309
sexual behaviour 601
shipping routes 127
Siam 64, 66, 82, 468 *see also*
  Thailand
Siberia 358
Sierra Leone 529

silicon chip 560–61, 562, 607
Singapore 115, 424, 468, 519, 603, 724
Single European Act (1987) 788–9
single European currency 809–11
Sinn Fein 285, 786
Six-Day War (1967) 680, 747
slavery 13, 18–19, 536
Slovakia 784–5
Slovenia 781, 782–3, 799, 808, 812
smallpox 582
Smuts, Jan Christiaan 209n
Social Democratic Party (SPD) (Germany) 149, 150, 159, 704
social welfare, provision of 600
socialism 147–51
solar power 559
Solidarity 754, 755, 756
Somalia 526, 804
Somaliland 530
Somme, battle of (1916) 249
South Africa 86, 524, 525, 526, 531–2, 734–8, 853
  Afrikaner domination in politics 531–2
  and Angola 533
  apartheid 532, 734, 735
  and Boer War see South African War
  changes under Botha 734–5
  dismantling of apartheid by de Klerk 735–6
  economic sanctions against 735
  elections (1994) 737
  establishment of Union (1910) 109
  gold and diamond industry 110
  Great Trek 107
  hostility of United Nations towards 734
  leaves Commonwealth 530
  political violence (1993) 736
  release of Mandela (1990) 736
  and Rhodesia 538
  and Second World war 531
  steps towards black majority rule 736–7
  suppression of rebellion against crown (1914) 252
  treatment of native populations by white settlers 95
South African war 106–10, 153, 179–80, 181, 187–8, 246, 247
South America see Latin America
South East Asia Treaty Organization (SEATO) 490
South Korea 504, 603, 724, 728, 816
  see also Korea
Southern Rhodesia 527, 530, 532–3
sovereignty, state 629
Soviet Union 293–303, 396, 647–52, 662–5, 710–11
  admiration of Stalin's regime by foreigners 403–4
  and Afghanistan 685, 733, 741, 746, 748, 751
  and Africa 526
  agriculture 295: collectivization 298–9, 398–9; decline in output 299; failure of 663–4
  and Albania 446, 492, 651
  armaments expenditure 711
  ascendancy and power of after Second World War 446–7
  attempted coup (1991) against Gorbachev 772–3
  and Brezhnev doctrine 651–2, 753–4
  and Britain 293, 332

Soviet Union – *cont.*
  changes and reforms under
    Gorbachev 748–9, 757–8
  and China *see* China
  and Chinese Civil War 363, 477
  civil war 294–5
  and Comintern 291–2, 455–6
  and CSCE 712–13
  and Cuba 658–9
  and Czechoslovakia: Prague
    Spring (1968) 651; withdrawal
    of forces from 761–2
  denouncement of Stalin's
    misdeeds by Khrushchev 649,
    663
  and Depression 343
  difficulties faced 741–2
  disintegration of 627, **756–60**,
    772–5, 779, 850, 853
  dissidence in 710
  and East Germany 653, 704
  and Berlin blockade and airlift
    463–4
  and eastern Europe 451, 592, 593,
    629, 649, 751
  economy 603, 663, 664, 758
  education 664
  and Germany: non-aggression
    treaty (1926) 331; opposition
    to a re-united Germany after
    the war 451, 452, 462; Rapallo
    agreement 328–9, 331; and
    reunification 763–4
  health service 664
  and Hungarian uprising (1956)
    546, 650
  and India 500, 502
  industrialization 295–6, 298,
    299–300, 398, 663
  and Israel 485, 549

  and Khrushchev 511, 647–8, 653,
    658, 659, 662–3
  and Korean War 487–9
  and League of Nations 277
  legacy of backwardness 664
  life expectancy at birth 114
  limits on freedom and rights of
    citizens 490, 665
  and Marshall Plan 455
  navy 733
  New Economic Policy (NEP)
    295–6
  nuclear accidents 578–9
  nuclear power stations 664
  nuclear weapons 450, 660, 774n
  and peasants 294, 297, 298
  and Poland 292, 416
  promotion and support for
    revolution elsewhere 301
  purges 399–400, 403, 465
  road to modernization 296
  and Romania 651
  ruthlessness of Bolshevik rule
    293–4, 294–5
  Second World War: battle on
    eastern front 425; casualties
    432, 437; enters Poland 426;
    invasion of by Germany
    416–18; mobilization 425; pact
    with Germany (1939) 409, 416;
    suffering caused by 449–50
  secret police 295
  seeking of diplomatic relations
    with other countries by
    Bolsheviks 329, 331–2
  setting up of labour camps 299
  and space programme 570, 571,
    572, 574, 664–5
  and Spanish Civil War 405,
    408

and Stalin *see* Stalin, Joseph
and Suez crisis 649
Terror 399–400
territories occupied after war 447
and Turkish treaty (1921) 329n
and United Nations 443, 444, 452
and United States *see* United
States
and World Council of Churches
621
and Yugoslavia 446, 465, 492,
649–50
see also Russia
space exploration 570–4, 577,
857–9
and American Space Shuttle 574
benefits of 573
cooperation between United
States and Soviet Union 574
criticism of 573
first landing on the moon (1969)
571–3
first 'space walk' 572
launching of Sputnik I by Soviet
Union 570, 652
rivalry between United States and
Soviet Union 571, 574, 652–3
Soviet achievements 664–5
and unmanned satellites 574
Spain 74, 697–8
and Africa 98n
authoritarianism in 316, 318
Basque terrorists 785
Civil War 378, 404–7, 408–9,
431, 437
communism in 401
and Cuban independence 76, 104,
657
joins European Community
(1986) 704, 788

and monarchy 698
political problems and unrest at
turn of century 157, 158
and Second World War 697
'Tragic Week' of Barcelona
(1909) 158
and United Nations 697
war with United States (1898) 96,
104, 105, 177, 318
and women's vote 631
Spanish Organic Law (1966) 623n
SPD *see* Social Democratic Party
Sputnik I 570, 652
Sputnik II 571
Sputnik V 571
Stalin, Joseph 302, 354, 485, 492
character 298
death 489, 647
denouncement of misdeeds by
Khrushchev 649, 663
and Germany 452
and industrialization 298
and KMT 363
and Korean War 487
legacy of 489–90
and Mao 511
purges 399, 465
ruthlessness of 297–8
and Second World War 418
and Spanish Civil War 408
and Yalta conference 439
state(s) 52–6, 623, 847–9
challenges to 628–31
intervention in economy 624
and nationalism 53–5, 627
power of 624–5
and sovereignty 629
virtual monopoly of main
instruments of physical control
624

state(s) – *cont.*
and welfare 624
steam 123, 126
steel industry 604–5
Stolypin, Peter 164
assassination (1912) 200
Straits of Constantinople *see*
Constantinople Straits
student demonstrations (1968)
643–4, 753
submarines, deployment in Great
War 254, 255, 256
Sudan
Anglo-Egyptian conquest and
proclamation of condominium
(1898/9) 97, 233
battle of Omdurman (1898) 92
civil war 738, 746
and Islam 688, 745
military coup (1989)745–6
Suez Canal 190
crisis (1956) 544–6, 649
importance to Britain 262, 306,
307, 483, 543
opening of (1869) 51, 232
suffragettes 155, 174
Sukarno, Achmed 479, 503, 504,
544
Sun Yat-sen 218, 221, 351, 640, 721
background 217
and CCP 359
death (1925) 360
and KMT 217, 348
and presidency of 'United
Provinces' 219
view of world 359–60
Surrealism 324
Sweden 57, 811, 812
Switzerland 174, 631
Syllabus of Errors 167

Syria 234
Ba'ath party takes power (1963)
680
and Egypt 546, 683
European cultural influences 234
and France 305, 308, 482, 483
and Gulf War 768
independence (1941) 483
paralysis in early 60s 546
and Second World War 424
and Six-Day War (1967) 680
and United States 549

Taft, President William 72, 377n,
822
Taiwan (formerly Formosa) 104n
728, 729, 793, 826
and China 815–16
expulsion from United Nations
676
GDP 603
and KMT 477, 510
and United States 510, 677
withdrawal of United States
forces 723, 815
Tajikistan 777
Tanganyika 92, 97, 526, 529
Tannu Tuva 512
Tanzania 529, 588
taxation 51, 624
technology 31, 123–5, 137, 555
effect of in Great War 246–7
and growth of imperialism 89–90
impact of new on women's lives
173
progress in 28
see also communications
technology; information
technology
telecommunications 560

telegraph 130, 134
telephone 28, 130
television 133–4, 560, 562, 564–5
Teng-Hui, President Lee 815
terrorism 686–7, 770
test-tube baby 569
Thailand 519, 724, 817 *see also* Siam
Thatcher, Margaret 714–15, 789–90
Third World 501–502, 650
'Three Emperors League' 178
Tiananmen Square massacre (1989) 565, **795–8**
Tibet 13, 193
    invasion of by Britain (1904) 24, 101, 215
    occupation of by Chinese (1951) 509–10
'tiger economies' 724, 816
Times 132
Titanic disaster (1912) 130
Tito, Marshall 465, 490, 492, 502, 782
Tokyo 611
trade 50–51, 122, 604
    effect on by Great War 280
    free trade doctrine 50–51, 492
    and globalization 611
    growth in world 591, 611
    liberalization of 610
    systems of 492–3
    and tariffs 591
'Tragic Week' of Barcelona (1909) 158
Transjordan *see* Jordan
'transnational advocacy networks' 630–31
Transylvania 284, 784
Triple Alliance (Germany/Austria-

Hungary/Italy) 178, 179, 185
Trotsky, Leon 297, 298
Truman Doctrine 454–5
Truman, President H. F. 450 452, 487, 488, 666
Tsolikovsky, K. E. 570
Tsushima Straits, battle of (1904) 213
tuberculosis 569
Tunis 89
Tunisia 526, 540, 544, 638
Turkey 482, 825
    abolition of polygamy (1926) 638
    attack on Muslim theocracy 310–11
    and EU 811, 812
    and Great War 248, 251
    and Iran 312
    and Kemal 308–11, 312, 811
    Kurdish nationalism 311
    and Lausanne Treaty (1923) 309
    and Sèvres Treaty (1920) 308
    treaty with Soviet Union (1921) 329
    United States aid to 454
    war with Britain (1914) 231
Twenty-one Demands (1915) 351, 352
Tzu Hsi, Empress 60–1, 215, 216, 217–18

Uganda 529
Ukraine 420, 437, 578–9, 760
Ulster 620, 786
unemployment 591, 601, 602
    and Depression 241–2, 341, 342, 343
    in nineteenth century 45–6, 143–4
United Arab Republic 546

United Kingdom *see* Britain
United Nations (UN) 427, 429, 628, 832, 849
  admission of China (1971) 676, 723
  and Bosnian crisis 799–800, 827
  establishment of 443
  expulsion of Taiwan 676
  first meeting of General Assembly (1946) 444
  and human rights 14n, 629
  importance of 444
  and Israel 681
  Japan joins (1956) 518, 727
  and Korea 487, 488
  organization and structure 443
  and South Africa 734
  and Soviet Union 443, 444, 452
  and Soviet veto 452
  and Spain 697
  veto power of permanent members of Security Council 443–4
United Nations Declaration (1942) 425n
United Nations Relief and Rehabilitation Administration *see* UNRRA
United States 48, 50, 67–74, 102–6, 332–5, 367–9, 666–71, 741–2, 820–28
  agriculture 70, 71, 118, 120
  and American Civil War (1861–5) 54, 67, 246
  annexation of Hawaii (1898) 104
  anti-imperialism 466–7, 478
  ascendancy and power of after war 446, 447–8
  and blacks 73, 668–70, 671, 825: ending of segregation in

  schools 669–70; 'ghetto' areas 671; problems in 1990s 820–21; rioting in Los Angeles (1965) 671
  bombing of Iraq over failure of UN weapons inspections 803–4, 804–5
  bombing of Libya (1986) 750
  and Bosnian crisis 800
  and China *see* China
  and Chinese civil war 476, 477
  and Clinton *see* Clinton, President Bill
  and Cuba 104, 106, 656–8, 660–61: 'Bay of Pigs' operation 658, 660; missile crisis 658–9, 660, 711, 741
  democracy 69–70
  and Depression 342, 343, 367
  dissipation of authority of presidency 821–2
  and Dominican Republic 661–2
  economy 679: abandonment of fixed-rate exchange or the dollar (1971) 602; effect of Great War on 279–80, 340; GDP 588t; growth 590, 820, 821; and Reagan 749
  and Egypt 544–5, 549
  emigration of Europeans to 43, 68
  and Europe 68, 445–6
  European investment 788
  and feminism 636
  and government intervention 666–7
  and Great War 73, 249, 254–5, 263, 332
  growth in geographical extent 86, 87

growth of 'Hispanic' Americans 821

growth in nineteenth century 68–9

growth of power 666

and Gulf War 765

impact on European culture 609

and imperialism 86, 102–6, 466–7

and India 502

and Indonesia 503

industrial power 49, 69, 70, 448, 666

and Iran 540, 684–5: hostage crisis 684–5, 685–6, 740, 741, 742; Iran-Contra affair (1987) 750; Iranian revolution 684, 685

isolation policy 67–8, 278, 332–3

and Israel 542, 549, 682, 825

and Japan see Japan

and Korean War 487–9, 490

and Kosovo crisis 826–7

and Latin America see Latin America

and League of Nations 276

life expectancy at birth 114

limits on immigration 335

Louisiana Purchase (1803) 67, 94, 454

and McCarthyism 667–8, 672

and Marshall Plan 455–6, 463, 490–91, 590, 591, 592, 696, 698

and Mexico 94, 106, 822

and Middle East peace process 823–4, 825

and NATO 779

and New Deal 368–9

nuclear accidents 579

nuclear weapons 490, 660, 823

number of states belonging 851

and oil crisis 683

and Panama canal 105

and Philippines 91n, 104, 214, 466–7

population growth 67, 586t, 666

populist challenge 70–71

and Progressivism 71–3

and Prohibition 334, 368

prosperity in 1920s 333, 340

and Reagan 742, 747–8, 749–50

role of government 625

Second World War: and Atlantic Charter 421–2, 429, 466; attack on Pearl Harbor 423–4; battles in the Pacific 425; declaration of war on by Germany 422, 424; and industrial power 448; and Lend-Lease 421, 441, 448, 449

slow progress in social reform 71

and Somalia 804

and Soviet Union 444–5, 460: deterioration of relations 450; new degree of cooperation between 711–12; origins of antagonism between 461–2; setting up of 'hot line' between 659–60

and space programme 570, 571–2, 573–4, 653

stock market crash (1929) 367

and Suez crisis 545

swing back to isolationism after Vietnam 678

and Taiwan 510, 677, 723, 815

and Truman Doctrine 454–5

and Vietnam 508

United States – *cont.*
  and Vietnam War *see* Vietnam
    War
  war with Spain (1898) 96, 104,
    105, 177, 318
  and women's vote 631
UNRRA (United Nations Relief
  and Rehabilitation
  Administration) 437, 438, 448
Upper Silesia 277
urbanization, growth in 117
Uruguay 375, 692
USSR (Union of Soviet Socialist
  Republics) *see* Soviet Union
Ustaša 439, 782

vaccinations 569
Vanishing Adolescent, The
  (Firedenberg) 642
Venezuela 76, 105, 373, 655
Versailles Treaty (1919) 328, 330,
  341
  Hitler's denouncement of 390,
    391
  and League of Nations 276
  resentment towards by Germany
    291, 388
  seeking of revision of by
    Germany 328, 389
  terms 273–4
  violation of by Germany 405
Victoria, Queen 9, 108, 225
Viet Minh 386, 480, 481
Vietcong 508
Vietnam
  aftermath of war 677–8
  American support of South
    Vietnam 508–9
  and China 509, 677, 794
  formation of new state of 480

and Indo-China war with French
  481, 507
partition of into North and
  South 508
Vietnam War **672–6**, 677, 678, 723,
  729, 741
  air attacks on North Vietnam
    and sending in of combat units
    to the South 673
  impact of on United States 675–6
  peace negotiations and ceasefire
    675
  protests against 643, 673–4
  withdrawal of American troops
    by Nixon 675
Vietnamese National Party 385
Voting and women 26, 27, 174, 284,
  631, 636

Wałesa, Lech 754–5, 756, 761
war crimes 835
warfare
  attempts to humanize in
    nineteenth century 165
wars
  attitude and views of in early
    twentieth century 187–8
Warsaw Pact 491, 492, 704, 779
wealth
  cultural consequences of increase
    in 608–10
  and dissatisfaction 579–80
  disparity in distribution of 588,
    595–6, 846
  growth in 45, 51, 117–20, 326–7,
    576–7, 587–9, 836, 839, 840
weapons
  and Great War 247, 249
  and imperialism 92
  see also nuclear weapons

welfare state 602, 625, 705

Wells, H. G., *The War in the Air* 209

West Berlin *see* Berlin

West Germany

  admittance to NATO 491, 701, 704

  currency reform 462–3

  economic growth 491

  and ECSC 700

  emergence of 464–5

  outflow of refugees from East Germany to 491, 653

  relations with East Germany 594, 709–10, 762

  and reunification 806

  under Adenauer 491

  unemployment 601

  see also Germany

Western European Union (WEU) 701

Wilhelm II, Kaiser 154, 160, 178, 185, 191

  abdication (1918) 265

  and Balkan wars 204

  on parliamentarians 162

Wilson, President Woodrow 73, 263, 274, 277, 278, 333

  election as president (1912) 72

  and First World War 283

  and Fourteen Points 255, 261, 263

  and League of Nations 276

  and Mexico 106

  re-election (1916) 255

wind energy 559

Windscale (later called Sellafield) reactor fire (1957) 578

wireless transmission 130 *see also* radio

women 25–7, 631–41, 837

  in 1901 25–6

  effect of contraception on lives of 173 *see also* Pill and employment 172, 602, 633

  in Europe 171–4

  and feminism 636

  impact of new technology and innovations on 173

  inequalities of 632

  influence of treatment by west on other countries 632–3

  and marriage law 632

  in non-western world 637–41

  and polygamy 637–8

  and voting 26, 27, 174, 284, 631, 636

Women's Movement 636, 640–41

Women's Rights Convention (1848) 26

World Bank 442, 590, 597

world civilization 844–8

World Council of Churches 621

World Health Organization 569

World Monetary and Economic Conference (1933) 344

World Trade Organization 826

World War I *see* Great War

World War II *see* Second World War

World Wide Web 563

Wright, Orville 129

Yalta conference (1945) 439, 450

Yeltsin, Boris 775, 777

  and attempted coup (1991) 773

  health 778

  and Kosovo crisis 802–3

  opposition to 776

  personal style 776

Yom Kippur war (1973) 602, 681, 682
Young Turks 194–7, 203, 235, 261
youth 609, 641–4, 845
   changes in awareness of 642
   and communism 643
   identification as lucrative market 642–3
   new freedom of 641–2
Yuan Shih-kai 219, 348, 351
Yugoslavia 490, 705
   attack on by Stalin 465
   Croat–Serb antagonism 782
   disintegration of 627, 780–84
   divisions within 780–81
   expulsion from Cominform 492, 649
   founding of 262, 265, 780
   murder of king by Croats (1936) 378
   murder of Serbians by Croats in aftermath of war 438–9
   and Second World War 417, 420
   and Soviet Union 446, 465, 492, 649–50

Zaire (was Congo) 525, 530
Zambia (was Northern Rhodesia) 525, 532, 533
Zanzibar 529
Zapata, Emilio 371
Zeppelin, Ferdinand 128
Zhao Ziyang 795
Zimbabwe 538, 734 *see also* Rhodesia